Get the eBook FREE!

(PDF, ePub, Kindle, and liveBook all included)

We believe that once you buy a book from us, you should be able to read it in any format we have available. To get electronic versions of this book at no additional cost to you, purchase and then register this book at the Manning website.

Go to https://www.manning.com/freebook and follow the instructions to complete your pBook registration.

That's it!
Thanks from Manning!

Microservices Security in Action

Microservices Security in Action

PRABATH SIRIWARDENA
AND NUWAN DIAS

MANNING
SHELTER ISLAND

For online information and ordering of this and other Manning books, please visit
www.manning.com. The publisher offers discounts on this book when ordered in quantity.
For more information, please contact

Special Sales Department
Manning Publications Co.
20 Baldwin Road
PO Box 761
Shelter Island, NY 11964
Email: orders@manning.com

Manning Publications Co.
20 Baldwin Road
PO Box 761
Shelter Island, NY 11964

Development editor:	Marina Michaels
Technical development editor:	Jonathan Thoms and Joshua White
Review editor:	Ivan Martinović
Production editor:	Deirdre S. Hiam
Copy editor:	Sharon Wilkey
Proofreader:	Keri Hales
Technical proofreader:	Thorsten P. Weber
Typesetter and cover designer:	Marija Tudor

ISBN 9781617295959
Printed in the United States of America

To Dr. Sanjiva Weerawarana,
our mentor for more than a decade
and for many more years to come!

brief contents

contents

ix

preface

While working at WSO2 for more than a decade, we've seen how the integration domain evolved over time from SOAP-based services to JSON/RESTful services and then to microservices. We spent most of our early days at WSO2 contributing to the Apache Axis2 project, which was a popular SOAP engine in those days, and to the Apache Rampart project, which implements many Organization for the Advancement of Structured Information Standards (OASIS) standards for web services security. Even though SOAP was quite promising in those days, it started to fade rapidly over time, and clearly JSON/RESTful services had won. Most of the microservice implementations we see today follow RESTful design principles.

In the last two to three years, we've seen a genuine interest from many companies we've worked with to move into microservices architecture, and projects starting from scratch are adopting microservices principles. Most of the early adopters of microservices just wanted to get things done, and worried mostly about implementing functional requirements. They didn't worry too much about security, although they should have. In many cases, securing microservices would mean securing the interactions among microservices with Transport Layer Security (TLS), and may be, for some, enforcing mutual TLS for service-to-service authentication. But none of them are quite adequate. There are two main reasons many didn't worry much about security: complexity and awareness.

Some time back, we found that most tools for securing microservices were not easy to use or couldn't address the challenges specific to microservices deployments. This complexity was a barrier to securing microservices. At the same time, people who didn't put much effort into security weren't fully aware of the risks. We started hearing these stories from many of our customers as well as from the extended open source community we work with. That motivated us to write this book on securing microservices. Bringing an idea from inception to reality takes considerable time and effort. We lived with this idea of writing a book for more than two years until Manning reached out to us. During that period, with the increased adoption of microservices, the infrastructure around microservices security also evolved.

Writing a book about a rapidly evolving domain is bit of a challenge; you never know when your book will be obsolete. After discussing this challenge with the publisher, we decided to put more weight on principles and patterns, and use tools just to demonstrate how to apply those principles and patterns in practice. This was our ground rule in picking up the technology stack for the book. We use Spring Boot / Java to develop all the samples, though we don't expect you to know either Java or Spring Boot in detail. If you have development experience in any programming language, you should be able to follow all the samples in the book with no difficulty.

Security itself is a larger domain. Securing microservices can mean different things to different people, based on their experiences and expectations. This fact was highlighted by one of the reviewers of the book, who comes from a security testing background. In our book, we wanted to focus on managing access to microservices. In other words, we wanted to focus on securing access to microservices with authentication and authorization. So, the book doesn't talk about protecting microservices against different types of attacks, such as SQL injection, cross-site scripting (XSS), cross-site request forgery, and so on.

After a marathon effort that spanned slightly more than two years, we are glad to see that our book on microservices security is out. We are also excited that this is the very first book on securing microservices. We hope you will enjoy reading it!

acknowledgments

This book would not have been possible without the support of many amazing people:

- Brian Sawyer, senior acquisitions editor at Manning, reached out to us and helped us structure our book proposal.
- Marina Michaels, development editor at Manning, was very patient and tolerant of us throughout the publishing process and provided invaluable advice during the writing process.
- To the rest of the staff at Manning: Deirdre Hiam, the project editor; Sharon Wilkey, the copyeditor; Keri Hales, the proofreader; and Ivan Martinović, the review editor.
- All the Manning Early Access Program (MEAP) subscribers of the book.
- Thorsten P. Weber, technical proofreader, who helped us review the code to make sure all the code samples work as expected.
- Tim Hinrichs, one of the creators of the Open Policy Agent (OPA) project, and Andrew Jessup, one of the creators of the SPIFFE project, who helped us by reviewing the appendices on OPA and SPIFFE.
- Sanjiva Weerawarana, the founder and CEO of WSO2, and Paul Fremantle, the CTO of WSO2, who have constantly mentored us for many years.
- To all the reviewers: Andrew Bovill, Björn Nordblom, Bruno Vernay, Eros Pedrini, Evgeny Shmarnev, Gerd Koenig, Gustavo Gomes, Harinath Mallepally, Joel Holmes, John Guthrie, Jonas Medina, Jonathan Levine, Jorge Ezequiel Bo, Leonardo Gomes da Silva, Lukáš Hozda, Massimo Siani, Matthew Rudy Jacobs, Mostafa Siraj, Philip Taffet, Raushan Jha, Salvatore Campagna, Simeon Leyzerzon, Srihari Sridharan, Stephan Pirnbaum, Thilo Käsemann, Tim van Deurzen, Ubaldo Pescatore, Yurii Bodarev—your suggestions helped make this a better book.

PRABATH SIRIWARDENA: My wife, Pavithra, and my little daughter, Dinadi, supported me throughout the writing process. Thank you very much, Pavithra and Dinadi. My parents and my sister are with me all the time. I am grateful to them for everything they have done for me. And also, my wife's parents—they were amazingly helpful.

NUWAN DIAS: My family, including my wife, Kasun, and son, Jason. I would not have been able to make the effort required to contribute to this book if not for their consistent support and patience throughout. My parents and in-laws are always a strength to me and back me up in everything I do.

about this book

Microservices Security in Action teaches you how to secure your microservices applications code and infrastructure. After a straightforward introduction to the challenges of microservices security, you'll learn fundamentals needed to secure both the application perimeter and service-to-service communications. Following a hands-on example, you'll explore how to deploy and secure microservices behind an API gateway as well as how to access microservices via a single-page application (SPA).

Along the way, the book highlights important concepts including throttling, analytics gathering, access control at the API gateway, and microservice-to-microservice communications. You'll also discover how to securely deploy microservices by using state-of-the-art technologies, including Kubernetes, Docker, and the Istio service mesh.

Lots of hands-on exercises secure your learning as you go, and this straightforward guide wraps up with a security process review and best practices. When you're finished reading, you'll be planning, designing, and implementing microservices applications with the priceless confidence that comes with knowing they're secure!

Who should read this book

Microservices Security in Action is for developers who are well versed in microservices design principles and have a basic familiarity with Java. Even if you are not a Java developer, but are familiar with any object-oriented programming language such as C++ or C#, and understand basic programming constructs well, you'll still get much out of this book. While some documents and blog posts exist online, this book brings together everything in a clear, easy-to-follow format that will benefit anyone wanting to get a thorough understanding of securing microservices.

How this book is organized: A roadmap

The book has five sections and 13 chapters. Part 1 takes you through the fundamentals in securing microservices:

- Chapter 1 teaches you why securing microservices is challenging, and takes you through the key principles in securing a microservices deployment.
- Chapter 2 teaches you how to build your first microservice in Spring Boot and secure it with OAuth 2.0. You will also learn how to set up an OAuth 2.0 token issuer.

Part 2 takes you through securing a microservice at the edge (or entry point) in a typical microservices deployment:

- Chapter 3 takes you through the consumer landscape of your microservices and teaches you how to deploy a Spring Boot microservice behind the Zuul API gateway. You will also learn how to enforce OAuth 2.0-based security at the Zuul API gateway.
- Chapter 4 teaches you how to develop a single-page application (SPA) with Angular. You will also learn how to secure a SPA with OpenID Connect.
- Chapter 5 teaches you how to extend the use case you built in chapter 4 by engaging throttling, monitoring, and access control at the Zuul API gateway.

Part 3 takes you through the process of securing interactions among microservices once a request from a client application passes through the security at the edge and enters into your microservices deployment:

- Chapter 6 teaches you how to secure communications among microservices that take place over HTTP, with mutual Transport Layer Security (mTLS).
- In chapter 7, you learn how to share contextual data (for example, the end user context) among microservices by using JSON Web Token (JWT).
- Chapter 8 teaches you how to secure communications among microservices that take place over gRPC, with mTLS and JWT.
- Chapter 9 teaches you how to secure reactive microservices. It also teaches you how to set up Kafka as a message broker, and how to enforce access-control policies for Kafka topics.

Part 4 takes you through deploying and securing microservices in a containerized environment:

- Chapter 10 teaches you how to deploy your microservices in Docker and to secure service-to-service interactions with mTLS and JWT. You also learn some of the built-in security features related to Docker.
- Chapter 11 teaches you how to deploy your microservices as Docker containers in Kubernetes and to secure service-to-service communications with JWT over mTLS.

- Chapter 12 teaches you how to offload the security processing overhead from your microservices by using the Istio service mesh.

Part 5 takes you through security testing in the development process:

- Chapter 13 teaches you how to automate security testing of your microservices with SonarQube, Jenkins, and OWASP ZAP.

In general, you should be sure to read the first two chapters so that you have the right mindset to take on the challenges of securing microservices and that you've gotten your feet wet and are ready to build more complex security patterns, which the book teaches you. The appendices provide information on OAuth 2.0, JWT, gRPC, Docker, Kubernetes, Istio, Open Policy Agent (OPA), and SPIFFE. This information supplements the chapters.

About the code

This book contains many examples of source code both in numbered listings and in line with normal text. In both cases, source code is formatted in a `fixed-width font like this` to separate it from ordinary text.

In many cases, the original source code has been reformatted; we've added line breaks and reworked indentation to accommodate the available page space in the book. In rare cases, even this was not enough, and listings include line-continuation markers (\). Additionally, comments in the source code have often been removed from the listings when the code is described in the text. Code annotations highlight important concepts and significant lines of code in many of the listings.

Source code for the examples in this book is available for download from the publisher's website at www.manning.com/books/microservices-security-in-action.

liveBook discussion forum

Purchase of *Microservices Security in Action* includes free access to a private web forum run by Manning Publications, where you can make comments about the book, ask technical questions, and receive help from the author and from other users. To access the forum and subscribe to it, point your web browser to www.manning.com/books/microservices-security-in-action. You can also learn more about Manning's forums and the rules of conduct at https://livebook.manning.com/#!/discussion.

Manning's commitment to our readers is to provide a venue where a meaningful dialogue between individual readers and between readers and the author can take place. It is not a commitment to any specific amount of participation on the part of the author, whose contribution to the forum remains voluntary (and unpaid). We suggest you try asking the authors some challenging questions lest their interest stray! The forum and the archives of previous discussions will be accessible from the publisher's website as long as the book is in print.

Other online resources

Need additional help?

- You can ask any questions related to the content of this book from the Microservices Security Slack channel: https://bit.ly/microservices-security.
- The OAuth IETF working group is a good place to ask any questions on OAuth 2.0 and related standards. You can subscribe to the OAuth IETF working group mailing list with the information available at https://datatracker.ietf.org/wg/oauth/about.
- The JOSE IETF working group is a good place to ask any questions on JSON Web Token (JWT) and the related standards. You can subscribe to the JOSE IETF working group mailing list with the information available at https://datatracker.ietf.org/wg/jose/about.
- You can ask any questions related to Kubernetes security from the Slack channel: https://slack.k8s.io/.
- You can ask any questions related to the Open Policy Agent (OPA) project from the Slack channel: https://slack.openpolicyagent.org/.
- You can ask any questions related to the SPIFFE project from the Slack channel: https://slack.spiffe.io/.
- To get updates on the conference/meetup talks the authors of this book do regularly, you can subscribe to the YouTube channel: http://vlog.facilelogin.com/.

about the authors

PRABATH SIRIWARDENA is the vice president of security architecture at WSO2, and has been working in the identity management and security domain since 2007.

NUWAN DIAS is the director of API architecture at WSO2 and has worked in the software industry since 2012, most of which he has spent focusing on the API management domain.

about the cover illustration

The figure on the cover of *Microservices Security in Action* is captioned "Homme Islandois," or a man from Iceland. The illustration is taken from a collection of dress costumes from various countries by Jacques Grasset de Saint-Sauveur (1757–1810), titled *Costumes de Différents Pays,* published in France in 1797. Each illustration is finely drawn and colored by hand. The rich variety of Grasset de Saint-Sauveur's collection reminds us vividly of how culturally apart the world's towns and regions were just 200 years ago. Isolated from each other, people spoke different dialects and languages. In the streets or in the countryside, it was easy to identify where they lived and what their trade or station in life was just by their dress.

The way we dress has changed since then, and the diversity by region, so rich at the time, has faded away. It is now hard to tell apart the inhabitants of different continents, let alone different towns, regions, or countries. Perhaps we have traded cultural diversity for a more varied personal life—certainly for a more varied and fast-paced technological life.

At a time when it is hard to tell one computer book from another, Manning celebrates the inventiveness and initiative of the computer business with book covers based on the rich diversity of regional life of two centuries ago, brought back to life by Grasset de Saint-Sauveur's pictures.

Part 1

Overview

Microservices are no longer a novelty. We're seeing large-scale microservices deployments with thousands of services. But whether we have one or two services or thousands, security is a top priority. This part of the book takes you through the fundamentals in securing microservices.

Chapter 1 teaches you why securing microservices is challenging, and takes you through the key principles in securing a microservices deployment.

Chapter 2 teaches you how to build your first microservice in Spring Boot and secure it with OAuth 2.0. You will also learn how to set up an OAuth 2.0 token issuer.

When you're finished with these two chapters, you'll have the right mindset to take on the challenges of securing microservices. After getting your feet wet in this part of the book, you'll be ready to build more complex security patterns (which we teach you in the rest of the book) on top of your first microservice.

Microservices security landscape 1

This chapter covers
- Why microservices security is challenging
- Principles and key elements of a microservices security design
- Edge security and the role of an API gateway
- Patterns and practices in securing service-to-service communications

Fail fast, fail often is a mantra in Silicon Valley. Not everyone agrees, but we love it! It's an invitation to experiment with new things, accept failures, fix problems, and try again. Not everything in ink looks pretty in practice. Fail fast, fail often is only hype unless the organizational leadership, the culture, and the technology are present and thriving.

We find microservices to be a key enabler for fail fast, fail often. Microservices architecture has gone beyond technology and architectural principles to become a culture. Netflix, Amazon, Lyft, Uber, and eBay are the front-runners in building that culture. Neither the architecture nor the technology behind microservices—but the discipline practiced in an organizational culture—lets your team build

3

stable products, deploy them in a production environment with less hassle, and introduce frequent changes with no negative impact on the overall system.

Speed to production and evolvability are the two key outcomes of microservices architecture. International Data Corporation (IDC) has predicted that by 2022, 90% of all apps will feature microservices architectures that improve the ability to design, debug, update, and leverage third-party code.[1]

We assume that you're well versed in microservices design principles, applications, and benefits. If you're new to microservices and have never been (or are only slightly) involved in development projects, we recommend that you read a book on microservices first, such as *Spring Microservices in Action* by John Carnell (Manning, 2017). *Microservices Patterns* by Chris Richardson (Manning, 2018) and *Microservices in Action* by Morgan Bruce and Paulo A. Pereira (Manning, 2018) are two other good books on the subject. *Microservices for the Enterprise: Designing, Developing, and Deploying* by Prabath Siriwardena (a coauthor of this book) and Kasun Indrasiri (Apress, 2018) is another beginner's book on microservices.

In this book, we focus on *microservices security*. When you make the decision to go ahead with microservices architecture to build all your critical business operations, security is of topmost importance. A security breach could result in many unpleasant outcomes, from losing customer confidence to bankruptcy. Emphasis on security today is higher than at any time in the past. Microservices are becoming key enablers of digital transformation, so microservices security must be consciously planned, designed, and implemented.

This book introduces you to the key fundamentals, security principles, and best practices involved in securing microservices. We'll be using industry-leading open source tools along with Java code samples developed with Spring Boot for demonstrations. You may pick better, competitive tools later in your production environment, of course.

This book will give you a good understanding of how to implement microservices security concepts in real life, even if you're not a Java developer. If you're familiar with any object-oriented programming language (such as C++ or C#) and understand basic programming constructs well, you'll still enjoy reading the book, even though its samples are in Java. Then again, security is a broader topic. It's a discipline with multiple subdisciplines. In this book, we mostly focus on application developers and architects who worry about managing access to their microservices. Access management itself is another broader subdiscipline of the larger security discipline. We do not focus on pen testing, developing threat models, firewalls, system-level configurations to harden security, and so on.

---

[1] You can read more about IDC's predictions for 2019 and beyond at https://www.forbes.com/sites/louiscolumbus/2018/11/04/idc-top-10-predictions-for-worldwide-it-2019.

1.1 *How security works in a monolithic application*

A monolithic application has few entry points. An *entry point* for an application is analogous to a door in a building. Just as a door lets you into a building (possibly after security screening), an application entry point lets your requests in.

Think about a web application (see figure 1.1) running on the default HTTP port 80 on a server carrying the IP address 192.168.0.1. Port 80 on server 192.168.0.1 is an entry point to that web application. If the same web application accepts HTTPS requests on the same server on port 443, you have another entry point. When you have more entry points, you have more places to worry about securing. (You need to deploy more soldiers when you have a longer border to protect, for example, or to build a wall that closes all entry points.) The more entry points to an application, the broader the attack surface is.

Most monolithic applications have only a couple of entry points. Not every component of a monolithic application is exposed to the outside world and accepts requests directly.

In a typical Java Platform, Enterprise Edition (Java EE) web application such as the one in figure 1.1, all requests are scanned for security at the application level by a servlet filter.[2] This security screening checks whether the current request is associated with a valid web session and, if not, challenges the requesting party to authenticate first.

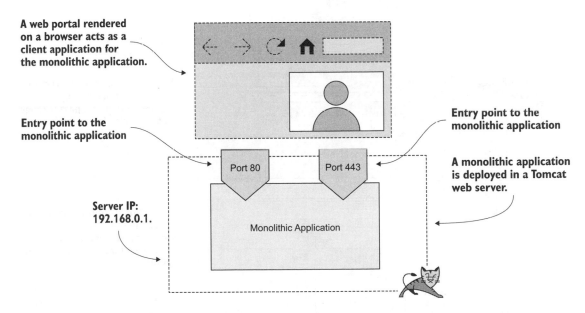

A web portal rendered on a browser acts as a client application for the monolithic application.

Entry point to the monolithic application

Entry point to the monolithic application

A monolithic application is deployed in a Tomcat web server.

Server IP: 192.168.0.1.

Port 80   Port 443

Monolithic Application

Figure 1.1   A monolithic application typically has few entry points. Here, there are two: ports 80 and 443.

---

[2]   If you aren't familiar with servlet filters, think of them as interceptors running in the same process with the web application, intercepting all the requests to the web application.

Further access-control checks may validate that the requesting party has the necessary permissions to do what they intend to do. The servlet filter (the interceptor) carries out such checks centrally to make sure that only legitimate requests are dispatched to the corresponding components. Internal components need not worry about the legitimacy of the requests; they can rightly assume that if a request lands there, all the security checks have already been done.

In case those components need to know who the requesting party (or user) is or to find other information related to the requesting party, such information can be retrieved from the web session, which is shared among all the components (see figure 1.2). The servlet filter injects the requesting-party information into the web session during the initial screening process, after completing authentication and authorization.

Once a request is inside the application layer, you don't need to worry about security when one component talks to another. When the Order Processing component talks to the Inventory component, for example, you don't necessarily need to enforce any additional security checks (but, of course, you can if you need to enforce more granular access-control checks at the component level). These are in-process calls and in most cases are hard for a third party to intercept.

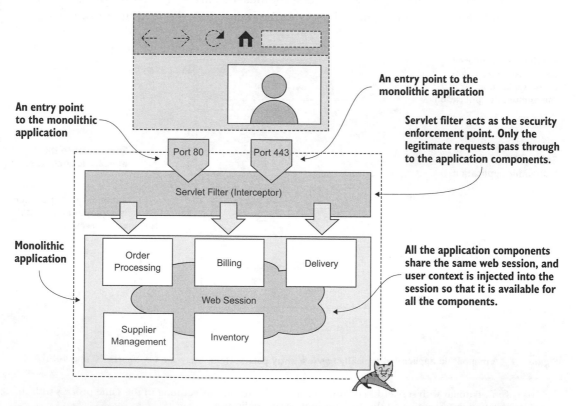

Figure 1.2   Multiple entry points (ports 80 and 443) are funneled to a single servlet filter. The filter acts as a centralized policy enforcement point.

In most monolithic applications, security is enforced centrally, and individual components need not worry about carrying out additional checks unless there is a desperate requirement to do so. As a result, the security model of a monolithic application is much more straightforward than that of an application built around microservices architecture.

1.2 Challenges of securing microservices

Mostly because of the inherent nature of microservices architecture, security is challenging. In this section, we discuss the challenges of securing microservices without discussing in detail how to overcome them. In the rest of the book, we discuss multiple ways to address these challenges.

1.2.1 The broader the attack surface, the higher the risk of attack

In a monolithic application, communication among internal components happens within a single process—in a Java application, for example, within the same Java Virtual Machine (JVM). Under microservices architecture, those internal components are designed as separate, independent microservices, and those in-process calls among internal components become remote calls. Also, each microservice now independently accepts requests or has its own entry points (see figure 1.3).

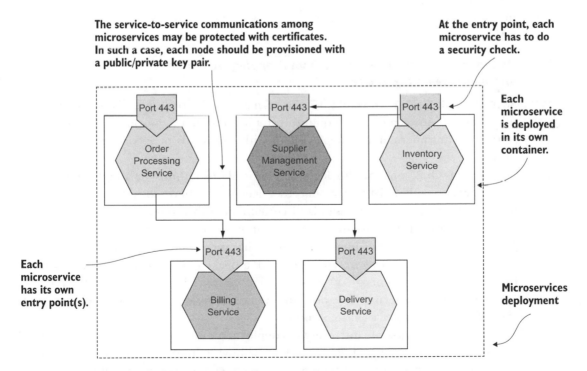

Figure 1.3 As opposed to a monolithic application with few entry points, a microservices-based application has many entry points that all must be secured.

Instead of a couple of entry points, as in a monolithic application, now you have a large number of entry points. As the number of entry points to the system increases, the attack surface broadens too. This situation is one of the fundamental challenges in building a security design for microservices. Each entry point to each microservice must be protected with equal strength. The security of a system is no stronger than the strength of its weakest link.

1.2.2   *Distributed security screening may result in poor performance*

Unlike in a monolithic application, each microservice in a microservices deployment has to carry out independent security screening. From the viewpoint of a monolithic application, in which the security screening is done once and the request is dispatched to the corresponding component, having multiple security screenings at the entry point of each microservice seems redundant. Also, while validating requests at each microservice, you may need to connect to a remote security token service (STS). These repetitive, distributed security checks and remote connections could contribute heavily to latency and considerably degrade the performance of the system.

Some do work around this by simply trusting the network and avoiding security checks at each and every microservice. Over time, trust-the-network has become an antipattern, and the industry is moving toward zero-trust networking principles. With zero-trust networking principles, you carry out security much closer to each resource in your network. Any microservices security design must take overall performance into consideration and must take precautions to address any drawbacks.

1.2.3   *Deployment complexities make bootstrapping trust among microservices a nightmare*

Security aside, how hard would it be to manage 10, 15, or hundreds of independent microservices instead of one monolithic application in a deployment? We have even started seeing microservices deployments with thousands of services talking to each other.

Capital One, one of the leading financial institutions in the United States, announced in July 2019 that its microservices deployment consists of thousands of microservices on several thousands of containers, with thousands of Amazon Elastic Compute Cloud (EC2) instances. Monzo, another financial institution based in the United Kingdom, recently mentioned that it has more than 1,500 services running in its microservices deployment. Jack Kleeman, a backend engineer at Monzo, explains in a blog (http://mng.bz/gyAx) how they built network isolation for 1,500 services to make Monzo more secure. The bottom line is, large-scale microservices deployments with thousands of services have become a reality.

Managing a large-scale microservices deployment with thousands of services would be extremely challenging if you didn't know how to automate. If the microservices concept had popped up at a time when the concept of containers didn't exist, few people or organizations would have the guts to adopt microservices. Fortunately, things didn't happen that way, and that's why we believe that microservices and containers are a match made in heaven. If you're new to containers or don't know what Docker is, think of containers as a way to make software distribution and deployment hassle-free. Microservices and containers (Docker) were born at the right time to complement each other nicely. We talk about containers and Docker later in the book, in chapter 10.

Does the deployment complexity of microservices architecture make security more challenging? We're not going to delve deep into the details here, but consider one simple example. Service-to-service communication happens among multiple microservices. Each of these communication channels must be protected. You have many options (which we discuss in detail in chapters 6 and 7), but suppose that you use certificates.

Now each microservice must be provisioned with a certificate (and the corresponding private key), which it will use to authenticate itself to another microservice during service-to-service interactions. The recipient microservice must know how to validate the certificate associated with the calling microservice. Therefore, you need a way to bootstrap trust between microservices. Also, you need to be able to revoke certificates (in case the corresponding private key gets compromised) and rotate certificates (change the certificates periodically to minimize any risks in losing the keys unknowingly). These tasks are cumbersome, and unless you find a way to automate them, they'll be tedious in a microservices deployment.

1.2.4 *Requests spanning multiple microservices are harder to trace*

Observability is a measure of what you can infer about the internal state of a system based on its external outputs. Logs, metrics, and traces are known as the *three pillars of observability.*

A *log* can be any event you record that corresponds to a given service. A log, for example, can be an audit trail that says that the Order Processing microservice accessed the Inventory microservice to update the inventory on April 15th, 2020, at 10:15.12 p.m. on behalf of the user Peter.

Aggregating a set of logs can produce *metrics.* In a way, metrics reflect the state of the system. In terms of security, the average invalid access requests per hour is a metric, for example. A high number probably indicates that the system is under attack or the first-level defense is weak. You can configure alerts based on metrics. If the number of invalid access attempts for a given microservice goes beyond a preset threshold value, the system can trigger an alert.

Traces are also based on logs but provide a different perspective of the system. Tracing helps you track a request from the point where it enters the system to the point where it leaves the system. This process becomes challenging in a microservices deployment. Unlike in a monolithic application, a request to a microservices deployment may enter the system via one microservice and span multiple microservices before it leaves the system.

Correlating requests among microservices is challenging, and you have to rely on distributed tracing systems like Jaeger and Zipkin. In chapter 5, we discuss how to use Prometheus and Grafana to monitor all the requests coming to a microservices deployment.

1.2.5   *Immutability of containers challenges how you maintain service credentials and access-control policies*

A server that doesn't change its state after it spins up is called an *immutable server*. The most popular deployment pattern for microservices is container based. (We use the terms *container* and *Docker* interchangeably in this book, and in this context, both terms have the same meaning.) Each microservice runs in its own container, and as a best practice, the container has to be an immutable server.[3] In other words, after the container has spun up, it shouldn't change any of the files in its filesystem or maintain any runtime state within the container itself.

The whole purpose of expecting servers to be immutable in a microservices deployment is to make deployment clean and simple. At any point, you can kill a running container and create a new one with the base configuration without worrying about runtime data. If the load on a microservice is getting high, for example, you need more server instances to scale horizontally. Because none of the running server instances maintains any runtime state, you can simply spin up a new container to share the load.

What impact does immutability have on security, and why do immutable servers make microservices security challenging? In microservices security architecture, a microservice itself becomes a security enforcement point.[4] As a result, you need to maintain a list of allowed clients (probably other microservices) that can access the given microservice, and you need a set of access-control policies.

These lists aren't static; both the allowed clients and access-control policies get updated. With an immutable server, you can't maintain such updates in the server's filesystem. You need a way to get all the updated policies from some sort of policy administration endpoint at server bootup and then update them dynamically in memory, following a push or pull model. In the *push model*, the policy administration endpoint pushes policy updates to the interested microservices (or security enforcement points). In the *pull model*, each microservice has to poll the policy administration endpoint periodically for policy updates. Section 1.5.2 explains in detail service-level authorization.

Each microservice also has to maintain its own credentials, such as certificates. For better security, these credentials need to be rotated periodically. It's fine to keep them

---

[3] In "What Is Mutable vs. Immutable Infrastructure," Armon Dadger explains the trade-offs between the two infrastructure types: http://mng.bz/90mr.

[4] This isn't 100% precise, and we discuss why in chapter 12. In many cases, it's not the microservice itself that becomes the security enforcement point, but another proxy, which is deployed collocated with the microservice itself. Still, the argument we present here related to immutability is valid.

with the microservice itself (in the container filesystem), but you should have a way to inject them into the microservice at the time it boots up. With immutable servers, maybe this process can be part of the continuous delivery pipeline, without baking the credentials into the microservice itself.

1.2.6 *The distributed nature of microservices makes sharing user context harder*

In a monolithic application, all internal components share the same web session, and anything related to the requesting party (or user) is retrieved from it. In microservices architecture, you don't enjoy that luxury. Nothing is shared among microservices (or only a very limited set of resources), and the user context has to be passed explicitly from one microservice to another. The challenge is to build trust between two microservices so that the receiving microservice accepts the user context passed from the calling microservice. You need a way to verify that the user context passed among microservices isn't deliberately modified.[5]

Using a JSON Web Token (JWT) is one popular way to share user context among microservices; we explore this technique in chapter 7. For now, you can think of a JWT as a JSON message that helps carry a set of user attributes from one microservice to another in a cryptographically safe manner.

1.2.7 *Polyglot architecture demands more security expertise on each development team*

In a microservices deployment, services talk to one another over the network. They depend not on each service's implementation, but on the service interface. This situation permits each microservice to pick its own programming language and the technology stack for implementation. In a multiteam environment, in which each team develops its own set of microservices, each team has the flexibility to pick the optimal technology stack for its requirements. This architecture, which enables the various components in a system to pick the technology stack that is best for them, is known as a *polyglot architecture*.

A polyglot architecture makes security challenging. Because different teams use different technology stacks for development, each team has to have its own security experts. These experts should take responsibility for defining security best practices and guidelines, research security tools for each stack for static code analysis and dynamic testing, and integrate those tools into the build process. The responsibilities of a centralized, organization-wide security team are now distributed among different teams. In most cases, organizations use a hybrid approach, with a centralized security team and security-focused engineers on each team who build microservices.

---

[5] User context carries information related to the user who invokes a microservice. This user can be a human user or a system, and the information related to the user can be a name, email address, or any other user attribute.

1.3   Key security fundamentals

Adhering to fundamentals is important in any security design. There's no perfect or unbreakable security. How much you should worry about security isn't only a technical decision, but also an economic decision. There's no point in having a burglar-alarm system to secure an empty garage, for example. The level of security you need depends on the assets you intend to protect. The security design of an e-commerce application could be different from that of a financial application.

In any case, adhering to security fundamentals is important. Even if you don't foresee some security threats, following the fundamentals helps you protect your system against such threats. In this section, we walk you through key security fundamentals and show you how they're related to microservices security.

1.3.1   Authentication protects your system against spoofing

Authentication is the process of identifying the requesting party to protect your system against spoofing. The requesting party can be a system (a microservice) or a system requesting access on behalf of a human user or another system (see figure 1.4). It's rather unlikely that a human user will access a microservice directly, though. Before creating a security design for a given system, you need to identify the audience. The authentication method you pick is based on the audience.

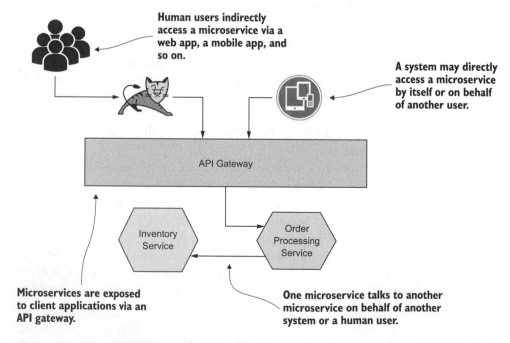

Figure 1.4   A system (for example, a web/mobile application), just by being itself or on behalf of a human user or another system, can access microservices via an API gateway.

If you're worried about a system accessing a microservice on behalf of a human user, you need to think about how to authenticate the system as well as the human user. In practice, this can be a web application, which is accessing a microservice, on behalf of a human user who logs into the web application. In these kinds of delegated use cases, in which a system requests access on behalf of another system or a human user, OAuth 2.0 is the de facto standard for security. We discuss OAuth 2.0 in detail in appendix A.

To authenticate the human user to a system (for example, a web application), you could request the username and password with another factor for multifactor authentication (MFA). Whether MFA is required is mostly a business decision, based on how critical your business assets are or how sensitive the data you want to share with users. The most popular form of MFA is the one-time passcode (OTP) sent over SMS. Even though it's not the best method in terms of security, it's the most usable form of MFA, mostly because a large portion of the world population has access to mobile phones (which don't necessarily need to be smartphones). MFA helps reduce account breaches by almost 99.99%.[6] Much stronger forms of MFA include biometrics, certificates, and Fast Identity Online (FIDO).

You have multiple ways to authenticate a system. The most popular options are certificates and JWTs. We discuss both these options in detail, with a set of examples, in chapters 6 and 7.

1.3.2 Integrity protects your system from data tampering

When you transfer data from your client application to a microservice or from one microservice to another microservice—depending on the strength of the communication channel you pick—an intruder could intercept the communication and change the data for their advantage. If the channel carries data corresponding to an order, for example, the intruder could change its shipping address to their own. Systems protected for integrity don't ignore this possibility; they introduce measures so that if a message is altered, the recipient can detect and discard the request.

The most common way to protect a message for integrity is to sign it. Any data in transit over a communication channel protected with Transport Layer Security (TLS), for example, is protected for integrity. If you use HTTPS for communications among microservices (that communication is, in fact, HTTP over TLS), your messages are protected for integrity while in transit.

Along with the data in transit, the data at rest must be protected for integrity. Of all your business data, audit trails matter most for integrity checks. An intruder who gets access to your system would be happiest if they could modify your audit trails to wipe out any evidence. In a microservices deployment based on containers, audit logs aren't kept at each node that runs the microservice; they're published in some kind of a distributed tracing system like Jaeger or Zipkin. You need to make sure that the data maintained in those systems is protected for integrity.

---

[6] See "Basics and Black Magic: Defending Against Current and Emerging Threats" by Alex Weinert at www .youtube.com/watch?v=Nmkeg0wPRGE for more details.

One way is to periodically calculate the message digests of audit trails, encrypt them, and store them securely. In a research paper, Gopalan Sivathanu, Charles P. Wright, and Erez Zadok of Stony Brook University highlight the causes of integrity violations in storage and present a survey of available integrity assurance techniques.[7] The paper explains several interesting applications of storage integrity checking; apart from security it also discusses implementation issues associated with those techniques.

1.3.3   *Nonrepudiation: Do it once, and you own it forever*

Nonrepudiation is an important aspect of information security that prevents you from denying anything you've done or committed. Consider a real-world example. When you lease an apartment, you agree to terms and conditions with the leasing company. If you leave the apartment before the end of the lease, you're obliged to pay the rent for the remaining period or find another tenant to sublease the apartment. All the terms are in the leasing agreement, which you accept by signing it. After you sign it, you can't dispute the terms and conditions to which you agreed. That's nonrepudiation in the real world. It creates a legal obligation. Even in the digital world, a signature helps you achieve nonrepudiation; in this case, you use a digital signature.

In an e-commerce application, for example, after a customer places an order, the Order Processing microservice has to talk to the Inventory microservice to update inventory. If this transaction is protected for nonrepudiation, the Order Processing microservice can't later deny that it updated inventory. If the Order Processing microservice signs a transaction with its private key, it can't deny later that the transaction was initiated from that microservice. With a digital signature, only the owner of the corresponding private key can generate the same signature; so make sure that you never lose the key!

Validating the signature alone doesn't help you achieve nonrepudiation, however. You also need to make sure that you record transactions along with the timestamp and the signature—and maintain those records for a considerable amount of time. In case the initiator disputes a transaction later, you'll have it in your records.

1.3.4   *Confidentiality protects your systems from unintended information disclosure*

When you send order data from a client application to the Order Processing microservice, you expect that no party can view the data other than the Order Processing microservice itself. But based on the strength of the communication channel you pick, an intruder can intercept the communication and get hold of the data. Along with the data in transit, the data at rest needs to be protected for confidentiality (see figure 1.5). An intruder who gets access to your data storage or backups has direct access to all your business-critical data unless you've protected it for confidentiality.

---

[7] See "Ensuring Data Integrity in Storage: Techniques and Applications" at http://mng.bz/eQVP.

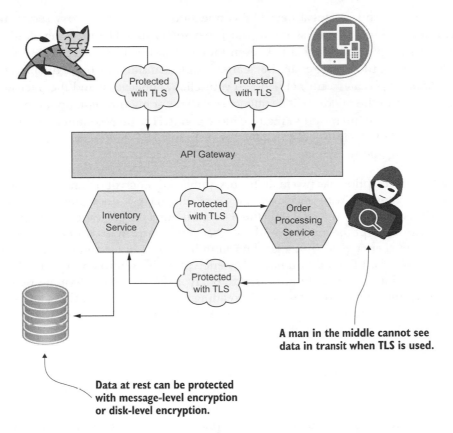

Figure 1.5 To protect a system for confidentiality, both the data in transit and at rest must be protected. The data in transit can be protected with TLS, and data at rest can be protected by encryption.

DATA IN TRANSIT

Encryption helps you achieve confidentiality. A cryptographic operation makes sure that the encrypted data is visible only to the intended recipient. TLS is the most popular way of protecting data for confidentiality in transit. If one microservice talks to another over HTTPS, you're using TLS underneath, and only the recipient microservice will be able to view the data in cleartext.

Then again, the protection provided by TLS is point to point. At the point where the TLS connection terminates, the security ends. If your client application connects to a microservice over a proxy server, your first TLS connection terminates at the proxy server, and a new TLS connection is established between the proxy server and the microservice. The risk is that anyone who has access to the proxy server can log the messages in cleartext as soon as the data leaves the first connection.

Most proxy servers support two modes of operation with respect to TLS: TLS bridging and TLS tunneling. *TLS bridging* terminates the first TLS connection at the proxy server, and creates a new TLS connection between the proxy server and the next destination of the message. If your proxy server uses TLS bridging, don't trust it and possibly put your data at risk, even though you use TLS (or HTTPS). If you use TLS bridging, the messages are in cleartext while transiting through the proxy server. *TLS tunneling* creates a tunnel between your client application and the microservices, and no one in the middle will be able to see what's going through, not even the proxy server. If you are interested in reading more about TLS, we recommend having a look at *SSL and TLS: Designing and Building Secure Systems* by Eric Rescorla (Addison-Wesley Professional, 2000).

> **NOTE** Encryption has two main flavors: public-key encryption and symmetric-key encryption. With *public-key encryption,* the data is encrypted using the recipient's public key, and only the party who owns the corresponding private key can decrypt the message and see what's in it. With *symmetric-key encryption,* the data is encrypted with a key known to both the sender and the recipient. TLS uses both flavors. Symmetric-key encryption is used to encrypt the data, while public-key encryption is used to encrypt the key used in symmetric-key encryption. If you are interested in reading more about encryption and cryptography, we recommend having a look at *Real-World Cryptography* by David Wong (Manning, to be published in 2021).

DATA AT REST

Encryption should also apply to data at rest to protect it from intruders who get direct access to the system. This data can be credentials for other systems stored in the filesystem or business-critical data stored in a database. Most database management systems provide features for automatic encryption, and disk-level encryption features are available at the operating-system level. Application-level encryption is another option, in which the application itself encrypts the data before passing it over to the filesystem or to a database.

Of all these options, the one that best fits your application depends on the criticality of your business operations. Also keep in mind that encryption is a resource-intensive operation that would have considerable impact on your application's performance unless you find the optimal solution.[8]

1.3.5 *Availability: Keep the system running, no matter what*

The whole point of building any kind of a system is to make it available to its users. Every minute (or even second) that the system is down, your business loses money. Amazon was down for 20 minutes in March 2016, and the estimated revenue loss was $3.75 million. In January 2017, more than 170 Delta Airlines flights were canceled because of a system outage, which resulted in an estimated loss of $8.5 million.

---

[8] See "Performance Evaluation of Encryption Techniques for Confidentiality of Very Large Databases" by Malik Sikander et al. at www.ijcte.org/papers/410-G1188.pdf.

It's not only the security design of a system that you need to worry about to keep a system up and running, but also the overall architecture. A bug in the core functionality of an application can take the entire system down. To some extent, these kinds of situations are addressed in the core design principles of microservices architecture. Unlike in monolithic applications, in a microservices deployment, the entire system won't go down if a bug is found in one component or microservice. Only that microservice will go down; the rest should be able to function.

Of all the factors that can take a system down, security has a key role to play in making a system constantly available to its legitimate stakeholders. In a microservices deployment, with many entry points (which may be exposed to the internet), an attacker can execute a denial-of-service (DoS) or a distributed denial-of-service (DDoS) attack and take the system down.

Defenses against such attacks can be built on different levels. On the application level, the best thing you could do is reject a message (or a request) as soon as you find that it's not legitimate. Having layered security architecture helps you design each layer to take care of different types of attacks and reject an attacker at the outermost layer.

As shown in figure 1.6, any request to a microservice first has to come through the *API gateway*. The API gateway centrally enforces security for all the requests entering the microservices deployment, including authentication, authorization, throttling, and message content validation for known security threats. We get into the details of each topic in chapters 3, 4, and 5.

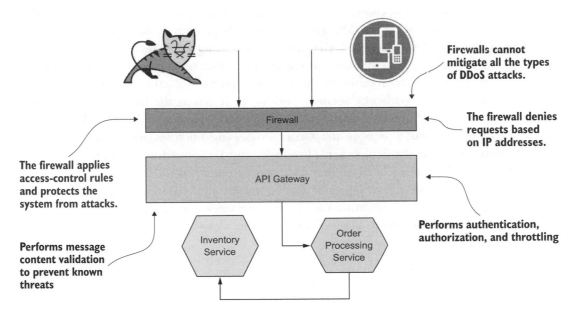

Figure 1.6 Multiple security enforcement points at multiple layers help improve the level of security of a microservices deployment.

The network perimeter level is where you should have the best defense against DoS/DDoS attacks. A firewall is one option; it runs at the edge of the network and can be used to keep malicious users away. But firewalls can't protect you completely from a DDoS attack. Specialized vendors provide DDoS prevention solutions for use outside corporate firewalls. You need to worry about those solutions only if you expose your system to the internet. Also, all the DDoS protection measures you take at the edge aren't specific to microservices. Any endpoint that's exposed to the internet must be protected from DoS/DDoS attacks.

1.3.6 Authorization: Nothing more than you're supposed to do

Authentication helps you learn about the user or the requesting party. *Authorization* determines the actions that an authenticated user can perform on the system. In an e-commerce application, for example, any customer who logs into the system can place an order, but only the inventory managers can update the inventory.

In a typical microservices deployment, authorization can happen at the edge (the entry point to the microservices deployment, which could be intercepted by a gateway) and at each service level. In section 1.4.3, we discuss how authorization policies are enforced at the edge and your options for enforcing authorization policies in service-to-service communication at the service level.

1.4 Edge security

In a typical microservices deployment, microservices are not exposed directly to client applications. In most cases, microservices are behind a set of APIs that is exposed to the outside world via an API gateway. The API gateway is the entry point to the microservices deployment, which screens all incoming messages for security.

Figure 1.7 depicts a microservices deployment that resembles Netflix's, in which all the microservices are fronted by the Zuul API gateway.[9] Zuul provides dynamic routing, monitoring, resiliency, security, and more. It acts as the front door to Netflix's server infrastructure, handling traffic from Netflix users around the world. In figure 1.7, Zuul is used to expose the Order Processing microservice via an API. Other microservices in the deployment, Inventory and Delivery, don't need to be exposed from the API gateway because they don't need to be invoked by external applications. A typical microservices deployment can have a set of microservices that external applications can access, and another set of microservices that external applications don't need to access; only the first set of microservices is exposed to the outside world via an API gateway.

---

[9] Zuul (https://github.com/Netflix/zuul) is a gateway service that provides dynamic routing, monitoring, resiliency, security, and more.

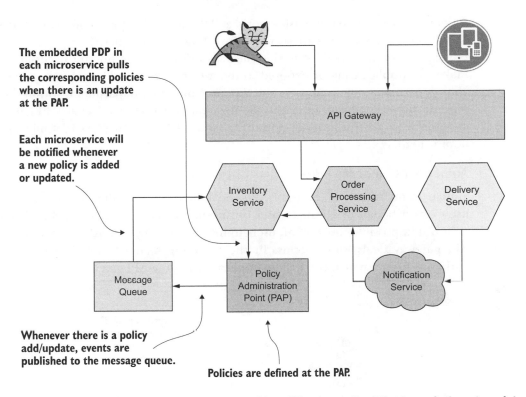

The embedded PDP in each microservice pulls the corresponding policies when there is an update at the PAP.

Each microservice will be notified whenever a new policy is added or updated.

Whenever there is a policy add/update, events are published to the message queue.

Policies are defined at the PAP.

Figure 1.7   A typical microservices deployment with an API gateway: the API gateway is the entry point, which screens all incoming messages for security.

1.4.1   *The role of an API gateway in a microservices deployment*

Over time, APIs have become the public face of many companies. We're not exaggerating by saying that a company without an API is like a computer without the internet. If you're a developer, you surely know how life would look with no internet!

APIs have also become many companies' main revenue-generation channel. At Expedia, for example, 90% of revenue comes through APIs; at Salesforce, APIs account for 50% of revenue; and at eBay, APIs account for 60% of revenue.[10] Netflix is another company that has heavily invested in APIs. Netflix accounts for a considerable percentage of all internet traffic in North America and also globally, all of which comes through Netflix APIs.

APIs and microservices go hand in hand. Most of the time, a microservice that needs to be accessed by a client application is exposed as an API via an API gateway. The key role of the API gateway in a microservices deployment is to expose a selected

---

[10] See "The Strategic Value of APIs" by Bala Iyer and Mohan Subramaniam at https://hbr.org/2015/01/the -strategic-value-of-apis.

set of microservices to the outside world as APIs and build quality-of-service (QoS) features. These QoS features are security, throttling, and analytics.

Exposing a microservice to the outside world, however, doesn't necessarily mean making it public-facing or exposed to the internet. You could expose it only outside your department, allowing users and systems from other departments within the same organizational boundary to talk to the upstream microservices via an API gateway. In chapter 3, we discuss in detail the role that an API gateway plays in a microservices deployment.

1.4.2   *Authentication at the edge*

Similar to microservices, even for APIs the audience is a system that acts on behalf of itself or on behalf of a human user or another system (see figure 1.8). It's unlikely (but not impossible) for human users to interact directly with APIs. In most cases, an API gateway deals with systems. In the following sections, we discuss options for authenticating a system (or a client application) at the API gateway.

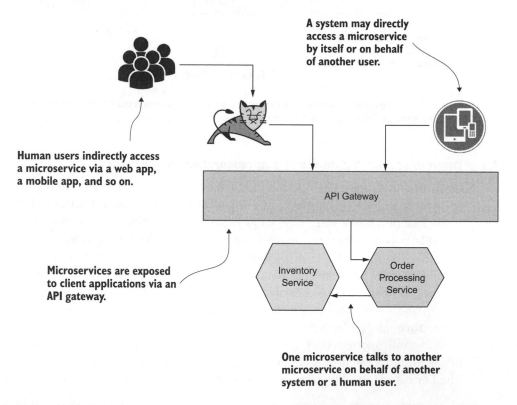

Figure 1.8   Authentication at the edge is enforced by the API gateway. Only the authenticated requests are dispatched to the upstream microservices.

CERTIFICATE-BASED AUTHENTICATION

Certificate-based authentication protects an API at the edge with mutual Transport Layer Security (mTLS). In the Netflix microservices deployment, access to the APIs is protected with certificates. Only a client provisioned with a valid certificate can access Netflix APIs. The role of the API gateway here is to make sure that only clients carrying a trusted certificate can access the APIs and that only those requests are routed to the upstream microservices. In chapter 3, we discuss how to secure APIs at the API gateway with mTLS.

OAUTH 2.0–BASED ACCESS DELEGATION

Anyone can create an application to consume Twitter and Facebook APIs. These can be web or mobile applications (refer to figure 1.8). An application can access an API as itself or on behalf of a human user. *OAuth 2.0*, which is an authorization framework for delegated access control, is the recommended approach for protecting APIs when one system wants to access an API on behalf of another system or a user.

We explain OAuth 2.0 in chapter 3 and appendix A; don't worry if you don't know what it is. Even if you don't know what OAuth 2.0 is, you use it if you use Facebook to log into third-party web applications, because Facebook uses OAuth 2.0 to protect its APIs.

> ### Cambridge Analytica/Facebook scandal
>
> The Cambridge Analytica/Facebook privacy scandal happened in early 2018, when public media accounts reported that British political consulting firm Cambridge Analytica had collected the personal Facebook data of more than 87 million people without their consent for use in targeted political campaign advertising. The data was collected by a third-party application called This Is Your Digital Life, created by researcher Alexander Kogan, and was sold to Cambridge Analytica.
>
> The third-party application acted as a system, accessing the Facebook API secured with OAuth 2.0, on behalf of legitimate Facebook users to collect their personal data. These Facebook users directly or indirectly delegated access to their personal data to this third-party application; users were under the impression they were taking a personality quiz that would be used by a university for academic purposes.

The role of the API gateway is to validate the OAuth 2.0 security tokens that come with each API request. The OAuth 2.0 security token represents both the third-party application and the user who delegated access to the third-party application to access an API on their behalf.

Those who know about OAuth 2.0 probably are raising their eyebrows at seeing it mentioned in a discussion of authentication. We agree that it's not an authentication protocol at the client application end, but at the resource server end, which is the API gateway. We discuss this topic further in appendix A.

1.4.3 Authorization at the edge

In addition to figuring out who the requesting party is during the authentication process, the API gateway could enforce corporatewide access-control policies, which are probably coarse-grained. More fine-grained access-control policies are enforced at the service level by the microservice itself (or by a proxy to the microservice, which we discuss in chapter 12). In section 1.5.2, we discuss service-level authorization in detail.

1.4.4 Passing client/end-user context to upstream microservices

The API gateway terminates all the client connections at the edge, and if everything looks good, it dispatches the requests to the corresponding upstream microservices. But you need a way to protect the communication channels between the gateway and the corresponding microservice, as well as a way to pass the initial client/user context. *User context* carries basic information about the end user, and *client context* carries information about the client application. This information probably could be used by upstream microservices for service-level access control.

As you may have rightly guessed, communication between the API gateway and the microservices is system to system, so you probably can use mTLS authentication to secure the channel. But how do you pass the user context to the upstream microservices? You have a couple of options: pass the user context in an HTTP header, or create a JWT with the user data. The first option is straightforward but raises some trust concerns when the first microservice passes the same user context in an HTTP header to another microservice. The second microservice doesn't have any guarantee that the user context isn't altered. But with JWT, you have an assurance that a man in the middle can't change its content and go undetected, because the issuer of the JWT signs it.

We explain JWT in detail in appendix B; for now, think of it as a signed payload that carries data (in this case, the user context) in a cryptographically safe manner. The gateway or an STS connected to the gateway can create a JWT that includes the user context (and the client context) and passes it to the upstream microservices. The recipient microservices can validate the JWT by verifying the signature with the public key of the STS that issued the JWT.

1.5 Securing service-to-service communication

The frequency of service-to-service communication is higher in a microservices deployment. Communication can occur between two microservices within the same trust domain or between two trust domains. A trust domain represents the ownership. Microservices developed, deployed, and managed together probably fall under one trust domain, or the trust boundaries can be defined at the organizational level by taking many other factors into account.

The security model that you develop to protect service-to-service communication should consider the communication channels that cross trust boundaries, as well as how the actual communication takes place between microservices: synchronously or asynchronously. In most cases, synchronous communication happens over HTTP. Asynchronous communication can happen over any kind of messaging system, such as

RabbitMQ, Kafka, ActiveMQ, or even Amazon Simple Queue Service (SQS). In chapters 6, 7, and 8, we discuss various security models to secure synchronous communication among microservices, and chapter 9 covers securing event-driven microservices.

1.5.1 Service-to-service authentication

You have three common ways to secure communications among services in a microservices deployment: trust the network, mTLS, and JWTs.

TRUST THE NETWORK

The *trust-the-network* approach is an old-school model in which no security is enforced in service-to-service communication; rather, the model relies on network-level security (see figure 1.9). Network-level security must guarantee that no attacker can intercept communications among microservices. Also, each microservice is a trusted system. Whatever it claims about itself and the end user is trusted by other microservices. You should make this deployment choice based on the level of security you expect and the trust you keep on every component in the network.

Another school of thought, known as the *zero-trust network* approach, opposes the trust-the-network approach. The zero-trust network approach assumes that the network is always hostile and untrusted, and it never takes anything for granted. Each

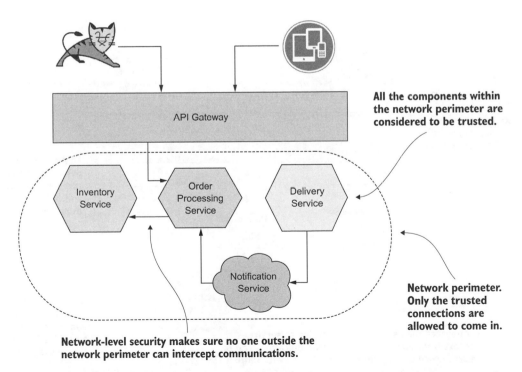

Figure 1.9 **The trusted network makes sure that communications among microservices are secured. No one on a system outside the trusted network can see the traffic flows among microservices in the trusted network.**

request must be authenticated and authorized at each node before being accepted for further processing. If you are interested in reading more about zero-trust networks, we recommend *Zero Trust Networks: Building Secure Systems in Untrusted Networks* by Evan Gilman and Doug Barth (O'Reilly Media, 2017).

MUTUAL TLS

Mutual TLS is another popular way to secure service-to-service communications in a microservices deployment (see figure 1.10). In fact, this method is the most common form of authentication used today. Each microservice in the deployment has to carry a public/private key pair and uses that key pair to authenticate to the recipient microservices via mTLS.

TLS provides confidentiality and integrity for the data in transit, and helps the client identify the service. The client microservice knows which microservice it's going to talk with. But with TLS (one-way), the recipient microservice can't verify the identity of the client microservice. That's where mTLS comes in. mTLS lets each microservice in communication identify the others.

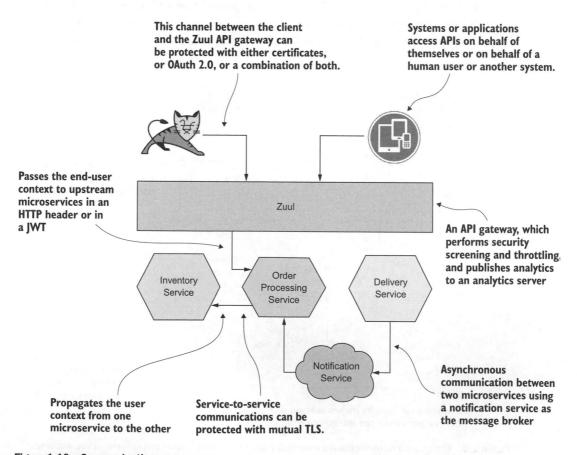

Figure 1.10 Communications among microservices are secured with mTLS. All the microservices that communicate with each other trust the certificate authority (CA) in the deployment.

Challenges in mTLS include bootstrapping trust and provisioning keys/certificates to workloads/microservices, key revocation, key rotation, and key monitoring. We discuss those challenges and possible solutions in detail in chapter 6.

JSON WEB TOKENS

JSON Web Token is the third approach for securing service-to-service communications in a microservices deployment (see figure 1.11). Unlike mTLS, JWT works at the application layer, not at the transport layer. JWT is a container that can carry a set of claims from one place to another.

These claims can be anything, such as end-user attributes (email address, phone number), end-user entitlements (what the user can do), or anything the calling microservice wants to pass to the recipient microservice. The JWT includes these claims and is signed by the issuer of the JWT. The issuer can be an external STS or the calling microservice itself.

The latter example is a self-issued JWT. As in mTLS, if we use self-issued JWT-based authentication, each microservice must have its own key pair, and the corresponding private key is used to sign the JWT. In most cases, JWT-based authentication works over TLS; JWT provides authentication, and TLS provides confidentiality and integrity of data in transit.

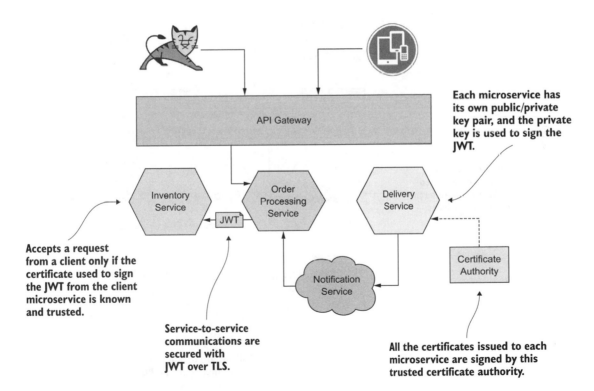

Figure 1.11 Communications among microservices are secured with JWT. Each microservice uses a certificate issued to it by the certificate authority to sign JWTs.

1.5.2   *Service-level authorization*

In a typical microservices deployment, authorization can happen at the edge (with the API gateway), at the service, or in both places. Authorization at the service level gives each service more control to enforce access-control policies in the way it wants. Two approaches are used to enforce authorization at the service level: the centralized policy decision point (PDP) model and the embedded PDP model.

In the *centralized PDP model*, all the access-control policies are defined, stored, and evaluated centrally (see figure 1.12). Each time the service wants to validate a request, it has to talk to an endpoint exposed by the centralized PDP. This method creates a lot of dependency on the PDP and also increases the latency because of the cost of calling the remote PDP endpoint. In some cases, the effect on latency can be prevented by caching policy decisions at the service level, but other than cache expiration time, there's no way to communicate policy update events to the service. In practice, policy updates happen less frequently, and cache expiration may work in most cases.

With *embedded PDPs*, policies are defined centrally but are stored and evaluated at the service level. The challenge with embedded PDPs is how to get policy updates from the centralized policy administration point (PAP).

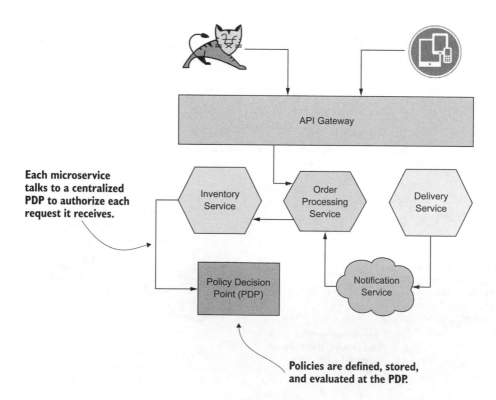

Figure 1.12   Each microservice is connected to a centralized PDP to authorize requests. All the access-control policies are defined, stored, and evaluated centrally.

There are two common methods. One approach is to poll the PAP continuously after a set period and then pull new and updated policies from PAP. The other approach is based on a push mechanism. Whenever a new policy or policy update is available, the PAP publishes an event to a topic (see figure 1.13). Each microservice acts as an event consumer and registers for the events it's interested in. Whenever a microservice receives an event for a registered topic, it pulls the corresponding policy from the PAP and updates the embedded PDP.

Some people believe that both these approaches are overkill, however. They load policies to the embedded PDP only when the server starts up from a shared location. Whenever a new policy or a policy update is available, each service has to restart.

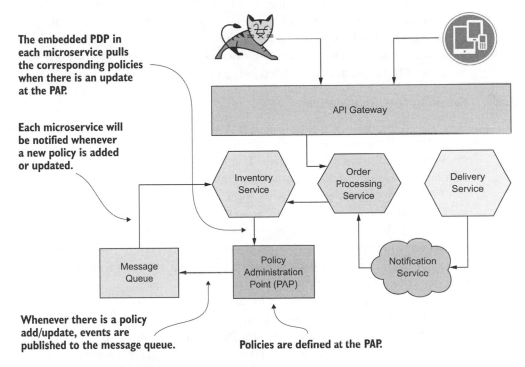

The embedded PDP in each microservice pulls the corresponding policies when there is an update at the PAP.

Each microservice will be notified whenever a new policy is added or updated.

Whenever there is a policy add/update, events are published to the message queue.

Policies are defined at the PAP.

Figure 1.13 Each microservice embeds a PDP. The embedded PDPs pull the policies from the policy administration point upon receiving a notification.

1.5.3 Propagating user context among microservices

When one microservice invokes another microservice, it needs to carry both the end-user identity and the identity of the microservice itself. When one microservice authenticates to another microservice with mTLS or JWT, the identity of the calling microservice can be inferred from the embedded credentials. There are three common ways to pass the end-user context from one microservice to another microservice:

- *Send the user context as an HTTP header.* This technique helps the recipient microservice identify the user but requires the recipient to trust the calling microservice. If the calling microservice wants to fool the recipient microservice, it can do so easily by setting any name it wants as the HTTP header.

- *Use a JWT.* This JWT carries the user context from the calling microservice to the recipient microservice and is also passed in the HTTP request as a header. This approach has no extra value in terms of security over the first approach if the JWT that carries the user context is self-issued. A self-issued JWT is signed by the calling service itself, so it can fool the recipient microservice by adding any name it wants to add.

- *Use a JWT issued by an external STS that is trusted by all the microservices in the deployment.* The user context included in this JWT can't be altered, as alteration would invalidate the signature of the JWT. This is the most secure approach. When you have the JWT from an external STS, the calling microservice can embed that JWT in the new JWT it creates to make a nested JWT (if JWT-based authentication is used among microservices) or pass the original JWT as-is, as an HTTP header (if mTLS is being used among microservices).

1.5.4 *Crossing trust boundaries*

In a typical microservices deployment, you find multiple trust domains. We can define these trust domains by the teams having control and governance over the microservices or organizational boundaries. The purchasing department, for example, might manage all its microservices and create its own trust domain.

In terms of security, when one microservice talks to another microservice, and both microservices are in the same trust domain, each microservice may trust one STS in the same domain or a certificate authority in the same domain. Based on this trust, the recipient microservice can validate a security token sent to it by a calling microservice. Typically, in a single trust domain, all the microservices trust one STS and accept only security tokens issued by that STS.

When one microservice wants to talk to another microservice in a different trust domain, it can take one of two primary approaches. In the first approach (see figure 1.14), the calling microservice (Order Processing) in the `foo` trust domain wants to talk to the recipient microservice (Delivery) of the `bar` trust domain. First, it has to obtain a security token that is trusted by all the microservices in the `bar` trust domain. In other words, it needs to obtain a security token from the STS of the recipient trust domain.

Here's the numbered flow shown in figure 1.14:

- *Step 1*—The API gateway routes the request from the client application to the Order Processing microservice in the `foo` trust domain, along with a JWT signed by the gateway (or by an STS attached to it). Because all the microservices in the `foo` trust domain trust the top-level STS (the one attached to the API gateway), the Order Processing microservice accepts the token as valid. The JWT has an attribute called `aud` that defines the target system of the JWT. In this case, the value of `aud` is set to the Order Processing microservice of the

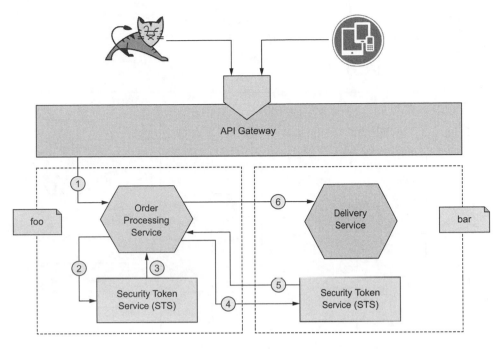

Figure 1.14   Cross-domain security between two trust domains behind a single trusted API gateway (and an STS). Each trust domain has its own STS.

foo trust domain. Ideally, if the Order Processing microservice receives a JWT with a different aud value, it must reject that JWT, even if its signature is valid. We discuss JWT in detail in appendix B.

- *Step 2*—The Order Processing microservice passes the original JWT that it got from the gateway (or STS at the top level) to the STS at the foo trust domain. Once again, the foo STS has to validate the aud value in the JWT it gets. If it cannot identify the audience of the token, the foo STS must reject it.
- *Step 3*—The foo STS returns a new JWT, which is signed by it and has an aud value targeting the STS in the bar trust domain.
- *Steps 4 and 5*—The Order Processing microservice accesses the STS of the bar trust domain and exchanges the JWT from step 3 to a new JWT signed by the STS of the bar trust domain, with an aud value targeting the Delivery microservice.
- *Step 6*—The Order Processing microservice accesses the Delivery microservice with the JWT obtained from step 5. Because the STS of the bar domain signs this JWT and has a matching aud value, the Delivery microservice will accept the token.

In the second approach, the Order Processing microservice from the foo trust domain doesn't talk directly to the Delivery microservice of the bar trust domain.

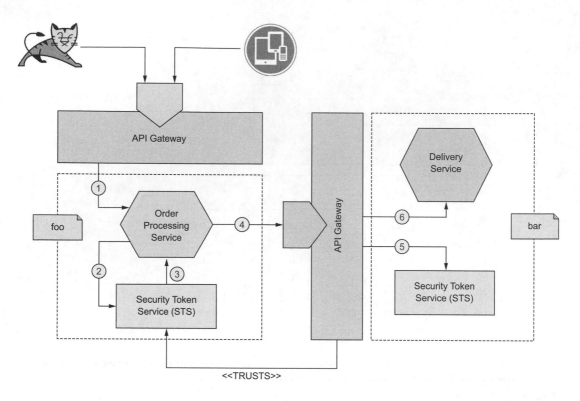

Figure 1.15   Cross-domain security between two trust domains behind two API gateways (and STSs)

Each trust domain has its own API gateway, and communication among microservices happens via the gateways (see figure 1.15).

Here's the numbered flow shown in figure 1.15:

- *Step 1*—The API gateway of the foo trust domain routes the request from the client application to the Order Processing microservice, along with a JWT signed by the gateway (or the foo STS, which is attached to the foo API gateway). Because all the microservices in the foo trust domain trust the foo STS, the Order Processing microservice accepts the token as valid.

- *Step 2*—The Order Processing microservice passes the original JWT that it got from the gateway (or the foo STS) to its own STS (which is also the foo STS).

- *Step 3*—The foo STS returns a new JWT, which is signed by it and has an aud value targeting the API gateway of the bar trust domain.

- *Step 4*—The Order Processing microservice accesses the Delivery microservice of the bar domain with the JWT obtained from step 3. Because the API gateway of the bar domain trusts the foo domain STS, it accepts the JWT as valid. The JWT is signed by the foo STS and has an aud value to match the bar API gateway.

- *Step 5*—The bar API gateway talks to the bar STS to create its own JWT (signed by the bar STS) with an aud value to match the Delivery microservice.

- *Step 6*—The `bar` API gateway forwards the request to the Delivery microservice along with the new JWT issued by the `bar` STS. Because the Delivery microservice trusts its own STS, the token is accepted as valid.

Summary

- Securing microservices is quite challenging with respect to securing a monolithic application, mostly because of the inherent nature of the microservices architecture.
- A microservices security design starts by defining a process to streamline development and engage security-scanning tools to the build system, so that we can discover the code-level vulnerabilities at a very early stage in the development cycle.
- We need to worry about edge security of a microservices deployment and securing communications among microservices.
- Edge security is about authenticating and authorizing requests coming into the microservices deployment from client applications, at the edge, probably with an API gateway.
- Securing communications among microservices is the most challenging part. We discussed multiple techniques in this chapter, and which you choose will depend on many factors, such as the level of security, the type of communication (synchronous or asynchronous), and trust boundaries.

First steps in
securing microservices

This chapter covers

- Developing a microservice in Spring Boot/Java
- Running and testing a Spring Boot/Java microservice with curl
- Securing a microservice at the edge with OAuth 2.0
- Enforcing authorization at the service level with OAuth 2.0 scopes

You build applications as a collection of smaller/modular services or components when you adhere to architectural principles of microservices. A system by itself, or a system on behalf of a human user or another system, can invoke a microservice. In all three cases, we need to properly authenticate and authorize all the requests that reach the microservice. A microservice may also consume one or more other microservices in order to cater to a request. In such cases, it is also necessary to propagate user context (from downstream services or client applications) to upstream microservices.

In this chapter, we explain how the security validation of the incoming requests happens, and in chapter 3, we discuss how to propagate the user context to upstream microservices. The focus of this chapter is to get you started with a straight-forward deployment. The design of the samples presented in this chapter is far from a production deployment. As we proceed in the book, we explain how to fill the gaps and how to build a production-grade microservices security design step by step.

2.1 *Building your first microservice*

In this section, we discuss how to write, compile, and run your first microservice using Spring Boot. You will learn some basics about the Spring Boot framework and how you can use it to build microservices. Throughout this book, we use a retail store application as an example, which we build with a set of microservices. In this section, we build our first microservice, which accepts requests to create and manage orders, using Spring Boot (https://spring.io/projects/spring-boot).

Spring Boot is a framework based on the Spring platform that allows you to convert functions written in the Java programming language to network-accessible functions, known as *services* or *APIs*, by decorating your code with a special set of annotations. If you're not familiar with Java, you still have nothing to worry about, because we don't expect you to write code yourself. All the code samples you see in this book are available on GitHub (https://github.com/microservices-security-in-action/samples). As long as you are or have been a software developer, you'll find it easy to understand the code.

Figure 2.1 shows a set of microservices, which are part of the retail store application we are building, with a set of consumer applications. The consumer applications, in fact, are the consumers of the microservices we build.

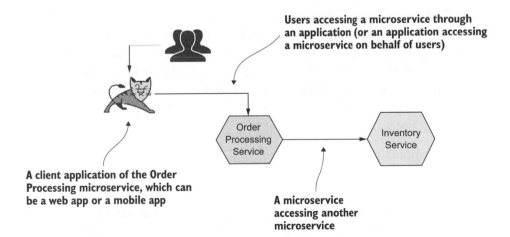

Figure 2.1   In this typical microservices deployment, consumer applications (a web app or a mobile app) access microservices on behalf of their end users, while microservices communicate with each other.

2.1.1   *Downloading and installing the required software*

To build and run samples we use in this chapter and throughout the rest of this book, you need to have a development environment set up with the Java Development Kit (JDK), Apache Maven, the curl command-line tool, and the Git command-line client.

INSTALLING THE JDK

The JDK is required to compile the source code in the samples. You can download the latest JDK from http://mng.bz/OMmo. We used Java version 11 to test all the samples.

INSTALLING APACHE MAVEN

Maven is a project management and comprehension tool that makes it easy to declare third-party (external) dependencies of your Java project required in the compile/build phase. It has various plugins such as the compiler plugin, which compiles your Java source code and produces the runnable artifact (binary). You can download Maven from the Apache website (https://maven.apache.org/download.cgi). Follow the installation instructions at https://maven.apache.org/install.html to install Maven on your operating system. We used Maven version 3.5 to test all the samples. To work with the samples in the book, we do not expect you to know Maven in detail, and where required, the book provides all the necessary commands. If you are interested in learning Maven, we recommend *Mastering Apache Maven 3* (Packt Publishing, 2014) by Prabath Siriwardena, a coauthor of this book.

INSTALLING CURL

Download and install the curl command-line tool from the curl website (https://curl.haxx.se/download.html). You use curl in the book as a client application to access microservices. Most of the operating systems do have curl installed out of the box.

INSTALLING THE GIT COMMAND-LINE TOOL

Download and install the Git command-line client on your computer, based on your operating system. You use the Git client only once to clone our *samples* Git repository. It's not a must to install the Git client; you can also download the complete sample Git repository as a zip file from https://github.com/microservices-security-in-action/samples. When you click the Clone or Download button, you will find a link to download a zip file.

2.1.2   *Clone samples repository*

Once you complete the steps in section 2.1.1, and you'd like to clone the samples Git repository, rather than download it as a zip file, you can run the following command. Once successfully executed, it creates a directory called samples in your local file-system, with all the samples we have for the book:

```
\> git clone \
https://github.com/microservices-security-in-action/samples.git
```

2.1.3 Compiling the Order Processing microservice

Once you complete the preceding steps, it's time to get your hands dirty and run your first microservice. First, open the command-line tool in your operating system, and navigate to the location on your filesystem where you cloned the samples repository; in the rest of the book, we identify this location as [samples]:

```
\> cd [samples]/chapter02/sample01
```

Inside the chapter02/sample01 directory, you'll find the source code corresponding to the Order Processing microservice. From within that directory, execute the following command to build the Order Processing microservice:

```
\> mvn clean install
```

If you run into problems while running the command, old and incompatible dependencies might reside in your local Maven repository. To get rid of such problems, try removing (or renaming) the .m2 directory that resides in your home directory (~/.m2/). The preceding command instructs Maven to compile your source code and produce a runnable artifact known as a Java Archive (JAR) file. Note that you need to have Java and Maven installed to execute this step successfully. If your build is successful, you'll see the message BUILD SUCCESS.

If this is the first time you're using Maven to build a Spring Boot project, Maven downloads all the Spring Boot dependencies from their respective repositories; therefore, an internet connection is required in the build phase. The first-time build is expected to take slightly longer than the next attempts. After the first build, Maven installs all the dependencies in your local filesystem, and that takes the build times down considerably for the subsequent attempts.

If the build is successful, you should see a directory named *target* within your current directory. The target directory should contain a file named com.manning .mss.ch02.sample01-1.0.jar. (Other files will be within the target directory, but you're not interested in them at the moment.) Then run the following command from the chapter02/sample01/ directory to spin up the Order Processing microservice. Here, we use a Maven plugin called spring-boot:

```
\> mvn spring-boot:run
```

If the microservice started successfully, you should see a bunch of messages being printed on the terminal. At the bottom of the message stack, you should see this message:

```
Started OrderApplication in <X> seconds
```

By default, Spring Boot starts the microservice on HTTP port 8080. If you have any other services running on your local machine on port 8080, make sure to stop them;

alternatively, you can change the default port of the Order Processing microservice by changing the value of the `server.port` property as appropriate in the chapter02/sample01/src/main/resources/application.properties file. But, then again, it would be much easier to follow the rest of the samples in the chapter, with minimal changes, if you keep the Order Processing microservice running on the default port.

2.1.4 *Accessing the Order Processing microservice*

By default, Spring Boot runs an embedded Apache Tomcat web server that listens for HTTP requests on port 8080. In this section, you access your microservice using curl as the client application. In case you run the Order Processing microservice on a custom port, make sure to replace the value of the port (8080) in the following command with the one you used. To invoke the microservice, open your command-line client and execute the following `curl` command:

```
\> curl  -v http://localhost:8080/orders \
-H 'Content-Type: application/json' \
--data-binary @- << EOF
{
  "items":[
    {
      "itemCode":"IT0001",
      "quantity":3
    },
    {
      "itemCode":"IT0004",
      "quantity":1
    }
  ],
  "shippingAddress":"No 4, Castro Street, Mountain View, CA, USA"
}
EOF
```

You should see this message on your terminal:

```
{
  "orderId":"1633c9bd-7b9b-455f-965e-91d41331063c",
  "items":[
    {
      "itemCode":"IT0001",
      "quantity":3
    },
    {
      "itemCode":"IT0004",
      "quantity":1
    }
  ],
  "shippingAddress":"No 4, Castro Street, Mountain View, CA, USA"
}
```

If you see this message, you've successfully developed, deployed, and tested your first microservice!

NOTE All samples in this chapter use HTTP (not HTTPS) endpoints to spare you from having to set up proper certificates and to make it possible for you to inspect messages being passed on the wire (network), if required. In production systems, we do not recommend using HTTP for any endpoint. You should expose all the endpoints only over HTTPS. In chapter 6, we discuss how to secure microservices with HTTPS.

When you executed the preceding command, curl initiated an HTTP POST request to the /orders resource located on the server localhost on port 8080 (local machine). The content (payload) of the request represents an order placed for two items to be shipped to a particular address. The Spring Boot server runtime (embedded Tomcat) dispatched this request to the placeOrder function (in the Java code) of your Order Processing microservice, which responded with the message.

2.1.5 *What is inside the source code directory?*

Let's navigate inside the sample01 directory and inspect its contents. You should see a file named pom.xml and a directory named src. Navigate to the src/main/java/com/manning/mss/ch02/sample01/service/ directory. You'll see two files: OrderApplication.java and OrderProcesingService.java.

Before you dig into the contents of these files, let us explain what you're trying to build here. As you'll recall, a *microservice* is a collection of network-accessible functions. In this context, *network-accessible* means that these functions are accessible over HTTP (https://tools.ietf.org/html/rfc2616) through applications such as web browsers and mobile applications, or software such as curl (https://curl.haxx.se/) that's capable of communicating over HTTP. Typically, a function in a microservice is exposed as an action over a REST resource (https://spring.io/guides/tutorials/rest/). Often, a resource represents an object or entity that you intend to inspect or manipulate. When mapped to HTTP, a resource is usually identified by a request URI, and an action is represented by an HTTP method; see sections 5.1.1 and 5.1.2 of the HTTP specification or RFC 2616 (https://tools.ietf.org/html/rfc2616#page-35).

Consider a scenario in which an e-commerce application uses a microservice to retrieve the details of an order. An HTTP request template that maps to that particular function in the microservice looks similar to the following:

```
GET /orders/{orderid}
```

GET is the HTTP method used in this case, since you're performing a data-retrieval operation. /orders/{orderid} is the resource path on the server that hosts the corresponding microservice. This path can be used to uniquely identify an order resource. {orderid} is a variable that needs to be replaced with proper values in the actual HTTP request. Something like GET /orders/d59dbd56-6e8b-4e06-906f-59990ce2e330 would ask the microservice to retrieve details of the order with ID d59dbd56-6e8b-4e06-906f-59990ce2e330.

2.1.6   *Understanding the source code of the microservice*

Now that you have a fair understanding of how to expose a microservice as an HTTP resource, let's look at the code samples to see how to develop a function in Java and use Spring Boot to expose it as an HTTP resource. Use the file browser in your operating system to open the directory located at sample01/src/main/java/com/manning/mss/ch02/sample01/service, and open the OrderProcessingService.java file in a text editor. If you're familiar with Java integrated development environments (IDEs) such as Eclipse, NetBeans, IntelliJ IDEA, or anything similar, you can import the sample as a Maven project to the IDE. The following listing shows what the content of the OrderProcessingService.java file looks like.

Listing 2.1   The content of the OrderProcessingService.java file

Informs the Spring Boot runtime that you're interested in exposing this class as a microservice

Specifies the path under which all the resources of the service exist

Informs the Spring Boot runtime to expose this function as a POST HTTP method

```java
@RestController
@RequestMapping("/orders")
public class OrderProcessingService {

    private Map<String, Order> orders = new HashMap<>();

    @PostMapping
    public ResponseEntity<Order> placeOrder(@RequestBody Order order) {

        System.out.println("Received Order For "
                        + order.getItems().size() + " Items");
        order.getItems().forEach((lineItem) ->
        System.out.println("Item: " + lineItem.getItemCode() +
                        " Quantity: " + lineItem.getQuantity()));

        String orderId = UUID.randomUUID().toString();
        order.setOrderId(orderId);
        orders.put(orderId, order);
        return new ResponseEntity<Order>(order, HttpStatus.CREATED);
    }
}
```

This code is a simple Java class with a function named `placeOrder`. As you may notice, we decorated the class with the `@RestController` annotation to inform the Spring Boot runtime that you're interested in exposing this class as a microservice. The `@RequestMapping` annotation specifies the path under which all the resources of the service exist. We also decorated the `placeOrder` function with the `@Post-Mapping` annotation, which informs the Spring Boot runtime to expose this function as a POST HTTP method (action) on the `/orders` context. The `@RequestBody` annotation says that the payload in the HTTP request is to be assigned to an object of type `Order`.

Another file within the same directory is named OrderApplication.java. Open this file with your text editor and inspect its content, which looks like the following:

```
@SpringBootApplication
public class OrderApplication {
    public static void main(String args[]) {
        SpringApplication.run(OrderApplication.class, args);
    }
}
```

This simple Java class has only the main function. The @SpringBootApplication annotation informs the Spring Boot runtime that this application is a Spring Boot application. It also makes the runtime check for Controller classes (such as the OrderProcessingService class you saw earlier) within the same package of the OrderApplication class. The main function is the function invoked by the JVM when you command it to run the particular Java program. Within the main function, start the Spring Boot application through the run utility function of the Spring-Application class, which resides within the Spring framework.

2.2   Setting up an OAuth 2.0 server

Now that you have your first microservice up and running, we can start getting to the main focus of this book: securing microservices. You'll be using OAuth 2.0 to secure your microservice at the edge.

If you are unfamiliar with OAuth 2.0, we recommend you first go through appendix A, which provides a comprehensive overview of the OAuth 2.0 protocol and how it works. In chapter 3, we discuss in detail why we opted for OAuth2.0 over options such as basic authentication and certificate-based authentication. For now, know that OAuth 2.0 is a clean mechanism for solving the problems related to providing your username and password to an application that you don't trust to access your data.

When combined with JWT, OAuth2.0 can be a highly scalable authentication and authorization mechanism, which is critical when it comes to securing microservices.[1] Those who know about OAuth 2.0 probably are raising their eyebrows at seeing it mentioned as a way of authentication. We agree that it's not an authentication protocol at the client application end, but at the resource server end, which is the microservice.

2.2.1   The interactions with an authorization server

In an OAuth 2.0 flow, the client application, the end user, and the resource server all interact directly with the authorization server, in different phases (see figure 2.2). Before requesting a token from an authorization server, the client applications have to register themselves with it.

---

[1] As you may recall from chapter 1, a JSON Web Token (JWT) is a container that carries different types of assertions or claims from one place to another in a cryptographically safe manner. If you are new to JWT, please check appendix B.

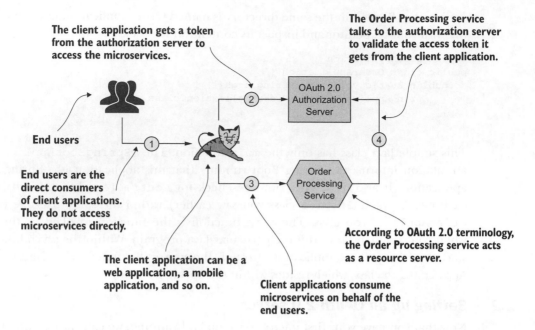

The client application gets a token from the authorization server to access the microservices.

The Order Processing service talks to the authorization server to validate the access token it gets from the client application.

End users

End users are the direct consumers of client applications. They do not access microservices directly.

The client application can be a web application, a mobile application, and so on.

Client applications consume microservices on behalf of the end users.

According to OAuth 2.0 terminology, the Order Processing service acts as a resource server.

Figure 2.2   Actors in an OAuth2.0 flow: in a typical access delegation flow, a client—on behalf of the end user—accesses a resource that is hosted on a resource server by using a token provided by the authorization server.

An authorization server issues tokens only for the client applications it knows. Some authorization servers support Dynamic Client Registration Protocol (https://tools.ietf.org/html/rfc7591), which allows clients to register themselves on the authorization server on the fly or on demand (see figure 2.3).

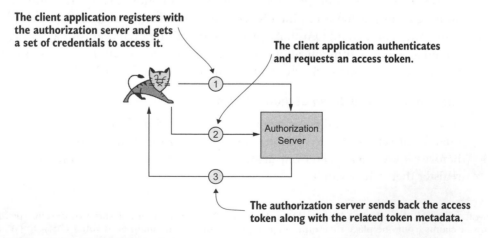

The client application registers with the authorization server and gets a set of credentials to access it.

The client application authenticates and requests an access token.

Authorization Server

The authorization server sends back the access token along with the related token metadata.

Figure 2.3   A client application is requesting an access token from the authorization server. The authorization server issues tokens to only known client applications. A client application must register at the authorization server first.

The Order Processing microservice, which plays the role of the resource server here, would receive the token issued by the authorization server from the client, usually as an HTTP header or as a query parameter when the client makes an HTTP request (see step 1 in figure 2.4). It's recommended that the client communicate with the microservice over HTTPS and send the token in an HTTP header instead of a query parameter. Because query parameters are sent in the URL, those can be recorded in server logs. Hence, anyone who has access to the logs can see this information.

Having TLS to secure the communication (or in other words, the use of HTTPS) between all the entities in an OAuth 2.0 flow is extremely important. The token (access token) that the authorization server issues to access a microservice (or a resource) must be protected like a password. We do not send passwords over plain HTTP and always use HTTPS. Hence we follow the same process when sending access tokens over the wire.

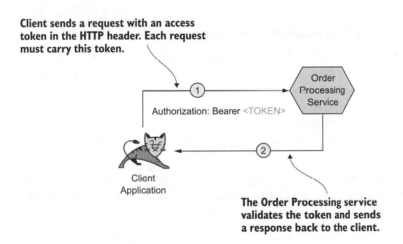

Figure 2.4   A client application is passing the OAuth access token in the HTTP Authorization header to access a resource from the resource server.

Upon receipt of the access token, the Order Processing microservice should validate it against the authorization server before granting access to its resources. An OAuth 2.0 authorization server usually supports the OAuth 2.0 token introspection profile (https://tools.ietf.org/html/rfc7662) or a similar alternative for resource servers to check the validity of an access token (see figure 2.5). If the access token is a self-contained JWT, the resource server can validate it, by itself, without talking to the authorization server. We discuss self-contained JWT in detail in chapter 6.

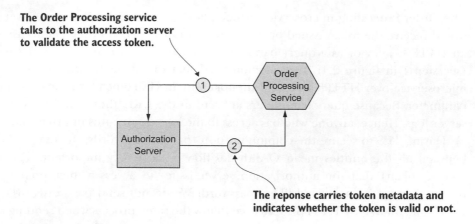

The Order Processing service talks to the authorization server to validate the access token.

The reponse carries token metadata and indicates whether the token is valid or not.

Figure 2.5   The Order Processing microservice (resource server) introspects the access token by talking to the authorization server.

2.2.2   *Running the OAuth 2.0 authorization server*

Many production-grade OAuth 2.0 authorization servers are out there, both proprietary and open source. However, in this chapter, we use a simple authorization server that's capable of issuing access tokens. It is built using Spring Boot. Within the Git repository you cloned earlier, you should find a directory named sample02 under the directory chapter02. There you'll find the source code of the simple OAuth 2.0 authorization server. First, compile and run it; then look into the code to understand what it does.

To compile, use your command-line client to navigate into the chapter02/ sample02 directory. From within that directory, execute the following Maven command to compile and build the runnable artifact:

```
\> mvn clean install
```

If your build is successful, you'll see the message BUILD SUCCESS. You should find a file named com.manning.mss.ch02.sample02-1.0.jar within a directory named target. Execute the following command from within the chapter02/sample02 directory, using your command-line client, to run the OAuth 2.0 authorization server:

```
\> mvn spring-boot:run
```

If you managed to run the server successfully, you should see this message:

```
Started OAuthServerApplication in <X> seconds
```

This message indicates that you successfully started the authorization server. By default, the OAuth 2.0 authorization server runs on HTTP port 8085. If you have any other services running on your local machine, on port 8085, make sure to stop them; alternatively, you can change the default port of the authorization server by changing the value of the `server.port` property as appropriate in the chapter02/sample02/ src/main/resources/application.properties file. But, then again, it would be much easier to follow the rest of the samples in the chapter, with minimal changes, if you keep the authorization server running on the default port.

> **NOTE** The OAuth 2.0 authorization server used in this chapter is running on HTTP, while in a production deployment it must be over HTTPS. In chapter 6, we discuss how to set up an authorization server over HTTPS.

2.2.3 *Getting an access token from the OAuth 2.0 authorization server*

To get an access token from the authorization server, use an HTTP client to make an HTTP request to the server. In the real world, the client application that is accessing the microservice would make this request. You'll be using curl for this purpose as the HTTP client. To request an access token from the authorization server (which runs on port 8085), run the following command, using your command-line client:

```
\> curl -u orderprocessingapp:orderprocessingappsecret \
-H "Content-Type: application/json" \
-d '{"grant_type": "client_credentials", "scope": "read write}' \
http://localhost:8085/oauth/token
```

Take a quick look at this request and try to understand it. You can think of `order-processingapp:orderprocessingappsecret` as the client application's user-name (`orderprocessingapp`) and password (`orderprocessingappsecret`). The only difference is that these credentials belong to an application, not a user. The application being used to request a token needs to bear a unique identifier and a secret that's known by the authorization server. The `-u` flag provided to curl instructs it to create a basic authentication header and send it to the authorization server as part of the HTTP request. Then curl base64-encodes the `orderprocessingapp` `:orderprocessingappsecret` string and creates the `Basic` authentication HTTP header as follows:

```
Authorization: Basic
b3JkZXJwcm9jZXNzaW5nYXBwOm9yZGVycHJvY2Vzc2luZ2FwcHNlY3JldA==
```

The string that follows the `Basic` keyword is the base64-encoded value of `order-processingapp:orderprocessingappsecret`. As you may have noticed, you're sending a `Basic` authentication header to the token endpoint of the OAuth2.0 autho-rization server because the token endpoint is protected with basic authentication (https://tools.ietf.org/html/rfc2617). Because the client application is requesting a token here, the `Basic` authentication header should consist of the credentials of the client application, not of a user. Note that basic authentication here isn't used for securing the resource server (or the microservice); you use OAuth 2.0 for that pur-pose. Basic authentication at this point is used only for obtaining the OAuth token required to access the microservice, from the authorization server.

In chapter 3, we discuss in detail why we chose OAuth 2.0 over protocols such as basic authentication and mTLS to secure your resource server. Even for securing the token endpoint of the OAuth 2.0 authorization server, instead of basic authentication, you can pick whichever authentication mechanism you prefer. For strong authentication, many prefer using certificates.

The parameter `-H "Content-Type: application/json"` in the preceding token request informs the authorization server that the client will be sending a request in JSON format. What follows the `-d` flag is the actual JSON content of the message, which goes in the HTTP body. In the JSON message, the `grant_type` specifies the protocol to be followed in issuing the token. We talk more about OAuth 2.0 grant types in chapter 3. For now, think of a *grant type* as the sequence of steps that the client application and the authorization server follow to issue an access token. In the case of the `client_credentials` grant type, the authorization server validates the `Basic` authentication header and issues an access token if it's valid.

The `scope` declares what actions the application intends to perform with a token. When issuing a token, the authorization server validates whether the requesting application is permitted to obtain the requested scopes and binds them to the token as appropriate. If the application identified by `orderprocessingapp` can perform only read operations, for example, the authorization server issues the corresponding token under the scope `read`. The URL http://localhost:8085/oauth/token is the endpoint of the authorization server that issues access tokens. Your curl client sends the HTTP request to this endpoint to obtain an access token. If your request is successful, you should see a response similar to this:

```
{
  "access_token":"8c017bb5-f6fd-4654-88c7-c26ccca54bdd",
  "token_type":"bearer",
  "expires_in":300,
  "scope":"read write"
}
```

2.2.4   *Understanding the access token response*

The following list provides details on the preceding JSON response from the authorization server. If you are new to OAuth 2.0, please check appendix A for further details.

- `access_token`—The value of the token issued by the authorization server to the client application (curl, in this case).
- `token_type`—The token type (more about this topic when we talk about OAuth 2.0 in appendix A). Most of the OAuth deployments we see today use bearer tokens.
- `expires_in`—The period of validity of the token, in seconds. The token will be considered invalid (expired) after this period.
- `scope`—The actions that the token is permitted to perform on the resource server (microservice).

2.3   *Securing a microservice with OAuth 2.0*

So far, you've learned how to develop your first microservice and how to set up an OAuth 2.0 authorization server to get an access token. In this section, you'll see how to secure the microservice you developed. Up to now, you've accessed it without any security in place.

2.3.1   *Security based on OAuth 2.0*

Once secured with OAuth 2.0, the Order Processing microservice now expects a valid security token (access token) from the calling client application. Then it will validate this access token with the assistance of the authorization server before it grants access to its resources. Figure 2.6 illustrates this scenario.

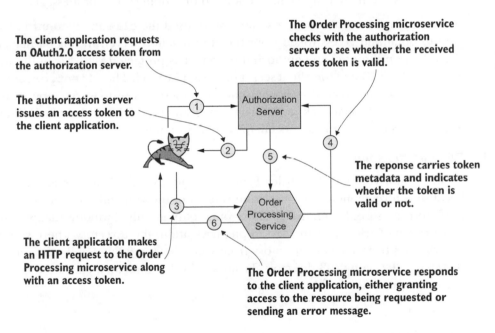

Figure 2.6   A client application accessing a secured microservice with an access token obtained from the authorization server. The Order Processing microservice talks to the authorization server to validate the token before granting access to its resources.

Here's what happens in each of the steps illustrated in figure 2.6:

1 The client application requests an OAuth2.0 access token from the authorization server.
2 In response to the request in step 1, the authorization server issues an access token to the client application.

3 The client application makes an HTTP request to the Order Processing micro-service. This request carries the access token obtained in step 2 as an HTTP header.

4 The Order Processing microservice checks with the authorization server to see whether the received access token is valid.

5 In response to the request in step 4, the authorization server checks to see whether the provided access token is an active token in the system (its state is active) and whether the token is valid for that particular moment (it isn't expired). Then it responds to the Order Processing microservice, indicating whether the access token is valid.

6 In response to the request in step 3, and based on the result in step 5, the Order Processing microservice responds to the client application, either granting access to the resource being requested or sending an error message.

In the examples in this chapter so far, you've used the `client_credentials` grant type to obtain an access token from the authorization server. In this particular case, the token endpoint of the authorization server is protected via basic authentication with the client ID and the client secret of the application. The `client_credentials` grant type is good when the client application doesn't need to worry about end users. If it has to, it should pick an appropriate grant type. The `client_credentials` grant type is used mainly for system-to-system authentication.

2.3.2   *Running the sample*

If you're still running the Order Processing microservice from section 2.1, stop it, because you're about to start a secured version of the same microservice on the same port. You can stop the microservice by going to the terminal window that is running it and pressing Ctrl-C. To run this sample, navigate to the directory where you cloned the samples from the Git repository from your command-line application, and go to the chapter02/sample03 directory. From within that directory, execute the following Maven command to build the sample:

```
\> mvn clean install
```

If the build is successful, you should see a directory named target within your current directory. The target directory should contain a file named com.manning.mss.ch02 .sample03-1.0.jar. (Other files will be within the target directory, but you're not interested in them at the moment.) Then run the following command from the chapter02/ sample03/ directory to spin up the secured Order Processing microservice. Here, we use a Maven plugin called `spring-boot`:

```
\> mvn spring-boot:run
```

If you managed to run the server successfully, you should see a message like this:

```
Started OrderApplication in <X> seconds
```

Now run the same curl command you used earlier in this chapter to access the Order Processing microservice:

```
\> curl  -v http://localhost:8080/orders \
-H 'Content-Type: application/json' \
--data-binary @- << EOF
{
  "items":[
    {
      "itemCode":"IT0001",
      "quantity":3
    },
    {
      "itemCode":"IT0004",
      "quantity":1
    }
  ],
  "shippingAddress":"No 4, Castro Street, Mountain View, CA, USA"
}
EOF
```

You should see an error message saying that the request was unsuccessful. The expected response message is as follows:

```
{
 "error":"unauthorized",
     "error_description":"Full authentication is
                         required to access this resource"
}
```

Your Order Processing microservice is now secured and can no longer be accessed without a valid access token obtained from the authorization server. To understand how this happened, look at the modified source code of your Order Processing microservice. Using your favorite text editor or IDE, open the file OrderProcessing-Service.java located inside the src/main/java/com/manning/mss/ch02/sample03/ service directory. This is more or less the same class file you inspected earlier with a function named placeOrder. One addition to this class is the annotation @Enable-WebSecurity. This annotation informs your Spring Boot runtime to apply security to the resources of this microservice. Following is the class definition:

```
@EnableResourceServer
@EnableWebSecurity
@RestController
@RequestMapping("/orders")
public class OrderProcessingService extends WebSecurityConfigurerAdapter {
}
```

If you further inspect this class, you should notice a method named tokenServices that returns an object of type ResourceServerTokenServices (see listing 2.2). Properties set in the RemoteTokenServices object (which is of the Resource-ServerTokenServices type) are the ones that the Spring Boot runtime uses to communicate with the authorization server to validate credentials received by the Order Processing microservice (the resource server, in this case).

If you go through the code of the `tokenServices` function, you'll see that it uses a method named `setCheckTokenEndpointUrl` to set the value `http://local-host:8085/oauth/check_token` as the `TokenEndpointURL` property in the `RemoteTokenServices` class. The `TokenEndpointURL` property is used by the Spring Boot runtime to figure out the URL on the OAuth 2.0 authorization server that it has to talk to, to validate any tokens it receives via HTTP requests. This is the URL the Order Processing microservice uses in step 4 of figure 2.6 to talk to the authorization server.

> **Listing 2.2 The `tokenServices` method from OrderProcessingService.java**

```
@Bean
public ResourceServerTokenServices tokenServices() {
    RemoteTokenServices tokenServices = new RemoteTokenServices();
    tokenServices.setClientId("orderprocessingservice");
    tokenServices.setClientSecret("orderprocessingservicesecret");
    tokenServices
      .setCheckTokenEndpointUrl("http://localhost:8085/oauth/check_token");
    return tokenServices;
}
```

The endpoint that does the validation of the token itself is secure; it requires a valid `Basic` authentication header. This header should consist of a valid client ID and a client secret. In this case, one valid client ID and client secret pair is `orderprocessing-service` and `orderprocessingservicesecret`, which is why those values are set in the `RemoteTokenServices` object. In fact, these credentials are hardcoded in the simple OAuth server we developed.

In section 2.4, you'll see how to use the token you obtained from the authorization server in section 2.2 to make a request to the now-secure Order Processing microservice.

2.4 *Invoking a secured microservice from a client application*

Before a client application can access your secured Order Processing microservice, it should obtain an OAuth2.0 access token from the authorization server. As explained in section 2.2.4, the client application at minimum requires a valid client ID and a client secret to obtain this token. The client ID and client secret registered on your OAuth 2.0 authorization server at the moment are `orderprocessingapp` and `orderprocessingappsecret`, respectively. As before, you can use the following curl command to obtain an access token:

```
\> curl -u orderprocessingapp:orderprocessingappsecret \
-H "Content-Type: application/json" \
-d '{ "grant_type": "client_credentials", "scope": "read write" }' \
http://localhost:8085/oauth/token
```

If the request is successful, you should get an access token in response, as follows:

```
{
  "access_token":"8c017bb5-f6fd-4654-88c7-c26ccca54bdd",
  "token_type":"bearer",
  "expires_in":300,
  "scope":"read write"
}
```

As discussed earlier, `8c017bb5-f6fd-4654-88c7-c26ccca54bdd` is the value of the access token you got, and it's valid for 5 minutes (300 seconds). This access token needs to be provided to the HTTP request you'll make to the Order Processing microservice. You need to send the token as an HTTP header named `Authorization`, and the header value needs to be prefixed by the string `Bearer`, as follows:

```
Authorization: Bearer 8c017bb5-f6fd-4654-88c7-c26ccca54bdd
```

The new curl command to access the Order Processing microservice is as follows:

```
\> curl  -v http://localhost:8080/orders \
-H 'Content-Type: application/json' \
-H "Authorization: Bearer 8c017bb5-f6fd-4654-88c7-c26ccca54bdd" \
--data-binary @- << EOF
{
  "items":[
    {
      "itemCode":"IT0001",
      "quantity":3
    },
    {
      "itemCode":"IT0004",
      "quantity":1
    }
  ],
  "shippingAddress":"No 4, Castro Street, Mountain View, CA, USA"
}
EOF
```

Note that the `-H` parameter is used to pass the access token as an HTTP header named `Authorization`. This time, you should see the Order Processing microservice responding with a proper message saying that the order was successful:

```
{
  "orderId":"d59dbd56-6e8b-4e06-906f-59990ce2e330",
  "items":[
    {
      "itemCode":"IT0001",
      "quantity":3
    },
    {
      "itemCode":"IT0004",
      "quantity":1
    }
  ],
  "shippingAddress":"No 4, Castro Street, Mountain View, CA, USA"
}
```

If you see this message, you've successfully created, deployed, and tested a secured microservice. Congratulations! The access token that the client application (curl) sent in the HTTP header to the Order Processing microservice was validated against the authorization server. This process is called *token introspection*. Because the result of the introspection operation ended up being a success, the Order Processing microservice granted access to its resources.

2.5 Performing service-level authorization with OAuth 2.0 scopes

You need a valid access token to access a microservice. Authentication is the first level of defense applied to a microservice to protect it from spoofing. The authentication step that occurs before granting access to the microservice ensures that the calling entity is a valid client (user, application, or both) in the system. Authentication, however, doesn't mention anything about the level of privileges the client has in the system.

A given microservice may have more than one operation. The Order Processing microservice, for example, has one operation for creating orders (POST /orders) and another operation for retrieving order details (GET /orders/{id}). Each operation in a microservice may require a different level of privilege for access.

A *privilege* describes the actions you're permitted to perform on a resource. More often than not, your role or roles in an organization describe which actions you're permitted to perform within that organization and which actions you're not permitted to perform. A privilege may also indicate status or credibility. If you've traveled on a commercial airline, you're likely familiar with the membership status of travelers who belong to airline frequent-flyer programs. Likewise, a privilege is an indication of the level of access that a user or an application possesses in a system.

In the world of OAuth 2.0, privilege is mapped to a scope. A *scope* is way of abstracting a privilege. A privilege can be a user's role, membership status, credibility, or something else. It can also be a combination of a few such attributes. You use scopes to abstract the implication of a privilege. A scope declares the privilege required by a calling client application to grant access to a resource. The place-Order operation, for example, requires a scope called write, and the getOrder operation requires a scope called read. The implications of write and read—whether they're related to user roles, credibility, or anything else—is orthogonal from a resource-server point of view.

2.5.1 Obtaining a scoped access token from the authorization server

The authorization server you built in this chapter contains two applications: one with client ID orderprocessingapp, which you used for accessing the microservice, and one with client ID orderprocessingservice. You configured these applications in such a way that the first application, with client ID orderprocessingapp, has privileges to obtain both scopes read and write, whereas the second application, with client ID orderprocessingservice, has privileges to obtain only scope read, as explained in the following listing:

```
clients.inMemory()
    .withClient("orderprocessingapp").secret("orderprocessingsecret")
    .authorizedGrantTypes("client_credentials", "password")
    .scopes("read", "write")
    .accessTokenValiditySeconds(3600)
    .resourceIds("sample-oauth")
    .and()
    .withClient("orderprocessingservice")
    .secret("orderprocessingservicesecret")
    .authorizedGrantTypes("client_credentials", "password")
    .scopes("read")
    .accessTokenValiditySeconds(3600)
    .resourceIds("sample-oauth");
```

This code indicates that anyone who uses orderprocessingapp is allowed to obtain an access token under both scopes read and write, whereas any user of order-processingservice is allowed to obtain an access token only under scope read. In all the requests so far to obtain an access token, you used orderprocessingapp as the client ID and requested both scopes read and write.

Now execute the same request to obtain an access token with orderprocessing-service as the client ID to see what the token response looks like. Execute this curl command to make the token request:

```
\> curl -u orderprocessingservice:orderprocessingservicesecret \
-H "Content-Type: application/json" \
-d '{ "grant_type": "client_credentials", "scopes": "read write" }' \
http://localhost:8085/oauth/token
```

If the token request was successful, you should see this response:

```
{
  "access_token":"47190af1-624c-48a6-988d-f4319d36b7f4",
  "token_type":"bearer",
  "expires_in":3599,
  "scope":"read"
}
```

Notice that although in the token request you requested both scopes read and write, the OAuth 2.0 authorization server issued a token with scope read only. One good thing about the OAuth 2.0 authorization server is that although you may not have the privileges to get all the scopes you request, instead of refusing to issue an access token, the server issues an access token bound to the scopes that you're entitled to. Then again, this may vary based on the authorization server you pick—and the OAuth 2.0 standard does not mandate a way that the authorization servers should handle such cases.

2.5.2 *Protecting access to a microservice with OAuth 2.0 scopes*

Now you have an idea of how an authorization server grants privileges to a token based on the scopes. In this section, you'll see how the resource server or the microservice enforces these scopes on the resources it wants to protect. The following listing (chapter02/sample03/src/main/java/com/manning/mss/ch02/sample03/service/ResourceServerConfig.java class file) explains how the resource server enforces these rules.

Listing 2.4   ResourceServerConfig.java

```
@Configuration
@EnableResourceServer
public class ResourceServerConfig extends ResourceServerConfigurerAdapter {

private static final String SECURED_READ_SCOPE =
                              "#oauth2.hasScope('read')";

private static final String SECURED_WRITE_SCOPE =
                              "#oauth2.hasScope('write')";

private static final String SECURED_PATTERN_WRITE = "/orders/**";

private static final String SECURED_PATTERN_READ = "/orders/{id}";

@Override
public void configure(HttpSecurity http) throws Exception {

http.requestMatchers()
.antMatchers(SECURED_PATTERN_WRITE).and().authorizeRequests()
.antMatchers(HttpMethod.POST,SECURED_PATTERN_WRITE)
.access(SECURED_WRITE_SCOPE)
.antMatchers(HttpMethod.GET,SECURED_PATTERN_READ)
.access(SECURED_READ_SCOPE);
}

@Override
public void configure(ResourceServerSecurityConfigurer resources) {
      resources.resourceId("sample-oauth");
}
}
```

As you can see, the code instructs the microservice runtime (Spring Boot) to check for the relevant scope for the particular HTTP method and request path. This line of code

```
.antMatchers(HttpMethod.POST,
      SECURED_PATTERN_WRITE).access(SECURED_WRITE_SCOPE)
```

checks for the scope `write` for any `POST` request made against the request path that matches the regular expression `/orders/**`. Similarly, this line of code checks for the scope `read` for `GET` requests on path `/orders/{id}`:

```
.antMatchers(HttpMethod.GET,
            SECURED_PATTERN_READ).access(SECURED_READ_SCOPE)
```

Now try to access the POST /orders resource with the token that has only a read scope. Execute the same curl command you used last time to access this resource, but with a different token this time (one that has read access only):

```
\> curl  -v http://localhost:8080/orders \
-H 'Content-Type: application/json' \
-H "Authorization: Bearer 47190af1-624c-48a6-988d-f4319d36b7f4" \
--data-binary @- << EOF
{
  "items":[
    {
      "itemCode":"IT0001",
      "quantity":3
    },
    {
      "itemCode":"IT0004",
      "quantity":1
    }
  ],
  "shippingAddress":"No 4, Castro Street, Mountain View, CA, USA"
}
EOF
```

When this command executes, you should see this error response from the resource server:

```
{
  "error":"insufficient_scope",
  "error_description":"Insufficient scope for this resource",
  "scope":"write"
}
```

This response says that the token's scope for this particular operation is insufficient and that the required scope is write.

Assuming that you still have a valid orderId (d59dbd56-6e8b-4e06-906f-59990ce2e330) from a successful request to the POST /orders operation, try to make a GET /orders/{id} request with the preceding token to see whether it's successful. You can use the following curl command to make this request. Note that the orderId used in the example won't be the same orderId you got when you tried to create an order yourself. Use the one that you received instead of the one used in this example. Also make sure to replace the value of the token in the Authorization header with what you got in section 2.5.1:

```
\> curl -H "Authorization: Bearer 47190af1-624c-48a6-988d-f4319d36b7f4" \
http://localhost:8080/orders/d59dbd56-6e8b-4e06-906f-59990ce2e330
```

This request should give you a successful response, as follows. The token that you obtained bears the read scope, which is what the GET /order/{id} resource requires, as declared on the resource server:

```
{
  "orderId":"d59dbd56-6e8b-4e06-906f-59990ce2e330",
```

```
"items":[
  {
    "itemCode":"IT0001",
    "quantity":3
  },
  {
    "itemCode":"IT0004",
    "quantity":1
  }
],
"shippingAddress":"No 4, Castro Street, Mountain View, CA, USA"
}
```

Throughout this chapter, we've covered the most primary mechanism of securing a microservice and accessing a secured microservice. As you may imagine, this chapter is only the beginning. Real-world scenarios demand a lot more than an application with a valid client ID and client secret to gain access to resources on a microservice. We discuss all these options throughout the rest of this book.

Summary

- OAuth 2.0 is an authorization framework, which is widely used in securing microservices deployments at the edge.
- OAuth 2.0 supports multiple grant types. The client credentials grant type, which we used in this chapter, is used mostly for system-to-system authentication.
- Each access token issued by an authorization server is coupled with one or more scopes. Scopes are used in OAuth 2.0 to express the privileges attached to an access token.
- OAuth 2.0 scopes are used to protect and enforce access-control checks in certain operations in microservices.
- All samples in this chapter used HTTP (not HTTPS) endpoints to spare you from having to set up proper certificates and to make it possible for you to inspect messages being passed on the wire (network), if required. In production systems, we do not recommend using HTTP for any endpoint.

Part 2

Edge security

The first microservice that you built and secured in part 1 is a good way to get started. But in practice, or in a production deployment, the approach you follow in securing a microservice is bit different from what you did in part 1. This part of the book takes you through securing a microservice at the edge (or at the entry point) in a typical microservices deployment. In most cases, microservices are behind a set of APIs that is exposed to the outside world via an API gateway. An API gateway is the entry point to the microservices deployment, which screens all incoming messages for security.

Chapter 3 takes you through the consumer landscape of your microservices and teaches you how to deploy a Spring Boot microservice behind the Zuul API gateway. You'll also learn how to enforce OAuth 2.0–based security at this gateway. At the end of the chapter, you'll have an API that is exposed to the client applications via the Zuul API gateway, and the Zuul API gateway will route the requests to the Spring Boot microservice.

Chapter 4 extends the use case that you built in chapter 3 by developing a single-page application (SPA) with Angular. You will also learn how to secure a SPA with OpenID Connect. Then you'll have an end-to-end use case working. A user can log into the SPA with OpenID Connect, and then the SPA talks to the Spring Boot microservice on behalf of the user via the Zuul API gateway.

Chapter 5 teaches you how to extend the use case you built in chapter 4 by engaging throttling, monitoring, and access control at the Zuul API gateway.

When you're finished with this part of the book, you'll know how to protect your microservices at the edge. You may not necessarily use the same set of tools we used in part 2, but you should be able to apply the techniques you learned with your preferred set of tools to protect your microservices at the edge in your production deployment.

Securing north/south
traffic with an API gateway

3

This chapter covers

- Understanding the role of an API gateway
- Improving architecture deficiencies from chapter 2
- Deploying a microservice behind the Zuul API gateway
- Using OAuth 2.0 for securing microservices at the edge

In chapter 2, we discussed how to secure microservices at the edge with OAuth 2.0. The focus of chapter 2 was to get things started with a straightforward deployment. The samples in that chapter were far from production-ready. Each microservice had to connect to an OAuth 2.0 authorization server for token validation and decide which OAuth 2.0 authorization server it wanted to trust. This is not a scalable model when you have hundreds of microservices and too much responsibility on the microservices developer.

In an ideal world, the microservices developer should worry only about the business functionality of a microservice, and the rest should be handled by specialized components with less hassle. The API Gateway and Service Mesh are two architectural patterns that help us reach that ideal. In this chapter, we discuss the API Gateway pattern, and in chapter 12, the Service Mesh pattern. The API Gateway pattern is mostly about edge security, while the Service Mesh pattern deals with service-to-service security. Or, in other words, the API Gateway deals with north/south traffic, while the Service Mesh deals with east/west traffic. We call the software that implements the API Gateway pattern an *API gateway*—and the software that implements the Service Mesh pattern, a *service mesh.*

Edge security is about protecting a set of resources (for example, a set of microservices) at the entry point to the deployment, at the API gateway. The API gateway is the only entry point to our microservices deployment for requests originating from outside. In the Service Mesh pattern, the architecture is much more decentralized. Each microservice has its own policy enforcement point much closer to the service—mostly it is a proxy, running next to each microservice. The API gateway is the centralized policy enforcement point to the entire microservices deployment, while in a service mesh, a proxy running along with each microservice provides another level of policy enforcement at the service level. In chapter 12, we discuss how to leverage the API Gateway pattern we discuss in this chapter, along with the Service Mesh pattern to build an end-to-end security solution.

3.1 The need for an API gateway in a microservices deployment

Having an API gateway in a microservices deployment is important. The API gateway is a crucial piece of infrastructure in our architecture, since it plays a critical role that helps us clearly separate the functional requirements from the nonfunctional ones. We'll extend chapter 2's use case (a retail store), look at a few of its problems, and explain how to solve them by using the API Gateway pattern.

In a typical microservices deployment, microservices are not exposed directly to client applications. In most cases, microservices are behind a set of APIs that is exposed to the outside world via an API gateway. The API gateway is the entry point to the microservices deployment, which screens all incoming messages for security and other QoS features.

Figure 3.1 depicts a microservices deployment that resembles Netflix's, in which all the microservices are fronted by the Zuul API gateway. Zuul provides dynamic routing, monitoring, resiliency, security, and more. It acts as the front door to Netflix's server infrastructure, handling traffic from Netflix users around the world. In figure 3.1, Zuul is used to expose the Order Processing microservice via an API. We do not expose Inventory and Delivery microservices from the API gateway, because external applications don't need access to those.

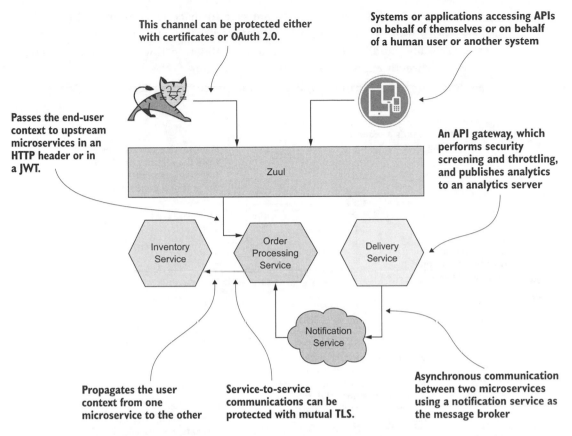

This channel can be protected either with certificates or OAuth 2.0.

Systems or applications accessing APIs on behalf of themselves or on behalf of a human user or another system

Passes the end-user context to upstream microservices in an HTTP header or in a JWT.

An API gateway, which performs security screening and throttling, and publishes analytics to an analytics server

Zuul

Inventory Service

Order Processing Service

Delivery Service

Notification Service

Propagates the user context from one microservice to the other

Service-to-service communications can be protected with mutual TLS.

Asynchronous communication between two microservices using a notification service as the message broker

Figure 3.1 A typical microservices deployment with an API gateway. The API gateway screens all incoming messages for security and other quality-of-service features.

3.1.1 *Decoupling security from the microservice*

One key aspect of microservices best practices is the *single responsibility principle*. This principle, commonly used in programming, states that every module, class, or function should be responsible for a single part of the software's functionality. Under this principle, each microservice should be performing only one particular function.

In the examples in chapter 2, the secured Order Processing microservice was implemented in such a way that it had to talk to the authorization server and validate the access tokens it got from client applications, in addition to the core business functionality of processing orders. As figure 3.2 shows, the Order Processing microservice had to worry about the multiple tasks listed here:

- Extracting the security header (token) from the incoming requests
- Knowing beforehand the location of the authorization server that it has to talk to in order to validate the security token

- Being aware of the protocol and message formats for communicating with the authorization server in order to validate the security token
- Gracefully handling errors in the token validation flow, because the microservice is directly exposed to the client application
- Performing the business logic related to processing orders

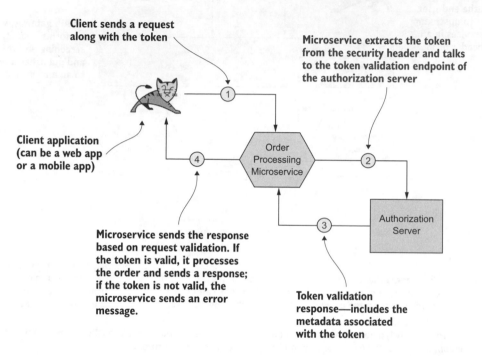

Figure 3.2   The interactions among the client application, microservice, and authorization server. The Order Processing microservice handles more functionality than it ideally should.

Executing all these steps becomes a problem because the microservice loses its atomic characteristics by performing more operations than it's supposed to. It would be ideal for the microservice to perform only the fifth task from the preceding list, which is the one that deals with the business logic for which we designed the microservice. The coupling of security and business logic introduces unwanted complexity and maintenance overhead to the microservice. For example, making changes in the security protocol would require changes in the microservice code, and scaling up the microservice would result in more connections to the authorization server.

CHANGES IN THE SECURITY PROTOCOL REQUIRE CHANGES IN THE MICROSERVICE

Someday, if you decide to move from OAuth 2.0 to something else as the security protocol enforced on the microservice, you have to make changes in the microservice, even though it may not have any changes related to its business logic. Also, if you find a bug in the current security implementation, you need to patch the microservice code to fix it. This unwanted overhead compromises your agility in designing, developing, and deploying your microservice.

SCALING UP THE MICROSERVICE RESULTS IN MORE CONNECTIONS TO THE AUTHORIZATION SERVER

In certain cases, you need to run more instances of the microservice to cater to rising demand. Think of Thanksgiving weekend, when people place more orders in your retail store than usual, which would require you to scale up your microservice to meet the demand. Because each microservice talks to the authorization server for token validation, scaling your microservice will also increase the number of connections to the authorization server.

There is a difference between 50 users using a single instance of a microservice, and 50 users using 10 instances of a microservice. To cater to these 50 users, a single microservice may maintain a connection pool of about 5 to communicate with the authorization server. When each instance of the microservice maintains a connection pool of 5 to connect to the authorization server, 10 instances of the microservice end up creating 50 connections on the authorization server as opposed to 5. Figure 3.3 illustrates scaling up a microservice to meet increased demand.

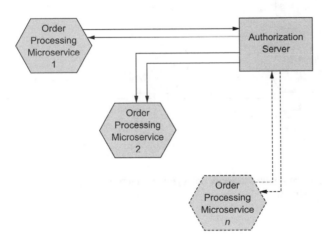

Figure 3.3   The effect on the authorization server when the microservice scales up, which results in more load on the authorization server

An API gateway helps in decoupling security from a microservice. It intercepts all the requests coming to a microservice, talks to the respective authorization, and dispatches only the legitimate requests to the upstream microservice. Otherwise, it returns an error message to the client application.

3.1.2 The inherent complexities of microservice deployments make them harder to consume

A microservices deployment typically consists of many microservices and many interactions among these microservices (figure 3.4).

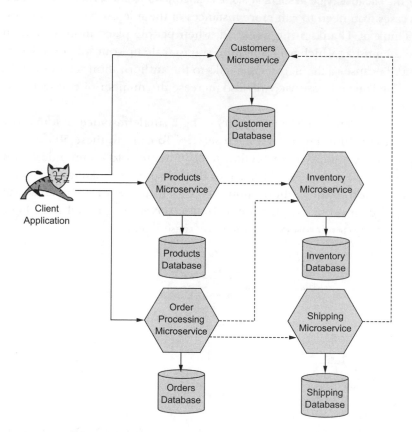

Figure 3.4   Architecture diagram of a microservices deployment, illustrating the services and connections among them

As you can see, an application that consumes microservices to build its own functionality must be capable of communicating with several microservices. Think of an organization with several teams, in which each team has the responsibility to develop one of the microservices shown in figure 3.4. Developers on each team could use their own technology stacks for the microservices as well as their own standards and practices. The nonuniformity of these microservices makes it hard for developers of the consuming application, who need to learn how to work with many inconsistent interfaces.

An API gateway solution, which usually comes as part of API management software, can bring consistency to the interfaces that are being exposed to the consuming applications. The microservices themselves could be inconsistent, because they're now hidden from the outside world, and the API gateway can deal with the complications of interacting with the microservices.

3.1.3 *The rawness of microservices does not make them ideal for external exposure*

Microservices can be as granular as they need to be. Suppose that you have two operations in your Products microservice: one for retrieving your product catalog and another for adding items to the catalog. From a REST point of view, the operation that retrieves the products would be modeled as GET on the /products resource, and the operation that adds products would be modeled as POST on the /products resource. GET /products gets the list of products (read operation). POST /products adds a new product to the list of products (write operation).

In practice, you could expect more requests for the read operation than the write operation, because on a retail website, people browse for products much more frequently than items are added to the catalog. Therefore, you could decide to implement the GET and POST operations on two different microservices—maybe even on different technology stacks—so that they can scale out the microservices independently. This solution increases robustness because the failure of one microservice doesn't affect the operations performed by the other microservice. From a consuming point of view, however, it would be odd for the consuming applications to have to talk to two endpoints (two APIs) for the add and retrieve operations. A strong REST advocate could argue that it makes more sense to have these two operations on the same API (same endpoint).

The API Gateway architectural pattern is an ideal solution to this problem. It provides the consuming application a single API with two resources (GET and POST). Each resource can be backed by a microservice of its own, providing the scalability and robustness required by the microservices layer (see figure 3.5).

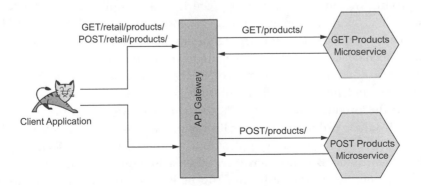

Figure 3.5 Multiple microservices are being exposed as a single API on the gateway. The client application needs to worry about only a single endpoint.

3.2   Security at the edge

In this section, we look at why OAuth 2.0 is the most appropriate protocol for securing your microservices at the edge. In a typical microservices deployment, we do not directly expose microservices to client applications. The API gateway, which is the entry point to the microservices deployment, selectively exposes microservices as APIs to the client applications.

In most cases, these API gateways use OAuth 2.0 as the security protocol to secure the APIs they expose at the edge. If you are interested in understanding OAuth 2.0 and API security in detail, we recommend *Advanced API Security: OAuth 2.0 and Beyond* by Prabath Siriwardena, a coauthor of this book (Apress, 2019). *OAuth 2 in Action* by Justin Richer and Antonio Sanso (Manning, 2017) is also a very good reference on OAuth 2.0.

3.2.1   Understanding the consumer landscape of your microservices

As discussed earlier in this chapter, the primary reason that organizations and enterprises adopt microservices is the agility that they provide for developing services. An organization wants to be agile to develop and deploy services as fast as possible. The pace is driven by the rise of demand in consumer applications. Today, people use mobile applications for most of their day-to-day activities, such as ordering pizza, grocery shopping, networking, interacting socially, and banking. These mobile applications consume services from various providers.

In an organization, both its internal and external (such as third-party) applications could consume microservices. External applications could be mobile applications, web applications on the public internet, applications running on devices or cars, and so on. For these types of applications to work, you need to expose your microservices over the public internet over HTTPS. As a result, you cannot just rely on network-level security policies to prevent access to these microservices. Therefore, you may always have to rely on an upper layer of security to control access. An *upper layer of security* here refers to the layers in the TCP/IP protocol stack (www.w3.org/People/Frystyk/thesis/TcpIp.html). You need to rely on security that's applied above the Network layer, such as Transport- or Application-layer protocols including TLS and HTTPS.

Applications running within the organization's computing infrastructure may consume both internal-facing and external-facing microservices. Internal-facing microservices may also be consumed by other microservices that are external-facing or internal-facing. As shown in figure 3.6, in the retail-store example, the microservice that's used for browsing the product catalog (the Products microservice) and the microservice that's used for taking orders (the Order Processing microservice) are external-facing microservices that are required by applications running outside the security perimeters of the organization. But the microservice that's used for updating the inventory—the Inventory microservice—doesn't need to be exposed outside the organization's security perimeters, because the inventory is updated only when an order is placed (via the Order Processing microservice) or when stocks are added to inventory through an internal application.

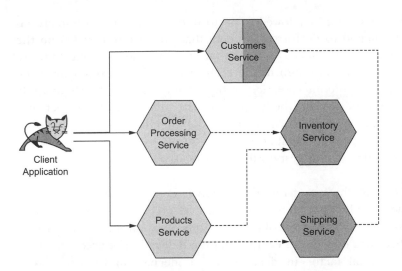

Figure 3.6
Internal microservices,
external microservices, and
hybrid microservices, each
communicating with others
to fulfill their functionality

3.2.2 Delegating access

A microservice is exposed to the outside world as an API. Similar to microservices, even for APIs the audience is a system that acts on behalf of itself, or on behalf of a human user or another system. It's unlikely (but not impossible) for human users to interact directly with APIs. This is where access delegation is important and plays a key role in securing APIs.

As we discussed briefly in chapter 2, multiple parties are involved in a typical flow to access a secured microservice. Even though we didn't worry about APIs in our previous discussions for simplicity, the flow doesn't deviate much even if we introduce an API between the client application and the Order Processing microservice, as shown in figure 3.7.

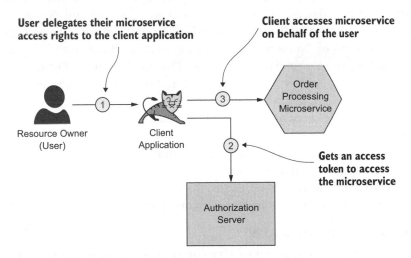

Figure 3.7   Multiple parties are involved in a typical flow to access a
microservice, protected with OAuth.

A user (resource owner) should be allowed to perform only the actions on microservices that they are privileged to perform. The data that the user retrieves from the microservice, or updates via the microservice, should be only the data that they are entitled to receive or update. Although this level of privilege is checked against the user, the entity that accesses the microservice on behalf of the user is the client application the user uses. In other words, the actions that the user is entitled to perform on the microservices are executed by a client application. In effect, the user delegates their access rights to an application that accesses the resources on the microservices. As a result, the application has a responsibility to deal with the delegated rights appropriately.

Therefore, the trustworthiness of the application is important. Especially when third-party applications are being used to access resources on your microservices, having a mechanism that allows you to control which actions the application can perform on your resources becomes important. Controlling the delegation of access to client applications is an essential factor in deciding on a mechanism to secure your microservices.

3.2.3   *Why not basic authentication to secure APIs?*

Basic authentication allows a user (or a system) with a valid username and password to access a microservice via an API. In fact, basic authentication (or basic auth) is a standard security protocol introduced with HTTP/1.0 in RFC 1945 a long time back. It allows you to pass the base64-encoded username and password, in the HTTP `Authorization` header, along with a request to an API. This model fails to meet access delegation requirements we discussed in section 3.2.2 in a microservices deployment, though, for a variety of reasons:

- *The username and password are static, long-living credentials.* If a user provides a username and password to an application, the application needs to retain this information for that particular user session to access the microservices. The time during which this information needs to be retained could be as long as the application decides. None of us likes having to authenticate into an application again and again to perform operations. Therefore, if basic authentication is used, the application has to retain this information for long durations of time. The longer this information is retained, the higher the chance of compromise. And because these credentials almost never change, a compromise of this information could have severe consequences.
- *No restrictions on what the application can do.* After an application gets access to the username and password of a user, it can do everything that user can do with the microservice. In addition to accessing the microservice, the application can do anything with those credentials, even on other systems.

3.2.4   *Why not mutual TLS to secure APIs?*

Mutual Transport Layer Security is a mechanism by which a client application verifies a server and the server verifies the client application by exchanging respective certificates and proving that each one owns the corresponding private keys. In chapter 6, we discuss mTLS in detail. For the moment, think of mTLS as a technique for building two-way trust between a client application and a server using certificates.

mTLS solves one of the problems with basic authentication by having a lifetime for its certificates. The certificates used in mTLS are time-bound, and whenever a certificate expires, it's no longer considered valid. Therefore, even if a certificate and the corresponding private key are compromised, its vulnerability is limited by its lifetime. In some situations, however, certificates have lifetimes as long as years, so the value of mTLS over protocols such as basic authentication is limited. Then again, unlike basic authentication (where you send your password over the wire), when you use mTLS, the corresponding private key never leaves its owner—or is never passed over the wire. That's the main advantage mTLS has over basic authentication.

However, just as in basic authentication, mTLS fails to meet access delegation requirements we discussed in section 3.2.2 in a microservices deployment. mTLS doesn't provide a mechanism to represent the end user who uses the corresponding application. You can use mTLS to authenticate the client application that talks to the microservice, but it does not represent the end user. If you want to pass the end user information with mTLS, you need to follow your own custom techniques, such as sending the username as a custom HTTP header, which is not recommended. Therefore, mTLS is mostly used to secure communication between a client application and a microservice, or communications among microservices. In other words, mTLS is mostly used to secure communications among systems.

3.2.5   *Why OAuth 2.0?*

To understand why OAuth 2.0 is the best security protocol for securing your microservices at the edge, first you need to understand your audience. You need to figure out who wants access to your resources, for what purpose, and for how long. You must properly understand the audience of your microservices through their characteristics and desires:

- *Who*—Ensure that only permitted entities are granted access to your resources
- *What purpose*—Ensure that the permitted entities can perform only what they're allowed to perform on your resources
- *How long*—Ensure that access is granted for only the desired period

As we've discussed a few times in the book already, the audience of a microservice is a system that acts on behalf of itself, or on behalf of a human user or another system. The owner of a microservice should be able to delegate access to the microservice it owns (or it has privileges to access), to a system. You may have a Netflix account, and to view the trending movies on Netflix on your smart TV, you need to delegate access from your Netflix account to your smart TV. Delegation is a key requirement in securing microservices—and out of all security protocols, OAuth 2.0, which is designed for access delegation, fits best in securing microservices at the edge.

> **NOTE**   Before running the samples in this chapter, please make sure that you have downloaded and installed all the required software as mentioned in section 2.1.1.

3.3   Setting up an API gateway with Zuul

In the first part of this chapter, we stated why an API gateway is an important component of a microservices deployment. In this section, you'll set up an API gateway for your Order Processing microservice, with Zuul (https://github.com/Netflix/zuul/wiki). Zuul is an open source proxy server built by Netflix, acting as the entry point for all of the company's backend streaming applications.

3.3.1   Compiling and running the Order Processing microservice

To begin, download the chapter 3 samples from GitHub (https://github.com/microservices-security-in-action/samples) to your computer. The examples in this chapter use Java version 11, but still should work with Java 8+. Before running the examples in this chapter, make sure that you've stopped running the examples from other chapters or elsewhere. You could experience port conflicts if you attempt to start multiple microservices on the same port.

Once you've downloaded all the samples from the GitHub repository, you should see a directory named sample01 inside the chapter03 directory. This is the same sample used in chapter 2; we repeat it here for the benefit of those who skipped that chapter. Navigate to the chapter03/sample01 directory from your command-line client application, and execute the following command to build the source code of the Order Processing microservice:

```
\> mvn clean install
```

If the build is successful, you should see a message on the terminal saying BUILD SUCCESS. If you see this message, you can start the microservice by executing the following command from the same location:

```
\> mvn spring-boot:run
```

If the service started successfully, you should see a log statement on the terminal that says Started OrderApplication in <X> seconds. If you see this message, your Order Processing microservice is up and running. Now send a request to it, using curl, to make sure that it responds properly:

```
\> curl  -v http://localhost:8080/orders \
-H 'Content-Type: application/json' \
--data-binary @- << EOF
{
  "items":[
    {
      "itemCode":"IT0001",
      "quantity":3
    },
    {
      "itemCode":"IT0004",
      "quantity":1
    }
  ],
  "shippingAddress":"No 4, Castro Street, Mountain View, CA, USA"
}
EOF
```

Upon successful execution of this request, you should see a response message:

```
{
  "orderId":"7c3fb57b-3198-4cf3-9911-6dd157b93333",
  "items":[
    {
      "itemCode":"IT0001",
      "quantity":3
    },
    {
      "itemCode":"IT0004",
      "quantity":1
    }
  ],
  "shippingAddress":"No 4, Castro Street, Mountain View, CA, USA"
}
```

This request gets curl (a client application) to access your Order Processing microservice directly, as shown in figure 3.8. Your client application sent a request to the Order Processing microservice to place an order. As you saw in the response message, the ID of the particular order is `7c3fb57b-3198-4cf3-9911-6dd157b93333`. Later, when you try to retrieve the same order by using the `GET /orders/{id}` resource, you should be able to get the details on the order you placed.

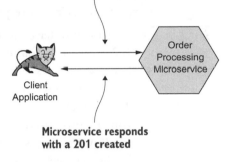

Client sends POST/orders request

Client Application

Order Processing Microservice

Microservice responds with a 201 created

Figure 3.8   The client application sends a request directly to the Order Processing microservice and gets a response back with an order ID.

3.3.2   *Compiling and running the Zuul proxy*

The next step is compiling and running Zuul as a proxy to the Order Processing microservice. To build the Zuul proxy, navigate to the chapter03/sample02 directory in your command-line client, and execute this command:

```
\> mvn clean install
```

You should see the BUILD SUCCESS message. Next, run the Zuul proxy by executing the following command from within the same directory:

```
\> mvn spring-boot:run
```

You should see the `server-start-successful` message. Now try to access your Order Processing microservice through the Zuul proxy. To do so, you'll be attempting to retrieve the details on the order you placed. Execute the following command from your terminal application (make sure to have the correct order ID from section 3.3.1):

```
\> curl \
http://localhost:9090/retail/orders/7c3fb57b-3198-4cf3-9911-6dd157b93333
```

If the request is successful, you should see a response like this:

```
{
  "orderId":"7c3fb57b-3198-4cf3-9911-6dd157b93333",
  "items":[
    {
      "itemCode":"IT0001",
      "quantity":3
    },
    {
      "itemCode":"IT0004",
      "quantity":1
    }
  ],
  "shippingAddress":"No 4, Castro Street, Mountain View, CA, USA"
}
```

This response should contain the details of the order you created earlier. Note several important points in this request:

- As you may have noticed, the port to which you sent the request this time (9090) isn't the same as the port of the Order Processing microservice (8080), because you're sending the request to the Zuul proxy instead of the Order Processing microservice directly.

- The request URL now starts with /retail, which is the base path in Zuul that you've configured to route requests to the Order Processing microservice. To see how routing is configured, open the application.properties file that resides in the sample02/src/main/resources directory by using a text editor. The following line you find there instructs the Zuul proxy to route requests received on /retail to the server running on http://localhost:8080:

```
zuul.routes.retail.url=http://localhost:8080
```

Figure 3.9 illustrates how Zuul does routing by dispatching a request it gets from the client application to the Order Processing microservice.

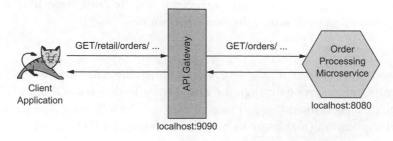

Figure 3.9   The Order Processing microservice is proxied via the Zuul gateway. All requests to the microservice need to go through the gateway.

3.3.3 *Enforcing OAuth 2.0–based security at the Zuul gateway*

Now that you've successfully proxied your Order Processing microservice via the Zuul gateway, the next step is enforcing security on the Zuul gateway so that only authenticated clients are granted access to the Order Processing microservice. First, you need an OAuth 2.0 authorization server (see appendix A), which is capable of issuing access tokens to client applications. In a typical production deployment architecture, the authorization server is deployed inside the organization's network, and only the required endpoints are exposed externally. Usually, the API gateway is the only component that's allowed access from outside; everything else is restricted within the local area network of the organization. In the examples in this section, the `/oauth2/ token` endpoint of the authorization server is exposed through the Zuul gateway so that clients can obtain access tokens from the authorization server. Figure 3.10 illustrates this deployment architecture.

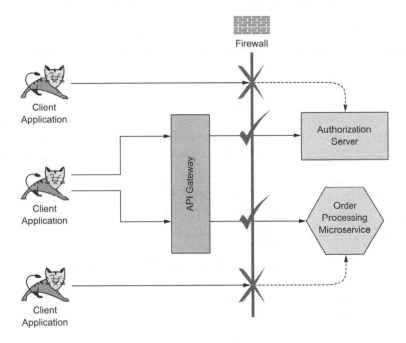

Figure 3.10   The firewall guarantees that access to the authorization server and microservice can happen only via the API gateway.

To build the authorization server, navigate to the chapter03/sample03 directory from your command-line client, and execute the following command:

```
\> mvn clean install
```

When the authorization server is built, you can start it by using the following command:

```
\> mvn spring-boot:run
```

When the authorization server starts successfully, you can request tokens from it via the Zuul gateway. However, we did not enforce OAuth 2.0 security screening at the Zuul gateway, which you started from sample02 in section 3.3.2. So, you'd need to stop it and build and run a new Zuul gateway from sample04, in which we have enforced OAuth 2.0 security screening.

Before you build sample04, first have a look at the following property in the sample04/src/main/resources/application.properties file. This property points to the token validation endpoint of the authorization server. The Zuul gateway talks to this endpoint to validate tokens. Make sure the value of the `authserver.intro-spection.endpoint` property correctly points to your authorization server:

```
authserver.introspection.endpoint=http://localhost:8085/oauth/check_token
```

To build the new Zuul gateway, open a new terminal window and navigate to the chapter03/sample04 directory and then execute the following command:

```
\> mvn clean install
```

When the gateway is built, you can start it by using the following command:

```
\> mvn spring-boot:run
```

Once the gateway has started successfully on port 9090, execute the following command on a new terminal window to get an access token from the authorization server, through the Zuul gateway. Here we use the OAuth 2.0 `client_credentials` grant type, with `application1` as the client ID and `application1secret` as the client secret:

```
\> curl -u application1:application1secret \
-H "Content-Type: application/x-www-form-urlencoded" \
-d "grant_type=client_credentials" \
http://localhost:9090/token/oauth/token
```

You should receive the access token in a response that looks like this:

```
{
  "access_token":"47190af1-624c-48a6-988d-f4319d36b7f4",
  "token_type":"bearer",
  "expires_in":3599
}
```

Open the application.properties file at sample04/src/main/resources/ by using a text editor. You will notice the following configuration that routes requests received on the /token endpoint of Zuul to the authorization server:

```
zuul.routes.token.url=http://localhost:8085
```

Once the client application gets an access token from the token endpoint of the authorization server, the client application accesses the Order Processing microservice via the Zuul gateway with this token. The purpose of exposing the Order Processing microservice via the Zuul gateway is to make the gateway enforce all security-related policies while the Order Processing microservice focuses only on the business logic it executes. This situation is in line with the principles of microservices, which state that a microservice should focus on doing only one thing. The Zuul gateway allows requests to the Order Processing microservice only if the requesting client bears a valid OAuth 2.0 access token.

Now, let's try to access the Order Processing microservice through the Zuul gateway as before with the following command (with no valid access token):

```
\> curl -v \
http://localhost:9090/retail/orders/7c3fb57b-3198-4cf3-9911-6dd157b93333
```

This command should now give you an authentication error message that looks like the following. This error message confirms that the Zuul gateway, with OAuth 2.0 security screening enforced, does not allow any request to pass through it without a valid token:

```
< HTTP/1.1 401
< Transfer-Encoding: chunked
<

{"error": true, "reason":"Authentication Failed"}
```

Zuul no longer grants open access to resources on the resource server. It mandates authentication. We are therefore required to use a valid token to access the Order Processing microservice via the Zuul gateway. Let's retry accessing the same Order Processing microservice by using the access token we just obtained through the /token endpoint. You can use the following command for this purpose. Make sure to have the correct order ID from section 3.3.1 and replace 7c3fb57b-3198-4cf3-9911-6dd157b93333 in the following command with it:

```
\> curl \
http://localhost:9090/retail/orders/7c3fb57b-3198-4cf3-9911-6dd157b93333 \
-H "Authorization: Bearer 47190af1-624c-48a6-988d-f4319d36b7f4"
```

You should see a successful response as shown here:

```
{
  "orderId":"7c3fb57b-3198-4cf3-9911-6dd157b93333",
  "items":[
    {
      "itemCode":"IT0001",
      "quantity":3
    },
    {
      "itemCode":"IT0004",
      "quantity":1
    }
  ],
      "shippingAddress":"No 4, Castro Street, Mountain View, CA, USA"
}
```

ENFORCING TOKEN VALIDATION AT THE ZUUL GATEWAY

In the previous example, the Zuul gateway talked to the authorization server (token issuer) to validate the token it got from the curl client application. As you learned in chapter 2, this process is known as *token introspection* (https://tools.ietf.org/html/rfc7662). The request flow from client to the Order Processing microservice is shown in figure 3.11.

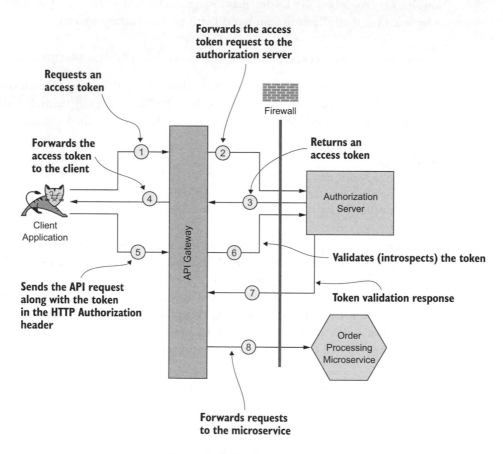

Figure 3.11   Message exchanges from the point where the client application gets a token to the point where it accesses the microservice

As you can see, the client application sends an OAuth 2.0 access token as a header to the Zuul gateway on the path on which the Order Processing microservice is exposed (/retail/orders). The gateway extracts the token from the header and introspects it through the authorization server. The authorization server responds with a valid or invalid status message; if the status is valid, the gateway allows the request to be passed to the Order Processing microservice.

To do this in Zuul, you use a request filter, which intercepts requests and performs various operations on them. A filter can be one of four types:

- *Prerequest filter*—Executes before the request is routed to the target service
- *Route filter*—Can handle the routing of a message
- *Post-request filter*—Executes after the request has been routed to the target service
- *Error filter*—Executes if an error occurs in the routing of a request

In this case, because you need to engage the validation before routing the request to the target service, you use a prerequest filter. You can find the source code of this filter in the following class:

```
sample04/src/main/java/com/manning/mss/ch03/sample04/filters/OAuthFilter.java
```

If you inspect the contents of this Java class, you notice a method named `filter-Type`. This method returns a string as `pre`. This string tells the Zuul runtime that it's a prerequest filter that needs to be engaged before the request is routed to the target service. The `run` method of this class contains the logic related to introspecting the token through the authorization server. If you look at that method, you'll notice that a few validations are performed on the Zuul gateway itself to check whether the client is sending the access token in an HTTP header named `Authorization` and whether the header is received in the correct format.

When all format checks are done, the gateway talks to the authorization server to check whether the token is valid. If the authorization server responds with an HTTP response status code of 200, it is a valid token:

```
int responseCode = connection.getResponseCode();

//If the authorization server doesn't respond with a 200.
if (responseCode != 200) {
log.error("Response code from authz server is " + responseCode);
handleError(requestContext);
}
```

If the server doesn't respond with 200, the authentication has failed. The authentication could have failed for many reasons. The token may have been incorrect, the token may have expired, the authorization server may have been unavailable, and so on. At this point, you're not concerned about the reason for the failure. Unless the authorization server responds with 200, consider that the authentication has failed.

> **NOTE** The preceding examples cover a fundamental mechanism for applying OAuth 2.0–based security on your microservices through an API gateway. You may not completely understand the source code in the samples; what is important is that you understand the pattern we are applying to secure your microservices.

OAUTH2.0 TOKEN INTROSPECTION PROFILE

We talked briefly about OAuth 2.0 token introspection (https://tools.ietf.org/html/rfc7662) in the preceding section. There the API gateway makes a request to the authorization server to validate a given token. Following is what the token introspection request looks like when the Zuul gateway talks to the authorization server to check the validity of an access token:

```
POST /oauth/check_token
Content-Type: application/x-www-form-urlencoded
Authorization: Basic YXBwbGljYXRpb24xOmFwcGxpY2F0aW9uMXNlY3JldA==

token=626e34e6-002d-4d53-9656-9e06a5e7e0dc&
token_type_hint=access_token&
```

As you can see, the introspection endpoint of the authorization server is protected with basic authentication. The introspection request is sent to the authorization server as a typical form submission with the content type `application/x-www-form-urlencoded`. The `token` field contains the value of the token that you want to check for validity. It is the only mandatory field in the introspection request as per the specification. The `token_type` field indicates to the authorization server whether this token is an `access_token` or `refresh_token`. When the authorization server completes the introspection, it responds with a payload similar to this:

```
HTTP/1.1 200 OK
Content-Type: application/json
Cache-Control: no-store

{
  "active": true,
  "client_id": "application1",
  "scope": "read write",
  "sub": "application1",
  "aud": "http://orders.ecomm.com"
}
```

The `active` field indicates that the token is active (not expired). The `client_id` is the identifier of the application for which the token was issued. The `scope` field includes the scopes bound to the token. The `sub` field contains the identifier of the entity that consented to the authorization server to share the token with the client application. When we use the OAuth 2.0 `client_credentials` grant type, the value of `sub` is the same as the value of `client_id`. The `aud` field indicates a list of identifiers of the entities that are considered to be valid receivers of this access token.

Using the information in the introspection response, the gateway can allow or refuse access to the resources. It can also perform fine-grained access control (authorization) based on the scopes as well as get to know which client application (from the `client_id`) is requesting access to its resources.

SELF-VALIDATION OF TOKENS WITHOUT INTEGRATING WITH AN AUTHORIZATION SERVER

The key benefit of using microservices for your architectures is the agility it provides developers in terms of developing and managing software systems. Microservices' ability to operate by themselves without affecting other components in the system/

architecture is one important factor that gives developers this agility. But the gateway component relies heavily on the authorization server to enable access to your microservices, so the gateway component is coupled with another entity. Although you may achieve agility on your microservices layer, the fronting layer (which is the API gateway) can't be managed with the same level of agility because of its reliance on the authorization server for token validations.

If you're a microservice developer who wants to put an API gateway in front of your microservice, this architecture doesn't give you the necessary flexibility; you have to come to an agreement with the administrator of the authorization server to get a set of credentials to access its introspection endpoint. If you're running this system in production and want to scale up your microservice and the API gateway to deal with a high number of requests, the performance of your authorization server will be affected, because the gateway will call it each time it wants to validate a token. An authorization server, unlike other services in an organization, usually is managed by a separate group of people who have special privileges because of the server's sensitivity. Therefore, you can't expect the same level of dynamic scaling capabilities on your authorization server to meet the demands of the API gateway.

The way to deal with this problem is to find a mechanism that enables the gateway to validate tokens by itself without the assistance of an authorization server. To see how, look at what an authorization server does when someone asks it to validate a token through an introspection call:

1 It checks to see whether that particular token exists in its token store (database). This step verifies that the token was issued by itself and that the server knows details about that token.
2 It checks whether the token is still valid (token state, expiry, and so on).
3 Based on the outcome of these checks, it responds to the requester with the information discussed under the "OAuth 2.0 token introspection profile" section.

If the access token received on the API gateway, instead of being an opaque meaningless string, contains all the information you need (including expiry details, scopes, client ID, user, and so on), the gateway could validate the token by itself. But anybody could create this string and send it along to the gateway. The gateway wouldn't know whether a trusted authorization server issued the token.

JWTs are designed to solve this problem (see appendix B for the details). A JSON Web Signature (JWS) is a JWT signed by the authorization server. By verifying the signature of the JWS, the gateway knows that this token was issued by a trusted party and that it can trust the information contained in the body. The standard claims described in the JWT specification (https://tools.ietf.org/html/rfc7519) don't have placeholders for all the information that's included in the introspection profile, such as the `client_id` and `scope`. The authorization server, however, can add any information it wants to the JWT as custom claims.[1] We discuss self-contained access tokens in detail in appendix A.

---

[1] At the time of this writing, a draft specification under the IETF OAuth working group defines the structure of a self-contained access token; see http://mng.bz/jgde.

PITFALLS OF SELF-VALIDATING TOKENS AND HOW TO AVOID THEM

The self-validating token mechanism discussed in the preceding section comes at a cost, with pitfalls that you have to be mindful of. If one of these tokens is prematurely revoked, the API gateway won't know that the token has been revoked, because the revocation happens at the authorization server end, and the gateway no longer communicates with the authorization server for the validation of tokens.

One way to solve this problem is to issue short-lived JWTs (tokens) to client applications to minimize the period during which a revoked token will be considered valid on the API gateway. In practice, however, applications with longer user sessions have to keep refreshing their access tokens when the tokens carry a shorter expiration.

Another solution is for the authorization server to inform the API gateway whenever a token has been revoked. The gateway and authorization server can maintain this communication channel via a pub/sub (https://cloud.google.com/pubsub/docs/overview) mechanism. This way, whenever a token is revoked, the gateway receives a message from the authorization server through a message broker. Then the gateway can maintain a list of revoked tokens until their expiry and before validating a given token check if it exists in the "revoked tokens" list. Revocations are rare, however. Figure 3.12 illustrates the revocation flow.

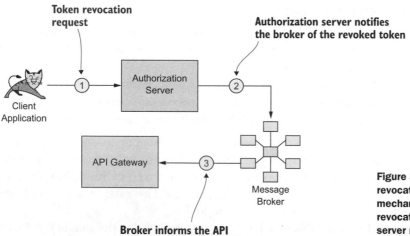

Figure 3.12   Executing the token revocation flow via a pub/sub mechanism. Upon a token revocation, the authorization server notifies the message broker, hence the API gateway.

Another problem with the self-contained access token is that the certificate used to verify a token signature might have expired. When this happens, the gateway can no longer verify the signature of an incoming JWT (as an access token). To solve this problem, you need to make sure that whenever a certificate is renewed, you deploy the new certificate on the gateway.

Sometimes, provisioning new certificates can be a little harder when you have a large-scale deployment with certificates having a short lifetime. In that case, you do not need to provision the token issuer's certificate to the gateway, but the certificate of the certificate authority (CA) corresponding to the token issuer's certificate. Then the gateway can fetch the token issuer's certificate dynamically from an endpoint exposed by the authorization server to do the JWT signature validation, and check whether that certificate is signed by a certificate authority it trusts. However, if the certificate issued to the authorization server by the certificate authority is revoked, then that decision too must be communicated to the API gateway—or the API gateway can rely on a certification revocation list.

3.4 Securing communication between Zuul and the microservice

So far, you've used the API Gateway pattern to secure access to your microservice. This pattern ensures that no one who lacks valid credentials (a token) gets access to your microservice through the API gateway. But you also have to consider what happens if someone accesses the microservice directly, bypassing the API gateway layer. In this section, we discuss how to secure access to your microservice in such a case.

3.4.1 Preventing access through the firewall

First and foremost, you need to make sure that your microservice isn't directly exposed to external clients, so you need to make sure that it sits behind your organization's firewall. That way, no external clients get access to your microservices unless they come in via the API gateway (see figure 3.13).

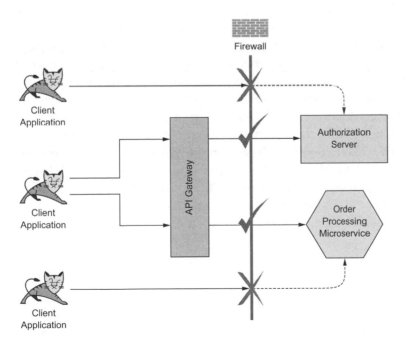

Figure 3.13 Direct access to the authorization server and microservice is prevented by the firewall, allowing only the API gateway to access them.

Although the API Gateway pattern ensures that no one outside the organization gets access to the microservice, a risk still exists that unintended internal clients may gain access to the microservice. The following section discusses how to prevent this situation.

3.4.2 Securing the communication between the API gateway and microservices by using mutual TLS

To make sure that your microservice is secure from internal clients and accessible only via the API gateway, you need to build a mechanism in which the microservice rejects any requests coming from clients other than the API gateway. The standard way is to enable mTLS between the API gateway and the microservice. When you use mTLS, you get the microservice to verify the client that talks to it. If the microservice trusts the API gateway, the API gateway can route requests to the microservice.

Under microservices principles, it's not a good idea for a microservice to be performing many operations. In fact, it's said that the microservice should focus on doing only one thing: executing the business logic that it's supposed to execute. You may think that you're burdening the microservice with extra responsibilities by expecting it to verify the client through mTLS. But mTLS verification happens at the Transport layer of the microservice and doesn't propagate up to the Application layer. Microservices developers don't have to write any application logic to handle the client verification, which is done by the underlying Transport-layer implementation. Therefore, mTLS verification doesn't affect the agility of developing the microservice itself and can be used safely without violating microservices principles.

If you're still worried about performing certificate validation as part of your microservice, chapter 12 covers an approach to avoid that, using the Service Mesh pattern. With the Service Mesh pattern, a proxy, which runs along with your microservice (each microservice has its own proxy), intercepts all the requests and does the security validation. The certificate validation can be part of that as well.

In chapter 6, we cover using client certificates to secure service-to-service communications. This scenario is essentially the one in which the API gateway becomes the source service and the microservice becomes the target service. We'll go into the details on setting up the certificates and building trust between clients and services in chapter 6. Figure 3.14 illustrates how both internal and external client applications are permitted to access a microservice only via the API gateway.

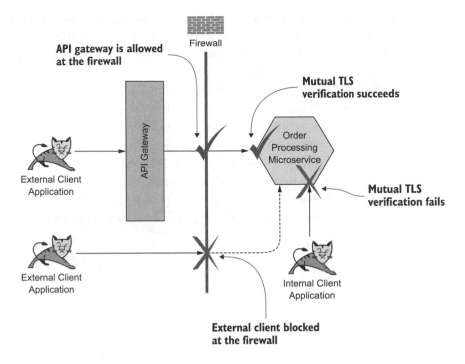

Figure 3.14 **Enabling mutual TLS at the microservice to prevent access by unintended parties. All the requests outside the firewall must be routed via the API gateway.**

Summary

- The API Gateway pattern is used to expose microservices to client applications as APIs.
- The API gateway helps to expose microservices of different flavors by using a consistent and easy-to-understand interface to the consumers of these microservices.
- We do not have to expose all microservices through the API gateway. Some microservices are consumed internally only, in which case they will not be exposed through the gateway to the outside world.
- Protocols such as basic authentication and mutual TLS are not sufficient to secure APIs, and microservices are exposed to the outside world via APIs.
- OAuth 2.0 is the de facto standard for securing APIs and microservices at the edge.
- OAuth 2.0 is an extensible authorization framework, which has a wide array of grant types. Each grant type defines the protocol indicating how a client application would obtain an access token to access an API/microservice.
- We need to choose the right OAuth 2.0 grant type for our client applications based on their security characteristics and trustworthiness.

- An access token can be a reference token or a self-contained token (JWT). If it is a reference token, the gateway has to talk to the issuer (or the authorization server) always to validate it. For self-contained tokens, the gateway can perform the validation by verifying the token signature.

- A self-contained access token has its own pitfalls, and one way to get around token revocation is to have short-lived JWTs for self-contained access tokens.

- The communication between the gateway and the microservice can be protected with either firewall rules or mutual TLS—or a combination of both.

- All samples in this chapter use HTTP (not HTTPS) endpoints to spare you from having to set up proper certificates and to make it possible for you to inspect messages being passed on the wire (network), if required. In production systems, we do not recommend using HTTP for any endpoint.

Accessing a secured microservice via a single-page application

In chapter 2, we discussed how to secure a microservice with OAuth 2.0 and directly invoked it with a curl client. Chapter 3 made further improvements by deploying the microservice behind an API gateway. The API gateway took over the OAuth 2.0 token validation responsibility from the microservice, and the communication between the API gateway and the microservice was secured with mTLS. The API gateway introduced a layer of abstraction between the client applications and microservices. All the communications with microservices had to go through the API gateway.

In this chapter, we discuss in detail how to build a *single-page application*, or *SPA* (pronounced spä), to invoke microservices via an API gateway. In case you're wondering why we're talking about building a SPA in a microservices security book, the reason is that understanding the constructs of a SPA is important in building an end-to-end security design. We believe in completing an end-to-end architecture with a microservices deployment, from data to screen. And SPAs are the most used client application type. If you are new to SPA architecture, we recommend you go through appendix C first. It will help you understand what a SPA is and the benefits it offers.

4.1 Running a single-page application with Angular

Suppose that you've chosen to adopt a SPA architecture to build your retail-store web application. In this section, you'll build a SPA by using Angular (https://angular.io/). *Angular* is a framework that helps you build web pages with dynamic HTML content. You'll implement a simple SPA to get firsthand experience with its characteristics and behaviors.

4.1.1 Building and running an Angular application from the source code

To start, you need the samples from the GitHub repo at https://github.com/microservices-security-in-action/samples. The samples related to this chapter are in the chapter04 directory. Make sure that none of the processes you may have started when trying samples from other chapters are running. Shut them down before you try any of the samples in this chapter. Also, make sure that you have downloaded and installed all the required software, as mentioned in section 2.1.1.

In addition, you need to have Node.js, npm, and the Angular command-line interface (CLI) installed to try out this chapter's samples. You can install Node.js and npm by following the instructions at http://mng.bz/pBKR. To install the Angular CLI, follow instructions at https://angular.io/guide/setup-local. The samples in this chapter have been tested on Node.js version 12.16.1, npm version 6.13.4, and Angular version 9.0.4. You can use the following three commands to check the versions you have in your local setup:

```
\> ng version
Angular CLI: 9.0.4
Node: 12.16.1

\> npm -v
6.14.3

\>node -v
v12.16.1
```

After you've set up the all dependencies and downloaded the relevant code onto your working environment, open a command-line client and navigate to the chapter04/sample01 directory. You will see two subdirectories within named resource and ui. The ui directory contains the code of the SPA (Angular application), while the resource directory contains the code of a Spring Boot application written in Java. Since we follow OAuth 2.0 terminology here, we call this Spring Boot application the *resource server*. Navigate to the resource directory and execute the following command to build the resource server:

```
\> mvn clean install
```

If the build is successful, you should see a message on the terminal saying BUILD SUCCESS. Execute the following command to run the resource server after the build is complete:

```
\> mvn spring-boot:run
```

This resource server has a resource under the URL /books that returns a list of book details in JSON format. You can try it out by sending a GET request to the /books endpoint by using curl:

```
\> curl http://localhost:8080/books
```

If this command returns a list of book details, our resource server is operating as expected. The next step is to run our Angular application that lists these books on a web page. Open a new terminal window and navigate to the samples/chapter04/sample01/ui directory and execute the following command:

```
\> ng serve
```

If the application runs successfully, you should see a message on the terminal saying Compiled successfully. When you see this message, open a web browser tab and navigate to http://localhost:4200. You should see a simple web page with a single button, as shown in figure 4.1. If the ng serve command results in the error [error] Error: Cannot find module '@angular-devkit/build-angular/package.json', you can follow the instructions at http://mng.bz/OMBj to overcome it. This could occur if you're upgrading Angular from an older version to 9.0.4.

Figure 4.1 On the Angular single-page application home page, the Load Books button loads the book list from the resource server.

Click the Load Books button. This should display a list of book titles on your web page, as shown in figure 4.2.

We have successfully executed our SPA on Angular. This application talked to a resource server (which is a Spring Boot application) to load a list of book titles onto a web page. In the next section, we take a closer look at the inner workings of this application.

4.1.2 Looking behind the scenes of a single-page application

In this section, we look at our SPA to see how it communicated with the resource server to display a list of book titles on a web page. Close the

Figure 4.2 The Angular app displays a list of books returned from the resource server.

browser window (or tab) from the previous section and open a new browser window, preferably in private/incognito mode, and then open the browser's developer tools so you can inspect what happens behind the scenes.

When the developer tools are open, go to the Network tab of the developer-tools window and click the Persist Logs button so you can observe the requests and responses exchanged by the web browser and the web server. Then type the URL http://localhost:4200 in the address bar of your browser, and press Enter. You should see the initial web page with the Load Books button as before.

If you observe the Network tab on your browser developer tools, you'll notice the browser making a GET request to http://localhost:4200. The response of this request is a bunch of HTML code that renders the title Book List App and the Load Books button on your browser web page. You should also see other requests to load a few JavaScript files onto the browser. These are not important for the concepts we teach in this chapter, so we can safely ignore them for the moment.

Next, click the Load Books button again and observe what happens on the Network tab of your browser development tools. You should see that the browser sends a GET request to http://localhost:8080/books. This request returns a list of book titles in JSON format, the exact response we noticed when we tested the resource server directly. Figure 4.3 illustrates the sequence of events that happens to load this web page with a list of book titles.

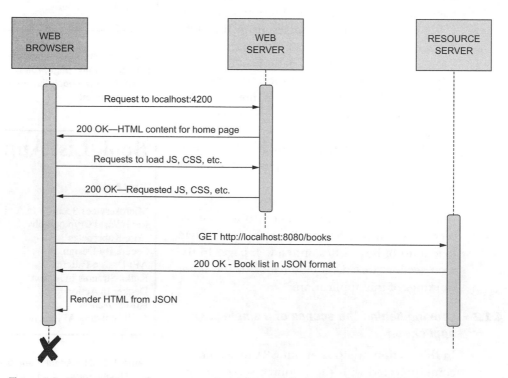

Figure 4.3 This sequence of message exchanges among the web browser, web server, and resource server displays a list of book titles on a web page in the Angular application.

The browser makes an initial request to `http://localhost:4200`, which loads the web application onto the web browser. The Angular-based web application is hosted on a Node.js server running on port 4200 in this sample. Once the application is loaded onto the browser, it renders the HTML content of the home page, which contains the Load Books button. Once this button is clicked, the browser initiates a request to load the list of books from the resource server running on `localhost:8080`. The resource server returns the list of books in JSON format. The JavaScript loaded on the web page then converts this JSON-formatted data into HTML, which results in us seeing the book titles on the web page.

Next, let's take a look at the source code that generates this content. As we mentioned earlier, you're using an Angular web application hosted on Node.js. In discussing the benefits of a SPA in appendix C, we mention that because SPAs have a simple design and content, they can be deployed on any simple HTTP hosting service. This web application, like any standard web application, has an index file named index.html. The file is located at sample01/ui/src/app/index.html. You can open this file with any text editor or an IDE. The interesting feature of this HTML file is the content of the `<body>` element:

```
<body>
  <app-root></app-root>
</body>
```

As you may notice, the `<app-root>` element isn't a standard DOCTYPE (www .w3schools.com/tags/ref_html_dtd.asp) in HTML. This particular index.html is loaded into the browser on the first request to the web server; then the browser replaces the content of the `<body>` element that's loaded into it, with new content based on how the user interacts with the application. The JavaScript code running on the browser performs this action, which is typical behavior of SPAs. Many applications are designed in such a way that index.html is the only static HTML file loaded into the browser. User actions (clicks) result in its contents being dynamically updated by the JavaScript running on the browser itself. Note that although some applications follow SPA architecture and principles, they could have more than one static HTML file loaded for different actions.

The request to the `/books` path of the resource server fetches the actual (dynamic) content to be displayed on the web page. If you observe the content of that response message in the browser's developer tools, you should see a JSON payload similar to the following:

```
[
  {
    "id":1,
    "name":"Microservices Security In Action",
    "author":null
  },
  {
    "id":2,
    "name":"Real World Cryptography",
```

```
        "author":null
    },
    . . . . .
]
```

The message you saw in your browser was constructed from the data contained in the preceding JSON string. When the browser made a request to the /books path to the resource server running on localhost:8080, it executed a method on your Spring Boot application. You can find that method in the file located at sample01/resource/ src/main/java/com/manning/mss/ch04/sample01/resource/BookController.java, shown in the following listing.

Listing 4.1   The content of the BookController.java file

```
@GetMapping("/books")
@CrossOrigin(origins = "http://localhost:4200")
public Collection<Book> getBooks() {
    System.out.println("Executing GET /books");
    return repository.findAll();
}
```

The method annotation @GetMapping("/books") instructs the Spring Boot runtime to execute the method getBooks when a GET request is received on /books. If you go through the rest of the method contents, you can figure out how it constructs the content of the JSON you saw earlier.

Another file that can help you understand the dynamic HTML content is the file located at sample01/ui/src/app/app.component.ts. This file contains code that will generate the HTML that will eventually replace the content of the <body> section of index.html (see the following listing).

Listing 4.2   The content of the app.component.ts file

```
@Component({
  selector: 'app-root',
  template: `<h1>Book List App</h1>
    <p>
      <button (click)='loadBooks()'>Load Books</button>
    </p>
    <span>
      <div *ngFor=\"let book of books\">{{book.name}}</div>
    </span>`,
  styles: []
})

export class AppComponent {
  books: Book[];

  constructor(private http: HttpClient) {
  }
```

```
loadBooks(){
    this.http
      .get<Book[]>('http://localhost:8080/books')
      .subscribe(data => {this.books = data});
    }
}
```

Notice the placeholder {book.name}, which will be replaced by the JSON content sent by the /books endpoint. The code inside the file sample01/ui/src/app/app.component.ts is a TypeScript file. The button click event triggers the loadBooks function that initiates the request to the /books endpoint, as the following piece of code shows:

```
loadBooks(){
    this.http
      .get<Book[]>('http://localhost:8080/books')
      .subscribe(data => {this.books = data});
}
```

Notice the HTTP GET request to the /books endpoint of the resource server. The response of the request is assigned to a variable named books.

In this particular example, your web server—the one that hosted the UI application—and the data endpoint (/books) are running on different hosts, localhost:4200 and localhost:8080, respectively. In most real-world scenarios, you would find a similar deployment, which leads us to a problem enforced by the same-origin policy on web browsers. In the next section, we talk about this policy in detail and discuss how we can resolve it by using cross-origin resource sharing.

4.2 Setting up cross-origin resource sharing

Suppose different teams in your organization are developing microservices that power a web application, such as an online retail store. These teams could be hosting their microservices in different domains (such as orders.retailstore.com and products.retailstore.com). In section 4.1, you built a SPA with the frontend and backend on different hosts. By default, web browsers will not allow an application hosted on one domain to access resources from another domain.

This was made possible in sample01 that we tried out in section 4.1 because of the cross-origin resource sharing (CORS) policy available in web browsers. Let's take a deeper look at the same-origin policy, its implications, and how CORS allows us to make cross-origin requests. If you are interested in learning about CORS in detail, we recommend *CORS in Action* (Manning, 2014) by Monsur Hossain.

4.2.1 Using the same-origin policy

The *same-origin policy* (https://en.wikipedia.org/wiki/Same-origin_policy) is a web security concept introduced to ensure that scripts running on a particular web page can make requests only to services running on the same origin. An origin of a given

URL consists of the URI scheme, hostname, and port. Given the URL http://localhost:8080/login, the following sections compose the origin:

- http—The URL scheme
- localhost—The hostname/IP-address
- 8080—The port

The sections after the port aren't considered to be part of the origin; therefore, /login isn't considered to be part of the origin. The same-origin policy exists to prevent a malicious script on one website from accessing data on other websites unintentionally. The same-origin policy applies only to data access, not to CSS, images, and scripts, so you could write web pages that consist of links to CSS, images, and scripts of other origins. Figure 4.4 illustrates this scenario.

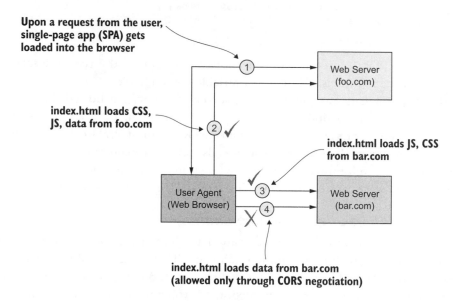

Figure 4.4   In a web browser, the same-origin policy ensures that scripts running on a particular web page can make requests only to services running on the same origin.

Here are the steps shown in figure 4.4:

1 The browser loads an HTML file (index.html) from the domain foo.com. This request is successful.
2 The index.html file loaded into the browser makes a request to the same domain (foo.com) to load CSS and JavaScript files; it also loads data (makes an HTTP request) from the domain foo.com. All requests are successful because everything is from the same domain as the web page itself.
3 The index.html file loaded into the browser makes a request to a domain named bar.com to load CSS and JavaScript files. This request, although made to

a different domain (bar.com) from a web page loaded from another domain (foo.com), is successful because it's loading only CSS and JavaScript.

4 The index.html file loaded into the browser loads data (makes an HTTP request) from an endpoint on domain bar.com. This request fails because, by default, the browser doesn't allow web pages in one domain (foo.com) to make HTTP requests to endpoints in other domains (bar.com) unless the request is for CSS, JavaScript, or images.

What is the danger of not having a same-origin policy?

Suppose you're logged into Gmail in your web browser. As you may know, Gmail uses cookies in your browser to maintain data related to your browser session. Someone sends you a link (via email or chat) that appears to be a link to an interesting website. You click this link, which results in loading that particular website in your browser.

If this website has a page with one or more scripts that access the Gmail APIs to retrieve your data, the lack of something similar to a same-origin policy would allow the script to be executed. Because you're already authenticated to Gmail, and your session data is stored locally on cookies, a request to Gmail APIs would submit these cookies as well. So effectively, a malicious website has authenticated to Gmail pretending to be you and is now capable of retrieving any data that the Gmail APIs/services provide.

Now you have a good understanding of the same-origin-policy in web browsers, its importance, and the risks of not having such a policy. But in practice, you still need this to work in certain scenarios, especially with a SPA, to invoke a set of APIs/services, which are outside the domain of the SPA. Let's take a look at how web browsers facilitate resource sharing among domains to support such legitimate use cases.

4.2.2 Using cross-origin resource sharing

Web browsers have an exception to the same-origin policy: *cross-origin resource sharing* (*CORS*), a specification that allows web browsers to access selected resources on different origins; see https://developer.mozilla.org/en-US/docs/Web/HTTP/CORS. CORS allows the SPA running on origin `localhost:4200` to access resources running on origin `localhost:8080`. Web browsers use the `OPTIONS` HTTP method along with special HTTP headers to determine whether to allow or deny a cross-origin request. Let's see how the protocol works.

Whenever the browser detects that it's about to execute a script that makes a request to a different origin, it sends an HTTP `OPTIONS` request to the resource on the particular origin. You can observe this request, known as a *preflight request*, by inspecting it on the Network tab of your browser's developer tools. The request includes the following HTTP headers:

- `Access-Control-Request-Headers`—Indicates the HTTP headers that the request is about to send to the server (such as `origin`, `x-requested-with`)

- `Access-Control-Request-Method`—Indicates the HTTP method about to be executed by the request (such as `GET`)
- `Origin`—Indicates the origin of the web application (such as `http://local-host:8080`)

The server responds to this preflight request with the following headers:

- `Access-Control-Allow-Credentials`—Indicates whether the server allows the request originator to send credentials in the form of authorization headers, cookies, or TLS client certificates. This header is a Boolean value that indicates `true` or `false`.
- `Access-Control-Allow-Headers`—Indicates the list of headers allowed by the particular resource on the server. If the server allows more than is requested via the `Access-Control-Request-Headers` header, it returns only what is requested.
- `Access-Control-Allow-Methods`—Indicates the list of HTTP methods allowed by the particular resource on the server. If the server allows more than is requested via the `Access-Control-Request-Method`, it returns only the one requested (such as `GET`).
- `Access-Control-Allow-Origin`—Indicates the cross-origin allowed by the server. The server may support more than one origin, but what is returned in this particular header is the value of the `Origin` header requested if the server supports cross-origin requests from the domain of the request originator (such as `http://localhost:8080`).
- `Access-Control-Max-Age`—Indicates for how long, in seconds, browsers can cache the response to the particular preflight request (such as 3600).

Upon receiving the response to the preflight request, the web browser validates the response headers to determine whether the target server allows the cross-origin request. If the response headers to the preflight request don't correspond to the request to be sent (perhaps the HTTP method isn't allowed, or one of the required headers is missing in the `Access-Control-Allow-Headers` list), the browser stops the cross-origin request from being executed.

4.2.3   *Inspecting the source that allows cross-origin requests*

In the directory chapter04/sample01/resource, open the file located at src/main/java/com/manning/mss/ch04/sample01/resource/BookController.java with a text editor or IDE. You should find a method named `getBooks` in this file and an annotation with the name `@CrossOrigin`:

```
@GetMapping("/books")
@CrossOrigin(origins = "http://localhost:4200")
public Collection<Book> getBooks() {
    System.out.println("Executing GET /books");
    return repository.findAll();
}
```

Behind the scenes, whenever the server receives an HTTP OPTIONS request to the /books resource, this piece of code uses the data specified within the @CrossOrigin annotation to build the corresponding HTTP response. By looking at the contents of the annotation, you should be able to figure out how they correspond to the preflight response headers discussed earlier. In the next section, you see how to offload CORS responsibilities to an API gateway layer so that your microservice is relieved from CORS-related duties.

4.2.4 *Proxying the resource server with an API gateway*

As you saw in section 4.2.3, you need code in your microservice to deal with CORS-specific configurations. According to microservices best practices and recommendations, you should try to avoid burdening the microservice with anything other than what it's primarily designed to do. Another alternative for dealing with the same-origin policy is using an API gateway to act as a reverse proxy to your microservices, which we discuss in this section.

Suppose that you have to expose the same microservice to other origins someday in the future. In the design discussed earlier, you would need to modify your microservice's @CrossOrigin annotation to allow additional origins, which requires rebuilding and redeploying the microservice to expose it to a consumer from a new origin. As mentioned earlier, this modification goes against the microservices recommendations and best practices. Therefore, it would be better to use an API gateway solution.

> **NOTE** You can also use any standard reverse-proxy solution such as NGINX (www.nginx.com) for the same requirement. We keep mentioning the API gateway because, when it comes to separating the consumer (UI) application from the backend, an API gateway becomes useful for much more than CORS negotiations alone.

To examine a practical example of this pattern, look at sample02 inside the chapter04 directory. Make sure to shut down running samples from the previous sections before you attempt to run samples in this section. You should see three subdirectories within sample02—namely ui, resource, and gateway. Use separate windows (or tabs) of your command-line tool to build and run the gateway and resource server processes. To build and run the gateway, execute the following two commands from the sample02/gateway directory:

```
\> mvn clean install
\> mvn spring-boot:run
```

To build and run the resource server, execute the following two commands from the sample02/resource directory:

```
\> mvn clean install
\> mvn spring-boot:run
```

These commands should start the gateway and resource server processes. The resource server would be running on port 8080 as before. The gateway process would be running on port 9090. Next, use your command line to navigate to sample02/ui and execute the following command to start the Angular web application:

```
\> ng serve
```

Once the application starts successfully, open a web browser with the browser developer tools switched on and navigate to http://localhost:4200. If the ng serve command results in the error [error] Error: Cannot find module '@angular-devkit/build-angular/package.json', you can follow the instructions at http://mng.bz/Mdr2 to overcome it. This could occur if you're upgrading Angular from an older version to 9.0.4.

Observe the Network tab of your browser developer tool and click the Load Books button. You should see that the browser now sends the GET /books request to local-host:9090 (to the gateway) instead of localhost:8080 (the resource server). If the request is successful, you should see the list of book titles on the web page.

Use a text editor or IDE to open the Java class declared in the file sample02/resource/src/main/java/com/manning/mss/ch04/sample02/resource/BookController.java. You will notice now that its getBooks function is no longer annotated with @Cross-Origin as in sample01. This is because we have removed CORS handling from the microservice and delegated that to the API gateway. Open the sample02/gateway/src/main/java/com/manning/mss/ch04/sample02/gateway/GatewayApplication.java file by using a text editor or IDE. Notice the code block in the following listing that configures CORS on the API gateway.

Listing 4.3   The code that handles CORS on the API gateway

```
@Bean
public WebMvcConfigurer corsConfigurer() {
    return new WebMvcConfigurer() {
        public void addCorsMappings(CorsRegistry registry) {
            registry.addMapping("/books/**")
                    .allowedOrigins("http://localhost:4200")
                    .allowedMethods("GET", "POST");
        }
    };
}
```

Open the file sample02/gateway/src/main/resources/application.yml with your text editor or IDE, and notice the following route instruction:

```
zuul:
  routes:
    path: /books/**
    url: http://localhost:8080/books
```

This route instruction tells the Zuul API gateway to route whatever requests it receives on path /books/** to URL http://localhost:8080/books. When your browser makes a GET request to http://localhost:9090/books, the Zuul gateway

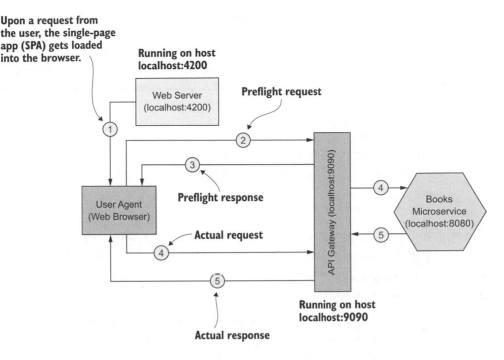

Figure 4.5   The API gateway handles preflight requests generated corresponding to a web application running on a different origin.

intercepts this request and forwards it to the resource server URL `http://local-host:8080/books`. However, Zuul does not forward the preflight `OPTIONS` requests on `/books`. The Zuul gateway responds to the preflight requests by itself, as configured in listing 4.3. Figure 4.5 illustrates this pattern of the API gateway handling preflight requests while forwarding the other requests to the resource server.

4.3   *Securing a SPA with OpenID Connect*

In this section, you'll see a practical example of using OpenID Connect to secure your SPA. *OpenID Connect* (*OIDC*) is an identity layer built on top of OAuth 2.0. If you are not familiar with OpenID Connect, we recommend you first go through appendix A. In all the preceding examples, we did not use any authentication to secure our SPA. In this section, we use OpenID Connect to authenticate users to the SPA. You can find the source code of this example in the chapter04/sample03 directory. Three components participate in this example:

- *The web server*—The UI server hosts the SPA and is also an OAuth client with a valid client ID and client secret.
- *The OAuth 2.0 authorization server*—This component plays the role of the authorization server, which also is the OpenID Connect provider.
- *The resource server*—This microservice provides the details of books.

To build the source code of these samples, navigate to the chapter04/sample03 directory by using your command-line client. You should see three subdirectories named ui, resource, and authz. The ui directory contains the code of the Angular-based web application, the resource directory contains code of our Books microservice, and the authz directory contains the code of our OIDC provider, also known as the *authorization server*. Open separate command-line windows (or tabs) and navigate to the resource directory in one of them, and to the authz directory in the other. Execute the following command in each window to build the code of the microservice and authorization server, respectively. To build and run the authorization server, execute the following commands from the sample03/authz directory:

```
\> mvn clean install
\> mvn spring-boot:run
```

To build and run the resource server, execute the following commands from the sample03/ resource directory:

```
\> mvn clean install
\> mvn spring-boot:run
```

You should now have the authorization server and the resource server up and running. Let's try to access the /books resource with an HTTP GET on the resource server. Open a new terminal window and execute the following command:

```
\> curl -v http://localhost:8080/books
```

This should return a 401 Unauthorized response, which looks like the following:

```
< HTTP/1.1 401
< Cache-Control: no-store
< Pragma: no-cache
< WWW-Authenticate: Bearer realm="oauth2-resource", error="unauthorized",
    error_description="Full authentication is required to access this
    resource"
```

As you can observe from the error response, the resource server is now expecting an OAuth 2.0 Bearer token to access this resource. In this next section, we take a look at how our web application goes through an OIDC login flow to obtain an access token and accesses this resource to get the list of books.

4.3.1 *Understanding the OpenID Connect login flow*

In this section, we look at the OIDC login flow in our Angular web application. We use the angular-oauth2-oidc library available for Angular applications; see https://github.com/manfredsteyer/angular-oauth2-oidc. This is an open source OpenID-certified library. Open a new command-line terminal, navigate to the sample03/ui directory, and execute the following command to run the web application:

```
\> ng serve
```

Once everything is running, open a private browsing session in your web browser, and go to http://localhost:4200/.

You should see the Book List application web page as in sample02, but this time with a Log In button instead of a Load Books button, as shown in figure 4.6.

Click the Log In button and you'll be redirected to a web page on the authorization server (localhost:8081) to enter your username and password. Provide the value user as the username, and password for the password, and then click the Sign In button, shown in figure 4.7.

Figure 4.6   The Book List App web page requires you to log in to view the list of book titles.

Figure 4.7   The login page of the authorization server

Once you provide the correct credentials and click the Sign In button, you'll be taken to a page to approve the request from the SPA to access the protected resources, as shown in figure 4.8.

OAuth Approval

Do you authorize "clientapp" to access your protected resources?

- scope.openid: ● Approve ○ Deny

Authorize

Figure 4.8   On the authorization page presented by the authorization server, chose the Approve option and proceed.

Select the Approve option and then click the Authorize button. You will then be taken back to the SPA's home page. Now, instead of the Log In button, you should see the Load Books button. Clicking this button should load the book titles to the web page, as shown in figure 4.9.

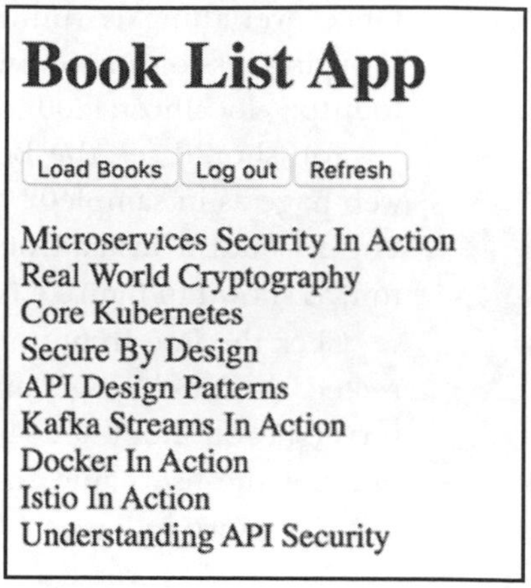

What we just went through was a typical OIDC login flow in an application to obtain an access token to access the GET /books resource on the resource server. Close the web browser that you just executed these steps on and reopen a new web browser in private browsing mode with the browser developer tools turned on. Repeat the steps that we just completed and observe the Network tab to see what happens behind the scenes when we try to log in to our web application.

Book List App

[Load Books] [Log out] [Refresh]

Microservices Security In Action
Real World Cryptography
Core Kubernetes
Secure By Design
API Design Patterns
Kafka Streams In Action
Docker In Action
Istio In Action
Understanding API Security

Figure 4.9   After you click the Load Books button, the web page shows the list of book titles.

When you click the Log In button, you'll notice that the browser initiates an authorization request to the /oauth/authorize endpoint of the authorization server. This passes a response_type parameter set to code, indicating that it is initializing an authorization code grant, in this case can also be called as an OIDC authorization code flow. The client_id is sent as a request parameter as well:

```
http://localhost:8081/oauth/authorize?
   response_type=code&
   client_id=clientapp&
   state=Ulg4V1pN.....&
   redirect_uri=http.....&
   scope=openid&
   nonce=Ulg4V1.....&
   audience=https...
```

As a response to this authorization request, the authorization server responds with a 302 redirect to the login page. You should notice the Location header in the response pointing to http://localhost:8081/login. The browser makes a GET request to this URL, and that request results in what you see on the login page of your browser. Figure 4.10 illustrates this scenario.

Once you provide the username and password on the login page, you will notice the browser submitting the data to the authorization server. The authorization server then redirects the browser to the content page, where you need to approve the web application's access to the protected resources on the resource server. Once the approval is provided, the authorization server redirects the browser back to the web application providing an authorization code. You can notice this in the Location header that comes as a response from the authorization request:

```
Location:
   http://localhost:4200/?code=rnRb4K&state=bEs1c.....
```

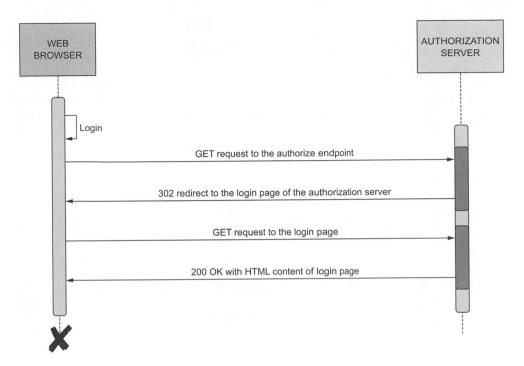

Figure 4.10 Sequence of events that present the login page of the authorization server during an OpenID Connect login flow

Once the browser receives this authorization code, it initiates a request to the /oauth/token endpoint of the authorization server to exchange the authorization code for an access token. You should see a request similar to the following being initiated from your web browser:

```
POST http://localhost:8081/oauth/token
grant_type=authorization_code&
code-rnRb4K&
redirect_uri=http://localhost:4200/&
client_id=clientapp&
client_secret=123456&
audience=https://bookstore.app
```

The response to this request is an access token, which can now be used by the web application to access resources on the resource server. The token response is JSON that looks similar to the following:

```
{
"access_token":"92ee7d17-cfab-4bad-b110-f287b4c2b630",
"token_type":"bearer",
"refresh_token":"dcce6ad7-9520-43fd-8170-a1a2857818b3",
"expires_in":1478,
"scope":"openid"
}
```

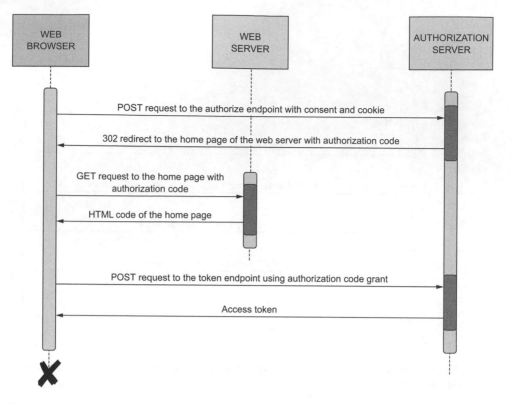

Figure 4.11   Sequence of events that exchanges the authorization code for an access token

Figure 4.11 illustrates this exchange of messages.

Once the web application has received the access token, it no longer displays the Log In button, but instead displays the Load Books button. Clicking this button to load books makes a request to the resource server to fetch the list of books and displays them on the web page. The difference between this and the previous sample is that in this case, the browser sends the access token it received in an `Authorization: Bearer` header to the resource server. The resource server validates the access token by talking to the authorization server. It returns the list of books only upon a successful validation of the access token. Figure 4.12 illustrates this scenario.

In the next section, we take a look at the code of our web application, resource server, and authorization server that enabled this flow.

4.3.2   *Inspecting the code of the applications*

In this section, we look at the code that allowed our applications to participate in the flow of events shown in figure 4.11 and figure 4.12 to secure our web application through an OIDC flow.

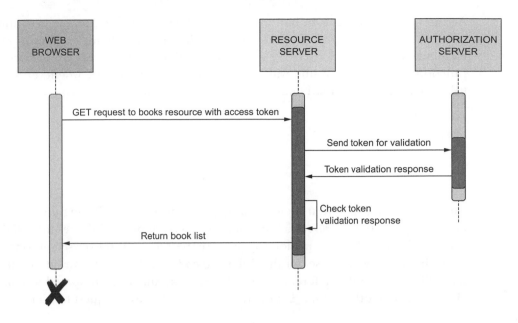

Figure 4.12 Sequence of events for the web application to display the list of book titles

CODE OF THE ANGULAR WEB APPLICATION

As mentioned previously in this chapter, we use the angular-oauth2-oidc library to secure the Angular application using OIDC. The following listing contains code from the sample03/ui/src/app/app.component.ts file.

Listing 4.4 The app.component.ts file that renders buttons on the web page

```
import { Component } from '@angular/core';
import { OAuthService, OAuthErrorEvent } from 'angular-oauth2-oidc';
import { HttpClient } from '@angular/common/http';

@Component({
  selector: 'app-root',
  template: `<h1>Book List App</h1>
    <p>
      <button *ngIf="!isLoggedIn()" (click)='login()'>Log In</button>
      <button *ngIf="isLoggedIn()" (click)='loadBooks()'>Load Books</button>
      <button (click)='logout()'>Log out</button>
      <button (click)='refresh()'>Refresh</button>
    </p>

    <span *ngIf="isLoggedIn()">
      <div *ngFor=\"let book of books\">{{book.name}}</div>
    </span>`,
  styles: []
})
```

As you can see, the Log In button is rendered whenever the `isLoggedIn` function returns `false`. The Load Books button and the book list items (within the `<span>` element) are rendered whenever the same function returns `true`. The `isLoggedIn` function, which you can find within the same file, returns `true` whenever an access token is available, as shown here:

```
isLoggedIn(){
  if (this.oauthService.getAccessToken() === null){
    return false;
  }
  return true;
}
```

Clicking the Log In button triggers the `login` function, and clicking the Load Books button triggers the `loadBooks` function. The `login` function initiates the OIDC flow, whereas the `loadBooks` function triggers a request to the resource server to fetch the list of books, as you can see in the following code block (which can be found in the same file). Notice the difference in the `loadBooks` function compared to sample02. Here, we also set the `Authorization: Bearer` token as a request header:

```
login() {
    this.oauthService.initCodeFlow();
}

loadBooks(){

 this.http
   .get<Book[]>('http://localhost:8080/books',
     { headers: {'Authorization': 'Bearer '+
                               this.oauthService.getAccessToken()}})
   .subscribe(data => {this.books = data});
}
```

The initialization of the angular-oauth2-oidc library with configuration parameters such as the `clientId` and `scope` can be found in the sample03/ui/src/app/app .module.ts file. The following listing presents the code block that sets these parameters.

Listing 4.5   Initialization of the angular-oauth2-oidc library with config parameters

```
const config: AuthConfig = {
  issuer: 'http://localhost:8080/',
  loginUrl: 'http://localhost:8081/oauth/authorize',
  tokenEndpoint: 'http://localhost:8081/oauth/token',
  dummyClientSecret: '123456',
  clientId: 'clientapp',
  disablePKCE: true,
  responseType: 'code',
  oidc: true,
  requireHttps: false,
  strictDiscoveryDocumentValidation: false,
  customQueryParams: { audience: 'https://bookstore.app' },
```

```
    redirectUri: window.location.origin + '/',
    silentRefreshRedirectUri: window.location.origin + '/silent-refresh.html',
    scope: 'openid',
    requestAccessToken: true,
    skipIssuerCheck: true,
    showDebugInformation: true,
};
```

CODE OF THE RESOURCE SERVER

The code of the resource server remains more or less similar to that of sample02. The inclusion of the following two dependencies in the pom.xml file found in the sample03/resource/ directory enables OAuth2.0–based security for the resources we expose through the resource server:

```
<dependency>
    <groupId>org.springframework.cloud</groupId>
    <artifactId>spring-cloud-starter-oauth2</artifactId>
    <version>2.2.0.RELEASE</version>
</dependency>
<dependency>
    <groupId>org.springframework.security.oauth.boot</groupId>
    <artifactId>spring-security-oauth2-autoconfigure</artifactId>
    <version>2.2.4.RELEASE</version>
</dependency>
```

Once these Spring OAuth 2.0 dependencies are included in our project, Spring Boot automatically mandates OAuth 2.0-based authentication for the resources. This is why we were unable to access the /books resource directly without a valid access token the previous time we attempted to access it using curl.

Next, take a look at the application.properties file located at sample03/resource/ src/main/resources. The first property in this file (security.oauth2.resource .token-info-uri) points to the endpoint on the authorization server that validates access tokens received on the resource server. The clientId and clientSecret properties in this file are credentials of the resource server granted by the authorization server itself. These are required to access the token validation endpoint (http:// localhost:8081/oauth/check_token). Note that these credentials are not the same as what was used by the web application to authenticate itself against the authorization server.

CODE OF THE AUTHORIZATION SERVER

The code of the authorization server is more or less the same as what we saw in chapter 3. The configure method found in the OAuth2AuthorizationServer.java file within the sample03/authz/src/main/java/com/manning/mss/ch04/sample03/ authz/config directory contains the code that configures our authorization server. In listing 4.6, observe how we have registered the two client applications: the first with client_id having the value clientapp, which is used by our web application; and the next with client_id having the value resourceclient, which is used by our resource server.

Listing 4.6   The authorization server registers the two client apps

```
public void configure(ClientDetailsServiceConfigurer clients) throws Exception {
    clients.inMemory()
            .withClient("clientapp")
            .secret(passwordEncoder.encode("123456"))
            .authorizedGrantTypes("password", "authorization_code",
                                                "refresh_token")
            .authorities("READ_ONLY_CLIENT")
            .scopes("openid", "read_profile_info")
            .resourceIds("oauth2-resource")
            .redirectUris("http://localhost:4200/")
            .accessTokenValiditySeconds(5000)
            .refreshTokenValiditySeconds(50000)
            .and()
            .withClient("resourceclient")
            .secret(passwordEncoder.encode("resourcesecret"));
}
```

The `configure` method in the SecurityConfig.java file in the same location lists the code where we register the valid users in the system:

```
protected void configure(AuthenticationManagerBuilder auth) throws Exception {
    auth.inMemoryAuthentication()
        .withUser("user")
        .password(passwordEncoder().encode("password"))
        .roles("USER");
}
```

4.4   *Using federated authentication*

In the preceding sections, we discussed building a SPA and securing it with OIDC. We discussed securing your resources with OAuth 2.0 in chapters 2 and 3, and we used the same mechanism to protect your resource server in this chapter. Figure 4.13 shows at a high level how the resource server is protected.

As we discussed in chapter 3, when the resource server (or the API gateway that sits in front of it) receives a self-contained access token, it doesn't have to talk to the authorization server to validate it. The resource server first validates the authenticity (proof of identity) of the access token by verifying its signature and then checks the validity of its contents (intended audience, expiry, scopes, and so on). To validate the authenticity of a self-contained access token (JWT), the resource server requires the public key of the authorization server that signed the token.

As you may have noticed, a trust relationship is required between the resource server and the authorization server. Even if you used an opaque token (also known as a reference token), so that the resource server would need to talk to the authorization server that issued the token to validate it, you still need a trust relationship between the resource server and the authorization server.

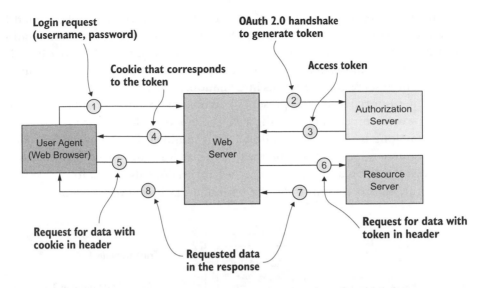

Figure 4.13   In this end-to-end authentication flow between the SPA and resource server, users authenticate to SPA with OpenID Connect, and the resource server protects all its APIs with OAuth 2.0.

> **NOTE**   Although we keep using the term *resource server* in this chapter to refer to a Spring Boot application that hosts a microservice, you could also call an *API gateway* a resource server. We're omitting a discussion of the API gateway to reduce the number of components discussed in this chapter.

The client application (SPA), authorization server, and resource server need to be in the same trust domain. Suppose that in your online retail store, you have to work with a third-party shipping service to make shipping requests for the orders that are placed and to get details on pending shipments. When a user logs in to your retail store, the user authenticates against your trust domain. But when the user inquires about the status of shipments, your web application needs to talk to a third-party shipping service. The shipping service needs to make sure that it gives details only to the relevant users (user A can't get details on orders placed by user B) and therefore needs to know the identity of the user who's logged in to the system. Because the shipping service is in a separate trust domain, by default it won't know how to validate a token issued by your own private trust domain. To access an API or a service from the shipping trust domain, first you need to get a token from an authorization server, which is trusted by the shipping trust domain.

4.4.1   Multiple trust domains

If a client application works across multiple trust domains, the preceding solution we discussed in section 4.3 won't work. When a resource server is presented a token issued by an authorization server of another trust domain (which the resource server does not trust), it won't be able to validate the token or accept it as valid.

If the presented token is a self-contained token in the form of a signed JWT, the resource server needs to know the public certificate used by the authorization server in the foreign trust domain to validate the signature of the token. Because the authorization server and resource server are separated by a trust domain, it's unlikely that the resource server will know this information.

If the resource server was presented an opaque token, it would need to contact the authorization server that issued the access token to validate it. Again, because these two servers belong to different trust domains, it's unlikely for this scenario to be possible. The resource server may not know where the relevant authorization server resides, and even if it does, it may not have the necessary credentials to talk to its token validation endpoint. Figure 4.14 illustrates the trust boundaries between systems.

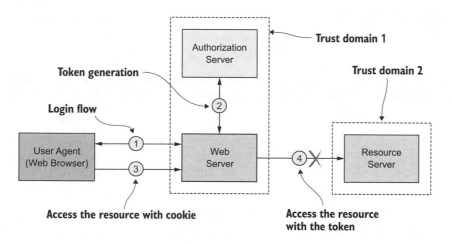

Figure 4.14   The authorization server and resource server are in two trust domains. The resource server in trust domain 2 does not know how to validate a token issued by the authorization server in trust domain 1.

As shown in figure 4.14, step 4 will fail because the token that's passed to the resource server at this point is obtained from trust domain 1. Because the resource server is in trust domain 2, it won't know how to validate the token that it receives; hence, the request will fail with an authentication error.

4.4.2 *Building trust between domains*

To solve the problem discussed in section 4.4.1, you need to build a mechanism that builds a trust relationship across domains. An authorization server itself usually defines a trust domain. A given trust domain has many resource servers, web applications, user stores, and so on, but it has only one authorization server that governs how each component or application in the particular domain should accept requests for processing. This authorization server is the single source of truth. Therefore, to build trust between domains, you need to build a chain of trust between the authorization servers of each domain. This chain of trust combined with the token exchange pattern (using the JWT grant type) can provide a solution to your problem (see figure 4.15).

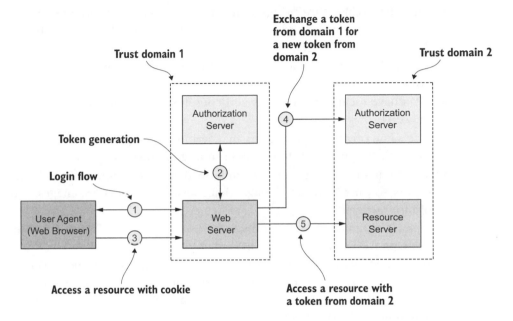

Figure 4.15 Token exchange pattern to obtain a token valid for domain 2. The authorization server in domain 2 trusts the authorization server in domain 1, but the resource server in domain 2 trusts only the authorization server in its own domain.

As shown in figure 4.15, before the service provider (web server) attempts to access resources from the resource server in domain 2, it should perform a token exchange from the authorization server in domain 2. Assuming that the token obtained from the authorization server in domain 1 is a JWT (not an opaque token), it can use the JWT bearer grant type (https://tools.ietf.org/html/rfc7523) to request an access token from the authorization server in domain 2.

The JWT bearer grant type (officially known as the *JWT profile* for OAuth2.0 client authentication and authorization grants) has a simple protocol. It accepts a JWT and performs the relevant validations on the token (verifying its signature, expiry, and so on); if the token is valid, it issues a valid OAuth 2.0 token to the client, which can be another JWT itself or even an opaque token string. The important thing in this scenario is the ability of the authorization server in domain 2 to validate the token (JWT) it receives and to exchange it for a new access token. For this purpose, you need to build a trust relationship between the authorization servers in domain 1 and domain 2. Building this trust relationship could be a matter of exchanging public certificates.

Summary

- Single-page applications perform better by reducing network chattiness as they perform all rendering on the web browser and by reducing the workload on the web server.
- The SPA architecture brings simplicity to microservices architectures because they do not require complex web application-hosting facilities such as JBoss or Tomcat.
- The SPA architecture abstracts out the data layer from the user experience layer.
- SPAs have security restrictions and complexities due to the same-origin policy on web browsers.
- The same-origin policy ensures that scripts running on a particular web page can make requests only to services running on the same origin.
- The same-origin policy applies only to data access, not to CSS, images, and scripts, so you can write web pages that consist of links to CSS, images, and scripts of other origins.
- OpenID Connect is an identity layer built on top of OAuth 2.0. Most SPAs use OpenID Connect to authenticate users.
- Because SPAs may consume APIs (data sources) from multiple trust domains, a token obtained from one trust domain may not be valid for another trust domain. We need to build token-exchange functionality when a SPA hops across multiple trust boundaries.
- All samples in this chapter used HTTP (not HTTPS) endpoints to spare you from having to set up proper certificates and to make it possible for you to inspect messages being passed on the wire (network), if required. In production systems, we do not recommend using HTTP for any endpoint.

5
Engaging throttling, monitoring, and access control

This chapter covers

- Setting up a Zuul proxy to enforce throttling
- Using Prometheus and Grafana to monitor microservices
- Applying access-control policies at the edge with Zuul and OPA

In chapter 3, we introduced the API Gateway architectural pattern and discussed its applicability in a microservices deployment. *Zuul* is an open source API gateway developed by Netflix to proxy all its microservices. Zuul provides dynamic routing, monitoring, resiliency, security, and more. It acts as the front door to Netflix's server infrastructure, handling traffic from Netflix users around the globe.

We also discussed in chapter 3 how to enforce security based on OAuth 2.0 for your microservices, using Zuul as the API gateway. In this chapter, we extend those samples to use Zuul to handle throttling and apply access-control policies, and we also discuss the monitoring aspects of a microservices deployment.

109

5.1   *Throttling at the API gateway with Zuul*

In this section, we discuss the types of threats a typical microservices deployment is exposed to by allowing too many requests within a particular time frame, and why it is important to throttle requests. Take a look at figure 5.1 to refresh your memory from chapter 3 on the participants of an API Gateway architecture pattern.

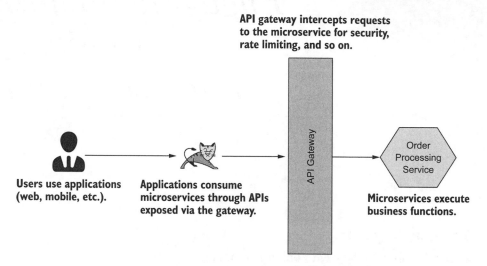

Figure 5.1   API gateways are used in microservices architectures to expose microservices for external consumption. Users use applications for various tasks, and these applications consume services exposed by API gateways.

As you can see, the client application accesses the API gateway, which in turn sends the requests to your target microservices (backend). The API gateway and the target service are both request-serving nodes in the system. Every request sent by a client application needs to be processed by the API gateway, and every valid request received by the API gateway needs to be sent to the target microservice for processing.

As requests from the client applications increase, the performance and scalability factors of the API gateway are negatively affected. The increased number of valid requests, which are authenticated and authorized, have a negative impact on the performance and scalability factors of the target microservices, unless the system is designed properly. The way we usually deal with a rising number of requests to process is to scale up the application layers (API gateway and target services).

Scaling up has two primary models: vertical scaling and horizontal scaling, as shown in figure 5.2. *Vertical scaling* increases the computing power on which our software runs, such as increasing the memory and CPU capacity of the corresponding servers. With horizontal scaling, we scale our deployment by adding more virtual machines, or VMs, (or computers) to our pool of resources where our software (microservices) runs and execute all of them in parallel.

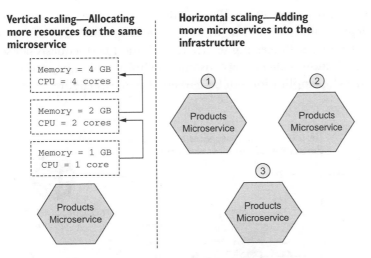

Figure 5.2 Vertical scaling versus horizontal scaling. The resources available on the host of the microservice limit vertical scaling. Horizontal scaling in theory is unlimited.

Scaling doesn't come for free. Whatever model of scaling we opt for, it comes at a cost. There is also a physical limit on how much we can scale our systems. This limit is sometimes defined by the amount of available physical hardware. And at other times, this is also limited by the ability of our software to scale horizontally. Especially when it comes to stateful software systems, such as a system that depends on a relational database, scaling the software beyond a certain level becomes harder and harder because of the complexities involved in scaling the relational database.

All of these complexities lead us to a point where it becomes necessary for us to limit the number of requests being served by our system. And we need to set those limits fairly so that all consumers of our services get a fair quota of the total amount of traffic we can handle. Limiting the number of requests can also help protect our systems from attackers who attempt to perform DoS and DDoS attacks by sending in a huge number of requests and thus preventing others from gaining access to the system. Let's now look at the various types of throttling we can apply on our systems.

5.1.1 Quota-based throttling for applications

In this section, we discuss how to apply throttling to our microservices based on request quotas allocated to specific client applications. Allocating request quotas becomes useful in cases such as monetizing microservices as well as when we want to prevent microservices from being consumed more than their capacity allows.

In our example in figure 5.3, some sort of application or device consumes the Order Processing microservice. Alternatively, more than one application could access the same microservice, such as the Order Processing microservice being accessed by a mobile device, a web application, and a desktop application. When the number of consumer applications of the Order Processing microservice increases, its performance could degrade unless you design the system properly. Let's assume for argument's sake that the Order Processing service can handle 1,000 requests per second. If all the mobile applications collectively consume the full 1,000 requests, the web application and the desktop application will be starved of requests (figure 5.3).

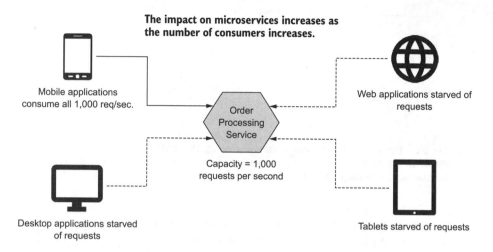

Figure 5.3   The more consumers a microservice has, the greater the capacity it must handle.

The way to solve this problem is to provide each application a quota, such as 200 requests per second, and to enforce this quota at the API gateway. This way, a given application or device will not be able to starve the rest of the consumers in the system. The maximum capacity each application can consume from the system would now be limited to 200 requests per second. This leaves room for other consumers to consume the remaining 800 requests within a given second. Hence this eliminates the risk of a single application causing a DoS or a DDoS attack.

For this mechanism to work, the API gateway must be able to identify the application from which each request originates. If the API gateway is unable to identify the application or device type, it should default to a common value, such as 100 requests per second. Assuming the APIs on the API gateway are secured using OAuth 2.0, each consumer application would need to have a unique client ID, as we discussed in chapter 3. When an application sends a request along with an access token to the API gateway, the gateway can then introspect the access token (by talking to the OAuth 2.0 authorization server) and retrieve the corresponding client ID. This client ID can be used to uniquely identify the application from which the request originated.

The API gateway would then count the number of requests being served within a time window of 1 second against each unique client ID, as shown in figure 5.4. When a given client ID goes beyond 200 requests per second, the API gateway would prevent further requests from that client ID from being sent to the target services until the time window has passed.

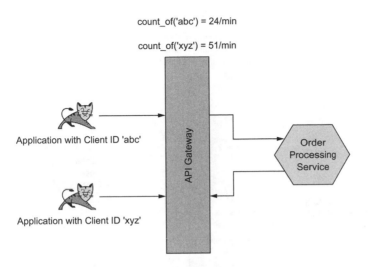

Figure 5.4 **The gateway keeps a count of the requests made by each application within the respective time windows. The ID of the application (`client_id` in the case of OAuth 2.0) is used as the unique identifier of the application.**

5.1.2 *Fair usage policy for users*

In this section, we discuss how to ensure that all users of applications are treated equally. We don't want certain users of an application to be denied access to a service because other users are consuming larger chunks of the quota.

As we discussed in section 5.1.1, we can apply a limit of requests for a given time window for each application. This prevents one or a few applications from consuming a majority of the capacity of our services, which could result in a denial of service for other applications. The same problem could occur for users of applications. Say, for example, an application has 20 users, and the application is given a quota of 200 requests per second. If a given user consumes all 200 requests within a time window of 1 second, the other users will not be left with anything to consume—thus resulting in a denial of service for those users. It is therefore important to impose a fair usage policy on an application to ensure that all users get a fair share of the quota given to the application, as shown in figure 5.5.

Inspecting the user's credential used to access the API gateway/microservice helps identify the user to apply fair usage policies. For example, if we use basic authentication to protect our APIs, we can have the username as the user identifier. If we use self-contained access tokens or JWTs to protect the APIs, we can have the sub claim that comes with the JWT as the user identifier. If the client application uses regular OAuth 2.0 tokens (or the reference tokens), we can find the corresponding user identifier by talking to the authorization server to introspect the token.

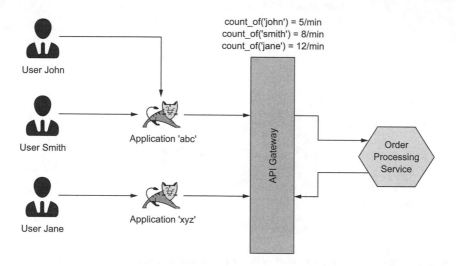

Figure 5.5   The API gateway ensures that fair usage is maintained across all users of the application so that one (or a few) users of the application cannot starve the other users of the application.

5.1.3 *Applying quota-based throttling to the Order Processing microservice*

Before we discuss further details on throttling, let's run through an exercise that gives you an idea of what it means to throttle requests by users. To begin, download the chapter 5 samples from GitHub (https://github.com/microservices-security-in-action/samples) to your computer.

> **NOTE**   The examples in this chapter use Java version 11 but still should work with Java 8+. Before executing the examples in this chapter, make sure that you've stopped running the examples from other chapters or elsewhere. You could experience port conflicts if you attempt to start multiple microservices on the same port.

Once you've downloaded all the samples from the GitHub repository, you should see a directory called sample01 inside the chapter05 directory. You will see three subdirectories within the sample01 directory:

- *oauth2_server*—Contains the code of the OAuth 2.0 authorization server. This is the same authorization server we used in chapter 3.

- *gateway*—Contains the source of the Zuul gateway, which applies throttling policies on our services. Just as it intercepted requests and applied security (in chapter 3), this gateway now performs throttling as well.
- *service*—Contains the source code of the Order Processing microservice, which actually hosts the business logic.

Navigate to the oauth2_server directory from your command-line client tool and execute the following command to build it:

```
\> mvn clean install
```

Once the code is successfully built, execute the following command to run the OAuth 2.0 authorization server:

```
\> mvn spring-boot:run
```

Execute the same two commands from the gateway and the service directories, but from different terminal tabs each, to build and run the Zuul gateway and the Order Processing microservice. Once all three processes are up and running, we can start using them to see what it looks like to rate-limit our services.

First let's get an access token to access the Order Processing microservice. We expose the Order Processing microservice via the Zuul API gateway, and it enforces OAuth 2.0-based security. So, we need a valid OAuth 2.0 access token to make requests to the API gateway. You can get an access token from the authorization server (via the gateway) by executing the following command from your command-line client:

```
\> curl -u application1:application1secret \
-H "Content-Type: application/x-www-form-urlencoded" \
-d "grant_type=client_credentials" \
'http://localhost:9090/token/oauth/token'
```

If the request is successful, you should get a response similar to this:

```
{
  "access_token":"c0f9c2c1-7f81-43e1-acac-05af147662bb",
  "token_type":"bearer",
  "expires_in":3599,
  "scope":"read write"
}
```

Once you have the token, we can access the Order Processing microservice via the Zuul API gateway. Let's run the following curl command to do an HTTP POST to the Order Processing microservice. Make sure to use the value of the same access token you received from the previous request. If not, you will receive an authentication failure error:

```
\> curl -v http://localhost:9090/retail/orders \
-H "Authorization: Bearer c0f9c2c1-7f81-43e1-acac-05af147662bb" \
-H "Content-Type: application/json" \
--data-binary @- << EOF
{  "customer_id":"101021",
```

```
  "payment_method":{
    "card_type":"VISA",
    "expiration":"01/22",
    "name":"John Doe",
    "billing_address":"201, 1st Street, San Jose, CA"
  },
  "items":[        {
    "code":"101",
    "qty":1
    },
    {
    "code":"103",
    "qty":5
    }
  ],
  "shipping_address":"201, 1st Street, San Jose, CA"
}
EOF
```

If the request is successful, you get a response as follows with the status code 200. This indicates that the Order Processing microservice has successfully created the order. The `orderId` in the response is the unique identifier of the newly created order. Take note of the `orderId` since we need it in the next step:

```
{
  "orderId":"cabfd67f-ac1a-4182-bd7f-83c06bd4b7bf",
  "items":[
    {
      "itemCode":"IT0001",
      "quantity":3
    },
    {
      "itemCode":"IT0004",
      "quantity":1
    }
  ],
  "shippingAddress":"No 4, Main Street, Colombo 1, Sri Lanka"
}
```

Next let's use the `orderId` to query our order information. Make sure to use the same access token and the same `orderId` as before. In our request, the `orderid` is `cabfd67f-ac1a-4182-bd7f-83c06bd4b7bf`:

```
\> curl -v \
-H "Authorization: Bearer c0f9c2c1-7f81-43e1-acac-05af147662bb" \
http://localhost:9090/retail/orders/cabfd67f-ac1a-4182-bd7f-83c06bd4b7bf
```

You should see a response with the status code 200 including the details of the order we placed before. Execute the same request three more times. You should observe the same response, with status code 200 being returned. If you execute the same request for the fourth time within a minute, you should see a response with the status code 429 saying the request is throttled out. The duration of the time window

(1 minute) is configured in a Java class that we will take a look at shortly. The response looks like this:

```
< HTTP/1.1 429
< X-Application-Context: application:9090
< Transfer-Encoding: chunked
< Date: Mon, 18 Mar 2019 13:28:36 GMT
<
{"error": true, "reason":"Request Throttled."}
```

In chapter 3, we used the API gateway to enforce security on our microservices. We extend the same gateway here to enforce throttling limits as well. In chapter 3, we used a Zuul filter on our gateway to enforce security. Here, we introduce another filter that executes after the security filter to enforce throttling limits.

Let's take a look at the code. The Java class file that implements throttling is ThrottlingFilter.java (listing 5.1), which you can find inside the gateway/src/main/ java/com/manning/mss/ch05/sample01/gateway/filters/ directory. If you open this file in a text editor or in your IDE, you will see three methods on this class, named `filterType`, `filterOrder`, and `shouldFilter`.

Listing 5.1   A code snippet extracted from ThrottlingFilter.java

```
public String filterType() {
    return "pre";
}
```
The filter-type pre indicates that this filter should execute before the request being processed.

```
public int filterOrder() {
    return 2;
}
```
The filter-order 2 indicates that this filter executes after the OAuthFilter, whose filter-order is 1.

```
public boolean shouldFilter() {
    return true;
}
```
The should-filter true indicates that this filter is active.

At the top of the ThrottlingFilter.java class file, we initialize a counter of the `Counter-Cache` type, which is an in-memory map. Each entry in this map holds a counter against its key. And each entry in the map resides for approximately 60 seconds, after which it is removed:

```
//Create a counter cache where each entry expires in 1 minute
//and the cache is cleared every 10 seconds.
//Maximum number of entries in the cache would be 10000.
private CounterCache counter = new CounterCache(60, 10, 10000);
```

The key in this map is quite important and is what we count our requests against. In this particular example, we use the access token as the key to count against. Since the access token itself is kind of a secret (or like a password), you might be able to use its hashed value rather than using it as it is. If you make two requests using the same access token within a 60-second time window, the counter of that token would be 2:

```
//Get the value of the token by splitting the Authorization header
String key = authHeader.split("Bearer ")[1];
Object count = counter.get(key);
```

We can similarly use any other key or even multiple keys to count against, depending on our use cases. For example, if we want to count the number of requests of an application, we would use the `client_id` as the key to count against. We can also use any attribute such as the user's username, IP address, OpenID Connect claims, and so on as a key.

5.1.4   *Maximum handling capacity of a microservice*

The gradual increase in applications and users accessing a given microservice demands to increase the capacity or the maximum number of requests that microservice can handle. Although we can apply quotas for applications and quotas for each individual user, a sudden increase in the number of applications or users might also cause our target services to be loaded beyond their capacity.

For example, assume that the maximum capacity tolerated by our target services is 1,500 transactions per second. If we allow each application to consume 100 transactions per second, we can tolerate a maximum of 15 applications at full capacity. Now imagine that more than 15 applications are each consuming at least 100 transactions per second. In this situation, each application would be well within its quota, but we'd still go beyond our maximum tolerance limit of 1,500. The same situation can occur when an application experiences a spike in usage from its users. See figure 5.6 for an illustration.

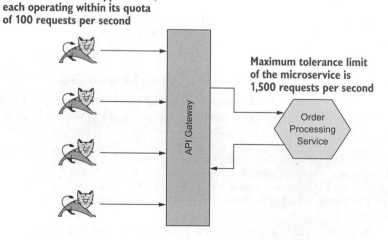

Figure 5.6   When more than 15 client applications are operating within their quota of 100 requests per second, the combined load causes the maximum tolerable limit to exceed at the microservice.

These types of spikes can usually occur during special events. For example, if you run an e-commerce application, you probably will experience similar occurrences on special events such as Thanksgiving and the Super Bowl. In most cases when the spike is predictable beforehand, you can scale up the target service layer for the relevant time period only.

We have worked with a customer running a ride-sharing business who rose in popularity and success in a very short time period, but unfortunately was unable to practically scale the target services layer because of design limitations. This unexpected growth caused an unusually high amount of traffic on Friday evenings and Saturdays. This caused the company's target services layer to fail, resulting in a total loss of business when the demand was at its most.

To handle these types of unprecedented surges, we need to have a maximum threshold limit for our target services. Having such a policy prevents potential crashes from sudden surges, resulting in a total loss of availability. But it also results in some users and applications being denied service even though they operate within the allowed quota. The trade-off here is that we operate at maximum possible capacity, servicing everyone possible instead of facing a total system failure, resulting in service unavailability for everybody.

The particular customer we mentioned previously who had a ride-sharing business used this solution until they could rectify the design limitations that caused services to be unscalable beyond a certain point. Figure 5.7 illustrates this scenario.

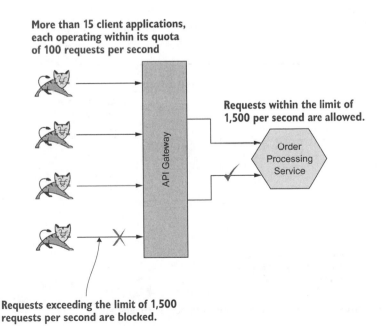

Figure 5.7   The gateway ensures that it does not allow more than the maximum tolerable limit of the microservice to pass through.

5.1.5   *Operation-level throttling*

An API hosted on the API gateway can provide a level of abstraction over one or more microservices. In other words, an API could have a one-to-many relationship with microservices. As we discussed in chapter 3, it sometimes makes sense to expose microservices as operations of a single API. When we do this, we sometimes require applying throttling per each operation of the API instead of applying for the entire API as a whole.

For example, in our Order Processing microservice, we may have one microservice that performs read operations on our orders, and another microservice that performs write operations. If these two microservices are exposed via the same API as two operations, one as a GET /orders and the other as a POST /orders operation, you would most likely want to allow different quotas for each.

We once worked with a customer in the ticketing industry. They had APIs with operations that allowed consumers to search for as well as to purchase tickets. They had an application that allowed users to perform these search and purchase operations. You had to be logged into the application (authenticated) in order to make a purchase, but you could perform search operations without logging in (anonymously). This customer served many more search operations than purchase operations. They therefore limited their quotas based on the operations they served to make sure that this usage pattern remained consistent with their observations and expectations. Although having more purchases can be a good thing in terms of revenue, they wanted to stay safe. Any abnormality had to be first prevented and then allowed based on validation of legitimacy. Figure 5.8 illustrates this scenario.

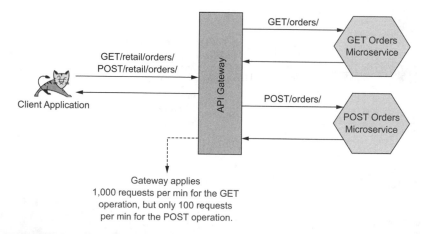

Figure 5.8   The gateway applies different levels of throttling to different operations of the same API.

5.1.6 *Throttling the OAuth 2.0 token and authorize endpoints*

We have so far been discussing throttling business operations of APIs. But how about the login operation or the API (or the endpoint) that we use to authenticate users? Throttling this endpoint is also very important because a DoS or a DDoS attack on the authentication endpoint alone could make it impossible for a legitimate user to obtain tokens to access APIs.

However, throttling these APIs is tricky. Unlike other APIs, these APIs are invoked at a preauthentication phase. Whoever is accessing these APIs is requesting to be logged in and therefore is not yet authenticated. Whatever credentials the users present at this point may or may not be valid. We can assess their legitimacy only after performing the necessary validations. If this is an attacker, the validations are the exact points the attacker wants to exhaust, resulting in a denial of service for all others. Therefore, things like application-based quotas or fair-usage quotas for users cannot be applied in practice for this use case. This is because any attempt to identify the application or user at this point is in vain, since we have no clue as to their legitimacy.

To uniquely identify the originator of these requests, we therefore need to drop down to IP addresses. We need to identify the source IP address from which each request is originating and apply quotas for the unique IP addresses. To identify these source IP addresses, we can use the X-Forwarded-For header.[1] Doing this at large scale and for internet-facing applications goes beyond the scope of an API gateway. In such cases, we use a web application firewall (WAF), which runs before the API gateway and intercepts all the requests. Imperva, Akamai Technologies, Cloudflare, and AWS WAF are some popular WAF solution providers that also provide DoS and DDoS prevention.

5.1.7 *Privilege-based throttling*

Enforcing throttling based on different user privilege levels is another common use case we see in the industry. A user with a higher privilege may be allowed a larger quota of requests compared to a user with lesser privileges. Most of us have come across scenarios in which a free account provides a limited quota of a particular service, whereas a paid account offers a larger quota of the service.

As we discussed in chapter 4 in detail, we can use OpenID Connect claims to determine the privilege level of the corresponding user and apply the relevant throttling limit to a client application. The API gateway intercepts the request originating from the client application and determines the privilege level of the end user. It can then enforce throttling limits on the client based on the end user's privilege level. The gateway would either receive the claims from the client application itself in the form of a JWT (a self-contained access token) or by querying information regarding the

---

[1] The X-Forwarded-For (XFF) HTTP header field is a common method for identifying the originating IP address of a client connecting to a web server through an HTTP proxy or load balancer.

access token using the /userinfo endpoint of the authorization server. If you are new to OpenID Connect, please check appendix A and chapter 4. Figure 5.9 illustrates this workflow.

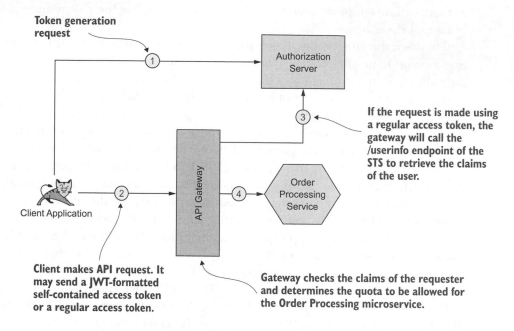

Figure 5.9   The workflow for applying privilege-based throttling for requests. The gateway determines the quota by inspecting the claims of the requester.

5.2   *Monitoring and analytics with Prometheus and Grafana*

The modern term for *monitoring and analytics* is known as *observability*. In appendix D, we discuss the importance of monitoring a microservices deployment and why it is critical to do so compared to monolithic applications. In this section, we discuss a few technologies for monitoring microservices, focusing on Prometheus and Grafana.

Prometheus is a popular open source monitoring tool for microservices. It helps us keep track of system metrics over a given time period and can be used to determine the health of a software system. Metrics include memory usage and CPU consumption.

Grafana is an open source data visualization tool. It can help you build dashboards to visualize the metrics being provided by Prometheus or any other data source. At this time of writing, Grafana is the most popular data-visualizing tool in the market. Although Prometheus has its own visualization capabilities, the features supported by Grafana are far superior. Its visualization effects are much more appealing than those of Prometheus.

5.2.1 *Monitoring the Order Processing microservice*

In this section, we discuss what it means to monitor the Order Processing microservice using Prometheus and Grafana. To run this exercise, you need to have Docker (www .docker.com) installed on your computer. We discuss Docker in detail in appendix E and therefore don't go through Docker's basics in this section. Here we are going to run the Order Processing microservice, which is developed with Spring Boot and exposes some system metrics over an endpoint (URL). We will then set up Prometheus to read these metrics from this endpoint. Once that is done, we will set up Grafana to visualize these metrics by getting the relevant information from Prometheus.

First check out the samples of this section from the chapter05/sample02 directory of the https://github.com/microservices-security-in-action/samples GitHub repository. Navigate to the chapter05/sample02 directory by using your command-line client tool and execute the following command to build the source code of the Order Processing microservice:

```
\> mvn clean install
```

Once the microservice is successfully built, you can start the service by executing this command:

```
\> mvn spring-boot:run
```

If you see a message like the following, the Order Processing microservice is up and running successfully:

```
Started OrderProcessingApp in 3.206 seconds
```

For Prometheus to be able to monitor the Order Processing microservice, the microservice needs to expose its metrics via a publicly accessible endpoint. Prometheus reads various metrics from the Order Processing microservice through this endpoint. This process is called *scraping*, and we will discuss it in detail later. To take a look at how these metrics are exposed, you can open your web browser and access http://localhost:8080/actuator/prometheus. You should see output that looks similar to the following listing.

> **Listing 5.2   The output from the actuator/Prometheus endpoint**

```
# TYPE system_load_average_1m gauge
system_load_average_1m 2.654296875
# HELP jvm_memory_max_bytes The maximum amount of memory in bytes that can be
# used for memory management
# TYPE jvm_memory_max_bytes gauge
jvm_memory_max_bytes{area="nonheap",id="Code Cache",} 2.5165824E8
jvm_memory_max_bytes{area="nonheap",id="Metaspace",} -1.0
jvm_memory_max_bytes{area="nonheap",id="Compressed Class Space",}
1.073741824E9
jvm_memory_max_bytes{area="heap",id="PS Eden Space",} 6.2652416E8
jvm_memory_max_bytes{area="heap",id="PS Survivor Space",} 4.456448E7
```

```
jvm_memory_max_bytes{area="heap",id="PS Old Gen",} 1.431830528E9
# HELP process_files_max_files The maximum file descriptor count
# TYPE process_files_max_files gauge
process_files_max_files 10240.0
# HELP process_start_time_seconds Start time of the process since unix epoch.
# TYPE process_start_time_seconds gauge
process_start_time_seconds 1.552603801488E9
# HELP system_cpu_usage The "recent cpu usage" for the whole system
# TYPE system_cpu_usage gauge
system_cpu_usage 0.0
```

You can observe and figure out the type of metrics being exposed in listing 5.2. For example, the metric `jvm_memory_max_bytes` indicates the amount of memory being consumed by the JVM. The metric `process_start_time_seconds` provides the time at which the process started, likewise. The following dependencies need to be added to the Spring Boot project of the Order Processing microservice for it to be able to expose this information. The dependencies are defined in the sample02/pom.xml file:

```
<dependency>
        <groupId>org.springframework.boot</groupId>
        <artifactId>spring-boot-starter-actuator</artifactId>
</dependency>
<dependency>
        <groupId>io.micrometer</groupId>
        <artifactId>micrometer-registry-prometheus</artifactId>
</dependency>
```

To enable exposure of the metrics at runtime, the following properties need to be enabled in the sample02/src/resources/application.properties file:

```
management.endpoints.web.exposure.include=prometheus,info,health
management.endpoint.prometheus.enabled=true
```

Now that we have our Order Processing microservice exposing the required metrics, the next step is to configure and start Prometheus so that it can read the exposed metrics. In this particular example, we have created a docker-compose script that first starts the Prometheus container and then the Grafana container. To run these containers, navigate to the sample02/monitoring directory by using your command-line client and execute the following command:

```
\> docker-compose -f docker-compose.yml up
```

If this is the first time you are starting these containers, it might take a few minutes for startup because it downloads the container images from Docker Hub (https://hub.docker.com/) and copies to your local Docker registry. These containers would start up in a matter of seconds in subsequent attempts. Once the containers have started successfully, you should see two messages as follows:

```
Starting prometheus ... done
Starting grafana    ... done
```

To see Prometheus in action, open a new tab in your web browser and navigate to http://localhost:9090. From the top menu, click the Status drop-down list and choose Targets. You should be able to see a target named order-processing with its state as UP. You should see the last scrape timestamp information as well. This means that Prometheus is able to read the metrics exposed by our Spring Boot service.

Next, click the Graph link from the top menu. This UI in Prometheus allows you to query various metrics if you know their names. To check how much memory the JVM consumes, enter the string `jvm_memory_used_bytes` in the provided text box and click the Execute button. The Graph tab gives you a view of the memory consumed over a period of time, and the Console tab shows you the exact values at that particular moment. The Graph view looks similar to figure 5.10.

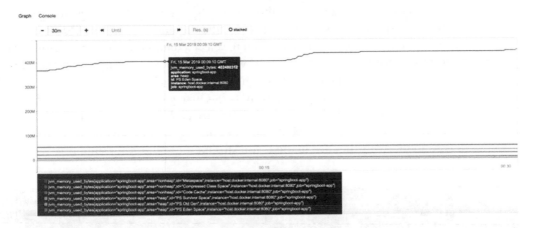

Figure 5.10 Graph view of the `jvm_memory_used_bytes` metric as displayed in the Prometheus UI.

To understand how Prometheus scrapes the Order Processing microservice for information, you can open the monitoring/prometheus/prometheus.yml file. This is the Prometheus configuration file. The scrape configurations shown in the following listing help Prometheus find the Order Processing microservice and its metrics.

Listing 5.3   The Prometheus scrape configuration

```
scrape_configs:
- job_name: 'order-processing'
  scrape_interval: 10s
  metrics_path: '/actuator/prometheus'
static_configs:
  - targets: ['host.docker.internal:8080']
    labels:
      application: 'order-processing-app'
```

Defines the frequency at which metrics should be collected from each target under the order-processing job

Defines the path under which the metrics of the Order Processing microservice are hosted

Specifies the hosts that require monitoring under this job

As you have noticed from using the Prometheus UI, we need to know the parameters to watch out for in order to use the default Prometheus UI for monitoring our microservices. In terms of having an overall view of the state of a microservices deployment, this experience/process does not help us a lot. This is where Grafana comes into the picture and helps us build dashboards for an overall view. Let's take a look at creating a dashboard in Grafana for a better view.

By now, our Grafana container is up and running. We can therefore use it directly. To do that, open a new tab in your browser console and navigate to http://localhost:3000. Enter `admin` as the username, and `password` as the password to log in to Grafana.

Next, we need to install a dashboard on Grafana. To do that, hover over the Create menu item on the left menu panel (it should be the first item in the menu) and click the Import link. In the page that appears, click the Upload .JSON File button and choose to upload the sample02/monitoring/grafana/dashboard.json file.

In the form that appears next, go with the defaults for all the fields except the Prometheus field, where you are expected to select a data source for this dashboard. Select Prometheus as the data source for its value and proceed to import this dashboard.

Next, under Dashboards in the left menu pane, click the Manage link. You should see a dashboard named JVM (Micrometer). Once you click this dashboard, you should see widgets being loaded onto the UI. They are categorized into sections such as Quick Facts, I/O Overview, and JVM Memory. At first, it might take a short while for the widgets to load. After they are loaded, you should see something similar to figure 5.11.

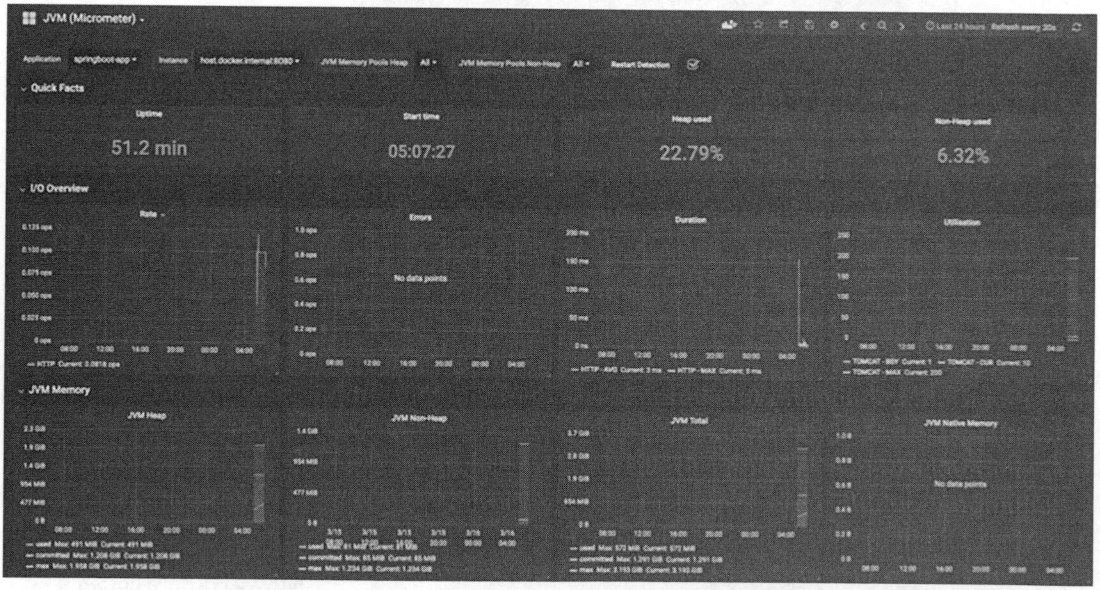

Figure 5.11   The Grafana dashboard for our microservice. The metrics exposed by our microservice are scraped by Prometheus periodically. Grafana queries Prometheus by using PromQL and visualizes the metrics.

As you can see, Grafana gives you a much more user-friendly view of the metrics exposed by the Order Processing microservice. To understand how Grafana queries data from Prometheus, you need to take a look at the sample02/monitoring/grafana/provisioning/datasources/datasource.yml file. This file contains the Prometheus URL so that Grafana can connect to it and query its data. The dashboard.json file located in the sample02/monitoring/grafana directory defines, in JSON format, the type of metrics to be visualized under each widget. For example, take a look at the following JSON, which visualizes the Uptime panel on this dashboard:

```
"targets": [
{
"expr": "process_uptime_seconds{application=\"$application\",
instance=\"$instance\"}",
          "format": "time_series",
          "intervalFactor": 2,
          "legendFormat": "",
          "metric": "",
          "refId": "A",
          "step": 14400
}
],
"thresholds": "",
"title": "Uptime",
```

We now have a bit of experience in using Prometheus to scrape metrics from our exposed microservice and in using Grafana to visualize these metrics.

5.2.2 *Behind the scenes of using Prometheus for monitoring*

Prometheus, an open source tool for system monitoring and alerting, is a standalone project maintained by the community itself. It is part of the Cloud Native Computing Foundation (CNCF) and the second hosted project in CNCF. As of this writing, only ten projects have graduated in CNCF, and Prometheus is one of them.

Prometheus is also the most popular open source monitoring tool available. When using Prometheus to monitor a microservices deployment, it's important to understand a few things regarding how Prometheus works.

SCRAPING DATA FROM MICROSERVICES TO MONITOR

Prometheus pulls metrics data from microservices on a periodic time interval. As you've learned, this is known as *scraping*. Each microservice needs to have an exposed endpoint, which contains details about the various metrics we need to monitor. The Prometheus server connects to these endpoints periodically and pulls down the information it needs for its monitoring purposes.

Prometheus also has a push-gateway for supporting short-lived processes. Processes that may not live long enough for Prometheus to scrape can push their metrics to a push gateway before dying off. The push gateway acts as a metrics cache for the processes that no longer exist.

WHAT IS TIME-SERIES DATA?

Prometheus stores metrics in a time-series database at millisecond precision. A time-series database contains a recording of various metrics against the time at which it was recorded. This data is stored for a period of time and is usually presented in line graphs against time.

DEFINING A METRIC IN PROMETHEUS

A *metric* in Prometheus is an immutable block of data identified using both the metric name and labels. A metric is stored against its timestamp. Given a metric name and labels, time series are identified using the following notion:

```
<metric_name>={<label_name>=<label_value>, . . . .}
```

For example, a metric used for getting the total number of HTTP requests would look like the following:

```
http_requests_total={method="POST", path="/menu", type="JSON"}
```

Figure 5.12 illustrates the architecture of Prometheus.

As you can see, each microservice needs to expose an endpoint from which Prometheus scrapes metrics information. When exposing this endpoint, we need to ensure that this endpoint is secured, using TLS so that the information passed on the

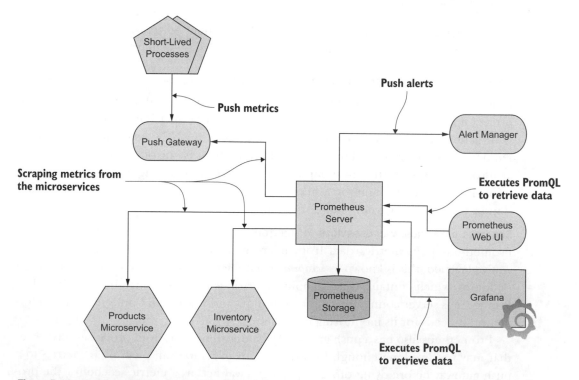

Figure 5.12   A Prometheus server scrapes the microservices and push gateway for metrics. It then uses these metrics to trigger alerts. The Prometheus web UI and Grafana use PromQL to retrieve data from Prometheus for visualization.

wire is kept safe from intruders, and using an authentication mechanism such as OAuth 2.0 or basic authentication.

5.3 Enforcing access-control policies at the API gateway with Open Policy Agent

In this section, we look at controlling access to the Order Processing microservice by using *Open Policy Agent (OPA)* at the API gateway. The API gateway here is acting as a policy enforcement point. OPA is a lightweight general-purpose policy engine that has no dependency on microservices. You can use OPA to define fine-grained access-control policies and enforce those policies at different places in a microservices deployment.

In chapter 2, we looked at using OAuth 2.0 scopes to control access to microservices. There we enforced OAuth 2.0 scope-based access control at the service level by modifying the service code, which is not a good practice. Access-control policies evolve as business requirements change—so every time we have to change our access-control policies, changing the microservice code is not a good practice.

OPA helps you externalize access-control policies and enforce them at any point in the request or response path. Figure 5.13 illustrates the sequence of events that happens when an API gateway intercepts client requests to apply authorization policies using OPA. The OPA engine runs as a different process, outside the API gateway, and the API gateway connects to the OPA engine over HTTP. Please check appendix F for more details on OPA.

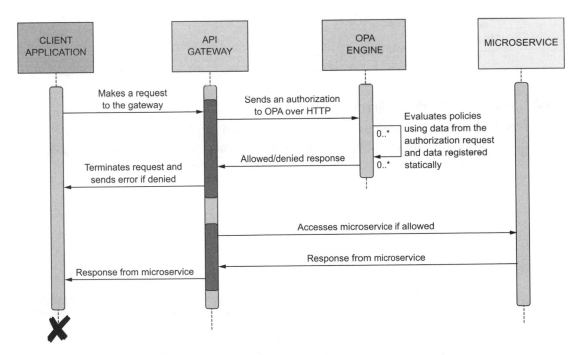

Figure 5.13 Sequence of events that happens when an API gateway intercepts client requests to apply authorization policies using OPA

5.3.1 *Running OPA as a Docker container*

Starting OPA as a Docker container is the most straightforward and easiest way to get started. As in the Prometheus example, you need Docker installed and running on your machine to try this out, along with the other prerequisites mentioned in chapter 2 for running samples in this book in general.

First check out the samples for this section from chapter05/sample03 at https://github.com/microservices-security-in-action/samples. As the first step of executing this sample, we need to start the OPA Docker container (if you are new to Docker, refer to appendix E). You can do this by using your command-line client to execute the following command from within the chapter05/sample03 directory. This script starts the OPA server on port 8181 and binds it to port 8181 of your local machine. So, make sure that no other process is running on port 8181. If you want to change the port, you can do so by editing the run_opa.sh file:

```
\> sh run_opa.sh
```

If your OPA container starts successfully, you should see a message in your terminal window as follows. Note that if this is the first time you are running this command, it might take a few minutes for the OPA Docker image to be downloaded from the Docker registry. Subsequent attempts will be much faster than the initial attempt:

```
{
  "addrs":[
    ":8181"
  ],
  "insecure_addr":"",
  "level":"info",
  "msg":"Initializing server.",
  "time":"2019-11-04T01:03:09Z"
}
```

5.3.2 *Feeding the OPA engine with data*

Now that our OPA engine is up and running and can be accessed on port 8181, it is time to register the data required for executing policies. As you can see, listing 5.4 is a declaration of a collection of resource paths. These resources represent one or more resources corresponding to the Order Processing microservice. Each resource has an id, path, method, and a collection of scopes that are associated with the resource. The OPA's REST APIs allow registering these types of data sets on it. You can find the content of listing 5.4 in the file chapter05/sample03/order_policy.json. This data set is a collection of service paths (resources), where each resource declares the scope required for accessing it.

> **Listing 5.4   A set of resources in Order Processing microservice, defined as OPA data**

```
[
{                                    An identifier for
  "id": "r1",          ⟵┘           the resource path
  "path": "orders",                       ⟵──  The resource path
```

```
    "method": "POST",          ⟵──── The HTTP method
    "scopes": ["create_order"]                ⟵─┐  To do an HTTP POST
  },                                             │  to the orders resource,
  {                                              │  you must have this scope.
    "id": "r2",
    "path": "orders",
    "method": "GET",
    "scopes": ["retrieve_orders"]
  },
  {
    "id": "r3",
    "path": "orders/{order_id}",
    "method": "PUT",
    "scopes": ["update_order"]
  }
]
```

You can register this data on the OPA server by running the following curl command from the chapter05/sample03 directory:

```
\> curl -v -H "Content-Type: application/json" \
-X PUT --data-binary @order_policy.json \
http://localhost:8181/v1/data/order_policy
```

You should see a response with status code 204 if the request was successful. Note that the order_policy element in the OPA endpoint, after the data element, is important. OPA uses order_policy to derive the package name for the data you pushed. In this case, the data you pushed to the OPA server is registered under the data.order_policy package name. You can find more details on this in appendix F.

To verify that your data has been successfully registered on the OPA engine, you can execute the following curl command. You should see the content of your resource definitions if the request is successful:

```
\> curl http://localhost:8181/v1/data/order_policy
```

Once the OPA engine has been initialized with the dataset required for our policies, the next step is to implement and deploy access-control policies on OPA.

5.3.3   *Feeding the OPA engine with access-control policies*

Let's see how to deploy authorization policies into the OPA server; these policies check whether a user/system that's accessing a resource with an access token bears the scopes required for accessing that resource. We'll use OPA policies to make authorization checks on the Order Processing microservice.

OPA policies are written using a declarative language called *Rego*. It has rich support for traversing nested documents and transforming data using syntax similar to Python and JSONPath. Each policy written in Rego is a collection of rules that need to be applied on your microservice.

Let's take a look at the policy defined in the following listing, which checks whether a token being used to access the Order Processing microservice bears the scopes required by the microservice.

Listing 5.5   OPA policy written in Rego

```
package authz.orders          ← The package name
                                of the policy

import data.order_policy as policies    ← Declares the set of statically
                                           registered data identified by
                                           order_policy, as in listing 5.4

default allow = false         ← All the requests by default are
                                disallowed. If this is not set and no
allow {          ← Declares the conditions to   allowed rules are matched, OPA
                   allow access to the resource  will return an undefined decision.
  policy = policies[_]        ← Iterates over values in the policies array
  policy.method = input.method   ←
  policy.path = input.path
  policy.scopes[_] = input.scopes[_]    ← For an element in the policies array, checks whether
}                                         the value of the method parameter in the input
                                          matches with the method element of the policy
```

Here, the package declaration is an identifier for the policy. If you want to evaluate this policy against certain input data, you need to make an HTTP POST request to the `http://localhost:8181/v1/data/authz/orders` endpoint, having the input data as a JSON payload. Here we refer to the policy in the URL by `/authz/orders`. This is exactly the same as the package declaration of the policy, with the period character (`.`) being replaced by forward slash (`/`).

You can find the policy we define in listing 5.5 in the sample03/orders.rego file. We can register this policy in OPA by executing the following command from within the chapter05/sample03 directory:

```
\> curl -v -X PUT --data-binary @orders.rego \
http://localhost:8181/v1/policies/orders
```

We can execute the following command to verify that our policy has been registered successfully. If it's successful, you should get the response with the content of your policy:

```
\> curl http://localhost:8181/v1/policies/orders
```

5.3.4   *Evaluating OPA policies*

Once we have the OPA policy engine running with data and policies, we can use its REST API to check whether a given entity is authorized to perform a certain action. To send a request to the OPA policy engine, first we need to create an OPA input document. An input document will let OPA know details of the resource being accessed and details of the user who is accessing it.

Such inputs are provided to the policy so that the policy can compare that with the set of statically defined data to make its decision. These inputs are provided in JSON format from the microservice (or the API gateway) to the OPA engine at the time of serving a business API request. The following listing shows an example of an input document that contains information of a particular request that is being served by the Order Processing microservice.

Listing 5.6 OPA input document

```
{
  "input":{
    "path":"orders",
    "method":"GET",
    "scopes":["retrieve_orders"]
  }
}
```

This input document tells OPA that the microservice is serving a request on the path orders for an HTTP GET method. And there's a scope named retrieve_orders that's associated with the user (or the token) accessing the Order Processing microservice. OPA will use this input data and the statically declared data to evaluate the rules declared in its policies.

Let's query the OPA engine by using its REST API to check whether a particular input results in a true or false evaluation. We first evaluate a true case by using the input defined in sample03/input_true.json. You can evaluate this by executing the following command from the chapter05/sample03 directory:

```
\> curl -X POST --data-binary @input_true.json \
http://localhost:8181/v1/data/authz/orders -v
```

This should give you an HTTP 200 OK response with the following response body. This means that the details we used in the input_true.json file match one of the rules in the policy registered on OPA. Note that, as we discussed before, the OPA endpoint is derived from the package name of the policy we want to evaluate, which is authz.orders (see listing 5.5):

```
{"result":{"allow":true}}
```

If you execute the same command using the input_false.json file, you would see a 200 OK response with the following content. This means that you do not have rights to access the given resource with the given scope:

```
{"result":{"allow":false}}
```

5.3.5 *Next steps in using OPA*

Let's discuss some of the limitations and next steps with respect to the OPA use case we've discussed. You can learn how to address these limitations in appendix F:

- The connection to the OPA server for evaluating policies is not properly secured. There are multiple options to secure OPA endpoints, which we discuss in appendix F.
- The OPA server runs as a Docker container, and all the policies and data pushed to the OPA server using APIs will be gone when you restart the server. Once again, in appendix F we discuss how to overcome that.
- In our example, we use only the curl client to evaluate OPA policies against a given request (or an input document). If you would like to engage OPA with

the Zuul API gateway, you need to write a Zuul filter, which is similar to the ThrottlingFilter we used in listing 5.1. This filter has to intercept the requests, create an input document, and then talk to the OPA endpoint to see whether the request is authorized.

Summary

- Quota-based throttling policies for applications help to monetize APIs/microservices and to limit a given application from overconsuming APIs/microservices.
- Fair-usage policies need to be enforced on applications to ensure that all users get a fair quota of requests.
- User privilege-based throttling is useful for allowing different quotas for users with different privilege levels.
- An API gateway can be used to apply throttling rules in a microservices deployment.
- Prometheus is the most popular open source monitoring tool available as of this writing.
- Grafana helps to visualize the data being recorded by Prometheus.
- Open Policy Agent (OPA) helps control access to a microservices deployment.
- OPA data, OPA input data, and OPA policies are used together to apply various access-control rules.
- All samples in this chapter used HTTP (not HTTPS) endpoints to spare you from having to set up proper certificates and to make it possible for you to inspect messages being passed on the wire (network), if required. In production systems, we do not recommend using HTTP for any endpoint.

Part 3

Service-to-service communications

In part 2, you learned how to protect your microservices at the edge. After a request from a client application passes through the security at the edge and enters into your microservices deployment, you'll need to secure the interactions among microservices. The chapters in this part of the book teach you those skills.

Chapter 6 teaches you how to secure communications among microservices that take place over HTTP, with mutual Transport Layer Security (mTLS).

In chapter 7, you'll learn how to share contextual data (for example, the end-user context) among microservices by using JSON Web Token (JWT).

Not all microservices use JSON over HTTP for service-to-service interactions, and gRPC is already a popular pick as an alternative. Chapter 8 teaches you how to secure communications among microservices that take place over gRPC, with mTLS and JWT.

Chapter 9 teaches you how to secure reactive microservices. It also teaches you how to set up Kafka as a message broker, and how to enforce access-control policies for Kafka topics.

When you're finished with this part of the book, you'll know how to protect service-to-service communications in your microservices deployment that take place over HTTP or gRPC, as well as how to protect reactive microservices.

Securing east/west
traffic with certificates

This chapter covers

- Generating keys/certificates and securing microservices with mTLS
- Challenges in provisioning certificates, bootstrapping trust, and revoking certificates

In chapters 3, 4, and 5, we discussed how to expose and secure a microservice as an API via an API gateway and to apply other quality-of-service features such as throttling and monitoring. That's all part of the edge security in a typical microservices deployment. *Edge security* deals with authenticating and authorizing the end user, which is a system accessing a microservice on behalf of a human user or another system. When the security screening at the edge is completed, the end-user context is passed to the upstream microservices.

In this chapter, we discuss securing communications among microservices with mutual Transport Layer Security (mTLS). mTLS is the most popular option for securing communications among microservices.

137

6.1   Why use mTLS?

When you buy something from Amazon, for example, all your credit card information flows from your browser to Amazon's servers over TLS, and no one in the middle can see what it is. When you log in to Facebook, your credentials flow from your browser to Facebook's servers over TLS, and no one in the middle can intercept the communications and find out what those are.

TLS protects communications between two parties for confidentiality and integrity. Using TLS to secure data in transit has been a practice for several years. Recently, because of increased cybersecurity threats, it has become a mandatory practice in any business that has serious concerns about data security. From July 2018 onward, the Google Chrome browser (version 68.0.0+) has indicated that any website that doesn't support TLS is insecure (http://mng.bz/GVNR).

Apart from protecting data in transit for confidentiality and integrity, TLS helps a client application identify the server that it communicates with. In the Amazon example, the browser is the client application, and when it talks to Amazon over TLS, it knows what it talks to as a result of the security model and the infrastructure built around TLS. If Amazon wants to expose its services over TLS, it must have a valid certificate that's trusted by all the client applications that want to communicate with it.

A certificate represents the corresponding server's public key and binds it to a common name. Amazon's public certificate (see figure 6.1 in the next section), for example, binds its public key to the www.amazon.com common name. The most important and challenging part of TLS is how we build trust between a client and a server.

6.1.1   Building trust between a client and a server with a certificate authority

How do you build trust between Amazon and all the browsers (client applications) that want to access it? A third party that's known to (and trusted by) all the client applications signs the certificates given to services such as Amazon. This third party is known as a *certificate authority* (*CA*). Anyone who wants to expose services that are protected with TLS over the web must get their certificates signed by a trusted CA.

Few trusted CAs are available globally, and their public keys are embedded in all browsers. When a browser talks to Amazon over TLS, it can verify that Amazon's certificate is valid (not forged) by verifying its signature against the corresponding CA's public key that's embedded in the browser. The certificate also includes the hostname of Amazon (which is the common name) so that the browser knows it's communicating with the right server. Figure 6.1 shows the certificate issued to www.amazon.com by the DigiCert Global CA.

6.1.2   Mutual TLS helps the client and the server to identify each other

TLS itself is also known as *one-way TLS*, mostly because it helps the client identify the server it's talking to, but not the other way around. Two-way TLS, or *mutual TLS* (mTLS), fills this gap by helping the client and the server identify themselves to each other. Just as the client knows which server it's talking to in one-way TLS, with mTLS, the server knows the client it's talking to as well (figure 6.2).

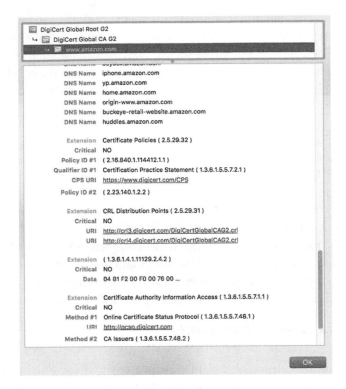

DNS Name   iphone.amazon.com
DNS Name   yp.amazon.com
DNS Name   home.amazon.com
DNS Name   origin-www.amazon.com
DNS Name   buckeye-retail-website.amazon.com
DNS Name   huddles.amazon.com

Extension   Certificate Policies (2.5.29.32)
Critical   NO
Policy ID #1   (2.16.840.1.114412.1.1)
Qualifier ID #1   Certification Practice Statement (1.3.6.1.5.5.7.2.1)
CPS URI   https://www.digicert.com/CPS
Policy ID #2   (2.23.140.1.2.2)

Extension   CRL Distribution Points (2.5.29.31)
Critical   NO
URI   http://crl3.digicert.com/DigiCertGlobalCAG2.crl
URI   http://crl4.digicert.com/DigiCertGlobalCAG2.crl

Extension   (1.3.6.1.4.1.11129.2.4.2)
Critical   NO
Data   04 81 F2 00 F0 00 76 00 ...

Extension   Certificate Authority Information Access (1.3.6.1.5.5.7.1.1)
Critical   NO
Method #1   Online Certificate Status Protocol (1.3.6.1.5.5.7.48.1)
URI   http://ocsp.digicert.com
Method #2   CA Issuers (1.3.6.1.5.5.7.48.2)

Figure 6.1 The certificate of www.amazon.com, issued by the DigiCert Global CA. This certificate helps clients talking to www.amazon.com properly identify the server.

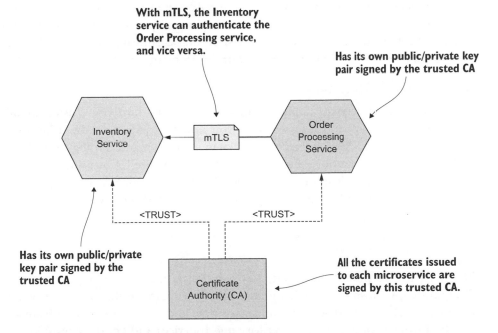

Figure 6.2 mTLS among microservices lets those services identify themselves. All the microservices in the deployment trust one CA.

To take part in a communication channel secured with mTLS, both the server and the client must have valid certificates, and each party must trust the issuer of the corresponding certificates. When mTLS is used to secure communications between two microservices, each microservice can legitimately identify who it talks to, in addition to achieving confidentiality and integrity of the data in transit between the two microservices.

6.1.3   HTTPS is HTTP over TLS

When you communicate with Amazon over TLS, the browser's address bar shows HTTPS instead of HTTP. HTTPS runs on TLS; HTTPS relies on TLS to provide security in the communication channel.

TLS can be used by any application-layer protocol to make communications secure, not just HTTPS. A Java program can talk to a database by using Java Database Connectivity (JDBC), for example. To secure the JDBC connection between the Java program and the database, you can use TLS. Also, when an email client wants to talk to a server over a secured communication channel, it can use Simple Mail Transfer Protocol (SMTP) over TLS. There are many such examples, and these are but a few.

6.2   Creating certificates to secure access to microservices

In this section, we explain how to create a public/private key pair for your microservice and how to get a trusted CA to sign it. In a typical microservices deployment, microservices aren't directly exposed to the public; the external clients interact mostly with microservices via APIs. If your microservice endpoints aren't public, you don't need to have a public CA sign the corresponding certificates. You can use your own CA, trusted by all the microservices in your deployment.

6.2.1   Creating a certificate authority

In a typical microservices deployment, you have your own CA, trusted by all your microservices. In appendix G, we show you how to create a CA by using OpenSSL (www.openssl.org). *OpenSSL* is a commercial-grade toolkit and cryptographic library for TLS, available for multiple platforms. Before we create the CA by using OpenSSL, let's prepare a working environment. You need a key pair for your CA, the Order Processing microservice, and the Inventory microservice. Create a directory structure as follows:

```
\> mkdir -p keys/ca
\> mkdir -p keys/orderprocessing
\> mkdir -p keys/inventory
```

To create a CA's public and private key pair, follow the steps in appendix G (section G.1) and copy those keys (ca_key.pem and ca_cert.pem) to the keys/ca directory you just created. In the next section, we discuss how to generate a public/private key pair for the Order Processing and Inventory microservices and get the keys signed by the CA you created in this section.

NOTE If you want to skip the detailed instructions in appendix G and generate all the keys for the CA, Order Processing, and Inventory microservices in one go, see section 6.2.4.

6.2.2 Generating keys for the Order Processing microservice

To generate a public and private key pair for the Order Processing microservice, you can follow the steps in appendix G (section G.2), and at the end of the process, copy the generated keystore file (app.jks) to the keys/orderprocessing directory. Then rename the file to orderprocessing.jks. This keystore file has the private and public key pair of the Order Processing microservice; the public key is signed by the CA created in section 6.2.1.

6.2.3 Generating keys for the Inventory microservice

You repeat the same process (described in section 6.2.2) for the Inventory microservice. You can follow the steps in appendix G (section G.2), and at the end of the process, copy the generated keystore file (app.jks) to the keys/inventory directory. Then rename the file to inventory.jks. This keystore file has the private and public key pair of the Inventory microservice; the public key is signed by the CA created in section 6.2.1.

Figure 6.3 shows the setup of keystores for both the Order Processing and Inventory microservices. Each keystore has its own private key, the public key signed by the CA, and the CA's public certificate. In section 6.3, we discuss how to use these two keystores to secure the communication between the two microservices over TLS.

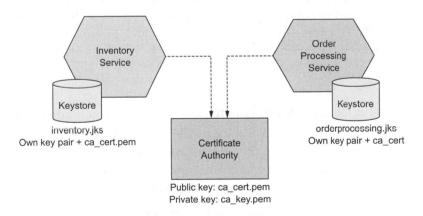

Figure 6.3 Keystore setup: each microservice has its own public/private key pair stored in a Java keystore file (.jks), along with the CA's public key.

6.2.4 Using a single script to generate all the keys

In this section, we introduce a single script to perform all the actions to create keys for the CA and the Order Processing and Inventory microservices. If you've already followed the instructions in sections 6.2.1, 6.2.2, and 6.2.3, you can safely skip this section.

NOTE   The source code related to all the samples used in this chapter is available at the https://github.com/microservices-security-in-action/samples GitHub repository, under the chapter06 directory.

First, copy the `gen-key.sh` script from the chapter06 directory to the keys directory that you created in section 6.2.1. Here we run OpenSSL in a Docker container. If you're new to Docker, see appendix E, but you don't need to be thoroughly familiar with Docker to follow the rest of this section. To spin up the OpenSSL Docker container, run the following `docker run` command from the keys directory.

Listing 6.1   Spinning up OpenSSL in a Docker container

```
\> docker run -it -v $(pwd):/export prabath/openssl
#
```

The `docker run` command starts OpenSSL in a Docker container with a bind mount, which maps the keys directory (or the current directory, which is indicated by `${pwd}`) from the host filesystem to the `/export` directory of the container filesystem. This bind mount lets you share part of the host filesystem with the container filesystem. When the OpenSSL container generates certificates, those are written to the `/export` directory of the container filesystem. Because we have a bind mount, everything inside the `/export` directory of the container filesystem is also accessible from the keys directory of the host filesystem.

When you run the command in listing 6.1 for the first time, it may take a couple of minutes to execute. It ends with a command prompt, where you can execute our script as in the following command to create all the keys. Once the command completes successfully, you can type `exit` at the command prompt to exit from the Docker container:

```
# sh /export/gen-key.sh
# exit
```

Now, if you look at the keys directory in the host filesystem, you'll find the following set of files:

- ca_key.pem and ca_cert.pem files in the keys/ca directory
- orderprocessing.jks file in the keys/orderprocessing directory
- inventory.jks file in the keys/inventory directory

If you want to understand what happens underneath the gen-key.sh script, check appendix G.

6.3   *Securing microservices with TLS*

In this section, you'll develop two microservices, Order Processing and Inventory, with Java, using Spring Boot.[1] Then you'll enable TLS to secure communication between those two microservices.

---

[1] Spring Boot (https://spring.io/projects/spring-boot) is one of the most popular frameworks for developing microservices.

6.3.1 *Running the Order Processing microservice over TLS*

The Spring Boot sample of the Order Processing microservice is available in the chapter06/sample01 directory in the Git repository. Before you delve deep into the code, let's try to build, deploy, and run the Order Processing microservice.

To build the sample, run the following Maven command from the chapter06/sample01 directory. When you run this command for the first time, its completion can take a considerable amount of time. During the build process, Maven fetches all the binary dependencies that the Order Processing microservice needs. If those dependencies aren't available in the local Maven repo, it talks to remote Maven repositories and downloads them. That's how Maven works. If everything goes well, a BUILD SUCCESS message is printed at the end:

```
\> mvn clean install

[INFO] BUILD SUCCESS
```

To run the microservice, use the following Maven command. Here you use the Spring Boot Maven plugin (https://docs.spring.io/spring-boot/docs/current/maven-plugin/reference/html/). If the service starts successfully, you'll find these two logs toward the end, saying that the Order Processing microservice is available on HTTP port 6443:

```
\> mvn spring-boot:run

INFO 21811 --- [main] s.b.c.e.t.TomcatEmbeddedServletContainer :
Tomcat started on port(s): 6443 (http)
INFO 21811 --- [main] c.m.m.ch06.sample01.OrderProcessingApp   :
Started OrderProcessingApp in 2.738 seconds (JVM running for 5.552)
```

Use the following `curl` command to test the Order Processing microservice. If everything goes well, the command returns a JSON response, which represents an order:

```
\> curl -v  http://localhost:6443/orders/11

{
   "customer_id":"101021",
   "order_id":"11",
   "payment_method":{
      "card_type":"VISA",
      "expiration":"01/22",
      "name":"John Doe",
      "billing_address":"201, 1st Street, San Jose, CA"
   },
   "items":[
      {
         "code":"101",
         "qty":1
      },
      {
         "code":"103",
            "qty":5
      }
   ],
   "shipping_address":"201,1st Street, San Jose, CA"
}
```

Now we'll show you how to enable TLS. First, press Ctrl-C to shut down the service. Then copy the orderprocessing.jks file that you created earlier from the keys/order-processing directory to the chapter06/sample01 directory, where we have the source code of the Order Processing microservice. This keystore file contains the public/private key pair of the Order Processing microservice. Next, you'll need to edit the application.properties file in the chapter06/sample01/src/main/resources/ directory and uncomment the following properties. If you used different values for those parameters while generating the keystore, replace them appropriately:

```
server.ssl.key-store: orderprocessing.jks
server.ssl.key-store-password: manning123
server.ssl.keyAlias: orderprocessing
```

In addition to these properties, you'll find a `server.port` property in the same file. By default, this property is set to 6443. If you want to start the service on a different port, feel free to change the value. Then you'll be all set. Rebuild the service and start it with the following commands:

```
\> mvn clean install
\> mvn spring-boot:run

INFO 21811 --- [main] s.b.c.e.t.TomcatEmbeddedServletContainer :
Tomcat started on port(s): 6443 (https)
INFO 21811 --- [main] c.m.m.ch06.sample01.OrderProcessingApp   :
Started OrderProcessingApp in 2.738 seconds (JVM running for 5.624)
```

If the service starts successfully, you'll find a log that says that the Order Processing microservice is available on HTTPS port 6443 (if you used that port). Use the following `curl` command to test it over TLS:

```
\> curl -v -k  https://localhost:6443/orders/11

{
    "customer_id":"101021",
    "order_id":"11",
    "payment_method":{
      "card_type":"VISA",
      "expiration":"01/22",
      "name":"John Doe",
      "billing_address":"201, 1st Street, San Jose, CA"
    },
    "items":[
      {
        "code":"101",
        "qty":1
      },
      {
        "code":"103",
        "qty":5
      }
    ],
    "shipping_address":"201, 1st Street, San Jose, CA"
}
```

Now you have your Order Processing microservice running on TLS (or over HTTPS).

Behind the scenes of a TLS handshake

When you use curl to invoke a microservice secured with TLS, curl acts as the TLS client, in the same way that a browser acted as a client to the Amazon web server. The microservice first shares its public certificate (along with the certificate chain up to the root CA) with the curl client before establishing a connection. This process happens during the TLS handshake.

The TLS handshake happens between a TLS client and a TLS service before they start communicating with each other, and during the handshake the client and the service share certain properties required to establish the secure communication. When the client gets the public certificate of the TLS service, it checks whether a CA that it trusts has issued it. The public key of the CA that issued the certificate to the TLS service must be with the TLS client.

In the example in this section, the Order Processing microservice is protected with a certificate issued by your own CA, and by default, curl doesn't know about its public key. You have two options: ask curl to accept any certificate it receives without validating whether the certificate is issued by a CA it trusts, or provide curl with the public key of your CA. In this example, you chose the first option, using –k in the `curl` command to instruct curl to avoid trust validation. Ideally, you shouldn't do this in a production deployment.

6.3.2 *Running the Inventory microservice over TLS*

To enable TLS for the Inventory microservice, follow the same process you did before in section 6.3.1. The Spring Boot sample of the Inventory microservice is available in the chapter06/sample02 directory. Before you build and run the service, copy the inventory.jks file that you created before from the keys/inventory directory to the samples/chapter06/sample02 directory. This keystore file contains the public/private key pair of the Inventory microservice. Then, to enable TLS, uncomment the following properties in the chapter06/sample02/src/main/resources/application.properties file. If you used different values for those parameters while generating the keystore, replace them appropriately:

```
server.ssl.key-store: inventory.jks
server.ssl.key-store-password: manning123
server.ssl.keyAlias: inventory
```

In addition to these properties, you'll find the `server.port` property in the same file. By default, it's set to 8443. If you want to start the service on a different port, feel free to change the value. Now you're all set to build the project and start the microservice with the following Maven commands:

```
\> mvn clean install
\> mvn spring-boot:run
```

```
INFO 22276 --- [main] s.b.c.e.t.TomcatEmbeddedServletContainer :
Tomcat started on port(s): 8443 (https)
INFO 22276 --- [main] c.m.m.ch06.sample02.InventoryApp         :
Started InventoryApp in 3.068 seconds (JVM running for 6.491)
```

If the service starts successfully, you see a log that says the Inventory microservice is available on HTTPS port 8443 (shown in the previous output). Use the following `curl` command to test it over TLS:

```
\> curl -k  -v -X PUT -H "Content-Type: application/json" \
       -d '[{"code":"101","qty":1},{"code":"103","qty":5}]' \
       https://localhost:8443/inventory
```

If everything works, the item numbers from the request are printed on the terminal where the Inventory microservice is running. Now you have both your Order Processing and Inventory microservices running on TLS (or over HTTPS). In the next section, you'll see how these two microservices talk to each other over TLS.

6.3.3   *Securing communications between two microservices with TLS*

You're a few steps from enabling TLS communication between the Order Processing and Inventory microservices. You need to make a few changes in both microservices, though, so shut them down for the moment (if they're running).

When the Order Processing microservice talks to the Inventory microservice over TLS, the Order Processing microservice is the TLS client (figure 6.4). To establish a

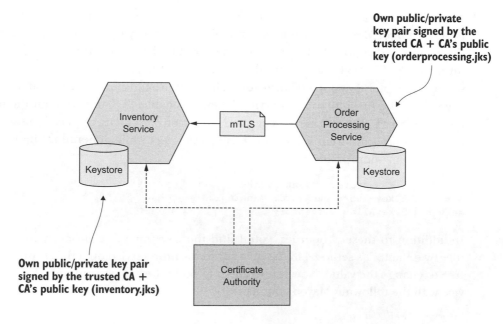

Figure 6.4   The Order Processing microservice talks to the Inventory microservice over TLS.

TLS connection, it has to trust the issuer of the server certificate that the Inventory microservice provides during the TLS handshake. In other words, the Order Processing microservice has to trust the CA that you created earlier in this chapter.

To trust a given CA in Java (and in Spring Boot), you need to explicitly specify a keystore in a system property called `javax.net.ssl.trustStore`. That property carries the location of the keystore file with the corresponding public key of the CA. You may recall that you imported the public key (ca_cert.pem) of your CA to both orderprocessing.jks and inventory.jks files. Now you need to set the location of the orderprocessing.jks keystore as a system property at the Order Processing microservice end. You don't need to set the same system property on the Inventory microservice side for the moment, because it doesn't do any calls to external microservices. Setting up the system property `javax.net.ssl.trustStore` is required only if a microservice acts as a TLS client. Uncomment the following code block (inside the `setEnvironment` method) in the OrderAppConfiguration.java file in the chapter06/sample01/src/main/java/com/manning/mss/ch06/sample01/ directory:

```
// points to the path where orderprocessing.jks keystore is.
System.setProperty("javax.net.ssl.trustStore", "orderprocessing.jks");
// password of the orderprocessing.jks keystore.
System.setProperty("javax.net.ssl.trustStorePassword", "manning123");
```

The following code snippet from the OrderProcessingService.java file (in the chapter06/sample01/src/main/java/com/manning/mss/ch06/sample01/service directory) shows how the Order Processing microservice talks to the Inventory microservice over TLS. When you POST an order to the Order Processing microservice, the Order Processing microservice talks to the Inventory microservice to update the item inventory. Here, you use the URL https://localhost:8443/inventory, which points to the Inventory microservice. The value of this URL is picked from the `inventory.service` property defined in the chapter06/sample01/src/main/resources/application.properties file:

```
if (order != null) {
  RestTemplate restTemplate = new RestTemplate();
  URI uri = URI.create(System.getProperty("inventory.service"));
  restTemplate.put(uri, order.getItems());

  order.setOrderId(UUID.randomUUID().toString());
  URI location = ServletUriComponentsBuilder
                    .fromCurrentRequest().path("/{id}")
                    .buildAndExpand(order.getOrderId()).toUri();
  return ResponseEntity.created(location).build();
}
```

What's the issue in this code snippet? You may recall that when you created the public certificate for the Inventory microservice following the steps in appendix G, you used `iv.ecomm.com` as the value of the Common Name (CN) attribute. Any TLS client that talks to the Inventory microservice must use `iv.ecomm.com` as the hostname in the URL, not `localhost`. Otherwise, a hostname verification failure results.

How do you fix this problem? The correct approach is to use the right hostname in the preceding code (or set it as the value of the `inventory.service` key in the application.properties file—currently, it is set to localhost). But then you need to have a DNS setting pointing to the IP address of the server that runs the Inventory microservice, which is what you should do in production. For the time being, you can use a little trick. When you uncomment the following code snippet (inside the static block) in the OrderProcessingApp.java file, the system automatically ignores the hostname verification:

```
HttpsURLConnection.setDefaultHostnameVerifier(new HostnameVerifier() {
        public boolean verify(String hostname, SSLSession session) {
            return true;
        }
});
```

Now try service-to-service communication between the Order Processing and Inventory microservices over TLS. First, build and start the Order Processing microservice with the following Maven commands from the chapter06/sample01 directory, which you're already familiar with:

```
\> mvn clean install
\> mvn spring-boot:run
```

Next, start the Inventory microservice. Run the following Maven commands from the chapter06/sample02 directory:

```
\> mvn clean install
\> mvn spring-boot:run
```

Now you have both services running again. Use the following `curl` command to POST an order to the Order Processing microservice, which internally talks to the Inventory microservice over TLS to update the inventory. The following `curl` command is formatted with line breaks for clarity:

```
\> curl -k -v https://localhost:6443/orders \
-H 'Content-Type: application/json' \
-d @- << EOF
{   "customer_id":"101021",
    "payment_method":{
       "card_type":"VISA",
       "expiration":"01/22",
       "name":"John Doe",
       "billing_address":"201, 1st Street, San Jose, CA"
    },
    "items":[   {
       "code":"101",
       "qty":1
       },
       {
       "code":"103",
       "qty":5
```

```
    }
  ],
    "shipping_address":"201, 1st Street, San Jose, CA"
}
EOF
```

If everything works, the item numbers from the request are printed on the terminal where the Inventory microservice is running.

6.4   *Engaging mTLS*

Now you have two microservices communicating with each other over TLS, but it's one-way TLS. Only the calling microservice knows what it communicates with, and the recipient has no way of identifying the client. This is where you need mTLS.

In this section, you'll see how to protect the Inventory microservice with mTLS. When you have TLS set up among microservices, enabling mTLS is straightforward. First, shut down both microservices if they're running. To enforce mTLS at the Inventory microservice end, uncomment the following property in the application.properties file in chapter06/sample02/src/main/resources/:

```
server.ssl.client-auth = need
```

Setting this property to need isn't sufficient, however. You also need to identify which clients to trust. In this example, you're going to trust any client with a certificate signed by your CA. To do that, set the value of the system property `javax.net` `.ssl.trustStore` to a keystore that carries the public certificate of your trusted CA. You already have the public certificate of the trusted CA in the inventory.jks keystore, so all you have to do is set the system property that points to that keystore. Uncomment the following code block (inside the `setEnvironment` method) in chapter06/sample02/src/main/java/com/manning/mss/ch06/sample02/Inventory AppConfiguration.java:

```
// points to the path where inventory.jks keystore is.
System.setProperty("javax.net.ssl.trustStore", "inventory.jks");
// password of inventory.jks keystore.
System.setProperty("javax.net.ssl.trustStorePassword", "manning123");
```

Next, build and spin up both microservices to see how the interservice communication works. Run the following commands from the chapter06/sample01 directory to start the Order Processing microservice:

```
\> mvn clean install
\> mvn spring-boot:run
```

Next, to start the Inventory microservice, run the following Maven commands from the chapter06/sample02 directory:

```
\> mvn clean install
\> mvn spring-boot:run
```

Now both services are running again. Use the following `curl` command to `POST` an order to the Order Processing microservice, which internally talks to the Inventory microservice over TLS to update the inventory. You might expect this request to fail because you enabled mTLS at the Inventory microservice end but didn't change the Order Processing microservice to authenticate to the Inventory microservice with its private key:

```
\> curl -k -v https://localhost:6443/orders \
-H 'Content-Type: application/json' \
-d @- << EOF
{   "customer_id":"101021",
    "payment_method":{
        "card_type":"VISA",
        "expiration":"01/22",
        "name":"John Doe",
        "billing_address":"201, 1st Street, San Jose, CA"
    },
    "items":[  {
        "code":"101",
        "qty":1
        },
        {
        "code":"103",
        "qty":5
        }
    ],
    "shipping_address":"201, 1st Street, San Jose, CA"
}
EOF
```

This request results in an error, and if you look at the terminal that runs the Order Processing microservice, you see the following error log:

```
javax.net.ssl.SSLHandshakeException: Received fatal alert: bad_certificate
```

The communication between the two microservices fails during the TLS handshake. To fix it, first take down the Order Processing service. Then uncomment the following code (inside the `setEnvironment` method) in the OrderAppConfiguration.java file (in chapter06/sample01/src/main/java/com/manning/mss/ch06/sample01/). This code asks the system to use its private key from orderprocessing.jks to authenticate to the Inventory microservice:

```
// points to the path where orderprocessing.jks keystore is located.
System.setProperty("javax.net.ssl.keyStore", "orderprocessing.jks");
// password of orderprocessing.jks keystore.
System.setProperty("javax.net.ssl.keyStorePassword", "manning123");
```

Next, run the following Maven commands from the chapter06/sample01 directory to build and start the Order Processing microservice:

```
\> mvn clean install
\> mvn spring-boot:run
```

Now use the following `curl` command again to POST an order to the Order Processing microservice. It should work this time!

```
\> curl -k -v https://localhost:6443/orders \
-H 'Content-Type: application/json' \
-d @- << EOF
{   "customer_id":"101021",
    "payment_method":{
        "card_type":"VISA",
        "expiration":"01/22",
        "name":"John Doe",
        "billing_address":"201, 1st Street, San Jose, CA"
    },
    "items":[   {
        "code":"101",
        "qty":1
        },
        {
        "code":"103",
        "qty":5
        }
    ],
    "shipping_address":"201, 1st Street, San Jose, CA"
}
EOF
```

You have two microservices secured with TLS, and the communication between them is protected with mTLS.

6.5 Challenges in key management

Ask any DevOps person to name the hardest part of the job, and eight out of ten would say *key management*. As the name implies, key management is about how you manage keys in your microservices deployment. It involves four main areas: bootstrapping trust and provisioning keys/certificates to workloads or microservices, key revocation, key rotation, and monitoring the key usage.

6.5.1 Key provisioning and bootstrapping trust

In a typical microservices deployment, each microservice is provisioned with a key pair, as you did manually by copying the Java keystore files to the Order Processing and Inventory microservices earlier in this chapter. Doing things manually won't work in a large-scale microservices deployment, however; everything must be automated. Ideally, during the continuous integration/continuous delivery (CI/CD) pipeline, the keys should be generated and provisioned to the microservices. When the keys are provisioned to all the microservices, the next challenge is building trust among microservices. Why would one microservice trust a request initiated from another microservice?

One approach is to have a single CA for a given deployment and have each microservice in the deployment trust this CA; during the boot-up process of each microservice, you need to provision the public certificate of the CA to each microservice. This

CA issues all the microservice-specific keys. When one microservice talks to another one secured with mTLS, the recipient microservice validates the caller's certificate and verifies whether it's issued by the trusted CA (of the deployment); if so, it accepts the request. You followed this model in the Spring Boot examples earlier in this chapter.

TYPICAL KEY-PROVISIONING PROCESS AT AN ENTERPRISE

The typical key-provisioning mechanics that most enterprises use today don't deviate much from the approach you followed in this chapter when creating keys for the Order Processing and Inventory microservices. The developer who wants to secure a service with TLS first has to generate a public/private key pair, and then create a certificate-signing request (CSR) and submit the CSR for approval to the team that maintains the corporate CA. If everything looks good, the signed certificate is handed over to the developer who initiated the signing request. Then the developer deploys the certificate and the keys to the microservice. But this process is painful in a microservices deployment with hundreds of services spinning up and down all the time.

KEY PROVISIONING AT NETFLIX

Netflix has thousands of microservices, and communication among those microservices is secured with mTLS. Netflix uses Lemur, an open source certificate management framework that acts as a broker (see figure 6.5) between the internal service deployment and the CA, and provides management tools to automate the key-provisioning process. During the process of continuous delivery, each microservice is injected with a set of credentials that are good enough to access the Lemur APIs. A tool called Metatron, which is internal to Netflix (not open source), does this credential

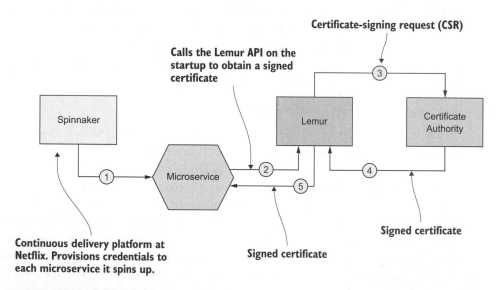

Figure 6.5   Key provisioning at Netflix. Each microservice at startup talks to Lemur to get a signed certificate from the CA in the domain.

bootstrapping. As each microservice boots up, it talks to the Lemur API and gets a signed certificate for its (microservice's) public/private key pair.

Lemur isn't a CA, but it knows how to integrate with a CA and generate a signed certificate. Microservices developers shouldn't worry about the certificate-signing process, but about talking to the Lemur API. Figure 6.5 illustrates the key-provisioning process.

GENERATING LONG-LIVED CREDENTIALS

In the key-provisioning model at Netflix, discussed in the preceding section, each microservice is provisioned with long-lived credentials that are used to connect to Lemur to get a signed certificate. This signed certificate, particularly in the Netflix environment, is a short-lived credential. We talk about short-lived credentials later in this chapter. Each microservice uses the same long-lived credentials to connect to Lemur to refresh the current signed certificate. This method is a common solution to the trust bootstrapping problem.

As discussed before, Netflix uses a tool called *Metatron* to do the credential bootstrapping. The internal details of Metatron aren't available yet for public access because the tool isn't open source. In this section, however, we propose a scalable approach to generate long-lived credentials:

1 Protect the API of the certificate issuer (such as Lemur) so that anyone who wants to access it must present a valid key.

2 Build a handler to intercept the continuous delivery (CD) pipeline that injects long-lived credentials into the microservices.

3 Write the intercept handler in such a way that it generates long-lived credentials as JWTs. The JWT will carry information about the microservice and will be signed by a key that's known to the certificate issuer. We discuss JWTs in detail in chapter 7.

4 At boot-up time, the microservice uses the injected long-lived credentials (JWT) to talk to the certificate issuer's API and to get a signed certificate. It can keep using the same long-lived credentials to rotate certificates.

SECURE PRODUCTION IDENTITY FRAMEWORK FOR EVERYONE

Secure Production Identity Framework for Everyone (SPIFFE) is an open standard that defines a way a microservice (or a *workload*, in SPIFFE terminology) can establish an identity. SPIFFE Runtime Environment (SPIRE) is the open source reference implementation of SPIFFE. While helping establish an identity for each microservice in a given deployment, SPIFFE solves the trust bootstrapping problem. We discuss SPIFFE in detail in appendix H.

6.5.2 *Certificate revocation*

Certificate revocation can happen for two main reasons: the corresponding private key is compromised or the private key of the CA that signed the certificate is compromised. The latter situation can be rare, but in an internal CA deployment, anything is possible. A certificate can also be revoked for a third reason, which isn't as common in a private certificate deployment: if a CA finds that the entity behind the signed certificate no longer represents the original entity at the time the certificate was issued, or if it finds the details provided along with the CSR are invalid, the CA can revoke the certificate.

The challenge in certificate revocation is how to communicate the revocation decision to the interested parties. If the Amazon certificate is revoked, for example, that decision must be propagated to all browsers. Over time, multiple approaches have been suggested to overcome the challenges in certificate revocation. We go through some of these approaches in the following sections.

CERTIFICATE REVOCATION LISTS

A certificate revocation list (CRL) was among one of the first approaches suggested to overcome issues related to certificate revocation as defined in RFC 2459 (www .ietf.org/rfc/rfc2459.txt). Each CA publishes an endpoint where the TLS client applications can query and retrieve the latest revoked certificate list from that CA. As shown in figure 6.6, this endpoint is known as the *CRL distribution point* and is embedded in the certificate by the CA. According to RFC 5280 (https://tools.ietf.org/html/rfc5280), a CRL distribution point is a noncritical extension in a certificate. If a CA decides not to include it, it's up to the TLS client application to find the endpoint related to the corresponding CRL by another means.

A CRL means overhead to a TLS client application. Each time the client application validates a certificate, it has to talk to the CRL endpoint of the corresponding CA,

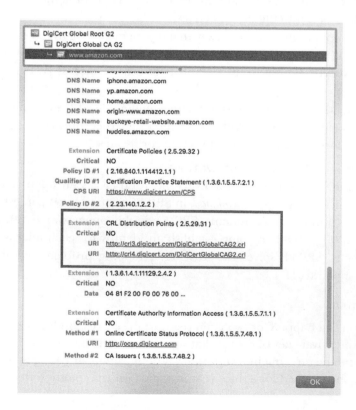

Figure 6.6   The Amazon certificate embeds the corresponding CRL distribution points.

retrieve the list of revoked certificates, and check whether the certificate in question is part of that list. The CRL can sometimes grow by megabytes. To avoid making frequent calls to the CA's CRL endpoint, client applications can follow a workaround in which they cache the CRLs by CA. Every time they see the same certificate, they don't need to retrieve the corresponding CRL from the CA.

This solution isn't good enough for highly security-concerned environments, however, because there's a possibility of making security decisions based on stale data. Also, CRLs create a coupling between the TLS client application and the CA. What would happen if the CRL endpoint of a given CA goes down? Should the TLS client application accept the certificates issued by that CA? This decision is tricky to make. With all these drawbacks and challenges, people started to move away from CRL-based certificate revocation.

ONLINE CERTIFICATE STATUS PROTOCOL

Unlike CRL, the Online Certificate Status Protocol (OCSP) doesn't build one bulky list of all the revoked certificates. Each time the TLS client application sees a certificate, it has to talk to the corresponding OCSP endpoint and check whether the certificate was revoked. As in CRL, the OCSP endpoint that corresponds to a given CA is also embedded in the certificate (see figure 6.7). Because the client application has to talk to the OCSP endpoint each time during the certificate validation process, the process creates a lot of traffic on the CA (or, to be precise, on the OCSP responder).

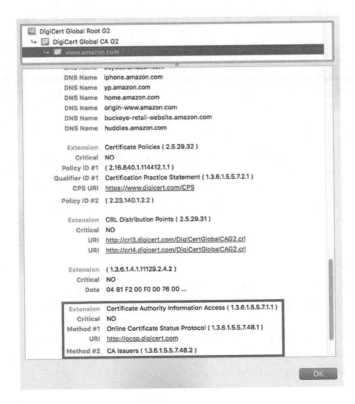

Figure 6.7   The Amazon certificate embeds the OCSP endpoint.

Once again, as with CRL, to avoid frequent calls to the OCSP endpoint, some clients cache the revocation decisions. This solution, however, has the same issue as CRLs: security decisions could be made based on stale data. Also, you still don't have a proper answer about what to do if the OCSP endpoint is down. Should the TLS client application accept the certificates issued by that CA?

OCSP makes certificate revocation a little better, but it doesn't fix all the challenges involved with CRLs. Google, in fact, decided not to support OCSP-based certificate validation in its Chrome browser; rather, it relies on frequent browser updates to share a list of revoked certificates.

Drawbacks in OCSP

"Towards Short-Lived Certificates" by Emin Topalovic et al. (http://bit.ly/2ZC9IS0) identifies four drawbacks in OCSP:

- OCSP validation increases client-side latency because verifying a certificate is a blocking operation requiring a round trip to the OCSP responder to retrieve the revocation status (if no valid response is found in the cache). A previous study indicates that 91.7% of OCSP lookups are costly, taking more than 100 ms to complete, thereby delaying HTTPS session setup.

- OCSP can provide real-time responses to revocation queries, but it's unclear whether the responses contain updated revocation information. Some OCSP responders may rely on cached CRLs on their backend. It was observed that DigiNotar's OCSP responder was returning good responses well after it was attacked.

- Like CRLs, OCSP validations can be defeated in multiple ways, including traffic filtering and bogus responses forged by network attackers. Most importantly, revocation checks in browsers fail open. When a browser can't verify a certificate through OCSP, most don't alert the user or change their UI; some even don't check the revocation status at all. We must note that failing open is necessary, however, because there are legitimate situations in which the browser can't reach the OCSP responder.

- OCSP also introduces a privacy risk: OCSP responders know which certificates are being verified by end users, so responders can, in principle, track which sites the user is visiting. OCSP stapling, which we discuss in the next section, is intended to mitigate this privacy risk, but it isn't often used.

OCSP STAPLING

OCSP stapling makes OCSP a little better. It takes the overhead of talking to the OCSP endpoint from the TLS client and hands it over to the server. This move is interesting, as it considerably reduces the traffic on the OCSP endpoint. Now the TLS server talks to the corresponding OCSP endpoint first, gets the signed response from the CA (or the OCSP responder), and attaches, or *staples*, the response to the certificate. The TLS client application looks at the OCSP response attached to the corresponding certificate to check whether the certificate is revoked.

This process may look a little tricky because the owner of the certificate attaches the OCSP response to the certificate. If the owner decides to attach the same OCSP response throughout, even after the certificate is revoked, it can possibly fool the TLS client applications. In practice, however, this scenario is impossible. Each signed OCSP response from the CA (or the OCSP responder) has a timestamp, and if that timestamp isn't relatively recent, the client must refuse to accept it.

OCSP STAPLING REQUIRED

Even with OCSP stapling, what would happen if no OCSP response is attached to the certificate? Should you reject the communication with the corresponding server or go ahead and accept it? This decision is hard to make. When OCSP stapling is required, the server guarantees that the server certificate exchanged during the TLS handshake includes the OCSP response. If the client doesn't find the OCSP response attached to the certificate, it can refuse to communicate with the server.

SHORT-LIVED CERTIFICATES

The common consensus on certificate revocation is that it's a hard one to address. The approach suggested by short-lived certificates ignores certificate revocation, relying instead on expiration. But what's a good value for certificate expiration? Is it years or a couple of days? If the expiration time is too long, in case of a key compromise, all the systems that depend on the compromised key are at risk for a long time as well, and the short-lived certificates suggest a short expiration, possibly a couple of days.

The concept of short-lived certificates is nothing new. It was initially discussed in 1998, but with microservices-based deployments, it's come back into the mainstream discussion. Research done at Carnegie Mellon University proposes using short-lived certificates to improve TLS performance (www.linshunghuang.com/papers/short-lived.pdf). According to this proposal, CAs could configure the validity period of short-lived certificates to match the average validity lifetime of an OCSP response measured in the real world, which is four days. Such certificates expire quickly, and most importantly, the TLS client application rejects any communication afterward, treating those as insecure without the need for a revocation mechanism. Further, according to this proposal, when a website purchases a year-long certificate, the CA's response is a URL that can be used to download on-demand, short-lived certificates. The URL remains active for the year, but the certificates that you download from that URL are valid for only a few days.

NETFLIX AND SHORT-LIVED CERTIFICATES

In the Netflix microservices deployment, service-to-service communication is secured with mTLS using short-lived certificates. Netflix uses a layered approach to build a short-lived certificate deployment: a system identity or long-lived credentials residing in a Trusted Platform Module (TPM) or an Intel Software Guard Extensions (SGX) chip tightens security. During the boot-up process, access to the long-lived credentials is provisioned to each microservice. Then each microservice uses those credentials to get short-lived credentials.

NOTE   TPM is a hardware chip that can securely store cryptographic keys, according to the TPM specification published by Trusted Computing Group (http://mng.bz/04Ml). SGX by Intel allows applications to execute code and protect secrets in their own trusted execution environments. SGX is designed to protect secrets from malicious software.

Metatron, a tool developed by Netflix for credential management (which we discussed briefly in section 6.5.1), does the credential bootstrap. At this writing, Metatron is in its beta version, and there are plans to open source it in the future. When the initial long-lived credentials are provisioned to microservices, they use those credentials to talk to Netflix Lemur to get the short-lived credentials.

Lemur (https://github.com/Netflix/lemur) is an open source certificate manager developed by Netflix (see figure 6.8). Each microservice can refresh the short-lived credentials periodically, using its long-lived credentials. Each time a microservice gets new short-lived credentials, the server environment must be updated with it. If you run your microservice on Spring Boot, for example, it should know how to update all its transport senders and listeners with the updated credentials without restarting the server.

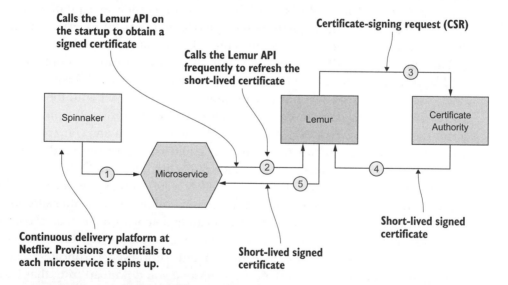

Figure 6.8   Netflix uses short-lived certificates with mTLS to secure service-to-service communications.

Why use long-lived credentials?

We assume that long-lived credentials are secure and hard to compromise. If that's the case, why are short-lived credentials necessary? Why not use the more secure long-lived credentials themselves?

The answer lies in performance. Long-lived credentials are secured with a TPM or an SGX chip. Loading such long-lived credentials frequently is a costly operation. Short-lived credentials, on the other hand, are kept in memory.

6.6 *Key rotation*

All the keys provisioned into microservices must be rotated before they expire. Not every enterprise is concerned about key rotation, however. Expiration times used to be higher, such as 5 to 10 years. You realize that you have to rotate certificates only when communication links start to fail because of an expired certificate. Some companies have key rotation policies stating that all the keys used in a deployment must be rotated every month or two. The short-lived certificate approach we discussed earlier in this chapter enforces certificate rotation in short intervals. Netflix, for example, rotates keys every 4 minutes in its microservices deployment. That interval may look crazy, but that's the level of security Netflix worries about. Then again, the key rotation policy differs from short-lived credentials to long-lived credentials.

The keys embedded in microservices can be short-lived and rotated frequently, but your corporate CA's private key doesn't need to be rotated. The overhead of rotating the CA's private key is much higher. You need to make sure that every service that trusts the CA has the updated key. If it's hard to rotate some keys frequently, you should find better ways of securing those keys. These ways usually are expensive, both financially and in terms of performance. Netflix, for example, uses TPM or an SGX chip with tightened security to secure its long-lived credentials.

Key rotation is more challenging in a microservices deployment with an increased number of services spinning on and off. Automation is the key to addressing this problem. Every microservices deployment requires an approach like the one Netflix uses with Lemur. SPIFFE is another approach, which we discuss in detail in appendix H.

6.7 *Monitoring key usage*

Observability, an essential ingredient of a typical microservices deployment, indicates how well you can infer the internal state of a system by looking at the external outputs. *Monitoring* is about tracking the state of a system. Unless you have a way to monitor the external outputs of a system, you'll never be able to infer its internal state. Only if a microservice is observable will you be able to infer its internal state. We discuss the observability of a system under three categories, which we call the *three pillars of observability*: logging, metrics, and tracing.

With *logging*, you can record any event happening in your system: a successful login event; a failed login event; success or failure in an access-control check; an event related to key provisioning, key rotation, or key revocation; and so on.

Metrics indicate the direction of a system. Logging events help you derive metrics. By tracking the time it takes to refresh keys in short intervals, for example, you can derive how much that process contributes to the average latency of the system. The latency of a system is reflected by the time interval between a request entering and exiting a system. You can derive another metric by tracking the number of failed login attempts against a service. If the number of failed login attempts is high or goes beyond a certain threshold, that service may be under attack, or a certificate may be expired or revoked.

Tracing is also derived from logs. Tracing is concerned with the order of events and the impact of one event on another. In a microservices deployment, if a request fails at the Inventory microservice, tracing helps you find the root cause and what happened to the same request in the Order Processing and Delivery microservices. You can also trace which keys are being used between which services and identify the patterns in key use, which helps you identify anomalous behaviors and raise alerts.

Monitoring a microservices deployment is challenging, as many service-to-service interactions occur. We use tools like Zipkin, Prometheus, and Grafana in a microservices deployment to monitor key use.

Summary

- There are multiple options in securing communications among microservices, including mutual TLS (mTLS) and JSON Web Tokens (JWTs).
- Transport Layer Security protects communications between two parties for confidentiality and integrity. Using TLS to secure data in transit has been a practice for several years.
- mTLS is the most popular way of securing interservice communications among microservices.
- TLS is also known as one-way TLS, mostly because it helps the client identify the server it's talking to, but not the other way around. Two-way TLS, or mTLS, fills this gap by helping the client and server identify themselves to each other.
- Key management in a microservices deployment is quite challenging, and we need to be concerned about bootstrapping trust and provisioning keys and certificates to workloads or microservices, key revocation, key rotation, and key use monitoring.
- Certificate revocation can happen for two main reasons: the corresponding private key is compromised, or the private key of the CA that signed the certificate is compromised.
- Using a certificate revocation list (CRL), defined in RFC 2459, was among one of the very first approaches suggested to overcome issues related to certificate revocation.
- Unlike CRL, the Online Certificate Status Protocol (OCSP) doesn't build one bulky list of all revoked certificates. Each time the TLS client application sees a certificate, it has to talk to the corresponding OCSP endpoint and check whether the certificate is revoked.
- OCSP stapling makes OCSP a little better. It takes the overhead of talking to the OCSP endpoint from the TLS client and hands it over to the server.
- The approach suggested by short-lived certificates ignores certificate revocation, relying instead on expiration.
- All the keys provisioned into microservices must be rotated before they expire.
- Observability is an essential ingredient of a typical microservices deployment. It's about how well you can infer the internal state of a system by looking at the external outputs. Monitoring is about tracking the state of a system.

7
Securing east/west traffic with JWT

This chapter covers

- Using JWTs in securing service-to-service communications
- Using JWT to carry user context among microservices
- Using JWT for cross-domain authentication

In chapter 6, we discussed securing service-to-service communications in a microservices deployment with mTLS. mTLS is, in fact, the most popular option for authenticating one microservice to another. *JSON Web Token* (*JWT*), which provides a way to carry a set of claims or attributes from one party to another in a cryptographically secure way, also plays a key role in securing service-to-service communications in a microservices deployment.

You can use JWT to carry the identity of the calling microservice, or the identity of the end user or system that initiated the request. JWT can also be used to propagate identity attributes between multiple trust domains. In this chapter, we explore the role that JWT plays in securing service-to-service communications in a

161

microservices deployment. If you're not familiar with JWT, we recommend you first read appendix B, which provides a comprehensive overview of JWT.

7.1   Use cases for securing microservices with JWT

JWT addresses two main concerns in a microservices security design: securing service-to-service communications and passing end-user context across microservices (figure 7.1). As we discussed in chapter 6, JWT isn't the most popular option for securing service-to-service communications; mTLS is. In this section, we discuss why you might pick JWT over mTLS to secure service-to-service communications, as well as other use cases of JWT in a microservices deployment. In practice, you use JWT along with mTLS, together, in most cases.

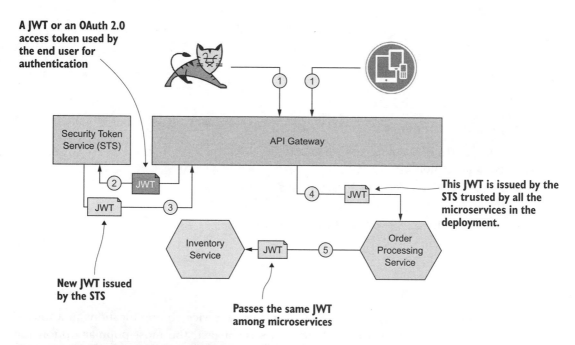

Figure 7.1   Propagating the end user's identity in a JWT among microservices. All the microservices in the deployment trust the STS. The API gateway exchanges the JWTs it gets from client applications for new JWTs from this STS.

7.1.1   Sharing user context between microservices with a shared JWT

When the identity of the microservice isn't relevant, but the identity of the end user (a system or a human) is, you should consider using JWT instead of mTLS. In this case, services themselves don't authenticate to one another. In every request, you need to carry the identity of the end user who initiates the message flow; if not, the recipient microservice rejects the request. But in practice, even though you do not worry about the service's identity, in terms of better security you should still use mTLS among microservices, along with the JWT protection. This will add a second layer of defense. The following walks you through the numbered request flow shown in figure 7.1:

1 An end user initiates the request flow. This end user can be a human or a system.

2 As discussed in chapters 1 and 3, the edge gateway authenticates the end user. The edge gateway intercepts the request from the end user, extracts the token (which can be an OAuth 2.0 reference or self-contained token), and then talks to the STS connected to it to validate the token. Then again, the token that the end user presents might not be issued by this STS; it can come from any other identity provider that this STS trusts. The details related to the end user authentication are discussed in chapter 3. The STS should know how to validate the token presented to it in this step.

3 After validating the token, the STS issues a new JWT signed by itself. This JWT includes the user details copied from the old JWT (from step 2). When the edge gateway passes the new JWT to the upstream microservices, those upstream microservices need only trust this STS to accept the token as valid. Typically, all the microservices within a single trust domain trust a single STS.

4 The API gateway passes the new JWT issued by the STS in an HTTP header (Authorization Bearer) over TLS to the Order Processing microservice. The Order Processing microservice validates the signature of the JWT to make sure that it's issued by the STS it trusts. Apart from the signature validation, the Order Processing microservice also does audience validation, checking whether the value of the provided JWT's aud is known to itself (more details in appendix B). For the pattern discussed in this section to work, all the microservices in the same trust domain (that trust a single STS) must accept a JWT with a wildcard audience value such as *.ecomm.com.

5 When the Order Processing microservice talks to the Inventory microservice, it passes the same JWT that it got from the API gateway. The Inventory microservice validates the signature of the JWT to make sure that it's issued by the STS it trusts. Also, it checks whether the value of the aud attribute in the JWT is *.ecomm.com.

In this approach, JWT helps you achieve two things. First, it helps you pass the end-user context across microservices in a manner that can't be forged. Because the claims set of the JWT is signed by the STS, no microservice can change its content without invalidating its signature. Also, JWT helps you secure service-to-service communications. One microservice can access another microservice only if it carries a valid JWT issued by the trusted STS. Any recipient microservice rejects any request without a valid JWT.

7.1.2 *Sharing user context with a new JWT for each service-to-service interaction*

The use case we discuss in this section is a slight variation of the one we discussed in section 7.1.1, but still only the end user's identity is relevant—not the identity of the microservice. Instead of passing the same JWT across all the microservices and accepting the same audience value at each microservice, you generate a new JWT for each service interaction. This approach is much more secure than using a shared JWT. But there's no such thing as absolute security. Everything depends on your use cases and the level of trust you have in your microservices deployment.

Figure 7.2 illustrates how this pattern works. It's the same flow discussed in section 7.1.1 except for steps 4a and 4b. In step 4a, before the Order Processing microservice talks to the Inventory microservice, it talks to the STS and does a token exchange. It passes the JWT it got from the API gateway (issued under `op.ecomm.com` audience) and requests a new JWT to access the Inventory microservice. In step 4b, STS issues a new JWT under the audience `iv.ecomm.com`. Thereafter, the flow continues as in the preceding section.

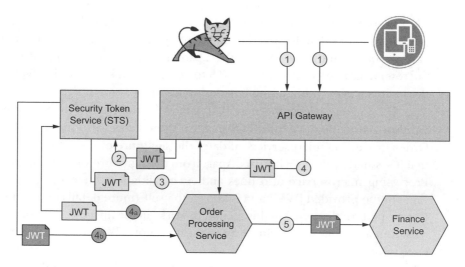

Figure 7.2   Propagating the end user's identity in a JWT among microservices with token exchange

Why do you need a new JWT with a new audience value when the Order Processing microservice talks to the Inventory microservice? Why is it more secure than sharing the same JWT coming from the API gateway across all the microservices in the deployment and accepting a single audience value? There are two valid reasons at minimum:

- When you have a one-to-one mapping between a microservice in your deployment and the audience value of the corresponding JWT issued by the STS, for a given JWT, you know exactly who the intended audience is. In step 4 of figure 7.2, for example, when the request is dispatched to the Order Processing microservice from the API gateway, it can make sure that the token goes to no other microservice but Order Processing. If the token goes to the wrong microservice, it will still be rejected by that microservice because of the audience mismatch.

- If the Order Processing microservice tries to reuse the token given to it as-is to access another service, such as the Finance microservice (which ideally, it shouldn't need access to), the request fails because the audience value in the original JWT doesn't work with the Finance microservice, which has its own audience value. The only way that the Order Processing microservice can talk to the Finance microservice is to pass its current JWT to the STS and exchange it for a new JWT with an audience value accepted by the Finance microservice. Now you have more control at the STS, and the STS can decide whether to let the Order Processing microservice access the Finance microservice.

One would argue, what's the point of doing access-control checks at the STS at the point of token exchange, while we can do it anyway at the edge of the microservice? Enforcing access control at the edge of a microservice is a common pattern, mostly with the Service Mesh architecture, which we discuss in chapter 12.

In this case, because we don't need to worry about the identity of the microservices, the recipient microservice has no way to figure out who the calling microservice is unless the STS embeds identity information about the calling microservice into the new JWT it created at the point of token exchange. However, STS always knows about the identity of the microservice that initiates the token exchange flow (step 4a in figure 7.2), as well as the identity of the first microservice it intends to call with the new token. So, the STS is in a better position to enforce access-control checks. It's better to do coarse-grained access-control checks at the STS, and push fine-grained access-control checks to the edge of the microservice.

7.1.3 *Sharing user context between microservices in different trust domains*

The use case in this section is an extension of the token exchange use case discussed in section 7.1.2. As figure 7.3 shows, most of the steps are straightforward. There's no change from the preceding section up to step 6. (Steps 5 and 6 in figure 7.3 are equivalent to steps 4a and 4b in figure 7.2.)

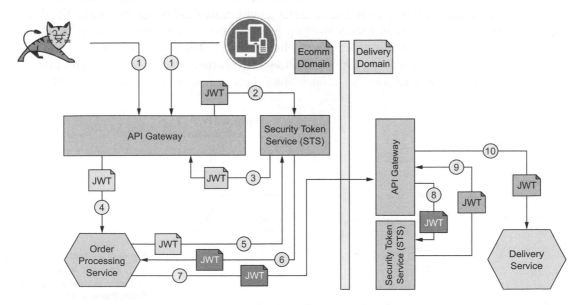

Figure 7.3   Cross-domain authentication and user context sharing among multiple trust domains. The STS in the delivery domain trusts the STS in the ecomm domain.

In step 7, the Order Processing microservice from the ecomm domain tries to access the Delivery microservice in the delivery domain via the delivery API gateway. The JWT carried in this request (step 7) is issued by the STS in the ecomm domain and has an audience value to match the Delivery microservice. In step 8, the API gateway of the Delivery domain talks to its own STS to validate the JWT. The validation passes only if the delivery STS trusts the ecomm STS. In other words, the corresponding public key of the signature in the JWT issued by the ecomm STS must be known to the delivery STS. If that's the case, in step 9, the delivery STS creates its own JWT and passes it over to the Delivery microservice via the API gateway. All the microservices in the delivery domain trust only their domain's own STS.

7.1.4   Self-issued JWTs

In the use cases discussed so far, we didn't need to worry about the identity of the microservice itself. Rather, we relied on a JWT issued by a trusted STS that carried the end user's identity. With self-issued JWTs (see figure 7.4), however, we do need to be concerned about the identity of microservices when they talk to one another, as in mTLS (discussed in chapter 6).

As in mTLS, and in this model, each microservice must have its own public/private key pair. Each microservice generates a JWT, signs it with its own private key, and passes it as an HTTP header (Authorization Bearer) along with the request to the recipient microservice over TLS. Because the JWT in this case is a bearer token, the use of TLS is highly recommended (or in other words, a must). The recipient microservice can identify the calling microservice after verifying the JWT signature by using the corresponding public key.

How does this process differ from mTLS? If what you're trying to achieve is only authentication between two microservices, neither method is superior. From the developer overhead point of view, setting up mTLS is more straightforward than using self-issued JWTs. Both techniques need to handle all the key management challenges discussed in chapter 6, along with service-to-service authentication. If you intend to share contextual data (not just the business data) between two microservices, the self-issued

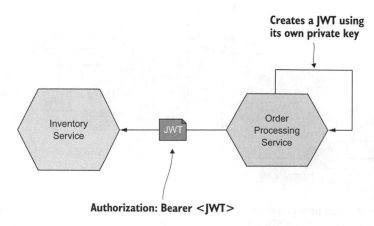

Figure 7.4   Self-issued JWT. The JWT is signed using the private key of the Order Processing microservice.

JWT is much better than mTLS. If the Order Processing microservice wants to share the order ID with the Inventory microservice as a correlation handle, for example, it can embed it in the JWT. In case of mTLS, you need to pass it as an HTTP header.

What's the difference? mTLS provides confidentiality and integrity of the data in transit, but not nonrepudiation. Nonrepudiation cryptographically binds an action to the person who initiated it so that they can't deny it later. With mTLS alone, you can't achieve nonrepudiation. But when you use a self-issued JWT, all the data added to it is bound to the owner of the corresponding private key that's used to sign the message, and helps you achieve nonrepudiation. Even if you use a self-issued JWT, in most cases the communication between the two microservices must happen over TLS (not mTLS), which protects the confidentiality and integrity of the communication. If you want to get rid of TLS, you can use a signed, encrypted JWT and still achieve those attributes. But you'll rarely want to get rid of TLS.

> **NOTE** A JWT is a bearer token. A bearer token is like cash. If someone steals $10 from you, they can use it at any Starbucks to buy a cup of coffee, and no one will ask for proof that they own the $10. Anyone who steals a bearer token can use it with no issue until the token expires. If you use JWT for authentication between microservices (or in other words, authenticate one microservice to another), you must secure the communication channel with TLS to minimize the risk of an intruder stealing the token. Also, make sure the JWT is short-lived. In that case, even if someone steals the token, the impact of the stolen token is minimal.

7.1.5 Nested JWTs

The use case in this section is an extension of the use case discussed in section 7.1.4. A *nested JWT* is a JWT that embeds another JWT (see figure 7.5). When you use a self-issued JWT to secure service-to-service communications between two microservices, for example, you can embed the JWT issued by the trusted STS that carries the end-user

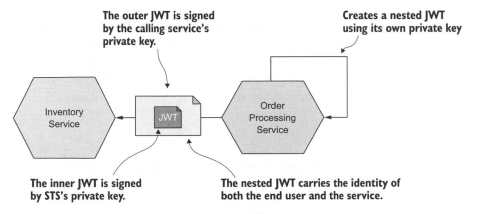

Figure 7.5 A nested JWT: the Order Processing microservice creates its own JWT and embeds in it the JWT it receives from the downstream microservice (or the API gateway).

context in the self-issued JWT itself and build a nested JWT. On the recipient side, the service has to validate the signature of the nested JWT with the public key corresponding to the calling microservice and validate the signature of the embedded JWT with the corresponding public key from the trusted STS. The nested JWT carries the identities of the end user and the calling microservice in a manner that can't be forged!

7.2   *Setting up an STS to issue a JWT*

In this section, we'll set up an STS to issue a JWT. We're going to use this JWT to access a secured microservice. The source code related to all the examples in this chapter is available in the https://github.com/microservices-security-in-action/samples Git-Hub repository, inside the chapter07 directory. The source code of the STS, which is a Spring Boot application developed with Java, is available in the chapter07/sample01 directory.

This STS is a simple STS and not production-ready. Many open source and proprietary identity management products can serve as an STS in a production microservices deployment.[1] Run the following Maven command from the chapter07/sample01 directory to build the STS. If everything goes well, you'll see the BUILD SUCCESS message at the end:

```
\> mvn clean install

[INFO] BUILD SUCCESS
```

To start the STS, run the following command from the same directory. The STS, by default, starts on HTTPS port 8443; make sure that no other services are running on the same port. When the server boots up, it prints the time it took to boot up on the terminal:

```
\> mvn spring-boot:run

INFO 30901 --- [main] s.b.c.e.t.TomcatEmbeddedServletContainer :
Tomcat started on port(s): 8443 (https)
INFO 30901 --- [main] c.m.m.ch07.sample01.TokenService         :
Started TokenService in 4.729 seconds (JVM running for 7.082)
```

Run the following curl command, which talks to the STS and gets a JWT. You should be familiar with the request, which is a standard OAuth 2.0 request following the password grant type. We use password grant type here only as an example, and for simplicity. In a production deployment, you may pick authorization code grant type or any other grant type that fits better for your use cases. (In appendix A, we discuss OAuth 2.0 grant types in detail.)

```
\> curl -v -X POST --basic -u applicationid:applicationsecret \
-H "Content-Type: application/x-www-form-urlencoded;charset=UTF-8" \
-k -d "grant_type=password&username=peter&password=peter123&scope=foo" \
https://localhost:8443/oauth/token
```

---

[1] Gluu, Keycloak, and WSO2 Identity Server are all open source, production-ready, identity management products that you can use as an STS.

You can think of this request as being generated by an external application, such as a web application, on behalf of an end user. In this example, the client ID and secret represent the web application, and the username and password represent the end user. Figure 7.6 illustrates this use case. For simplicity, we have removed the API gateway from figure 7.6.

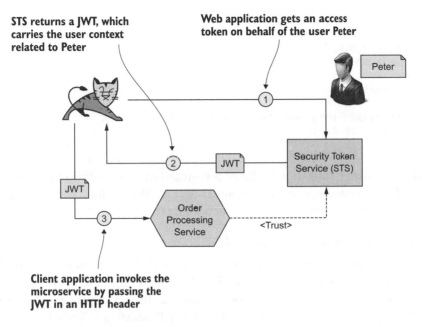

STS returns a JWT, which carries the user context related to Peter

Web application gets an access token on behalf of the user Peter

Client application invokes the microservice by passing the JWT in an HTTP header

Figure 7.6   STS issues a JWT access token to the web application.

In this command, `applicationid` is the client ID of the web application, and `applicationsecret` is the client secret. If everything works, the STS returns an OAuth 2.0 access token, which is a JWT (or a JWS, to be precise):

```
{"access_token":"eyJhbGciOiJSUzI1NiIsInR5cCI6IkpXVCJ9.eyJzdWIiOiJwZXRlciIsI
mF1ZCI6IiouZWNvbW0uY29tIiwidXNlcl9uYW1lIjoicGV0ZXIiLCJzY29wZSI6WyJmb28iXSwi
aXNzIjoic3RzLmVjb21tLmNvbSIsImV4cCI6MTUzMzI4MDAyNCwiaWF0IjoxNTMzMjc5OTY0LCJ
hdXRob3JpdGllcyI6WyJST0xFX1VTRVIiXSwianRpIjoiYjJjMzkxZjItMWI4MC00ZTgzLThlYjEt
NGE1ZmZmNDRlNjkyIiwiY2xpZW50X2lkIjoiMTAxMDEwMTAifQ.MBPq2ngesDB3eCjAQg_ZZd
sTd7_Vw4aRocS-ig-UHa92xe4LvEl7vADr7SUxPuWrCSre4VkMwN8uc7KAxJYWH2i0Hfb5haL3j
P7074POcRlKzoSoEB6ZJu7VhW5TVY4hsOJXWeldHqPccHTJNKbloUWBDyGYnnRyMG47wmQb2MMan
YURFCFKwFZdO3eEOz0BRV5BX-PsyESgK6qwOV5C6MErVe_Ga_dbVjUR5BGjgjMDlmCoDf4O3gX
K2ifzh_PYlGgx9eHKPZiq9Tll3yWSvribNgIs9donciJHh6WSxT_SFyg7gS-CD66PgOuA8YRJ5g
g3vW6kJVtqsgS8oMYjA",
"token_type":"bearer",
"refresh_token":"",
"expires_in":1533280024,
"scope":"foo"}
```

Following is the payload of the decoded JWT access token. If you are not familiar with JWT, please check appendix B:

```
{
  "sub": "peter",
  "aud": "*.ecomm.com",
  "user_name": "peter",
  "scope": [
    "foo"
  ],
  "iss": "sts.ecomm.com",
  "exp": 1533280024,
  "iat": 1533279964,
  "authorities": [
    "ROLE_USER"
  ],
  "jti": "b2c391f2-1b80-4e83-8eb1-4a5fff44e692",
  "client_id": "10101010"
}
```

You can find more details about the STS configuration and the source code in the README file available inside the chapter07/sample01 directory. In the next section, you see how to use this JWT to access a secured microservice.

7.3   *Securing microservices with JWT*

In this section, you first secure a microservice with JWT and then use a curl client to invoke it with a JWT obtained from the STS that you set up in the preceding section. You can find the complete source code related to this example in the chapter07/ sample02 directory. Here, we'll build the Order Processing microservice written in Java with Spring Boot and secure it with JWT. First, we'll build the project from the chapter07/sample02 directory with the following Maven command. If everything goes well, you should see the BUILD SUCCESS message at the end:

```
\> mvn clean install

[INFO] BUILD SUCCESS
```

To start the Order Processing microservice, run the following command from the same directory. When the server boots up, it prints the time that it took to boot up on the terminal. Per the default setting, the Order Processing microservice runs on HTTPS port 9443:

```
\> mvn spring-boot:run

INFO 32024 --- [main] s.b.c.e.t.TomcatEmbeddedServletContainer  :
Tomcat started on port(s): 9443 (https)
INFO 32024 --- [main] c.m.m.ch07.sample02.OrderProcessingApp    :
Started OrderProcessingApp in 6.555 seconds (JVM running for 9.62)
```

Now let's invoke the Order Processing microservice with the following `curl` command with no security token. As expected, you should see an error message:

```
\> curl -k  https://localhost:9443/orders/11

{"error":"unauthorized","error_description":
        "Full authentication is required to access this resource"}
```

To invoke the Order Processing microservice with proper security, you need to get a JWT from the STS using the following `curl` command. This example assumes that the security token service discussed in the preceding section still runs on HTTPS port 8443. For clarity, we removed the long JWT in the response and replaced it with the value `jwt_access_token`:

```
\> curl -v -X POST --basic -u applicationid:applicationsecret \
-H "Content-Type: application/x-www-form-urlencoded;charset=UTF-8" \
-k -d "grant_type=password&username=peter&password=peter123&scope=foo" \
https://localhost:8443/oauth/token

{
"access_token":"jwt_access_token",
"token_type":"bearer",
"refresh_token":"",
"expires_in":1533280024,
"scope":"foo"
}
```

Now let's invoke the Order Processing microservice with the JWT we got from the `curl` command. Set the same JWT in the HTTP Authorization Bearer header using the following `curl` command and invoke the Order Processing microservice. Because the JWT is a little lengthy, you can use a small trick when using the `curl` command. First, export the JWT to an environmental variable (`TOKEN`), and then use that environmental variable in your request to the Order Processing microservice:

```
\> export TOKEN=jwt_access_token

\> curl -k -H "Authorization: Bearer $TOKEN" \
https://localhost:9443/orders/11

{
   "customer_id":"101021",
   "order_id":"11",
   "payment_method":{
      "card_type":"VISA",
      "expiration":"01/22",
      "name":"John Doe",
      "billing_address":"201, 1st Street, San Jose,CA"
   },
   "items":[{"code":"101","qty":1},{"code":"103","qty":5}],
   "shipping_address":"201, 1st Street, San Jose, CA"
}
```

You can find more details about the Order Processing microservice configuration and the source code in the README file available in the chapter07/sample02 directory.

7.4   *Using JWT as a data source for access control*

The example in this section is an extension of the example in section 7.3. Here, we use the same codebase to enforce access control at the Order Processing microservice's end by using the data that comes with the JWT itself. If you're already running the Order Processing microservice, first take it down (but keep the STS running). Open the OrderProcessingService.java file in the directory sample02/src/main/java/com/manning/mss/ch07/sample02/service/ and uncomment the method-level annotation @PreAuthorize("#oauth2.hasScope('bar')") from the getOrder method so that the code looks like the following:

```
@PreAuthorize("#oauth2.hasScope('bar')")
@RequestMapping(value = "/{id}", method = RequestMethod.GET)
public ResponseEntity<?> getOrder(@PathVariable("id") String orderId) {

}
```

Rebuild and spin up the Order Processing microservice from the chapter07/sample02 directory by using the following two Maven commands:

```
\> mvn clean install
\> mvn spring-boot:run
```

After the Order Processing microservice boots up, you need to get a JWT again from the STS and use it to access the Order Processing microservice. One important thing to notice is that when the client application talks to the STS, it's asking for an access token for the scope foo. You'll find the value foo in both the curl request and in the response. Also, if you decode the JWT in the response from the STS, that too includes an attribute called scope with the value foo:

```
\> curl -v -X POST --basic -u applicationid:applicationsecret \
-H "Content-Type: application/x-www-form-urlencoded;charset=UTF-8" \
-k -d "grant_type=password&username=peter&password=peter123&scope=foo" \
https://localhost:8443/oauth/token

{
"access_token":"jwt_access_token",
"token_type":"bearer",
"refresh_token":"",
"expires_in":1533280024,
"scope":"foo"
}
```

Now you have a JWT with the foo scope from the STS. Try to invoke the Order Processing microservice, which asks for a token with the bar scope. Ideally, the request should fail with an access-denied message:

```
\> export TOKEN=jwt_access_token
\> curl -k -H "Authorization: Bearer $TOKEN" \
```

```
https://localhost:9443/orders/11
```

```
{"error":"access_denied","error_description":"Access is denied"}
```

It failed as expected. Try the same thing with a valid scope. First, request a JWT with the bar scope from the STS:

```
\> curl -v -X POST --basic -u applicationid:applicationsecret \
-H "Content-Type: application/x-www-form-urlencoded;charset=UTF-8" \
-k -d "grant_type=password&username=peter&password=peter123&scope=bar" \
https://localhost:8443/oauth/token

{
"access_token":"jwt_access_token",
"token_type":"bearer",
"refresh_token":"",
"expires_in":1533280024,
"scope":"bar"
}
```

Now invoke the Order Processing microservice with the right token, and we should get a positive response:

```
\> curl -k -H "Authorization: Bearer $TOKEN" \
https://localhost:9443/orders/11

{
   "customer_id":"101021",
   "order_id":"11",
   "payment_method":{
      "card_type":"VISA",
      "expiration":"01/22",
      "name":"John Doe",
      "billing_address":"201, 1st Street, San Jose,CA"
   },
   "items":[{"code":"101","qty":1},{"code":"103","qty":5}],
   "shipping_address":"201, 1st Street, San Jose, CA"
}
```

In this particular example, when the curl client asks for a token with foo or bar scopes from the STS, STS didn't do any access-control checks to see whether the user (peter) in the request is authorized to get a token under the requested scope. Ideally, in a production deployment, when you use a production-ready STS, you should be able to enforce access-control policies at the STS to carry out such validations.

7.5   *Securing service-to-service communications with JWT*

Now you have the STS and the Order Processing microservice secured with JWT. In this section, we introduce the Inventory microservice, which is also secured with JWT. We'll show you how to pass the same JWT that the Order Processing microservice got from the client application to the Inventory microservice. You'll keep both the Order Processing microservice and the STS running and introduce the new Inventory microservice. First, build the project from the chapter07/sample03 directory with the following Maven command. If everything goes well, you should see the BUILD SUCCESS message at the end:

```
\> mvn clean install

[INFO] BUILD SUCCESS
```

To start the Inventory microservice, run the following command from the same directory. After the server boots up, it prints the time that it took to boot up on the terminal. Per the default setting, the Inventory microservice runs on HTTPS port 10443:

```
\> mvn spring-boot:run

INFO 32024 --- [main] s.b.c.e.t.TomcatEmbeddedServletContainer :
Tomcat started on port(s): 10443 (https)
INFO 32024 --- [main] c.m.m.ch07.sample03.InventoryApp         :
Started InventoryApp in 6.555 seconds (JVM running for 6.79)
```

Now we want to get a JWT from the STS by using the following curl command, which is the same one you used in the preceding section. For clarity, we removed the long JWT in the response and replaced it with the value jwt_access_token:

```
\> curl -v -X POST --basic -u applicationid:applicationsecret \
-H "Content-Type: application/x-www-form-urlencoded;charset=UTF-8" \
-k -d "grant_type=password&username=peter&password=peter123&scope=bar" \
https://localhost:8443/oauth/token

{
"access_token":"jwt_access_token",
"token_type":"bearer",
"refresh_token":"",
"expires_in":1533280024,
"scope":"foo"
}
```

Now let's post an order to the Order Processing microservice with the JWT you got from the preceding curl command. First, export the JWT to an environmental variable (TOKEN) and then use that environmental variable in your request to the Order Processing microservice. If everything goes well, the Order Processing microservice validates the JWT, accepts it, and then talks to the Inventory microservice to update the inventory. You'll find the item numbers printed on the terminal that runs the Inventory microservice:

```
\> export TOKEN=jwt_access_token
\> curl -k -H "Authorization: Bearer $TOKEN" \
-H 'Content-Type: application/json' \
-v https://localhost:9443/orders \
-d @- << EOF
{   "customer_id":"101021",
    "payment_method":{
        "card_type":"VISA",
```

```
      "expiration":"01/22",
      "name":"John Doe",
      "billing_address":"201, 1st Street, San Jose, CA"
   },
   "items":[{"code":"101","qty":1},{"code":"103","qty":5}],
   "shipping_address":"201, 1st Street, San Jose, CA"
}
EOF
```

You can find more details about the Inventory microservice configuration and the source code in the README file available inside the chapter07/sample05 directory.

7.6 *Exchanging a JWT for a new one with a new audience*

Token exchange is a responsibility of the STS. In this section, you'll see how to exchange a JWT to a new one by talking to the STS we spun up in section 7.2. Make sure that STS is up and running. Figure 7.7 illustrates the complete flow of what we're trying to do here. In step 1, the client application gets a JWT access token on behalf of the user.

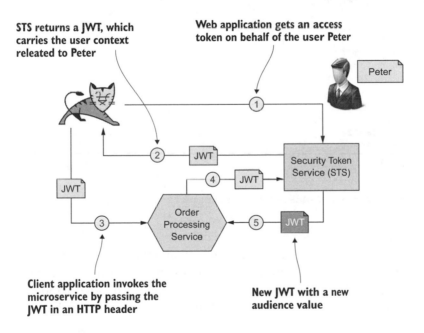

Figure 7.7 Token exchange with STS

Now run the following curl command, which talks to the STS and gets a JWT:

```
\> curl -v -k -X POST --basic -u applicationid:applicationsecret \
-H "Content-Type: application/x-www-form-urlencoded;charset=UTF-8" \
-d "grant_type=password&username=peter&password=peter123&scope=bar" \
https://localhost:8443/oauth/token
```

In this command, `applicationid` is the client ID of the web application, and `applicationsecret` is the client secret. If everything works, the STS returns an OAuth 2.0 access token that's a JWT (or a JWS, to be precise):

```
{"access_token":"eyJhbGciOiJSUzI1NiIsInR5cCI6IkpXVCJ9.eyJzdWIiOiJwZXRlciIsI
mF1ZCI6IiouZWNvbW0uY29tIiwidXNlcl9uYW1lIjoicGV0ZXIiLCJzY29wZSI6WyJmb28iXSwi
aXNzIjoic3RzLmVjb21tLmNvbSIsImV4cCI6MTUzMzI4MDAyNCwiaWF0IjoxNTMzMjc5OTY0LCJ
hdXRob3JpdGllcyI6WyJST0xFX1VTRVIiXSwianRpIjoiYjJjMzkxZjItMWI4MC00ZTgzLThlYjEt
NGE1ZmZmNDRlNjkyIiwiY2xpZW50X2lkIjoiMTAxMDEwMTAifQ.MBPq2ngesDB3eCjAQg_ZZd
sTd7_Vw4aRocS-ig-UHa92xe4LvEl7vADr7SUxPuWrCSre4VkMwN8uc7KAxJYWH2i0Hfb5haL3j
P7074POcRlKzoSoEB6ZJu7VhW5TVY4hsOJXWeldHqPccHTJNKbloUWBDyGYnnRyMG47wmQb2MManY
URFCFKwFZdO3eEOz0BRV5BX-PsyESgK6qwOV5C6MErVe_Ga_dbVjUR5BGjgjMDlmCoDf4O3gX
K2ifzh_PYlGgx9eHKPZiq9Tll3yWSvribNgIs9donciJHh6WSxT_SFyg7gS-CD66PgOuA8YRJ5g
g3vW6kJVtqsgS8oMYjA",
"token_type":"bearer",
"refresh_token":"",
"expires_in":1533280024,
"scope":"foo"}
```

The following is the payload of the decoded JWT access token that carries the audience value `*.ecomm.com`:

```
{
  "sub": "peter",
  "aud": "*.ecomm.com",
  "user_name": "peter",
  "scope": [
    "foo"
  ],
  "iss": "sts.ecomm.com",
  "exp": 1533280024,
  "iat": 1533279964,
  "authorities": [
    "ROLE_USER"
  ],
  "jti": "b2c391f2-1b80-4e83-8eb1-4a5fff44e692",
  "client_id": "10101010"
}
```

Now you're done with steps 1 and 2 (figure 7.7), and the client application has a JWT access token. In step 3, the client application talks to the Order Processing microservice with this JWT. We're going to skip that step and show you what happens in steps 4 and 5—the two most important steps, which show you how token exchange happens.

> **NOTE** The STS we use in this chapter has not implemented the token exchange functionality (RFC 8693). So, you won't be able to see how the token exchange works with that STS, as explained in the rest of the section. Most of the production-ready STS implementations support RFC 8693, and you can use one of them in your real production deployment. Since the token exchange is a standard API exposed by an STS following RFC 8693, the curl commands we explain in the rest of the section will still work with any STS that supports RFC 8693.

Suppose that the Order Processing microservice makes the following call with the JWT it got in step 3. An STS that supports the token-exchange functionality in a standard way must implement the OAuth 2.0 Token Exchange specification (https:// tools.ietf.org/html/rfc8693). Run the following `curl` command, which exchanges the JWT we have to a new one by talking to the STS. First, export the JWT you already got from the STS (step 3 in figure 7.7) to an environmental variable (TOKEN) and then use that environmental variable in your token exchange request:

```
\> export TOKEN=jwt_access_token
\> curl -v -X POST https://localhost:8443/oauth/token \
--basic -u applicationid:applicationsecret \
-H "Content-Type: application/x-www-form-urlencoded;charset=UTF-8" -k \
-d @- << EOF
grant_type=urn:ietf:params:oauth:grant-type:token-exchange&
subject_token=$TOKEN&
subject_token_type=urn:ietf:params:oauth:token-type:jwt&
audience=inventory.ecomm.com
EOF
```

In the request to the token endpoint of the STS, we need to send the original JWT in the `subject_token` argument, and the value of the `subject_token_type` argument must be set to `urn:ietf:params:oauth:token-type:jwt`. For clarity, in the preceding `curl` command, we used the TOKEN environmental variable to represent the original JWT. Another important argument we use here is `grant_type` with the value `urn:ietf:params:oauth:grant-type:token-exchange`.

The STS validates the provided JWT, and if everything looks good, it returns a new JWT with the requested audience value as in the following. Now the Order Processing microservice can use this JWT to talk to the Inventory microservice:

```
{
  "access_token":"new_jwt_access_token",
  "issued_token_type":"urn:ietf:params:oauth:token-type:jwt",
  "token_type":"Bearer",
  "expires_in":60
}
```

If you run the preceding curl command against the STS that comes with this chapter, it will fail and will result in the following error, because that STS does not support the token exchange functionality:

```
{
  "error":"unsupported_grant_type",
  "error_description":
    "Unsupported grant type: urn:ietf:params:oauth:grant-type:token-exchange"
}
```

NOTE In chapter 12, we discuss how to use JWT to secure service-to-service communications in a service mesh deployment with Istio. *Istio* is a service mesh developed by Google that runs on Kubernetes. A *service mesh* is a decentralized application-networking infrastructure between microservices in a particular deployment that provides resiliency, security, observability, and routing control.

Summary

- A JWT, which provides a way to carry a set of claims or attributes from one party to another in a cryptographically secure way, plays a key role in securing service-to-service communications in a microservices deployment.

- You can use a JWT to carry the identity of the calling microservice, or the identity of the end user or system that initiated the request.

- JWT addresses two main concerns in a microservices security design: securing service-to-service communications and passing end-user context across microservices.

- When the identity of the microservice isn't relevant, but the identity of the end user (system or human) is, you should prefer using JWT over mTLS. But still, in practice you will use JWT with mTLS together to build a second layer of defense.

- Having a different or new JWT for each interaction among microservices is a more secure approach than sharing the same JWT among all the microservices.

- JWT can be used for cross-domain authentication and attribute sharing.

- A self-issued JWT is issued by a microservice itself and used for authentication among microservices.

- A nested JWT is a JWT that embeds another JWT. It carries the identity of both the calling microservice and the end user.

Securing east/west
traffic over gRPC

8

This chapter covers

- The role of gRPC in interservice communications
  in a microservices deployment
- Securing interservice communications that
  happen over gRPC using mTLS
- Securing interservice communications that
  happen over gRPC using JWTs

In chapters 6 and 7, we discussed how to secure communications among microservices with mTLS and JWT. All the examples in those chapters assumed that the communication between the calling microservice and the recipient microservice happens over HTTP in a RESTful manner with JSON messages. JSON over HTTP is a common way of communicating among microservices. But another school of thought believes that is not the optimal way.

The argument is that human-readable, well-structured data interchange format is of no value when the communication happens between two systems (or microservices). This is true, since you need human-readable message formats only for troubleshooting purposes and not when your systems are running live. Instead of a text-based protocol like JSON, you can use a binary protocol like Protocol Buffers (Protobuf). It provides a way of encoding structured data in an efficient manner when communications happen among microservices.

gRPC (https://grpc.io/) is an open source remote procedure call framework (or a library), originally developed by Google. It's the next generation of a system called Stubby, which Google has been being using internally for over a decade. gRPC achieves efficiency for communication between systems using HTTP/2 as the transport and Protocol Buffers as the interface definition language (IDL). In this chapter, we discuss how to secure communications between two microservices that happen over gRPC. If you are new to gRPC, we recommend you first go through appendix I, which covers gRPC fundamentals.

8.1 Service-to-service communications over gRPC

In this section, we discuss the basics of establishing a communication channel between two parties over gRPC. We teach you how to run a simple gRPC client and a server in Java. You can find the source code for this example in the chapter08/sample01 directory of the https://github.com/microservices-security-in-action/samples GitHub repository.

Our use case is something that simulates a service-to-service communication. The popular scenario used throughout this book is an example of a retail store. We discuss various use cases of this retail store in different chapters. In this section's use case, a customer makes an order by using our system. When a customer places an order, the system needs to update its inventory to make sure the relevant product items that were ordered are removed from the database.

Our system is built in such a way that all major functions are separated into individual microservices. We have microservices for getting product information, processing orders, updating inventory, shipping orders, and so on. In this particular use case, you can assume that the Order Processing microservice is exposed to our clients via an API gateway. When a client application makes a call to place an order, the Order Processing microservice takes on the responsibility of making sure the order is properly placed. Within this process, it performs a set of coordinated actions, such as processing the payment, updating inventory, initiating the shipping process, and so on.

The Inventory microservice is implemented as a gRPC service. Therefore, when the Order Processing microservice needs to update the inventory while processing an order, it needs to make a gRPC request to the Inventory microservice. Figure 8.1 illustrates this use case.

As you can see, the communication between the Order Processing microservice and Inventory microservice happens over gRPC. We will be focusing on the communication between only these two microservices in this section of the chapter.

Let's first look at the interface definition of the Inventory microservice, which uses Protocol Buffers as its IDL. You can find the IDL of the Inventory microservice at

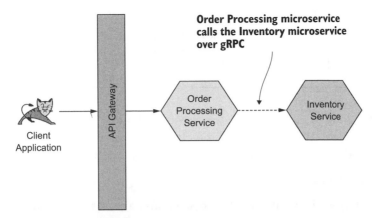

Figure 8.1 The client application places an order through an API exposed on the API gateway. The client's request is then delegated to the Order Processing microservice. The Order Processing microservice calls the Inventory microservice after the order is placed. The communication between the Order Processing microservice and the Inventory microservice happens over gRPC.

chapter08/sample01/src/main/proto/inventory.proto. Here's the service definition of the Inventory microservice:

```
service Inventory {
    rpc UpdateInventory (Order) returns (UpdateReply) {}
}
```

This defines the Inventory microservice as having a single RPC method named `UpdateInventory`. It accepts a message of type `Order` and returns a message of type `UpdateReply`. The `Order` and `UpdateReply` message types are defined further in the following listing.

Listing 8.1 The Protobuf definition of the `Order` and `UpdateReply` messages

```
message Order {
    int32 orderId = 1;            ◁── An Order has an ID and consists
    repeated LineItem items = 2;       of a collection of LineItem objects.
}

message LineItem {               ◁── Each LineItem has a
    Product product = 1;              quantity and a product.
    int32 quantity = 2;
}

message Product {
    int32 id = 1;
    string name = 2;
```

```
        string category = 3;
        float unitPrice = 4;
}

message UpdateReply {
        string message = 1;
}
```

The message sent as a response to the inventory update. The UpdateReply message has a variable of type string.

Let's compile the code to autogenerate the service stub and client stub of the Inventory microservice. To do that, navigate to the chapter08/sample01 directory by using your command-line client and execute the following command:

```
\> ./gradlew installDist
```

If the stubs are successfully built, you should see a message saying BUILD SUCCESS-FUL. You should also see a new directory being created with the name *build*. This directory has the autogenerated stub classes from the sample01/src/main/proto/inventory.proto file.

Open the InventoryGrpc.java file in the build/generated/source/proto/main/grpc/com/manning/mss/ch08/sample01 directory by using a text editor or IDE. Within this file, you'll find an inner class named InventoryImplBase with the following class definition:

```
public static abstract class InventoryImplBase implements
io.grpc.BindableService {
```

This is our Inventory microservice's server stub. To provide the actual implementation of the UpdateInventory RPC, we need to extend this class and override the updateInventory method. Let's take a quick look at how to run the inventory server (which is the Inventory microservice) and inventory client now. To run the server, navigate back to the chapter08/sample01 directory from your command-line client and execute the following command:

```
\> ./build/install/sample01/bin/inventory-server
```

It should output a message saying the server has started on port 50051. Once the server is started, we can execute our client program. To do that, open a new terminal window, navigate to the chapter08/sample01 directory, and execute the following command:

```
\> ./build/install/sample01/bin/inventory-client
```

If the client runs successfully, you should see a message on your terminal saying INFO: Message: Updated inventory for 1 products. What happened here is that the inventory client program executed the UpdateInventory RPC running on a different port/process (not a different host, because we've been using the same machine for both client and server). The server process received the message from the client and executed its UpdateReply method to send back the reply.

Now that we've seen how a typical client server interaction happens, let's take a look at the server and client source code. To understand the client code, open up the chapter08/sample01/src/main/java/com/manning/mss/ch08/sample01/Inventory Client.java file by using a text editor or IDE. The client class in this case is instantiated using its constructor in the manner shown in the following listing.

Listing 8.2   Instantiating the gRPC client

```
public InventoryClient(String host, int port) {  ◀──┐

    this(ManagedChannelBuilder.forAddress(host, port)  ◀──┐
      .usePlaintext()
      .build());
}

private InventoryClient(ManagedChannel channel) {  ◀──────
    this.channel = channel;
    inventoryBlockingStub = InventoryGrpc.newBlockingStub(channel);
}
```

Construct the client connecting to the InventoryServer with the provided hostname and the port.

Channels are secure by default (via TLS). We disable TLS to avoid needing certificates.

Instantiate the InventoryClient for accessing the InventoryServer.

What happens in listing 8.2 is that when the client is instantiated, a Channel is created between the client and server. A gRPC Channel provides a connection to a gRPC server on a specified host and port. In this particular example, we are disabling TLS to keep things simple. You may notice that we explicitly set usePlaintext to indicate that we are not doing TLS or mTLS on this Channel. We look at TLS specifics later in this chapter. The created Channel is then used to instantiate a stub, named InventoryBlockingStub. This stub will be used to communicate with the server when RPCs are being executed. The reason this is called a *blocking stub* is because, in this particular case, we're using a stub that blocks the running thread until the client receives a response or raises an error. The other alternative is to use the Inventory-FutureStub, which is a stub that does not block the running thread and expects the server to respond later.

The communication between the client and server happens in the update-Inventory method in the InventoryClient class. This method receives an object of type OrderEntity, which contains the details of the confirmed order. It converts the OrderEntity object into its respective RPC object and passes the RPC object to the server:

```
public void updateInventory(OrderEntity order) {
UpdateReply updateResponse;
try {
updateResponse =
inventoryBlockingStub.updateInventory(orderBuilder.build());
} catch (StatusRuntimeException e) {
    logger.log(Level.WARNING, "RPC failed: {0}", e.getStatus());
    return;
  }
}
```

The inventoryBlockingStub.updateInventory(. .) statement transports the Order object to the server and gets the response from the server. The server code of the Inventory microservice is relatively simpler. To see what the server code looks like, open the sample01/src/main/java/com/manning/mss/ch08/sample01/ InventoryServer.java file by using a text editor or IDE. The start method of the InventoryServer.java file contains the code that starts the server, as shown in the following listing.

Listing 8.3   Starting the gRPC server

```java
private void start() throws IOException {
int port = 50051;
server = ServerBuilder.forPort(port)
        .addService(new InventoryImpl())          // Adds gRPC services to be
        .build()                                   // hosted on this server process
        .start();

Runtime.getRuntime().addShutdownHook(new Thread() {
        @Override
        public void run() {
            InventoryServer.this.stop();
            System.err.println("Server shut down");  // Shutting down gRPC server
        }                                            // since JVM is shutting down
});
}
```

This code starts the server on port 50051. It then adds gRPC services to be hosted on this server process. In this particular example, we add only the Inventory microservice by using the Java class InventoryImpl. This is an inner class declared within the InventoryServer class, as shown in the following listing. It extends the autogenerated InventoryImplBase class and overrides the updateInventory method.

Listing 8.4   The implementation of the Inventory microservice

```java
static class InventoryImpl extends InventoryGrpc.InventoryImplBase {

@Override
public void updateInventory(Order req,
            StreamObserver<UpdateReply> responseObserver) {

  UpdateReply updateReply = UpdateReply.newBuilder()
            .setMessage("Updated   inventory for " + req.getItemsCount()
            + " products").build();
  responseObserver.onNext(updateReply);                // Updates the inventory
  responseObserver.onCompleted();                      // upon receiving a message
}
}
```

When the InventoryClient class executes its updateInventory method, the client stub is transported over the network through the Channel that was created between the client and server and executes the updateInventory method on the server. In this example, the updateInventory method on the server simply replies to the client, saying the inventory was updated with the number of items received on the order request. In a typical scenario, this would probably update a database and remove the items that were ordered from the stock.

8.2 Securing gRPC service-to-service communications with mTLS

In this section, we look at securing a channel between two parties that communicate over gRPC, using mTLS. In section 8.1, we discussed a simple communication channel between a client and server over gRPC. We discussed a retail-store use case where the Order Processing microservice communicates with the Inventory microservice to update the inventory. In a traditional monolithic application architecture pattern, processing orders and updating the inventory would have been done via two functions within the same process/service. The scope of the updateInventory function would be designed in such a way that it is directly (within the same process) accessible only from the orders function.

As you can see in figure 8.2, the only entry point into the monolith application is through the /orders endpoint, which is exposed via the API gateway. The update-Inventory function is directly inaccessible by anyone else.

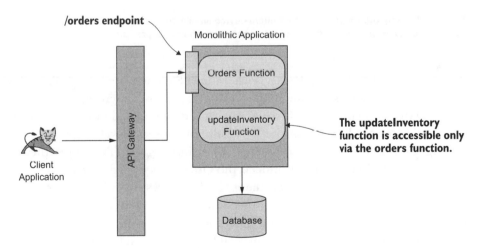

Figure 8.2 In a monolithic application, functions that are not exposed over a network do not have direct access unless within the application itself.

In microservices architecture, the Inventory microservice is deployed independently. Therefore, anyone with direct access to the microservice at the network level can invoke its functions. From our use case point of view, we need to prevent this. We need to ensure that the inventory is updated only upon processing an order. We therefore need to ensure that only the Order Processing microservice can execute the functions on the Inventory microservice, even if others have direct access to it. Figure 8.3 illustrates this scenario.

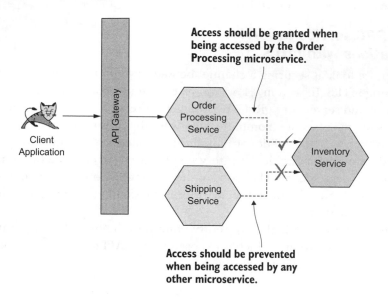

Figure 8.3   Only the Order Processing microservice should be able to access the Inventory microservice. All other accesses should be prevented.

As we discussed in chapter 6, this is where mTLS comes into play. mTLS allows us to build an explicit trust between the Order Processing microservice and Inventory microservice by using certificates. Whenever a communication happens between the two parties over mTLS, the Order Processing microservice validates that it is actually talking to the Inventory microservice by using regular TLS. And the Inventory microservice validates that it is indeed the Order Processing microservice that calls it by validating the certificate of the client (Order Processing microservice).

Let's run the same example as in section 8.1, but with mTLS enabled between the Order Processing microservice and Inventory microservice. You can find the samples for this section in the chapter08/sample02 directory. In addition to the prerequisites defined in section 2.1.1, you also need to install OpenSSL on your computer.

> **NOTE**   If you do not want the pain of installing OpenSSL, you can run OpenSSL as a Docker container, in the way we discussed in section 6.2.4.

You can check whether you already have OpenSSL installed by executing the following command on your command-line tool:

```
\> openssl version
```

The output of this command indicates the version of OpenSSL on your computer if you have it installed. Check out the samples from the GitHub repository to your computer and use your command-line client to navigate to the chapter08/sample02 directory. Execute the following command to compile the source code and build the binaries for the client and server:

```
\> ./gradlew installDist
```

If the source is successfully built, you should see a message saying BUILD SUCCESSFUL. You should also see a directory named *build* being created inside the sample02 directory.

As the next step, we need to create the certificates and keys required for the inventory client and inventory server (which is the Inventory microservice). In chapter 6, we discussed in detail the fundamentals of mTLS, including the steps required to create keys and certificates. We therefore will not repeat the same steps here. The mkcerts.sh script (in the sample02 directory) will create the required certificates for us in one go.

Note that you need to have OpenSSL installed on your computer for the script to work. Execute the script from sample02 directory by using this command:

```
\> ./mkcerts.sh
```

The preceding command creates the required certificates in the /tmp/sslcert directory. Once the certificates are successfully created, we can start the inventory server, which hosts the Inventory microservice by using the following command:

```
\> ./build/install/sample02/bin/inventory-server localhost 50440 \
/tmp/sslcert/server.crt /tmp/sslcert/server.pem /tmp/sslcert/ca.crt
```

If the server starts successfully, you should see the following message:

```
INFO: Server started, listening on 50440
```

As you can observe from the command we just executed, we pass in five parameters to the process. Their values, along with their usages, are listed here:

- localhost—The host address to which the server process binds to
- 50440—The port on which the server starts
- /tmp/sslcert/server.crt—The certificate chain file of the server, which includes the server's public certificate
- /tmp/sslcert/server.pem—The private key file of the server
- /tmp/sslcert/ca.crt—The trust store collection file, which contains the certificates to be trusted by the server

NOTE If you need to know the importance of the certificate files and private key file listed here, see chapter 6, which explains their importance in detail.

To start the client process, open a new terminal window and navigate to the chapter08/sample02 directory and then execute this command:

```
\> ./build/install/sample02/bin/inventory-client localhost 50440 \
/tmp/sslcert/ca.crt /tmp/sslcert/client.crt /tmp/sslcert/client.pem
```

Similar to the way we executed the server process, we need to pass in similar parameters to the client process as well. The parameters are as follows:

- `localhost`—The host address of the server
- `50440`—The port of the server
- `/tmp/sslcert/client.crt`—The certificate chain file of the client, which includes the client's public certificate
- `/tmp/sslcert/client.pem`—The private key file of the client
- `/tmp/sslcert/ca.crt`—The trust store collection file, which contains the certificates to be trusted by the client

If the client executes successfully, you should see a message on your terminal:

```
INFO: Message: Updated inventory for 1 products
```

Let's look at the source code to understand how we enabled mTLS on our server and client processes. To look at the server code, open the sample02/src/main/java/com/manning/mss/ch08/sample02/InventoryServer.java file by using a text editor or IDE. Let's first take a look at the start method, which starts the server process.

Listing 8.5   Starting the server to listen on the provided port over TLS

The InventoryImpl constructor builds and adds the Inventory microservice to the server process by using the addService function.

```
private void start() throws IOException {
server = NettyServerBuilder.forAddress(new InetSocketAddress(host, port))
        .addService(new InventoryImpl())
        .sslContext(getSslContextBuilder().build())
        .build()
        .start();

Runtime.getRuntime().addShutdownHook(new Thread() {
    @Override
    public void run() {
        System.err.println("Shutting down gRPC server since JVM is shutting down");
        InventoryServer.this.stop();
        System.err.println("*** server shut down");
    }
});
}
```

This sslContext that is passed in contains information such as the server certificate file, private key file, and trust store file.

As you can see, we start the inventory server process by binding it to the host, which is the first argument we passed to the server-starting command. The process is started on the passed-in port. The following listing shows the `getSslContextBuilder` method.

Listing 8.6   Building the server SSL context

```
private SslContextBuilder getSslContextBuilder() {
    SslContextBuilder sslClientContextBuilder =
                SslContextBuilder.forServer(new File(certChainFilePath),
                                    new File(privateKeyFilePath));
```

```
    if (trustCertCollectionFilePath != null) {
      sslClientContextBuilder.trustManager(
                        new File(trustCertCollectionFilePath));
      sslClientContextBuilder.clientAuth(ClientAuth.REQUIRE);
    }
    return GrpcSslContexts.configure(sslClientContextBuilder,
                            SslProvider.OPENSSL);
}
```

This sets some context variables, which define the behavior of the server process. By setting `sslClientContextBuilder.clientAuth(ClientAuth.REQUIRE)`, we are mandating that the client application present its certificate to the server for verification (mandating mTLS). Let's now look at the client code and see the changes we had to make in order for it to work over mTLS. First let's recall a part of the client code from listing 8.1; here's how we implemented the constructor of the client class:

```
public InventoryClient(String host, int port) {
    this(ManagedChannelBuilder.forAddress(host, port)
            .usePlaintext()
            .build());
}
```

You may notice that we explicitly set `usePlaintext` to indicate that we are not doing TLS or mTLS on this channel. The same constructor has been enhanced as follows to enable TLS/mTLS:

```
public InventoryClient(String host, int port, SslContext sslContext)
throws SSLException {
    this(NettyChannelBuilder.forAddress(host, port)
            .negotiationType(NegotiationType.TLS)
            .sslContext(sslContext)
            .build());
}
```

We now have `sslContext` being set instead of using `usePlaintext`. The `ssl-Context` bears information about the trust store file, client certificate chain file, and the private key of the client. The following listing shows how the client `sslContext` is built.

> **Listing 8.7 Building client SSL context**

If a collection of trusted certificates is provided, build the TrustManager. This is required for any TLS connection.

```
private static SslContext buildSslContext(String trustCertCollectionFilePath,
String clientCertChainFilePath, String clientPrivateKeyFilePath)
throws SSLException {
    SslContextBuilder builder = GrpcSslContexts.forClient();
    if (trustCertCollectionFilePath != null) {
        builder.trustManager(new File(trustCertCollectionFilePath));    ⟵
    }
    if (clientCertChainFilePath != null
```

```
          && clientPrivateKeyFilePath != null) {
          builder.keyManager(new File(clientCertChainFilePath),
                             new File(clientPrivateKeyFilePath));
      }
    return builder.build();
}
```

If the client's public/private keys are provided, build the KeyManager. This is required for mTLS.

The client is built in a way that you could run it with mTLS, with TLS, or without anything at all. If you do not pass values to `trustCertCollectionFilePath`, `clientCertChainFilePath`, and `clientPrivateKeyFilePath` in listing 8.7, the client supports neither TLS nor mTLS. If you do not pass values to `clientCertChainFilePath` and `clientPrivateKeyFilePath`, but to `trustCertCollectionFilePath`, then the client supports only TLS. If you pass values to all three parameters, the client supports mTLS. When you tried out the client previously in this section, you passed values to all three parameters, and that's why it could successfully connect to the Inventory microservice, which has mTLS enabled.

Let's try to run the client with just TLS (not mTLS) and see how our server responds. Assuming your server process is still running, rerun the client process as follows (with fewer arguments):

```
\> ./build/install/sample02/bin/inventory-client localhost 50440 \
/tmp/sslcert/ca.crt
```

Here, we are providing only the trust store collection to the client, which makes the client work in TLS mode only. After executing this command, you should notice an error indicting the connection was refused. This is because on the server side we have mandated mTLS, as we discussed in this section. In this mode, the server expects the client to present its certificate information, and we have executed the client process without specifying its own certificate and private key information.

8.3   Securing gRPC service-to-service communications with JWT

In this section, we discuss in detail how to secure a communication channel between two parties over gRPC using JWTs. In chapter 7, we discussed securing service-to-service communications using JWTs. The same fundamentals apply throughout this section as well. We'll use the knowledge we gained in chapter 7 to understand how the same concepts apply in the context of a gRPC communication channel.

Also in chapter 7, we discussed the use cases for securing microservices with JWT, the benefits of JWT over mTLS, and how both JWT and mTLS complement each other. In this section, we use a practical scenario to demonstrate how you can use JWTs effectively over gRPC.

As shown in figure 8.4, we have the Order Processing microservice, which exchanges the JWT it receives from the client application for another (second) JWT

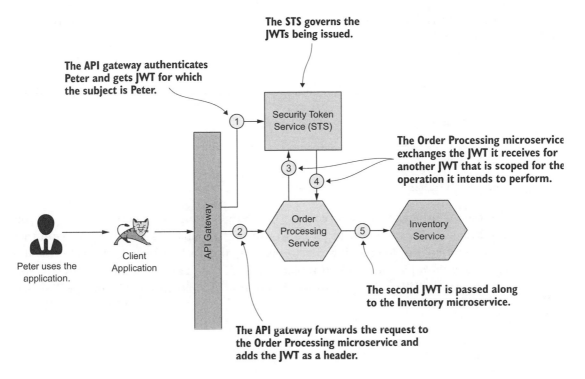

Figure 8.4 The JWT received by the Order Processing microservice is exchanged for a secondary JWT, which is scoped to access the relevant operations on the Inventory microservice.

with the help of an STS. This new JWT will then be passed along to the Inventory microservice.

When the Order Processing microservice performs the JWT exchange in step 3, the STS has complete control over the JWT being issued. The STS can therefore decide who the audience of the JWT should be, what other information to include/exclude in the JWT, the scopes of the JWT, and so on. By specifying the scopes associated to the JWT, the STS determines which operations this JWT is allowed to perform on the respective audience.

You can find the source code related to the sample we discuss in this section inside the chapter08/sample03 directory. This sample implements steps 3, 4, and 5 in figure 8.4. In the sample03 directory, you'll find two subdirectories: one named sts and the other named client_server. Let's start by compiling and running the STS for us to get a JWT.

Open a command-line client tool, navigate to the sample03/sts directory, and execute the following command to compile the source code of the STS:

```
\> mvn clean install
```

If the build is successful, you'll see a BUILD SUCCESS message. Run the following command to spin up the STS:

```
\> mvn spring-boot:run
```

If the STS starts properly, you should see a message similar to Started Token-Service in 3.875 seconds. After the STS is started, open a new terminal tab and use the following command to generate a JWT:

```
\> curl -v -X POST --basic -u applicationid:applicationsecret \
-H "Content-Type: application/x-www-form-urlencoded;charset=UTF-8" -k \
-d "grant_type=password&username=peter&password=peter123&scope=foo" \
https://localhost:8443/oauth/token
```

This command makes a token request to the STS by using Peter's credentials. And you should get an access token in JWT form in the response, as shown next. Note that we've omitted the long string that represents the JWT (which is the value of the access_token parameter) and replaced it with jwt_token_value for brevity. You can inspect the JWT token via https://jwt.io. It will show you the decoded JWT string. Here's the response:

```
{
  "access_token":"jwt_token_value",
  "expires_in":5999,
  "scope":"foo",
  "jti":"badc4a65-b6d6-4a1c-affc-3d0565cd2b55"
}
```

Once we have a JWT access token, we can use it to access the Inventory microservice. To begin our gRPC service, first navigate to the chapter08/sample04/client_server directory and execute the following command:

```
\> ./gradlew installDist
```

If the program compiles successfully, you should see a BUILD SUCCESSFUL message. Let's start the server process by executing the following command:

```
\> ./build/install/client_server/bin/inventory-server localhost 50440 \
/tmp/sslcert/server.crt /tmp/sslcert/server.pem
```

If the server starts successfully, you should see a message saying INFO: Server started, listening on 50440. Note that we are using TLS only (not mTLS) for this sample. We are using JWT as the client verification process. The next step would be to start the client process. As per figure 8.4, this client process simulates the Order Processing microservice. Before starting the client process, open a new terminal window, navigate to the chapter08/sample03/client_server directory, and set the value of the access token as an environment variable by using the following command. Make sure to replace jwt_token_value with your token's actual value:

```
\> export TOKEN=jwt_token_value
```

Next, execute the following command on the same terminal window to execute the gRPC client. Note that we are providing the value of the obtained JWT access token to the gRPC client as an argument:

```
\> ./build/install/client_server/bin/inventory-client localhost 50440 \
/tmp/sslcert/ca.crt $TOKEN
```

If the client executes successfully, you should see a message saying `INFO: Message: Updated inventory for 1 products`. Ideally, you can think of this as a request initiated from the Order Processing microservice to the Inventory microservice. Let's now execute the same gRPC client without providing the JWT access token as an argument. Execute the following command on the same terminal window:

```
\> ./build/install/client_server/bin/inventory-client localhost 50440 \
/tmp/sslcert/ca.crt
```

You should see an error message: `WARNING: RPC failed: Status {code=UNAU-THENTICATED, description=JWT Token is missing from Metadata, cause=null}`. This is because the Inventory microservice is expecting a valid client JWT, and when it doesn't receive it, it throws an error.

Unlike in HTTP, gRPC doesn't have headers. gRPC supports sending metadata between client and server. The *metadata* is a key-value pair map; the key is a string, and the value can be a string or in binary form. Keys that contain binary data as the values need to be suffixed with the string `-bin`; for example, `key-bin`. In the example we just executed, we used metadata to transfer the JWT access token from client to server. We used something called a `ClientInterceptor`, which intercepts the messages being passed from client to server on the channel to inject the JWT access token as gRPC metadata. The code for the `ClientInterceptor` can be found in the chapter08/sample03/client_server/src/main/java/com/manning/mss/ch08/sample03/JWT ClientInterceptor.java file. Its `interceptCall` method is the one that's executed on each message passed. The following listing shows what it looks like.

Listing 8.8 Method that executes on each message to inject the JWT

```
@Override
public <ReqT, RespT> ClientCall<ReqT, RespT> interceptCall(
  MethodDescriptor<ReqT, RespT> methodDescriptor,
  CallOptions callOptions, Channel channel) {
    return new ForwardingClientCall
    .SimpleForwardingClientCall<ReqT, RespT>(channel.newCall(
                        methodDescriptor, callOptions)) {
      @Override
      public void start(Listener<RespT> responseListener, Metadata headers)
      {
          headers.put(Constants.JWT_KEY, tokenValue);      ⟵─┐ Sets the value of the
          super.start(responseListener, headers);             │ JWT access token
      }                                                        │ to request metadata
    };
}
```

To understand how the `JWTClientInterceptor` class is set to the gRPC client, take a look at the method in the following listing. This method is found in the `Inventory-Client` class under the same package as the `JWTClientInterceptor` class.

Listing 8.9   Setting the `JWTClientInterceptor` class to the gRPC client

```
public InventoryClient(String host,
                       int port,
                       SslContext sslContext,
                       JWTClientInterceptor clientInterceptor) throws
                                                          SSLException {
    this(NettyChannelBuilder.forAddress(host, port)
            .negotiationType(NegotiationType.TLS)
            .sslContext(sslContext)
            .intercept(clientInterceptor)             ◁────  The client interceptor is set
            .build());                                        to the channel being created
}                                                             between the client and server.
```

We follow a similar approach on the server side to validate the JWT access token. The server too uses an interceptor, called `ServerInterceptor`, to intercept incoming messages and perform validations on them. The server interceptor class can be found in the file chapter08/sample03/client_server/src/main/java/com/manning/mss/ch08/sample03/JWTServerInterceptor.java. Its `interceptCall` method, shown in the following listing, is executed on each message. We retrieve the JWT access token from the metadata and validate it at this point.

Listing 8.10   Method that executes on each message to validate the JWT

```
                                                Gets token from the request metadata. This
                                                way, we can use gRPC metadata to pass in
                                                an access token from client to server.
@Override
public <ReqT, RespT> ServerCall.Listener<ReqT>
  interceptCall(ServerCall<ReqT, RespT> serverCall,
                Metadata metadata,
                ServerCallHandler<ReqT, RespT> serverCallHandler) {
    String token = metadata.get(Constants.JWT_KEY);          ◁──
                                                    ┌── Validates
    if (!validateJWT(token)) {               ◁──────┘   the token
        serverCall.close(Status.UNAUTHENTICATED
        .withDescription("JWT Token is missing from Metadata"), metadata);
        return NOOP_LISTENER;
    }

    return serverCallHandler.startCall(serverCall, metadata);
}
```

Summary

- In a microservices deployment, given that many interactions happen over the network among microservices, JSON over HTTP/1.1 is not efficient enough.

- gRPC operates over HTTP/2, which is significantly more efficient than HTTP/1.1 because of request response multiplexing, binary encoding, and header compression.
- Unlike in HTTP/1.1, HTTP/2 supports bidirectional streaming, which is beneficial in microservice architectures.
- gRPC supports mTLS, which you can use to secure communication channels among microservices.
- mTLS does not necessarily address the full spectrum of security we need to ensure on microservice architectures; we therefore need to resort to JWTs in certain cases.
- Unlike HTTP, gRPC does not have a concept of headers, so we have to use metadata fields in gRPC to send JWTs.
- The client interceptors and server interceptors available in gRPC help to send JWTs from clients to servers and to validate them.

Securing reactive
microservices

9

This chapter covers

- Using Kafka as a message broker for interservice communications
- Using TLS in Kafka to secure messages in transit
- Using mTLS to authenticate microservices connecting to Kafka
- Controlling access to Kafka topics using access control lists
- Using NATS for reactive microservices

In chapter 6 and chapter 7, we discussed how to secure service-to-service communications with mTLS and JWT. Chapter 8 extended that discussion and explained how mTLS and JWT can be used to secure communications happening over gRPC. In all those cases, our examples assumed synchronous communications between the calling microservice and the recipient microservice. The security model that you develop to protect service-to-service communications should consider how the actual communications take place among microservices: synchronously or asynchronously.

In most cases, synchronous communications happen over HTTP. Asynchronous communications can happen over any kind of messaging system such as RabbitMQ, Apache Kafka, NATS, ActiveMQ, or even Amazon SQS. In this chapter, we discuss how to use Kafka and NATS as a message broker, which enables microservices to communicate with each other in an event-driven fashion, and how to secure the communication channels.

Kafka is the most popular messaging system used in many microservice deployments. If you're interested in learning more about Kafka, we recommend *Kafka in Action* by Dylan Scott (Manning, 2020). *NATS* is an open source, lightweight, high-performing messaging system designed for cloud-native applications, which is also an alternative to Kafka. If you're interested in learning more about NATS, we recommend *Practical NATS* by Waldemar Quevedo (Apress, 2018).

9.1 Why reactive microservices?

In this section, we discuss the need to have reactive microservices in your microservices deployment. A microservice is considered to be *reactive* when it can react to events that occur in a system without explicitly being called by the event originator; the recipient microservice is decoupled from the calling microservice. The microservice that generates events doesn't necessarily need to know which microservices consume those events.

Let's take the example of a typical order-placement scenario. As we discussed in chapter 8, multiple actions occur when an order is placed, some of which include the following:

- Preparing the invoice and processing the payment
- Updating the inventory to reduce the items in stock
- Processing the shipment to the customer who placed the order
- Sending an email notification to the customer regarding the status of the order

In a typical microservices deployment, each of these actions is performed by an independent microservice. That way, each operation is independent from the other, and a failure in one doesn't cause an impact on others. For example, if a bug in the Shipping microservice causes it to go out of memory, it doesn't impact the rest of the functionality when processing the order, and the order can still be completed.

In previous chapters, we looked at how the Order Processing microservice becomes the triggering point for the rest of the actions that take place. When an order is processed by the Order Processing microservice, it initiates the rest of the actions that take place, such as updating the inventory, initializing the shipment, and so on. This way, the Order Processing microservice becomes the orchestrator for the rest of the actions related to processing an order. Figure 9.1 illustrates this pattern further.

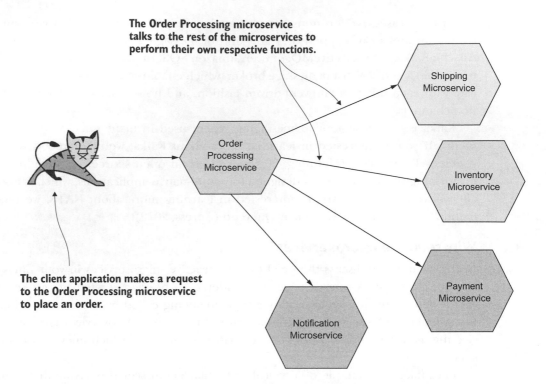

The Order Processing microservice talks to the rest of the microservices to perform their own respective functions.

Shipping Microservice

Order Processing Microservice

Inventory Microservice

Payment Microservice

Notification Microservice

The client application makes a request to the Order Processing microservice to place an order.

Figure 9.1   The Order Processing microservice talks to other microservices to initiate events related to processing an order, such as paying for the order, updating the inventory, and so on.

As you can see, the Order Processing microservice calls out to all the other microservices so that they can perform their own respective actions. These types of interactions between microservices elicit two types of actions: synchronous and asynchronous:

- *The synchronous actions are those types that need to be completed in real time.* For example, the payment needs to be successfully concluded before the order can be considered completed. Also, the Order Processing microservice needs to update the system's database to record an order successfully.

- *The asynchronous actions are those types that can be performed later.* The order can be considered complete even if these actions (for example, updating the inventory, processing the shipment, and sending an email to the customer) aren't performed in real time. These are the actions that we can perform offline, asynchronous to the main operation.

For the Order Processing microservice to be the orchestrator that calls to the respective microservices to perform the remaining actions related to processing an order, it needs to know how to invoke these microservices. This might include the connectivity information of the relevant microservices, the parameters that need to be passed in, and so on. Take a look at the following listing for a code sample showing how the Order Processing microservice would have to invoke functions to trigger the rest of the actions to be performed.

Listing 9.1 Order Processing microservice calls other services synchronously

```
try {
    updateResponse = inventoryStub.updateInventory(orderBuilder.build());
} catch (StatusRuntimeException e) {
    logger.log(Level.WARNING,
    "Unable to update inventory. RPC failed: {0}", e.getStatus());
    return;
}

try {
    updateResponse = shippingStub.makeShipment(orderBuilder.build());
} catch (StatusRuntimeException e) {
    logger.log(Level.WARNING,
    "Unable to make shipment. RPC failed: {0}", e.getStatus());
    return;
}

try {
    updateResponse = notificationsStub.sendEmail(orderBuilder.build());
} catch (StatusRuntimeException e) {
    logger.log(Level.WARNING,
    "Unable to send email to customer. RPC failed: {0}", e.getStatus());
    return;
}
```

Imagine a situation where we need a new action to be performed when an order is being processed. Say, for example, we introduce a new feature that tracks the buying patterns of each customer so that we can provide recommendations to other buyers. If we introduce this new feature as a separate microservice, we would need to update the Order Processing microservice to invoke this new microservice as well. This causes us to make code changes to the Order Processing microservice and to redeploy it in order to consume the features the new microservice provides.

As you may have observed, the Order Processing microservice becomes a trigger for multiple actions being performed. It's responsible for initiating the shipment, sending email, and updating the inventory. But although these actions must be performed for an order to be complete, having the Order Processing microservice perform so many actions is not ideal, as per the principles of microservices architecture.

The two main things that are mandatory for the order to be successfully recorded are the payment processing and the database update (which records the transactions). The rest of the actions can be performed asynchronously after the two main actions are complete. This is where reactive microservices become useful.

Reactive microservices work in such a way that the microservices are attentive to events that occur in the system and act accordingly, based on the type of event that occurs. In our example, the Order Processing microservice, when finished recording the customer's order, emits an event to the system with the details of the order. The rest of the microservices, which are paying attention to these events, receive the order event and react to it accordingly. By reacting, they perform their respective operations upon receiving the event. For example, when the Shipping microservice receives the order event, it performs the actions necessary to ship the order to the customer who placed it.

Reactive microservices create a loose coupling between the source microservice that initiates the event and the target microservices that receive and react to the event. As we saw in figure 9.1, in the older, traditional way of performing these actions, there's a direct link from the Order Processing microservice to the rest of the microservices (Inventory, Shipping, and so on). With reactive microservices, this link becomes indirect. This happens by introducing a message broker solution into our microservices deployment. Figure 9.2 illustrates this solution.

As you see, the Order Processing microservice emits an event (sends a message) to the message broker. All other microservices interested in knowing about the orders being processed in the system are subscribed to the particular topic on the broker.

> ### Topics vs. Queues
> In messaging systems, the message producers publish messages to either a queue or a topic. Consumers of the message subscribe to the queues or topics of interest to receive the messages. A topic is used when we want all the subscribers to receive the event and process it. A queue is used when an event needs to be processed by one subscriber only, the first subscriber to receive it.

Upon receiving an order event, the consumer microservices start executing their processes to complete the tasks they are responsible for. For example, when the Inventory microservice receives the order event, it starts executing its code to update the inventory as per the details in the order. The key benefit in this architecture is the loose coupling between the source and the target microservices. This loose coupling allows the Order Processing microservice to focus on its main responsibility, which is to ensure that the payment is properly processed (synchronously) via the Payment microservice and the recording of the order itself in the system.

Another major benefit with event-driven architecture is that it allows us to add new functionality to the system without affecting the current code. Referring to the same example we discussed earlier, imagine that we want to introduce a feature that tracks a user's buying patterns. With the older architecture, if we had to introduce a new microservice to track the buying patterns, we also had to change the Order Processing microservice so that it could talk to the Buying History microservice.

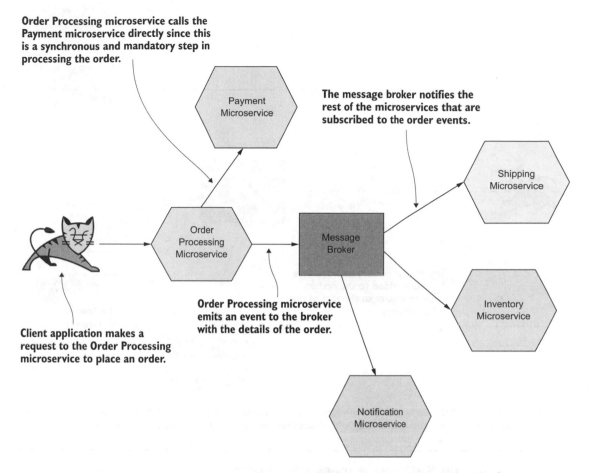

Order Processing microservice calls the Payment microservice directly since this is a synchronous and mandatory step in processing the order.

The message broker notifies the rest of the microservices that are subscribed to the order events.

Order Processing microservice emits an event to the broker with the details of the order.

Client application makes a request to the Order Processing microservice to place an order.

Figure 9.2 Introducing a message broker into the architecture. The Order Processing microservice calls the Payment microservice directly because payment is a mandatory and synchronous step in processing the order. It then emits an event to the message broker that delivers the order details to the rest of the microservices asynchronously. This makes the link between the Order Processing microservice and the other microservices indirect.

But with the reactive architecture, all we need to do is to make the Buying History microservice aware of the order event by linking it to a message broker. This way, the Buying History microservice gets to know the details of each order when an order is processed. This gives us the flexibility to add new functionality to the system without having to change and redeploy old code. Figure 9.3 illustrates the introduction of the Buying History microservice into this architecture.

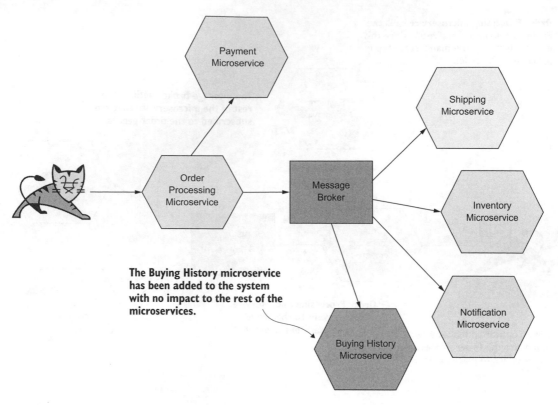

Figure 9.3   Introducing the Buying History microservice to the system so that we can benefit from its capabilities without having to make any changes in the Order Processing microservice or in anything else

9.2   *Setting up Kafka as a message broker*

In this section, we look at how to set up Apache Kafka as a message broker in our microservices deployment to receive streams of data events from some microservices and deliver them to other microservices in an asynchronous fashion. We discuss how to install Kafka, create a topic, and then transfer a message from a message producer to a receiver.

Apache Kafka is an open source, distributed streaming platform. One microservice can publish streams of records to topics in Kafka, and another microservice can subscribe to one or more topics in Kafka and consume streams of records. Kafka can receive, process, and store streams of data.

To set up Kafka on your local machine, first go to https://kafka.apache.org/downloads and download it. The version we use in this chapter is 2.5.0 (with Scala version 2.13), the latest version as of this writing. Kafka 2.5.0, released in April 2020, is the first Kafka version to support TLS 1.3 (along with Java 11 support). Once you have downloaded it, extract the zip archive to a location of your choice. Use your command-line tool to navigate to the location where you extracted Kafka and navigate inside the Kafka directory; we refer to this location as kafka_home.

Note that we'll use the Linux executables in Kafka for the examples in this chapter. If you're operating in a Windows environment, the corresponding executables (alternatives for the .sh files) can be found in the kafka_home/bin/windows directory. For example, the alternative for the executable bin/zookeeper-server-start.sh for Windows is bin/windows/zookeeper-server-start.bat.

Kafka requires a ZooKeeper server to run. *Apache ZooKeeper* (https://zookeeper .apache.org/) is a centralized service that provides various capabilities for managing and running distributed systems. Some of these capabilities include distributed synchronization, grouping services, naming services, and so on. Figure 9.4 illustrates how ZooKeeper coordinates across the Kafka cluster.

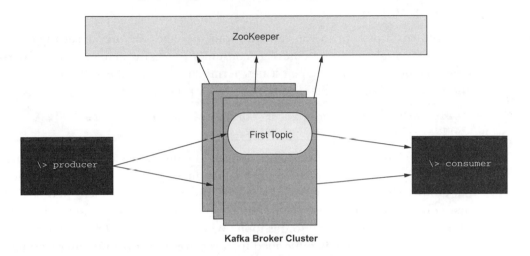

Figure 9.4   ZooKeeper coordinates the nodes in the Kafka cluster.

To run ZooKeeper, execute the following command by using your command-line terminal from within the kafka_home directory:

```
\> bin/zookeeper-server-start.sh config/zookeeper.properties
```

Once ZooKeeper is up and running, we can start the Kafka server. Open a new tab on your command-line client and navigate to the kafka_home directory; then execute the following command:

```
\> bin/kafka-server-start.sh config/server.properties
```

Once the Kafka server is running, we can create our topic for publishing messages. Kafka, by default, comes with a utility tool that helps us to create topics easily. Open a new tab on your command-line client and navigate to the kafka_home directory as before. Let's create our first topic by executing the following command. Note that we'll use `firsttopic` as the name of the topic we're creating:

```
\> bin/kafka-topics.sh --create --bootstrap-server localhost:9092 \
--replication-factor 1 --partitions 1 --topic firsttopic
```

To see whether the topic was created successfully, you can execute the following command in your command-line client. It should list the topic that we just created in the output:

```
\> bin/kafka-topics.sh --list --bootstrap-server localhost:9092
```

Now that Kafka is up and running and a topic is created on it, we can start to send and receive messages from Kafka. Open a new tab in your command-line client from the kafka_home directory and execute the following command to start a console process that we can type a message into:

```
\> bin/kafka-console-producer.sh --broker-list localhost:9092 \
--topic firsttopic
```

This returns a prompt so you can type your messages. Before we start typing in any message, though, let's start a message consumer process as well, so we can observe the messages being typed in. Open a new terminal tab from the kafka_home directory and execute this command to start a consumer process:

```
\> bin/kafka-console-consumer.sh --bootstrap-server localhost:9092 \
--topic firsttopic --from-beginning
```

Now go back to the previous prompt and start typing in messages. Press the Enter key after each message. You should notice that the messages you type appear on the terminal tab on which you started the consumer process. What happens here is that your first command prompt delivers a message to a topic named `firsttopic`. The consumer process is subscribed to this topic. When a message is delivered to a topic that the consumer process has subscribed to, it receives the corresponding message. And, in this particular case, the consumer process simply outputs the received message to the console. This is illustrated in figure 9.5.

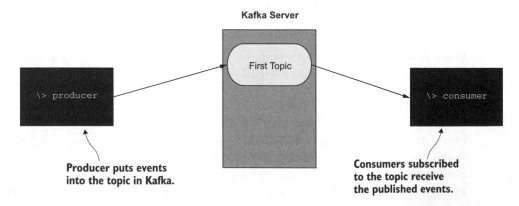

Figure 9.5   The producer process puts events into the topic in the Kafka server. The consumer process receives the events.

Once you've tried out this part, you can close the console process that you typed messages into and the consumer process that displayed the messages. But keep the Kafka processes up and running because we need Kafka for trying out the examples in section 9.3.

9.3   *Developing a microservice to push events to a Kafka topic*

In this section, we discuss how to develop a microservice in Spring Boot to push events to a Kafka topic. The microservice receives messages via HTTP, and those messages are then converted into events and pushed to a topic on Kafka. You can find all the samples in the https://github.com/microservices-security-in-action/samples GitHub repository. Navigate to the chapter09/sampe01 directory by using your command-line tool and execute the following command from within the sample01 directory to build the Order Processing microservice:

```
\> mvn clean install
```

Make sure that you have Kafka running as per the instructions given in section 9.2. Execute the following command to run the Order Processing microservice:

```
\> mvn spring-boot:run
```

Once the Order Processing microservice starts, you should see a topic named ORDERS being created on Kafka. You can verify that it's there by listing the topics in Kafka. Execute the following command in a new terminal window from within the kafka_home location:

```
\> bin/kafka-topics.sh --list --bootstrap-server localhost:9092
```

Let's now open a new console process that prints the messages sent to the ORDERS topic. As in section 9.2, we execute this command from within the kafka_home directory:

```
\> bin/kafka-console-consumer.sh --bootstrap-server localhost:9092 \
--topic ORDERS --from-beginning
```

Once the console process is running, we can send a message to the Order Processing microservice and observe its behavior. Open a new terminal window and navigate to the sample01 directory and execute the following curl command to send a request to the Order Processing microservice to place an order:

```
\> curl http://localhost:8080/order -X POST -d @order.json \
-H "Content-Type: application/json" -v
```

The order.json file (which is inside the sample01 directory) contains the message (in JSON format) that we sent to the Order Processing microservice. If the order was placed successfully, you should get an HTTP 201 response code to the request. If you observe the console process that prints messages on the ORDERS topic, you should see that the content within the order.json file (request payload) has been printed on the console.

What happened here was that we used curl to send an HTTP request to the Order Processing microservice to place an order. While the Order Processing microservice took care of the business logic related to placing the order, it also sent an event (message) to the Kafka ORDERS topic. Any process that subscribes to the ORDERS topic now receives the order details via the topic and can execute their respective actions. In our case, the console process printed the order details to the output. Figure 9.6 illustrates this scenario. In section 9.4, we discuss a process that listens to these order events and performs some actions.

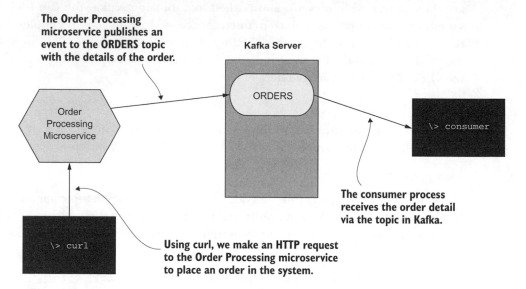

Figure 9.6   curl makes an HTTP request to the Order Processing microservice to place an order. After processing its logic, the Order Processing microservice puts an event into the ORDERS topic in Kafka with the details of the order. The consumer process subscribed to the ORDERS topic receives the order's details through Kafka.

Let's take a look at the code that processes the order. The OrderProcessing.java file found in sample01/src/main/java/com/manning/mss/ch09/sample01/service hosts the Order Processing microservice code. Its `createOrder` method is executed when it receives the HTTP request to place the order, as the following listing shows.

Listing 9.2   The `createOrder` method in the Order Processing microservice

```
@RequestMapping(method = RequestMethod.POST)
public ResponseEntity<?> createOrder(@RequestBody Order order) {
    if (order != null) {
        order.setOrderId(UUID.randomUUID().toString());
        URI location = ServletUriComponentsBuilder
                        .fromCurrentRequest().path("/{id}")
```

```
                     .buildAndExpand(order.getOrderId()).toUri();
      publisher.publish(order);
      return ResponseEntity.created(location).build();
    }
    return ResponseEntity.status(HttpStatus.BAD_REQUEST).build();
}
```

**Publishes the message to the
Kafka topic after the order-
processing logic completes**

The `publish` method used in listing 9.2 is declared in the OrderPublisher.java file, as shown in the following listing.

Listing 9.3   Publishing the order to the Kafka topic

```
@Service
public class OrderPublisher {
  @Autowired
  private Source source;
  public void publish(Order order){
    source.output().send(MessageBuilder
                  .withPayload(order).build());
  }
}
```

We use Spring Cloud's Binders (http://mng.bz/zjZ6) to bind the Order Processing microservice to Kafka. Spring's Binder abstractions allow us to bind our program to different types of streaming implementations. To find out how it connects to the Kafka server, take a look at the applications.properties file in the chapter09/sample01/src/main/resources directory, also listed here:

```
spring.cloud.stream.bindings.output.destination:ORDERS
spring.cloud.stream.bindings.output.content-type:application/json
spring.cloud.stream.kafka.binder.zkNodes:localhost
spring.cloud.stream.kafka.binder.zkNodes.brokers: localhost
```

You'll see several properties. One property tells our program which topic in Kafka to connect to (in this case, `ORDERS`), and two other properties specify the ZooKeeper connection details (in this case, `localhost`). You may notice that we haven't specified the ZooKeeper ports. That's because we're working with the default ports in Zoo-Keeper (2181). If you want to use nondefault ports, you need to specify the connection details in the format `<host>:<port>` (`localhost:2181`).

9.4   Developing a microservice to read events from a Kafka topic

In this section, we discuss how to create a microservice that reads and acts upon the events received from our Order Processing microservice. In section 9.3, we discussed how we could get the Order Processing microservice to send events to a topic in Kafka when an order is processed. In this section, we discuss how to implement our Buying

History microservice to track customers' buying patterns. This service listens on the ORDERS topic in Kafka. When it receives an order event, it acts on the event and executes its logic related to analyzing and recording the purchase. Figure 9.7 illustrates this architecture.

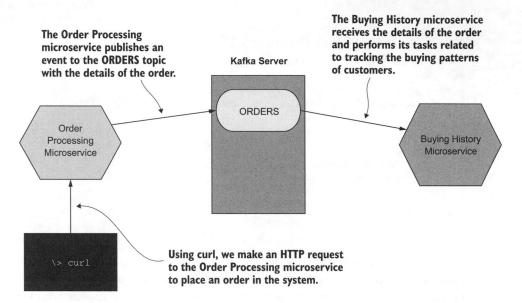

Figure 9.7   The Buying History microservice now receives the order details via Kafka. It then starts processing its task related to tracking the buying patterns of customers. This task is done asynchronously to the processing of the order.

Let's first run the Buying History microservice sample to see how the interactions shown in figure 9.7 work. You can find the code related to the Buying History microservice inside the chapter09/sample02 directory. You need to have both the Kafka server (from section 9.2) and the Order Processing microservice up and running.

The Order Processing microservice is the event source to the Kafka topic. The Buying History microservice is the one that consumes the events received on the Kafka topic. Open your command-line tool and navigate to the sample02 directory and then execute the following command to build this example:

```
\> mvn clean install
```

Once it's built, execute this command to start the Buying History microservice:

```
\> mvn spring-boot:run
```

When the Buying History microservice starts, it subscribes to the Kafka topic named ORDERS. Once the Buying History microservice is running, you can send an HTTP request to the Order Processing microservice to create an order. Open a new tab on your command-line tool and navigate to the sample02 directory. Execute the following command to make an order request (note the Order Processing microservice from section 9.3 handles this request):

```
\> curl http://localhost:8080/order -X POST -d @order.json \
-H "Content-Type: application/json" -v
```

If successful, this command returns a 201 response code. If you observe the console output of the terminal tab that runs the Buying History microservice, you should see the following message:

```
Updated buying history of customer with order: <order_id>
```

The Buying History microservice received the order details via the Kafka topic ORDERS. On receiving this event, it executes its logic to track the purchase history of the customer. In this particular case, it prints a message to the console saying it received the order event and processed it. Figure 9.8 illustrates the sequence of events.

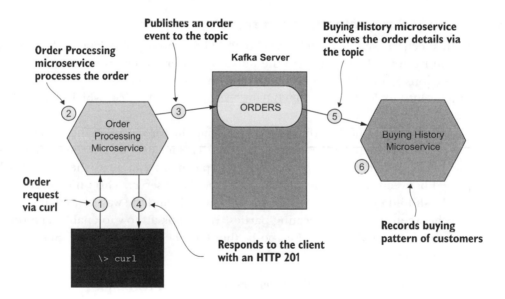

Figure 9.8   The sequence of events that happen when a client (curl) makes a request to place an order. Note that steps 4 and 5 can happen in parallel because they're on two independent processes.

Let's take a look at the code of the Buying History microservice, which received the message from Kafka when the order was placed. The BuyingHistoryMicroservice.java file located in the sample02/src/main/java/com/manning/mss/ch09/sample02 directory contains the code of the Buying History microservice. The following listing provides this code.

Listing 9.4   Microservice code that reads messages from Kafka

```
@SpringBootApplication
@EnableBinding(Sink.class)
public class BuyingHistoryMicroservice {

    public static void main(String[] args) {
        SpringApplication.run(BuyingHistoryMicroservice.class, args);
    }

    @StreamListener(Sink.INPUT)
    public void updateHistory(Order order) {
        System.out.println(
        "Updated buying history of customer with order: "
        + order.getOrderId());
    }
}
```

> Tells the Spring runtime to trigger this method when a message is received on the topic it's listening to

As we discussed in section 9.3, the Spring runtime is configured to connect to Kafka through the properties defined in the applications.properties file located in the sample02/src/main/resources directory.

9.5   *Using TLS to protect data in transit*

In this section, we teach you how to enable TLS to protect the data that's being passed to and from the Kafka server to the Kafka producers and consumers (microservices). In sections 9.3 and 9.4, we implemented the Order Processing microservice, which sent events to Kafka, and the Buying History microservice, which received events from Kafka.

In both cases, the data that was passed along the wire between the Kafka server and the respective microservices was in plaintext. This means that anyone having access to the network layer of the microservices deployment can read the messages being passed between the two microservices and the Kafka server. This isn't ideal.

We should encrypt data passed via the network, and the way to do that is to enable TLS between the communicating parties. We'll look at how to enable TLS on Kafka, and how to enable TLS for both the Order Processing and Buying History microservices.

9.5.1   *Creating and signing the TLS keys and certificates for Kafka*

In this section, we discuss how to create a key and a certificate for the Kafka server to enable TLS communication. We also discuss how to sign the Kafka certificate by using a self-generated CA. To create the CA and other related keys, you can use the gen-key.sh file in the chapter09/keys directory, which includes a set of OpenSSL commands.

OpenSSL is a commercial-grade toolkit and cryptographic library for TLS that's available for multiple platforms. Here we run OpenSSL as a Docker container, so you don't need to install OpenSSL on your computer, but you should have Docker installed. If you're new to Docker, check appendix E, but you don't need to know

Docker to follow the rest of this section. To spin up the OpenSSL Docker container, run the following command from the chapter09/keys directory.

Listing 9.5 Spinning up OpenSSL in a Docker container

```
\> docker run -it -v $(pwd):/export prabath/openssl
#
```

This `docker run` command starts OpenSSL in a Docker container with a bind mount that maps the keys directory (or the current directory, which is indicated by `${pwd}`) from the host filesystem to the /export directory of the container filesystem. This bind mount lets you share part of the host filesystem with the container filesystem. When the OpenSSL container generates certificates, it writes those to the /export directory of the container filesystem. Because we have a bind mount, everything inside the /export directory of the container filesystem is also accessible from the keys directory of the host filesystem.

When you run the command in listing 9.5 for the first time, it can take a couple of minutes to execute and ends with a command prompt, where we can execute our script to create all the keys. The following command that runs from the Docker container executes the gen-key.sh file, which is inside the export directory of the container. It's the same script that's inside the keys directory of your local filesystem:

```
# sh /export/gen-key.sh
# exit
```

Now, if you look at the keys directory in the host filesystem, you'll find a set of files as shown in the following listing. If you want to understand what happens underneath the script, check out appendix G.

Listing 9.6 Generated keys and certificates

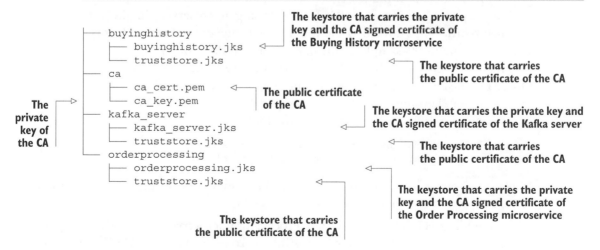

9.5.2   *Configuring TLS on the Kafka server*

In this section, we discuss how to enable TLS on the Kafka server. This requires changing a few configuration parameters and restarting the Kafka server.

To enable TLS on Kafka, first make sure the Kafka server is shut down if it's already running, but keep the ZooKeeper server running (from section 9.2). You need to press Ctrl-C on your keyboard on the respective command-line terminal process. After the process shuts down, use your command-line client tool or file explorer to navigate to the kafka_home/config directory. Open the server.properties file by using your text editor of choice and add the following properties to the file.

Listing 9.7   Content of server.properties file

Tells the Kafka server to listen on ports 9092 for plaintext (nonsecure) connections and port 9093 for secure connections

```
listeners=PLAINTEXT://:9092,SSL://:9093        ⬅
ssl.keystore.location=chapter09/keys/kafka_server/kafka_server.jks        ⬅┐
ssl.keystore.password=manning123
ssl.enabled.protocols=TLSv1.2,TLSv1.1,TLSv1
ssl.keystore.type=JKS
ssl.secure.random.implementation=SHA1PRNG
```

Provides the absolute path to the kafka_server.jks file. Make sure to change this value appropriately.

Once the configurations are done, as shown in listing 9.7, you can save and close the file and start the Kafka server. Use your command-line client and navigate to the kafka_home directory and execute this command to start Kafka:

```
\> bin/kafka-server-start.sh config/server.properties
```

9.5.3   *Configuring TLS on the microservices*

In this section, we discuss how to enable TLS on our Order Processing and Buying History microservices. We need to enable a few properties and provide these microservices with the details of the truststore.jks file that we created in section 9.5.1. You can find the updated code of the Order Processing microservice in the chapter09/sample03/orders_ms directory, and the updated code of the Buying History microservice in the chapter09/sample03/buying_history_ms directory.

First, we need to configure the keystores that we created in section 9.5.1 with the Order Processing and Buying History microservices. Let's copy the keystore files from the chapter09/keys directory to the corresponding microservice by executing the following commands from the chapter09 directory:

```
\> cp keys/orderprocessing/*.jks sample03/orders_ms/
\> cp keys/buyinghistory/*.jks sample03/buying_history_ms/
```

When configuring keystores with the Order Processing and Buying History microservices, we need to consider two things:

- Enabling HTTPS for the Order Processing microservice so the client applications that talk to the Order Processing microservice must use HTTPS. We don't need to do the same for the Buying History microservice because we don't expose it over HTTP.

- Configuring both Order Processing and Buying History microservices to trust the public certificate of the CA that signed the public certificate of the Kafka server. The Order Processing microservice connects to the Kafka server to publish messages, and the Buying History microservice connects to the Kafka server to read messages. Both of these communications now happen over TLS, and both the microservices have to trust the CA who issued the public certificate of the Kafka server.

Use your file editor of choice to open the application.properties file located in sample03/orders_ms/src/main/resources and then provide the proper values for the properties spring.kafka.ssl.trust-store-location and spring.kafka.ssl.trust-store-password. These are the properties that instruct Spring Boot to trust the CA who issued the public certificate of the Kafka server.

Also check the values of server.ssl.key-store and server.ssl.key-store-password properties. These two properties enable HTTPS transport for the Order Processing microservice. Save and close the file after these changes are done. If you accept the default values we used in our examples, as shown in the following listing, you don't need to make any changes.

> **Listing 9.8 Content of application.properties file**

The password
of the keystore

The location of the keystore that carries
the keys to enable HTTPS communication

Instructs the microservice to connect
to the TLS port (9093) of Kafka. If no
port is specified, the microservice
connects to the default Kafka port 9092,
which is the plaintext port (no TLS).

```
server.ssl.key-store: orderprocessing.jks
server.ssl.key-store-password: manning123
spring.kafka.bootstrap-servers:localhost:9093
spring.kafka.properties.security.protocol=SSL
spring.kafka.properties.ssl.endpoint
                    .identification.algorithm=
spring.kafka.ssl
          .trust-store-location=file:truststore.jks
spring.kafka.ssl.trust-store-password=manning123
spring.kafka.ssl.trust-store-type=JKS
```

Sets the protocol to SSL, which
enables TLS communication

The location of the
keystore that carries
the CA's public certificate

By leaving this empty, we effectively get our
microservice to ignore the hostname verification
of the server certificate. In a production
deployment, you shouldn't do this.

The type of
trust store

The password of
the trust store

> **NOTE** By setting the `ssl.endpoint.identification.algorithm` property as empty in listing 9.8, we effectively get our microservice to ignore the hostname verification of the server certificate. In a real production system, we wouldn't ideally do this. A production server should have a proper DNS setup for the Kafka server, and it should be exposed using a valid hostname (not localhost). We could use the hostname in our server certificate and enforce hostname

verification on the client (microservice), but for now, because we don't have a proper hostname to use, we'll skip the hostname verification on the client.

Do the same for the application.properties file located at buying_history_ms/src/main/resources and save and close the file. Once both these changes are done, use your command-line client and navigate to the sample03/orders_ms directory. Execute the following command to build the new Order Processing microservice:

```
\> mvn clean install
```

Once the build is successful, execute the following command to run the Order Processing microservice. Make sure you have the Kafka server running before you execute this command. In case you're still running the Order Processing microservice from section 9.3, make sure you shut it down as well:

```
\> mvn spring-boot:run
```

Let's now do the same for our Buying History microservice. In a new terminal tab, navigate to the sample03/buying_history_ms directory and execute the following command to build the Buying History microservice:

```
\> mvn clean install
```

Once the build is successful, execute the following command to run the Buying History microservice. In case you're still running the Buying History microservice from section 9.4, make sure you shut it down as well:

```
\> mvn spring-boot:run
```

As in section 9.4, we can now make an order request using curl. Open a new terminal tab on your command-line client, navigate to the sample03/orders_ms directory, and execute the following command:

```
\> curl -k https://localhost:8080/order -X POST -d @order.json \
-H "Content-Type: application/json" -v
```

If you observe the console output of the terminal tab on which you ran the Buying History microservice, you should see this output:

```
Updated buying history of customer with order: <order_id>
```

The preceding output means that the curl client has talked successfully to the Order Processing microservice over TLS, and then the Order Processing microservice has published an event to the ORDERS topic on Kafka over TLS, and finally, the Buying History microservice has read the order details from the ORDERS topic on Kafka over TLS.

9.6   *Using mTLS for authentication*

In section 9.5, we looked at enabling TLS between the microservices and the Kafka server. In this section, we discuss how to protect communications between the Order Processing microservice and the Kafka server, as well as the communications between the Buying History microservice and the Kafka server with mTLS for client authentication.

By enabling TLS between the microservices and Kafka, we ensure that the data being transmitted over the network among these parties is encrypted. Nobody sniffing into the network would be able to read the data being transmitted unless they had access to the server's (Kafka) private key. By enabling TLS, we also made sure that the microservices (clients) are connected to the intended/trusted Kafka server and not to anyone or anything pretending to be the server.

One problem that still remains, however, is that anyone that has network access to the Kafka server and that trusts the CA that signed Kafka's certificate can publish and receive events to and from the Kafka server. For example, anyone could impersonate the Order Processing microservice and send bogus order events to Kafka. Figure 9.9 illustrates this scenario.

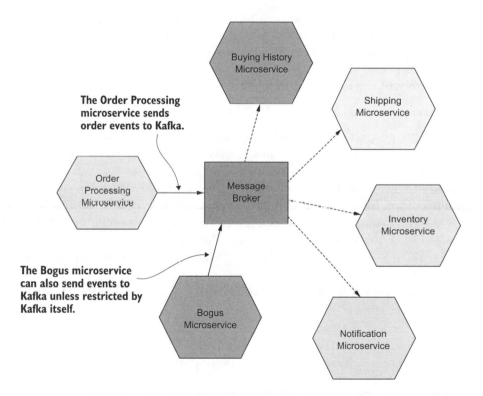

Figure 9.9   The Bogus microservice impersonates the Order Processing microservice by sending order events to Kafka. This makes the other microservices process these order events. Kafka needs to explicitly allow only the trusted microservices to connect to it.

Here, the Bogus microservice is also sending events to Kafka, which would trigger false events in the system and make the other microservices act on it. This would cause our system to break. To prevent this from happening, we need to make sure that only the trusted Order Processing microservice and other trusted microservices are permitted to send and receive events from Kafka.

In section 9.5, we used TLS to establish this trust one way; the client was made to trust the server before sending events to it. We now need to enable trust both ways, so the server also trusts the clients connecting to it through mTLS. Let's see how to enable this on Kafka.

Make sure your Kafka server is stopped. (You can stop it by pressing Ctrl-C on the terminal process that's running the Kafka server process.) Then open the server.properties file located at `kafka_home/config` with your text editor. Add the following two configuration properties to it. Make sure to provide the absolute path pointing to chapter09/keys/kafka_server/trustore.jks as the value of the `ssl.truststore.location` property (we created the `truststore.jks` in section 9.5.1):

```
ssl.truststore.location=chapter09/keys/kafka_server/truststore.jks
ssl.truststore.password=manning123
```

Change the value of the property `ssl.client.auth` to `required` (in the same server.properties file), as shown next. If this property is not there in the server.properties file, you need to add it. This tells the Kafka server to authenticate the clients connecting to Kafka before establishing a connection with them:

```
ssl.client.auth=required
```

Once these properties are set, save and close the file and start the Kafka server. The Kafka server is now ready to accept requests from clients who can authenticate themselves. If you attempt to run the microservices from section 9.5, those would fail because we've mandated client authentication on Kafka. The microservices from section 9.5 didn't have mTLS configurations enabled, hence the failure.

The next step would be to configure the Order Processing and Buying History microservices to be able to authenticate themselves when connecting to the Kafka server. You can take a look at the code that's related to the microservices in the chapter09/sample03 directory.

Let's see how to enable mTLS authentication support for the Order Processing microservice. Open the application.properties file located in the chapter09/samole03/orders_ms/src/main/resources directory. You should see three new properties added, compared to the same in listing 9.8. Those are commented out by default, so let's uncomment them. The following listing shows the updated configuration.

Listing 9.9   Content of application.properties file with mTLS support

```
spring.kafka.ssl.
    key-store-location=file:orderprocessing.jks  ←──┐ The location of the keystore that
spring.kafka.ssl.key-store-password=manning123          carries the microservice's public
spring.kafka.ssl.key-store-type=JKS                     certificate and the private key. We
                                                        created this keystore in section 9.5.1.
```

The type of the keystore

The password of the keystore

Do the same for the Buying History microservice as well. You can find the application.properties file corresponding to the Buying History microservice located in the chapter09/sample03/buying_history_ms/src/main/resources directory. There we need to use buyinghistory.jks as the location of the keystore file. (We created the buyinghistory.jks file in section 9.5.1 and copied it to the chapter09/sample03/buying _history_ms directory in section 9.5.3.)

Once both the `application.properties` files are updated, we can build and run the two microservices. Make sure you aren't running the microservices from previous sections before you execute the next steps. Build the Order Processing microservice by executing the following command using your command-line client within the sample03/orders_ms directory:

```
\> mvn clean install
```

Once the microservice is built, execute the following command to run the Order Processing microservice:

```
\> mvn spring-boot:run
```

Perform the same steps to build and run the Buying History microservice from the sample03/buying_history_ms directory and then execute the following `curl` command from sample03/orders_ms to make an order request to the Order Processing microservice:

```
\> curl -k https://localhost:8080/order -X POST -d @order.json \
-H "Content-Type: application/json" -v
```

You should receive a successful response from this command, and you should notice the following message printed on the terminal tab that's running the Buying History microservice:

```
Updated buying history of customer with order: <order_id>
```

9.7   *Controlling access to Kafka topics with ACLs*

In this section, we discuss how to control client (microservice) access to topics in Kafka with access control lists (ACLs). In section 9.6, we discussed how to enable client authentication using mTLS. We discussed how we could control connections to the Kafka server by using mTLS. We made sure that only trusted clients could connect to Kafka. We used mutually trusted certificates both on the client (microservice) and the Kafka server to achieve this. We did that by getting a mutually trusted CA to sign the certificates of both parties (the client and the server).

We now want to get to a state where only selected microservices are given selective permissions to Kafka topics. For example, we need to ensure that only the Order Processing microservice can publish events into the ORDERS topic in Kafka, and only the Buying History microservice should be permitted to read events from the ORDERS topic. We can't achieve this with mTLS only. Because the Buying History microservice from section 9.6 was granted connection rights through mTLS, it can technically

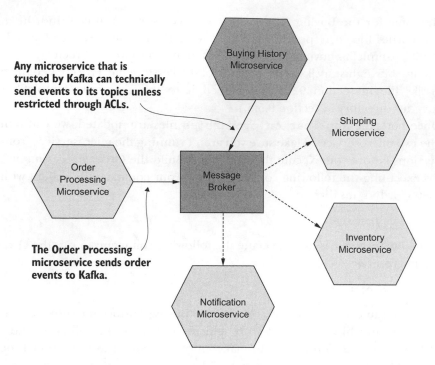

Figure 9.10   The Buying History microservice sends events to Kafka topics. Any microservice that's trusted by Kafka can technically send events to its topics unless restricted by ACLs. These events are delivered to microservices that are subscribed to the Kafka topic unless they have been restricted by ACLs.

publish events to the ORDERS topic even though the code examples we used didn't. Figure 9.10 illustrates this scenario.

Let's take a look at how to prevent this from happening. What we have so far achieved in this chapter is client and server authentication. To enforce more fine-grained access control on Kafka topics, we need to implement authorization on Kafka. Kafka provides a way of implementing authorization using ACLs. An *ACL* is basically a rule on Kafka that either permits or denies a particular entity from performing an action on a Kafka resource. Kafka ACLs are defined in the following format:

```
Principal P is [Allowed/Denied] Operation O From Host H
on any Resource R matching ResourcePattern RP
```

where

- Principal represents the entity (the client) that attempts to perform an operation.
- Operation can be any one of several actions including creating a topic, writing events to a topic, reading events from a topic, and so on.
- Host is the IP address/hostname of the Kafka client.

- `Resource` is an entity on Kafka, such as a topic, a consumer group, and so on.
- `ResourcePattern` is a pattern that's used to identify the resources on which the rule is to be applied.

9.7.1 Enabling ACLs on Kafka and identifying the clients

In this section, we discuss how to enable ACLs on Kafka by changing configuration settings. Before you make these changes to the configuration file, make sure your Kafka server is shut down.

> **NOTE** We're continuing our configurations from the previous sections. If you've directly jumped to this section, you need to first enable mTLS on Kafka by reading through sections 9.5 and 9.6.

Open the server.properties file located at kafka_home/config with your text editor and add the following properties to it:

```
authorizer.class.name=kafka.security.auth.SimpleAclAuthorizer
allow.everyone.if.no.acl.found=true
ssl.principal.mapping.rules=RULE:^CN=(.*?)$/$1/L,DEFAULT
```

The `authorizer.class.name` property contains the name of the class that executes the authorization logic in Kafka. In this case, we use the default class that ships with Kafka itself. If required, you can override the default implementation and add your custom authorization class name to the configuration file. By adding this property to the configuration file, we enable ACLs on Kafka.

The `allow.everyone.if.no.acl.found` property specifies the action to be performed in case an ACL isn't found for a given resource. By default, Kafka denies access to resources (topics) if no ACLs are declared on it. By setting this to `true`, we override that behavior by saying unless a rule is applied on a resource via an ACL, let anyone access it without restriction.

The `ssl.principal.mapping.rules` property defines the patterns to identify the principal (Kafka client). Because we use mTLS to authenticate clients (microservices), the Kafka server identifies a client through the properties in the corresponding client certificate. We can have multiple rules defined in the `ssl.principal` `.mapping.rules` property, and each rule is defined using the following format:

```
RULE:pattern/replacement/[LU]
```

This pattern is a regular expression that identifies the principal from the provided credentials (for example, a client certificate). By default, when we use an X509 certificate for authentication (or mTLS), the principal identifier is its *distinguished name* (or *DN*). The distinguished name of a certificate is a string that combines the certificate details as key-value pairs delimited by commas. For a certificate having the common name (or CN) `orders.ecomm.com`, the distinguished name could look like the following:

```
CN=orders.ecomm.com,OU=Unknown,O=Unknown,L=Unknown,ST=Unknown,C=Unknown
```

Unless the `ssl.principal.mapping.rules` property is specified, Kafka checks for the full distinguished name (as previously shown) when applying its ACLs. This property lets you override the default behavior with a principal mapping rule such as that shown here:

```
RULE:^CN=(.*?),OU=(.*?),O=(.*?),L=(.*?),ST=(.*?),C=(.*?)$/$1/L
```

We effectively instruct Kafka to accept any certificate (through the regular expression) and consider only the value of its CN (`$1`) in lowercase (`L`) when matching declared ACLs. We do that by setting the replacement string to `$1` and by setting the optional case matcher to `L` to indicate lowercase. For example, for a client (microservice) that has a certificate whose distinguished name matches

```
CN=orders.ecomm.com,OU= Unknown,O=Unknown,L=Unknown,ST=Unknown,C=Unknown
```

Kafka identifies the client as `orders.ecomm.com`, and we need to set ACLs against that name. When we created certificates for the Order Processing and Buying History microservices in section 9.5.1, we used `orders.ecomm.com` and `bh.ecomm.com`, respectively, as the CN for each microservice.

Once the preceding configurations are done, save and close the server.properties file and restart Kafka. Now that we have enabled ACLs on Kafka, the next step is to define the ACLs on it.

9.7.2   Defining ACLs on Kafka

In this section, we use our command-line tool to define ACLs on Kafka. Because we now have the ACLs enabled on Kafka and the server is up and running, we can proceed to define the rules we need to apply to the relevant topics. We'll set up two rules:

- Allow only the Order Processing microservice to publish events to the `ORDERS` topic (or to be the producer of the `ORDERS` topic).
- Allow only the Buying History microservice to consume events from the `ORDERS` topic (or to be a consumer of the `ORDERS` topic).

Open your command-line tool, navigate to the kafka_home directory, and execute the following command:

```
\> bin/kafka-acls.sh --authorizer-properties \
zookeeper.connect=localhost:2181 \
--add --allow-principal User:"orders.ecomm.com" --producer --topic ORDERS
```

This shows you output similar to the following:

```
Adding ACLs for resource `ResourcePattern(resourceType=TOPIC, name=ORDERS,
patternType=LITERAL)`:
  (principal=User:orders.ecomm.com, host=*, operation=DESCRIBE,
  permissionType=ALLOW)
  (principal=User:orders.ecomm.com, host=*, operation=CREATE,
  permissionType=ALLOW)
  (principal=User:orders.ecomm.com, host=*, operation=WRITE,
  permissionType=ALLOW)
```

As you can observe from the output, we now have an ACL that says the user `orders.ecomm.com` is allowed to create, write to, and describe the `ORDERS` topic. By *create*, it indicates that `orders.ecomm.com` is allowed to create the topic if it doesn't exist. By *write*, it indicates that `orders.ecomm.com` is allowed to publish events to the topic, and by *describe*, it indicates that `orders.ecomm.com` is allowed to view the details of the topic. These operations are allowed from any host because we haven't explicitly mentioned which hosts to restrict these operations to. In case you want to remove the ACL we just created, you can use the following command, but don't run it until we complete this chapter:

```
\> bin/kafka-acls.sh --authorizer-properties \
zookeeper.connect=localhost:2181 --remove \
--allow-principal User:"orders.ecomm.com" --producer --topic ORDERS
```

Next, execute the following command to enable read access to the `ORDERS` topic for our Buying History microservice that has a certificate with the CN `bh.ecomm.com`:

```
\> bin/kafka-acls.sh --authorizer-properties \
zookeeper.connect=localhost:2181 --add \
--allow-principal User:"bh.ecomm.com" --operation Read --topic ORDERS
```

This shows you output similar to the following:

```
Adding ACLs for resource `ResourcePattern(resourceType=TOPIC, name=ORDERS,
patternType=LITERAL)`:
 (principal=User:bh.ecomm.com, host=*, operation-READ, permissionTypc=ALLOW)
```

If you want to remove the ACL we just created, you can use the following command, but don't run it until we complete this chapter:

```
\> bin/kafka-acls.sh --authorizer-properties \
zookeeper.connect=localhost:2181 --remove \
--allow-principal User:"bh.ecomm.com" --operation Read --topic ORDERS
```

You can list the ACLs on the `ORDERS` topic by executing the following command:

```
\> bin/kafka-acls.sh --authorizer-properties \
zookeeper.connect=localhost:2181 --list --topic ORDERS
```

This displays all the ACLs applied on the `ORDERS` topic. You should see output similar to the following:

```
Current ACLs for resource `ResourcePattern(resourceType=TOPIC, name=ORDERS,
patternType=LITERAL)`:
 (principal=User:orders.ecomm.com, host=*, operation=DESCRIBE,
 permissionType=ALLOW)
 (principal=User:orders.ecomm.com, host=*, operation=CREATE,
 permissionType=ALLOW)
 (principal=User:orders.ecomm.com, host=*, operation=WRITE,
 permissionType=ALLOW)
 (principal=User:bh.ecomm.com, host=*, operation=READ,
 permissionType=ALLOW)
```

We now have in place all the ACLs that control access to the ORDERS topic. Assuming that both the Order Processing and Buying History microservices that we created in section 9.6 are running, stop and then restart both. This is required because we restarted the Kafka server.

To test how ACLs work with Kafka, run the following curl command from the chapter09/sample03/orders_ms directory to make an order request to the Order Processing microservice:

```
\> curl -k https://localhost:8080/order -X POST -d @order.json \
-H "Content-Type: application/json" -v
```

You should receive a successful response from this command. Notice the following message printed on the terminal tab that's running the Buying History microservice:

```
Updated buying history of customer with order: <order_id>
```

9.8 Setting up NATS as a message broker

In this section, we take a look at *NATS*, an alternative message broker to Kafka, which can be used by event-driven microservices to exchange messages/events. NATS (https://nats.io/) is an open source, lightweight messaging system designed for cloud-native applications. It is a project of the CNCF.

Similar to Kafka, it too has a concept of publishers and subscribers. NATS publishers send messages to subjects, and subscribers connected to those subjects can receive the messages. A *subject* in NATS is just a string identifier that publishers and subscribers use to find each other. Figure 9.11 illustrates how subjects are used by NATS publishers and subscribers.

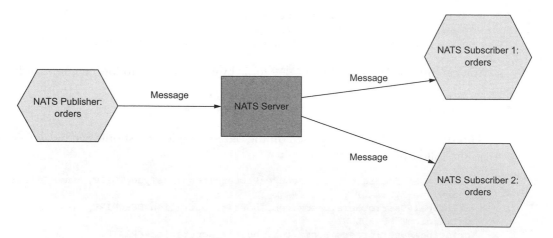

Figure 9.11   Publishers and subscribers connecting to the NATS server on the subject orders

NATS offers an *at-most-once* quality of service for its messages: it will deliver messages only to subscribers connected to and listening on the respective subject. Unlike in Kafka, NATS core does not offer persistent message delivery. If the receiver is not connected to the NATS server at the time of message delivery, it will not receive the message after it reconnects. It is basically a fire-and-forget message delivery system. If the clients require higher levels of message delivery guarantees, you either need to build guarantees into the client applications themselves or use NATS streaming (https:// docs.nats.io/nats-streaming-concepts/intro).

NATS is designed to perform fast processing of small messages, ideally less than 1 MB. However, teams have used NATS in production to exchange messages larger than that, in the 10 MB range. Let's take a quick look at setting up a NATS server and getting a publisher and subscriber to connect to it.

We will be using the NATS Docker image for this, so Docker is a prerequisite to run this sample. Setting up a NATS server through Docker is simple. If you have Docker installed, you just have to open a command-line terminal session and execute the following command:

```
\> docker run -p 4222:4222 -p 8222:8222 -p 6222:6222 \
--name nats-server -ti nats:latest
```

If this is the first time you are running this command, this will download the NATS server Docker image to your local Docker repository and run the Docker container. You should see the following messages after the process has started:

```
Listening for client connections on 0.0.0.0:4222
Server is ready
Listening for route connections on 0.0.0.0:6222
```

We are now ready to connect to the NATS server for sending and receiving messages. To stop the NATS server, you can execute the following command in a new terminal tab:

```
\> docker stop nats-server
```

To start the NATS server again, you can execute the following command:

```
\> docker start nats-server
```

Now that we have the NATS server up and running, the next step is to execute the NATS client and server, which communicate with each other. The code of the client and server can be found in the chapter09/sample05 directory. Open a new command-line terminal, navigate to the sample05/natssub directory, and execute the following command to compile the code of the subscriber (message receiver):

```
\> mvn clean install
```

Once the code is built, you should see a BUILD SUCCESS message on the terminal. You should also see a directory named target being created within the natssub directory.

Execute the following command on your terminal from within the natssub directory to run the NATS subscriber process:

```
\> java -jar target/com.manning.mss.ch09.sample05.natssub-1.0.0.jar
```

This will start the NATS subscriber process, which will be listening on NATS for messages. Next, open a new command-line terminal, navigate to the sample05/natspub directory, and execute the following command to compile the code of the NATS publisher process:

```
\> mvn clean install
```

Once the build is successful, execute the following command to run the NATS publisher:

```
\> java -jar target/com.manning.mss.ch09.sample05.natspub-1.0.0.jar
```

This process will send a message to the NATS server. The NATS subscriber process should receive the message that was sent. If you observe the terminal on which you ran the NATS subscriber process, you should now see a message as follows:

```
Received message: Welcome to NATS
```

To take a look at the code that produced the message, open the file sample05/natspub/src/main/java/com/manning/mss/ch09/sample05/natspub/NatsPublisher.java with a text editor. You will see that the code in the following listing performs this action.

Listing 9.10 Publishing a message via NATS

```
try {
  natsConnection = Nats.connect("nats://localhost:4222");     ⊲──┐ Connects to the
  natsConnection.publish("updates", "Welcome to                    NATS server
                  NATS".getBytes(StandardCharsets.UTF_8));   ⊲──┐ Pushes message to
  natsConnection.flush(Duration.ZERO);              ⊲──                subject "updates"
}
                        Makes sure the message goes
                        through before we close
```

Similarly, open the file sample05/natssub/src/main/java/com/manning/mss/ch09/sample05/natssub/NatsSubscriber.java with a text editor and observe the code in the following listing that prints the message received via NATS.

Listing 9.11 Consuming a message via NATS

```
try {
  natsConnection = Nats.connect("nats://localhost:4222");     ⊲──┐ Connects to the
  Subscription sub = natsConnection.subscribe("updates");    ⊲──┐ NATS server
  Message msg = sub.nextMessage(Duration.ZERO);                    Subscribes to
                                                                   subject "updates"
```

```
    String str = new String(msg.getData(), StandardCharsets.UTF_8);
    System.out.print("Received message: ");
    System.out.println(str);                    <─┐  Prints the
}                                                  │  received message
```

Similar to the options we discussed in securing a Kafka server, the connections to a NATS server can be protected for confidentiality with TLS, and we can use mTLS or JWT to authenticate client applications, which connect to the NATS server. We did not talk about NATS security in detail in this book, but you can always refer to the NATS documentation at https://docs.nats.io/nats-server/configuration/securing_nats.

Summary

- In a typical microservices deployment, the microservice that accepts requests from a client application becomes a trigger for the rest of the microservices involved in the flow of execution. This microservice can initiate both synchronous and asynchronous types of events to other microservices to trigger their execution.
- Reactive programming is a declarative programming paradigm that relies on data streams and the propagation of change events in a system.
- A microservice being directly connected to another microservice causes scalability and maintenance inefficiencies due to its dependency hierarchy. For asynchronous events, we can build reactive microservices that are capable of reacting to events that occur in a system, which reduces dependencies among microservices.
- Apache Kafka is a distributed stream platform that operates similar to message queues.
- In a microservices deployment, we use Kafka as a message broker to deliver events from source microservices to target microservices asynchronously.
- With the reactive pattern, we eliminate direct links between microservices and increase operational efficiencies. This pattern further reduces the response times of the microservices for the users and provides a better foundation for introducing new functionality into the system.
- TLS is used between the microservices and Kafka to encrypt messages being transferred between them.
- Kafka uses mTLS to control which microservices are permitted to connect to it, to authenticate the clients connecting to Kafka.
- Kafka uses ACLs as an authorization mechanism, which either permits or denies various microservices performing different types of actions on Kafka resources such as topics.
- Similar to Kafka, NATS is another popular open source technology that can be used to build reactive microservices.

Part 4

Secure deployment

In part 3, you learned how to secure service-to-service communications in a microservices deployment. But you still have all your microservices deployed on your physical machine. In this part of the book, you'll learn how to extend the samples you had in part 3 so you can deploy them in a containerized environment.

Chapter 10 teaches you how to deploy your microservices in Docker and to secure service-to-service interactions with mTLS and JWT. Also in chapter 10, you'll learn some of the built-in security features related to Docker.

Chapter 11 teaches you how to deploy your microservices as Docker containers in Kubernetes and to secure service-to-service communications with JWT over mTLS.

In chapters 10 and 11, each microservice by itself must worry about doing security processing. In short, each microservice embeds a set of Spring Boot libraries to do security processing. In chapter 12, you'll learn how to offload the security processing overhead from your microservices by using the Istio service mesh.

When you're finished with this part of the book, you'll know how to deploy your microservices in a containerized environment and protect service-to-service communications by using the Istio service mesh.

Conquering container security with Docker

10

This chapter covers

- Securing service-to-service communications with JWT and mTLS in a containerized environment
- Managing secrets in a containerized environment
- Signing and verifying Docker images with Docker Content Trust
- Running Docker Bench for Security

The benefits of microservices architecture come at a cost. Unless you have the proper infrastructure to support microservices development and deployment with a CI/CD pipeline, chances are that you'll more than likely fail to meet your objectives. Let us reiterate: one key objective of microservices architecture is the speed to production. With hundreds of microservices, management becomes a nightmare unless you have the right tools for automation. Packaging, distribution, and testing of microservices in various environments before getting into production in an efficient, less error-prone way is important.

Over time, *Docker* has become the most popular tool (or platform) for packaging and distributing microservices. It provides an abstraction over the physical machine. Docker not only packages your software, but all its dependencies too.

229

In this chapter, we discuss deploying and securing microservices in a containerized environment with Docker. We cover basic constructs of Docker in appendix E, so if you're new to Docker, look at that appendix first. Even if you're familiar with Docker, we still recommend you at least skim through appendix E, as the rest of the chapter assumes you have the basic knowledge it presents.

In practice, you don't have only Docker; Docker is used within a container orchestration framework. A *container orchestration framework* (such as Kubernetes or Docker Swarm) is an abstraction over the network. Container orchestration software like Kubernetes lets you deploy, manage, and scale containers in a highly distributed environment with thousands of nodes or more. In chapter 11, we discuss the role of a container orchestration framework (Kubernetes) in securing microservices. We wanted to highlight this at the beginning of this chapter to set your expectations correctly.

The security of a microservices deployment should be thought of in the context of a container orchestration framework, not just as container security in isolation. Also, an important pattern we see in a containerized deployment is the *Service Mesh* pattern. At a very high level, the Service Mesh pattern deals with service-to-service communications and helps to take most of the burden from microservices and delegate security processing to a proxy. Istio is the most popular service mesh implementation, and in chapter 12, we discuss securing microservices in a containerized environment with Istio. Once again, this is another reason we shouldn't think about container security in isolation when securing microservices.

10.1 Running the security token service on Docker

In chapter 7, you learned about JWT and how to secure microservices with a JWT issued by an STS. The use case from chapter 7 is illustrated in figure 10.1. In this section, we build the same use case, but we deploy STS on Docker.

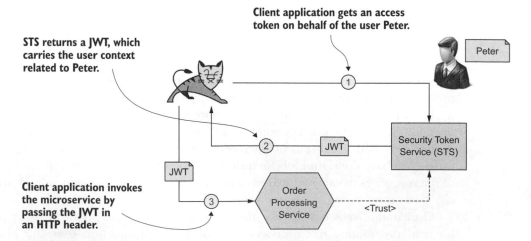

Figure 10.1   The STS issues a JWT self-contained access token to the web application (probably following OAuth 2.0). The web application uses the token to access the Order Processing microservice on behalf of Peter.

The source code related to all the samples in this chapter is available in the https://github.com/microservices-security-in-action/samples GitHub repository, inside the chapter10 directory. The source code of the STS, which is a Spring Boot application developed in Java, is available in the chapter10/sample01 directory.

To build the STS project and create a Docker image, run the first two commands in listing 10.1 from the chapter10/sample01 directory. Then run the third command in listing 10.1 to spin up the STS Docker container from the image you built. (Make sure that you have no other services running on port 8443 on your local machine.) These are standard commands that you'd use in any Docker project (section E.4 of appendix E explains these in detail in case you're not familiar with Docker).

Listing 10.1 Building the STS and creating a Docker image

```
\> mvn clean install
\> docker build -t com.manning.mss.ch10.sample01:v1 .
\> docker run -p 8443:8443 com.manning.mss.ch10.sample01:v1
```

Now let's test the STS with the following `curl` command. This is the same `curl` command we used in section 7.6:

```
\> curl -v -X POST --basic -u applicationid:applicationsecret \
-H "Content-Type: application/x-www-form-urlencoded;charset=UTF-8" \
-k -d "grant_type=password&username=peter&password=peter123&scope=foo" \
https://localhost:8443/oauth/token
```

In this command, the client ID of the web application is `applicationid`, and the client secret (which is hardcoded in the STS) is `applicationsecret`. If everything works fine, the STS returns an OAuth 2.0 access token, which is a JWT (or a JWS, to be precise):

```
{
"access_token":"eyJhbGciOiJSUzI1NiIsInR5cCI6IkpXVCJ9.eyJleHAiOjE1NTEzMTI
zNzYsInVzZXJfbmFtZSI6InBldGVyIiwiYXV0aG9yaXRpZXMiOlsiUk9MRV9VU0VSIl0sImp0
aSI6IjRkMmJiNjQ4LTQ2MWQtNGVlYy1hZTljLTVlYWUxZjA4ZTJhMiIsImNsaWVudF9pZCI6I
mFwcGxpY2F0aW9uaWQiLCJzY29wZSI6WyJmb28iXX0.tr4yUmGLtsH7q9Ge2i7gxyTsOOa0RS
0Yoc2uBuAW5OVIKZcVsIITWV3bDN0FVHBzimpAPy33tvicFROhBFoVThqKXzzG00SkURN5bnQ
4uFLAP0NpZ6BuDjvVmwXNXrQp2lVXl4lQ4eTvuyZozjUSCXzCI1LNw5EFFi22J73g1_mRm2j-
dEhBp1TvMaRKLBDk2hzIDVKzu5oj_gODBFm3a1S-IJjYoCimIm2igcesXkhipRJtjNcrJSegB
bGgyXHVak2gB7I07ryVwl_Re5yX4sV9x6xNwCxc_DgP9hHLzPM8yz_K97jlT6Rr1XZBlVeyjf
Ks_XIXgU5qizRm9mt5xg",
"token_type":"bearer",
"refresh_token":"",
"expires_in":5999,
"scope":"foo",
"jti":"4d2bb648-461d-4eec-ae9c-5eae1f08e2a2"
}
```

10.2 *Managing secrets in a Docker container*

When we created a Docker image for the STS in section 10.1, we missed something very important: we embedded all the keys and the credentials to access the keys in the image itself. When we push this to a Docker registry, anyone having access to the image can figure out all our secrets; oh no, it's the end of the world! Let's see how that's possible.

We've already published the insecure STS Docker image we created in section 10.1 to the Docker Hub as `prabath/insecure-sts-ch10:v1`, and it's available to the public. Anyone can execute the following `docker run` command to fetch the insecure STS image and run it locally. (If you're new to Docker, appendix E teaches you how to publish a Docker image to Docker Hub.)

```
\> docker run -d prabath/insecure-sts-ch10:v1

34839d0c9e3b32b5f4fa6a8b4f7f52c134ed3e198ad739b722ca556903e74fbc
```

Once the container starts, we can use the following command to connect to the container with the container ID and access the running shell. (Use the full container ID from the output of the previous `docker run` command.)

```
\> docker exec -it 34839d0c9e3b32b5f4fa6a8b4f7f52c134… sh
#
```

Now we're on the container's shell and have direct access to its filesystem. Let's first list all the files under the root of the container filesystem:

```
# ls
bin                                        proc
com.manning.mss.ch10.sample01-1.0.0.jar    root
dev                                        run
etc                                        sbin
home                                       srv
keystore.jks                               sys
lib                                        tmp
media                                      usr
mnt                                        var
opt
```

Now we can unzip the com.manning.mss.ch10.sample01-1.0.0.jar file and find all the secrets in the application.properties file:

```
# jar -xvf com.manning.mss.ch10.sample01-1.0.0.jar
# vi  BOOT-INF/classes/application.properties
```

The command displays the content of the application.properties file, which includes the credentials to access the private key that's used by the STS to sign the JWTs it issues, as shown in the following listing.

Listing 10.2   The content of the application.properties file

```
server.port: 8443
server.ssl.key-store: /opt/keystore.jks
server.ssl.key-store-password: springboot          ◁─┐  Keeps the private and public
server.ssl.keyAlias: spring                            keys of the service to use
spring.security.oauth.jwt: true                        in TLS communications
```

```
spring.security.oauth.jwt.keystore.password: springboot
spring.security.oauth.jwt.keystore.alias: jwtkey
spring.security.oauth.jwt.keystore.name: /opt/jwt.jks
```
Keeps the private key, which is used by the STS to sign the JWTs it issues

10.2.1 Externalizing secrets from Docker images

In this section, let's externalize the configuration files from the Docker image we created for the STS. We need to externalize both the keystores (keystore.jks and jwt.jks) and the application.properties files, where all our secrets reside.

Let's create a directory called config under chapter10/sample01 and *move* (not just copy) the application.properties file from the chapter10/sample01/src/main/resources/ directory to the new directory (chapter10/sample01/config). The sample you downloaded from the GitHub already has the config directory; probably you can delete it and create a new one. Then, let's run the following two commands in listing 10.3 from the chapter10/sample01 directory to build a new JAR file without the application.properties file and create a Docker image. This new Docker image won't have the two keystores (keystore.jks and jwt.jks) and the application.properties file in it.

> **Listing 10.3 Building the STS and creating a Docker image with externalized secrets**

```
\> mvn clean install

[INFO] BUILD SUCCESS

\> docker build -t com.manning.mss.ch10.sample01:v2 -f Dockerfile-2 .

Step 1/4 : FROM openjdk:8-jdk-alpine
 ---> 792ff45a2a17
Step 2/4 : ADD target/com.manning.mss.ch10.sample01-1.0.0.jar
com.manning.mss.ch10.sample01-1.0.0.jar
 ---> 2be952989323
Step 3/4 : ENV SPRING_CONFIG_LOCATION=/application.properties
 ---> Running in 9b62fdebd566
Removing intermediate container 9b62fdebd566
 ---> 97077304dbdb
Step 4/4 : ENTRYPOINT ["java", "-jar",
        "com.manning.mss.ch10.sample01-1.0.0.jar"]
 ---> Running in 215919f70683
Removing intermediate container 215919f70683
 ---> e7090e36543b
Successfully built e7090e36543b
Successfully tagged com.manning.mss.ch10.sample01:latest
```

You may notice a difference in this command from the command we ran in listing 10.1 to create a Docker image. In listing 10.3, we pass an extra argument, called -f, with the value Dockerfile-2. This is how we can instruct Docker to use a custom file as the manifest to create a Docker image instead of looking for a file with the name Dockerfile. Let's have a look at the content of Dockerfile-2, as shown in the following listing.

Listing 10.4   The content of `Dockerfile-2`

```
FROM openjdk:8-jdk-alpine
ADD target/com.manning.mss.ch10.sample01-1.0.0.jar \
          com.manning.mss.ch10.sample01-1.0.0.jar
ENV SPRING_CONFIG_LOCATION=/opt/application.properties
ENTRYPOINT ["java", "-jar", \
            "com.manning.mss.ch10.sample01-1.0.0.jar"]
```

The first line of `Dockerfile-2` instructs Docker to fetch the Docker image called `openjdk:8-jdk-alpine` from the Docker registry and, in this case, from the public Docker Hub. This is the base image of the Docker image we want to create. The second line instructs Docker to copy the file com.manning.mss.ch10.sample01-1.0.0.jar from the target directory of the host filesystem to the root of the container filesystem. The third line instructs Docker to create an environment variable called `SPRING _CONFIG_LOCATION` and point it to the /opt/application.properties file. The process running inside the container reads this environment variable to find the location of the application.properties file; then it looks for the file under the /opt directory of the container filesystem. Finally, the fourth line tells Docker the entry point to the container, or which process to run when we start the container.

Unlike the image we created in section 10.1, we don't add any keystore to the image here, and there's no application.properties file inside the image. When we spin up a container from this image, we need to specify from where in the host filesystem the container has to load those three files (two keystores and the application.properties file).

Let's run the commands in the following listing from the chapter10/sample01 directory to spin up a container from the Docker image we just created. If you've carefully looked into the command (listing 10.3) we used to build the Docker image, we tagged it this time with v2, so we need to use the image in the following listing with the v2 tag.

Listing 10.5   Running a Docker container with externalized files

Path from the container filesystem to the keystore that carries TLS keys

Path from the host machine to the keystore that carries TLS keys

Path from the host machine to the keystore that carries the keys to sign JWTs

```
\> export JKS_SOURCE="$(pwd)/keystores/keystore.jks"
\> export JKS_TARGET="/opt/keystore.jks"
\> export JWT_SOURCE="$(pwd)/keystores/jwt.jks"
\> export JWT_TARGET="/opt/jwt.jks"
\> export APP_SOURCE="$(pwd)/config/application.properties"
\> export APP_TARGET="/opt/application.properties"
```

Path from the container filesystem to the keystore that carries the keys to sign JWTs

Path from the host machine to the application.properties file

Path from the container filesystem to the application.properties file

```
\> docker run -p 8443:8443 \
--mount type=bind,source="$JKS_SOURCE",target="$JKS_TARGET" \
--mount type=bind,source="$JWT_SOURCE",target="$JWT_TARGET" \
```

```
--mount type=bind,source="$APP_SOURCE",target="$APP_TARGET" \
com.manning.mss.ch10.sample01:v2
```

This looks different from the `docker run` command we executed in section 10.1. Here we pass three extra `--mount` arguments. The Docker image we used in section 10.1 to run the container had keystore.jks, jwt.jks, and application.properties files built in. Now, because we don't have those files inside the image, each time we execute `docker run`, we need to tell Docker how to load those files from the host filesystem; that's what the `--mount` argument does.

The first `--mount` argument binds the keystore/keystore.jks file from the host filesystem to the /opt/keystore.jks file in the container filesystem; the second `--mount` argument binds the keystore/jwt.jks file from the host filesystem to the /opt/jwt.jks file in the container filesystem; and the third `--mount` argument binds the /config/ application.properties file from the host filesystem to the /opt/application.properties file in the container filesystem. Once we start the container successfully, we see the following logs printed on the terminal:

```
INFO 30901 --- [main] s.b.c.e.t.TomcatEmbeddedServletContainer :
Tomcat started on port(s): 8443 (https)
INFO 30901 --- [main] c.m.m.ch10.sample01.TokenService          :
Started TokenService in 4.729 seconds (JVM running for 7.082)
```

Now let's test the STS with the following `curl` command. This is the same `curl` command we used in section 10.1.2:

```
\> curl -v -X POST --basic -u applicationid:applicationsecret \
-H "Content-Type: application/x-www-form-urlencoded;charset=UTF-8" \
-k -d "grant_type=password&username=peter&password=peter123&scope=foo" \
https://localhost:8443/oauth/token
```

10.2.2 *Passing secrets as environment variables*

Once we externalize the configuration files and keystores from the Docker image, no one will be able to find any secrets in it. But we still have secrets hardcoded in a configuration file that we keep in the host filesystem. Anyone who has access to the host filesystem will be able to find those. In this section, let's see how to remove the secrets from the configuration file (application.properties) and pass them to the container as arguments at runtime.

Let's copy the content from the chapter10/sample01/application.properties file and replace the content in the chapter10/sample01/config/application.properties file with it. The following listing shows the updated content of the chapter10/ sample01/config/application.properties file.

> **Listing 10.6 The sample01/config/application.properties file**

```
server.port: 8443
server.ssl.key-store: /opt/keystore.jks
server.ssl.key-store-password: ${KEYSTORE_SECRET}
```
⟵ **A placeholder to read the password of the keystore.jks file**

```
server.ssl.keyAlias: spring
spring.security.oauth.jwt: true
spring.security.oauth.jwt.keystore.password: ${JWT_KEYSTORE_SECRET}    ◁──┐
spring.security.oauth.jwt.keystore.alias: jwtkey
spring.security.oauth.jwt.keystore.name: /opt/jwt.jks
```
A placeholder to
read the password
of the jwt.jks file

Here, we've removed all the secrets from the application.properties file and replaced
them with two placeholders: `${KEYSTORE_SECRET}` and `${JWT_KEYSTORE
_SECRET}`. Because our change is only in a file we've already externalized from the
Docker image, we don't need to build a new image. Let's spin up a container of the STS
Docker image with the command in the following listing (run from the chapter10/
sample01 directory) with the updated application.properties file.

Listing 10.7   Running a Docker container with externalized files and credentials

```
\> export JKS_SOURCE="$(pwd)/keystores/keystore.jks"
\> export JKS_TARGET="/opt/keystore.jks"
\> export JWT_SOURCE="$(pwd)/keystores/jwt.jks"
\> export JWT_TARGET="/opt/jwt.jks"
\> export APP_SOURCE="$(pwd)/config/application.properties"
\> export APP_TARGET="/opt/application.properties"

\> docker run -p 8443:8443 \
--mount type=bind,source="$JKS_SOURCE",target="$JKS_TARGET" \
--mount type=bind,source="$JWT_SOURCE",target="$JWT_TARGET" \
--mount type=bind,source="$APP_SOURCE",target="$APP_TARGET" \
-e KEYSTORE_SECRET=springboot \
-e JWT_KEYSTORE_SECRET=springboot \
com.manning.mss.ch10.sample01:v2
```
Password to
access the
keystore.jks file

Password to access
the jwt.jks file

Here we pass the values corresponding to the placeholders we kept in the applica-
tion.properties file as an argument to the `docker run` command under the name `-e`.
Once we start the container successfully, we'll see the following logs printed on the
terminal:

```
INFO 30901 --- [main] s.b.c.e.t.TomcatEmbeddedServletContainer :
Tomcat started on port(s): 8443 (https)
INFO 30901 --- [main] c.m.m.ch10.sample01.TokenService        :
Started TokenService in 4.729 seconds (JVM running for 7.082)
```

Now let's test the STS with the following `curl` command. This is the same `curl` command we used in section 10.2.1:

```
\> curl -v -X POST --basic -u applicationid:applicationsecret \
-H "Content-Type: application/x-www-form-urlencoded;charset=UTF-8" \
-k -d "grant_type=password&username=peter&password=peter123&scope=foo" \
https://localhost:8443/oauth/token
```

10.2.3 *Managing secrets in a Docker production deployment*

Both approaches we discussed in sections 10.2.1 and 10.2.2 are fundamental for managing secrets in a production containerized deployment. But neither approach provides a clean solution. In both cases, we keep credentials in cleartext.

As we discussed at the beginning of the chapter, when we deploy Docker in a production setup, we do that with some kind of a container orchestration framework. Kubernetes is the most popular container orchestration framework, while Docker Swarm is the container orchestration framework built into Docker. Both provide better solutions to manage secrets in a containerized environment. In chapter 11, we discuss in detail how to manage secrets with Kubernetes. If you are new to Kubernetes, appendix J provides a comprehensive overview.

10.3 *Using Docker Content Trust to sign and verify Docker images*

In this section, we discuss how to use *Docker Content Trust* (*DCT*) to sign and verify Docker images. DCT uses Notary (https://github.com/theupdateframework/notary) for image signing and verification. *Notary* is an open source project that doesn't have a direct dependency on Docker.

You can use Notary to sign and verify any content, not necessarily only Docker images. As a best practice, when you publish a Docker image to a Docker registry (say, for example, Docker Hub), you need to sign it so anyone who pulls it can verify its integrity before use. Notary is an opinionated implementation of The Update Framework (TUF) that we discuss in section 10.3.1, which makes better security easy.[1]

10.3.1 *The Update Framework*

In 2009, a set of security researchers implemented TUF, which was based on security flaws identified in Linux package managers. It aimed to help developers maintain the security of a software update system, even against attackers who compromise the repository or signing keys.[2] The first referenced implementation of the TUF specification is called Thandy, which is an application updater for the popular software Tor (www.torproject.org). If you're interested in learning TUF in detail, we recommend having a look at the TUF specification available at https://github.com/theupdateframework/specification.

---

[1] An *opinionated implementation* guides you through something in a well-defined way with a concrete set of tools; it gives you fewer options and dictates how to do something. This helps in a way, because when you are given multiple options to pick from, you might struggle to find what is the best.

[2] The Update Framework is a framework for securing software update systems; see https://theupdateframework.github.io/.

10.3.2 *Docker Content Trust*

DCT integrates Notary with Docker (from Docker 1.8 release onward) in an opinionated way. In doing that, DCT doesn't support all the functions Notary does, but only a subset. If you'd like to do some advanced tasks related to key management, you'd still need to use Notary, and a Notary command-line tool comes with the Docker distribution. Once the DCT is set up, it lets developers use `pull`, `push`, `build`, `create`, and `run` Docker commands in the same way as before, but behind the scenes, DCT makes sure all the corresponding images that are published to the Docker registry are signed and that only signed images are pulled from a Docker registry.

When you publish an image to the Docker registry, it's signed by the publisher's (or your) private key. When you interact with a Docker image for the first time (via `pull`, `run`, and so forth), you establish trust with the publisher of that image, and the image's signature is verified against the corresponding public key (of the publisher). If you've used SSH, this model of bootstrapping trust is similar to that. When you SSH a server for the first time, you're asked whether to trust the server, and for subsequent interactions, the SSH client remembers your decision.

10.3.3 *Generating keys*

Let's use the following command to generate keys for signing with DCT. The `docker trust key generate` command generates a public/private key pair with a key ID and stores the corresponding public key in the filesystem under the same directory where you ran the command. You can find the corresponding private key under ~/.docker/ trust/private directory. The key ID is generated by the system and is mapped to the given name of the signer (in this example, `prabath` is the name of the signer). Also, while generating the key, you will be asked to enter a passphrase and will need to know the passphrase when you use the generated key later:

```
\> docker trust key generate prabath

Generating key for prabath...
Enter passphrase for new prabath key with ID 1a60acb:XXXXX
Repeat passphrase for new prabath key with ID 1a60acb: XXXXX
Successfully generated and loaded private key. \
Corresponding public key available: \
                    /Users/prabathsiriwardana/dct/prabath.pub
```

The key generated by the command is called a *delegation key*, which you can find under the same location you ran the command. Since we use `prabath` as the signer in the command, the generated key carries the name `prabath.pub`.

Next, we need to associate the public key of the delegation key with a Docker repository (don't get it confused with a Docker registry; if you're new to Docker, see appendix E for the definition). Run the following command from the same location that you ran the previous one to associate the public key of the delegation key with the `prabath/`

`insecure-sts-ch10` repository. You should use your own repository (instead of `prabath/insecure-sts-ch10`) in the following command, with your own key (instead of `prabath.pub`) and your own signer name (instead of `prabath`). We've already created this repository in Docker Hub with the image we built in section 10.1.

If you get a 401 error response when you run the following command, that means you have not logged into the Docker Hub—and you can use the `docker login` command to log in. When we run the following command for the first time, it generates two more key pairs: the *root key pair* and the *target key pair*, and during the key generation process, for each key pair you will be asked to enter a passphrase:

```
\> docker trust signer add --key prabath.pub prabath \
prabath/insecure-sts-ch10

Adding signer "prabath" to prabath/insecure-sts-ch10...
Initializing signed repository for prabath/insecure-sts-ch10...
You are about to create a new root signing key passphrase. This passphrase
will be used to protect the most sensitive key in your signing system. Please
choose a long, complex passphrase and be careful to keep the password and the
key file itself secure and backed up. It is highly recommended that you use a
password manager to generate the passphrase and keep it safe. There will be no
way to recover this key. You can find the key in your config directory.
Enter passphrase for new root key with ID 494b9b7: XXXXX
Repeat passphrase for new root key with ID 494b9b7: XXXXX
Enter passphrase for new repository key with ID 44f0da3: XXXXX
Repeat passphrase for new repository key with ID 44f0da3: XXXXX
Successfully initialized "prabath/insecure-sts-ch10"
Successfully added signer: prabath to prabath/insecure-sts-ch10
```

The `--key` argument takes the public key (`prabath.pub`) of the delegation key as the value and then the name of the signer (`prabath`). Finally, at the end of the command, you can specify one or more repositories delimited by a space. DCT generates a target key pair for each repository. Because we specify only one repository in the command, it generates only one target key pair. The root key signs each of these target keys. Target keys are also known as *repository keys*. All the generated private keys corresponding to the root, target, and delegation keys in the previous code example are, by default, available in the ~/.docker/trust/private directory. The following shows the scrambled private keys:

```
-----BEGIN ENCRYPTED PRIVATE KEY-----
role: root

MIHuMEkGCSqGSIb3DQEFDTA8MBsGCSqGSIb3DQEFDDAOBAgwNkfrd4OJDQICCAAw
==
-----END ENCRYPTED PRIVATE KEY-----

-----BEGIN ENCRYPTED PRIVATE KEY-----
gun: docker.io/prabath/manning-sts
role: targets
```

MIHuMEkGCSqGSIb3DQEFDTA8MBsGCSqGSIb3DQEFDDAOBAhs5CaEbLT65gICCAAw
==
-----END ENCRYPTED PRIVATE KEY-----

-----BEGIN ENCRYPTED PRIVATE KEY-----
role: prabath

MIHuMEkGCSqGSIb3DQEFDTA8MBsGCSqGSIb3DQEFDDAOBAiX8J+5px9aogICCAAw
==
-----END ENCRYPTED PRIVATE KEY-----

10.3.4 *Signing with DCT*

Let's use the following command to sign the `prabath/insecure-sts-ch10:v1`
Docker image with the delegation key that we generated in the previous section under
the name `prabath`. This is, in fact, the signer's key and you should use your own
image (instead of `prabath/insecure-sts-ch10:v1`) in the following command.
Also please note that here we are signing a Docker image with a tag, not a repository:

```
\> docker trust sign prabath/insecure-sts-ch10:v1

Signing and pushing trust data for local image
prabath/insecure-sts-ch10:v1, may overwrite remote trust data
The push refers to repository [docker.io/prabath/insecure-sts-ch10]
be39ecbbf21c: Layer already exists
4c6899b75fdb: Layer already exists
744b4cd8cf79: Layer already exists
503e53e365f3: Layer already exists
latest: digest:
    sha256:a3186dadb017be1fef8ead32eedf8db8b99a69af25db97955d74a0941a5fb502
size: 1159
Signing and pushing trust metadata
Enter passphrase for prabath key with ID 706043c: XXXXX
Successfully signed docker.io/prabath/insecure-sts-ch10:v1
```

Now we can use the following command to publish the signed Docker image to
Docker Hub:

```
\> docker push prabath/insecure-sts-ch10:v1

The push refers to repository [docker.io/prabath/insecure-sts-ch10]
be39ecbbf21c: Layer already exists
4c6899b75fdb: Layer already exists
744b4cd8cf79: Layer already exists
503e53e365f3: Layer already exists
latest: digest:
    sha256:a3186dadb017be1fef8ead32eedf8db8b99a69af25db97955d74a0941a5fb502
size: 1159
Signing and pushing trust metadata
Enter passphrase for prabath key with ID 706043c:
Passphrase incorrect. Please retry.
Enter passphrase for prabath key with ID 706043c:
Successfully signed docker.io/prabath/insecure-sts-ch10:v1
```

Once we publish the signed image to Docker Hub, we can use the following command to inspect the trust data associated with it:

```
\> docker trust inspect --pretty prabath/insecure-sts-ch10:v1

Signatures for prabath/insecure-sts-ch10:v1
SIGNED TAG          DIGEST                          SIGNERS
v1                  0f99bb308437528da436c13369      prabath


List of signers and their keys for prabath/insecure-sts-ch10:v1

SIGNER              KEYS
prabath             706043cc4ae3


Administrative keys for prabath/insecure-sts-ch10:v1

Repository Key
44f0da3f488ff4d4870b6a635be2af60bcef78ac15ccb88d91223c9a5c3d31ef
Root Key
5824a2be3b4ffe4703dfae2032255d3cbf434aa8d1839a2e4e205d92628fb247
```

10.3.5 *Signature verification with DCT*

Out-of-the-box content trust is disabled on the Docker client side. To enable it, we need to set the DOCKER_CONTENT_TRUST environment variable to 1, as shown in the following command:

```
\> export DOCKER_CONTENT_TRUST=1
```

Once content trust is enabled, the Docker client makes sure all the push, build, create, pull, and run Docker commands are executed only against signed images. The following command shows what happens if we try to run an unsigned Docker image:

```
\> docker run  prabath/insecure-sts-ch10:v2

docker: Error: remote trust data does not exist for
docker.io/prabath/insecure-sts-ch10:v2: notary.docker.io does not have trust
data for docker.io/prabath/insecure-sts-ch10:v2.
```

To disable content trust, we can override the value of the DOCKER_CONTENT_TRUST environment variable to be empty, as shown in the following command:

```
\> export DOCKER_CONTENT_TRUST=
```

10.3.6 *Types of keys used in DCT*

DCT uses five types of keys: the root key, the target key, the delegation key, the timestamp key, and the snapshot key. So far, we know about only the root, the target, and the delegation keys. The target key is also known as repository key. Figure 10.2 shows the hierarchical relationship among the different types of keys.

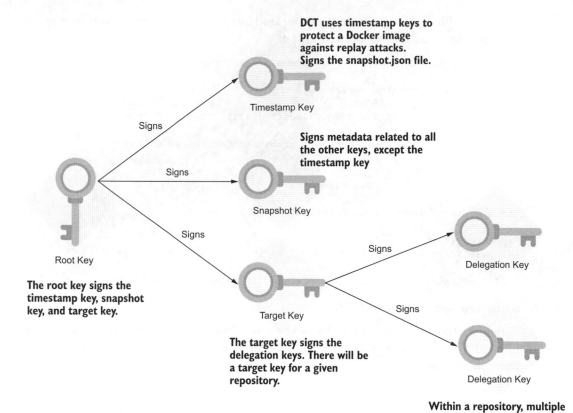

DCT uses timestamp keys to protect a Docker image against replay attacks. Signs the snapshot.json file.

Timestamp Key

Signs metadata related to all the other keys, except the timestamp key

Snapshot Key

Signs

Signs

Signs

Root Key

The root key signs the timestamp key, snapshot key, and target key.

Signs

Target Key

Signs

Signs

Delegation Key

Delegation Key

The target key signs the delegation keys. There will be a target key for a given repository.

Within a repository, multiple delegation keys can be used. A given delegation key signs an image tag.

Figure 10.2   DCT uses a key hierarchy to sign and verify Docker images.

The *root key*, which is also known as the *offline* key, is the most important key in DCT. It has a long expiration and must be protected with highest security. It's recommended to keep it offline (that's how the name *offline key* was derived), possibly in a USB or another kind of offline device. A developer or an organization owns the root key and uses it to sign other keys in DCT.

When you sign a Docker image with a delegation key, a set of trust data gets associated with that image, which you can find in your local filesystem in the ~/.docker/trust/tuf/docker.io/[repository_name]/metadata directory. Also, you will find the same set of files in the same location of your filesystem when you pull a signed Docker image. For example, the metadata for prabath/insecure-sts-ch10 is in the ~/.docker/trust/tuf/docker.io/prabath/insecure-sts-ch10/metadata directory. The following shows the list of files available in the metadata directory:

```
\> cd ~/.docker/trust/tuf/docker.io/prabath/insecure-sts-ch10/metadata
\> ls
```

```
root.json snapshot.json targets targets.json timestamp.json
\> ls targets
prabath.json releases.json
```

The root key signs the root.json file, which lists all the valid public keys corresponding to the `prabath/insecure-sts-ch10` repository. These public keys include the root key, target key, snapshot key, and timestamp key.

The target key (referred from the root.json file) signs the target.json file, which lists all the valid delegation keys. Inside the target.json file, you will find a reference to the delegation key that we generated before under the name `prabath`. DCT generates a *target key* per each Docker repository, and the root key signs each target key. Once we generate the root key, we need it again only when we generate target keys. A given repository has one target key, but multiple delegation keys.

DCT uses these *delegation keys* to sign and push images to repositories. You can use different delegation keys to sign different tags of a given image. If you look at the metadata/target directory, you will find a file named under the delegation key we generated: `prabath.json`. This file, which is signed by the delegation key, carries the hash of the `insecure-sts-ch10:v1` Docker image. If we sign another tag, say `insecure-sts-ch10:v2` with the same delegation key, DTC will update the prabath .json file with the v2 hash.

The *snapshot key* (which is referred from the root.json file) generated by DCT signs the snapshot.json file. This file lists all the valid trust metadata files (except timestamp.json), along with the hash of each file.

The *timestamp key* (which is referred from the root.json file) signs the timestamp.json file, which carries the hash of the currently valid snapshot.json file. The timestamp key has a short expiration period, and each time DCT generates a new timestamp key, it re-signs the timestamp.json file. DCT introduced the timestamp key to protect client applications from replay attacks, and we discuss in the next section how DCT does that.

10.3.7 *How DCT protects the client application from replay attacks*

An attacker can execute a replay attack by replaying previously valid trust metadata files, which we discussed in section 10.3.6, along with an old Docker image. This old Docker image could have some vulnerabilities, which are fixed by the latest image published to the registry by the publisher. However, because of the replay attack by the attacker, the victim would think they had the latest version of the Docker image, which is also properly signed by its publisher.

When you pull an image from a Docker registry, you also get the trust metadata associated with it, which you can find in your local filesystem in the ~/.docker/trust/tuf/docker.io/[repository_name]/metadata directory. However, if the attacker manages to replay old metadata files to your system, you won't have access to the latest. As we discussed in section 10.3.6, DCT introduced the timestamp metadata file to fix this issue.

DCT generates a timestamp file, with an updated timestamp and a version, every time the publisher publishes a Docker image to the corresponding repository. The timestamp key signs this timestamp file, and the timestamp file includes the hash of the snapshot.json file. And, the snapshot.json file includes the hash of the updated (or the new) Docker image.

Whenever a Docker image gets updated at the client side, DCT will download the latest timestamp.json file from the corresponding repository. Then it will validate the signature of the downloaded file (which was replayed by the attacker in this case) and will check whether the version in the downloaded timestamp file is greater than the one in the current timestamp file. If the downloaded file, which is replayed by the attacker, has an older version, DCT will abort the update operation, and will protect the system from the replay attack, which tries to downgrade your Docker image to an older version with vulnerabilities.

10.4 *Running the Order Processing microservice on Docker*

In this section, you'll first build and then deploy the Order Processing microservice on Docker. The Order Processing microservice we use here is the same one that we used in section 7.7. It's a secured microservice; to access it, we need a valid JWT from the STS that we discussed in section 10.1. You can find the complete source code related to the Order Processing microservice in the chapter10/sample02 directory.

First, let's build the project from the chapter10/sample02 directory with the following Maven command. If everything goes well, you should see the BUILD SUCCESS message at the end:

```
\> mvn clean install
[INFO] BUILD SUCCESS
```

Now, let's run the following command to build a Docker image for the Order Processing microservice from the chapter10/sample02 directory. This command uses the Dockerfile manifest, which is inside the chapter10/sample02 directory:

```
\> docker build -t com.manning.mss.ch10.sample02:v1 .
```

Before we proceed further, let's revisit our use case. As illustrated in figure 10.3, we try to invoke the Order Processing microservice from a token issued by the STS. The client application has to get a token from the STS and then pass it to the Order Processing microservice. Next, the Order Processing microservice talks to the STS to get its public key, which corresponds to the private key used by the STS to sign the token it issued. This is the only communication that happens between the Order Processing microservice and the STS. If you check the application.properties file in the chapter10/sample02/config directory, you'll find a property called security.oauth2 .resource.jwt.keyUri, which points to the STS.

To enable direct communication between the containers running the Order Processing microservice and the STS, we need to create a user-defined network. When two Docker containers are in the same user-defined network, they can talk to each other by using the container name. The following command creates a user-defined

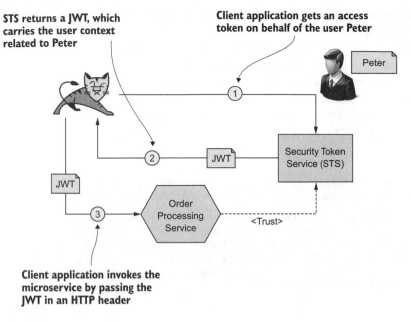

STS returns a JWT, which carries the user context related to Peter

Client application gets an access token on behalf of the user Peter

Client application invokes the microservice by passing the JWT in an HTTP header

Figure 10.3 STS issues a JWT access token to the web application. The web application uses it to access the microservice on behalf of the user, Peter.

network called `manning-network`. (If you're new to Docker, appendix E provides more Docker networking options.)

```
\> docker network create manning-network

06d1307dc12d01f890d74cb76b5e5a16ba75c2e8490c718a67f7d6a02c802e91
```

Now let's spin up the STS from the chapter10/sample01 directory with the commands in the following listing, which attach it to the `manning-network` we just created.

Listing 10.8 Running a Docker container attached to a custom network

```
\> export JKS_SOURCE="$(pwd)/keystores/keystore.jks"
\> export JKS_TARGET="/opt/keystore.jks"
\> export JWT_SOURCE="$(pwd)/keystores/jwt.jks"
\> export JWT_TARGET="/opt/jwt.jks"
\> export APP_SOURCE="$(pwd)/config/application.properties"
\> export APP_TARGET="/opt/application.properties"

\> docker run -p 8443:8443 \
--name sts --net manning-network  \            ◁── Defines a name of the
--mount type=bind,source="$JKS_SOURCE",target="$JKS_TARGET" \   container and attaches it
--mount type=bind,source="$JWT_SOURCE",target="$JWT_TARGET" \   to the manning-network
--mount type=bind,source="$APP_SOURCE",target="$APP_TARGET" \
-e KEYSTORE_SECRET=springboot \
-e JWT_KEYSTORE_SECRET=springboot \
com.manning.mss.ch10.sample01:v2
```

Here we use the `--net` argument to specify the name of the network, and the `--name` argument to specify the name of the container. This container is now accessible using the container name by any container in the same network. Also, the command uses the STS image we published to Docker Hub in section 10.2. Make sure that your `--mount` arguments in the previous command point to the correct file locations. If you run the command from chapter10/sample01, it should work just fine.

Next, let's spin up the Order Processing microservice from the image we created at the beginning of this section. Execute the commands in the following listing from within the chapter10/sample02 directory.

Listing 10.9   Running the Order Processing microservice attached to a custom network

```
\> export JKS_SOURCE="$(pwd)/keystores/keystore.jks"
\> export JKS_TARGET="/opt/keystore.jks"
\> export TRUST_SOURCE="$(pwd)/keystores/trust-store.jks"
\> export TRUST_TARGET="/opt/trust-store.jks"
\> export APP_SOURCE="$(pwd)/config/application.properties"
\> export APP_TARGET="/opt/application.properties"


\> docker run -p 9443:9443 \                              ◁──── Attaches to the
--net manning-network  \                                        manning-network
--mount type=bind,source="$JKS_SOURCE",target="$JKS_TARGET" \
--mount type=bind,source="$TRUST_SOURCE",target="$TRUST_TARGET" \
--mount type=bind,source="$APP_SOURCE",target="$APP_TARGET" \
-e KEYSTORE_SECRET=springboot \
-e TRUSTSTORE_SECRET=springboot \
com.manning.mss.ch10.sample02:v1
```

We pass the keystore.jks, trust-store.jks, and application.properties files as `--mount` arguments. If you look at the application.properties file in the chapter10/sample02/config directory, you'll find a property called `security.oauth2.resource.jwt` `.keyUri`, which points to the endpoint `https://sts:8443/oauth/token_key` with the hostname of the STS container (`sts`).

To invoke the Order Processing microservice with proper security, you need to get a JWT from the STS using the following `curl` command. For clarity, we removed the long JWT in the response and replaced it with the value `jwt_access_token`:

```
\> curl -v -X POST --basic -u applicationid:applicationsecret \
-H "Content-Type: application/x-www-form-urlencoded;charset=UTF-8" \
-k -d "grant_type=password&username=peter&password=peter123&scope=foo" \
https://localhost:8443/oauth/token

{
"access_token":"jwt_access_token",
"token_type":"bearer",
"refresh_token":"",
"expires_in":1533280024,
"scope":"foo"
}
```

Now let's invoke the Order Processing microservice with the JWT you got from this `curl` command. Using the following `curl` command, set the same JWT we got from the STS, in the HTTP Authorization Bearer header and invoke the Order Processing microservice. Because the JWT is a little lengthy, you can use a small trick when using the `curl` command. First, export the JWT to an environment variable (`TOKEN`). Then use that environment variable in your request to the Order Processing microservice:

```
\> export TOKEN=jwt_access_token
\> curl -k -H "Authorization: Bearer $TOKEN" \
https://localhost:9443/orders/11

{
  "customer_id":"101021",
  "order_id":"11",
  "payment_method":{
    "card_type":"VISA",
    "expiration":"01/22",
    "name":"John Doe",
    "billing_address":"201, 1st Street, San Jose,CA"
  },
  "items":[
    {
      "code":"101",
      "qty":1
    },
    {
      "code":"103",
      "qty":5
    }
  ],
  "shipping_address":"201, 1st Street, San Jose, CA"
}
```

10.5 Running containers with limited privileges

In any operating system, there's a super user or an administrator who can basically do anything. This user is called *root* in most of the Linux distributions. Traditionally, in the Linux kernel, there are two types of processes: privileged processes and unprivileged processes. Any *privileged process* runs with the special user ID 0, which belongs to the root user. Any process carrying a nonzero user ID is an *unprivileged process*. When performing a task, a privileged process bypasses all the kernel-level permission checks, while all the unprivileged processes are subjected to a permission check. This approach gives too much power to the root user; in any case, too much power is dangerous.

All Docker containers, by default, run as the root user. Does that mean anyone having access to the container can do anything to the host filesystem from a container? In appendix E (section E.13.4), we discuss how Docker provides process isolation with six namespaces. In Linux, a namespace partitions kernel resources so that each running process has its own independent view of those resources. The mount namespace (one of the six namespaces) helps isolate one container's view of the filesystem from other containers, as well from the host filesystem.

Each container sees its own /usr, /var, /home, /opt, and /dev directories. Any change you make as the root user within a container remains inside the container filesystem. But when you use a volume (see appendix E, section E.12), which maps a location in the container filesystem to the host filesystem, the root user can be destructive. Also, an attacker having access to a container running as root can use root privileges to install tools within the container and use those tools to find any vulnerability in other services in the network. In the following sections, we explore the options available to run a container as an unprivileged process.

10.5.1 *Running a container with a nonroot user*

There are two approaches to running a container with a nonroot user. One way is to use the flag `--user` (or `-u`) in the `docker run` command. The other way is to define the user you want to run the container in the Dockerfile itself. Let's see how the first approach works. In the following command, we start a Docker container from the `prabath/insecure-sts-ch10:v1` image that we've already published to Docker Hub:

```
\> docker run --name insecure-sts prabath/insecure-sts-ch10:v1
```

Let the container run, and use the following command from a different terminal to connect to the filesystem of the running container (`insecure-sts` is the name of the container we started in the previous command):

```
\> docker exec -it insecure-sts sh
#
```

Now you're connected to the container filesystem. You can try out any available commands in Alpine Linux there. The `id` command gives you the user ID (`uid`) and the group ID (`gid`) of the user who runs the container:

```
# id
uid=0(root) gid=0(root)
```

Let's exit from the container, and remove `insecure-sts` with the following command run from a different terminal. The `-f` option in the command removes the container forcefully, even if it is not stopped:

```
\> docker rm -f insecure-sts
```

The following command runs `insecure-sts` from the `prabath/insecure-sts-ch10:v1` image with the `--user` flag. This flag instructs Docker to run the container with the user having the user ID `1000` and the group ID `800`:

```
\> docker run --name insecure-sts --user 1000:800 \
prabath/insecure-sts-ch10:v1
```

Again, let the container run and use the following command from a different terminal to connect to the filesystem of the running container to find the user ID (`uid`) and the group ID (`gid`) of the user who runs the container:

```
\> docker exec -it insecure-sts sh

# id
uid=1000 gid=800
```

The second approach to run a container as a nonroot user is to define the user we want to run the container in the Dockerfile itself. This is a good approach if you're the developer who builds the Docker images, but it won't help if you're just the user. The first approach helps in such a case. In the following listing, let's have a look at the Dockerfile we used in section 10.1. You can find the source code related to this sample inside the chapter10/sample01 directory.

Listing 10.10 The content of the Dockerfile

```
FROM openjdk:8-jdk-alpine
ADD target/com.manning.mss.ch10.sample01-1.0.0.jar \
com.manning.mss.ch10.sample01-1.0.0.jar
ENV SPRING_CONFIG_LOCATION=/application.properties
ENTRYPOINT ["java", "-jar", "com.manning.mss.ch10.sample01-1.0.0.jar"]
```

In the code, there's no instruction to define a user to run this container in the Dockerfile. In such a case, Docker looks for the base image, which is openjdk:8-jdk-alpine. You can use the following docker inspect command to find out the details of a Docker image. It produces a lengthy output, but if you look for the User element under the ContainerConfig element, you can find out who the user is:

```
\> docker inspect openjdk:8-jdk-alpine

[
  {
    "ContainerConfig": {
      "User": ""
    }
  }
]
```

According to the output, even the base image (openjdk:8-jdk-alpine) doesn't instruct Docker to run the corresponding container as a nonroot user. In such a case, by default, Docker uses the root user to run the container. To fix that, we need to update our Dockerfile with the USER instruction, which asks Docker to run the corresponding container as a user with the user ID 1000.

Listing 10.11 The updated content of the Dockerfile with the USER instruction

```
FROM openjdk:8-jdk-alpine
ADD target/com.manning.mss.ch10.sample01-1.0.0.jar \
com.manning.mss.ch10.sample01-1.0.0.jar
ENV SPRING_CONFIG_LOCATION=/application.properties
USER 1000
ENTRYPOINT ["java", "-jar", "com.manning.mss.ch10.sample01-1.0.0.jar"]
```

10.5.2 *Dropping capabilities from the root user*

Linux kernel 2.2 introduced a new feature called *capabilities*, which categorizes all the privileged operations a root user can perform. For example, the `cap_chown` capability lets a user execute the `chown` operation, which can be used to change the user ID (uid) and/or group ID (gid) of a file. All these capabilities can be independently enabled or disabled on the root user. This approach lets you start a Docker container as the root user, but with a limited set of privileges.

Let's use the Docker image we created in section 10.1 to experiment with this approach. The following command starts a Docker container from the `prabath/insecure-sts-ch10:v1` image, which we already published to Docker Hub:

```
\> docker run --name insecure-sts prabath/insecure-sts-ch10:v1
```

Let the container run, and use the following command (as in section 10.5.1) from a different terminal to connect to the filesystem of the running container to find the user ID (uid) and the group ID (gid) of the user who runs the container:

```
\> docker exec -it insecure-sts sh

# id
uid=0(root) gid=0(root)
```

To find out which capabilities the root user has on the system, we need to run a tool called getpcaps, which comes as part of the libcap package. Because the default distribution of Alpine Linux does not have this tool, we'll use the Alpine package manager (apk) to install libcap with the following command. Because we're still inside the container filesystem, this installation has no impact on the host filesystem:

```
# apk add libcap

fetch http://dl-cdn.alpinelinux.org/alpine/v3.9/main/x86_64/APKINDEX.tar.gz
fetch http://dl-cdn.alpinelinux.org/alpine/v3.9/community/x86_64/
      APKINDEX.tar.gz
(1/1) Installing libcap (2.26-r0)
Executing busybox-1.29.3-r10.trigger
OK: 103 MiB in 55 packages
```

Once the installation completes successfully, we can use the following command to find out the capabilities associated with the root user:

```
# getpcaps root

Capabilities for `root': =
cap_chown,cap_dac_override,cap_fowner,cap_fsetid,cap_kill,cap_setgid,
cap_setuid,cap_setpcap,cap_net_bind_service,cap_net_raw,cap_sys_chroot,
cap_mknod,cap_audit_write,cap_setfcap+eip
```

Let's remove `insecure-sts` with the following command run from a different terminal:

```
\> docker rm -f insecure-sts
```

The following command runs the `insecure-sts` container from the `prabath/insecure-sts-ch10:v1` image, with the `--cap-drop` flag. This flag instructs Docker to drop the `chown` capability from the root user who runs the container. The Linux kernel prefixes all capability constants with `cap_`; for example, `cap_chown`, `cap_kill`, `cap_setuid`, and so on. Docker capability constants aren't prefixed with `cap_` but otherwise match the kernel's constants; for example, `chown` instead of `cap_chown`:

```
\> docker run --name insecure-sts --cap-drop chown \
prabath/insecure-sts-ch10:v1
```

Let the container run, and use the following command from a different terminal to connect to the filesystem of the running container:

```
\> docker exec -it insecure-sts sh
```

Because we started a new container, and because the container filesystem is immutable, we need to install libcap again using the following command:

```
# apk add libcap
```

If you check the capabilities of the root user again, you'll see that the `cap_chown` capability is missing:

```
# getpcaps root
```

```
Capabilities for `root': =
cap_dac_override,cap_fowner,cap_fsetid,cap_kill,cap_setgid,cap_setuid,
cap_setpcap,cap_net_bind_service,cap_net_raw,cap_sys_chroot,cap_mknod,
cap_audit_write,cap_setfcap+eip
```

One main benefit of capabilities is that you don't need to know the user who runs the container. The capabilities you define in the `docker run` command are applicable to any user who runs the container.

Just as we dropped some capabilities in the `docker run` command, we can also add those. The following command drops all the capabilities and adds only one capability:

```
\> docker run --name insecure-sts --cap-drop ALL \
--cap-add audit_write  prabath/insecure-sts-ch10:v1
```

10.6 *Running Docker Bench for security*

Docker Bench for Security is a script that checks a Docker deployment for common, well-known best practices as defined by the Center for Internet Security (CIS) in the Docker Community Edition Benchmark document (https://downloads.cisecurity .org). It's maintained as an open source project in the Git repository: https://github .com/docker/docker-bench-security.

This script can be executed either by itself or as a Docker container. The following command uses the second approach, where we run Docker Bench for Security with the Docker image docker/docker-bench-security. It checks the Docker host configuration, Docker daemon configuration, all the container images available in the host machine, and container runtimes for possible vulnerabilities. Here we've truncated the output to show you only the important areas covered by the Docker for Security Bench at a high level:

```
\> docker run -it --net host --pid host \
--cap-add audit_control -v /var/lib:/var/lib \
-v /var/run/docker.sock:/var/run/docker.sock \
-v /etc:/etc --label docker_bench_security \
docker/docker-bench-security

# ------------------------------------------------------------------------
# Docker Bench for Security v1.3.0
#
# Docker, Inc. (c) 2015-
#
# Checks for dozens of common best practices around deploying Docker
containers in production.
# Inspired by the CIS Docker 1.13 Benchmark.
# ------------------------------------------------------------------------
[INFO] 1 - Host Configuration
[WARN] 1.1  - Create a separate partition for containers
[INFO] 1.2  - Harden the container host
[PASS] 1.3  - Keep Docker up to date

[INFO] 2 - Docker Daemon Configuration
[WARN] 2.1  - Restrict network traffic between containers
[PASS] 2.2  - Set the logging level
[PASS] 2.3  - Allow Docker to make changes to iptables

[INFO] 3 - Docker Daemon Configuration Files
[INFO] 3.1  - Verify that docker.service file ownership is
set to root:root
[INFO]       * File not found
[INFO] 3.2  - Verify that docker.service file permissions
are set to 644 or more restrictive
[INFO]       * File not found

[INFO] 4 - Container Images and Build Files
[WARN] 4.1  - Create a user for the container
[WARN]       * Running as root: affectionate_lichterman
[INFO] 4.2  - Use trusted base images for containers

[INFO] 5 - Container Runtime
[WARN] 5.1  - Do not disable AppArmor Profile
[WARN]       * No AppArmorProfile Found: affectionate_lichterman
[WARN] 5.2  - Verify SELinux security options, if applicable

[INFO] 6 - Docker Security Operations
[INFO] 6.1  - Perform regular security audits of your
host system and containers
[INFO] 6.2  - Monitor Docker containers usage, performance
and metering
```

Apart from Docker Bench for Security, a few other alternatives can scan Docker images for known vulnerabilities. Clair is one such open source project (https://github.com/quay/clair) backed by CoreOS (and now RedHat). Anchore (https://github.com/anchore/anchore-engine) is another popular open source project for analyzing vulnerabilities in containers.

10.7 *Securing access to the Docker host*

In appendix E, section E.3, we discuss the high-level architecture of Docker. If you're new to Docker, we recommend you read through that first.

Figure 10.4 (copied from appendix E) illustrates the communication between a Docker client and a Docker host. If you want to intercept the communication between the client and host and see what's going on, you can use a tool like socat (see appendix E, section E.15).

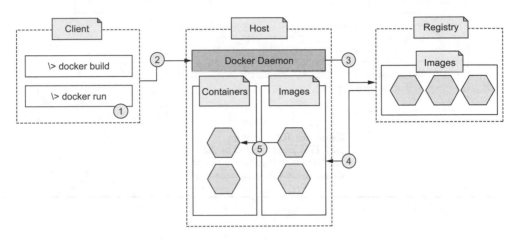

Figure 10.4 In this high-level Docker component architecture, the Docker client talks to the Docker daemon running on the Docker host over a REST API to perform various operations on Docker images and containers.

So far in this chapter, most of the Docker commands we used via the Docker client assumed we ran both the Docker client and the daemon in the same machine. In this section, we discuss how to set up a Docker host to accept requests securely from a remote Docker client. In practice, this isn't the case when we run Docker with Kubernetes (see appendix J). You don't need direct access to the Docker daemon, but only to the Kubernetes API server. In chapter 11, we discuss securing access to the Kubernetes API server. Still, many people run Docker without Kubernetes; for example, those who use the CI/CD tools to spin up Docker containers that connect remotely to a Docker host. In such cases, we need to expose the Docker daemon securely to the remote clients.

10.7.1 *Enabling remote access to the Docker daemon*

The Docker daemon supports listening on three types of sockets: UNIX, TCP, and FD (file descriptor). Enabling the *TCP socket* lets your Docker client talk to the daemon remotely. But if you run the Docker host on a Mac, you'll find it hard to enable the TCP socket on the Docker daemon. Here, we follow a workaround that works across any operating system and gives you more flexibility to control access to Docker APIs. Figure 10.5 illustrates what we want to build.

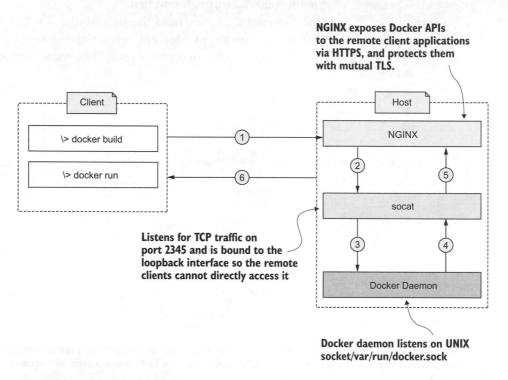

Figure 10.5   Exposing Docker APIs securely to remote clients via NGINX. Socat is used as a traffic forwarder between NGINX and the Docker daemon.

As per figure 10.5, we run socat as a traffic-forwarder on the same machine that runs the Docker daemon. It listens for TCP traffic on port 2345 and forwards that to the UNIX socket that the Docker daemon listens to. Then we have a NGINX (http:// nginx.org/en/docs/) instance, which acts as a reverse proxy to socat. All the external Docker clients talk to the Docker daemon via NGINX.

In this section, we're going to set up NGINX and socat with Docker Compose. If you're new to Docker Compose, we recommend you read through section E.16 of appendix E. The following listing shows the complete docker-compose.yaml file. You can find the same in the chapter10/sample03 directory.

Listing 10.12 The docker-compose.yaml file

```
version: '3'
services:
 nginx:
  image: nginx:alpine
  volumes:
  - ./nginx.conf:/etc/nginx/nginx.conf
  ports:
  - "8080:8080"
  depends_on:
  - "socat"
 socat:
  image: alpine/socat
  volumes:
  - /var/run/docker.sock:/var/run/docker.sock
  ports:
  - "2345:2345"
  command: TCP-L:2345,fork,reuseaddr,bind=socat UNIX:/var/run/docker.sock
```

This defines two services: one for NGINX and the other for socat. The NGINX service uses the `nginx:alpine` Docker image, and the socat service uses the `alpine/socat` Docker image. For the NGINX image, we have a bind mount that mounts the nginx.conf file from the chapter10/sample03 directory of the host filesystem to the /etc/nginx/nginx.conf file of the container filesystem. This is the main NGINX configuration file that forwards all the traffic it gets to socat. The following listing shows the NGINX configuration.

Listing 10.13 The nginx.conf file

```
events {}
http {
    server {
        listen 8080;
        location / {
            proxy_pass          http://socat:2345/;
            proxy_redirect      off;
            proxy_set_header    Host $host;
            proxy_set_header    X-Real-IP $remote_addr;
            proxy_set_header    X-Forwarded-For $proxy_add_x_forwarded_for;
            proxy_set_header    X-Forwarded-Host $server_name;
        }
    }
}
```

For the socat image, we have a bind mount that mounts the /var/run/docker.sock file from the host filesystem to the /var/run/docker.sock file of the container filesystem. This is the file that represents the UNIX socket the Docker daemon listens to on the host machine. When we do this bind mounting, the container that runs socat can write directly to the UNIX socket on the host filesystem so that the Docker daemon gets the messages. Let's have a look at the following line, which is the last line in listing 10.12:

```
command: TCP-L:2345,fork,reuseaddr,bind=socat UNIX:/var/run/docker.sock
```

The TCP-L:2345 flag instructs socat to listen on port 2345 for TCP traffic. The fork flag enables socat to handle each arriving packet by its own subprocess. When we use fork, socat creates a new process for each newly accepted connection. The bind=127.0.0.1 flag instructs socat to listen only on the loopback interface, so no one outside the host machine can directly talk to socat. UNIX:/var/run/docker .sock is the address of the UNIX socket where the Docker daemon accepts connections. In effect, the command asks socat to listen for TCP traffic on port 2345, log it, and then forward it to the UNIX socket /var/run/docker.sock. Let's run the following command from the chapter10/sample03 directory to start both the NGINX and socat containers:

```
\> docker-compose up

Pulling socat (alpine/socat:)...
latest: Pulling from alpine/socat
ff3a5c916c92: Pull complete
abb964a97c4c: Pull complete
Pulling nginx (nginx:alpine)...
alpine: Pulling from library/nginx
e7c96db7181b: Already exists
f0e40e45c95e: Pull complete
Creating sample03_socat_1 ... done
Creating sample03_nginx_1 ... done
Attaching to sample03_socat_1, sample03_nginx_1
```

To make sure everything works fine, you can run the following command from the Docker client machine with the proper NGINX hostname. It should return a JSON payload that carries Docker image details:

```
\> curl http://nginx-host:8080/v1.39/images/json
```

10.7.2 Enabling mTLS at the NGINX server to secure access to Docker APIs

In this section, we'll see how to secure the APIs exposed by the NGINX server with mTLS, so that all the Docker APIs will be secured too. To do that, we need to create a public/private key pair for the NGINX server as well as for the Docker client. The Docker client uses its key pair to authenticate to the NGINX server.

GENERATING KEYS AND CERTIFICATES FOR THE NGINX SERVER AND THE DOCKER CLIENT

Here we introduce a single script to perform all the actions to create keys for the CA, NGINX server, and Docker client. The CA signs both the NGINX certificate and Docker client's certificate. We run OpenSSL in a Docker container to generate keys. OpenSSL is a commercial-grade toolkit and cryptographic library for TLS, available for multiple platforms. Refer to appendix G to find more details on OpenSSL and key generation. To spin up the OpenSSL Docker container, run the following command from the chapter10/sample03/keys directory:

```
\> docker run -it -v $(pwd):/export prabath/openssl
#
```

This `docker run` command starts OpenSSL in a Docker container with a bind mount, which maps the chapter10/sample03/keys directory (or the current directory, which is indicated by `$(pwd)`) from the host filesystem to the /export directory of the container filesystem. This bind mount lets you share part of the host filesystem with the container filesystem. When the OpenSSL container generates certificates, those are written to the /export directory of the container filesystem. Because we have a bind mount, everything inside the /export directory of the container filesystem is also accessible from the chapter10/sample03/keys directory of the host filesystem.

When you run the `docker run` command for the first time, it can take a couple of minutes to execute and should end with a command prompt where you can execute this script to create all the keys:

```
# sh /export/gen-key.sh
# exit
```

Now, if you look at the chapter10/sample03/keys directory in the host filesystem, you'll find the following set of files. If you want to understand what happens in the script, check appendix G:

- *ca_key.pem and ca_cert.pem in the chapter10/sample03/keys/ca directory*—ca_key.pem is the private key of the CA, and ca_cert.pem is the public key.
- *nginx_key.pem and nginx_cert.pem in the chapter10/sample03/keys/nginx directory*—nginx_key.pem is the private key of the NGINX server, and nginx_cert.pem is the public key, which is signed by the CA.
- *docker_key.pem and docker_cert.pem in the chapter10/sample03/keys/docker directory*—docker_key.pem is the private key of the Docker client, and docker_cert.pem is the public key, which is signed by the CA. The Docker client uses these keys to authenticate to the NGINX server

PROTECTING THE NGINX SERVER WITH MTLS

In this section, we set up NGINX to work with mTLS with the keys we generated in the previous section. If you're running the NGINX container from section 10.7.1, stop it first by pressing Ctrl-C on the terminal that runs the container.

Listing 10.14 shows the content from the nginx-secured.conf file in the chapter10/sample03 directory. This is the same file in listing 10.13 with some new parameters related to the TLS configuration. The parameter `ssl_certificate` instructs NGINX to look for the server certificate at the /etc/nginx/nginx_cert.pem location in the container filesystem.

> **Listing 10.14 The nginx-secured.conf file**

```
events {}
http {
    server {
        listen              8443 ssl;
        server_name         nginx.ecomm.com;
```

```
ssl_certificate            /etc/nginx/nginx_cert.pem;
ssl_certificate_key        /etc/nginx/nginx_key.pem;
ssl_protocols              TLSv1.2;
ssl_verify_client          on;
ssl_client_certificate  /etc/nginx/ca_cert.pem;
location / {
    proxy_pass             http://socat:2345/;
    proxy_redirect         off;
    proxy_set_header       Host $host;
    proxy_set_header       X-Real-IP $remote_addr;
    proxy_set_header       X-Forwarded-For $proxy_add_x_forwarded_for;
    proxy_set_header       X-Forwarded-Host $server_name;
}
    }
}
```

Because we keep all the key files in the host filesystem in the updated docker-compose configuration file (listing 10.15), we have a new set of bind mounts. From the host filesystem, we map sample03/keys/nginx/nginx_cert.pem to the /etc/nginx/nginx_cert .pem file in the container filesystem. In the same way, we have a bind mount for the private key (ssl_certificate_key) of the NGINX server. To enable mTLS, we set the value of ssl_verify_client to on as in listing 10.14, and the ssl_client _certificate parameter points to a file that carries the public keys of all trusted CAs. In other words, we allow any client to access the Docker API if the client brings a certificate issued by a trusted CA.

Now, we need to update the docker-compose configuration to use the new nginx-secured.conf file. The following listing shows the updated docker-compose configuration, which is also available in the chapter10/sample03/docker-compose-secured .yaml file.

Listing 10.15   The updated docker-compose-secured.yaml file

```
services:
 nginx:
  image: nginx:alpine
  volumes:
  - ./nginx-secured.conf:/etc/nginx/nginx.conf
  - ./keys/nginx/nginx_cert.pem:/etc/nginx/nginx_cert.pem
  - ./keys/nginx/nginx_key.pem:/etc/nginx/nginx_key.pem
  - ./keys/ca/ca_cert.pem:/etc/nginx/ca_cert.pem
  ports:
  - "8443:8443"
  depends_on:
  - "socat"
 socat:
  image: alpine/socat
  volumes:
  - /var/run/docker.sock:/var/run/docker.sock
  ports:
  - "2345:2345"
  command: TCP-L:2345,fork,reuseaddr,bind=socat UNIX:/var/run/docker.sock
```

Let's run the following command to start both the secured NGINX and socat containers from the chapter10/sample03 directory. This command points to the docker-compose-secured.yaml file, which carries the new Docker Compose configuration:

```
\> docker-compose -f docker-compose-secured.yaml up
```

To make sure everything works fine, you can run the following command from the chapter10/sample03 directory of the Docker client machine with the proper NGINX hostname. Here we use the –k option to instruct curl to ignore any HTTPS server certificate validation. Still, this command will fail because we've now secured all Docker APIs with mTLS:

```
\> curl -k https://nginx-host:8443/v1.39/images/json
```

The following command shows how to use curl with the proper client-side certificates. Here, we use the key pair that we generated for the Docker client. This should return a JSON payload that carries the Docker image details:

```
\> curl --cacert keys/ca/ca_cert.pem --cert keys/nginx/nginx_cert.pem \
--key keys/nginx/nginx_key.pem \
--resolve 'nginx.ecomm.com:8443:10.0.0.128' \
https://nginx.ecomm.com:8443/v1.39/images/json
```

The --cacert argument in the command points to the public key of the CA, and the --cert and --key parameters point to the public key and the private key, respectively, that we generated in the previous section for the Docker client. In the API endpoint, the hostname we use must match the CN of the certificate we use for NGINX; otherwise, certificate validation fails. Then again, because we don't have a DNS entry for this hostname, we instruct curl to resolve it to the IP address 10.0.0.128 by using the --resolve argument; you probably can use 127.0.0.1 as the IP address if you run curl from the same machine where the Docker daemon runs.

CONFIGURING THE DOCKER CLIENT TO TALK TO THE SECURED DOCKER DAEMON

In this section, we configure the Docker client to talk to the Docker daemon via the secured NGINX server. The following command instructs the Docker client to use nginx.ecomm.com as the Docker host and 8443 as the port:

```
\> export DOCKER_HOST=nginx.ecomm.com:8443
```

Because we haven't set up nginx.ecomm.com in a DNS server, we need to update the /etc/hosts file of the machine, which runs the Docker client, with a hostname-to-IP-address mapping. If you run both the Docker daemon and the client on the same machine, you can use 127.0.0.1 as the IP address of the Docker daemon:

```
10.0.0.128 nginx.ecomm.com
```

Now run the following Docker client command from the same terminal where you exported the DOCKER_HOST environment variable. The tlsverify argument instructs the Docker client to use TLS to connect to the Docker daemon and verify the remote certificate. The `tlskey` and `tlscert` arguments point to the private key and the public key of the Docker client, respectively. These are the keys that we generated in the previous section. The `tlscacert` argument points to the public key of the CA:

```
\> docker --tlsverify --tlskey keys/docker/docker_key.pem \
--tlscert keys/docker/docker_cert.pem \
--tlscacert keys/ca/ca_cert.pem images
```

If you want to make the command look simple, we can replace the default keys that come with the Docker client, with the ones we generated. Replace the following:

- ~/.docker/key.pem with keys/docker/docker_key.pem
- ~/.docker/cert.pem with keys/docker/docker_cert.pem
- ~/.docker/ca.pem with keys/ca/ca_cert.pem

Now you can run your Docker client command as shown here:

```
\> docker --tlsverify  images
```

> **Ten layers of container security**
>
> The Red Hat whitepaper "Ten Layers of Container Security" talks about 10 elements of security for containers: container host multitenancy, container content, container registries, building containers, deploying containers, container orchestration, network isolation, storage, API management, and federated clusters. Though the focus of this whitepaper is on the Red Hat Enterprise Linux and Red Hat OpenShift platforms, it's still an excellent read; see www.redhat.com/en/resources/container-security-openshift-cloud-devops-whitepaper for details.

10.8 *Considering security beyond containers*

In a typical microservices deployment, containers don't act alone. Even though some people deploy microservices with just containers, most of the scalable microservices deployments use containers within a container orchestration framework such as Kubernetes. Securing a microservices deployment depends on the security constructs provided by your container orchestration framework. A few container orchestration frameworks exist, but the world is defaulting to Kubernetes. We discuss Kubernetes in detail in appendix J and chapter 11.

Apart from Kubernetes, the service mesh also plays a key role in securing a microservices deployment. A *service mesh* is a decentralized application-networking infrastructure between microservices, which provides resiliency, security, observability, and routing control. If you're familiar with software-defined networking (SDN), you can think of a service mesh as SDN too. Multiple popular service mesh implementations are available, but the one most used is Istio. In appendix K and chapter 12, we discuss in detail how to secure microservices with Istio.

Summary

- Docker containers have become the de facto standard to package, distribute, test, and deploy microservices.
- As a best practice, no secrets must be embedded in Docker images, and secrets must be externalized. Container orchestration frameworks, such as Kubernetes and Docker Swarm, provide better ways to manage secrets in a containerized environment.
- When securing microservices, the security of a microservices deployment should be thought of in the context of a container orchestration framework, not just container security in isolation.
- DCT is used to sign and verify Docker images. This makes sure that you run only trusted containers in your deployment and helps developers who rely on Docker images developed by you to validate them.
- As a best practice, you shouldn't run a container as the root user. One approach is to define the user who you want to run the container in the Dockerfile itself or to pass it as an argument to the `docker run` command. The other approach is to use capabilities to restrict what a user can do within a container.
- Sometimes you need to expose the Docker daemon to remote clients. In such cases, you must protect all Docker APIs to make sure only legitimate users have access.
- Docker Bench for Security checks a Docker deployment for common, well-known best practices, as defined by the CIS in the Docker Community Edition Benchmark document (https://downloads.cisecurity.org), and then validates your Docker environment.

Securing microservices
on Kubernetes

11

This chapter covers

- Securing service-to-service communications of a microservices deployment
- Managing secrets in Kubernetes
- Creating service accounts and associating them with Pods
- Protecting access to the Kubernetes API server with RBAC

In chapter 10, we discussed how to deploy and secure microservices on Docker containers. In a real production deployment, you don't have only containers; containers are used within a container orchestration framework. Just as a container is an abstraction over the physical machine, the container orchestration framework is an abstraction over the network. *Kubernetes* is the most popular container orchestration framework to date.

Understanding the fundamentals of Kubernetes and its security features is essential to any microservices developer. We cover basic constructs of Kubernetes in appendix J, so if you're new to Kubernetes, read that appendix first. Even if you're

262

familiar with Kubernetes, we still recommend you at least skim through appendix J, because the rest of this chapter assumes you have the knowledge contained in it.

11.1 Running an STS on Kubernetes

In this section, we deploy the Docker container that we built in chapter 10 with the STS in Kubernetes. This Docker image is already published to the Docker Hub as `prabath/insecure-sts-ch10:v1`. To deploy a container in Kubernetes, first we need to create a Pod. If you read appendix J, you learned that developers or DevOps don't directly work with Pods but with Deployments. So, to create a Pod in Kubernetes, we need to create a Deployment.

11.1.1 Defining a Kubernetes Deployment for the STS in YAML

A *Deployment* is a Kubernetes object that we represent in a YAML file. Let's create the following YAML file (listing 11.1) with the `prabath/insecure-sts-ch10:v1` Docker image. The source code related to all the samples in this chapter is available in the GitHub repository at https://github.com/microservices-security-in-action/ samples in the chapter11 directory. You can also find the same YAML configuration shown in the following listing in the chapter11/sample01/sts.deployment.yaml file.

Listing 11.1 The sts.deployment.yaml file

```yaml
apiVersion: apps/v1
kind: Deployment
metadata:
  name: sts-deployment
  labels:
    app: sts
spec:
  replicas: 1          ◁─┐  Instructs Kubernetes to run one
  selector:              └─ replica of the matching Pods
    matchLabels:        ◁─── This Deployment will carry a matching Pod
      app: sts               as per the selector. This is an optional
  template:             ◁─   section, which can carry multiple labels.
    metadata:
      labels:                A template describes how each Pod in
        app: sts             the Deployment should look. If you
    spec:                    define a selector/matchLabels, the Pod
      containers:            definition must carry a matching label.
      - name: sts
        image: prabath/insecure-sts-ch10:v1
        ports:
        - containerPort: 8443
```

11.1.2 Creating the STS Deployment in Kubernetes

In this section, we create a Deployment in Kubernetes for the STS that we defined in the YAML file in the above listing. We assume you have access to a Kubernetes cluster. If not, follow the instructions in appendix J, section J.5, to create a Kubernetes cluster with the

GKE.[1] Once you have access to a Kubernetes cluster, go to the chapter11/sample01 directory and run the following command from your local machine to create a Deployment for STS:

```
\> kubectl apply -f sts.deployment.yaml

deployment.apps/sts-deployment created
```

Use the following command to find all the Deployments in your Kubernetes cluster (under the current namespace). If everything goes well, you should see one replica of the STS up and running:

```
\> kubectl get deployment sts-deployment

NAME             READY   UP-TO-DATE   AVAILABLE   AGE
sts-deployment   1/1     1            1           12s
```

11.1.3 *Troubleshooting the Deployment*

Not everything goes fine all the time. Multiple things can go wrong. If Kubernetes complains about the YAML file, it could be due to an extra space or an error when you copy and paste the content from the text in the e-book. Rather than copying and pasting from the e-book, always use the corresponding sample file from the GitHub repo.

Also, in case you have doubts about your YAML file, you can use an online tool like YAML Lint (www.yamllint.com) to validate it, or use kubeval (www.kubeval.com), which is an open source tool. YAML Lint validates only the YAML file, while kubeval also validates your configurations against the Kubernetes schema.

Even though the `kubectl apply` command executes successfully, when you run `kubectl get deployments`, it may show that none of your replicas are ready. The following three commands are quite useful in such cases:

- The `kubectl describe` command shows a set of metadata related to the deployment:

  ```
  \> kubectl describe deployment sts-deployment
  ```

- The `kubectl get events` command shows all the events created in the current Kubernetes namespace. If something goes wrong while creating the Deployment, you'll notice a set of errors or warnings:

  ```
  \> kubectl get events
  ```

- Another useful command in troubleshooting is `kubectl logs`. You can run this command against a given Pod. First, though, you can run `kubectl get pods` to find the name of the Pod you want to get the logs from, and then use

---

[1] All the examples in this book use Google Cloud, which is more straightforward and hassle-free when trying out the examples, rather having your own local Kubernetes environment. If you still need to try out the examples locally, you can either use Docker Desktop or Minikube to set up a local, single-node Kubernetes cluster.

the following command with the Pod name (`sts-deployment-799fdff46f-hdp5s` is the Pod name in the following command):

```
\> kubectl logs sts-deployment-799fdff46f-hdp5s -follow
```

Once you identify the issue related to your Kubernetes Deployment, and if you need help to get that sorted out, you can either reach out to any of the Kubernetes community forums (https://discuss.kubernetes.io) or use the Kubernetes Stack Overflow channel (https://stackoverflow.com/questions/tagged/kubernetes).

11.1.4 Exposing the STS outside the Kubernetes cluster

In this section, we create a Kubernetes Service that exposes the STS outside the Kubernetes cluster. If you're new to Kubernetes Services, remember to check appendix J.

Here, we use a Kubernetes Service of LoadBalancer type. If there are multiple replicas of a given Pod, the Service of LoadBalancer type acts as a load balancer. Usually, it's an external load balancer provided by the Kubernetes hosting environment, and in our case, it's the GKE. Let's have a look at the YAML file to create the Service (listing 11.2). The same YAML file is available at chapter11/sample01/sts.service.yaml.

The Service listens on port 443 and forwards the traffic to port 8443. If you look at listing 11.1, you'll notice that when we create the Deployment, the container that carries the STS microservice is listening on port 8443. Even though it's not 100% accurate to say that a Service listens on a given port, it's a good way to simplify what's happening underneath. As we discussed in appendix J, what really happens when we create a Service is that each node in the Kubernetes cluster updates the corresponding iptables, so any request destined to a Service IP address/name and port will be dispatched to one of the Pods it backs.

Listing 11.2 The sts.service.yaml file

```
apiVersion: v1
kind: Service
metadata:
  name: sts-service
spec:
 type: LoadBalancer
 selector:
  app: sts
 ports:
 - protocol: TCP
   port: 443
   targetPort: 8443
```

To create the Service in the Kubernetes cluster, go to the chapter11/sample01 directory and run the following command from your local machine:

```
\> kubectl apply -f sts.service.yml

service/sts-service created
```

Use the following command to find all the Services in your Kubernetes cluster (under the current namespace):[2]

```
\> kubectl get services
NAME           TYPE          CLUSTER-IP       EXTERNAL-IP    PORT(S)          AGE
kubernetes     ClusterIP     10.39.240.1      <none>         443/TCP          134m
sts-service    LoadBalancer  10.39.244.238    <pending>      443:30993/TCP    20s
```

It takes Kubernetes a few minutes to assign an external IP address for the sts-service we just created. If you run the same command, you'll notice the following output after a couple of minutes, with an external IP address assigned to the sts-service:

```
\> kubectl get services
NAME           TYPE          CLUSTER-IP       EXTERNAL-IP    PORT(S)          AGE
kubernetes     ClusterIP     10.39.240.1      <none>         443/TCP          135m
sts-service    LoadBalancer  10.39.244.238    34.82.103.6    443:30993/TCP    52s
```

Now let's test the STS with the following curl command run from your local machine. This is exactly the same curl command we used in section 7.2. The IP address in the command is the external IP address corresponding to the sts-service from the previous command:

```
\> curl -v -X POST --basic -u applicationid:applicationsecret \
-H "Content-Type: application/x-www-form-urlencoded;charset=UTF-8" \
-k -d "grant_type=password&username=peter&password=peter123&scope=foo" \
https://34.82.103.6/oauth/token
```

In this command, applicationid is the client ID of the web application, and applicationsecret is the client secret (these are hardcoded in the STS). If everything works, the STS returns an OAuth 2.0 access token, which is a JWT (or a JWS, to be precise):

```
{
"access_token":"eyJhbGciOiJSUzI1NiIsInR5cCI6IkpXVCJ9.eyJleHAiOjE1NTEzMTIzNz
YsInVzZXJfbmFtZSI6InBldGVyIiwiYXV0aG9yaXRpZXMiOlsiUk9MRV9VU0VSIl0sImp0aSI6I
jRkMmJiNjQ4LTQ2MWQtNGVlYy1hZTljLTVlYWUxZjA4ZTJhMiIsImNsaWVudF9pZCI6ImFwcGxp
Y2F0aW9uaWQiLCJzY29wZSI6WyJmb28iXX0.tr4yUmGLtsH7q9Ge2i7gxyTsOOa0RS0Yoc2uBuA
W5OVIKZcVsIITWV3bDN0FVHBzimpAPy33tvicFROhBFoVThqKXzzG00SkURN5bnQ4uFLAP0NpZ6
BuDjvVmwXNXrQp2lVXl4lQ4eTvuyZozjUSCXzCI1LNw5EFFi22J73g1_mRm2jdEhBp1TvMaRKLB
Dk2hzIDVKzu5oj_gODBFm3a1S-IJjYoCimIm2igcesXkhipRJtjNcrJSegBbGgyXHVak2gB7I07
ryVwl_Re5yX4sV9x6xNwCxc_DgP9hHLzPM8yz_K97jlT6Rr1XZBlveyjfKs_XIXgU5qizRm9mt5
xg",
"token_type":"bearer",
"refresh_token":"",
"expires_in":5999,
"scope":"foo",
"jti":"4d2bb648-461d-4eec-ae9c-5eae1f08e2a2"
}
```

---

[2] If you're new to the namespace concept in Kubernetes, check appendix J. All the samples in this chapter use the default namespace.

Here, we talk to the STS running in Kubernetes over TLS. The STS uses TLS certificates embedded in the `prabath/insecure-sts-ch10:v1` Docker image, and the Kubernetes load balancer just tunnels all the requests it gets to the corresponding container.[3]

11.2 *Managing secrets in a Kubernetes environment*

In section 11.1, we used a Docker image called `prabath/insecure-sts-ch10:v1`. We named it `insecure-sts` for a reason. In chapter 10, we had a detailed discussion on why this image is insecure. While creating this image, we embedded all the keys and the credentials to access the keys into the image itself. Because this is in Docker Hub, anyone having access to the image can figure out all our secrets—and that's the end of the world! You can find the source code of this insecure STS in the chapter10/sample01 directory.

To make the Docker image secure, the first thing we need to do is to externalize all the keystores and credentials. In chapter 10, we discussed how to externalize the application.properties file (where we keep all the credentials) from the Docker image as well as the two keystore files (one keystore includes the key to secure the TLS communication, while the other keystore includes the key to sign JWT access tokens that the STS issues). We published this updated Docker image to Docker Hub as `prabath/secure-sts-ch10:v1`. To help you understand how this Docker image is built, the following listing repeats the Dockerfile from listing 10.4.

> **Listing 11.3   The Dockerfile used to build the secure STS**

```
FROM openjdk:8-jdk-alpine
ADD target/com.manning.mss.ch10.sample01-1.0.0.jar \
        com.manning.mss.ch10.sample01-1.0.0.jar
ENV SPRING_CONFIG_LOCATION=/opt/application.properties
ENTRYPOINT ["java", "-jar", "com.manning.mss.ch10.sample01-1.0.0.jar"]
```

We've externalized the application.properties file. Spring Boot reads the location of the application.properties file from the `SPRING_CONFIG_LOCATION` environment variable, which is set to `/opt/application.properties`. So Spring Boot expects the application.properties file to be present in the /opt directory of the Docker container. Because our expectation here is to externalize the application.properties file, we can't put it to the container filesystem.

In chapter 10, we used Docker bind mounts, so Docker loads the application .properties file from the host machine and maps it to the /opt directory of the container filesystem. Following is the command we used in chapter 10 to run the Docker container with bind mounts (only for your reference; if you want to try it, follow the instructions in section 10.2.2):

```
\> export JKS_SOURCE="$(pwd)/keystores/keystore.jks"
\> export JKS_TARGET="/opt/keystore.jks"
```

---

[3]   In addition to TLS tunneling, we can also do TLS termination at the Kubernetes load balancer. Then a new connection is created between the load balancer and the corresponding microservice.

```
\> export JWT_SOURCE="$(pwd)/keystores/jwt.jks"
\> export JWT_TARGET="/opt/jwt.jks"
\> export APP_SOURCE="$(pwd)/config/application.properties"
\> export APP_TARGET="/opt/application.properties"

\> docker run -p 8443:8443 \
--mount type=bind,source="$JKS_SOURCE",target="$JKS_TARGET" \
--mount type=bind,source="$JWT_SOURCE",target="$JWT_TARGET" \
--mount type=bind,source="$APP_SOURCE",target="$APP_TARGET" \
-e KEYSTORE_SECRET=springboot \
-e JWT_KEYSTORE_SECRET=springboot \
prabath/secure-sts-ch10:v1
```

In the command, we use bind mounts to pass not only the application.properties file, but also the two keystore files. If you look at the keystore locations mentioned in the application.properties file (listing 11.4), Spring Boot looks for the keystore.jks and jwt.jks files inside the /opt directory of the container filesystem. Also, in this listing, you can see that we've externalized the keystore passwords. Now, Spring Boot reads the password of the keystore.jks file from the `KEYSTORE_SECRET` environment variable, and the password of the jwt.jks file from the `JWT_KEYSTORE_SECRET` environment variable, which we pass in the `docker run` command.

> **Listing 11.4   The content of the application.properties file**

```
server.port: 8443
server.ssl.key-store: /opt/keystore.jks
server.ssl.key-store-password: ${KEYSTORE_SECRET}
server.ssl.keyAlias: spring
spring.security.oauth.jwt: true
spring.security.oauth.jwt.keystore.password: ${JWT_KEYSTORE_SECRET}
spring.security.oauth.jwt.keystore.alias: jwtkey
spring.security.oauth.jwt.keystore.name: /opt/jwt.jks
```

11.2.1   *Using ConfigMap to externalize configurations in Kubernetes*

When you run a container in a Kubernetes environment, you can't pass configuration files from your local filesystem as we did with Docker in section 11.2. Kubernetes introduces an object called ConfigMap to decouple configuration from containers or microservices running in a Kubernetes environment. In this section, you'll learn how to represent the application.properties file, the keystore.jks file, the jwt.jks file, and the keystore passwords as ConfigMap objects.

A ConfigMap is not the ideal object to represent sensitive data like keystore passwords. In such cases, we use another Kubernetes object called Secret. In section 11.3, we'll move keystore passwords from ConfigMap to a Kubernetes Secret. If you're new to Kubernetes ConfigMaps, see appendix J for the details and to find out how it works internally.

11.2.2   *Defining a ConfigMap for application.properties file*

Kubernetes lets you create a ConfigMap object with the complete content of a configuration file. Listing 11.5 shows the content of the application.properties file under the data element with the `application.properties` as the key. The name of the key must match the name of the file that we expect to be in the container filesystem. You can find the complete ConfigMap definition of the application.properties file in the chapter11/sample01/sts.configuration.yaml file.

Listing 11.5   The definition of application-properties-config-map

```
apiVersion: v1
kind: ConfigMap
metadata:                                     Creates a ConfigMap object of
  name: sts-application-properties-config-map   a file with a text representation
data:
  application.properties: |                   The name of the key must match
    [                                         the name of the file we expect to
      server.port: 8443                       be in the container filesystem.
      server.ssl.key-store: /opt/keystore.jks
      server.ssl.key-store-password: ${KEYSTORE_SECRET}
      server.ssl.keyAlias: spring
      spring.security.oauth.jwt: true
      spring.security.oauth.jwt.keystore.password: ${JWT_KEYSTORE_SECRET}
      spring.security.oauth.jwt.keystore.alias: jwtkey
      spring.security.oauth.jwt.keystore.name: /opt/jwt.jks
    ]
```

Once we define the ConfigMap in a YAML file, we can use the kubectl client to create a ConfigMap object in the Kubernetes environment. We defer that until section 11.2.5, when we complete our discussion on the other three ConfigMap objects as well (in sections 11.2.3 and 11.2.4).

11.2.3   Defining ConfigMaps for keystore.jks and jwt.jks files

Kubernetes lets you create a ConfigMap object of a file with a text representation (listing 11.5) or with a binary representation. In listing 11.6, we use the binary representation option to create ConfigMaps for the keystore.jks and jwt.jks files. The base 64-encoded content of the keystore.jks file is listed under the key `keystore.jks` under the element `binaryData`. The name of the key must match the name of the file we expect to be in the /opt directory of the container filesystem.

You can find the complete ConfigMap definition of the keystore.jks and jwt.jks files in the chapter11/sample01/sts.configuration.yaml file. Also, the keystore.jks and jwt.jks binary files are available in the chapter10/sample01/keystores directory in case you'd like to do file-to-base64 conversion yourself.[4]

Listing 11.6   The definition of ConfigMap for keystore.jks and jwt.jks

```
apiVersion: v1
kind: ConfigMap
metadata:
  name: sts-keystore-config-map
```

---

[4]   To convert a binary file to a base64-encoded text file, you can use an online tool like Browserling (www .browserling.com/tools/file-to-base64).

```
binaryData:
  keystore.jks: [base64-encoded-text]
---
apiVersion: v1
kind: ConfigMap
metadata:
  name: sts-jwt-keystore-config-map
binaryData:
  jwt.jks:[base64-encoded-text]
```

⟵ **Creates a ConfigMap object of a file with a binary representation**

11.2.4 Defining a ConfigMap for keystore credentials

First, *don't do this in a production deployment!* Kubernetes stores anything that you store in a ConfigMap in cleartext. To store credentials in a Kubernetes deployment, we use a Kubernetes object called Secret instead of a ConfigMap. We talk about Secrets later in section 11.3. Until then, we'll define keystore credentials in a ConfigMap.

Listing 11.7 shows the definition of the `sts-keystore-credentials` ConfigMap. There we pass the password to access the keystore.jks file under the `KEYSTORE_PASSWORD` key, and the password to access the jwt.jks file under the `JWT_KEYSTORE_PASSWORD` key, both under the `data` element. You can find the complete ConfigMap definition of keystore credentials in the chapter11/sample01/sts.configuration.yaml file.

Listing 11.7   The definition of keystore credentials

```
apiVersion: v1
kind: ConfigMap
metadata:
  name: sts-keystore-credentials
data:
  KEYSTORE_PASSWORD: springboot
  JWT_KEYSTORE_PASSWORD: springboot
```

11.2.5 Creating ConfigMaps by using the kubectl client

In the file chapter11/sample01/sts.configuration.yaml, you'll find ConfigMap definitions of all four ConfigMaps we've discussed in this section thus far. You can use the following `kubectl` command from the chapter11/sample01 directory to create ConfigMap objects in your Kubernetes environment:

```
\> kubectl apply -f sts.configuration.yaml

configmap/sts-application-properties-config-map created
configmap/sts-keystore-config-map created
configmap/sts-jwt-keystore-config-map created
configmap/sts-keystore-credentials created
```

The following `kubectl` command lists all the ConfigMap objects available in your Kubernetes cluster (under the current namespace):

```
\> kubectl get configmaps

NAME                                          DATA    AGE
sts-application-properties-config-map         1       50s
sts-keystore-config-map                       0       50s
sts-jwt-keystore-config-map                   0       50s
sts-keystore-credentials                      2       50s
```

11.2.6 Consuming ConfigMaps from a Kubernetes Deployment

In this section, we'll go through the changes we need to introduce to the Kubernetes Deployment, that we created in listing 11.1, to read the values from the ConfigMaps we created in section 11.2.5. You'll find the complete updated definition of the Kubernetes Deployment in the chapter11/sample01/sts.deployment.with.configmap.yaml file.

We'll focus on two types of ConfigMaps. For one, we want to read the content of a file from a ConfigMap and mount that file into the container filesystem. For the other one, we want to read a value from a ConfigMap and set that as an environment variable in the container. The following listing shows part of the Deployment object that carries the configuration related to the containers.

Listing 11.8 Part of the STS Deployment definition

```
spec:
  containers:
  - name: sts
    image: prabath/secure-sts-ch10:v1
    imagePullPolicy: Always
    ports:
    - containerPort: 8443
    volumeMounts:                                    ◁── Defines the volume mounts used by this Kubernetes Deployment
    - name: application-properties                   ◁── The name of the volume, which refers to the volumes section
      mountPath: "/opt/application.properties"       ◁── Location of the container filesystem to mount this volume
      subPath: "application.properties"
    - name: keystore
      mountPath: "/opt/keystore.jks"
      subPath: "keystore.jks"
    - name: jwt-keystore                             ◁── Defines the set of environment variables read by the Kubernetes Deployment
      mountPath: "/opt/jwt.jks"
      subPath: "jwt.jks"
    env:
    - name: KEYSTORE_SECRET                          ◁── The name of the environment variable. This is the exact name you find in application.properties file.
      valueFrom:
        configMapKeyRef:
          name: sts-keystore-credentials            ◁── The name of the ConfigMap to read the value for this environment variable
          key: KEYSTORE_PASSWORD                     ◁── The name of the key corresponding to the value we want to read from the corresponding ConfigMap
    - name: JWT_KEYSTORE_SECRET
      valueFrom:
        configMapKeyRef:
          name: sts-keystore-credentials
          key: JWT_KEYSTORE_PASSWORD
  volumes:
  - name: application-properties                     ◁── The name of the volume. This is referred by the name element under the volumeMounts section of the Deployment.
    configMap:
      name: sts-application-properties-config-map    ◁── The name the ConfigMap, which carries the data related to application.properties file
```

```
     - name: keystore
       configMap:
         name: sts-keystore-config-map
     - name: jwt-keystore
       configMap:
         name: sts-jwt-keystore-config-map
```

You can use the following `kubectl` command from the chapter11/sample01 directory to update the Kubernetes Deployment with the changes annotated in listing 11.8:

```
\> kubectl apply -f sts.deployment.with.configmap.yaml

deployment.apps/sts-deployment configured
```

The Kubernetes Service we created in section 11.1.4 requires no changes. Make sure it's up and running with the correct IP address by using the `kubectl get services` command. Now let's test the STS with the following `curl` command run from your local machine:

```
\> curl -v -X POST --basic -u applicationid:applicationsecret \
-H "Content-Type: application/x-www-form-urlencoded;charset=UTF-8" \
-k -d "grant_type=password&username=peter&password=peter123&scope=foo" \
https://34.82.103.6/oauth/token
```

In this command, `applicationid` is the client ID of the web application, and `applicationsecret` is the client secret. If everything works, the STS returns an OAuth 2.0 access token, which is a JWT (or a JWS, to be precise):

```
{
"access_token":"eyJhbGciOiJSUzI1NiIsInR5cCI6IkpXVCJ9.eyJleHAiOjE1NTEzMTIzNz
YsInVzZXJfbmFtZSI6InBldGVyIiwiYXV0aG9yaXRpZXMiOlsiUk9MRV9VU0VSIl0sImp0aSI6I
jRkMmJiNjQ4LTQ2MWQtNGVlYy1hZTljLTVlYWUxZjA4ZTJhMiIsImNsaWVudF9pZCI6ImFwcGxp
Y2F0aW9uaWQiLCJzY29wZSI6WyJmb28iXX0.tr4yUmGLtsH7q9Ge2i7gxyTsOOa0RS0Yoc2uBuA
W5OVIKZcVsIITWV3bDN0FVHBzimpAPy33tvicFROhBFoVThqKXzzG00SkURN5bnQ4uFLAP0NpZ6
BuDjvVmwXNXrQp2lVX14lQ4eTvuyZozjUSCXzCI1LNw5EFFi22J73g1_mRm2jdEhBp1TvMaRKLB
Dk2hzIDVKzu5oj_gODBFm3a1S-IJjYoCimIm2igcesXkhipRJtjNcrJSegBbGgyXHVak2gB7I07
ryVwl_Re5yX4sV9x6xNwCxc_DgP9hHLzPM8yz_K97jlT6Rr1XZBlveyjfKs_XIXgU5qizRm9mt5
xg",
"token_type":"bearer",
"refresh_token":"",
"expires_in":5999,
"scope":"foo",
"jti":"4d2bb648-461d-4eec-ae9c-5eae1f08e2a2"
}
```

11.2.7 *Loading keystores with an init container*

In Kubernetes, we can run more than one container in a Pod, but as a practice, we run only one application container. Along with an application container, we can also run one or more init containers. If you're familiar with Java (or any other programming language), an *init container* in Kubernetes is like a constructor in a Java class. Just as the constructor in a Java class runs well before any other methods, an init container in a Pod must run and complete before any other application containers in the Pod start.

This is a great way to initialize a Kubernetes Pod. You can pull any files (keystores, policies, and so forth), configurations, and so on with an init container. Just as with any other application container, we can have more than one init container in a given Pod; but unlike an application container, each init container must run to completion before the next init container starts.

Listing 11.9 modifies the STS Deployment to load keystore.jks and jwt.jks files from a Git repository by using an init container instead of loading them from a ConfigMap object (as in listing 11.8). You can find the complete updated definition of the Kubernetes Deployment in the chapter11/sample01/sts.deployment.with.initcontainer.yaml file. The following listing shows part of the updated STS deployment, corresponding to the init container.

> ### Listing 11.9 The STS Deployment with an init container

```
initContainers:              ◁──┐ Lists out all the
- name: init-keystores            init containers
  image: busybox:1.28
  command:
    - "/bin/sh"
    - "-c"
    - "wget ...sample01/keystores/jwt.jks \
       -O /opt/jwt.jks | wget ...sample01/keystores/keystore.jks \
       -O /opt/keystore.jks"
  volumeMounts:
  - name: keystore
    mountPath: "/opt/keystore.jks"
    subPath: "keystore.jks"
  - name: jwt-keystore
    mountPath: "/opt/jwt.jks"
    subPath: "jwt.jks"
```

Lists out all the init containers

The name of the Docker image used as the init container to pull the keystores from a Git repository

The Docker container executes this command at startup. The jwt.jks and keystore.jks files are copied to the opt directory of the container.

Defines a volume mount, so that the keystores loaded by the init container can be used by other containers in the Pod

Path to the keystore

Any container in the Pod that refers to the same volume mount must use the same name.

The subPath property specifies a subpath inside the referenced volume instead of its root.

We've created the init container with the `busybox` Docker image. Because the `busybox` container is configured as an init container, it runs before any other container in the Pod. Under the `command` element, we specified the program the `busybox` container should run. There we got both keystore.jks and jwt.jks files from a Git repo and copied both keystore.jks and jwt.jks files to the `/opt` directory of the `busybox` container filesystem.

The whole objective of the init container is to get the two keystores into the Docker container that runs the STS. To do that, we need to have two volume mounts; both volumes (`keystore` and `jwt-keystore`) are mapped to the `/opt` directory. Because we already have volume mounts with these two names (under the `secure-sts` container in the following listing), the two keystores are also visible to the `secure-sts` container filesystem.

Listing 11.10 Volume mounts in secure-sts container

```
volumeMounts:
- name: application-properties
  mountPath: "/opt/application.properties"
  subPath: "application.properties"
- name: keystore
  mountPath: "/opt/keystore.jks"
  subPath: "keystore.jks"
- name: jwt-keystore
  mountPath: "/opt/jwt.jks"
  subPath: "jwt.jks"
```

Finally, to support init containers, we also need to make one more change to the original STS Deployment. Earlier, under the `volumes` element of the STS Deployment, we pointed to the corresponding ConfigMaps, and now we need to point to a special volume called `emptyDir`, as shown here. The `emptyDir` volume gets created empty when Kubernetes creates the corresponding Pod, and the keystore files pulled from a Git repo by the init container populates it. You will lose the content of an `emptyDir` volume when you delete the corresponding Pod:

```
volumes:
- name: application-properties
  configMap:
  name: sts-application-properties-config-map
- name: keystore
  emptyDir: {}
- name: jwt-keystore
  emptyDir: {}
```

Let's use the following `kubectl` command with the chapter11/sample01/sts.deployment .with.init.containers.yaml file to update the STS deployment to use init containers:

```
\> kubectl apply -f sts.deployment.with.initcontainer.yaml

deployment.apps/sts-deployment configured
```

11.3 *Using Kubernetes Secrets*

As we discussed in section 11.2.4, ConfigMap is not the right way of externalizing sensitive data in Kubernetes. Secret is a Kubernetes object, just like ConfigMap, that carries name/value pairs but is ideal for storing sensitive data. In this section, we discuss Kubernetes Secrets in detail and see how to update the STS Deployment with Kubernetes Secrets, instead of using ConfigMaps, to externalize keystore credentials.

11.3.1 *Exploring the default token secret in every container*

Kubernetes provisions a Secret to each container of the Pod it creates. This is called the *default token secret*. To see the default token secret, run the following `kubectl` command:

```
\> kubectl get secrets

NAME                    TYPE                                  DATA  AGE
default-token-19fj8     kubernetes.io/service-account-token   3     10d
```

Listing 11.11 shows the structure of the default token secret returned by kubectl in YAML format. The name/value pairs under the `data` element carry the confidential data in base64-encoded format. The default token secret has three name/value pairs: `ca.crt`, `namespace`, and `token`. This listing shows only part of the values for `ca.crt` and `token`.

Listing 11.11 The default Kubernetes Secret

```
\> kubectl get secret default-token-19fj8 -o yaml

apiVersion: v1
kind: Secret
metadata:
  annotations:
    kubernetes.io/service-account.name: default
    kubernetes.io/service-account.uid: ff3d13ba-d8ee-11e9-a88f-42010a8a01e4
  name: default-token-19fj8
  namespace: default
type: kubernetes.io/service-account-token
data:
  ca.crt: LS0tLS1CRUdJTiBDRRVJUSUZJQ...
  namespace: ZGVmYXVsdA==
  token: ZXlKaGJHY2lPaUpTVXpJMU5pSX...
```

The value of `ca.crt` is, in fact, the root certificate of the Kubernetes cluster. You can use an online tool like Base64 Decode Online (https://base64.guru/converter/decode/file) to convert base64-encoded text to a file. You'll see something similar to the following, which is the PEM-encoded root certificate of the Kubernetes cluster:

```
-----BEGIN CERTIFICATE-----
MIIDCzCCAfOgAwIBAgIQdzQ6l91oRfLI141a9hEPoTANBgkqhkiG9w0BAQsFADAv
MS0wKwYDVQQDEyRkMWJjZGU1MC1jNjNkLTQ5MWYtOTZlNi0wNTEwZDliOTI5ZTEw
HhcNMTkwOTE3MDA1ODI2WhcNMjQwOTE1MDE0ODI2WjAvMS0wKwYDVQQDEyRkMWJj
ZGU1MC1jNjNkLTQ5MWYtOTZlNi0wNTEwZDliOTI5ZTEwggEiMA0GCSqGSIb3DQEB
AQUAA4IBDwAwggEKAoIBAQChdg15gweIqZZraHBFH3sB9FKfv2lDZ03/MAq6ek3J
NJj+7huiJUy6PuP9t5rOiGU/JIvRI7iXipqc/JGMRjmMVwCmSv6D+5N8+JmvhZ4i
uzbjUOpiuyozRsmf3hzbwbcLbcA94Y1d+oK0TZ+lYs8XNhX0RCM+gDKryC5MeGnY
zqd+/MLS6zajG3qlGQAWn9XKClPpRDOJh5h/uNQs+r2Y9Uz4oi4shVUvXibwOHrh
0MpAt6BGujDMNDNRGH8/dK1CZ1EYJYoUaOTOeF21RSJ2y82AFS5eA17hSxY4j6x5
```

```
3ipQt1pe49j5m7QU5s/VoDGsBBge6vYd0AUL9y96xFUvAgMBAAGjIzAhMA4GA1Ud
DwEB/wQEAwICBDAPBgNVHRMBAf8EBTADAQH/MA0GCSqGSIb3DQEBCwUAA4IBAQB4
331sGOSU2z6PKLdnZHrnnwZq44AH3CzCQ+M6cQPTU63XHXWcEQtxSDcjDTm1xZqR
qeoUcgCW4mBjdG4dMkQD+MuBUoGLQPkv5XsnlJg+4zRhKTD78PUEI5ZF8HBBX5Vt
+3IbrBelVhREuwDGClPmMR0/081ZlwLZFrbFRwRAZQmkEgCtfcOUGQ3+HLQw1U2P
xKFLx6ISUNSkPfO5pkBW6Tg3rJfQnfuKUPxUFI/3JUjXDzl2XLx7GFF1J4tW812A
T6WfgDvYS2Ld9o/rw3C036NtivdjGrnb2QqEosGeDPQOXs53sgFT8LPNkQ+f/8nn
G0Jk4TNzdxezmyyyvxh2
-----END CERTIFICATE-----
```

To get something meaningful out of this, you can use an online tool like the Report URI PEM decoder (https://report-uri.com/home/pem_decoder) to decode the PEM file, resulting in something similar to the following:

```
Common Name: d1bcde50-c63d-491f-96e6-0510d9b929e1
Issuing Certificate: d1bcde50-c63d-491f-96e6-0510d9b929e1
Serial Number: 77343A97DD6845F2C8D78D5AF6110FA1
Signature: sha256WithRSAEncryption
Valid From: 00:58:26 17 Sep 2019
Valid To: 01:58:26 15 Sep 2024
Key Usage: Certificate Sign
Basic Constraints: CA:TRUE
```

The `token` under the `data` element in listing 11.11 carries a JSON Web Token (see appendix B for details on JWT). This JWT is itself base64 encoded. You can use an online tool like Base64 Encode and Decode (www.base64decode.org) to base64-decode the `token`, and an online JWT decoder like JWT.IO (http://jwt.io) to decode the JWT. The following shows the decoded payload of the JWT:

```
{
  "iss": "kubernetes/serviceaccount",
  "kubernetes.io/serviceaccount/namespace": "default",
  "kubernetes.io/serviceaccount/secret.name": "default-token-l9fj8",
  "kubernetes.io/serviceaccount/service-account.name": "default",
  "kubernetes.io/serviceaccount/service-account.uid":
                       "ff3d13ba-d8ee-11e9-a88f-42010a8a01e4",
  "sub": "system:serviceaccount:default:default"
}
```

Each container in a Kubernetes Pod has access to this JWT from the /var/run/secrets/kuberenetes.io/serviceaccount directory, in its own container filesystem. If you want to access the Kubernetes API server from a container, you can use this JWT for authentication. In fact, this JWT is bound to a Kubernetes service account. We discuss service accounts in detail in section 11.6.

11.3.2 *Updating the STS to use Secrets*

In section 11.2, we updated the STS Deployment to use ConfigMaps to externalize configuration data. Even for keystore credentials, we used ConfigMaps instead of Secrets. In this section, we're going to update the STS Deployment to use Secrets to represent keystore credentials. First, we need to define the Secret object as shown in listing 11.12. The complete definition of the Secret object is in the chapter11/sample01/sts.secrets.yaml file.

Listing 11.12 The definition of the Secret object that carries keystore credentials

```
apiVersion: v1
kind: Secret
metadata:
  name: sts-keystore-secrets
stringData:
  KEYSTORE_PASSWORD: springboot
  JWT_KEYSTORE_PASSWORD: springboot
```

To create the Secret in the Kubernetes environment, run the following command from the chapter11/sample01 directory:

```
\> kubectl apply -f sts.secrets.yaml

secret/sts-keystore-secrets created
```

In listing 11.12, we defined keystore credentials under the `stringData` element. Another option is to define credentials under the `data` element. In listing 11.16 (later in the chapter), we have an example.

When you define credentials under the `data` element, you need to base64-encode the values. If you mostly use binary credentials like private keys, you need to use the `data` element. For text credentials, the `stringData` element is the preferred option. Another important thing to notice is that Kubernetes has designed the `stringData` element to be write-only. That means, when you try to view a Secret you defined with `stringData`, it won't return as a `stringData` element; instead, Kubernetes base64-encodes the values and returns those under the `data` element. You can use the following `kubectl` command to list the definition of the Secret object we created in listing 11.12 in YAML format:

```
\> kubectl  get secret sts-keystore-secrets -o yaml

apiVersion: v1
kind: Secret
metadata:
  name: sts-keystore-secrets
data:
  KEYSTORE_PASSWORD: c3ByaW5nYm9vdA==
  JWT_KEYSTORE_PASSWORD: c3ByaW5nYm9vdA==
```

Now let's see how to update the STS Deployment to use the Secret object we created. You can find the updated YAML configuration for the STS Deployment in the chapter11/sample01/sts.deployment.with.secrets.yaml file. The following listing shows part of the complete STS Deployment, which reads keystore credentials from the Secret object and populates the environment variables.

Listing 11.13   Part of the STS Deployment definition using Secrets

```
env:
- name: KEYSTORE_SECRET
  valueFrom:
    secretKeyRef:
      name: sts-keystore-secrets
        key: KEYSTORE_PASSWORD
- name: JWT_KEYSTORE_SECRET
  valueFrom:
    secretKeyRef:
      name: sts-keystore-secrets
      key: JWT_KEYSTORE_PASSWORD
```

Let's run the following `kubectl` command from chapter11/sample01 to update the STS Deployment:

```
\> kubectl apply -f sts.deployment.with.secrets.yaml

deployment.apps/sts-deployment configured
```

11.3.3 Understanding how Kubernetes stores Secrets

You have to pick Secrets over ConfigMaps to store sensitive data because of the way Kubernetes internally handles Secrets. Kubernetes makes sure that the sensitive data Kubernetes represents as Secrets are accessible only to the Pods that need them, and even in such cases, none of the Secrets are written to disk, but only kept in memory. The only place Kubernetes writes Secrets to disk is at the master node, where all the Secrets are stored in etcd (see appendix J), which is the Kubernetes distributed key-value store. From the Kubernetes 1.7 release onward, etcd stores Secrets only in an encrypted format.

11.4   Running the Order Processing microservice in Kubernetes

In this section, we're going to deploy the Order Processing microservice in Kubernetes. As in figure 11.1, the Order Processing microservice trusts the tokens issued by the STS, which we now have running in Kubernetes. Once the client application passes the JWT to the Order Processing microservice, the Order Processing microservice talks to the STS to retrieve its public key to validate the signature of the JWT. This is the only communication that happens between the Order Processing microservice and the STS. In fact, to be precise, the Order Processing microservice doesn't wait until it gets a request to talk to the STS; it talks to the STS at startup to get its public key and stores it in memory.

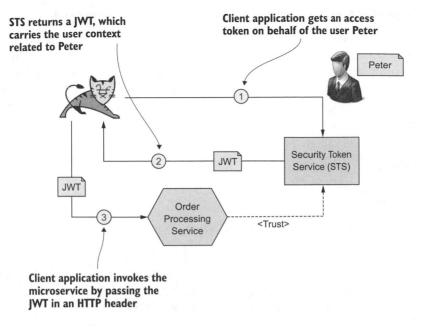

Figure 11.1 An STS issues a JWT access token to the client application, and the client application uses it to access the microservice on behalf of the user, Peter.

In chapter 10, we explained how to run the Order Processing microservice as a Docker container. This is the Docker command we used in section 10.4, which externalized the application.properties file, the keystore (keystore.jks), the trust store (trust-store.jks), the keystore credentials, and the trust store credentials. You don't need to run this command now; if you want to try it out, follow the instructions in chapter 10:

```
\> export JKS_SOURCE="$(pwd)/keystores/keystore.jks"
\> export JKS_TARGET-"/opt/keystore.jks"
\> export JWT_SOURCE="$(pwd)/keystores/jwt.jks"
\> export JWT_TARGET="/opt/jwt.jks"
\> export APP_SOURCE="$(pwd)/config/application.properties"
\> export APP_TARGET="/opt/application.properties"


\> docker run -p 8443:8443 \
--name sts --net manning-network  \
--mount type=bind,source="$JKS_SOURCE",target="$JKS_TARGET" \
--mount type=bind,source="$JWT_SOURCE",target="$JWT_TARGET" \
--mount type=bind,source="$APP_SOURCE",target="$APP_TARGET" \
-e KEYSTORE_SECRET=springboot \
-e JWT_KEYSTORE_SECRET=springboot \
prabath/order-processing:v1
```

To deploy the Order Processing microservice in Kubernetes, we need to create a Kubernetes Deployment and a Service. This is similar to what we did before when deploying the STS in Kubernetes.

11.4.1 *Creating ConfigMaps/Secrets for the Order Processing microservice*

In this section, we create three ConfigMaps to externalize the application.properties file and two keystores (keystore.jks and trust-store.jks) and a Secret to externalize the keystore credentials. Listing 11.14 shows the definition of the ConfigMap for the application.properties file. The value of security.oauth2.resource.jwt.key-uri in this listing carries the endpoint of the STS. Here the `sts-service` hostname is the name of Kubernetes Service we created for the STS.

Listing 11.14   The application.properties ConfigMap

```
apiVersion: v1
kind: ConfigMap
metadata:
  name: orders-application-properties-config-map
data:
  application.properties: |
    [
      server.port: 8443
      server.ssl.key-store: /opt/keystore.jks
      server.ssl.key-store-password: ${KEYSTORE_SECRET}
      server.ssl.keyAlias: spring
      server.ssl.trust-store: /opt/trust-store.jks
      server.ssl.trust-store-password: ${TRUSTSTORE_SECRET}
      security.oauth2.resource.jwt.key-uri: https://sts-service/oauth/
      token_key
      inventory.service: https://inventory-service/inventory
      logging.level.org.springframework=DEBUG
      logging.level.root=DEBUG
    ]
```

Listing 11.15 shows the ConfigMap definition for the keystore.jks and trust-store.jks files. Each `binaryData` element in each ConfigMap definition in this listing carries the base64-encoded text of the corresponding keystore file.

Listing 11.15   The keystore ConfigMaps

```
apiVersion: v1
kind: ConfigMap
metadata:
  name: orders-keystore-config-map
binaryData:
  keystore.jks: [base64-encoded-text]
---
apiVersion: v1
kind: ConfigMap
metadata:
  name: orders-truststore-config-map
binaryData:
  trust-store.jks: [base64-encoded-text]
```

Listing 11.16 shows the Secret definition of the credentials in the keystore.jks and trust-store.jks files. The value of each key under the `data` element in this listing carries the base64-encoded text of corresponding credentials. You can use the following command on a Mac terminal to generate the base64encoded value of a given text:

```
\> echo -n "springboot" | base64

c3ByaW5nYm9vdA==
```

Listing 11.16 The keystore credentials Secret

```
apiVersion: v1
kind: Secret
metadata:
  name: orders-key-credentials
type: Opaque
data:
  KEYSTORE_PASSWORD: c3ByaW5nYm9vdA==
  TRUSTSTORE_PASSWORD: c3ByaW5nYm9vdA==
```

In the chapter11/sample02/order.processing.configuration.yaml file, you'll find ConfigMap and Secret definitions of all that we discussed in this section. You can use the following `kubectl` command from the chapter11/sample02 directory to create ConfigMap and Secret objects in your Kubernetes environment:

```
\> kubectl apply -f order.processing.configuration.yaml

configmap/orders-application-properties-config-map created
configmap/orders-keystore-config-map created
configmap/orders-truststore-config-map created
secret/orders-key-credentials created
```

The following two `kubectl` commands list all the ConfigMap and Secret objects available in your Kubernetes cluster (under the current namespace):

```
\> kubectl get configmaps

NAME                                          DATA   AGE
orders-application-properties-config-map      1      50s
orders-keystore-config-map                    0      50s
orders-truststore-config-map                  0      50s

\> kubectl get secrets

NAME                     DATA   AGE
orders-key-credentials   2      50s
```

11.4.2 Creating a Deployment for the Order Processing microservice

In this section, we create a Deployment in Kubernetes for the Order Processing microservice that we defined in the order.processing.deployment.with.configmap.yaml file found in the chapter11/sample02/ directory. You can use the following `kubectl` command from the chapter11/sample02 directory to create the Kubernetes Deployment:

```
\>kubectl apply -f order.processing.deployment.with.configmap.yaml

deployment.apps/orders-deployment created
```

11.4.3 *Creating a Service for the Order Processing microservice*

To expose the Kubernetes Deployment we created in section 11.4.2 for the Order Processing microservice, we also need to create a Kubernetes Service. You can find the definition of this Service in the YAML file in the chapter11/sample02/order .processing.service.yml file. Use the following kubectl command from the chapter11 /sample02 directory to create the Kubernetes Service:

```
\> kubectl apply -f order.processing.service.yml

service/orders-service created
```

Then use the following command to find all the Services in your Kubernetes cluster (under the current namespace). It takes a few minutes for Kubernetes to assign an external IP address for the order-service we just created. After a couple of minutes, you'll notice the following output with an external IP address assigned to the Service. That is the IP address you should be using to access the Order Processing microservice:

```
\> kubectl get services
```

NAME	TYPE	CLUSTER-IP	EXTERNAL-IP	PORT(S)	AGE
kubernetes	ClusterIP	10.39.240.1	<none>	443/T	5d21h
orders-service	LoadBalancer	10.39.249.66	35.247.11.161	443:32401/TCP	72s
sts-service	LoadBalancer	10.39.255.168	34.83.188.72	443:31749/TCP	8m39s

Both the Kubernetes Services we created in this chapter for the STS and the Order Processing microservices are of LoadBalancer type. For a Service of the LoadBalancer type to work, Kubernetes uses an external load balancer. Since we run our examples in this chapter on GKE, GKE itself provides this external load balancer.

11.4.4 *Testing the end-to-end flow*

In this section, we test the end-to-end flow (figure 11.2, which is the same as figure 11.1, but we repeat here for convenience). We need to first get a token from the STS and then use it to access the Order Processing microservice. Now we have both microservices running on Kubernetes. Let's use the following curl command, run from your local machine, to a get a token from the STS. Make sure you use the correct external IP address of the STS:

```
\> curl -v -X POST --basic -u applicationid:applicationsecret \
-H "Content-Type: application/x-www-form-urlencoded;charset=UTF-8" \
-k -d "grant_type=password&username=peter&password=peter123&scope=foo" \
https://34.83.188.72/oauth/token
```

In this command, applicationid is the client ID of the web application, and applicationsecret is the client secret. If everything works, the STS returns an OAuth 2.0 access token, which is a JWT (or a JWS, to be precise):

```
{
"access_token":"eyJhbGciOiJSUzI1NiIsInR5cCI6IkpXVCJ9.eyJleHAiOjE1NTEzMTIzNz
YsInVzZXJfbmFtZSI6InBldGVyIiwiYXV0aG9yaXRpZXMiOlsiUk9MRV9VU0VSIl0sImp0aSI6I
jRkMmJiNjQ4LTQ2MWQtNGVlYy1hZTljLTVlYWUxZjA4ZTJhMiIsImNsaWVudF9pZCI6ImFwcGxp
```

```
Y2F0aW9uaWQiLCJzY29wZSI6WyJmb28iXX0.tr4yUmGLtsH7q9Ge2i7gxyTsOOa0RS0Yoc2uBuA
W5OVIKZcVsIITWV3bDN0FVHBzimpAPy33tvicFROhBFoVThqKXzzG00SkURN5bnQ4uFLAP0NpZ6
BuDjvVmwXNXrQp2lVXl4lQ4eTvuyZozjUSCXzCI1LNw5EFFi22J73g1_mRm2jdEhBp1TvMaRKLB
Dk2hzIDVKzu5oj_gODBFm3a1S-IJjYoCimIm2igcesXkhipRJtjNcrJSegBbGgyXHVak2gB7I07
ryVwl_Re5yX4sV9x6xNwCxc_DgP9hHLzPM8yz_K97jlT6Rr1XZBlveyjfKs_XIXgU5qizRm9mt5
xg",
"token_type":"bearer",
"refresh_token":"",
"expires_in":5999,
"scope":"foo",
"jti":"4d2bb648-461d-4eec-ae9c-5eae1f08e2a2"
}
```

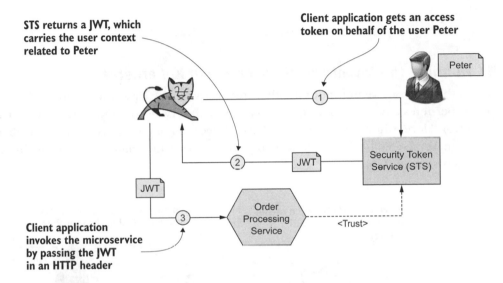

Figure 11.2   The STS issues a JWT access token to the client application, and the client application uses it to access the microservice on behalf of the user, Peter.

Now try to invoke the Order Processing microservice with the JWT you got from the previous `curl` command. Set the same JWT we got, in the HTTP Authorization Bearer header, using the following `curl` command, and invoke the Order Processing microservice. Because the JWT is a little lengthy, you can use a small trick when using the `curl` command in this case. Export the value of the JWT to an environmental variable (`TOKEN`) and then use that environmental variable in your request to the Order Processing microservice, as shown here:

```
\> export TOKEN=jwt_access_token
\> curl -k -H "Authorization: Bearer $TOKEN" \
https://35.247.11.161/orders/11

{
  "customer_id":"101021",
  "order_id":"11",
  "payment_method":{
```

```
  "card_type":"VISA",
  "expiration":"01/22",
  "name":"John Doe",
  "billing_address":"201, 1st Street, San Jose, CA"
},
"items":[
{
  "code":"101",
  "qty":1
},
{
  "code":"103",
  "qty":5
}
],
"shipping_address":"201, 1st Street, San Jose, CA"
}
```

11.5   *Running the Inventory microservice in Kubernetes*

In this section, we introduce another microservice, the Inventory microservice, to our Kubernetes environment and see how service-to-service communication works (figure 11.3). Here, when you invoke the Order Processing microservice with a JWT obtained from the STS, the Order Processing microservice internally talks to the Inventory microservice.

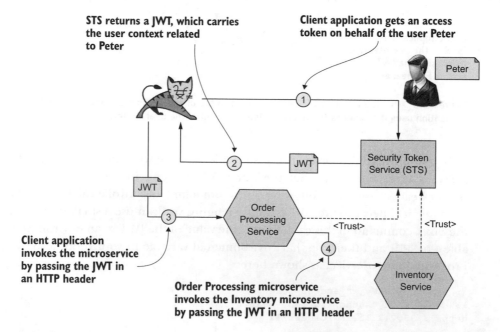

Figure 11.3   STS issues a JWT access token to the client application, and the client application uses it to access the Order Processing microservice on behalf of the user, Peter. The Order Processing microservice uses the same JWT it got from the client application to access the Inventory microservice.

Because the process of deploying the Inventory microservice on Kubernetes is similar to the process we followed while deploying the Order Processing microservice, we won't go into details. The only key difference is that the Kubernetes Service corresponding to the Inventory microservice is of `ClusterIP` type (or the default Service type) because we don't want external client applications to directly access it.

Let's run the following `kubectl` command from the chapter11/sample03 directory to create a Kubernetes Deployment for the Inventory microservice. This command creates a set of ConfigMaps, a Secret, a Deployment, and a Service:

```
\> kubectl apply -f .

configmap/inventory-application-properties-config-map created
configmap/inventory-keystore-config-map created
configmap/inventory-truststore-config-map created
secret/inventory-key-credentials created
deployment.apps/inventory-deployment created
service/inventory-service created
```

Use the following command to find all the Services in your Kubernetes cluster (under the current namespace). Because the Inventory microservice is a Service of `ClusterIP` type, you won't find an external IP address for it:

```
\> kubectl get services

NAME               TYPE          CLUSTER-IP     EXTERNAL-IP    PORT(S)
inventory-service  ClusterIP     10.39.251.182  <none>             443/TCP
orders-service     LoadBalancer  10.39.245.40   35.247.11.161  443:32078/TCP
sts-service        LoadBalancer  10.39.252.24   34.83.188.72   443:30288/TCP
```

Let's test the end-to-end flow (figure 11.3). We need to first get a token from the STS and then use it to access the Order Processing microservice. Now we have all three microservices running on Kubernetes. Let's use the following `curl` command, run from your local machine, to a get a token from the STS. Make sure you use the correct external IP address of the STS:

```
\> curl -v -X POST --basic -u applicationid:applicationsecret \
-H "Content-Type: application/x-www-form-urlencoded;charset=UTF-8" \
-k -d "grant_type=password&username=peter&password=peter123&scope=foo" \
https://34.83.188.72/oauth/token
```

In this command, `applicationid` is the client ID of the web application, and `applicationsecret` is the client secret. If everything works, the STS returns an OAuth 2.0 access token, which is a JWT (or a JWS, to be precise):

```
{
"access_token":"eyJhbGciOiJSUzI1NiIsInR5cCI6IkpXVCJ9.eyJleHAiOjE1NTEzMTIzNz
YsInVzZXJfbmFtZSI6InBldGVyIiwiYXV0aG9yaXRpZXMiOlsiUk9MRV9VU0VSIl0sImp0aSI6I
jRkMmJiNjQ4LTQ2MWQtNGVlYy1hZTljLTVlYWUxZjA4ZTJhMiIsImNsaWVudF9pZCI6ImFwcGxp
Y2F0aW9uaWQiLCJzY29wZSI6WyJmb28iXX0.tr4yUmGLtsH7q9Ge2i7gxyTsOOa0RS0Yoc2uBuA
W5OVIKZcVsIITWV3bDN0FVHBzimpAPy33tvicFROhBFoVThqKXzzG00SkURN5bnQ4uFLAP0NpZ6
BuDjvVmwXNXrQp2lVX14lQ4eTvuyZozjUSCXzCI1LNw5EFFi22J73g1_mRm2jdEhBp1TvMaRKLB
```

```
Dk2hzIDVKzu5oj_gODBFm3a1S-IJjYoCimIm2igcesXkhipRJtjNcrJSegBbGgyXHVak2gB7I07
ryVwl_Re5yX4sV9x6xNwCxc_DgP9hHLzPM8yz_K97jlT6Rr1XZBlveyjfKs_XIXgU5qizRm9mt5
xg",
"token_type":"bearer",
"refresh_token":"",
"expires_in":5999,
"scope":"foo",
"jti":"4d2bb648-461d-4eec-ae9c-5eae1f08e2a2"
}
```

Now let's invoke the Order Processing microservice with the JWT you got from the previous curl command. Set the same JWT you got, in the HTTP Authorization Bearer header using the following curl command and invoke the Order Processing microservice. Because the JWT is a little lengthy, you can use a small trick when using the curl command. Export the JWT to an environment variable (TOKEN), then use that environment variable in your request to the Order Processing microservice:

```
\> export TOKEN=jwt_access_token
\> curl -v -k https://35.247.11.161/orders \
-H "Authorization: Bearer $TOKEN" \
-H "Content-Type: application/json" \
-d @- << EOF
{   "customer_id":"101021",
    "payment_method":{
        "card_type":"VISA",
        "expiration":"01/22",
        "name":"John Doe",
        "billing_address":"201, 1st Street, San Jose, CA"
    },
    "items":[
      {
          "code":"101",
          "qty":1
      },
      {
          "code":"103",
          "qty":5
      }
    ],
    "shipping_address":"201, 1st Street, San Jose, CA"
}
EOF
```

In the previous command, we do an HTTP POST to the Order Processing microservice so that the Order Processing microservice can talk to the Inventory microservice. In return, you won't get any JSON payload, but only an HTTP 201 status code. When the Order Processing microservice talks to the Inventory microservice, the Inventory microservice prints the item codes in its logs. You can tail the logs with the following command that includes the Pod name corresponding to the Inventory microservice:

```
\> kubectl logs inventory-deployment-f7b8b99c7-4t56b --follow
```

11.6   *Using Kubernetes service accounts*

Kubernetes uses two types of accounts for authentication and authorization: user accounts and service accounts. The user accounts aren't created or managed by Kubernetes, while the service accounts are. In this section, we discuss how Kubernetes manages service accounts and associates those with Pods.

In appendix J, we talked about the high-level Kubernetes architecture and how a Kubernetes node communicates with the API server. Kubernetes uses service accounts to authenticate a Pod to the API server. A service account provides an identity to a Pod, and Kubernetes uses the ServiceAccount object to represent a service account. Let's use the following command to list all the service accounts available in our Kubernetes cluster (under the default namespace):

```
\> kubectl get serviceaccounts

NAME      SECRETS   AGE
default   1         11d
```

By default, at the time you create a Kubernetes cluster, Kubernetes also creates a service account for the default namespace. To find more details about the default service account, use the following `kubectl` command. It lists the service account definition in YAML format. There you can see that the default service account is bound to the default token secret that we discussed in section 11.3.1:

```
\> kubectl get serviceaccount default -o yaml

apiVersion: v1
kind: ServiceAccount
metadata:
  creationTimestamp: "2019-09-17T02:01:00Z"
  name: default
  namespace: default
  resourceVersion: "279"
  selfLink: /api/v1/namespaces/default/serviceaccounts/default
  uid: ff3d13ba-d8ee-11e9-a88f-42010a8a01e4
secrets:
- name: default-token-19fj8
```

Kubernetes binds each Pod to a service account. You can have multiple Pods bound to the same service account, but you can't have multiple service accounts bound to the same Pod (figure 11.4). For example, when you create a Kubernetes namespace, by default Kubernetes creates a service account. That service account is assigned to all the Pods that are created in the same namespace (unless you create a Pod under a specific service account). Under each namespace, you'll find a service account called `default`.

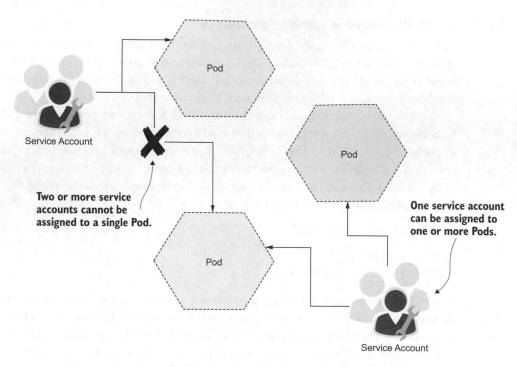

Figure 11.4   A service account in Kubernetes can be assigned to one or more Pods, while a Pod at any given time can be bound to only a single service account.

11.6.1 *Creating a service account and associating it with a Pod*

In this section, we create a service account called `ecomm`, and update the STS Deployment to use it. We want all the Pods running under the STS Deployment to run under the `ecomm` service account. Let's use the following `kubectl` command to create the `ecomm` service account:

```
\> kubectl create serviceaccount ecomm

serviceaccount/ecomm created
```

At the time of creating the service account, Kubernetes also creates a token secret and attaches it to the service account. When we update the STS Deployment to run under the `ecomm` service account, all the Pods under the STS Deployment can use this token secret (which is a JWT) to authenticate to the API server. The following command shows the details of the `ecomm` service account in YAML format:

```
\> kubectl get  serviceaccount ecomm -o  yaml

apiVersion: v1
kind: ServiceAccount
metadata:
  name: ecomm
```

```
    namespace: default
secrets:
- name: ecomm-token-92p7g
```

Now let's set the `ecomm` service account for the STS Deployment. The complete updated definition of the STS Deployment is in the chapter11/sample01/sts.deployment .with.service.account.yaml file. We are introducing these new changes on top of the STS Deployment created in section 11.3.2. As shown in the following listing, the only change was to add the `serviceAccountName` element under the `spec` element (corresponding to the Pod) of the Deployment.

Listing 11.17 Attaching a service account to a Pod

```
spec:
  serviceAccountName: ecomm
  containers:
  - name: sts
    image: prabath/secure-sts-ch10:v1
    imagePullPolicy: Always
    ports:
    - containerPort: 8443
```

Let's use the following command from the chapter11/sample01 directory to update the STS Deployment:

```
\> kubectl apply -f sts.deployment.with.service.account.yaml

deployment.apps/sts-deployment configured
```

If you run the `kubectl describe` pod command against the Pod Kubernetes created under the STS Deployment now, you'll find that it uses the token secret Kubernetes automatically created for the `ecomm` service account.

11.6.2 Benefits of running a Pod under a custom service account

If you don't specify a service account under the Pod spec of a Deployment (listing 11.17), Kubernetes runs all the corresponding Pods under the same default service account, created under the corresponding Kubernetes namespace.[5]

> **NOTE** Having different service accounts for each Pod or for a group of Pods helps you isolate what each Pod can do with the Kubernetes API server. Also, it helps you enforce fine-grained access control for the communications among Pods.

This is one security best practice we should follow in a Kubernetes Deployment. Then again, even if you have different service accounts for different Pods, if you don't

---

[5] The Pod spec in a Kubernetes Deployment object defines the parameters for the corresponding Pod.

enforce authorization checks at the API server, it adds no value. GKE enables role-based access control by default.

If your Kubernetes cluster doesn't enforce authorization checks, there's another option. If you don't want your Pod to talk to the API server at all, you can ask Kubernetes not to provision the default token secret to that corresponding Pod. Without the token secret, none of the Pods will be able to talk to the API server. To disable the default token provisioning, you need to set the `automountServiceAccountToken` element to `false` under the Pod `spec` of the Deployment (listing 11.17).

11.7   *Using role-based access control in Kubernetes*

Role-based access control (*RBAC*) in Kubernetes defines the actions a user or a service (a Pod) can perform in a Kubernetes cluster. A *role*, in general, defines a set of permissions or capabilities. Kubernetes has two types of objects to represent a role: Role and ClusterRole. The Role object represents capabilities associated with Kubernetes resources within a namespace, while ClusterRole represents capabilities at the Kubernetes cluster level.

Kubernetes defines two types of bindings to bind a role to one or more users (or services): RoleBinding and ClusterRoleBinding. The RoleBinding object represents a binding of namespaced resources to a set of users (or services) or, in other words, it binds a Role to a set of users (or services). The ClusterRoleBinding object represents a binding of cluster-level resources to a set of users (or services) or, in other words, it binds a ClusterRole to a set of users (or services). Let's use the following command to list all the ClusterRoles available in your Kubernetes environment. The truncated output shows the ClusterRoles available in GKE by default:

```
\> kubectl get clusterroles
```

```
NAME                                          AGE
admin                                         12d
cloud-provider                                12d
cluster-admin                                 12d
edit                                          12d
gce:beta:kubelet-certificate-bootstrap        12d
gce:beta:kubelet-certificate-rotation         12d
gce:cloud-provider                            12d
kubelet-api-admin                             12d
system:aggregate-to-admin                     12d
system:aggregate-to-edit                      12d
system:aggregate-to-view                      12d
```

To view the capabilities of a given ClusterRole, let's use the following `kubectl` command. The output in YAML format shows that under the `rules` section, the `cluster -admin` role can perform any verb (or action) on any resource belongs to any API group. In fact, this role provides full access to the Kubernetes cluster:

```
\> kubectl get clusterrole cluster-admin -o yaml

apiVersion: rbac.authorization.k8s.io/v1
kind: ClusterRole
```

```
metadata:
  annotations:
    rbac.authorization.kubernetes.io/autoupdate: "true"
  labels:
    kubernetes.io/bootstrapping: rbac-defaults
  name: cluster-admin
rules:
- apiGroups:
  - '*'
  resources:
  - '*'
  verbs:
  - '*'
- nonResourceURLs:
  - '*'
  verbs:
  - '*'
```

Let's use the following command to list all the ClusterRoleBindings available in your Kubernetes environment. The truncated output shows the ClusterRoleBindings available in GKE by default:

```
\> kubectl get clusterrolebinding
```

```
NAME                                          AGE
cluster-admin                                 12d
event-exporter-rb                             12d
gce:beta:kubelet-certificate-bootstrap        12d
gce:beta:kubelet-certificate-rotation         12d
gce:cloud-provider                            12d
heapster-binding                              12d
kube-apiserver-kubelet-api-admin              12d
kubelet-bootstrap                             12d
```

To view the users and services attached to a given ClusterRoleBinding, let's use the following `kubectl` command. The output of the command, in YAML, shows that under the `roleRef` section, `cluster-admin` refers to the `cluster-admin` Cluster-Role, and under the `subjects` section, the `system:masters` group is part of the role binding. Or, in other words, the `cluster-admin` ClusterRoleBinding binds the `system:masters` group to the `cluster-admin` ClusterRole, so anyone in the `system:masters` group has full access to the Kubernetes cluster:

```
\> kubectl get clusterrolebinding cluster-admin -o yaml
```

```
apiVersion: rbac.authorization.k8s.io/v1
kind: ClusterRoleBinding
metadata:
  annotations:
    rbac.authorization.kubernetes.io/autoupdate: "true"
  labels:
    kubernetes.io/bootstrapping: rbac-defaults
  name: cluster-admin
roleRef:
  apiGroup: rbac.authorization.k8s.io
```

```
  kind: ClusterRole
  name: cluster-admin
subjects:
- apiGroup: rbac.authorization.k8s.io
  kind: Group
  name: system:masters
```

As we discussed in section 11.5, Kubernetes has two types of accounts: users and service accounts, and users aren't managed by Kubernetes. Also, you can use a construct called a *group* to group both the users and service accounts. In this case, we have a group called `system:masters`.

Kubernetes has a plugin architecture to authenticate and authorize requests. Once an authentication plugin completes authenticating a request, it returns the username and the group information with respect to the corresponding account (a user or a service account) to the authorization plugin chain. How the authentication plugin finds the user's group information depends on how the plugin is implemented. Kubernetes needs to not maintain group information internally; the authentication plugin can connect to any external source to find the account-to-group mapping. That being said, Kubernetes also manages a set of predefined groups for service accounts. For example, the group `system:serviceaccounts:default` assumes all the service accounts under the default namespace.

Let's go through a practical example to understand how Kubernetes uses groups. Some time ago, when the developers of Docker Desktop decided to add Kubernetes support, they wanted to promote all the service accounts in the Kubernetes environment to cluster admins. To facilitate that, they came up with a ClusterRoleBinding called `docker-for-desktop-binding`, which binds the `cluster-admin` Cluster-Role to the group `system:serviceaccounts`. The `system:serviceaccounts` group is a built-in Kubernetes group that assumes all the system accounts in the Kubernetes cluster are members of it. The following shows the definition of the `docker-for-desktop-binding` ClusterRoleBinding:

```
apiVersion: rbac.authorization.k8s.io/v1
kind: ClusterRoleBinding
metadata:
  name: docker-for-desktop-binding
roleRef:
  apiGroup: rbac.authorization.k8s.io
  kind: ClusterRole
  name: cluster-admin
subjects:
- apiGroup: rbac.authorization.k8s.io
  kind: Group
  name: system:serviceaccounts
```

11.7.1 *Talking to the Kubernetes API server from the STS*

Let's say, for example, we need the STS to talk to the API server. Ideally, we'll do that in the STS code itself. Because this is just an example, we'll use curl from a container that runs the STS. Use the following `kubectl` command to directly access the shell of an STS Pod. Because we have only one container in each Pod, we can simply use the Pod name (`sts-deployment-69b99fc78c-j76tl`) here:

```
\> kubectl -it exec sts-deployment-69b99fc78c-j76tl sh
#
```

After you run the command, you end up with a shell prompt within the corresponding container. Also, we assume that you've followed along in section 11.6.1 and updated the STS Deployment, where now it runs under the `ecomm` service account.

Because we want to use curl to talk to the API server, we need to first install it with the following command in the STS container. And because the containers are immutable, if you restart the Pod during this exercise, you'll need to install curl again:

```
# apk add --update curl && rm -rf /var/cache/apk/*
```

To invoke an API, we also need to pass the default token secret (which is a JWT) in the HTTP authorization header. Let's use the following command to export the token secret to the `TOKEN` environment variable. As we've previously mentioned, the default token secret is accessible to every container from the /var/run/secrets/kubernetes.io /serviceaccount/token file:

```
# export TOKEN=$(cat /var/run/secrets/kubernetes.io/serviceaccount/token)
```

The following `curl` command talks to the Kubernetes API server to list all the metadata associated with the current Pod. Here, we pass the default token secret, which we exported to the `TOKEN` environment variable, in the HTTP authorization header. Also, inside a Pod, Kubernetes itself populates the value of the `HOSTNAME` environment variable with the corresponding Pod name, and the `kubernetes.default` `.svc` hostname is mapped to the IP address of the API server running in the Kubernetes control plane:

```
# curl -k -v -H "Authorization: Bearer $TOKEN" \
https://kubernetes.default.svc/api/v1/namespaces/default/pods/$HOSTNAME
```

In response to this command, the API server returns the HTTP 403 code, which means the `ecomm` service account isn't authorized to access this particular API. In fact, it's not only this specific API; the `ecomm` service account isn't authorized to access any of the APIs on the API server! That's the default behavior of GKE. Neither the default service account that Kubernetes creates for each namespace nor a custom service account you create are associated with any roles.

11.7.2 *Associating a service account with a ClusterRole*

Associating a service account with a ClusterRole gives that particular service account the permissions to do certain tasks authorized under the corresponding ClusterRole. There are two ways to associate the `ecomm` service account with a ClusterRole.

One way to associate a service account with a ClusterRole is to create a new Cluster-RoleBinding; the other way is to update an existing ClusterRoleBinding. In this section, we follow the first approach and create a new ClusterRoleBinding called `ecomm-cluster-admin` in GKE. You can find the definition of the `ecomm-cluster-admin` ClusterRoleBinding in the chapter11/sample01/ecomm.cluster-role.binding.yaml file (and in the following listing).

> **Listing 11.18   The definition of ecomm-cluster-admin**

```
apiVersion: rbac.authorization.k8s.io/v1
kind: ClusterRoleBinding
metadata:
  labels:
    addonmanager.kubernetes.io/mode: Reconcile
    kubernetes.io/cluster-service: "true"
  name: ecomm-cluster-admin
roleRef:
  apiGroup: rbac.authorization.k8s.io
  kind: ClusterRole
  name: cluster-admin
subjects:
- kind: ServiceAccount
  namespace: default
  name: ecomm
```

Let's use the following command from the chapter11/sample01 directory to update the Kubernetes environment with the new ClusterRoleBinding:

```
\> kubectl apply -f ecomm.clusterrole.binding.yaml

clusterrolebinding.rbac.authorization.k8s.io/kube-apiserver-kubelet-api-admin
configured
```

Now if you redo the exercise in section 11.7.1, you'll get a successful response from the API server, as the `ecomm` service account, which is now associated with a ClusterRole, is authorized to list all the metadata associated with the current Pod.

If you'd like to know more about the authorization model of Kubernetes, refer to the online documentation at https://kubernetes.io/docs/reference/access-authn-authz/authorization/.

Summary

- Kubernetes uses ConfigMaps to externalize configurations from the application code, which runs in a container, but it's not the correct way of externalizing sensitive data in Kubernetes.
- The ideal way to store sensitive data in a Kubernetes environment is to use Secrets; Kubernetes stores the value of a Secret in its etcd distributed key-value store in an encrypted format.
- Kubernetes dispatches Secrets only to the Pods that use them, and even in such cases, the Secrets are never written to disk, only kept in memory.

- Each Pod, by default, is mounted with a token secret, which is a JWT. A Pod can use this default token secret to talk to the Kubernetes API server.
- Kubernetes has two types of accounts: users and service accounts. The user accounts aren't created or managed by Kubernetes, while the service accounts are.
- By default, each Pod is associated with a service account (with the name `default`), and each service account has its own token secret.
- It's recommended that you always have different service accounts for different Pods (or for a group of Pods). This is one of the security best practices we should always follow in a Kubernetes Deployment.
- If you have a Pod that doesn't need to access the API server, it's recommended that you not provision the token secret to such Pods.
- Kubernetes uses Roles/ClusterRoles and RoleBindings/ClusterRoleBindings to enforce access control on the API server.

Securing microservices with Istio service mesh 12

This chapter covers

- Terminating TLS at the Istio Ingress gateway
- Securing service-to-service communications with mTLS in an Istio environment
- Securing service-to-service communications with JWT in an Istio environment
- Enforcing RBAC with Istio
- Managing keys in an Istio deployment

In chapter 6, we discussed how to secure service-to-service communications with certificates; and in chapter 7, we extended that discussion to use JWTs to secure service-to-service communications. Then in chapters 10 and 11, we discussed how to deploy a set of microservices as Docker containers in Kubernetes and to secure service-to-service communications with JWT over mTLS. In all of these cases, each microservice by itself had to worry about doing security processing. Or in other words, each microservice embedded a set of Spring Boot libraries to do security processing. This violates one key aspect of microservices architecture, the single responsibility principle, under which a microservice should be performing only one particular function.

A *service mesh* is a result of the gradual progress in implementing the single responsibility principle in microservices architecture. It is, in fact, an architectural pattern that brings in best practices in resiliency, security, observability, and routing control to your microservices deployment, which we discussed in appendix K in detail. Istio is an *out-of-process service mesh* implementation that runs apart from your microservice, transparently intercepts all the traffic coming into and going out from your microservice, and enforces security and other quality of service (QoS) controls.

> **NOTE** If you are new to the Service Mesh pattern and Istio, see appendix K first. This chapter assumes you understand the Service Mesh pattern and Istio, and have gone through all the samples in appendix K.

In this chapter, we are going to redo some of the examples we discussed in chapter 6 and chapter 7, following the Service Mesh architecture with Istio.

12.1 Setting up the Kubernetes deployment

In this section, we are going to set up a Kubernetes deployment (figure 12.1) that is similar to what we had in section 11.5. The only difference is that here we have removed the JWT verification and mTLS from the Order Processing and Inventory

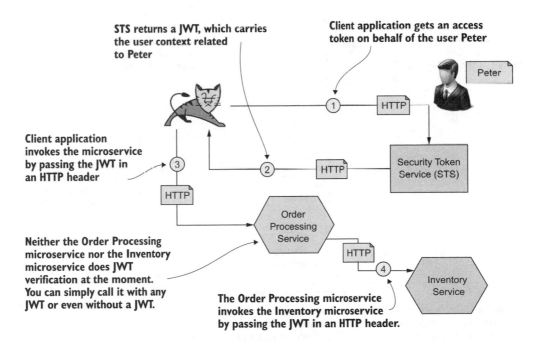

Figure 12.1 STS issues a JWT access token to the client application, and the client application uses it to access the Order Processing microservice on behalf of the user, Peter. The Order Processing microservice uses the same JWT it got from the client application to access the Inventory microservice.

microservices. Also, we have removed TLS support from all three microservices (figure 12.1). If you aren't familiar with Kubernetes, or if it's been a while since you've worked with it, see appendix J, which is an overview of the Kubernetes basics.

12.1.1 *Enabling Istio autoinjection*

To add Istio support for the microservices we are about to deploy—or, in other words, to autoinject Envoy as a sidecar proxy to the microservice deployment—run the following `kubectl` command. Figure 12.2 gives you a high-level understanding of what the deployment will look like. Here, we enable autoinjection for the `default` namespace (in appendix K, we discuss how to install Istio in Kubernetes and sidecar autoinjection in detail). If you are using a fresh Kubernetes cluster on Google Kubernetes Engine (GKE), make sure that you have enabled the Istio add-on for your cluster (see appendix K for the details):

```
\> kubectl label namespace default istio-injection=enabled
```

To try out the samples in this chapter, you can use either the Kubernetes cluster you created on GKE in appendix K (or chapter 11) or your local Kubernetes cluster running on Docker Desktop. At the time of this writing, the latest GKE cluster version is 1.14.10-gke.27, and it supports only Istio 1.2.10. Istio 1.2.10 was released in December 2019, and at the time of this writing, the latest Istio release is 1.6.2, which was released

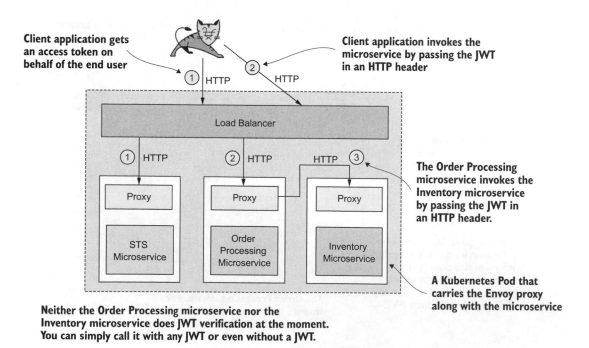

Figure 12.2   Istio introduces the Envoy sidecar proxy to each Pod, along with the container that carries the microservice.

in June 2020. There is always a time gap in GKE to support the latest version of Istio. So, if you are using GKE, you won't be able to test the new features introduced in Istio 1.5.*x* or later releases. In this chapter, we talk about some of the new security features Istio introduced in version 1.5.0, and you would need to switch from GKE to your local Istio installation on Docker Desktop to test them, unless GKE is upgraded to Istio 1.5.*x* at the time you read the book. You can find the GKE-to-Istio version mapping at https://cloud.google.com/istio/docs/istio-on-gke/versions.

12.1.2 *Clean up any previous work*

If you have already run the samples in appendix K or chapter 11, let's run the following command from the chapter12/sample01 directory to clean those Deployments. (If you have not, it's not a must to run those samples in appendix K or chapter 11.) If the script returns any errors saying some resources are not found, you can simply ignore them. All the source code related to the samples in this chapter is available in the https://github.com/microservices-security-in-action/samples GitHub repository, in the chapter12 directory. The clean.sh script deletes all the Kubernetes Services, Deployments, ConfigMaps, and Secrets we created in appendix K and chapter 11:

```
\> sh clean.sh
```

12.1.3 *Deploying microservices*

To create three Kubernetes Deployments and the corresponding Services with respect to the STS, Order Processing, and Inventory microservices, run the following command from the chapter12/sample01 directory:

```
\> kubectl apply -f .

configmap/inventory-application-properties-config-map created
deployment.apps/inventory-deployment created
service/inventory-service created
configmap/orders-application-properties-config-map created
deployment.apps/orders-deployment created
service/orders-service created
configmap/sts-application-properties-config-map created
configmap/sts-jwt-keystore-config-map created
secret/sts-keystore-secrets created
deployment.apps/sts-deployment created
service/sts-service created
```

Let's run the following command to verify the environment. This shows three Pods, each one corresponding to a microservice. In each Pod, we see two containers, one for the microservice and the other for the Envoy proxy:

```
\> kubectl get pods

NAME                                     READY   STATUS    RESTARTS
inventory-deployment-7848664f49-x9z7h    2/2     Running   0
orders-deployment-7f5564c8d4-ttgb2       2/2     Running   0
sts-deployment-85cdd8c7cd-qk2c5          2/2     Running   0
```

Next, you can run the following command to list the available Services. Here, we have `orders-service` and `sts-service` of the LoadBalancer type.[1] That means these two Services are publicly accessible. When we use Istio, we do not need to make these Services of LoadBalancer type, because we are going to use the Istio Ingress gateway anyway—and all the traffic should flow through it. If we have a Service of Load-Balancer type, and expose that via the Istio Ingress gateway, we create two entry points for that microservice. You can access the microservice with the external IP address of the Service, as well as with the IP address of the Istio Ingress gateway, which does not sound good:

```
\> kubectl get services

NAME                TYPE          CLUSTER-IP      EXTERNAL-IP     PORT(S)
inventory-service   ClusterIP     10.39.243.179   <none>          80/TCP
orders-service      LoadBalancer  10.39.242.8     35.247.11.161   80:32515/TCP
sts-service         LoadBalancer  10.39.243.231   35.199.169.214  80:31569/TCP
```

If you look at the `PORT` column in the preceding output, you'll notice that all three Services are running on HTTP on port 80 (not over TLS), which is not good in terms of security. In section 12.2, we discuss how to use the Istio Ingress gateway to protect these Services with TLS. Also in section 12.2, we are going to redeploy both the `orders-service` and `sts-service` Services as `ClusterIP` Services, so they won't be directly accessible outside the Kubernetes cluster.

12.1.4 *Redeploying Order Processing and STS as NodePort Services*

You need to follow this section only if you are using a local Kubernetes cluster on Docker Desktop or Minikube, where the Services of LoadBalancer type won't still let you access them outside the cluster, as you do not have an external load balancer in your environment. In that case, you can change the Service type of the Order Processing and STS microservices to NodePort type. Then you can access both the microservices with the port of the node and the corresponding node IP address (which is localhost or 127.0.0.1).

To do that, run the following command from chapter12/sample01/docker-desktop directory. This will delete the `orders-service` and `sts-service` Services (if already there) and redeploy both as NodePort type Services. As per the output of the command, the node port of the `orders-service` is 32485, and the node port of the `sts-service` is 31310:

```
\> sh deploy-locally.sh

NAME                TYPE        CLUSTER-IP      EXTERNAL-IP   PORT(S)
inventory-service   ClusterIP   10.97.213.70    <none>        80/TCP
orders-service      NodePort    10.96.187.28    <none>        80:32485/TCP
sts-service         NodePort    10.97.191.229   <none>        80:31310/TCP
```

---

[1] If you are not familiar with the various Kubernetes service types, see appendix J.

12.1.5 *Testing end-to-end flow*

In this section, we are going to test the end-to-end flow, as shown in figure 12.1. Because the Order Processing microservice is secured with JWT, first we need to get a JWT from the STS, which the Order Processing microservice trusts. Let's run the following curl command to talk to the STS and get a JWT. Here, we use curl to represent your client application; in the command, make sure to use the external IP address corresponding to your STS. If you followed section 12.1.4, you need to use the corresponding node port and localhost as the hostname:

```
\> curl -v -X POST --basic -u applicationid:applicationsecret \
-H "Content-Type: application/x-www-form-urlencoded;charset=UTF-8" \
-k -d "grant_type=password&username=peter&password=peter123&scope=foo" \
http://35.199.169.214/oauth/token
```

The following command does an HTTP GET to the Order Processing microservice. We do not need to pass the JWT we obtained from the previous command, because we are not doing JWT verification at the service level. Later in the chapter, we discuss how to do JWT verification with Istio. In the following command, make sure to use the external IP address corresponding to your Order Processing microservice. If you followed section 12.1.4, you need to use the corresponding node port and localhost as the hostname:

```
\> curl -k http://35.247.11.161/orders/11
```

Finally, let's run the following command to POST to the Order Processing microservice, which internally calls the Inventory microservice. Again, in the curl command, make sure to use the external IP address corresponding to your Order Processing microservice; or if you followed section 12.1.4, you need to use the corresponding node port and localhost as the hostname:

```
\> curl -k -v http://35.247.11.161/orders \
-H 'Content-Type: application/json' \
-d @- << EOF
{
   "customer_id":"101021",
   "payment_method":{
      "card_type":"VISA",
      "expiration":"01/22",
      "name":"John Doe",
      "billing_address":"201, 1st Street, San Jose, CA"
   },
   "items":[
      {
         "code":"101",
         "qty":1
      },
      {
         "code":"103",
         "qty":5
      }
```

```
    ],
    "shipping_address":"201, 1st Street, San Jose, CA"
}
EOF
```

All these communications happen over HTTP. This is an incomplete setup to verify that our Kubernetes environment works fine; in an ideal production setup, we should not expose any of the microservices just over HTTP. As we move forward in this chapter, we discuss how to make this incomplete setup more complete and secure.

12.2   Enabling TLS termination at the Istio Ingress gateway

In this section, we are going to expose the three microservices we deployed in Kubernetes in section 12.1 via the Istio Ingress gateway over TLS. The Istio Ingress gateway runs at the edge of the Kubernetes cluster; all the traffic coming to your service mesh ideally should go through the Ingress gateway (figure 12.3). Here, we enable TLS only at the Ingress gateway (each microservice will still run on HTTP). The Ingress gateway terminates TLS at the edge and then routes traffic over HTTP to the corresponding

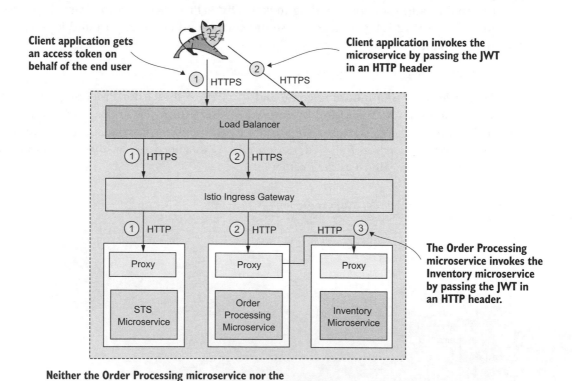

Figure 12.3   The Istio Ingress gateway intercepts all the requests coming to the microservice and terminates the TLS connection.

microservices. In section 12.3, we discuss how to enable mTLS between the Ingress gateway and the microservices—and also among microservices.

12.2.1 *Deploying TLS certificates to the Istio Ingress gateway*

In this section, we teach you how to enable TLS at the Istio Ingress gateway. To enable TLS, first we need to create a public/private key pair. Here, we use OpenSSL to generate the keys. OpenSSL is a commercial-grade toolkit and cryptographic library for TLS that's available for multiple platforms. Appendix G covers how to generate keys with OpenSSL in detail.

The following command uses an OpenSSL Docker image, which we can use to generate keys, so you don't need to worry about installing OpenSSL locally. Run the following command from the chapter12/sample02 directory, and when the OpenSSL container spins up, it provides a prompt to execute the OpenSSL commands:

```
\> docker run -it -v $(pwd):/export prabath/openssl
#
```

Run the following OpenSSL command to generate a public/private key pair; you can find the generated keys inside the chapter12/sample02/gateway-keys directory. When you pull the samples from the GitHub repository, the keys are already in the chapter12/sample02/gateway-keys directory—so before executing the following command, make sure to delete them. Alternatively, you can skip the key generation and use the keys from the GitHub repository. To exit from the OpenSSL Docker container, type exit:

```
# openssl req  -nodes -new -x509 -keyout /export/gateway-keys/server.key \
-out /export/gateway-keys/server.cert -subj "/CN=gateway.ecomm.com"
```

Istio introduced a feature called Secret Discovery Service (SDS) with Istio 1.1.0 under the sds profile for key provisioning and rotation (we discuss this in detail in section 12.6.3). So, if you are using Istio 1.1.0 or any release after that, but prior to 1.5.0, with the default profile, you will not see SDS support. If you check the Istio feature status available at the Istio website (https://istio.io/about/feature-stages/#security-and -policy-enforcement), you can find the status of the SDS feature. It was in the alpha phase prior to 1.5.0 and became stable since that. In the following sections, we discuss how to deploy the keys we generated in this section at the Ingress gateway, with and without the SDS support.

INGRESS GATEWAY WITH NO SDS

In this section, we discuss how to set up TLS keys for the Istio Ingress gateway with no SDS support. If you are using Istio 1.5.0 or later, you can move to the next section, which explains how to do the same with SDS support.

The Istio Ingress gateway (with no SDS support) reads the public/private key pair for the TLS communication from a well-defined Kubernetes Secret called istio-ingressgateway-certs. In fact, the Istio Ingress gateway is an Envoy proxy, running within a Pod, under the istio-system namespace, in the Kubernetes cluster.

You can run the following command to list all the Pods available in the `istio-system` namespace and find the name of the Istio Ingress gateway Pod. The output of the command is truncated to show only the Istio Ingress gateway Pod:

```
\> kubectl get pods -n istio-system

NAME                                      READY   STATUS    RESTARTS
istio-ingressgateway-6d8f9d87f8-sc2ch     1/1     Running   0
```

To learn more about the Istio Ingress gateway Pod, let's use the following command in listing 12.1 with the correct Pod name. This listing shows only a truncated output with the volume mounts (which we discussed in appendix J and chapter 11), and the code annotations explain some important elements.

Listing 12.1   The volume mounts of the Istio Ingress gateway Pod

```
\> kubectl get pod -n istio-system \
istio-ingressgateway-6d8f9d87f8-sc2ch -o yaml

volumeMounts:
- mountPath: /etc/certs                                  ◁──  Mount path from the Envoy local
  name: istio-certs                                            filesystem for the keys used by Envoy
  readOnly: true                                               when talking to upstream services
- mountPath: /etc/istio/ingressgateway-certs            ◁──  protected with mTLS, identified by
  name: ingressgateway-certs                                   the volume name istio-certs
  readOnly: true
- mountPath: /etc/istio/ingressgateway-ca-certs                 Mount path from the Envoy local
  name: ingressgateway-ca-certs                                 filesystem for the private/public
  readOnly: true                                                key pair to enable TLS for the
- mountPath: /var/run/secrets/kubernetes.io/serviceaccount      downstream clients
  name: istio-ingressgateway-service-account-token-qpmwf       ◁──
  readOnly: true
```

The public certificates of trusted certificate authorities corresponding to downstream clients authenticate to Ingress gateway using mTLS

The mount path to the default token secret (JWT) associated with the corresponding service account, which is provisioned by Kubernetes—not specific to Istio

To create the `istio-ingressgateway-certs` from the private/public keys we created at the beginning of the section 12.2.1, let's run the following command from the chapter12/sample02 directory:

```
\> kubectl create secret tls istio-ingressgateway-certs \
--key gateway-keys/server.key --cert gateway-keys/server.cert \
-n istio-system

secret/istio-ingressgateway-certs created
```

Finally, to enable TLS at the Ingress gateway, we need to define a Gateway resource. This resource, introduced by Istio, instructs the load balancer on how to route traffic to the Istio Ingress gateway. You can find more details on the Gateway resource in appendix K. Since the Ingress gateway is running in the `istio-system` namespace, we also create the Gateway resource in the same namespace. Ideally, you need to have only one Gateway resource for your Kubernetes cluster. That is only a common practice. Another practice is to have a Gateway resource in every namespace, but all of them pointing to the same Istio Ingress gateway Pod running in the `istio-system` namespace.

Listing 12.2 shows the definition of the Gateway resource. The `ecomm-gateway` Gateway resource instructs the load balancer to route traffic on HTTPS port 443 and HTTP port 80 to the Istio Ingress gateway Pod, which is an Envoy proxy.

Listing 12.2 The definition of the Gateway resource with no SDS

```
apiVersion: networking.istio.io/v1alpha3
kind: Gateway
metadata:
  name: ecomm-gateway
  namespace: istio-system          The Gateway resource is created
                                   in the istio-system namespace.
spec:
  selector:
    istio: ingressgateway          Associates the Istio Ingress gateway
                                   Pod with the Gateway resource
  servers:
  - port:                          Instructs the load balancer to route traffic on
      number: 443                  port 443 on HTTPS to the Ingress gateway
      name: https
      protocol: HTTPS                                    The volume mount
    tls:                           Enables TLS           of the public certificate
      mode: SIMPLE                                       for TLS communication
      serverCertificate: /etc/istio/ingressgateway-certs/tls.crt   with downstream clients
      privateKey: /etc/istio/ingressgateway-certs/tls.key
    hosts:                                               The volume mount of
    - "*"                          Instructs the load balancer to route   the private key for the
  - port:                          traffic on port 443 on HTTPS to the    TLS communication with
      number: 80                   Ingress gateway for any hostname       downstream clients
      name: http
      protocol: HTTP
    hosts:                         Instructs the load balancer to route
    - "*"                          traffic on port 80 on HTTP to the
    tls:                           Ingress gateway for any hostname
      httpsRedirect: true          Redirects any HTTP traffic
                                   to the HTTPS endpoint
```

Here, we use `SIMPLE` as the `tls/mode`. In addition, Istio supports four more modes, as table 12.1 describes.

To deploy the Gateway resource shown in listing 12.2 under the `istio-system` namespace, run the following command from the chapter12/sample02 directory:

```
\> kubectl apply -f istio.public.gateway.yaml

gateway.networking.istio.io/ecomm-gateway created
```

Once we enable TLS at the Ingress gateway, all the traffic that comes to the service mesh is protected for confidentiality. Next, to expose the Order Processing microservice and the STS via the Ingress gateway, we need to create two VirtualServices. Before that in the next section, we discuss how to set up TLS at the Istio Ingress gateway with SDS support. The way you set up VirtualServices for two microservices does not change, whether you use Istio with SDS support or not.

Table 12.1   TLS modes enforced by Istio Ingress gateway

Mode	Description
SIMPLE	Enables one-way TLS communication between the client applications and the Ingress gateway. You need to have a public/private key pair for the gateway.
PASSTHROUGH	Just passes through the traffic to the corresponding Pod, based on the Server Name Indication (SNI).[a] In appendix K, listing K.7, we discuss a sample that uses PASSTHROUGH mode. With this mode, you do not need to configure any public/private key pair for the gateway.
MUTUAL	Enables mTLS communication between the client applications (downstream applications) and the Ingress gateway. You need to have a public/private key pair for the gateway along with a set of trusted CA certificates. Only client applications carrying a valid certificate signed by any of the trusted CAs can access the Ingress gateway. To enable mTLS, we need to create a Secret with the name istio-ingressgateway-ca-certs that carries the trusted CA certificates, and define a new element called caCertificates under the tls element of the Gateway resource, which carries the value /etc/istio/ingressgateway-ca-certs/ca-chain.cert.pem.
AUTO_PASSTHROUGH	Under PASSTHROUGH mode, the Ingress gateway expects an Istio VirtualService to present and read the configuration data from the corresponding VirtualService to route the traffic to the upstream Pod. Under AUTO_PASSTHROUGH mode, we do not need to have a VirtualService, and the Ingress gateway expects all the required routing information to be encoded into the SNI value.
ISTIO_MUTUAL	Just like MUTUAL mode, this too enables mTLS communication between the client applications (downstream applications) and the Ingress gateway. Unlike in MUTUAL mode, this mode uses the certificates provisioned by Istio itself, which are available under the /etc/certs location of the Envoy filesystem.

[a] Server Name Indication (SNI) is a TLS extension that a client application can use before the start of the TLS handshake to indicate to the server which hostname it intends to talk to. The Istio gateway can route traffic by looking at this SNI parameter.

INGRESS GATEWAY WITH SDS

In this section, we discuss how to set up TLS keys (which we created at the beginning of section 12.2.1) for the Istio Ingress gateway with SDS support. If you already followed the instructions in the previous section on how to set up TLS keys for an Ingress gateway with no SDS, you can skip this section and proceed to section 12.2.2.

In this section, we assume you are using Istio 1.5.0 or later. At the time of this writing, the Istio default installation on GKE does not support Istio 1.5.0, so in that case you would need to have your own local Kubernetes cluster with Istio 1.5.0 or later on Docker Desktop. In appendix K, section K.5.1, we discuss how to set up Istio on Docker Desktop.

To set up TLS keys with SDS at the Istio Ingress gateway, first we need to enable SDS at the Ingress gateway with the following command.[2] This command uses the `istioctl` command-line utility (https://istio.io/docs/reference/commands/istioctl/), which comes with the Istio distribution. Here we generate an Istio install manifest by setting the `values.gateways.istio-ingressgateway.sds.enabled` property to `true`, and save the updated manifest in our local filesystem in the file `istio-ingressgateway.yaml`:

```
\> istioctl manifest generate \
--set values.gateways.istio-ingressgateway.sds.enabled=true > \
istio-ingressgateway.yaml
```

From the same location you ran the previous command, run the following to apply the updated Istio configuration:

```
\> kubectl apply -f istio-ingressgateway.yaml
```

Now we can create a Kubernetes Secret from the keys we created at the beginning of section 12.2.1. You should be able to find those keys in the chapter12/sample02/gateway-keys directory: the server.cert file is the public key, and server.key is the private key. Run the following command from the chapter12/sample02/gateway-keys directory to create the Kubernetes Secret. We create this Secret under the same namespace, where the Istio Ingress gateway is running (`istio-system`) and name it `ecomm-credentials`:

```
\> kubectl create  n istio-system secret generic ecomm-credential \
--from-file=key=server.key --from-file=cert=server.cert
```

Finally, to enable TLS at the Ingress gateway (with the SDS support), we need to define a Gateway resource. This resource, introduced by Istio, instructs the load balancer on how to route traffic to the Istio Ingress gateway. You can find more details on the Gateway resource in appendix K. Since the Ingress gateway is running in the `istio-system` namespace, we also create the Gateway resource in the same namespace. Ideally, you need to have only one Gateway resource for your Kubernetes cluster. That is only a common practice. Another practice is to have a Gateway resource in every namespace, but all of them pointing to the same Istio Ingress gateway Pod running in the `istio-system` namespace.

Listing 12.3 shows the definition of the Gateway resource. The `ecomm-gateway` Gateway resource instructs the load balancer to route traffic on HTTPS port 443 and HTTP port 80 to the Istio Ingress gateway Pod, which is an Envoy proxy. The Gateway definition in the following listing is very similar to what we had in listing 12.2 (with no SDS). The only difference is in the way we refer to TLS keys. Here, we use the name of the Kubernetes Secret we created before (`ecomm-credential`) to identify TLS keys.

---

[2] Even though SDS is enabled by default since Istio 1.5.0, the Istio Ingress gateway still does not use SDS by default.

Listing 12.3 The definition of the Gateway resource with SDS

```
apiVersion: networking.istio.io/v1alpha3
kind: Gateway
metadata:
  name: ecomm-gateway
  namespace: istio-system          ◁——  The Gateway resource is created
                                         in the istio-system namespace.
spec:
  selector:                        Associates the Istio Ingress gateway
    istio: ingressgateway      ◁—— Pod with the Gateway resource
  servers:
  - port:        ◁——  Instructs the load balancer to route traffic on
      number: 443     port 443 on HTTPS to the Ingress gateway
      name: https
      protocol: HTTPS
    tls:                    Enables TLS
      mode: SIMPLE     ◁——                  Points to a Kubernetes Secret,
      credentialName: ecomm-credential  ◁—— which carries TLS keys
    hosts:
    - "*"
  - port:        ◁——  Instructs the load balancer to route
      number: 80       traffic on port 443 on HTTPS to the
      name: http       Ingress gateway for any hostname
      protocol: HTTP
    hosts:      Instructs the load balancer to route
    - "*"       traffic on port 80 on HTTP to the
    tls:        Ingress gateway for any hostname     Redirects any HTTP traffic
      httpsRedirect: true      ◁——                  to the HTTPS endpoint
```

To deploy the Gateway resource shown in listing 12.3 under the `istio-system` namespace, run the following command from the chapter12/sample02 directory:

```
\> kubectl apply -f istio.public.gateway.sds.yaml
```

```
gateway.networking.istio.io/ecomm-gateway created
```

Once we enable TLS at the Ingress gateway, all the traffic that comes to the service mesh is protected for confidentiality. Next, to expose the Order Processing microservice and the STS via the Ingress gateway, we need to create two VirtualServices. The way you set up VirtualServices for two microservices does not change, whether you use Istio with SDS support or not.

12.2.2 *Deploying VirtualServices*

In this section, we are going to define and deploy two Istio VirtualServices for the STS and Order Processing microservices. These are two microservices we want the client applications to access through the Istio Ingress gateway. Since the Inventory microservice is invoked by only the Order Processing microservice within the cluster, we do not need to create a VirtualService for it.

Before creating the VirtualServices, we need to update the Kubernetes Service definition of the STS and the Order Processing microservices, which we created in section 12.1. There we used the LoadBalancer Service type (and in the Docker Desktop, we used the NodePort Service type), because we wanted to test the end-to-end flow from the curl client outside the Kubernetes cluster. When we expose these microservices through the Ingress gateway, we don't want the client applications to access them also via the Kubernetes Service directly. We want the Istio Ingress gateway to be the single entry point to our microservices from clients outside the Kubernetes cluster.

Run the commands in listing 12.4 from the chapter12/sample02 directory to update the two microservices to run as a `ClusterIP` Service (this is the default Service type in Kubernetes, when you have no type defined). First, we delete the two Services and then create them.

Listing 12.4   Updating the Service definition of STS and Order Processing microservice

```
\> kubectl delete service sts-service

service "sts-service" deleted

\> kubectl delete service orders-service

service "orders-service" deleted

\> kubectl apply -f order.processing.yaml

configmap/orders-application-properties-config-map unchanged
deployment.apps/orders-deployment unchanged
service/orders-service created

\> kubectl apply -f sts.yaml

configmap/sts-application-properties-config-map unchanged
configmap/sts-jwt-keystore-config-map unchanged
secret/sts-keystore-secrets configured
deployment.apps/sts-deployment unchanged
service/sts-service created
```

Now we can create two VirtualServices, one for the STS and the other for the Order Processing microservice. These two VirtualServices read the routing information from the corresponding Kubernetes Services. The following listing shows the VirtualService definition corresponding to the Order Processing microservice.

Listing 12.5   The VirtualService definition of the Order Processing microservice

```
apiVersion: networking.istio.io/v1alpha3
kind: VirtualService
metadata:
  name: orders-virtual-service
spec:
  hosts:
  - orders.ecomm.com
  gateways:
  - ecomm-gateway.istio-system.svc.cluster.local
  http:
```

This VirtualService is applicable only for requests coming to the orders.ecomm.com hostname.

The fully qualified name of the Gateway resource created in the istio-system namespace

```
- route:
  - destination:
      host: orders-service
      port:
        number: 80
```

Routes the traffic to the orders-service
Service on port 80. Istio finds the
Cluster IP of the orders-service Service
and routes the traffic there.

The VirtualService definition corresponding to the STS looks similar to the Order Processing microservice's definition, which you can find in the chapter12/sample02/virtualservices.yaml file. It's important to highlight that for Istio traffic rules to work, we must use named ports (listing 12.6) in the Kubernetes Service definition corresponding to the destination routes in the VirtualService. Also, these named ports should carry predefined values, as explained at https://istio.io/docs/setup/additional-setup/requirements/.

Listing 12.6 The Service definition of the Order Processing microservice

```
apiVersion: v1
kind: Service
metadata:
  name: orders-service
spec:
  selector:
    app: orders
  ports:
  - name: http
    protocol: TCP
    port: 80
    targetPort: 8443
```

This must be a named port for
Istio routing rules to work.

To deploy the VirtualServices under the `default` namespace, run the following command from the chapter12/sample02 directory:

```
\> kubectl apply -f virtualservices.yaml

virtualservice.networking.istio.io/sts-virtual-service created
virtualservice.networking.istio.io/orders-virtual-service created
```

Once we have created the two VirtualServices for the Order Processing microservice and the STS, the Istio Ingress gateway can route the traffic it gets from client applications over TLS to the corresponding microservice. Since our plan in this section is to terminate TLS at the Ingress gateway, next we need to instruct Istio to not enforce mTLS between the Ingress gateway and the upstream microservices, or among microservices.

12.2.3 Defining a permissive authentication policy

In this section, we are going to define a policy to instruct Istio not to enforce mTLS among microservices, or between the Istio Ingress gateway and the microservices. We want the Ingress gateway to terminate the TLS connection. The policy in the following listing uses `PERMISSIVE` as the `mtls/mode`, so Istio won't enforce mTLS or TLS for any requests to the Services defined under the `spec/target` element in the following listing.

Listing 12.7 The permissive authentication policy

```
apiVersion: authentication.istio.io/v1alpha1
kind: Policy
metadata:
  name: ecomm-authn-policy
spec:                          This policy is applicable
  targets:                     to only these targets.
  - name: orders-service                 Must match the name of a
  - name: inventory-service              Kubernetes Service name
  peers:
  - mtls:                  Instructs Istio to accept plaintext traffic as
      mode: PERMISSIVE     well as mutual TLS traffic at the same time
```

When we define mTLS `mode` to be `PERMISSIVE` as in listing 12.7, Istio lets the microservices that are deployed in the service mesh accept requests both over plain HTTP and over HTTPS protected with mTLS. That means your microservices in the service mesh can still communicate with each other over a channel protected with mTLS; at the same time, when those microservices want to talk to legacy microservices (or the microservices with no Envoy proxy fronting), then they can use plain HTTP.

Istio 1.5.0 by default enables mTLS among Istio-controlled microservices. Even though you set the mTLS `mode` to be `PERMISSIVE`, you will still see communications among microservices happen over mTLS. Prior to Istio 1.5.0, to enable mTLS, you need to define a DestinationRule, which we discuss in section 12.3.

Run the following command from the chapter12/sample02 directory to apply the authentication policy defined in listing 12.7:

```
\> kubectl apply -f authentication.policy.yaml
```

```
policy.authentication.istio.io/ecomm-authn-policy created
```

NOTE Istio 1.5.0 introduced a new custom resource definition (CRD) called *PeerAuthentication*, which you can use to define policies to protect service-to-service communications over mTLS. In a future Istio release, this new CRD will replace the policy we discussed in listing 12.7. You will learn more about the PeerAuthentication CRD in section 12.4.3.

12.2.4 *Testing end-to-end flow*

In this section, we are going to test the end-to-end flow, as shown in figure 12.4, with the Istio Ingress gateway secured with TLS. Here we use curl as the client application, which first talks to the STS microservice and gets a JWT. Then the client application talks to the Order Processing microservice via the Istio Ingress gateway, passing the JWT it got from the STS.

All the communications between the curl client and the microservices now happen via the Ingress gateway. Let's run the following two commands to find the external IP

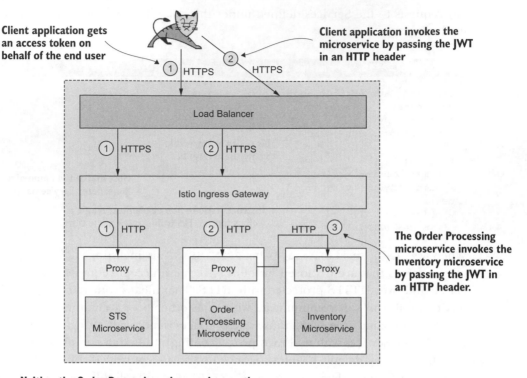

Client application gets an access token on behalf of the end user

Client application invokes the microservice by passing the JWT in an HTTP header

The Order Processing microservice invokes the Inventory microservice by passing the JWT in an HTTP header.

Neither the Order Processing microservice nor the Inventory microservice does JWT verification at the moment. You can simply call it with any JWT or even without a JWT.

Figure 12.4 STS issues a JWT access token to the client application, and the client application uses it to access the Order Processing microservice on behalf of the user, Peter. The Order Processing microservice uses the same JWT it got from the client application to access the Inventory microservice. The Istio Ingress gateway intercepts all the requests coming to the microservice and terminates the TLS connection.

address and the HTTPS port of the Istio Ingress gateway, which runs under the `istio-system` namespace. The first command finds the external IP address of the `istio-ingressgateway` Service and exports it to the `INGRESS_HOST` environment variable, and the second command finds the HTTPS port of the `istio-ingress-gateway` Service and exports it to the `INGRESS_HTTPS_PORT` environment variable. If you use a local Kubernetes deployment on Docker Desktop with no load balancer, then instead of the external IP, you need to use the node IP address (probably 127.0.0.1) along with the corresponding port (probably 443):

```
\> export INGRESS_HOST=$(kubectl -n istio-system \
get service istio-ingressgateway \
-o jsonpath='{.status.loadBalancer.ingress[0].ip}')
```

```
\> export INGRESS_HTTPS_PORT=$(kubectl -n istio-system \
get service istio-ingressgateway \
-o jsonpath='{.spec.ports[?(@.name=="https")].port}')
```

You can use the following `echo` command to make sure that we captured the right values for the two environment variables:

```
\> echo $INGRESS_HOST
34.83.117.171
\> echo $INGRESS_HTTPS_PORT
443
```

Let's use the following curl command to talk to the STS and get a JWT. We use the environment variables that we defined before for the hostname and the port of the `istio-ingressgateway` Service. Because we are using hostname-based routing at the Istio gateway and there is no DNS mapping to the hostnames `sts.ecomm.com` or `orders.ecomm.com`, we are using the `--resolve` parameter in curl to define the hostname-to-IP mapping:

```
\> curl -v -X POST --basic -u applicationid:applicationsecret \
-H "Content-Type: application/x-www-form-urlencoded;charset=UTF-8" \
-k -d "grant_type=password&username=peter&password=peter123&scope=foo" \
--resolve sts.ecomm.com:$INGRESS_HTTPS_PORT:$INGRESS_HOST \
https://sts.ecomm.com:$INGRESS_HTTPS_PORT/oauth/token
```

In this command, `applicationid` is the client ID of the web application, and `applicationsecret` is the client secret. If everything works fine, the STS returns an OAuth 2.0 access token, which is a JWT (or a JWS, to be precise):

```
{
"access_token":"eyJhbGciOiJSUzI1NiIs… ",
"token_type":"bearer",
"refresh_token":"",
"expires_in":5999,
"scope":"foo",
"jti":"4d2bb648-461d-4eec-ae9c-5eae1f08e2a2"
}
```

The following command does an HTTP `GET` to the Order Processing microservice. Before talking to the microservice, let's export the JWT we got from the previous command (under the value of the `access_token` parameter) to an environmental variable (`TOKEN`). Then use that environmental variable in your request to the Order Processing microservice to carry the JWT along with the HTTP request. Even though we pass the JWT, we are still not doing any JWT verification at the service level. Later in the chapter, we discuss how to do JWT verification with Istio. Here is the command:

```
\> export TOKEN=jwt_access_token
\> curl -k -H "Authorization: Bearer $TOKEN" \
--resolve orders.ecomm.com:$INGRESS_HTTPS_PORT:$INGRESS_HOST \
https://orders.ecomm.com:$INGRESS_HTTPS_PORT/orders/11
```

Finally, let's do an HTTP POST to the Order Processing microservice, which internally calls the Inventory microservice:

```
\> curl -k -v https://orders.ecomm.com:$INGRESS_HTTPS_PORT/orders \
-H "Content-Type: application/json" \
-H "Authorization: Bearer $TOKEN" \
--resolve orders.ecomm.com:$INGRESS_HTTPS_PORT:$INGRESS_HOST \
-d @- << EOF
{
  "customer_id":"101021",
  "payment_method":{
      "card_type":"VISA",
      "expiration":"01/22",
      "name":"John Doe",
      "billing_address":"201, 1st Street, San Jose, CA"
  },
  "items":[
      {
      "code":"101",
      "qty":1
      },
      {
      "code":"103",
      "qty":5
      }
  ],
  "shipping_address":"201, 1st Street, San Jose, CA"
}
EOF
```

TROUBLEHOOTING   If you get any errors for the preceding commands, see appendix K, section K.10.5, for troubleshooting tips.

12.3 Securing service-to-service communications with mTLS

This section helps you understand how mTLS works with Istio prior to version 1.5.0. We'll extend the use case in section 12.2 by enforcing mTLS between the Istio Ingress gateway and the microservices, as well as among microservices (figure 12.5). We assume you have successfully completed all the samples in section 12.2.

NOTE   If you are on Istio 1.5.0 or later, mTLS is enabled for all your microservices in the service mesh by default, and you do not need to do anything.

To enforce mTLS among microservices in an Istio deployment, we need to worry about two ends: the client and the server. A given microservice can play the role of an mTLS client as well as an mTLS server under different contexts. In our case, the Istio Ingress gateway is a client to the Order Processing microservice, and the Order Processing microservice is a client to the Inventory microservice. In the same way, the Order Processing microservice is a server to the Ingress gateway, and the Inventory microservice is a server to the Order Processing microservice.

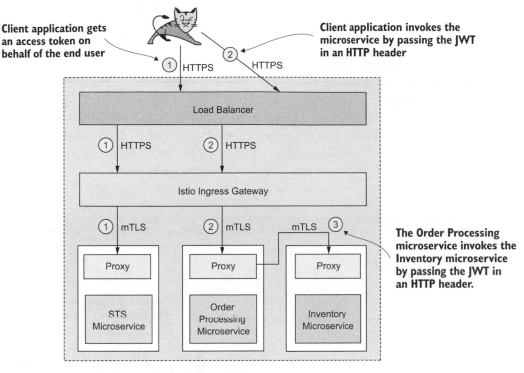

Client application gets an access token on behalf of the end user

Client application invokes the microservice by passing the JWT in an HTTP header

The Order Processing microservice invokes the Inventory microservice by passing the JWT in an HTTP header.

Neither the Order Processing microservice nor the Inventory microservice does JWT verification at the moment. You can simply call it with any JWT or even without a JWT.

Figure 12.5   The Istio Ingress gateway intercepts all the requests coming to the microservice and terminates the TLS connection. The communications between the Ingress gateway and microservices, as well as among microservices, are protected with mTLS.

To enforce mTLS at the server end, we will first update the authentication policy in listing 12.7 (which used PERMISSIVE) to use STRICT as the tls/mode, as shown in the following listing. Now, no client application can communicate with the Order Processing and Inventory microservices bypassing mTLS.

Listing 12.8   The strict mTLS authentication policy

```
apiVersion: authentication.istio.io/v1alpha1
kind: Policy
metadata:
  name: ecomm-authn-policy
spec:
  targets:
  - name: orders-service
  - name: inventory-service
```

```
peers:
  - mtls:
      mode: STRICT
```

◁───── **Instructs Istio to enforce mTLS for any traffic that comes to the Kubernetes Services defined under the targets element**

To use mTLS at the client side when one microservice talks to another microservice, Istio introduces a new resource type called *DestinationRule*.[3] The DestinationRule we have in the following listing enables mTLS for all the communications with all the hosts (indicated by the Kubernetes Service name) in the default namespace. We run the Order Processing and Inventory microservices in the default namespace, and this DestinationRule will enable mTLS between those two. As we highlighted at the beginning of this section, if you are using Istio 1.5.0 or later, you do not need to do any of these things to enable mTLS among microservices; it's enabled by default.

Listing 12.9   The DestinationRule enforces mTLS among all the services

```
apiVersion: networking.istio.io/v1alpha3
kind: DestinationRule
metadata:
  name: ecomm-authn-service-mtls
spec:
  host: "*.default.svc.cluster.local"          ◁───── Specifies the hosts, using
  trafficPolicy:                                        Kubernetes Service names
    tls:
      mode: ISTIO_MUTUAL
```

◁───── **Enables mTLS by using the certificates provisioned to each Envoy proxy by Istio itself, which are available under the /etc/certs location of the Envoy filesystem**

To use mTLS at the client side when the Istio Ingress gateway talks to a microservice in the default Kubernetes namespace, we use the DestinationRule defined in the following listing. We deploy this DestinationRule in the `istio-system` namespace.

Listing 12.10   The DestinationRule enforces mTLS between the gateway and services.

```
apiVersion: networking.istio.io/v1alpha3
kind: DestinationRule
metadata:
  name: ecomm-authn-istio-gateway-mtls
  namespace: istio-system            ◁───── This DestinationRule is deployed
spec:                                         under the istio-system namespace.
  host: "*.default.svc.cluster.local"       ◁───── Specifies the hosts, using
  trafficPolicy:                                    Kubernetes Service names
    tls:
      mode: ISTIO_MUTUAL
```

◁───── **Enables mTLS using the certificates provisioned to each Envoy proxy by Istio itself, which are available under the /etc/certs location of the Envoy filesystem**

---

[3]   A DestinationRule is used not only to configure mTLS for any outbound traffic from a microservice, but also to define policies for load balancing, connection pooling, and so on. More information on DestinationRules is available at https://istio.io/docs/reference/config/networking/destination-rule.

Let's run the following command from the chapter12/sample03 directory to apply the DestinationRules defined in listings 12.9 and 12.10 as well as the authentication policy defined in listing 12.8:

```
\> kubectl apply -f authentication.policy.yaml
```

```
policy.authentication.istio.io/ecomm-authn-policy configured
destinationrule.networking.istio.io/ecomm-authn-istio-gateway-mtls created
destinationrule.networking.istio.io/ecomm-authn-service-mtls created
```

To test the end-to-end flow after enforcing mTLS, follow the steps defined in section 12.2.4.

12.4 Securing service-to-service communications with JWT

This section extends the use case we discussed in section 12.3 by enforcing JWT verification at each microservice. We assume you have successfully completed all the samples we discussed in that section. Here, we use JWT to carry the end-user context, while using mTLS for service-to-service authentication.

> **NOTE** Istio 1.5.0 introduced two new CRDs for authentication: *PeerAuthentication* and *RequestAuthentication*. As you will learn in section 12.4.1, prior to Istio 1.5.0, you had to use the same policy to define both mTLS and JWT authentication methods. With the introduction of two new CRDs, Istio 1.5.0 provides a much cleaner way of defining authentication policies based on mTLS and JWT. You can use the PeerAuthentication CRD to define mTLS-based policies, and the RequestAuthentication CRD to define JWT-based policies. If you are on Istio 1.5.0 or later, this method is more recommended than the approach we discuss in section 12.4.1. In section 12.4.3, we discuss PeerAuthentication and RequestAuthentication in detail.

12.4.1 Enforcing JWT authentication

The authentication policy in listing 12.8 enforces only mTLS for the Order Processing and Inventory microservices, so we need to update it to enforce JWT authentication. The following listing shows the updated authentication policy, which is applicable for any requests coming to the Order Processing and Inventory microservices.

Listing 12.11 The JWT plus mTLS authentication policy

```
apiVersion: authentication.istio.io/v1alpha1
kind: Policy
metadata:
  name: ecomm-authn-policy
spec:
  targets:                        ◁——┐  This policy is applicable only to
  - name: orders-service              │  these targets, which are identified
  - name: inventory-service           │  by Kubernetes Service names.
  peers:
  - mtls:
```

```
    mode: STRICT
origins:
- jwt:
    issuer: "sts.ecomm.com"    ◁─┐
    audiences:
    - "*.ecomm.com"
    jwksUri: .../chapter12/sample04/jwtkey.jwk    ◁─
principalBinding: USE_ORIGIN    ◁─
```

The value of the iss attribute in the JWT in the request (or the issuer of the JWT) must exactly match this value.

The value of the aud attribute in the JWT in the request must exactly match this value.

Sets the authenticated principle from origin authentication or the subject of the JWT in the request

The URL to fetch the JSON Web Key, corresponding to the signature of the JWT in the request

Let's run the following command from the chapter12/sample04 directory to update the authentication policy as defined in listing 12.11:

```
\> kubectl apply -f authentication.policy.yaml
```

```
policy.authentication.istio.io/ecomm-authn-policy configured
```

To test the end-to-end flow after enforcing JWT authentication, follow the steps defined in the next section.

12.4.2 *Testing end-to-end flow with JWT authentication*

In this section, we are going to test the end-to-end flow, as shown in figure 12.6. The steps you follow here are exactly the same as those you followed in section 12.2.4—except if you send an invalid JWT, Istio will reject the request.

We use curl as the client application, which first talks to the STS microservice and gets a JWT. Then the client application talks to the Order Processing microservice via the Istio Ingress gateway, passing the JWT it got from the STS.

Let's run the following two commands to find the external IP address and the HTTPS port of the Istio Ingress gateway, which runs under the `istio-system` namespace. The first command finds the external IP address of the `istio-ingress-gateway` Service and exports it to the `INGRESS_HOST` environment variable, and the second command finds the HTTPS port of the `istio-ingressgateway` Service and exports it to the `INGRESS_HTTPS_PORT` environment variable. If you use a local Kubernetes deployment on Docker Desktop with no load balancer, then instead of the external IP, you need to use the node IP address (probably 127.0.0.1) along with the corresponding port (probably 443):

```
\> export INGRESS_HOST=$(kubectl -n istio-system \
get service istio-ingressgateway \
-o jsonpath='{.status.loadBalancer.ingress[0].ip}')
```

```
\> export INGRESS_HTTPS_PORT=$(kubectl -n istio-system \
get service istio-ingressgateway \
-o jsonpath='{.spec.ports[?(@.name=="https")].port}')
```

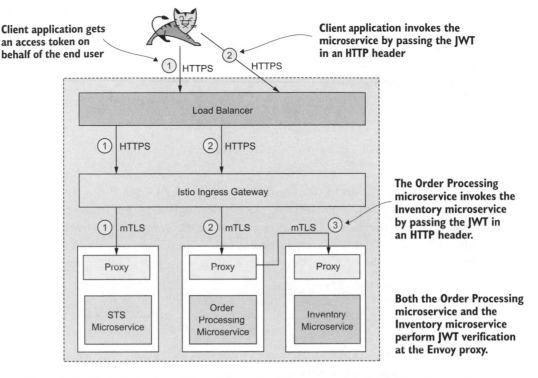

Figure 12.6 **The Istio Ingress gateway intercepts all the requests coming to the microservice and terminates the TLS connection. The communications between the Ingress gateway and microservices, as well as among microservices, are protected with mTLS. The Envoy proxy does JWT verification for the Order Processing and Inventory microservices.**

You can use the following `echo` command to make sure that we captured the right values for the two environment variables:

```
\> echo $INGRESS_HOST
34.83.117.171
\> echo $INGRESS_HTTPS_PORT
443
```

Let's use the following curl command to talk to the STS and get a JWT. We use the environment variables, which we defined before for the hostname and the port of the `istio-ingressgateway` Service. Since we are using hostname-based routing at the Istio gateway and there is no DNS mapping to the hostnames `sts.ecomm.com` or `orders.ecomm.com`, we are using the `--resolve` parameter in curl to define the hostname-to-IP mapping:

```
\> curl -v -X POST --basic -u applicationid:applicationsecret \
-H "Content-Type: application/x-www-form-urlencoded;charset=UTF-8" \
-k -d "grant_type=password&username=peter&password=peter123&scope=foo" \
--resolve sts.ecomm.com:$INGRESS_HTTPS_PORT:$INGRESS_HOST \
https://sts.ecomm.com:$INGRESS_HTTPS_PORT/oauth/token
```

In this command, `applicationid` is the client ID of the web application, and `applicationsecret` is the client secret. If everything works fine, the security token service returns an OAuth 2.0 access token, which is a JWT (or a JWS, to be precise):

```
{
"access_token":"eyJhbGciOiJSUzI1NiIs… ",
"token_type":"bearer",
"refresh_token":"",
"expires_in":5999,
"scope":"foo",
"jti":"4d2bb648-461d-4eec-ae9c-5eae1f08e2a2"
}
```

The following command does an HTTP `GET` to the Order Processing microservice. Before talking to the microservice, let's export the JWT we got from the previous command (under the value of the `access_token` parameter) to an environmental variable (`TOKEN`). Then use that environmental variable in our request to the Order Processing microservice to carry the JWT along with the HTTP request:

```
\> export TOKEN=jwt_access_token
\> curl -k -H "Authorization: Bearer $TOKEN" \
--resolve orders.ecomm.com:$INGRESS_HTTPS_PORT:$INGRESS_HOST \
https://orders.ecomm.com:$INGRESS_HTTPS_PORT/orders/11
```

Finally, let's do an HTTP `POST` to the Order Processing microservice, which internally calls the Inventory microservice:

```
\> curl -k -v https://orders.ecomm.com:$INGRESS_HTTPS_PORT/orders \
-H "Content-Type: application/json" \
-H "Authorization: Bearer $TOKEN" \
--resolve orders.ecomm.com:$INGRESS_HTTPS_PORT:$INGRESS_HOST \
-d @- << EOF
{
  "customer_id":"101021",
  "payment_method":{
      "card_type":"VISA",
      "expiration":"01/22",
      "name":"John Doe",
      "billing_address":"201, 1st Street, San Jose, CA"
  },
  "items":[
      {
      "code":"101",
      "qty":1
      },
      {
      "code":"103",
      "qty":5
      }
  ],
  "shipping_address":"201, 1st Street, San Jose, CA"
}
EOF
```

12.4.3 *Peer authentication and request authentication*

As we mentioned before in this chapter, PeerAuthentication and RequestAuthentication are two new CRDs introduced by Istio 1.5.0. You can use the PeerAuthentication CRD to define mTLS-based policies to authenticate one microservice to another, while the RequestAuthentication CRD to define JWT-based policies to authenticate end users.

PEERAUTHENTICATION CRD

In section 12.3, we mentioned that if you are on Istio 1.5.0 or later, mTLS is enabled for all your microservices in the service mesh by default, and you do not need to do anything. What does this really mean? Istio 1.5.0 does not enforce mTLS by default for all the microservices, but only enables those microservices to communicate with each other over mTLS, with no additional configuration. This also means that if a client application or a legacy microservice (with no Istio) wants to access those microservices over plain HTTP (or with no mTLS, but with HTTPS), you still can do it. But yet, the communications among Istio-controlled microservices happen over HTTPS with mTLS.

Prior to Istio 1.5, if you want to strictly enforce mTLS among all the microservices, you can do it at the service mesh level, using the MeshPolicy CRD (appendix K, listing K.6), by setting mtls/mode as STRICT. The MeshPolicy CRD is now deprecated and will be removed from a future Istio release. Also, if you want to strictly enforce mTLS at the service level (not at the service mesh level), you can do it as in listing 12.8. But, if you are using Istio 1.5 or later, the recommended approach is to use the PeerAuthentication CRD to define mTLS policies. The following listing shows the PeerAuthentication policy equivalent to what you find in listing 12.8.

> **Listing 12.12 PeerAuthentication policy to strictly enforce mTLS**

```
apiVersion: security.istio.io/v1beta1
kind: PeerAuthentication
metadata:
  name: default
  namespace: default            ◁── This policy is deployed in
spec:                                 the default namespace.
  selector:
    matchLabels:                     This policy is applicable to a Deployment
      app: orders                    that carries the label orders: the Order
      app: inventory         ◁──┐    Processing microservice.
  mtls:                           This policy is applicable to a
    mode: STRICT                  Deployment that carries the label
                                  inventory: the Inventory microservice.
```

Let's run the following command from the chapter12/sample04 directory to set up the authentication policy as defined in listing 12.12, under an Istio 1.5 or later deployment:

```
\> kubectl apply -f peer.authentication.policy.yaml

peerauthentication.security.istio.io/default created
```

You can read more variations of how you can apply PeerAuthentication policies at https://istio.io/docs/reference/config/security/peer_authentication.

REQUESTAUTHENTICATION CRD

As discussed at the beginning of this section, you can use the RequestAuthentication CRD to define JWT-based policies to authenticate end users. In section 12.4.1, we discussed how to enable access control based on the attributes a JWT carries, using the authentication policy in listing 12.11. If you revisit that policy, you'll notice that it's a bit bloated, and carries both JWT and mTLS settings. That's the way you did things prior to Istio 1.5.0.

As Istio 1.5.0 decouples peer authentication (mTLS) from request authentication (JWT), here we use RequestAuthentication CRD to define an access-control policy against the JWT in the request. Listing 12.13 defines the RequestAuthentication policy equivalent to that in listing 12.11, except for one change. The policy in listing 12.11 is applicable to both the Order Processing and Inventory microservices, but the policy in the following listing is applicable to only the Order Processing microservice. You can define a similar policy for the Inventory microservice with the label `app:inventory`.

Listing 12.13   RequestAuthentication policy to enforce JWT verification

```
apiVersion: security.istio.io/v1beta1
kind: RequestAuthentication
metadata:
  name: orders-req-authn-policy
spec:
  selector:
    matchLabels:
      app: orders
  jwtRules:
  - issuer: "sts.ecomm.com"
    audiences:
    - "*.ecomm.com"
    jwksUri: .../chapter12/sample04/jwtkey.jwk
```

> This policy is applicable to a Deployment, which carries the label orders: the Order Processing microservice.

> The value of the iss attribute in the JWT in the request (or the issuer of the JWT) must exactly match this value.

> The value of the aud attribute in the JWT in the request must exactly match this value.

> The URL to fetch the JSON Web Key, corresponding to the signature of the JWT in request

---

It is important to understand the behavior of the RequestAuthentication CRD. If the request carries an invalid JWT, which does not match the criteria defined in the policy, then Istio rejects the request. But if the request does not carry any JWT at all, Istio will not reject the request. That's bit strange, but that's the behavior at the time of this writing.

Since this behavior of the RequestAuthentication CRD can introduce some security risks, we must use another authorization policy, defined using the AuthorizationPolicy CRD along with it. The AuthorizationPolicy CRD was introduced in Istio 1.4.0, and in section 12.5.4 we discuss it in detail. The policy in the following listing rejects any request that does not have a valid subject associated with it. In other words, if a request does not carry a JWT, even if it passes through the RequestAuthentication policy, it will fail here, since there is no subject associated with the request.

Listing 12.14　AuthorizationPolicy CRD

```
apiVersion: security.istio.io/v1beta1
kind: AuthorizationPolicy
metadata:
 name: orders-services-policy
spec:
 selector:
   matchLabels:
     app: orders
 rules:
 - from:
   - source:
       requestPrincipals: ["*"]
```

Let's run the following command from the chapter12/sample04 directory to set up the authorization policy based on JWT in the request, as defined in listings 12.13 and 12.14, under an Istio 1.5 or later deployment:

```
\> kubectl apply -f request.authentication.policy.yaml
```

```
requestauthentication.security.istio.io/orders-req-authn-policy created
authorizationpolicy.security.istio.io/orders-services-policy configured
requestauthentication.security.istio.io/inventory-req-authn-policy created
authorizationpolicy.security.istio.io/inventory-services-policy created
```

To test the end-to-end flow after enforcing JWT authentication, follow the steps defined in section 12.4.2.

You can read more variations of how you can apply RequestAuthentication policies at https://istio.io/docs/reference/config/security/request_authentication/.

12.4.4　How to use JWT in service-to-service communications

In sections 12.4.1 and 12.4.3, we protected both the Order Processing and the Inventory microservices with JWT. For the Order Processing microservice, the client application has to send the JWT along with the HTTP request, and then, when the Order Processing microservice talks to the Inventory microservice, it passes the same JWT it got from the client application. (This is one of the use cases for securing microservices with JWT, which we discussed in detail in section 7.1.1. You can also find the limitations of this approach in section 7.1.2.)

However, Istio does not support this use case at the time of this writing; Istio does not support propagating a JWT that one microservice gets to another upstream microservice. So, while implementing this in our sample in sections 12.4.1 and 12.4.3, we did that at the code level. We modified the Order Processing microservice to read the incoming JWT from the HTTP header (which Envoy passes through to the microservice behind, after verification) and attached it to the HTTP request, when the Order Processing microservice talks to the Inventory microservice. You can find the code with respect to this in the chapter12/services/order/src/main/java/com/manning/mss/ch12/order/client/InventoryClient.java class file.

12.4.5   *A closer look at JSON Web Key*

In listing 12.11, the Envoy proxy uses a JSON Web Key Set endpoint to fetch a document, which carries a set of JSON Web Keys. A *JSON Web Key* (*JWK*) is a JSON representation of a cryptographic key, and a *JSON Web Key Set* (*JWKS*) is a representation of multiple JWKs. RFC 7517 (https://tools.ietf.org/html/rfc7517) provides the structure and the definition of a JWK. As per listing 12.13, the Envoy proxy gets the JWKS from https://raw.githubusercontent.com/microservices-security-in-action/samples/master/chapter12/sample04/jwtkey.jwk.

   The JWKS in listing 12.15 carries the information related to the public key of an issuer of a JWT. The recipient of a JWT can use the information in this listing to find the corresponding public key and validate the signature of the JWT. If you'd like to delve more deeply into the details of JWK, see RFC 7517. If you have a PEM-encoded X.509 certificate, you can use an online tool like JWK to PEM Converter Online (https://8gwifi.org/jwkconvertfunctions.jsp) to convert it to a JWK. Let's have a look at the content of the jwtkey.jwk file in the following listing; the code annotations explain each element.

Listing 12.15   JSON Web Key Set

```
{ "keys":[                               The parent element, which
  {"e":"AQAB",                           represents an array of JWKs      A cryptographic parameter
   "kid":"d7d87567-1840-4f45-9614-49071fca4d21",                         corresponding to the RSA algorithm
   "kty":"RSA",                                                     The key identifier. This
   "n":"-WcBjPsrFvGOwqVJd8vpV "                                     should match the kid
  }                                                                 value in the JWT header.
 ]                  A cryptographic parameter       Defines the key type. The RFC 7518
}                   corresponding to the RSA algorithm   defines the possible values.
```

12.5   *Enforcing authorization*

This section extends the use case in section 12.4 by enforcing authorization at each microservice. To follow this section, first you need to successfully complete all the samples in the preceding section. Here, we use JWT to carry the end-user attributes, while using mTLS for service-to-service authentication—and enforce access-control policies based on the attributes in the JWT.

12.5.1   *A closer look at the JWT*

Let's have a closer look at the JWT you got from the STS while running the end-to-end sample in section 12.4.2. What you get from the STS is a base64url-encoded string; you can use an online tool like JWT.IO (https://jwt.io) to decode it. Listing 12.16

shows the decoded JWT payload. Once you decode the token, the content of the token becomes readable. In appendix B, we discuss in detail the structure of a JWT. In Istio, we can define access-control policies against any of these attributes.

Listing 12.16 The base64url-decoded JWT payload

```
{
    "sub": "peter",            ←── The user or the principal
                                    associated with this JWT—
                                    or the authenticated user
    "aud": "*.ecomm.com",      ←── Identifies the recipient(s)
                                    of the JWT
    "user_name": "peter",
    "scope": [                 ←── Scopes associated with the JWT
      "foo"                        or what you can do with this JWT
    ],
    "iss": "sts.ecomm.com",    ←── Identifies the
    "exp": 1572480488,             issuer of the JWT
    "iat": 1572474488,
    "authorities": [           ←── The roles associated with
      "ROLE_USER"                  the subject of the JWT
    ],
    "jti": "88a5215f-7d7a-45f8-9632-ca78cbe05fde",    ←── Identifies the client
    "client_id": "applicationid"                          application, which sends
}                                                         this JWT to the microservice
```

12.5.2 *Enforcing role-based access control*

In this section, we define role-based access control (RBAC) policies for the Order Processing and Inventory microservices. In general terms, a *role* is a collection of permissions. A *permission* is a combination of a resource and an action. For example, the ability to do an HTTP GET on the Order Processing microservice is a permission. The HTTP GET is the action, and the Order Processing microservice is the resource.

Similarly, the ability to do an HTTP POST to the Order Processing microservice is another permission. Now we can combine these two permissions and call it a *role*, and anyone in this role can do an HTTP GET or POST to the Order Processing microservice.

> **NOTE** Istio introduced major changes to role-based access control in its 1.4.0 release, which we discuss in section 12.5.4. The ServiceRole, ServiceRole-Binding, ClusterRoleBinding CRDs we discuss in this section are now deprecated, and are removed from Istio 1.6.0. But still we thought of having them in this chapter, as at the time of this writing many people are still using Istio releases prior to 1.4.0. The latest GKE cluster version at the time of this writing is 1.14.10-gke.27, and it supports only Istio 1.2.10 by default. If your Istio version is 1.4 or later, you can move to section 12.5.4 directly.

Istio introduces a resource type (a CRD) called ServiceRole, which defines a set of rules. For example, take a look at the ServiceRole definition in listing 12.17. The `services` element represents a set of resources, and the `methods` element represents the allowed actions against those resources. In plain English, this says, if someone has the order-viewer role, they can do an HTTP GET to the orders-service microservice running in the Kubernetes default namespace.

Listing 12.17   The order-viewer ServiceRole

```
apiVersion: "rbac.istio.io/v1alpha1"
kind: ServiceRole
metadata:
  name: order-viewer
spec:
  rules:
  - services: ["orders-service.default.svc.cluster.local"]
    methods: ["GET"]
```

> An array of Services, with the fully qualified name, where this rule is applicable

> An array of HTTP verbs, where this rule is applicable

Let's take a look at another example in the following listing. It says, if someone has the order-admin role, they can do an HTTP POST to the orders-service microservice running in the Kubernetes default namespace.

Listing 12.18   The order-admin ServiceRole

```
apiVersion: "rbac.istio.io/v1alpha1"
kind: ServiceRole
metadata:
  name: order-admin
spec:
  rules:
  - services: ["orders-service.default.svc.cluster.local"]
    methods: ["POST"]
```

To attach or bind a ServiceRole to a user, Istio introduces a resource type called ServiceRoleBinding (figure 12.7). Listing 12.19 shows an example. There we *bind* (or *map*) a user having a role called ROLE_USER to the order-viewer ServiceRole. The way Istio finds the role of the user is by looking at the authorities attribute (which is a JSON array) from the JWT (listing 12.16). The issuer of the JWT or the STS finds the roles of the user from an enterprise identity store (an LDAP, a database) connected to it and embeds those to the JWT under the attribute name authorities.

Listing 12.19   The order-viewer-binding ServiceRoleBinding

```
apiVersion: "rbac.istio.io/v1alpha1"
kind: ServiceRoleBinding
metadata:
  name: order-viewer-binding
spec:
  subjects:
  - properties:
      request.auth.claims[authorities]: "ROLE_USER"
  roleRef:
    kind: ServiceRole
    name: order-viewer
```

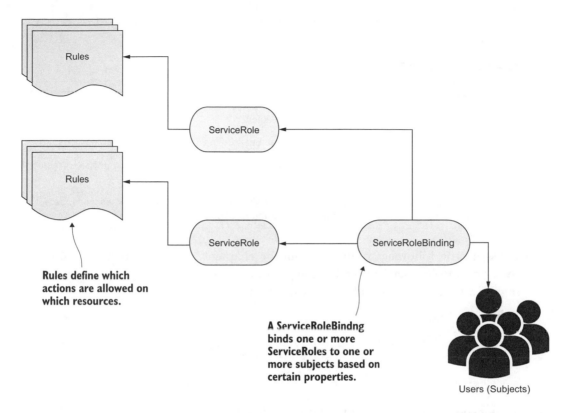

Figure 12.7 A ServiceRole binds a set of actions to a set of resources, and a ServiceRoleBinding binds a set of ServiceRoles to one or more subjects based on certain properties.

Once we have ServiceRoles and ServiceRoleBindings, to enable RBAC in Istio, we need to define a ClusterRbacConfig. The ClusterRbacConfig in the following listing enables RBAC for all the Services under the Kubernetes default namespace.

Listing 12.20 Defining the ClusterRbacConfig resource

```
apiVersion: "rbac.istio.io/v1alpha1"
kind: ClusterRbacConfig
metadata:
  name: default
spec:
  mode: ON_WITH_INCLUSION
  inclusion:                          Enables RBAC only for the Services
    namespaces: ["default"]       ◁── in the Kubernetes default namespace
```

Istio defines four possible values for the mode element in listing 12.20, as shown in table 12.2.

Table 12.2   RBAC config modes

Value	Description
OFF	RBAC is completely disabled.
ON	Enables RBAC for all the Services in all the Kubernetes namespaces.
ON_WITH_INCLUSION	Enables RBAC only for the Services in the Kubernetes namespaces mentioned under the inclusion element.
ON_WITH_EXCLUSION	Enables RBAC for the Services in all the Kubernetes namespaces, except those mentioned under the exclusion element.

Let's run the following command from the chapter12/sample05 directory to create the ServiceRoles, ServiceRoleBinding, and the ClusterRbacConfig, as defined in listings 12.17, 12.18, 12.19, and 12.20, respectively:

```
\> kubectl apply -f .

clusterrbacconfig.rbac.istio.io/default created
servicerole.rbac.istio.io/order-viewer created
servicerole.rbac.istio.io/order-admin created
servicerolebinding.rbac.istio.io/order-viewer-binding created
```

To test the end-to-end flow after enforcing RBAC, follow the steps defined in the next section.

12.5.3   *Testing end-to-end flow with RBAC*

In this section, we are going to test the end-to-end flow, as shown in figure 12.8. The steps you follow here are exactly the same as those you followed in section 12.2.4. Here, you will be able to do an HTTP GET to the Order Processing microservice, but will fail when doing an HTTP POST. The HTTP POST fails because the subject of the JWT that comes along with the request carries only the role ROLE_USER, and only a member of the order-viewer ServiceRole, not the order-admin ServiceRole. Only a member of order-admin ServiceRole can do an HTTP POST to the Order Processing microservice.

Here we use curl as the client application, which first talks to the STS microservice and gets a JWT. Then the client application talks to the Order Processing microservice via the Istio Ingress gateway, passing the JWT it got from the STS.

Let's run the following two commands to find the external IP address and the HTTPS port of the Istio Ingress gateway, which runs under the istio-system namespace. The first command finds the external IP address of the istio-ingress-gateway Service and exports it to the INGRESS_HOST environment variable, and the second command finds the HTTPS port of the istio-ingressgateway Service and

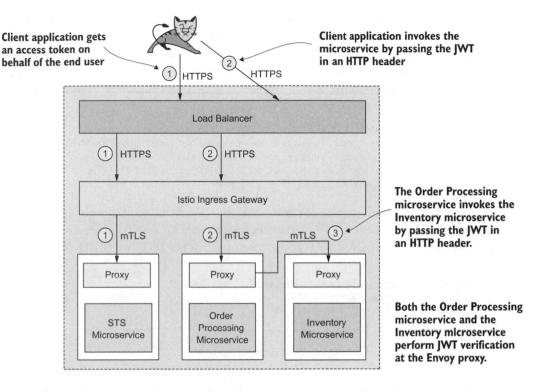

Figure 12.8 The Istio Ingress gateway intercepts all the requests coming to the microservice and terminates the TLS connection. The communications between the Ingress gateway and microservices, as well as among microservices, are protected with mTLS. The Envoy proxy does JWT verification for the Order Processing and Inventory microservices.

exports it to the INGRESS_HTTPS_PORT environment variable. In case you use a local Kubernetes deployment on Docker Desktop with no load balancer, then instead of the external IP, you need to use the node IP address (probably 127.0.0.1) along with the corresponding port (probably 443):

```
\> export INGRESS_HOST=$(kubectl -n istio-system \
get service istio-ingressgateway \
-o jsonpath='{.status.loadBalancer.ingress[0].ip}')

\> export INGRESS_HTTPS_PORT=$(kubectl -n istio-system \
get service istio-ingressgateway \
-o jsonpath='{.spec.ports[?(@.name=="https")].port}')
```

You can use the following echo commands to make sure that we captured the right values for the two environment variables:

```
\> echo $INGRESS_HOST
34.83.117.171
\> echo $INGRESS_HTTPS_PORT
443
```

Let's use the following curl command to talk to the STS and get a JWT. We use the environment variables, which we defined before for the hostname and the port of the istio-ingressgateway Service. Since we are using hostname-based routing at the Istio gateway and there is no DNS mapping to the hostnames sts.ecomm.com or orders.ecomm.com, we are using the --resolve parameter in curl to define the hostname-to-IP mapping:

```
\> curl -v -X POST --basic -u applicationid:applicationsecret \
-H "Content-Type: application/x-www-form-urlencoded;charset=UTF-8" \
-k -d "grant_type=password&username=peter&password=peter123&scope=foo" \
--resolve sts.ecomm.com:$INGRESS_HTTPS_PORT:$INGRESS_HOST \
https://sts.ecomm.com:$INGRESS_HTTPS_PORT/oauth/token
```

In this command, applicationid is the client ID of the web application, and applicationsecret is the client secret. If everything works fine, the security token service returns an OAuth 2.0 access token, which is a JWT (or a JWS, to be precise):

```
{
"access_token":"eyJhbGciOiJSUzI1NiIs… ",
"token_type":"bearer",
"refresh_token":"",
"expires_in":5999,
"scope":"foo",
"jti":"4d2bb648-461d-4eec-ae9c-5eae1f08e2a2"
}
```

The following command does an HTTP GET to the Order Processing microservice. Before talking to the microservice, let's export the JWT we got from the previous command (under the value of the access_token parameter) to an environmental variable (TOKEN). Then use that environmental variable in our request to the Order Processing microservice to carry the JWT along with the HTTP request:

```
\> export TOKEN=jwt_access_token
\> curl -k -H "Authorization: Bearer $TOKEN" \
--resolve orders.ecomm.com:$INGRESS_HTTPS_PORT:$INGRESS_HOST \
https://orders.ecomm.com:$INGRESS_HTTPS_PORT/orders/11
```

Finally, let's do an HTTP POST to the Order Processing microservice, which internally calls the Inventory microservice. This request will result in an HTTP 403 status code. Only a member of the order-admin ServiceRole can do an HTTP POST to the Order Processing microservice, so Istio will reject the request because the subject of the JWT, which comes along with the request, does not belong to that ServiceRole:

```
\> curl -k -v https://orders.ecomm.com:$INGRESS_HTTPS_PORT/orders \
-H "Content-Type: application/json" \
-H "Authorization: Bearer $TOKEN" \
--resolve orders.ecomm.com:$INGRESS_HTTPS_PORT:$INGRESS_HOST \
-d @- << EOF
{
  "customer_id":"101021",
  "payment_method":{
      "card_type":"VISA",
```

```
        "expiration":"01/22",
        "name":"John Doe",
        "billing_address":"201, 1st Street, San Jose, CA"
    },
    "items":[
        {
        "code":"101",
        "qty":1
        },
        {
        "code":"103",
        "qty":5
        }
    ],
    "shipping_address":"201, 1st Street, San Jose, CA"
}
EOF
```

12.5.4 *Improvements to role-based access control since Istio 1.4.0*

Istio has deprecated the ServiceRole, ServiceRoleBinding, and ClusterRoleBinding CRDs, which we discussed in section 12.5.2, since Istio version 1.4.0 and introduced a new CRD called AuthorizationPolicy as a replacement. Listing 12.21 defines an authorization policy for the Order Processing microservice, using the AuthorizationPolicy CRD. Here, it says, allow (action) to (to) do an HTTP GET or a POST (operation/method), on the Oder Processing microservice (matchLabel) when (when) the value of the user_name attribute is peter and the scope value is foo and the value of authorities attribute is ROLE_USER. The values of the attributes are picked from the claims set of the JWT that comes along with the request.

> **Listing 12.21 Defining an authorization policy with the AuthorizationPolicy CRD**

```
apiVersion: security.istio.io/v1beta1
kind: AuthorizationPolicy
metadata:
 name: orders-services-policy
 namespace: default
spec:
 selector:
   matchLabels:
     app: orders          ◁        This policy is applicable to a Deployment,
 action: ALLOW                     which carries the label orders: the Order
 rules:                            Processing microservice.
 - to:
   - operation:           ◁        If the criteria defined by this
       methods: ["GET", "POST"]    policy is satisfied, the policy
   when:                           allows the request to proceed.
   - key: request.auth.claims[user_name]
     values: ["peter"]    ◁        The value of the user_name attribute
                                   picked from the JWT that comes
```

Defines the HTTP methods allowed on the Order Processing microservice

The value of the user_name attribute picked from the JWT that comes with the request must be peter.

```
    - key: request.auth.claims[scope]
      values: ["foo"]
    - key: request.auth.claims[authorities]
          values: ["ROLE_USER"]
```

The value of the scope attribute picked from the JWT that comes with the request must be foo.

The value of the authorities attribute picked from the JWT that comes with the request must be ROLE_USER.

When Istio introduced AuthorizationPolicy CRD in the 1.4.0 release, it supported only ALLOW actions. But from version 1.5.0 onward, Istio supports both ALLOW and DENY actions. In an environment where you have multiple policies defined against the same microservice, with both ALLOW and DENY actions, Istio first evaluates the policies with DENY actions. If any one of those policies matches the request, Istio denies the action of the requester.

AuthorizationPolicy is not only based on request authentication with JWT, but you can also use it with peer authentication. Listing 12.22 shows a sample Authorization-Policy, which restricts access to the Inventory microservice, only for the requests coming from the Order Processing microservice. This check is done using the service account name associated with the Pod that carries the Order Processing microservice. Istio provisions certificates to each Pod in the service mesh, under the corresponding service account name. So, when we enforce peer authentication with mTLS for the Inventory microservice, looking at the certificate of the requester, Istio can identify the corresponding service account.

Listing 12.22   Defining an AuthorizationPolicy with peer authentication

```
apiVersion: security.istio.io/v1beta1
kind: AuthorizationPolicy
metadata:
 name: inventory-services-policy
 namespace: default
spec:
 selector:
   matchLabels:
     app: inventory
 action: ALLOW
 rules:
 - from:
   - source:
       principals: ["cluster.local/ns/default/sa/ecomm"]
   to:
   - operation:
       methods: ["PUT"]
```

Let's run the following commands from the chapter12/sample05/1.4.0 directory to set up the authorization policies we discussed in listings 12.21 and 12.22, under an Istio 1.5 or later deployment:

```
\> kubectl apply -f request.authz.policy.yaml

authorizationpolicy.security.istio.io/orders-services-policy configured
```

```
\> kubectl apply -f peer.authz.policy.yaml

serviceaccount/ecomm configured
deployment.apps/orders-deployment configured
authorizationpolicy.security.istio.io/inventory-services-policy configured
```

When you apply peer.authz.policy.yaml, which corresponds to listing 12.22, it also creates a service account called ecomm, and redeploys the Order Processing microservice under that. To test the end-to-end flow after enforcing authorization policies, follow the steps defined in section 12.4.2.

You can read more details about the AuthorizationPolicy at https://istio.io/docs/reference/config/security/authorization-policy/.

> **TROUBLEHOOTING** After applying peer.authz.policy.yaml in your Istio distribution, if the Pod corresponding to the Order Processing microservice does not start properly, please see the troubleshooting tips at https://github.com/microservices-security-in-action/samples/blob/master/chapter12/troubleshooting.md.

12.6 *Managing keys in Istio*

In an Istio deployment, *Citadel*—the Istio control plane component—provisions keys/certificates to each workload it manages. A Pod in a Kubernetes environment is a workload for Istio. Istio attaches an Envoy proxy for each Pod. So, when we say Citadel provisions keys/certificates to each workload it manages, what internally happens is that Citadel provisions keys/certificates to each Envoy proxy running in the corresponding Pod.

By provisioning keys/certificates, Citadel helps each workload that runs under Istio to maintain an identity and also facilitates secure communications among workloads. Further, Citadel rotates the keys/certificates it provisions to each Envoy proxy.

When you enable mTLS in an Istio deployment, Envoy uses the keys provisioned to it to authenticate to other Envoy proxies (or workloads). However, since Istio version 1.1, the way this works has changed significantly. In the following sections, we discuss various approaches Istio uses to provision and rotate keys/certificates.

12.6.1 *Key provisioning and rotation via volume mounts*

Prior to Istio 1.1.0, provisioning of keys/certificates to Envoy proxies happen via Citadel, with volume mounts. Even after Istio 1.1.0, prior to 1.5.0, if you don't have the sds Istio profile enabled, the provisioning of keys/certificates to Envoy proxies will still happen via Citadel, with volume mounts.[4] Listing 12.23 shows the volume mounts associated with Envoy (or the Istio proxy), which runs in the Order Processing Pod.

---

[4] Installation configuration profiles for Istio 1.4.0, includes sds as an independent profile: https://archive.istio.io/v1.4/docs/setup/additional-setup/config-profiles/.

If you run the command in the listing, you need to replace the Pod name (`orders-deployment-f7bc58fbc-bbhwd`) with the one that runs in your Kubernetes cluster. The Envoy proxy can access the certificates/keys provisioned to it by Citadel from the `/etc/certs` location of its local filesystem. Citadel keeps track of the expiration time of each key/certificate it provisions and then rotates them before expiration.

Listing 12.23 The volume mounts of the Istio ingress gateway Pod

```
\> kubectl get pod orders-deployment-f7bc58fbc-bbhwd -o yaml

volumeMounts:
- mountPath: /etc/istio/proxy
  name: istio-envoy
- mountPath: /etc/certs/
  name: istio-certs
  readOnly: true
- mountPath: /var/run/secrets/kubernetes.io/serviceaccount
  name: default-token-9h45q
  readOnly: true
```

> Mount path from the Envoy local filesystem for the keys used by Envoy proxy

> The default token secret (a JWT), which is provisioned by Kubernetes—not specific to Istio

Let's use the following command to print the PEM-encoded certificate provisioned to the Envoy proxy associated with the Order Processing microservice. Make sure to have the correct Pod name corresponding to your environment in the command:

```
\> kubectl exec -it  orders-deployment-f7bc58fbc-bbhwd \
-c istio-proxy cat /etc/certs/cert-chain.pem
```

You can decode the output from the preceding command by using an online tool like the Report URI Decode PEM Data tool (https://report-uri.com/home/pem _decoder). The decoded output is shown in the following listing. You can see the lifetime of the certificate is 90 days, and it is issued for a service account (see the Subject Alternative Names attribute).

Listing 12.24 The certificate provisioned to Envoy by Citadel

```
Issued By: cluster.local
Serial Number: 3BF3584E3780C0C46B9731D561A42032
Signature: sha256WithRSAEncryption
Valid From: 23:29:16 10 May 2020
Valid To: 23:29:16 08 Aug 2020
Key Usage: Digital Signature, Key Encipherment
Extended Key Usage: TLS Web Server Authentication,
                    TLS Web Client Authentication
```

> The issuer of the certificate

> A unique number associated with this certificate

> The CA signs the public key associated with this certificate, following this signature algorithm.

> This certificate can be used for mTLS authentication.

> This certificate can be used to sign a message or encrypt a key, but cannot be used to encrypt data.

```
Basic Constraints: CA:FALSE
Subject Alternative Names:
        URI:spiffe://cluster.local/ns/default/sa/default
```

The SPIFFE identifier corresponding to the service account associated with this istio proxy

When you create a Pod in a Kubernetes environment, you can associate a Pod with a service account. Multiple Pods can be associated with the same service account. If you do not specify which service account you want to associate with a Pod, Kubernetes uses the default service account. In section 11.6, we discuss service accounts in detail. Citadel adds the service account name to the certificate under the `Subject Alternative Names` field following the SPIFFE standard (for more information, see appendix H).

12.6.2 *Limitations in key provisioning and rotation via volume mounts*

If you use Istio add-ons within GKE to run the samples in this chapter, the key provisioning and rotation works in the way explained in section 12.6.1.[5] But this approach has limitations or risks, including the following:

- Whenever Citadel provisions/rotates keys/certificates by updating the corresponding Kubernetes Secret, the corresponding Envoy proxies have to restart to load the new key/certificate.
- The private keys are generated by Citadel outside the Kubernetes node, where the Envoy proxy that uses those keys runs. One potential security issue is that these keys can be compromised when they are transferred from Citadel to the Kubernetes node, which hosts the corresponding Pod.

To overcome these limitations, since version 1.1.0, Istio introduced the Secret Discovery Service, which we discuss next.

12.6.3 *Key provisioning and rotation with SDS*

In this section, we discuss how key provisioning and rotation in Istio works with the *Secret Discovery Service* (*SDS*). Istio introduced the SDS feature with Istio 1.1.0 under the `sds` profile. So, if you are using Istio 1.1.0 or a later release prior to 1.5.0, but still with the `default` profile, you will not see SDS support. With Istio 1.5.0 onward, SDS is enabled by default. If you check the Istio feature status available at the Istio website (https://istio.io/about/feature-stages/#security-and-policy-enforcement), you can find the status of the SDS feature. Since the Istio 1.5.0 release, it is in the stable phase.

When you enable the `sds` profile prior to Istio 1.5.0 release, you can find an SDS node agent running in every Kubernetes node under the `istio-system` namespace. Figure 12.9 explains how the Istio node agent (also known as the *SDS server*) facilitates key provisioning. However, since Istio 1.5.0 onward, this node agent is removed, and its functionality has been moved to the Envoy proxy itself.

---

[5] At the time of this writing, the latest GKE cluster version is 1.14.10-gke.27, and it supports only Istio 1.2.10.

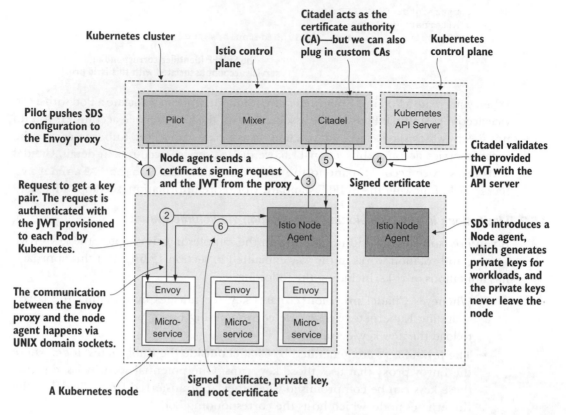

Figure 12.9   SDS introduces a node agent (prior to version 1.5.0), which runs on each Kubernetes node. This node agent generates a key pair for each workload (proxy) in the corresponding node and gets those signed by Citadel.

Let's have a look at how each step works:

1 The Pilot, which runs on the Istio control plane, keeps track of all the Pods Kubernetes spins up. When it finds a new Pod, the Pilot talks to the corresponding Envoy proxy and passes the SDS configuration along with other configurations. For example, this includes how the Envoy proxy could talk to the node agent via UNIX domain sockets (https://en.wikipedia.org/wiki/Unix_domain _socket).

2 The Envoy proxy talks to the node agent via UNIX domain sockets to request a key pair. Along with this request, Envoy also passes the JWT provisioned to its Pod by Kubernetes. This JWT is attached to the service account associated with the corresponding Pod.

3 The node generates a key pair—and then a CSR—and sends the CSR along with the JWT it got from the proxy to Citadel. When generating the certificate, the node agent uses the service account name associated with the provided JWT

to derive the Subject Alternative Name (listing 12.24) and embeds that to the certificate. This generated certificate is compliant with the SPIFFE standard, which we discuss in appendix H.

4 Citadel talks to the API server to validate the provided JWT and confirms that this workload carries the correct JWT and is running on the correct Kubernetes node.

5 Citadel returns the signed certificate to the node agent.

6 The node agent returns the signed certificate, the private key, and the root certificate to the Envoy proxy (or the workload).

After the keys are provisioned to workloads, the node agent keeps track of their expiration. It runs a timer job, which iterates over all the cached keys to find the keys closer to expiry. If a key is close to expiring, the node agent sends a message to the corresponding Envoy proxy, and the proxy will start the same process as in figure 12.7 to get the new keys. One main advantage of using SDS to provision and rotate keys is that we do not need to restart the Envoy proxy to reload new keys.

Summary

- Service Mesh is an architectural pattern that highlights the need for decoupling security, observability, routing control, and resiliency from the microservices implementation to another level of abstraction.
- Istio uses the Envoy service proxy, which is deployed alongside the microservice at the data plane to intercept ingress and egress traffic to and from a microservice and enforce security policies.
- Istio Citadel is a control plane component that provisions certificates to each service proxy in a microservices deployment and takes care of certificate rotation.
- The Istio Ingress gateway runs at the edge of the Kubernetes cluster and terminates TLS and can also establish an mTLS connection with upstream microservices.
- Istio introduced a new resource type called DestinationRule. This is used to instruct Envoy proxies at the client side to use mTLS for all the communications with the corresponding hosts. However, from Istio 1.5.0 onward you do not need to do anything to enable mTLS among microservices; it's enabled by default.
- Istio 1.5.0 introduced two new resource types for authentication: PeerAuthentication and RequestAuthentication. You can use PeerAuthentication resource type to define mTLS-based policies, and RequestAuthentication resource type to define JWT-based policies.
- Istio introduces two custom resource types: ServiceRole and ServiceRoleBinding to perform authorization, and ServiceRoleBinding is used to map a role/authority to a ServiceRole. However, if you are using Istio 1.4.0 or later, you should use the AuthorizationPolicy resource type.

- Since Istio 1.1.0 onward with the `sds` profile, Istio does key provisioning and rotation with the SDS. From Istio 1.5.0 onward, SDS is supported by default.
- When you use SDS, the private keys associated with workloads never leave the corresponding Kubernetes nodes. And during key rotation, we do not need to restart Envoy proxies to reload keys.

Part 5

Secure development

Speed to production is one of the key motivations behind the microservices architecture. Automating security testing in the development process helps you catch bugs as early as possible in the development cycle, and minimizes the effort in fixing them. This part of the book teaches you how to automate security testing of your microservices with SonarQube, Jenkins, and OWASP ZAP.

Secure coding practices and automation

This chapter covers

- OWASP top 10 API security vulnerabilities
- Performing static analysis of code by using SonarQube
- Automating code analysis by integrating with Jenkins
- Performing dynamic analysis of code by using OWASP ZAP

The complexity of the source code or the system design is a well-known vector of security vulnerabilities. According to published research, after some point, the number of defects in an application increases as the number of code lines increases. The defect increase is exponential and not linear, meaning that the rate of defects increases much faster compared to the rate of code being added. Unless you have good test coverage for both functionality and security, you won't be able to deploy changes into production frequently with confidence.

Two main kinds of security tests are integrated into the development life cycle: static code analysis and dynamic testing. You can integrate both tests to run automatically after each daily build. In the rest of this chapter, we look at the top 10 API security vulnerabilities as categorized by the Open Web Application Security Project (OWASP) and then take a look at tools we can use to perform static and dynamic analysis of our code.[1] If you'd like to learn more about security best practices, we recommend *Agile Application Security: Enabling Security in a Continuous Delivery Pipeline* (O'Reilly Media, 2017) by Laura Bell et al.

13.1 OWASP API security top 10

OWASP API Security (www.owasp.org/index.php/OWASP_API_Security_Project) is an open source project that's aimed at preventing organizations from deploying potentially vulnerable APIs. As we've discussed throughout this book, APIs expose microservices to consumers. It's therefore important to focus on how to make these APIs safer and avoid known security pitfalls. Let's take a look at the OWASP top 10 list of API security vulnerabilities:

1 Broken object-level authorization
2 Broken authentication
3 Excessive data exposure
4 Lack of resources and rate limiting
5 Broken function-level authorization
6 Mass assignment
7 Security misconfiguration
8 Injection
9 Improper asset management
10 Insufficient logging and monitoring

13.1.1 Broken object-level authorization

Broken object-level authorization is a vulnerability that's present when using identifiers (IDs) to retrieve information from APIs. Users authenticate to APIs via applications using protocols like OAuth 2.0.[2] An application can use object IDs to fetch data from an API. Let's take a look at an example API from Facebook, where we get user details by using an ID:

```
\> curl -i -X GET "https://graph.facebook.com/{user-id} \
?fields=id,name&access_token={your-user-access-token}"
```

This example shows an API that's used to retrieve details of a user identified by an ID. We pass the `user-id` in the request as a path parameter to get details of the corresponding user. We also pass in the access token of the user who's authenticated to the

---

[1] The Open Web Application Security Project (OWASP) is a nonprofit foundation that works to improve the security of software, https://owasp.org/.
[2] OAuth 2.0 is an authorization framework, but it also helps authenticating users at the resource end—or at the API gateway, which intercepts all the traffic coming to an API.

API in a query parameter. Unless Facebook checks whether the consumer of the API (the owner of the access token) has permissions to access details of the user to whom the ID belongs, an attacker can gain access to details of any user they prefer; for example, getting details of a user who's not in your Friends list (figure 13.1). This authorization check needs to happen for every API request.

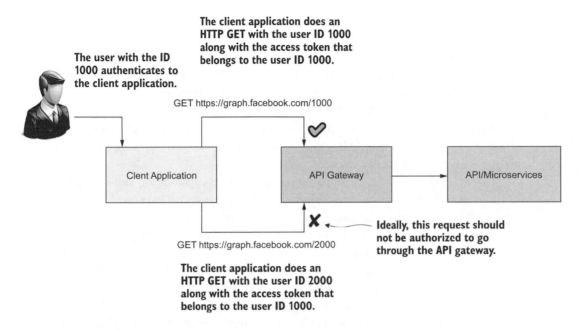

Figure 13.1 A client application under an attack could exploit the broken object-level authorization vulnerability in an API to retrieve one user's details with an access token that belongs to another user.

To reduce this type of attack, you should either avoid passing the user-id in the request or use a random (nonguessable) ID for your objects. If your intention is to expose only the details of the user who's authenticating to the API with the access token, you can remove the user-id from the API and use an alternative ID such as /me. For example:

```
\> curl -i -X GET "https://graph.facebook.com/me?fields=id,name&\
access_token={your-user-access-token}"
```

In case you can't omit passing in the user-id and need to allow getting details of different users, use a random nonguessable ID for your users. Assume that your user identifiers were an autoincrementing integer in your database. In certain cases, you'll pass in something like the value 5 as the user ID and, in another case, something like 976. This provides hints to the consumers of your API that you have user IDs ranging from 5 to maybe something like a 1000 in your system, and they can therefore randomly request user details. It's therefore best to use a nonguessable ID. If your system is already built, and you can't change IDs, use a random identifier in your API layer and an internal mapping system to map externally exposed random strings to the internal IDs. This way, the actual ID of the object (user) remains hidden from the consumers of the API.

13.1.2 *Broken authentication*

Broken authentication is a vulnerability that occurs when the authentication scheme of your APIs isn't strong enough or isn't implemented properly. Throughout this book, you've learned that OAuth 2.0 is the de facto standard for securing APIs. However, OAuth 2.0 as a framework provides multiple options for developers to secure their APIs. You need to pick the right grant type for your application, along with the right expiration times for the tokens. The expiration time you pick for the access token, for example, can depend on the risk associated with token leakage, duration of the underlying access grant (SAML grant or JWT grant), the time required for an attacker to guess or produce a valid token.

OAuth 2.0 works on opaque (reference) access tokens or self-contained JWT-formatted tokens. As we discussed in chapter 3, when we use a reference access token to access an API deployed on an API gateway, the gateway validates the token against the token issuer (or the STS). The token issuer of a reference access token has to make sure that the length of the token is greater than or equal to 128 bits and constructed from a cryptographically strong random or pseudorandom number sequence. In chapter 7, we talked about JWT and its attributes. If a JWT is used as an access token, the gateway can validate the token by itself. In either case, the gateway needs to make sure the validation of the token is done properly. For example, in the case of a JWT, the gateway needs to validate the token and check for the following:

- The token is signed properly with a strong signing algorithm and a key.
- The issuer of the token is trusted.
- The audience of the token is correct.
- The token isn't expired.
- The scopes bound to the token permit it to access the requested resource.

Failure to implement the security scheme properly can lead to APIs being left vulnerable to attacks that can exploit them. The OAuth 2.0 Security Best Current Practice document (https://tools.ietf.org/html/draft-ietf-oauth-security-topics-14), developed by the OAuth working group under IETF, shares security best practices related to OAuth 2.0 and extends the best practices defined in the OAuth 2.0 Threat Model and Security Considerations document (https://tools.ietf.org/html/rfc6819). The JSON Web Token Best Current Practices (https://tools.ietf.org/html/rfc8725) document from the same OAuth working group defines the best practices in issuing and verifying a JWT. All these are recommended readings, if you are keen on understanding OAuth 2.0 security in depth.

13.1.3 *Excessive data exposure*

APIs should return only the data that's relevant and required for its consumers. For example, if an application (consumer) requires to know whether a particular user is older than the age of 18, instead of exposing the user's date of birth or age, the API should return only true or false, that indicates whether the user is older than 18. This is also true for other software systems and websites, not just for APIs.

Software systems or websites shouldn't expose the technology or versions of the technologies they run on. It's quite common to find technologies used in websites by viewing the HTML page source. If the website runs on a particular platform, often the JavaScript libraries or CSS that appear in the HTML source contain the names and versions of the technology platform. This isn't a good practice because it allows attackers to mine for vulnerabilities of the mentioned technologies and attack the system by using that information.

It was not so long ago that an excessive data exposure vulnerability was uncovered in a mobile application called 3Fun, a location-based, online dating application.[3] Using location data that its API exposed unnecessarily, attackers could find dating preferences of the app's users in the White House, Supreme Court, and major cities in the world. By using the birthdate it exposed, attackers could pinpoint the exact users and hack into their personal photos!

We mostly see excessive data exposure happen in error handling, which provides a complete stack-trace in the API response of an internal error occurring in the API implementation. The exception shielding is one common pattern used to handle errors in a secure way. Rather than sharing an error as it is with the client application, the exception-shielding pattern shields the error with an error code, and shares the error code only with the client application, via the API response.

13.1.4 *Lack of resources and rate limiting*

APIs often don't impose limits on the number of requests they serve within a given time nor limit the amount of data returned. This can lead to attackers performing DDoS attacks that make the system unavailable to legitimate users. Imagine an API like the following that allows retrieving details of users:

```
https://findusers.com/api/v2?limit=10000000
```

If the API doesn't impose a limit on the maximum number of users that can be queried in a single API request, consumers could set a very large value on the limit. This would make the system fetch details of so many users that it would run the risk of consuming all resources it has and become unable to serve requests from legitimate users. A setting for the maximum number of records to be retrieved can be implemented at the application layer itself or by using an API gateway.

---

[3] Group dating app 3Fun exposed sensitive data of 1.5 million users; see https://techcrunch.com/2019/08/08/group-dating-app-3fun-security-flaws/ for more details.

Similarly, attackers could perform DDoS attacks by sending a large number of requests within a very short time; for example, sending a million requests per second using distributed attack clients. This too would make the system unavailable for legitimate users. Preventing such attacks is typically done at the network perimeter by using WAF solutions.

13.1.5   *Broken function-level authorization*

The *broken function-level authorization* vulnerability is about the lack of fine-grained authorization at an API. An API can consist of multiple operations (resources); for example, `GET /users/{user-id}` for retrieving user information and `DELETE /users/{user-id}` for removing a particular user. Both operations are part of a single API called `/users`. Authorization for this API should be done by operation, not only at an API level.

Performing authorization at the API level results in anyone with permissions to retrieve user information (`GET`) to also implicitly have permissions to remove user information (`DELETE`), which isn't correct. You could use OAuth 2.0 scopes for this, as we discussed in chapter 2. Different scopes could be bound to the different resources, and only users with the relevant permissions should be granted the scope when requesting OAuth 2.0 access tokens.

In some cases, the permissions are delegated to the consuming application of an API, such as with SPAs, as we discussed in chapter 4. The SPA can use OIDC to obtain the roles of the user and hide the relevant actions (`DELETE`, for example) from the UI if the user doesn't have the proper role. This isn't a proper design because the functionality is still exposed at the API level and therefore remains vulnerable.

As mentioned before, authorization checks should be enforced at the resource by using OAuth 2.0 scopes or something similar. There are also recommendations to make such operations that require fine-grained authorizations nonguessable; for example, using `GET /users/{user-id}?action=delete` instead of `DELETE /users/{user-id}`. This again isn't good design. It not only messes up your API design, but also doesn't solve the actual problem. This is called *security by obscurity*, which is not a good practice.

13.1.6   *Mass assignment*

Mass assignment is a vulnerability that's exposed when APIs blindly bind to JSON objects received via clients without being selective about the attributes they bind to. Let's assume we have some JSON that represents user attributes, including roles. A possible `GET /users/{user-id}` operation returns the following:

```
{"user":
    {
    "id": "18u-7uy-9j3",
    "username": "robert",
    "fullname": "Robert Smith",
    "roles": ["admin", "employee"]
    }
}
```

As you can observe, this operation returns the details of the user, including their roles. Now imagine using the same JSON to create or modify a user in the system. This is typically done by a POST /users or PUT /users/{user-id} to the /users API and by passing in the JSON message. If the API assigns user roles by reading them from the JSON message that's passed in, anyone having permissions to add or modify users can assign roles to users or even themselves. Imagine a sign-up form to a particular system being powered by such an API. This would enable anyone to assign themselves to the admin role of the system. To avoid such errors, the API should be selective about what fields it picks from the input message to assign to its entities. Ideally, you can define different JSON objects by the corresponding operation.

13.1.7 Security misconfiguration

Security misconfigurations on APIs can occur for various reasons. These misconfigurations mainly occur because of insecure default configurations. The following are some examples of these misconfigurations:

- Not disabling HTTP when allowing only HTTPS on your APIs
- Allowing unnecessary HTTP methods on API resources (for example, allowing POST on a resource when only a GET is required)
- Including stack traces on error messages that reveal the internals of a system
- Permissive CORS that allows access to APIs from unnecessary domains

Preventing these types of errors requires attention to both the design time of APIs and the runtime. We need to use tools that check our API specifications to make sure they adhere to API design best practices. This prevents design-time errors such as allowing unnecessary HTTP methods on APIs. Tools like the API contract security auditor (https://apisecurity.io/tools/audit/) provided by APISecurity.io let you check your API definitions (open API files) for vulnerabilities and malpractices in API design.

Runtime strengthening of the system needs to happen by automated mechanisms as much as possible. For example, when deploying an API, we'd typically expose the API on HTTPS only (disabling HTTP). Instead of expecting an administrator to disable HTTP, the deployer scripts of the APIs themselves should be automated to disable HTTP. In addition to this, the software should always be run on servers that have been hardened for security, and where all the security patches have been applied. You should also build strong verifications (tests), which verify that all necessary runtime configurations are applied. Netflix's Security Monkey (https://github.com/Netflix/security_monkey) is one such tool to make sure their AWS and GCP accounts always run on secure configurations, though it is now in maintenance mode.

13.1.8 Injection

Injection flaws such as Structured Query Language (SQL) injections and command injections can occur when APIs accept data and pass it on to interpreters to execute as a part of a query or a command. For example, imagine that a search operation on the user's API accepts a name to search and passes it to a SQL statement. The API would look like the following:

```
GET /search/users?name=robert
```

The name extracted from the query parameter would then be passed on to a SQL query that looks like this:

```
SELECT * FROM USERS WHERE NAME = robert;
```

Now if the name passed in is changed from `robert;` to `robert; DELETE FROM USERS WHERE ID = 1;`, the resulting SQL statement would be as follows and would remove a user from the system:

```
SELECT * FROM USERS WHERE NAME = robert; DELETE FROM USERS WHERE ID = 1;
```

To mitigate these types of attacks, user inputs should always be sanitized. Static code analysis tools are also capable of detecting whether input parameters have been directly used in SQL statements. WAF solutions are also capable of detecting and preventing such attacks at runtime. Programming languages too have their own mechanisms for preventing such attacks. For example, Java provides the `PreparedStatement` construct that can be used to execute SQL statements. It takes care of such vulnerabilities and prevents injection attacks.

13.1.9 *Improper asset management*

Platforms such as Kubernetes and containers have made it easy for developers to deploy APIs into various environments. But this has brought a new challenge—a lot of APIs tend to get deployed easily and forgotten over time. When APIs are forgotten and newer versions of APIs deployed, the older versions get less attention.

Organizations can miss applying security patches and other fixes to old APIs that may still be in operation under the radar. Unless they're properly documented and maintained, people may forget the details of these APIs and therefore be unwilling to make changes to them. Older APIs could remain unpatched and vulnerable. It's therefore important to document and maintain these APIs by using a proper API management system.

Red Hat's 3scale (www.redhat.com/en/technologies/jboss-middleware/3scale) and WSO2's API Manager (https://wso2.com/api-management/) are two examples of open source API management solutions. These systems enforce best practices on APIs when deployed and give an indication of which APIs are being used and which are old enough to retire. These systems also maintain the test scripts of APIs and help you with testing APIs when necessary.

13.1.10 *Insufficient logging and monitoring*

All actions performed in systems need to be logged, monitored, and analyzed for abnormalities. The lack of logs and monitoring results in not knowing what's going on in a system.

Assume, for example, that a user is accessing an API by using a token from an IP address from the United Kingdom. Now, if the same token is being used by a user from the United States a few minutes later, the token is likely to have been hacked by an intruder. Our authentication and authorization layers won't detect anything wrong with these requests because they contain valid credentials to access APIs.

We therefore need other mechanisms to detect such abnormalities. This is another instance where a proper API management system can help. A system that analyzes user behavior and processes behavioral data to find abnormalities and suspicious patterns is the only way of detecting and preventing such vulnerabilities.

13.2 *Running static code analysis*

In this section, we look at a practical example of running static code analysis by using SonarQube (www.sonarqube.org). *SonarQube* is an open source tool that helps you scan your code to check for security vulnerabilities, code smells, and bugs. It can be integrated with your build process so that it scans your code continuously (on each build). It can also be integrated with automated build tools such as Jenkins, which is something we'll look at later in this chapter.

Static code analysis is a method of code debugging without executing the code itself (without running the program). Static analysis helps to check whether the code adheres to industry best practices and prevents bad practices. Static analysis of code is important because it can reveal errors in code (by running the code) before an incident occurs. Automated tools such as SonarQube can assist developers in performing static analysis on their code.

Static analysis is, however, only the first step in software quality analysis. Dynamic analysis is also typically performed to ensure comprehensive coverage of the code. This section focuses on static code analysis. We'll discuss dynamic code analysis in section 13.4. You can find the examples of this chapter at https://github.com/microservices-security-in-action/samples/tree/master/chapter13. Download the code from this location to a directory of your choice. You'll need Docker (www.docker.com) installed on your machine to run these samples. We run SonarQube on a Docker container locally.

Execute the following steps to run the first example of this section. Make sure you have your Docker process up and running. Running the following command from the command line in a terminal window prints the version of Docker that's running:

```
\> docker --version
```

If Docker is running, execute the following command in your command-line tool to download (pull) the Docker image of SonarQube to your local workstation:

```
\> docker pull owasp/sonarqube
```

Once this command completes, you have the SonarQube Docker image on your local Docker repository. The next step is to run the Docker container by executing the following command from your command-line terminal:

```
\> docker run -d -p 9000:9000 -p 9092:9092 owasp/sonarqube
```

When this command completes, you should see a random ID printed to your console that indicates that SonarQube is now running on your machine. Run the following command to get a list of the running Docker processes on your machine:

```
\> docker ps
```

You should see a Docker image with the name `owasp/sonarqube`. You can now open a web browser and navigate to http://localhost:9000 to open the SonarQube dashboard. If you haven't run any code scans yet, you should see a message at the top right that says `0 projects scanned`.

The next step is to enable SonarQube scanning on our Maven installation and run a scan of our code. To enable SonarQube scanning on our Maven projects, we need to add the following section to the settings.xml file located in your $MAVEN_HOME/ conf directory (for example, /usr/local/apache-maven-3.5.2/conf). You can find a sample settings.xml file inside the chapter13 directory:

```
<settings>
    <pluginGroups>
        <pluginGroup>org.sonarsource.scanner.maven</pluginGroup>
    </pluginGroups>
    <profiles>
        <profile>
            <id>sonar</id>
            <activation>
                <activeByDefault>true</activeByDefault>
            </activation>
            <properties>
                <sonar.host.url>
                  http://localhost:9000
                </sonar.host.url>
            </properties>
        </profile>
    </profiles>
</settings>
```

Once this section is added to settings.xml, save and close the file, and use your command-line terminal to navigate to the chapter13/sample01 directory. This directory contains source code from our Order Processing microservice example from chapter 3. We'll scan this code to find potential security vulnerabilities. To do that, execute the following command at the prompt:

```
\> mvn clean verify sonar:sonar
```

Once the build succeeds, use your web browser to navigate to http://localhost:9000 (or refresh the page you visited previously). You should now see at the top right of the page that you have one project scanned. Click the number 1 to view details of the scanned project. A page appears that gives you the project name, `com.manning .mss.ch13.sample01`, which was scanned. This project doesn't have any security vulnerabilities as of this writing. It reports six code smells, however (figure 13.2).

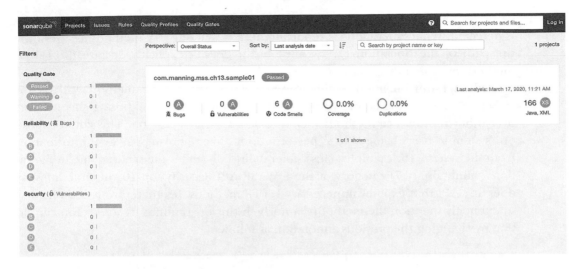

Figure 13.2 The SonarQube page shows the scan results of a project.

As newer versions of SonarQube are released with the capacity to uncover newer vulnerabilities and malpractices, it's possible for SonarQube to report vulnerabilities in this code as well. Click the name of the project to view the details of the code smells. By navigating through these links, you can view the details of each code smell and figure out the causes. SonarQube explains the details of these nicely and provides recommendations for fixes as well.

Because the code doesn't have any interesting security vulnerabilities, let's now try out an example that does. In the chapter13/sample02 directory, we have a new microservice that accepts credit card payments from users. This microservice has one method named pay. You can find the code of this service in the sample02/src/main/java/com/manning/mss/ch13/sample02/service/PaymentsService.java file. You'll notice that this method is annotated with @RequestMapping("/payment"). This annotation indicates that this operation is exposed over a path named /payment. Use your command-line terminal tool and navigate to the chapter13/sample02 directory and execute the same command as before:

```
\> mvn clean verify sonar:sonar
```

Once the build completes, refresh the SonarQube dashboard in your web browser. You'll notice that the number of projects scanned has now increased to two. Click number 2 (or the number of projects shown on the UI) to view the details of the scanned projects. You should see the second project with the name com.manning.mss.ch13.sample02 appearing in the project list.

The project in sample02 has one security vulnerability. Click the project name and then click the vulnerability to view more-detailed information. You should see the following message:

```
Add a "method" parameter to this "@RequestMapping" annotation.
```

Clicking this message takes you to the exact point in the code where this vulnerability is detected. What SonarQube is reporting here is that our `pay` method declares only the path of the operation (`/payment`) but it doesn't explicitly declare the HTTP methods on which this operation is exposed.

Although our intention originally was to make the payments method available on HTTP `POST` only, the failure to declare this explicitly is now exposing this method over other unintended methods such as `GET`, `DELETE`, and so on. This could expose our system to users being able to perform things like removing payment information from the system, for example. This vulnerability falls under the security misconfiguration (vulnerability 7) category of the OWASP API Security top 10 vulnerabilities, as does any API that exposes unnecessary HTTP methods. It's therefore recommended to explicitly mention the method(s) on which this operation is exposed. You can do that by changing the previous annotation as follows:

```
@RequestMapping(value = "/payment", method = RequestMethod.POST)
```

By using this annotation, we explicitly declare that the HTTP method (`POST`) be bound to the resource. Note that you need to import the `RequestMethod` class by adding the following `import` statement to the top of the class, along with the other `import` statements:

```
import org.springframework.web.bind.annotation.RequestMethod;
```

Next, rerun the `mvn clean verify sonar:sonar` command from your command-line prompt and observe the SonarQube dashboard. You'll need to refresh the web page. You should now notice that the earlier reported vulnerability is no longer being reported.

13.3 *Integrating security testing with Jenkins*

Jenkins is an open source automation server. It provides plugins to support many build, deployment, and automation processes. At this point, we need to integrate security testing of our code with our build pipelines. A *build pipeline* is a sequence of steps that happens in your build process (figure 13.3). The primary idea here is that we scan our code for vulnerabilities before the actual build happens.

You learned how to scan your code for vulnerabilities by using SonarQube, and now you'll learn how to automate this process by using Jenkins and why it's important

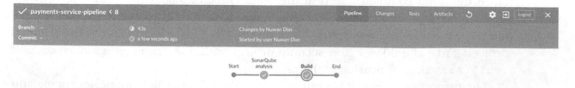

Figure 13.3   In this Jenkins build pipeline, the first step is to perform a code scan by using SonarQube and then to start the build process.

to do so. This is part of CI/CD: we scan our code before each build step to ensure that our code is free from vulnerabilities.

In most situations, we work as teams and collaboratively work on projects in which several people contribute code to a shared repository. In such situations, it's not practical for us to depend on each individual to contribute bug- and vulnerability-free code. We need mechanisms to verify the code being contributed and to alert us when someone checks in code with vulnerabilities. Identifying and preventing vulnerabilities as early as possible in our development life cycle helps us more easily fix them.

Let's take a look at how to set up Jenkins and configure a build pipeline to perform code scanning using SonarQube. Be sure to have your SonarQube server running as instructed in section 13.2.

13.3.1 *Setting up and running Jenkins*

In this section, we set up Jenkins on a Docker container and in section 13.3.2 configure a simple build pipeline that compiles the source code of a microservice. You'll need Docker to run the examples. The code for these examples is at https://github.com/microservices-security-in-action/chapter13. Note that this repository isn't the same repository where we had code for other examples. We need a separate repository because Jenkins requires a configuration file (Jenkinsfile) to be present in the root of the repository. Having this code in a repository that's separate from the rest of the samples in this book makes it easier to teach and for you to try out the examples. The following command shows how to clone the new repository into your local machine:

```
\> git clone \
https://github.com/microservices-security-in-action/chapter13.git
```

Check out (pull) the code from the repository and use the following instructions to set up Jenkins. Make sure to have Docker running on your machine. Open your command-line tool and execute this command to run the Docker image of Jenkins in a container:

```
\> docker run --rm -u root -p 7070:8080 \
-v jenkins-data:/var/jenkins_home \
-v /var/run/docker.sock:/var/run/docker.sock \
-v "$HOME":/home jenkinsci/blueocean
```

With the argument `-p 7070:8080`, we map port 7070 on our host (our machine) to the Jenkins port of 8080 that runs inside the container. The `-v "$HOME":/home` option mounts the home directory of our host machine to path `/home` of the image within the container. If you're on Windows, the command should be as follows. Note that the home path mount argument (`$HOME`) has changed:

```
\> docker run --rm -u root -p 7070:8080 \
-v jenkins-data:/var/jenkins_home \
-v /var/run/docker.sock:/var/run/docker.sock \
-v "%HOMEDRIVE%%HOMEPATH%":/home jenkinsci/blueocean
```

This command starts the Jenkins process on the terminal session you ran it on. You should see an ID printed between two sets of asterisks in your command-line output, as shown next. This ID (`2ud7j28ojr9jhaa8wljhue8skiuq8nm`) is required for getting started with Jenkins. You can save the ID for future use; alternatively, on your first login to Jenkins, you can create an admin user with your own credentials:

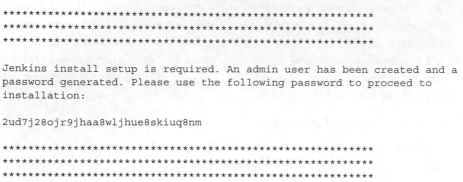

```
************************************************************
************************************************************
************************************************************

Jenkins install setup is required. An admin user has been created and a
password generated. Please use the following password to proceed to
installation:

2ud7j28ojr9jhaa8wljhue8skiuq8nm


************************************************************
************************************************************
************************************************************
```

Once the process is started, open your browser and navigate to http://localhost:7070, where you'll see the Unlock Jenkins page and will be prompted to enter the administrator password. Copy the ID (`2ud7j28ojr9jhaa8wljhue8skiuq8nm`) printed between the two sets of asterisks on your command line and paste it in the field that prompts for the admin password. Then proceed by clicking Continue.

Next, you'll see the Customize Jenkins page. Click the Install Suggested Plugins option to install the default set of plugins recommended by Jenkins. The installation may take a few minutes. Once the process is complete, you'll be prompted to create a new admin user. Provide the account details you'd like to create and complete the initial setup process.

You'll now be directed to the home page of Jenkins. To install the SonarQube plugin, click the Manage Jenkins link in the lefthand menu and then click Manage Plugins, as shown in figure 13.4.

On the page that appears, click the Available tab and filter all the plugins related to SonarQube by typing `SonarQube` in the Filter input box at the top right. Select the plugin named SonarQube Scanner and then select Install Without Restart.

Once completed, go back to the Manage Jenkins page and click Configure System to configure SonarQube for our build processes. You should now see a section named SonarQube servers. Click the Add SonarQube button, and then fill in the details on the presented form. Use `SonarScanner` as the name and `http://host.docker .internal:9000` as the Server URL, as shown in figure 13.5. Make sure that you have no blank spaces before or after the value of the Server URL. Note that the reason we provide host.docker.internal as the host is that Jenkins is running within a Docker container, and for it to connect to a port on the host machine (where SonarQube is running), localhost doesn't work. Also make sure to tick the check box, Enable

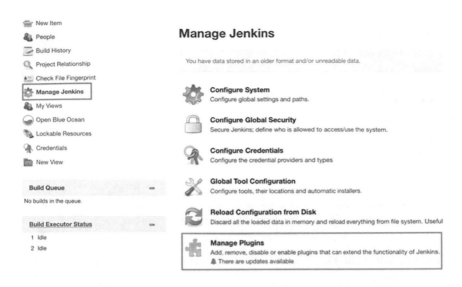

Figure 13.4 The Manage Jenkins page lets you install plugins for Jenkins.

Injection of SonarQube Server Configuration as Build Environment Variables (figure 13.5). Once completed, click the Save button to save your configurations.

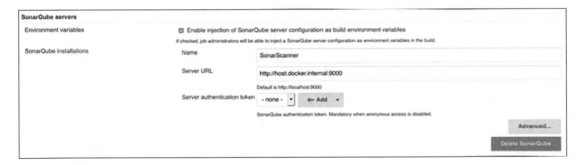

Figure 13.5 To set up the SonarQube plugin on Jenkins for the examples in this section, use host.docker.internal as the SonarQube host URL to connect to a port on the host machine where the Jenkins Docker container is running.

The next step is to create our Jenkins build pipeline, which we discuss in the next section.

13.3.2 *Setting up a build pipeline with Jenkins*

A pipeline in Jenkins is the configuration that instructs Jenkins on the steps to perform when executing an automation process. To do that, go to the Jenkins home page (http://localhost:7070/) and click New Item at the top left. Specify a name for your

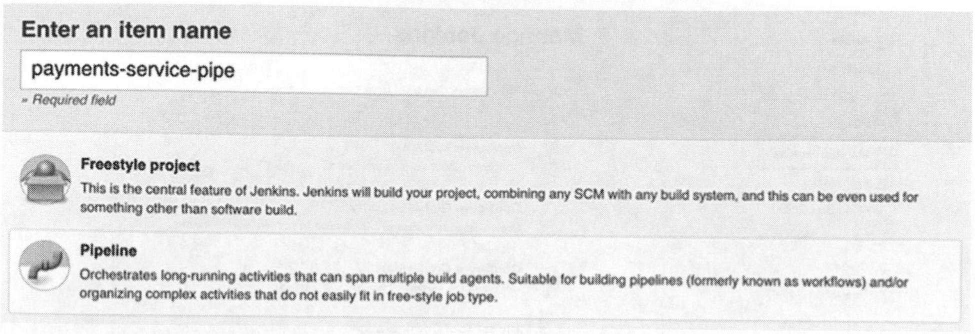

Enter an item name

payments-service-pipe

» *Required field*

Freestyle project
This is the central feature of Jenkins. Jenkins will build your project, combining any SCM with any build system, and this can be even used for something other than software build.

Pipeline
Orchestrates long-running activities that can span multiple build agents. Suitable for building pipelines (formerly known as workflows) and/or organizing complex activities that do not easily fit in free-style job type.

Figure 13.6   To create a Jenkins pipeline for our project, provide a name for the pipeline and then click the Pipeline option. Proceed by clicking the OK button at the bottom left.

pipeline and select the Pipeline option, as shown in figure 13.6; then click the OK but-ton at the bottom left.

Once this pipeline is created, we can navigate to the page where we can configure the newly created pipeline. Access the Pipeline tab, shown in figure 13.7. Pick the Pipeline Script from SCM option from the Definition drop-down box, and select Git as the SCM.

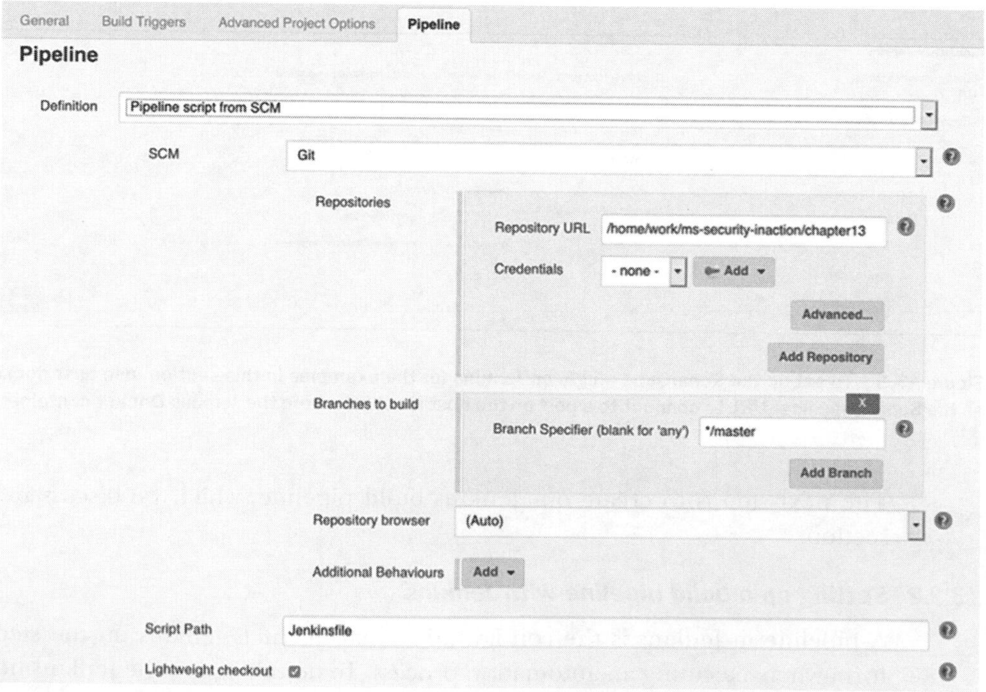

| General | Build Triggers | Advanced Project Options | **Pipeline** |

Pipeline

Definition   Pipeline script from SCM

SCM   Git

Repositories

Repository URL   /home/work/ms-security-inaction/chapter13

Credentials   - none -   ← Add ▾

Advanced...

Add Repository

Branches to build

Branch Specifier (blank for 'any')   */master

Add Branch

Repository browser   (Auto)

Additional Behaviours   Add ▾

Script Path   Jenkinsfile

Lightweight checkout ☑

Figure 13.7   In the Jenkins pipeline configuration, note that the path to the repository URL has been provided. Provide details as shown here and proceed by clicking the Save button at the bottom left.

Note that the path to the Repository URL has been provided. This should be the directory path where you cloned the repository containing the examples for this section, where /home maps to the $HOME path on your host machine. For example, if you cloned the repository to the /Users/roger/code/ms-security-inaction/chapter13 directory, and /Users/roger is your $HOME path, the Repository URL should be provided as /home/code/ms-security-inaction/chapter13.

Also notice the Script Path option that specifies Jenkinsfile as its value. This is the most important configuration file in this pipeline. This file should reside in the root of the aforementioned repository URL. It contains the steps to execute in the pipeline. When you cloned the repository for this section, you would have received a copy of this file as well. Let's take a look at the content of the Jenkinsfile in the following listing.

Listing 13.1   The Jenkinsfile

```
pipeline {
    agent {                                    ◁──  The agent is typically a machine or container
        docker {                                    that executes tasks when instructed by
            image 'maven:3-alpine'                  Jenkins. In this case, we use a Docker image
            args '-v /root/.m2:/root/.m2'           of Maven to execute our build. This means
        }                                           that when you run your Jenkins pipeline, a
    }                                               Docker image of Maven will be executed.
    stages {                ◁──  The stages of the
        stage('SonarQube analysis') {   build pipeline
            steps {
                withSonarQubeEnv(installationName: 'SonarScanner') {
                    sh 'mvn clean verify sonar:sonar'
                }
            }
        }
        stage('Build') {        ◁──  The Build
            steps {                  stage
                sh 'mvn -B clean package'    ◁──  Execute a Maven build.
            }                                     The -B argument is used to run
        }                                         the build in a noninteractive mode.
    }
}
```

SonarQube analysis stage

The stages define various phases in our Jenkins pipeline (figure 13.8). In our case, we have two stages: the first stage runs the SonarQube analysis, and the next stage performs the build of our code. You can provide any name for the stage (SonarQube analysis, for example). However, the installationName parameter should be the same as what you provided when configuring the SonarQube plugin for Jenkins (SonarScanner, in this case). The script provided within a step should be the same script we'd execute when performing the relevant action manually. You can see that we execute the same instruction from section 13.2 to scan our code for vulnerabilities here (listing 13.1) as well: sh 'mvn clean verify sonar:sonar'.

Once the preceding details have been provided, you can proceed to save the pipeline configuration. You should see your pipeline appearing on the home page of

Jenkins. Click the pipeline and then click the Open Blue Ocean link on the left. On the page that appears, click the Run button to run your pipeline, but make sure to have SonarQube running before running the pipeline. You can click the relevant item to view the progress of your build.

The first execution of the pipeline can take a few minutes to complete, depending on the speed of your internet connection. This is because the Maven container that executes your build is brand new. Maven downloads all of the dependencies of your project to its local repository before it can execute the build. Builds after the first execution would be faster because the dependencies exist on the local Maven repo of the container. However, because Jenkins too is running on a container, once the Jenkins container restarts, the first build that executes after that will be equal to our first build as well.

You can view the progress of each stage. Clicking a particular stage displays the logs relevant to the action (script) being performed. Once the build completes, you should see the progress bar shown in figure 13.8.

Figure 13.8 **After the build is successful, this progress bar shows the result of your SonarQube scan.**

You should now be able to visit the SonarQube application by pointing your browser to http://localhost:9000. The code we just scanned is the same as that inside the samples/chapter13/sample02 directory. We have, however, modified that code by fixing the vulnerability that was present in that example.

We just completed setting up our first Jenkins pipeline that scans our code using SonarQube and then builds it. We executed the pipeline manually by clicking the Run button on the Jenkins pipeline. In ideal situations, this pipeline will be run through automated processes. You can find the options for running this pipeline automatically by visiting the Build Trigger section under the Configure option of your pipeline.

Jenkins allows us to run these pipelines by using GitHub hooks (https://developer .github.com/webhooks/) on periodic intervals. We could also get our build job to fail if the relevant quality gates on SonarQube don't pass. This can be done by slightly advanced configurations on our Jenkinsfile as described in the SonarQube docs (http://mng.bz/WP2l). Jenkins could also be configured to trigger email and other notifications when builds fail. This way, we could configure a fully automated build process for our projects that would also send out notifications upon failures.

13.4 Running dynamic analysis with OWASP ZAP

Dynamic analysis of code checks your code through automated and manual processes while it's executing. You can perform dynamic analysis on your applications by using OWASP ZAP (www.owasp.org/index.php/OWASP_Zed_Attack_Proxy_Project). ZAP, short for *Zed Attack Proxy*, is an open source tool that helps find security vulnerabilities in web applications.

Dynamic code analysis is a software testing mechanism that evaluates a program during real-time execution. Unlike static code analysis, the software needs to be run (and used) either by a human or by automated scripts for tools. This process tests various execution paths of a program by automatically generating various types of input parameters that would trigger different execution flows. Dynamic analysis is of great use to software developers and testers because it can greatly increase the efficiency of the software testing process.

ZAP, a tool that acts as a proxy between the client application (web browser) and server, analyzes the requests and responses to identify potential vulnerabilities in the application. Figure 13.9 illustrates the pattern.

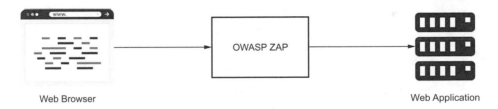

Figure 13.9 OWASP ZAP acts as a proxy between the web browser and the web application. It intercepts all request and response exchanges between the two.

13.4.1 Passive scanning vs. active scanning

Penetration testing is the process of testing a computer system, network, or web application for vulnerabilities that could be exploited. If you are new to penetration testing, we recommend *The Art of Network Penetration Testing* (Manning, 2020) by Royce Davis.

When it comes to penetration testing, a *passive scan* is a harmless scan that looks only for responses and checks them against known vulnerabilities. It doesn't modify the website's data, so it's safe to use against sites where you don't have permission. Passive scanning, however, isn't effective. Because it looks only at existing traffic and tries to identify threats and vulnerabilities by looking at passing data, the chances of detecting vulnerabilities are less. Some examples of passive scans are looking for software and patch versions of software against public databases that report known vulnerabilities in software, inspecting the messages being passed between communicating parties to identify malpractices in data patterns, and so on.

Active scanning, on the other hand, is much more effective because it deliberately tries to penetrate the system by using known techniques to find vulnerabilities. For example, you can exploit an SQL injection vulnerability that can be used to modify the system's database by executing a malicious SQL statement. It not only updates the application's data, but also can insert malicious scripts into the system. It's therefore important to perform active scanning tests only on systems where you're permitted. These tests should be performed in dedicated environments (QA, Production, for example) so that they don't affect users of other environments.

13.4.2 *Performing penetration tests with ZAP*

In this section, we'll use ZAP to perform a penetration test against an intentionally vulnerable website. You'll need Java version 11+ to run the exercises in this section. Download OWASP ZAP for your operating system from www.zaproxy.org/download/ and install it. Then run the software. We use ZAP 2.9.0 for the examples in this section. You'll see a screen that asks to persist the ZAP session, as shown in figure 13.10. Select the option to not persist the session and click the Start button.

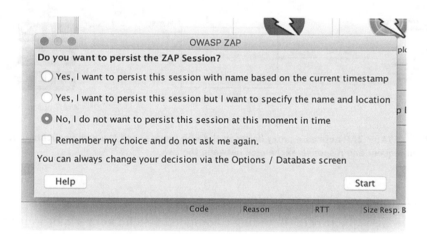

Figure 13.10 The ZAP start screen asks whether to persist the ZAP session. The exercises in this section don't require you to persist the session.

Next, we need a web application to scan for. We'll use the WebGoat application from OWASP. This open source web application is purposely designed to contain vulnerabilities, so it's useful for learning about the various types of vulnerabilities in web applications. You can download the latest available version of the application from https://github.com/WebGoat/WebGoat/releases. At the time of this writing, the latest version is v.8.0.0.M26, and that's what we'll run the exercises against. This application requires Java 11+. You can check the Java version installed by running the command `java -version` in your command-line tool.

WARNING   The WebGoat application contains many vulnerabilities; it's therefore recommended that you disconnect from the internet when running it. This is to prevent any chance of an attacker making you execute malicious scripts that could steal information or harm the system in any way.

Once you've downloaded the webgoat-server-<version>.jar file, copy it to a preferred location and navigate to that location by using your command-line tool. Then execute the following command to run the WebGoat web application. Make sure to have the correct file name of the JAR file in the command:

```
\> java -jar webgoat-server-8.0.0.M26.jar --server.port=9090 \
--server.address=localhost
```

You should see a message that looks like the following text after the WebGoat application has started successfully:

```
Started StartWebGoat in 14.386 seconds
```

Once the application has started, open a web browser and navigate to http://localhost:9090/WebGoat. You should see a login screen and a link to register a new user. Click the link to create an account to use WebGoat and log in. You could browse through the various links provided on the website. This is a website primarily designed by the OWASP community for learning purposes and, therefore, it contains lots of valuable information and teaching material about various types of attacks and remedies. Let's now look at how we can attack this site by using ZAP.

We'll first perform an automated scan on the website to look for any obvious misconfigurations or vulnerabilities. Go back to the ZAP UI, and on the Welcome page, click the Automated Scan option shown in figure 13.11.

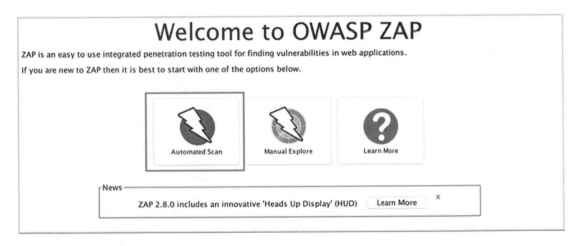

Figure 13.11   On the ZAP Welcome page, click the Automated Scan option to perform an automated scan on the WebGoat application.

On the next screen that appears, provide `http://localhost:9090/WebGoat` as the URL of the application to attack. For the Use Ajax Spider option, select Firefox (or pick a browser of your choice, but you'd need the corresponding driver installed), as shown in figure 13.12.

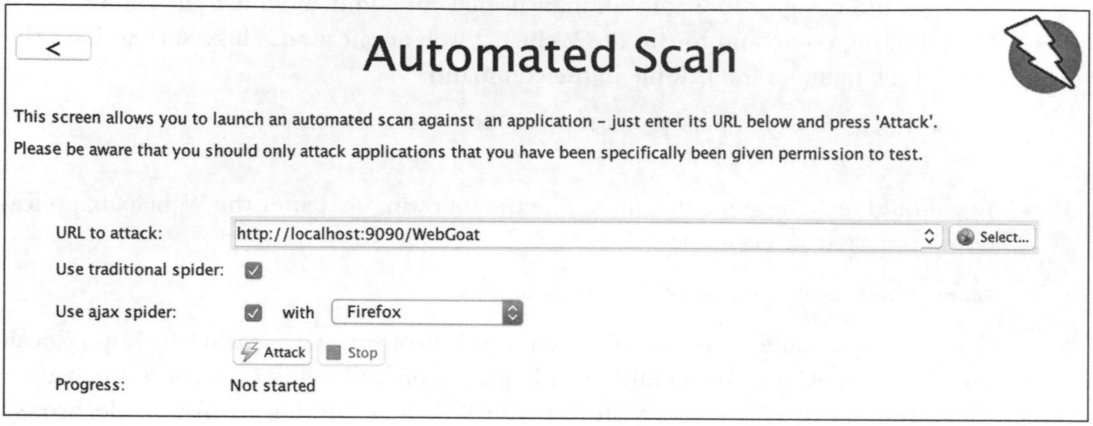

Automated Scan

This screen allows you to launch an automated scan against an application – just enter its URL below and press 'Attack'.

Please be aware that you should only attack applications that you have been specifically been given permission to test.

URL to attack:	http://localhost:9090/WebGoat ⬍ 🌐 Select...
Use traditional spider:	☑
Use ajax spider:	☑ with [Firefox ⬍]
	⚡ Attack ◼ Stop
Progress:	Not started

Figure 13.12   **Use the Automated Scan screen in ZAP to obtain details of the WebGoat application and attack using Firefox.**

Once the required information is provided, click the Attack button to start attacking the website. This temporarily opens a web browser and runs a series of attacks on the pages of the website. You can observe the progress of the attacks by selecting the Active Scan tab. Once the attack is complete (progress is shown as 100%), check the Alerts tab to view details of the discovered vulnerabilities and warnings.

The Alerts section should display a few yellow flags. You can click each of the alerts to discover the details reported. Because the WebGoat application requires a login to work, the automated scan can't proceed beyond the login and user registration pages. This is true for many of the sensitive web applications in use.

You can verify the details of the pages that were scanned by selecting the AJAX Spider tab and observing the URLs of the scanned pages. You'll notice that it consists mainly of links to CSS files, JavaScript files, images, and paths of the login page and the user registration page. The automated scan isn't effective when it comes to applications that require user logins to perform its actions. For your penetration tests to be more effective, you need to manually navigate the application in a way that covers as many features and combinations as possible.

Let's navigate back to the Welcome page of ZAP by clicking the < button and then select the Manual Explore option. Provide the URL of the WebGoat application to attack as http://localhost:9090/WebGoat and select Firefox as the browser to launch the application. Then click the Launch Browser button, shown in figure 13.13.

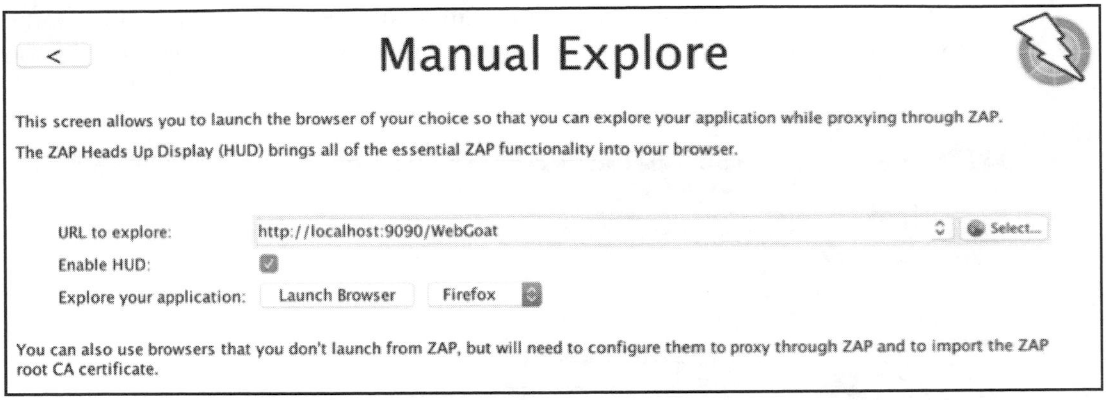

Manual Explore

This screen allows you to launch the browser of your choice so that you can explore your application while proxying through ZAP. The ZAP Heads Up Display (HUD) brings all of the essential ZAP functionality into your browser.

URL to explore: http://localhost:9090/WebGoat   ◇ ⊕ Select...

Enable HUD: ☑

Explore your application: Launch Browser   Firefox ▾

You can also use browsers that you don't launch from ZAP, but will need to configure them to proxy through ZAP and to import the ZAP root CA certificate.

Figure 13.13   On the Manual Explore screen in ZAP, provide the details as shown here and then click the Launch Browser button.

This launches a Firefox browser, and you'll be presented with an option to either go through the tutorials or continue to the target. Select the option to continue to the target. You'll then see the screen to log in to WebGoat. Log in with the account you created previously on WebGoat. Next, you'll be presented with the WebGoat home page, shown in figure 13.14.

We are now going to visit a vulnerable web page on this website and perform actions on it to see how ZAP identifies the vulnerabilities. Click the Cross Site Scripting link

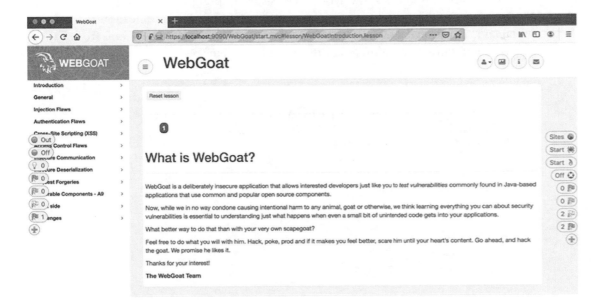

Figure 13.14   On the WebGoat home page, various tutorials are navigable from the lefthand menu.

from the left menu and then click the first link that appears beneath. You'll see the screen shown in figure 13.15. Click the number 7 that appears on the menu at the top of the screen.

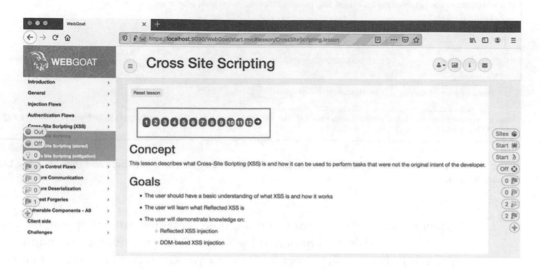

Figure 13.15   On the Cross Site Scripting page, you can learn all about XSS attacks and how to prevent them.

Step 7 in this tutorial lets you try out a reflected cross-site scripting (XSS) attack on a form. A *reflected XSS attack* is a type of cross-site scripting attack in which a malicious script sent via a link to a user executes on a web page of an application that's being attacked. This tutorial has a form that allows you to check out a few items from a shopping cart. Figure 13.16 shows what this form looks like.

Shopping Cart

Shopping Cart Items -- To Buy Now	Price	Quantity	Total
Studio RTA - Laptop/Reading Cart with Tilting Surface - Cherry	69.99	1	$0.00
Dynex - Traditional Notebook Case	27.99	1	$0.00
Hewlett-Packard - Pavilion Notebook with Intel Centrino	1599.99	1	$0.00
3 - Year Performance Service Plan $1000 and Over	299.99	1	$0.00

The total charged to your credit card: $0.00   UpdateCart

Enter your credit card number: 4128 3214 0002 1999

Enter your three digit access code: 111

Purchase

Figure 13.16   On the shopping cart form that's vulnerable to reflected XSS attacks, click the Purchase button to make ZAP detect the vulnerability.

Click the Purchase button. You'll see a warning appearing on the page that informs you about an XSS attack. This is because ZAP detected that this page is vulnerable to reflected XSS after you submitted the form.

To see the details of the vulnerability and see which field in the form is vulnerable, let's go back to the ZAP UI and select the Alerts section. You should see a red flag on the Alerts section that mentions an XSS vulnerability. If you click the relevant vulnerability, you can view the details and figure out which field in the form is vulnerable. Figure 13.17 illustrates what the ZAP UI should look like now.

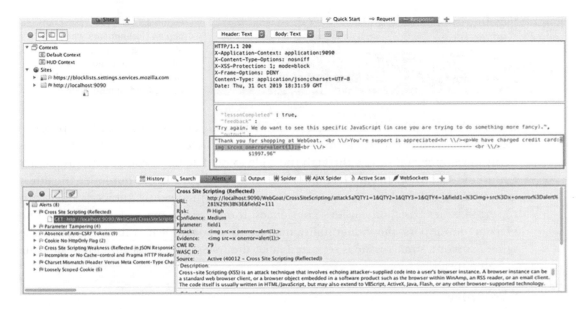

Figure 13.17 ZAP reports an XSS vulnerability on the page: the area that prints out the credit card number is vulnerable.

The highlighted text box in figure 13.17 shows that an area on the page is vulnerable to XSS; this area seems to print the credit card number when the Purchase button is clicked. We can verify that by manually entering JavaScript code into the field that accepts the credit card number. Go back to the Firefox browser from which you submitted the form and enter the following text in the credit card number field and then click the Purchase button:

```
<script>alert("Attacked");</script>
```

You should see a pop up that displays a JavaScript alert, which says Attacked, as shown in figure 13.18.

ZAP can similarly be used to detect various kinds of dynamic attacks on web applications that can't be identified by static code analysis tools. It also provides recommendations for remedies in the tool itself.

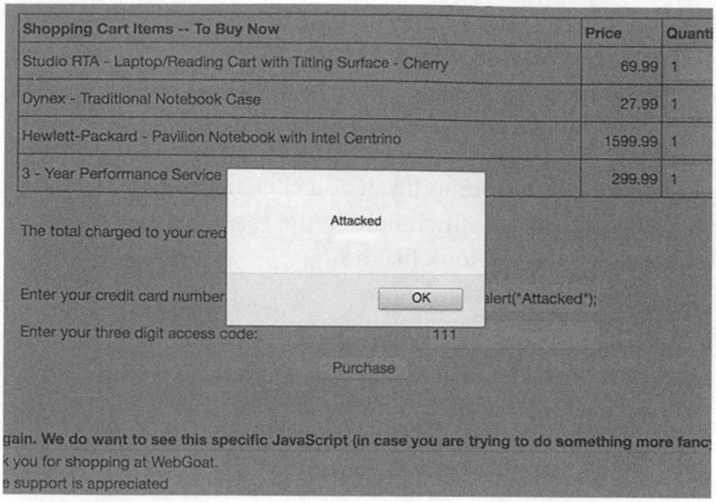

Figure 13.18   The JavaScript pop up that appears when attempting the purchase. It's clear that the page tries to print the user input entered in the Credit Card Number field.

One challenge with tools that perform dynamic and static scans is that they produce lots of false positives: most of the issues reported by these tools are invalid, but it takes many developer hours to go through the code to validate those issues. This problem is common in both open source and commercial tools. One way to minimize the effect is to build a vulnerability management system that intelligently knows to reject any reported issues based on earlier experiences. If one issue is marked as invalid by one of your developers, the vulnerability management system learns from it. When the same issue or a similar issue is reported later, the system automatically closes the issue as being invalid.

Summary

- The OWASP top 10 API security vulnerabilities describe the most common vulnerabilities discovered in APIs and recommended mitigation mechanisms for each identified vulnerability.
- You can use static analysis to debug code without execution to identify potential bugs and security vulnerabilities. SonarQube is an open source tool that you can use to scan and debug code without execution.
- It's important to integrate your code-scanning processes with automation tools such as Jenkins. These tools provide automated mechanisms for running code analysis through build pipelines and triggering notifications when failures occur, either due to code build failures or code not passing software's quality gates.
- Dynamic analysis checks your code through automated and manual processes while it's executing. Dynamic analysis generates different combinations of artificial inputs that can test various execution paths of code to identify bugs and vulnerabilities.
- OWASP ZAP is an open source tool that you can use to perform dynamic analysis of code.

appendix A
OAuth 2.0 and
OpenID Connect

OAuth 2.0 is an authorization framework developed by the Internet Engineering Task Force (IETF) OAuth working group. It's defined in RFC 6749. The fundamental focus of OAuth 2.0 is to fix the access delegation problem. *OpenID Connect* (OIDC) is an identity layer built on top of OAuth 2.0, and the OpenID Foundation developed the OpenID Connect specification.

In chapter 2, we briefly discussed OAuth 2.0 and how to use it to protect a microservice and to do service-level authorization with OAuth 2.0 scopes. Then in chapter 3, we discussed how to use the Zuul API gateway for OAuth 2.0 token validation. In chapter 4, we discussed how to log in to a SPA with OpenID Connect and then access the Order Processing microservice, which is protected with OAuth 2.0. In this appendix, we delve into the OAuth 2.0 and OpenID Connect fundamentals that you'll need to understand as a microservices developer.

If you're interested in understanding OAuth 2.0 and API security in detail, we recommend *Advanced API Security: OAuth 2.0 and Beyond* (Apress, 2019) by Prabath Siriwardena (a coauthor of this book). *OAuth 2 in Action* (Manning, 2017) by Justin Richer and Antonio Sanso is also a good reference.

A.1 The access delegation problem

If you want someone else to access a resource (a microservice, an API, and so on) on your behalf and do something with the resource, you need to delegate the corresponding access rights to that person (or thing). For example, if you want a third-party application to read your Facebook status messages, you need to give that third-party application the corresponding rights to access the Facebook API. There are two models of access delegation:

- Access delegation via credential sharing
- Access delegation with no credential sharing

If we follow the first model, we need to share our Facebook credentials with the third-party application so it can use the Facebook API, authenticate with our credentials, and read our Facebook status messages. This is quite a dangerous model (we are using Facebook just as an example; however, it does not support this model).

Once you share your credentials with a third-party application, it can do anything, not just read your Facebook status messages. It can read your friends list, view your photos, and chat with your friends via Messenger. This is the model many applications used before OAuth. FlickrAuth, Google AuthSub, and Yahoo BBAuth all tried to fix this problem in their own proprietary way: to undertake access delegation with no credential sharing. OAuth 1.0, released in 2007, was the first effort to crack this problem in a standard way. OAuth 2.0 followed the direction set by OAuth 1.0, and in October, 2012, became RFC 6749.

A.2   *How does OAuth 2.0 fix the access delegation problem?*

OAuth 1.0 and OAuth 2.0 both fix the access delegation problem in the same way, conceptually. The main difference is that OAuth 2.0 is more extensible than OAuth 1.0. OAuth 1.0 is a concrete protocol, whereas OAuth 2.0 is an authorization framework. In the rest of the appendix, when we say *OAuth*, we mean *OAuth 2.0*.

Figure A.1 illustrates a request/response flow in which a third-party web application follows the *access delegation with the no credential-sharing* model to get access to the Facebook API.

With OAuth 2.0, the third-party web application first redirects the user to Facebook (where the user belongs). Facebook authenticates and gets the user's consent to share a temporary token with a third-party web application, which is only good enough to read the user's Facebook status messages for a limited time. Once the web application gets the token from Facebook, it uses the token along with the API calls to Facebook.

The temporary token Facebook issues has a limited lifetime and is bound to the Facebook user, the third-party web application, and the purpose. The purpose of the token here is to read the user's Facebook status messages, and the token should be only good enough to do just that and no more. The OAuth 2.0 terminology is as follows:

- The Facebook user is called the *resource owner*. The resource owner decides who should have which level of access to the resources owned by that resource owner.
- Facebook, which issues the token, is called the *authorization server*. The authorization server knows how to authenticate (or identify) the resource owner, and grants access to third-party applications to access resources owned by the resource owner, with their consent.
- The Facebook API is called the *resource server*. The resource server guards the resources owned by the resource owner, and lets someone access a resource only if the access request comes along with a valid token issued by the authorization server.
- The third-party web application is called the *client*. The client consumes a resource on behalf of the resource owner.

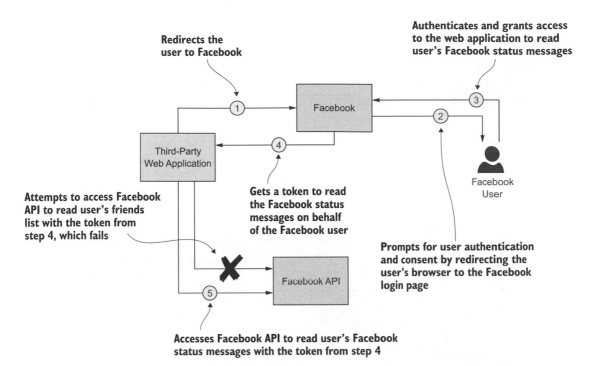

Figure A.1   A third-party application follows the model of access delegation with no credential sharing in order to get a temporary token from Facebook, which is only good enough to read a user's status messages.

- The token Facebook issues to the third-party web application is called the *access token*. The authorization server issues access tokens, and the resource server validates those. To validate an access token, the resource server may talk to the authorization server.
- The purpose of the token is called the *scope*. The resource server makes sure a given token can be used only for the scope attached to it. If the third-party application tries to write to the user's Facebook wall with the access token it got to read the status messages, that request will fail.
- The flow of events that happens while the third-party web application gets the token is called a *grant flow*, which is defined by a *grant type*. OAuth 2.0 defines a set of grant types, which we discuss in section A.4.

In the rest of the appendix, we discuss OAuth 2.0 concepts in detail.

A.3   Actors of an OAuth 2.0 flow

In OAuth 2.0, we mainly talk about four actors, based on the role each plays in an access delegation flow (see figure A.2). We talked briefly about them in section A.2:

- The resource server
- The client

- The end user (also known as the resource owner)
- The authorization server

In a typical access delegation flow, a client accesses a resource that's hosted on a resource server on behalf of an end user (or a resource owner) with a token provided by an authorization server. This token grants access rights to the client to access a resource on behalf of the end user.

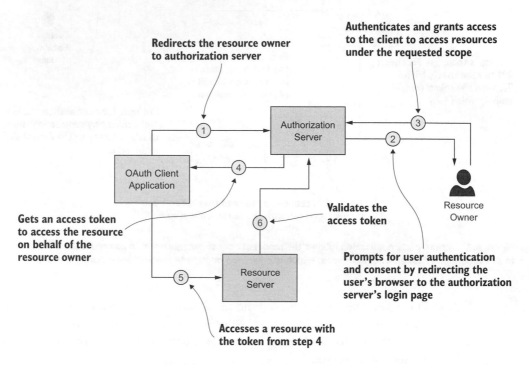

Redirects the resource owner to authorization server

Authenticates and grants access to the client to access resources under the requested scope

Gets an access token to access the resource on behalf of the resource owner

Validates the access token

Prompts for user authentication and consent by redirecting the user's browser to the authorization server's login page

Accesses a resource with the token from step 4

Figure A.2   In a typical OAuth 2.0 access delegation flow, a client accesses a resource that's hosted on a resource server, on behalf of the end user, with a token provided by the authorization server.

A.3.1   *The role of the resource server*

The *resource server* hosts the resources and decides who can access which resources based on certain conditions. If we take Flickr, the famous image- and video-hosting service, all the images and videos that you upload to Flickr are resources. Because Flickr hosts them all, Flickr is the resource server. In the Facebook example we discussed in section A.2, the server that hosts the Facebook API is the resource server. The Facebook wall, the friends list, videos, and photos are the resources exposed by the Facebook API.

In a microservices deployment, we can consider a microservice (for example, the Order Processing microservice that you developed and tested earlier in the book) as a resource server, and the orders as the resources. The Order Processing microservice is the entity that's responsible for managing orders. Also, you can consider the API gateway that exposes all your microservices to the external client applications as a resource server. As we discussed in chapter 5, the API gateway enforces throttling and access-control policies centrally, against all the APIs it hosts.

A.3.2 The role of the client application

The *client* is the consumer of the resources. If we extend the same Flickr example that we discussed in section A.3.1, a web application that wants to access your Flickr photos is a client. It can be any kind of an application: a mobile, web, or even a desktop application. In the Facebook example we discussed in section A.2, the third-party application that wanted to read Facebook status messages is also a client application.

In a microservices deployment, the application from which you'd consume the Order Processing microservice is the client application. The client application is the entity in an OAuth flow that seeks the end user's approval to access a resource on their behalf.

A.3.3 The role of the resource owner

The *resource owner* (or the *end user*) is the one who owns the resources. In our Flickr example, you're the resource owner (or the end user) who owns your Flickr photos. In the Facebook example we discussed in section A.2, the Facebook user is the resource owner.

In a microservices deployment, the person who places orders via the client application (which internally talks to the Order Processing microservice) is the end user. In some cases, the client application itself can be the end user, which simply accesses the microservice, just as itself with no other party involved.

A.3.4 The role of the authorization server

In an OAuth 2.0 environment, the *authorization server* issues tokens (commonly known as *access tokens*). An *OAuth 2.0 token* is a key issued by an authorization server to a client application to access a resource (for example, a microservice or an API) on behalf of an end user. The resource server talks to the authorization server to validate the tokens that come along with the access requests. The authorization server should know how to authenticate the end user, as well as how to validate the identity of the client application, before issuing an access token.

A.4 Grant types

In this section, we talk about OAuth 2.0 grant types and show you how to pick the correct one for your applications. Because this book is about microservices, we focus our discussion on those, but please keep in mind that OAuth 2.0 isn't just about microservices.

Different types of applications bearing different characteristics can consume your microservices. The way an application gets an access token to access a resource on behalf of a user depends on these application characteristics. The client application picks a request/response flow to get an access token from the authorization server, which is known as a *grant type* in OAuth 2.0.

The standard OAuth 2.0 specification identifies five main grant types. Each grant type outlines the steps for obtaining an access token. The result of executing a particular grant type is an access token that can be used to access resources on your microservices. The following are the five main grant types highlighted in the OAuth 2.0 specification:

- *Client credentials*—Suitable for authentication between two systems with no end user (we discuss this in section A.4.1)
- *Resource owner password*—Suitable for trusted applications (we discuss this in section A.4.2)
- *Authorization code*—Suitable for almost all the applications with an end user (we discuss this in section A.4.4)
- *Implicit*—Don't use it! (we discuss this in section A.4.5)
- *Refresh token*—Used for renewing expired access tokens (we discuss this in section A.4.3)

The OAuth 2.0 framework isn't restricted to these five grant types. It's an extensible framework that allows you to add grant types as needed. The following are two other popular grant types that aren't defined in the core specification but are in related profiles:

- *SAML Profile for OAuth 2.0 Client Authentication and Authorization Grants*— Suitable for applications having single sign-on using SAML 2.0 (defined in RFC 7522)
- *JWT Profile for OAuth 2.0 Client Authentication and Authorization Grants*—Suitable for applications having single sign-on using OpenID Connect (defined in RFC 7523)

A.4.1   *Client credentials grant type*

With a *client credentials grant type*, we have only two participants in the grant flow: the client application and the authorization server. There's no separate resource owner; the client application itself is the resource owner.

Each client carries its own credentials, known as the *client ID* and the *client secret*, issued to it by the authorization server. The *client ID* is the identifier of the client application; the *client secret* is the client's password. The client application should securely store and use the client secret. For example, you should never store a client secret in cleartext; instead, encrypt it and store it in persistent storage (such as a database).

As shown in figure A.3, in the client credentials grant type, the client application has to send its client ID and client secret to the authorization server over HTTPS to get an access token. The authorization server validates the combination of the ID and secret and responds with an access token.

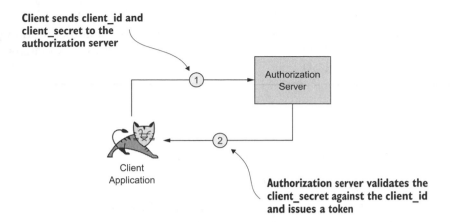

Figure A.3 The client credentials grant type lets an application obtain an access token with no end user; the application itself is the end user.

Here's a sample `curl` command for a client credentials grant request (this is just a sample, so don't try it out as-is):

```
\> curl \
-u application_id:application_secret \
-H "Content-Type: application/x-www-form-urlencoded" \
-d "grant_type=client_credentials" https://localhost:8085/oauth/token
```

The value `application_id` is the client ID, and the value `application_secret` is the client secret of the client application in this case. The `-u` parameter instructs curl to perform a base64-encoded operation on the string `application_id:application_secret`. The resulting string that's sent as the HTTP Authorization header to the authorization server would be YXBwbGljYXRpb25faWQ6YXBwbGljYXRpb25fc2VjcmV0. The authorization server validates this request and issues an access token in the following HTTP response:

```
{
  "access_token":"de09bec4-a821-40c8-863a-104dddb30204",
  "token_type":"bearer",
  "expires_in":3599
}
```

Even though we use a client secret (`application_secret`) in the `curl` command to authenticate the client application to the token endpoint of the authorization server, the client application can use mTLS instead if stronger authentication is required. In that case, we need to have a public/private key pair at the client application end, and the authorization server must trust the issuer of the public key or the certificate.

The client credentials grant type is suitable for applications that access APIs and that don't need to worry about an end user. Simply put, it's good when you need not be concerned about access delegation, or in other words, the client application accesses an API just by being itself, not on behalf of anyone else. Because of this, the client credentials grant type is mostly used for system-to-system authentication when an application, a periodic task, or any kind of a system directly wants to access your microservice over OAuth 2.0.

Let's take a weather microservice, for example. It provides weather predictions for the next five days. If you build a web application to access the weather microservice, you can simply use the client credentials grant type because the weather microservice isn't interested in knowing who uses your application. It is concerned with only the application that accesses it, not the end user.

A.4.2 Resource owner password grant type

The *resource owner password grant type* is an extension of the client credentials grant type, but it adds support for resource owner authentication with the user's username and password. This grant type involves all four parties in the OAuth 2.0 flow—resource owner (end user), client application, resource server, and authorization server.

The resource owner provides the client application their username and password. The client application uses this information to make a token request to the authorization server, along with the client ID and client secret embedded within itself. Figure A.4 illustrates the resource owner password grant type.

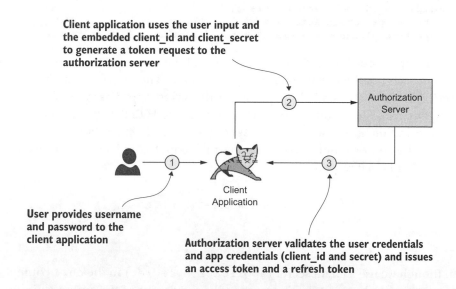

Figure A.4   The password grant type allows an application to obtain an access token.

The following is a sample `curl` command for a password grant request made to the authorization server (this is just a sample, so don't try it out as-is):

```
\> curl \
-u application_id:application_secret \
```

```
-H "Content-Type: application/x-www-form-urlencoded" \
-d "grant_type=password&username=user&password=pass" \
https://localhost:8085/oauth/token
```

As with the client credentials grant, the `application_id` and `application_secret` are sent in base64-encoded form in the HTTP Authorization header. The request body contains the grant type string, the user's username, and the user's password. Note that because you're passing sensitive information in plaintext format in the request header and body, the communication must happen over TLS (HTTPS). Otherwise, any intruder into the network would be able to see the values being passed.

In this case, the authorization server validates not only the client ID and secret (`application_id` and `application_secret`) to authenticate the client application, but also the user's credentials. The issuance of the token happens only if all four fields are valid. As with the client credentials grant type, upon successful authentication, the authorization server responds with a valid access token as shown here:

```
{
  "access_token":"de09bec4-a821-40c8-863a-104dddb30204",
  "refresh_token":" heasdcu8-as3t-hdf67-vadt5-asdgahr7j3ty3",
  "token_type":"bearer",
  "expires_in":3599
}
```

The value of the `refresh_token` parameter you find in the response can be used to renew the current access token before it expires. (We discuss refresh tokens in section A.6.) You might have noticed that we didn't get a `refresh_token` in the client credentials grant type.

With the password grant type, the resource owner (user of the application) needs to provide their username and password to the client application. Therefore, this grant type should be used only with client applications that are trusted by the authorization server. This model of access delegation is called *access delegation with credential sharing*. It is, in fact, what OAuth 2.0 wanted to avoid using. Then why is it in the OAuth 2.0 specification? The only reason the password grant type was introduced in the OAuth 2.0 specification was to help legacy applications using HTTP Basic authentication migrate to OAuth 2.0; otherwise, you should avoid using the password grant type where possible.

As with the client credentials grant type, the password grant type requires the application to store the client secret securely. It's also critically important to deal with the user credentials responsibly. Ideally, the client application must not store the end user's password locally, using it only to get an access token from the authorization server and then forgetting it. The access token the client application gets at the end of the password grant flow has a limited lifetime. Before this token expires, the client application can get a new token by using the `refresh_token` received in the token response from the authorization server. This way, the client application doesn't have to prompt for the user's username and password every time the token on the application expires.

A.4.3   *Refresh token grant type*

The *refresh token grant* is used to renew an existing access token. Typically, it's used when the current access token expires or is near expiry, and the application needs a new access token to work with without having to prompt the user of the application to log in again. To use the refresh token grant, the application should receive an access token and a refresh token in the token response.

Not every grant type issues a refresh token along with its access token, including the client credentials grant and the implicit grant (discussed later in section A.4.5). Therefore, the refresh token grant type is a special grant type that can be used only with applications that use other grant types to obtain the access token. Figure A.5 illustrates the refresh token grant flow.

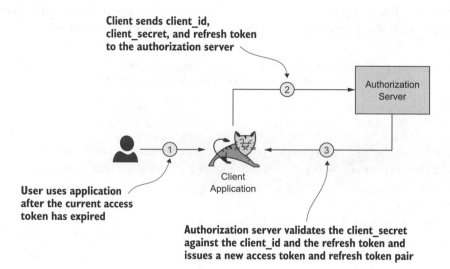

Figure A.5   The refresh token grant type allows a token to be renewed when it expires.

The following `curl` command can be used to renew an access token with the refresh token grant (this is just a sample, so don't try it out as-is):

```
\> curl \
-u application_id:application_secret \
-H "Content-Type: application/x-www-form-urlencoded" \
-d "grant_type=refresh_token&
    refresh_token=heasdcu8-as3t-hdf67-vadt5-asdgahr7j3ty3" \
https://localhost:8085/oauth/token
```

As in the earlier cases, the application's client ID and client secret (`application_id` and `application_secret`) must be sent in base64-encoded format as the HTTP Authorization header. You also need to send the value of the refresh token in the request payload (body). Therefore, the refresh token grant should be used only with the applications that can store the client secret and refresh token values securely, without any risk of compromise.

The refresh token usually has a limited lifetime, but it's generally much longer than the access token lifetime, so an application can renew its token even after a significant duration of idleness. When you refresh an access token in the response, the authorization server sends the renewed access token, along with another refresh token. This refresh token may or may not be the same refresh token you get in the first request from the authorization server. It's up to the authorization server; it's not governed by the OAuth 2.0 specification.

A.4.4 Authorization code grant type

The *authorization code grant* is used with desktop applications and in web applications (accessed via a web browser) or native mobile applications that are capable of handling HTTP redirects. In the authorization code grant flow, the client application first initiates an authorization code request to the authorization server. This request provides the client ID of the application and a redirect URL to redirect the user when authentication is successful. Figure A.6 illustrates the flow of the authorization code grant.

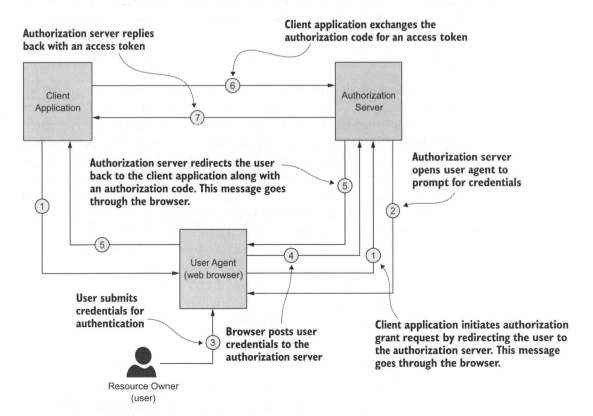

Figure A.6 The authorization code grant type allows a client application to obtain an access token on behalf of an end user (or a resource owner).

As shown in figure A.6, the first step of the client application is to initiate the authorization code request. The HTTP request to get the authorization code looks like the following (this is just a sample, so don't try it out as-is):

```
GET   https://localhost:8085/oauth/authorize?
            response_type=code&
            client_id=application_id&
            redirect_uri=https%3A%2F%2Fweb.application.domain%2Flogin
```

As you can see, the request carries the `client_id` (`application_id`), the `redirect_uri`, and the `response_type` parameters. The `response_type` indicates to the authorization server that an authorization code is expected as the response to this request. This authorization code is provided as a query parameter in an HTTP redirect (https://developer.mozilla.org/en-US/docs/Web/HTTP/Redirections) on the provided `redirect_uri`. The `redirect_uri` is the location to which the authorization server should redirect the browser (user agent) upon successful authentication.

In HTTP, a redirect happens when the server sends a response code between 300 and 310. In this case, the response code would be 302. The response would contain an HTTP header named `Location`, and the value of the `Location` header would bear the URL to which the browser should redirect. A sample `Location` header looks like this:

```
Location: https://web.application.domain/login?code=hus83nn-8ujq6-7snuelq
```

The `redirect_uri` should be equal to the `redirect_uri` provided when registering the particular client application on the authorization server. The URL (host) in the `Location` response header should be equal to the `redirect_uri` query parameter in the HTTP request used to initiate the authorization grant flow. One optional parameter that's not included in the authorization request in this example is `scope`. When making the authorization request, the application can request the scopes it requires on the token to be issued. We discuss scopes in detail in section A.5.

Upon receiving this authorization request, the authorization server first validates the client ID and the `redirect_uri`; if these parameters are valid, it presents the user with the login page of the authorization server (assuming that no valid user session is already running on the authorization server). The user needs to enter their username and password on this login page. When the username and password are validated, the authorization server issues the authorization code and provides it to the user agent via an HTTP redirect. The authorization code is part of the `redirect _uri` as shown here:

```
https://web.application.domain/login?code=hus83nn-8ujq6-7snuelq
```

Because the authorization code is provided to the user agent via the `redirect_uri`, it must be passed over HTTPS. Also, because this is a browser redirect, the value of the authorization code is visible to the end user, and also may be logged in server logs. To reduce the risk that this data will be compromised, the authorization code usually has a short lifetime (no more than 30 seconds) and is a one-time-use code. If the code is used more than once, the authorization server revokes all the tokens previously issued against it.

Upon receiving the authorization code, the client application issues a token request to the authorization server, requesting an access token in exchange for the authorization code. The following is a `curl` command of such a request (step 6 in figure A.6):

```
\> curl \
-u application1:application1secret \
-H "Content-Type: application/x-www-form-urlencoded" \
-d "grant_type=authorization_code&
    code=hus83nn-8ujq6-7snuelq&
    redirect_uri=https%3A%2F%2Fweb.application.domain%2Flogin" \
https://localhost:8085/oauth/token
```

Like the other grant types discussed so far, the authorization code grant type requires the client ID and client secret (optional) to be sent as an HTTP Authorization header in base64-encoded format. It also requires the `grant_type` parameter to be sent as `authorization_code`; the value of the code itself and the `redirect_uri` are sent in the payload of the HTTP request to the authorization server's token endpoint. Upon validation of these details, the authorization server issues an access token to the client application in an HTTP response:

```
{
  "access_token":"de09bec4-a821-40c8-863a-104dddb30204",
  "refresh_token":" heasdcu8-as3t-hdf67-vadt5-asdgahr7j3ty3",
  "token_type":"bearer",
  "expires_in":3599
}
```

Prior to returning an authorization code (step 5 in figure A.6), the authorization server validates the user by verifying the user's username and password. In step 6 in figure A.6, the authorization server validates the client application by verifying the application's client ID and secret. The authorization code grant type doesn't mandate authenticating the application. So, it's not a must to use the application secret in the request to the token endpoint to exchange the authorization code for an access token. This is the recommended approach when you use the authorization code grant type with SPAs, which we discuss in chapter 4.

As you've seen, the authorization code grant involves the user, client application, and authorization server. Unlike the password grant, this grant type doesn't require the user to provide their credentials to the client application. The user provides their credentials only on the login page of the authorization server. This way, you prevent the client application from learning the user's login credentials. Therefore, this grant type is suitable to provide user credentials for web, mobile, and desktop applications that you don't fully trust.

A client application that uses this grant type needs to have some prerequisites to use this protocol securely. Because the application needs to know and deal with sensitive information, such as the client secret, refresh token, and authorization code, it needs to be able to store and use these values with caution. It needs to have mechanisms for encrypting the client secret and refresh token when storing and to use HTTPS, for example, for secure communication with the authorization server. The communication between the client application and the authorization server needs to happen over TLS so that network intruders don't see the information being exchanged.

A.4.5   *Implicit grant type*

The *implicit grant type* is similar to the authorization code grant type, but it doesn't involve the intermediary step of getting an authorization code before getting the access token. Instead, the authorization server issues the access token directly in response to the implicit grant request. Figure A.7 illustrates the implicit grant flow.

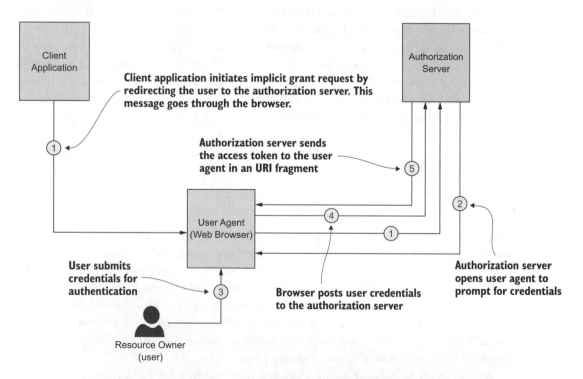

Figure A.7   The implicit grant type allows a client application to obtain an access token.

With the implicit grant type, when the user attempts to log in to the application, the client application initiates the login flow by creating an implicit grant request. This request should contain the client ID and the `redirect_uri`. The `redirect_uri`, as with the authorization code grant type, is used by the authorization server to redirect the user agent back to the client application when authentication is successful. The following is a sample implicit grant request (this is just a sample, so don't try it out as-is):

```
GET https://localhost:8085/oauth/authorize?
            response_type=token&
            client_id=application_id&
            redirect_uri=https%3A%2F%2Fweb.application.domain%2Flogin
```

As you can see in the HTTPS request, the difference between the authorization code grant's initial request and the implicit grant's initial request is the fact that the `response_type` parameter in this case is `token`. This indicates to the authorization server that you're interested in getting an access token as the response to the implicit request. As with the authorization code grant, here too `scope` is an optional parameter that the user agent can provide to ask the authorization server to issue a token with the required scopes.

When the authorization server receives this request, it validates the client ID and the `redirect_uri`, and if those are valid, it presents the user the login page of the authorization server (assuming that no active user session is running on the browser against the authorization server). When the user enters their credentials, the authorization server validates them and presents to the user a consent page to acknowledge that the application is capable of performing the actions denoted by the `scope` parameter (only if `scope` is provided in the request). Note that the user provides credentials on the login page of the authorization server, so only the authorization server gets to know the user's credentials. When the user has consented to the required scopes, the authorization server issues an access token and provides it to the user agent on the `redirect_uri` itself as a URI fragment. The following is an example of such a redirect:

```
https://web.application.domain/login#access_token=jauej28slah2&
            expires_in=3599
```

When the user agent (web browser) receives this redirect, it makes an HTTPS request to the `web.application.domain/login` URL. Because the `access_token` field is provided as a URI fragment (denoted by the # character in the URL), that particular value doesn't get submitted to the server on `web.application.domain`. Only the authorization server that issued the token and the user agent (web browser) get to know the value of the access token. The implicit grant doesn't provide a refresh token to the user agent. As we discussed earlier in this chapter, because the value of the access token is passed in the URL, it will be in the browser history and also possibly logged into server logs.

The implicit grant type doesn't require your client application to maintain any sensitive information, such as a client secret or a refresh token. This fact makes it a good candidate for use in SPAs, where rendering the content happens on web browsers through JavaScript. These types of applications execute mostly on the client side (browser); therefore, these applications are incapable of handling sensitive information such as client secrets. But still, the security concerns in using the implicit grant type is much higher than its benefits, and it's no longer recommended, even for SPAs.

As discussed in the previous section, the recommendation is to use the authorization code grant type with no client secret, even for SPAs.

A.5   *Scopes bind capabilities to an OAuth 2.0 access token*

Each access token that an authorization server issues is associated with one or more scopes. A *scope* defines the purpose of a token. A token can have more than one purpose; hence, it can be associated with multiple scopes. A scope defines what the client application can do at the resource server with the corresponding token.

When a client application requests a token from the authorization server, along with the token request, it also specifies the scopes it expects from the token (see figure A.8). That doesn't necessarily mean the authorization server has to respect that request and issue the token with all requested scopes. An authorization server can decide on its own, also with the resource owner's consent, which scopes to associate with the access token. In the token response, it sends back to the client application the scopes associated with the token, along with the token.

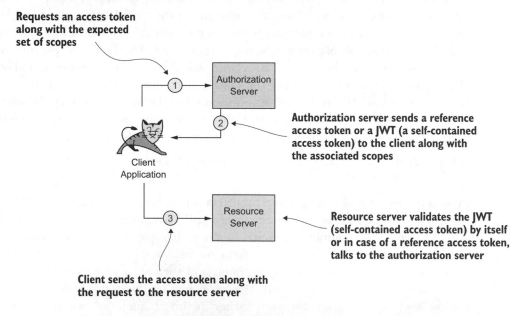

Figure A.8   The client application requests an access token along with the expected set of scopes. When the access token is a self-contained JWT, the resource server validates the token by itself, without talking to the authorization server.

A.6   *Self-contained access tokens*

An access token can be either a reference token or a self-contained token. A *reference token* is just a string, and only the issuer of the token knows how to validate it. When the resource server gets a reference token, it has to talk to the authorization server all the time to validate the token.

In contrast, if the token is a *self-contained token*, the resource server can validate the token itself; there's no need to talk to the authorization server (see figure A.8). A self-contained token is a signed JWT or a JWS (see appendix B). The JWT Profile for OAuth 2.0 Access Tokens (which is in its fifth draft at the time of writing), developed under the IETF OAuth working group, defines the structure for a self-contained access token.

A.7 *What is OpenID Connect?*

OpenID Connect is built on top of OAuth 2.0 as an additional identity layer. It uses the concept of an ID token. An *ID token* is a JWT that contains authenticated user information, including user claims and other relevant attributes. When an authorization server issues an ID token, it signs the contents of the JWT (a signed JWT is called a *JWS*, or *JSON Web Signature*), using its private key. Before any application accepts an ID token as valid, it should verify its contents by validating the signature of the JWT.

> **NOTE** An *ID token* is consumed by an application to get information, such as a user's username, email address, phone number, and so on. An *access token* is a credential used by an application to access a secured API on behalf of an end user or just by being itself. OAuth 2.0 provides only an access token, whereas OpenID Connect provides both an access token and an ID token.

The following is an example of a decoded ID token (payload only) that includes the standard claims as defined by the OpenID Connect specification (http://mng.bz/yyWo):

```
{
    "iss":"http://server.example.com",
    "sub":"janedoe@example.xom",
    "aud":"8ajduw82swiw",
    "nonce":"82jd27djuw72jduw92ksury",
    "exp":1311281970,
    "iat":1311280970,
    "auth_time":1539339705,
    "acr":"urn:mace:incommon:iap:silver",
    "amr":"password",
    "azp":"8ajduw82swiw"
}
```

Details on these attributes are in the OIDC specification. The following lists a few important ones:

- `iss`—The identifier of the issuer of the ID token (usually, an identifier to represent the authorization server that issued the ID token).
- `sub`—The subject of the token for which the token was issued (usually, the user who authenticated at the authorization server).
- `aud`—The audience of the token; a collection of identifiers of entities that are supposed to use the token for a particular purpose. It must contain the OAuth 2.0 `client_id` of the client application, and zero or more other identifiers (an

array). If a particular client application uses an ID token, it should validate whether it's one of the intended audiences of the ID token; the client application's `client_id` should be one of the values in the aud claim.

- iat—The time at which the ID token was issued.
- exp—The time at which the ID token expires. An application must use an ID token only if its exp claim is later than the current timestamp.

An ID token usually is obtained as part of the access token response. OAuth 2.0 providers support various grant types for obtaining access tokens, as we discussed in section A.5. An ID token usually is sent in the response to a request for an access token by using a grant type. You need to specify `openid` as a scope in the token request to inform the authorization server that you require an ID token in the response. The following is an example of how to request an ID token in an authorization request when using the authorization_code grant type:

```
GET https://localhost:8085/oauth/authorize?
            response_type=code&
            scope=openid&
            client_id=application1&
            redirect_uri=https%3A%2F%2Fweb.application.domain%2Flogin
```

The ID token is sent in the response to the token request in following form:

```
{
  "access_token": "sdfj82j7sjej27djwterh720fnwqudkdnw72itjswnrlvod92hvkwyfp",
  "expires_in": 3600,
  "token_type": "Bearer",
  "id_token": "sdu283ngk23rmas….."
}
```

The `id_token` is a JWT, which is built with three base64 URL-encoded strings, each separated by a period. We omitted the full string in the example for readability. In chapter 3, you see how to use OpenID Connect in practice with a SPA.

A.8   *More information about OpenID Connect and OAuth 2.0*

If you are interested in learning more about OpenID Connect and OAuth 2.0, the following list provides a set of YouTube videos presented by Prabath Siriwardena (a coauthor of this book):

- *OAuth 2.0 with curl* (www.youtube.com/watch?v=xipHJSW93KI)—This video takes you through all the core OAuth 2.0 grant types, using curl as a client application.
- *OAuth 2.0 Access Token versus OpenID Connect ID Token* (www.youtube.com/watch?v=sICt5aS7wzk)—This video explains the difference between an OAuth 2.0 access token and an OpenID Connect ID token.
- *OAuth 2.0 Response Type versus Grant Type* (www.youtube.com/watch?v=Qdjuavr33E4)—This video explains the difference between the response_type parameter and the grant_type parameter that you find in an OAuth 2.0 flow.

- *OAuth 2.0 Token Introspection* (www.youtube.com/watch?v=CuawoBrs_6k)—This video explains the OAuth 2.0 token introspection RFC, which is used by the resource server to talk to the authorization server to validate an access token.
- *OAuth 2.0 Token Revocation* (www.youtube.com/watch?v=OEab8UoEUow)—This video explains the OAuth 2.0 token revocation RFC, which is used by the client application to revoke an access token.
- *Proof Key for Code Exchange* (www.youtube.com/watch?v=2pJShFKYoJc)—This video explains the Proof Key for Code Exchange RFC, which helps you protect your applications from code interception attack.
- *Securing Single-Page Applications with OpenID Connect* (www.youtube.com/watch?v=tmKD2famPJc)—This video explains the internals of OpenID Connect and how to use OpenID Connect to secure a SPA.

appendix B
JSON Web Token

We've discussed JSON Web Token (JWT) many times in this book. In chapter 2, we talked about how we can use a JWT as an OAuth 2.0 self-contained access token, and in chapter 4, we described how OpenID Connect uses a JWT as its ID token to transfer user claims from the OpenID provider to the client application. In chapter 7, we discussed how to pass end-user context in a JWT among services in a microservices deployment. In chapter 11, we examined how each pod in Kubernetes uses a JWT to authenticate to the Kubernetes API server. In chapter 12, we showed how an Istio service mesh uses JWT to verify the end-user context at the Envoy proxy. Finally, in appendix F, we described how an Open Policy Agent (OPA) uses JWT to carry policy data along with the authorization request.

All in all, JWT is an essential ingredient in securing a microservices deployment. In this appendix, we discuss JWT in detail. If you are interested in understanding further internals of JWT, we recommend *Advanced API Security: OAuth 2.0 and Beyond* (Apress, 2019) by Prabath Siriwardena (a coauthor of this book), and the YouTube video JWT Internals and Applications (www.youtube.com/watch?v=c-jsKk1OR24), presented by Prabath Siriwardena.

B.1 What is a JSON Web Token?

A *JWT* (pronounced *jot*) is a container that carries different types of assertions or claims from one place to another in a cryptographically safe manner. An *assertion* is a strong statement about someone or something issued by an entity. This entity is also known as the issuer of the assertion.

Imagine that your state's Department of Motor Vehicles (DMV) can create a JWT (to represent your driver's license) with your personal information, which includes your name, address, eye color, hair color, gender, date of birth, license expiration date, and license number. All these items are attributes, or claims, about you and are also known as *attribute assertions*. The DMV is the issuer of the JWT.

Anyone who gets this JWT can decide whether to accept what's in it as true, based on the level of trust they have in the issuer of the token (in this case, the DMV). But before accepting a JWT, how do you know who issued it? The issuer of a JWT signs it by using the issuer's private key. In the scenario illustrated in figure B.1, a bartender, who is the recipient of the JWT, can verify the signature of the JWT and see who signed it.

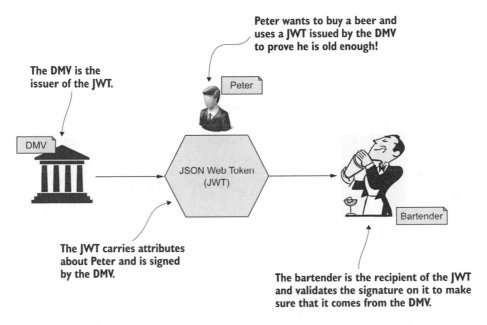

Figure B.1   **A JWT is used as a container to transport assertions from one place to another in a cryptographically safe manner. The bartender, who is the recipient of the JWT, accepts the JWT only if they trust the DMV, the issuer of the JWT.**

In addition to attribute assertions, a JWT can carry authentication and authorization assertions. In fact, a JWT is a container; you can fill it with anything you need. An authentication assertion might be the username of the user and how the issuer authenticates the user before issuing the assertion. In the DMV use case, an authentication assertion might be your first name and last name (or even your driver's license number), or how you are known to the DMV.

An *authorization assertion* is about the user's entitlements, or what the user can do. Based on the assertions the JWT brings from the issuer, the recipient can decide how to act. In the DMV example, if the DMV decides to embed the user's age as an attribute in the JWT, that data is an attribute assertion, and a bartender can do the math to calculate whether the user is old enough to buy a beer. Also, without sharing the user's age with a bartender, the DMV may decide to include an authorization assertion stating that the user is old enough to buy a beer. In that case, a bartender will accept the

JWT and let the user buy a beer. The bartender wouldn't know the user's age, but the DMV authorized the user to buy beer.

In addition to carrying a set of assertions about the user, a JWT plays another role behind the scenes. Apart from the end user's identity, a JWT also carries the issuer's identity, which is the DMV in this case. The issuer's identity is implicitly embedded in the signature of the JWT. By looking at the corresponding public key while validating the signature of the token, the recipient can figure out who the token issuer is.

B.2   What does a JWT look like?

Before we delve deep into the JWT use cases within a microservices deployment, take a closer look at a JWT. Figure B.2 shows the most common form of a JWT. This figure may look like gibberish unless your brain is trained to decode base64url-encoded strings.

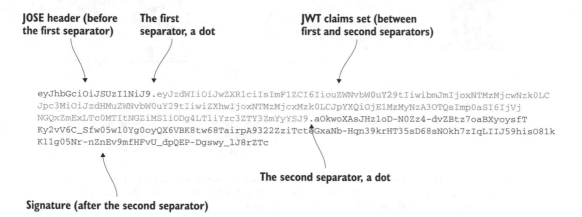

Figure B.2   A base64url-encoded JWT, which is also a JWS

What you see in figure B.2 is a *JSON Web Signature* (*JWS*), which we discuss in detail in section B.3. The JWS, which is the most commonly used format of a JWT, has three parts, with a dot (.) separating each part:

- The first part is known as the *JSON Object Signing and Encryption* (*JOSE*) *header.*
- The second part is the *claims set,* or *body* (or *payload*).
- The third part is the *signature.*

The JOSE header is a base64url-encoded JSON object, which expresses the metadata related to the JWT, such as the algorithm used to sign the message. Here's the base64url-decoded JOSE header:

```
{
  "alg": "RS256",
}
```

The JWT claims set is a base64url-encoded JSON object, which carries the assertions (between the first and second separators). Following is the base64url-decoded claims set:

```
{
  "sub": "peter",
  "aud": "*.ecomm.com",
  "nbf": 1533270794,
  "iss": "sts.ecomm.com",
  "exp": 1533271394,
  "iat": 1533270794,
  "jti": "5c4d1fa1-7412-4fb1-b888-9bc77e67ff2a"
}
```

The JWT specification (RFC 7519) defines seven attributes: `sub`, `aud`, `nbf`, `iss`, `exp`, `iat`, and `jti`. None of these are mandatory—and it's up to the other specifications that rely on JWT to define what is mandatory and what is optional. For example, the OpenID Connect specification makes the `iss` attribute mandatory. These seven attributes that the JWT specification defines are registered in the Internet Assigned Numbers Authority (IANA) Web Token Claims registry. However, you can introduce your own custom attributes to the JWT claims set. In the following sections, we discuss these seven attributes in detail.

B.2.1 The issuer of a JWT

The `iss` attribute in the JWT claims set carries an identifier corresponding to the *issuer,* or asserting party, of the JWT. The JWT is signed by the issuer's private key. In a typical microservices deployment within a given trust domain, all the microservices trust a single issuer, and this issuer is typically known as the *security token service (STS)*.

B.2.2 The subject of a JWT

The `sub` attribute in the JWT claims set defines the *subject* of a JWT. The subject is the owner of the JWT—or in other words, the JWT carries the claims about the subject. The applications of the JWT can further refine the definition of the `sub` attribute. For example, the OpenID Connect specification makes the `sub` attribute mandatory, and the issuer of the token must make sure that the `sub` attribute carries a unique identifier.

B.2.3 The audience of a JWT

The `aud` attribute in the JWT claims set specifies the *audience,* or intended recipient, of the token. In figure B.2, it's set to the string value `*.ecomm.com`. The value of the `aud` attribute can be any string or a URI that's known to the microservice or the recipient of the JWT.

Each microservice must check the value of the `aud` parameter to see whether it's known before accepting any JWT as valid. If you have a microservice called `foo` with the audience value `foo.ecomm.com`, the microservice should reject any JWT carrying the `aud` value `bar.ecomm.com`, for example. The logic in accepting or rejecting a JWT based on audience is up to the corresponding microservice and to the overall microservices security design. By design, you can define a policy to agree that any microservice will accept a token with the audience value `<microservice identifier>.ecomm .com` or `*.ecomm.com`, for example.

B.2.4   *JWT expiration, not before and issued time*

The value of the `exp` attribute in the JWT claims set expresses the time of expiration in seconds, which is calculated from 1970-01-01T0:0:0Z as measured in Coordinated Universal Time (UTC). Any recipient of a JWT must make sure that the time represented by the `exp` attribute is not in the past when accepting a JWT—or in other words, the token is not expired. The `iat` attribute in the JWT claims set expresses the time when the JWT was issued. That too is expressed in seconds and calculated from 1970-01-01T0:0:0Z as measured in UTC.

The time difference between `iat` and `exp` in seconds isn't the lifetime of the JWT when there's an `nbf` (not before) attribute present in the claims set. You shouldn't start processing a JWT (or accept it as a valid token) before the time specified in the `nbf` attribute. The value of `nbf` is also expressed in seconds and calculated from 1970-01-01T0:0:0Z as measured in UTC. When the nbf attribute is present in the claims set, the lifetime of a JWT is calculated as the difference between the `exp` and `nbf` attributes. However, in most cases, the value of `nbf` is equal to the value of `iat`.

B.2.5   *The JWT identifier*

The `jti` attribute in the JWT claims set defines a unique identifier for the token. Ideally, the token issuer should not issue two JWTs with the same `jti`. However, if the recipient of the JWT accepts tokens from multiple issuers, a given `jti` will be unique only along with the corresponding issuer identifier.

B.3   *JSON Web Signature*

The JWT explained in section B.2 (and, as a reminder, shown in figure B.3) is also a JSON Web Signature. JWS is a way to represent a signed message. This message can be anything, such as a JSON payload, an XML payload, or a binary.

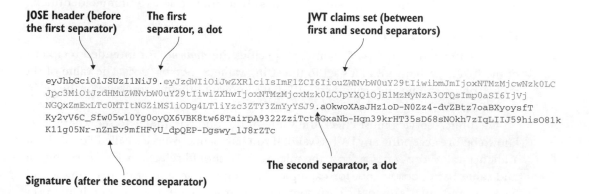

Figure B.3   Base64url-encoded JWT, which is also a JWS

A JWS can be serialized in two formats, or represented in two ways: compact serialization and JSON serialization. We don't call every JWS a JWT. A JWS becomes a JWT only when it follows compact serialization and carries a JSON object as the payload. Under JWT

Figure B.4   A JWT that is a compact-serialized JWS with a JOSE header, a claims set, and a signature

terminology, we call this payload the *claims set*. Figure B.4 shows a compact-serialized JWS—or a JWT. Section B.3 details the meaning of each component in figure B.4.

With JSON serialization, the JWS is represented as a JSON payload (see figure B.5). It's not called a JWT. The `payload` parameter in the JSON-serialized JWS can carry any value. The message being signed and represented in figure B.5 is a JSON message with all its related metadata.

```
{ ⊟
    "payload":"eyJpc3MiOiJqb2UiLA0KICJleHAiOjEzMDA4MTkzOD",
    "signatures":[ ⊟
        { ⊟
            "protected":"eyJhbGciOiJSUzI1NiJ9",
            "header":{ ⊟
                "kid":"2014-06-29"
            },
            "signature":"cC4hiUPoj9Eetdgtv3hF80EGrhuB"
        },
        { ⊟
            "protected":"eyJhbGciOiJFUzI1NiJ9",
            "header":{ ⊟
                "kid":"e909097a-ce81-4036-9562-d21d2992db0d"
            },
            "signature":"DtEhU3ljbEg8L38VWAfUAqOyKAM"
        }
    ]
}
```

Figure B.5   A JWS with JSON serialization that includes related metadata

Unlike in a JWT, a JSON serialized JWS can carry multiple signatures corresponding to the same payload. In figure B.5, the `signatures` JSON array carries two elements, and each element carries a different `signature` of the same payload. The `protected` and `header` attributes inside each element of the `signatures` JSON array define the metadata related to the corresponding signature.

Let's see how to use the open source Nimbus (https://connect2id.com/products/nimbus-jose-jwt) Java library to create a JWS. The source code related to all the samples used in this appendix is available in the https://github.com/microservices-security-in-action/samples GitHub repository, inside the appendix-b directory.

NOTE   Before running the samples in this appendix, make sure that you have downloaded and installed all the required software as mentioned in section 2.1.1.

Let's build the sample, which builds the JWS, and run it. Run the following Maven command from the appendix-b/sample01 directory. It may take a couple of minutes to finish the build process when you run this command for the first time. If everything goes well, you should see the BUILD SUCCESS message at the end:

```
\> mvn clean install
[INFO] BUILD SUCCESS
```

Now run your Java program to create a JWS with the following command (from the appendix-b/sample01/lib directory). If it executes successfully, it prints the base64url-encoded JWS:

```
\> java  -cp "../target/com.manning.mss.appendixb.sample01-1.0.0.jar:*" \
com.manning.mss.appendixb.sample01.RSASHA256JWTBuilder
```

eyJhbGciOiJSUzI1NiJ9.**eyJzdWIiOiJwZXRlciIsImF1ZCI6IiouZWNvbW0uY29tIiwibmJmIj
oxNTMzMjcwNzk0LCJpc3MiOiJzdHMuZWNvbW0uY29tIiwiZXhwIjoxNTMzMjcxMzk0LCJpYXQiO
jE1MzMyNzA3OTQsImp0aSI6IjVjNGQxZmExLTc0MTItNGZiMS1iODg4LTliYzc3ZTY3ZmYyYSJ9
**.aOkwoXAsJHz1oD-N0Zz4-dvZBtz7oaBXyoysfTKy2vV6C_Sfw05w10Yg0oyQX6VBK8tw68Tair
pA9322ZziTcteGxaNb-Hqn39krHT35sD68sNOkh7zIqLIIJ59hisO81kK11g05Nr-nZnEv9mfHF
vU_dpQEP-Dgswy_lJ8rZTc

You can decode this JWS by using the JWT decoder available at https://jwt.io. The following is the decoded JWS claims set, or payload:

```
{
  "sub": "peter",
  "aud": "*.ecomm.com",
  "nbf": 1533270794,
  "iss": "sts.ecomm.com",
  "exp": 1533271394,
  "iat": 1533270794,
  "jti": "5c4d1fa1-7412-4fb1-b888-9bc77e67ff2a"
}
```

NOTE   If you get any errors while executing the previous command, check whether you executed the command from the correct location. It has to be from inside the appendix-b/sample01/lib directory, not from the appendix-b/sample01 directory. Also make sure that the value of the –cp argument is within double quotes.

Take a look at the code that generated the JWT. It's straightforward and self-explanatory with comments. You can find the complete source code in the sample01/src/main/java/com/manning/mss/appendixb/sample01/RSASHA256JWTBuilder.java file.

The following method does the core work of JWT generation. It accepts the token issuer's private key as an input parameter and uses it to sign the JWT with RSA-SHA256.

Listing B.1 The RSASHA256JWTBuilder.java file

```java
public static String buildRsaSha256SignedJWT(PrivateKey privateKey)
                                          throws JOSEException {

    // build audience restriction list.
    List<String> aud = new ArrayList<String>();
    aud.add("*.ecomm.com");

    Date currentTime = new Date();

    // create a claims set.
    JWTClaimsSet jwtClaims = new JWTClaimsSet.Builder().
    // set the value of the issuer.
    issuer("sts.ecomm.com").
    // set the subject value - JWT belongs to this subject.
    subject("peter").
    // set values for audience restriction.
    audience(aud).
    // expiration time set to 10 minutes.
    expirationTime(new Date(new Date().getTime() + 1000 * 60 * 10)).
    // set the valid from time to current time.
    notBeforeTime(currentTime).
    // set issued time to current time.
    issueTime(currentTime).
    // set a generated UUID as the JWT identifier.
    jwtID(UUID.randomUUID().toString()).build();
    // create JWS header with RSA-SHA256 algorithm.

    JWSHeader jswHeader = new JWSHeader(JWSAlgorithm.RS256);

    // create signer with the RSA private key..
    JWSSigner signer = new RSASSASigner((RSAPrivateKey) privateKey);

    // create the signed JWT with the JWS header and the JWT body.
    SignedJWT signedJWT = new SignedJWT(jswHeader, jwtClaims);

    // sign the JWT with HMAC-SHA256.
    signedJWT.sign(signer);

    // serialize into base64url-encoded text.
    String jwtInText = signedJWT.serialize();

    // print the value of the JWT.
    System.out.println(jwtInText);

    return jwtInText;
}
```

B.4   *JSON Web Encryption*

In the preceding section, we stated that a JWT is a compact-serialized JWS. It's also a compact-serialized *JSON Web Encryption* (*JWE*). Like JWS, a JWE represents an encrypted message using compact serialization or JSON serialization. A JWE is called a JWT only when compact serialization is used. In other words, a JWT can be either a JWS or a JWE, which is compact serialized. JWS addresses the integrity and nonrepudiation aspects of the data contained in it, while JWE protects the data for confidentiality.

A compact-serialized JWE (see figure B.6) has five parts; each part is base64url-encoded and separated by a dot (.). The JOSE header is the part of the JWE that carries metadata related to the encryption. The JWE encrypted key, initialization vector, and authentication tag are related to the cryptographic operations performed during the encryption. We won't talk about those in detail here. If you're interested, we recommend the blog "JWT, JWS, and JWE for Not So Dummies" at http://mng.bz/gya8. Finally, the ciphertext part of the JWE includes the encrypted text.

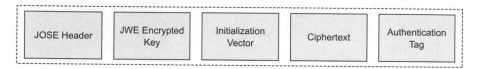

Figure B.6   A JWT that's a compact-serialized JWE

With JSON serialization, the JWE is represented as a JSON payload. It isn't called a JWT. The `ciphertext` attribute in the JSON-serialized JWE carries the encrypted value of any payload, which can be JSON, XML or even binary. The actual payload is encrypted and represented in figure B.7 as a JSON message with all related metadata.

```
{ ⊟
    "protected":"eyJlbmMiOiJBMTI4Q0JDLUhTMjU2In0",
    "unprotected":{ ⊟
        "jku":"https://server.example.com/keys.jwks"
    },
    "recipients":[ ⊟
        { ⊟
            "header":{ ⊟
                "alg":"RSA1_5",
                "kid":"2011-04-29"
            },
            "encrypted_key":"UGhIOguC7IuEvf_NPVaXsGMoLOmwvc1GyqlI9XShH59_i8J0PH5ZZyNfGy2xGd"
        },
        { ⊟
            "header":{ ⊟
                "alg":"A128KW",
                "kid":"7"
            },
            "encrypted_key":"6KB707dM9YTIgHtLvtgWQ8nKwboJW3of9locizkDTHzBC2IlrT1oOQ"
        }
    ],
    "iv":"AxY8DCtDaGlsbGljb3RoZQ",
    "ciphertext":"KDlTtXchhZTGufMYmOYGS4HffxPSUrfmqCHXaI9wOGY",
    "tag":"Mz-VPPyU4RlcuYv1IwIvzw"
}
```

Figure B.7   A JWE with JSON serialization and all related metadata

Let's see how to use the open source Nimbus Java library to create a JWE. The source code related to all the samples used in this appendix is available in the https://github.com/microservices-security-in-action/samples Git repository inside the appendix-b directory. Before you delve into the Java code that you'll use to build the JWE, try to build the sample and run it. Run the following Maven command from the appendix-b/sample02 directory. If everything goes well, you should see the BUILD SUCCESS message at the end:

```
\> mvn clean install
[INFO] BUILD SUCCESS
```

Now run your Java program to create a JWE with the following command (from the appendix-b/sample02/lib directory). If it executes successfully, it prints the base64url-encoded JWE:

```
\> java  -cp "../target/com.manning.mss.appendixb.sample02-1.0.0.jar:*" \
com.manning.mss.appendixb.sample02.RSAOAEPJWTBuilder
```

eyJlbmMiOiJBMTI4R0NNIiwiYWxnIjoiUlNBLU9BRVAifQ.Cd0KjNwSbq5OPxcJQ1ESValmRGPf
7BFUNpqZFfKTCd-9XAmVE-zOTsnv78SikTOK8fuwszHDnz2eONUahbg8eR9oxDi9kmXaHeKXyZ9
Kq4vhg7WJPJXSUonwGxcibgECJySEJxZaTmA1E_8pUaiU6k5UHvxPUDtE0pnN5XD82cs.0b4jWQ
HFbBaM_azM.XmwvMBzrLcNW-oBhAfMozJlmESfG6o96WT958BOyfjpGmmbdJdIjirjCBTUATdOP
kLg6-YmPsitaFm7pFAUdsHkm4_K1ZrE5HuP43VM0gBXSe-41dDDNs7D2nZ5QFpeoYH7zQNocCjy
bseJPFPYEw311nBRfjzNoDEzvKMsxhgCZNLTv-tpKh6mKIXXYxdxVoBcIXN90UUYi.mVLD4t-85
qcTiY8q3J-kmg

Following is the decrypted JWE payload:

```
JWE Header:{"enc":"A128GCM","alg":"RSA-OAEP"}
JWE Content Encryption Key: Cd0KjNwSbq5OPxcJQ1ESValmRGPf7BFUNpqZFfKTCd-9
XAmVE-zOTsnv78SikTOK8fuwszHDnz2eONUahbg8eR9oxDi9kmXaHeKXyZ9Kq4vhg7WJPJXS
UonwGxcibgECJySEJxZaTmA1E_8pUaiU6k5UHvxPUDtE0pnN5XD82cs
Initialization Vector: 0b4jWQHFbBaM_azM
Ciphertext: XmwvMBzrLcNW-oBhAfMozJlmESfG6o96WT958BOyfjpGmmbdJdIjirjCBTUA
TdOPkLg6-YmPsitaFm7pFAUdsHkm4_K1ZrE5HuP43VM0gBXSe-41dDDNs7D2nZ5QFpeoYH7z
QNocCjybseJPFPYEw311nBRfjzNoDEzvKMsxhgCZNLTv-tpKh6mKIXXYxdxVoBcIXN90UUYi
Authentication Tag: mVLD4t-85qcTiY8q3J-kmg
Decrypted Payload:
{
  "sub":"peter",
  "aud":"*.ecomm.com",
  "nbf":1533273878,
  "iss":"sts.ecomm.com",
  "exp":1533274478,
  "iat":1533273878,
  "jti":"17dc2461-d87a-42c9-9546-e42a23d1e4d5"
}
```

NOTE If you get any errors while executing the previous command, check whether you executed the command from the correct location. It has to be from inside the appendix-b/sample02/lib directory, not from the appendix-b/sample02 directory. Also make sure that the value of the –cp argument is within double quotes.

Now take a look at the code that generated the JWE. It's straightforward and self-explanatory with code comments. You can find the complete source code in the sample02/src/main/java/com/manning/mss/appendixb/sample02/RSAOAEPJWT Builder.java file. The method in the following listing does the core work of JWE encryption. It accepts the token recipient public key as an input parameter and uses it to encrypt the JWE with RSA-OAEP.

Listing B.2   The RSAOAEPJWTBuilder.java file

```java
public static String buildEncryptedJWT(PublicKey publicKey)
                            throws JOSEException {

    // build audience restriction list.
    List<String> aud = new ArrayList<String>();

    aud.add("*.ecomm.com");

    Date currentTime = new Date();

    // create a claims set.
    JWTClaimsSet jwtClaims = new JWTClaimsSet.Builder().

    // set the value of the issuer.
    issuer("sts.ecomm.com").
    // set the subject value - JWT belongs to this subject.
    subject("peter").
    // set values for audience restriction.
    audience(aud).
    // expiration time set to 10 minutes.
    expirationTime(new Date(new Date().getTime() + 1000 * 60 * 10)).
    // set the valid from time to current time.
    notBeforeTime(currentTime).
    // set issued time to current time.
    issueTime(currentTime).
    // set a generated UUID as the JWT identifier.
    jwtID(UUID.randomUUID().toString()).build();
    // create JWE header with RSA-OAEP and AES/GCM.
    JWEHeader jweHeader = new JWEHeader(JWEAlgorithm.RSA_OAEP,
                                EncryptionMethod.A128GCM);

    // create encrypter with the RSA public key.
    JWEEncrypter encrypter = new RSAEncrypter((RSAPublicKey) publicKey);

    // create the encrypted JWT with the JWE header and the JWT payload.
    EncryptedJWT encryptedJWT = new EncryptedJWT(jweHeader, jwtClaims);

    // encrypt the JWT.
    encryptedJWT.encrypt(encrypter);

    // serialize into base64url-encoded text.
    String jwtInText = encryptedJWT.serialize();

    // print the value of the JWT.
    System.out.println(jwtInText);

    return jwtInText;
}
```

appendix C
Single-page application architecture

In chapter 4, we discussed how to create a single-page application (SPA) with Angular and then talked about accessing the Order Processing microservice from the SPA. SPA is already a popular architectural pattern for building applications against a set of APIs. In fact, the rise of API adoption had a great influence in moving developers to build SPAs. In this appendix, we discuss the basic principles behind the SPA architecture. If you are interested in learning the SPA architecture in depth, we recommend *SPA Design and Architecture* (Manning, 2015) by Emmit A. Scott, Jr.

C.1 What is single-page application architecture?

A *single-page application* (*SPA*) is an architectural pattern used to develop frontend, user-facing web applications. In a traditional multiple-page application (MPA) architecture, when a web browser makes a request to the web server, the web server first loads the data (content) required for the requested web page (by reading a database, talking to other external services, and so on), generates the HTML content, and provides it to the web browser for rendering.

Notice the word *HTML* in the preceding sentence. In this case, the server is responsible for generating multiple HTML pages for the browser to render, which is why these types of applications are known as *multipage* applications. As illustrated in figure C.1, when the web browser makes a request for a particular page, the web server requests data from a data source and generates the HTML content using that data. This HTML content is then sent back to the web browser.

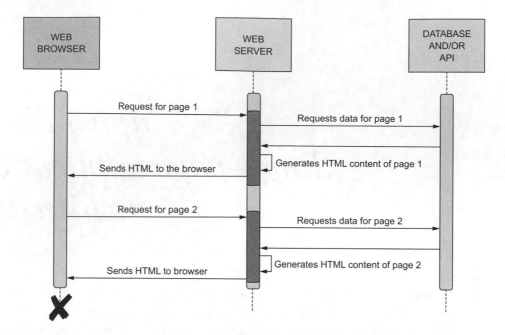

Figure C.1   An MPA loads content to the browser with multiple page reloads.

A SPA, on the other hand, loads the initial HTML, Cascading Style Sheets (CSS), and JavaScript to the browser when loading the application for the first time. On requests to fetch further data, the SPA directly downloads the actual data—in JavaScript Object Notation (JSON) or whatever the data format is—from the web server. The generation of dynamic HTML content happens on the browser itself through the JavaScript that's already loaded (and cached). Figure C.2 illustrates the flow of actions for a SPA.

Most of the modern websites you use today follow this pattern. If you've used Gmail, Google Maps, Facebook, Twitter, Airbnb, Netflix, PayPal, and the like, you've used a SPA. All these websites use this design to load content into your web browser.

A typical difference between an MPA and a SPA is that in an MPA, each request for new content reloads the web page. But in a SPA, after the application has been loaded into the browser, no page reloads happen. All new content is rendered on the browser itself without any requests to the web server. The SPA talks to different endpoints (APIs) to retrieve new content, but the rendering of that content happens in the browser.

The reason these are called *single-page applications* is that most of them have only one HTML file (a single page) for the entire application. The content of the website is rendered by dynamically changing the HTML of the file upon user actions.

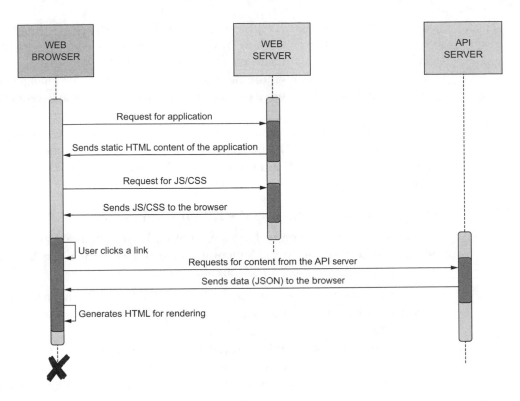

Figure C.2 Any web application that follows this architectural pattern is known as a SPA. A SPA loads content to the browser with no page reloads.

C.2 Benefits of a SPA over an MPA

A SPA has several benefits compared to an MPA, some of which are specifically useful for microservices architectures:

- Beyond the initial loading of the application, page rendering is faster because the generation of HTML happens on the client side (browser) and the amount of data being downloaded is reduced (no HTML; mostly JSON content). The HTML, CSS, and JavaScript are loaded once throughout the lifespan of the application.
- The load on the web server is reduced because the server has been relieved of the responsibility to generate HTML content. This thereby reduces the need for the web application to scale, saving a lot of problems related to handling sessions. Each request to backend APIs will carry a token (for authentication), and it's the responsibility of each API endpoint to manage how it wants to handle sessions.

- Because the application design is simple (HTML, CSS, and JavaScript only), the application can be hosted in any type of environment that can be accessed over HTTP and doesn't require advanced web server capabilities.
- The application becomes more flexible because it can easily be changed to talk to any number of microservices (via APIs) for fetching data and rendering as appropriate.
- Because SPAs retrieve data mostly from standard HTTP-based REST APIs, they can cache data effectively and use that data offline. A well-implemented REST API supports HTTP ETags and similar cache validations, making it easy for browsers to store, validate, and use client-side caches effectively.[1]

C.3   *Drawbacks of a SPA compared with an MPA*

SPAs don't come for free, however. They have drawbacks that you need to think about carefully before committing to implementing them. Luckily, engineers have found ways to overcome the limitations in SPA architectures:

- The rendering of content happens through JavaScript. If the pages contain heavy or unresponsive JavaScript, these can affect the browser process of the application user.
- Because the application relies on JavaScript, it becomes more prone to cross-site scripting (XSS) attacks; therefore, developers have to be extra cautious.
- SPAs won't work on browsers that have JavaScript disabled. Workarounds exist for these cases, but these don't help you reap the benefits of a SPA.
- The initial loading of the application into the browser can be slow because it involves loading all the HTML, CSS, and JavaScript. Workarounds are available to improve the loading time, however.
- The application would find it hard to deal with sensitive information such as user credentials or tokens because it works primarily on the client side (browser).

---

[1] An HTTP ETag (entity tag) is one of several mechanisms HTTP provides for web cache validation.

appendix D
Observability in a microservices deployment

In chapter 5, we discuss in detail how to monitor a microservices deployment with Prometheus and Grafana. The modern term for monitoring and analytics is *observability*. In this appendix, we discuss why observability is so critical in a microservices deployment as compared to monolithic applications.

D.1 *The need for observability*

Compared to a traditional monolithic application, microservices-backed applications are heavily distributed. In a traditional monolithic application, when function foo calls function bar, the chances of the function invocation failing because of external factors are rare. This is because in a monolithic application, both functions reside on the same process. If a failure occurs in the process, the application will fail as a whole, reducing the chances of partial failures. Figure D.1 illustrates a traditional retail application composed of many functions within the same process.

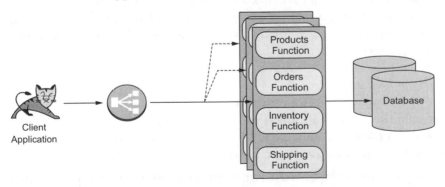

Figure D.1   In a scalable monolithic application, all functions of the application are within the same process. A failure of the application results in a failure of all functions.

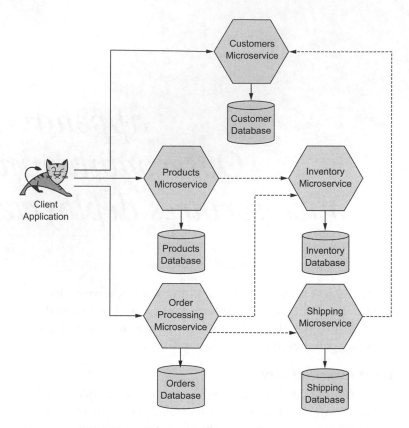

Figure D.2   In this microservices-based architecture of a retail store, individual functions are divided into independent microservices.

If we break this monolithic application into a microservices-driven architecture, we'll probably end up with an architecture that looks like figure D.2.

As you can see, a request made from a client can go through multiple hops of microservices in a typical microservices deployment. This calls for resiliency, robustness, and recovery factors to be built into our microservices to minimize failures as much as possible. Let's look at a real example and see why it's important to have stringent monitoring in place.

When a client makes a request to query the available products through the Products microservice, the Products microservice makes a query to the Inventory microservice to get the list of available product stock. At this point, the Inventory microservice can fail for various reasons, such as these:

- The Inventory microservice is running under high resource utilization and, therefore, is slow to respond. This can cause a time-out on the connection between the Products microservice and the Inventory microservice.
- The Inventory microservice is currently unavailable. The process has either crashed or has been stopped by someone.

- The Inventory microservice seems pretty healthy in terms of resource utilization; however, it takes a long time to respond because of a few slow-running database queries.
- Some data inconsistency on the inventory database is causing a failure on the code of the Inventory microservice, resulting in the code being unable to execute successfully, thus generating an error/exception.

In all four types of failures, the Products microservice needs to fall back to an alternative, such as presenting the list of products without providing details on stock availability, for example. As you can see, these types of partial failures of our microservices require immediate attention to be rectified and fixed. And that's what makes observability a critical factor in our microservices.

D.2 The four pillars of observability

The four main pillars of observability are metrics, tracing, logging, and visualization. Each factor is important in monitoring our microservices effectively. Let's take a look at why we need to pay attention to each of them.

D.2.1 The importance of metrics in observability

Metrics are a set of data values that are recorded over a period of time. These are mostly numeric values that are constantly recorded as min, max, average, and percentile. Metrics are usually used to measure the efficiency of the software process. These can be things like memory usage of a particular process, CPU usage of a process, load average, and so forth (figure D.3).

Metrics come in handy when troubleshooting and taking precautionary actions to minimize the impact of the failures described in the first and second bullet points of the preceding section. When a particular microservice is running under heavy resource utilization, monitoring the metrics of the relevant microservice would help trigger alerts to enable our DevOps personnel to take relevant actions. Systems such as

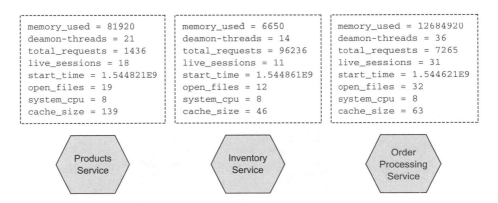

Figure D.3   Recording metrics of a microservice based on various attributes such as memory, sessions, and so forth

Kubernetes (see appendix J) monitor these types of metrics to perform autohealing and autoscaling activities so that these failures have minimal business impact.

The downside of metrics is that they are useful only to monitor a given microservice in isolation, based on a limited set of attributes. There are no technical barriers to adding any number of attributes to your metrics. However, adding a lot of metrics requires a lot of storage, making the microservice harder to manage. Metrics also don't give you a view of the problems that happen because of a request spanning across multiple microservices and other third-party systems. This is when distributed tracing comes to the rescue.

D.2.2 *The importance of tracing in observability*

A *trace* is a sequence of related distributed events. A single trace will have a unique identifier (UID), which spans across all the parties involved in the trace. A trace is like a collection of logs that spans across several components of a system. Each log record has a UID that makes it possible to correlate the data of a single request (event), which spans across various components of the system. Each record in a trace can contain information relevant to tracing and troubleshooting a request, such as entry point timestamps, latency information, or any other information that might be useful to identify the source of a request or to troubleshoot a request flow.

If you take a look at the third bullet point in section D.1, which talks about a microservice (the Inventory microservice) taking a long time to respond to a request because of a few slow-running database queries, you'll see that metrics don't help us a lot in that case because the vitals of the systems remain intact. In this scenario, the Inventory microservice as a whole remains healthy, but a particular function within it that accesses the database takes a longer time to complete, causing the Products microservice to fail partially. If we instrument the code of the Inventory microservice to emit a record with the latency details of the database query, this would help us to identify the particular section in the request flow that causes the problem. Let's take a deeper look at this in figure D.4.

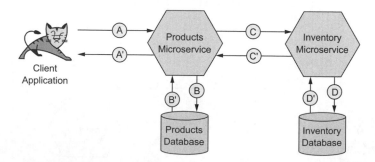

Figure D.4 The points in the request flow at which the spans are started and stopped

As you can see, when a client application makes a request to the Products microservice, it initiates a trace with a UID. The following is a rough sequence of events that happens to serve this request:

1. The client application initiates a request to the Products microservice. Because there's no trace prior to this point, the Products microservice begins the trace by creating the first span (A).[1]

2. The Products microservice executes a function to retrieve the list of products from the products database. The Products microservice creates a new span for this (B to B') and adds it to the trace started in the previous step. Because this particular span ends at this point, the span details are emitted from the microservice itself.

3. The Products microservice gets the IDs of the relevant products and passes them to the Inventory microservice for retrieving the inventory details of each product item. At this point, the Products microservice creates a new span (C) and adds it to the same trace.

4. The Inventory microservice queries the Inventory database for the inventory details of each product and responds to the Products microservice. The Inventory microservice creates a new span (D to D') and adds it to the trace started by the Products microservice. Once the function completes, the span details are emitted.

5. The Products microservice creates an aggregated response, which contains the product and inventory details of each product to be sent back to the client application. At this point, the span (C) is completed, and the span details are emitted.

6. The Products microservice responds to the client application with the information. Before sending the response to the client application, the Products microservice finishes span A, and the span details are emitted.

Each hop along this flow is represented as a span. When the execution flow reaches a particular point in the instrumentation, a span record is emitted, which contains details about the execution. Each span belongs to the same trace bearing the UID that was generated by the Products microservice at the point of initiating the processing of the request. If we assume the complete request takes about 1 second to complete, the database query in the Inventory microservice consumes about 700 milliseconds. If that's the case, the spans would look like those in figure D.5.

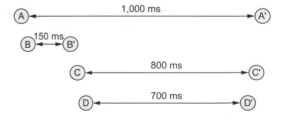

Figure D.5 By analyzing the time taken in each span, it becomes evident that the database operation that happens in the Inventory microservice consumes the largest chunk of request time.

---

[1] A *span* represents an individual unit of work performed in a distributed system.

Although this description matches the general pattern of tracing distributed events, we would need all our microservices to conform to a single pattern when emitting their traces. This would make it easier and consistent for querying them. As such, it would be perfect to have a global standard for all microservices worldwide when emitting their traces. OpenTracing (https://opentracing.io/) is such a vendor-neutral specification for distributed tracing requirements, supported by the Cloud Native Computing Foundation (CNCF). It provides instrumentation libraries for various programming languages. OpenCensus (https://opencensus.io/) provides another approach for collecting traces. This project started at Google and also got support from Microsoft and VMWare. OpenCensus too provides libraries for various programming languages to collect metrics and distributed traces. However, in May 2019 CNCF announced that it's merging both the OpenTracing and OpenCensus projects to create a new project called OpenTelemetry (https://opentelemetry.io/). You can think of OpenTelemetry as the next major version upgrade of both OpenTracing and OpenCensus projects.

> **NOTE**   Jaeger (www.jaegertracing.io) and Zipkin (https://zipkin.io/) are two of the most popular open source distributed tracing solutions that conform to the OpenTracing specification.

One major challenge with tracing is that it's hard to retrofit into an existing system. You need to add instrumentation code to a lot of places all across your microservices. And on top of that, it may not even be possible to instrument some of the services involved in the flow, because they may be out of your control. Failure to instrument all components in a given flow may not give you the optimal results you're looking for. And in some cases, if you're unable to trace an entire flow end to end, you may not be able to use whatever traces you have on hand as well.

Service meshes (see appendix K) can sometimes be a savior when you're unable to instrument your microservices for tracing (or something else). Service meshes attach a sidecar (figure D.6) to your microservice, which adds tracing capabilities (and other capabilities) to it.[2] This way, you can strap on tracing to any microservice without having to modify the microservice at all. Istio and Linkerd are two popular service mesh implementations that can help with your microservices architecture.

---

[2] A sidecar proxy is an architecture pattern that abstracts certain features such as security and traceability away from the main process (microservice).

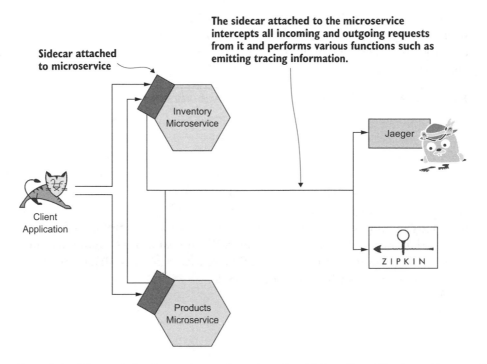

Figure D.6 Sidecars help microservices emit tracing-related information without requiring any changes to the microservices themselves

D.2.3 *The importance of logging in observability*

A *log* is a timestamped record of a particular event. It could be an acknowledgement of a request notifying the starting of a particular process or the recording of an error/exception, for example. Most readers, by experience, know the importance of a log record.

Metrics and traces are both used for observing statistical information about your microservices, either in isolation or spanning across several microservices. In many instances, however, this statistical information isn't useful for identifying the root cause of an issue, as in the failure scenario we discussed under the fourth bullet point in section D.1, which talks about data inconsistency of a database causing a failure on the code of a microservice. In this case, a particular inconsistency in the database was causing a problem in our microservice. This is a type of failure that we may not be able to capture or troubleshoot by using metrics or tracing only. From a statistical point of view, the microservice would have executed the function without delays or would have added resource usage. However, the code would have failed with exceptions being printed on the logs. This is why it becomes important to monitor your logs by using log collection and analysis tools.

A technology such as Fluentd can be used for the aggregation of logs from all of your microservices. It plugs into systems such as Elasticsearch and Splunk and can be used for the analysis and querying of log records. Fluentd can also be configured to trigger alerts based on connectors to send email, SMS notifications, and instant messages.

D.2.4 *The importance of visualization in observability*

Another key important factor in observability is being able to visualize the data and streams you collect from your microservices. *Visualization* is, of course, for humans only. We may have automated systems in place that are capable of acting based on failures or risks of failures. But in reality, most organizations still require some level of human intervention to fix things when they go wrong.

Therefore, having dashboards that constantly display the state of your systems can help a great deal. Kibana and Grafana are two popular technologies for visualizing statistics related to monitoring your systems. We discuss using Grafana in detail to monitor microservices in chapter 5. At the time of this writing, Grafana is the most popular open source data visualization tool available.

appendix E
Docker fundamentals

As a software developer, you've probably experienced the pain of distributing software and then finding out that it didn't work in certain environments. This is where the popular developer cry of "it works on my machine" was born. Docker helps you overcome this problem to some extent by packaging your software, along with all its dependencies, for distribution. In chapter 10, we discuss securing microservices deployed in a Docker environment. If you're new to Docker, this appendix lays the right foundation for you to follow chapter 10.

E.1 Docker overview

Docker is an open source project that simplifies software packaging, distribution, and execution. It's also the name of a private company, founded in 2010, that's behind the Docker open source project and that also maintains a commercial version of it. To avoid any confusion, when we talk about Docker the company, we use *Docker Inc*. When we say just *Docker*, we mean the software produced by the Docker open source project.

Docker builds a layer of abstraction over the infrastructure (host machine). Any software that runs on Docker can be easily decoupled from the infrastructure and distributed. Docker's core capabilities are built on top of Linux kernel features. The Linux kernel helps with building an isolated environment for a running process. We call this isolated environment a *container*.

A process running in a container has its own view of the filesystem, process identifiers, hostname, domain name, network interface, and so on, which doesn't conflict with the view of another process running in a container on the same host operating system. For example, two independent processes, each running in its own container, can listen on the same port even though they run on the same host operating system. You'll learn more about the level of isolation that containers bring in as we move forward in this appendix.

E.1.1   *Containers prior to Docker*

Docker brought containers into the mainstream, but the concept is a few decades old (figure E.1). In 1979, we could change the root directory of a running process with the chroot system call, introduced in UNIX V7 and added to the Berkeley Software Distribution (BSD) in 1982. To limit the visibility of the filesystem to a running process, chroot is still popular today and is considered a best practice by system administrators.

After almost two decades later, in 2000, FreeBSD added support for FreeBSD Jails. Jails, built on top of the chroot concept, allowed dividing a given host environment into multiple isolated partitions. Each partition is called a *jail.* A jail has its own set of users, and a process running in one jail can't interact with another process running in another jail.

Linux-VServer followed a similar concept, and by 2001, it was possible to partition a Linux-VServer so that each partition had its own, isolated filesystem, network, and memory.

In 2004, Solaris 10 introduced a new feature called Solaris Containers (also known as Solaris Zones). Like FreeBSD Jails, Solaris Containers provided operating system-level virtualization. Then Google introduced Process Containers in 2006 as a way of building isolation over the CPU, disk I/O, memory, and network. A year later, Process Containers were renamed and added to Linux Kernel 2.6.24 as control groups (cgroups). In 2008, Linux Containers (LXC) developed a container technology on top of cgroups and namespaces. The cgroups and namespaces are fundamental to the

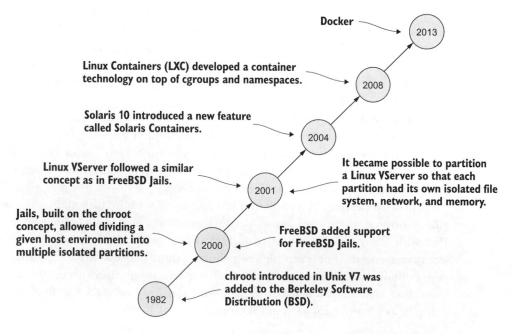

Figure E.1   The evolution of containers started in 1982 by introducing chroot to the Berkeley Software Distribution (BSD).

containers we see today. Docker, up to version 1.10, is based on LXC (more details in section E.13). We further discuss cgroups and namespaces in detail and how these are related to Docker in sections E.13.4 and E.13.5.

E.1.2 *Docker adding value to Linux containers*

The main value Docker provides over traditional Linux containers is portability. Docker makes Linux containers portable among multiple platforms (not just Linux) and builds an ecosystem to share and distribute containers. Docker does this by defining a common format to package an application (or a microservice) and all its dependencies into an artifact called Docker image. Developers can use a Docker image on any platform that runs Docker, and Docker makes sure it provides the same environment for the containers to run, regardless of the underlying infrastructure.

E.1.3 *Virtual machines vs. containers*

A virtual machine (VM) provides a virtualized environment over the infrastructure. In general, a VM operates in two modes: with a type-1 hypervisor and with a type-2 hypervisor. A *hypervisor* is software that runs VMs, or in other words, manages the life cycle of a VM. VMs with a type-2 hypervisor are the most common model. When you run VirtualBox (www.virtualbox.org) as a VM (or even VMWare Workstation Player or Parallels Desktop for Mac), it operates with a type-2 hypervisor.

As shown in figure E.2, the type-2 hypervisor runs on top of a host operating system, and all the VMs run on the hypervisor. The type-1 hypervisor doesn't require a

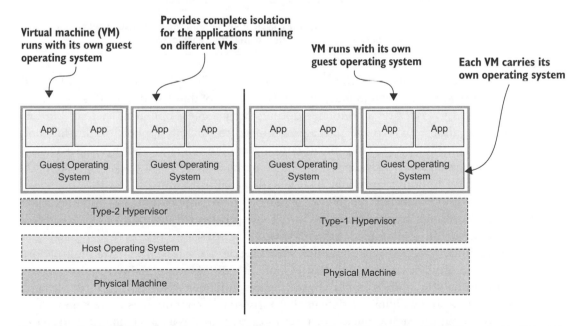

Figure E.2 A side-by-side comparison of a type-2 hypervisor and type-1 hypervisor. Each VM running on the host operating system carries its own guest operating system. The type-2 hypervisor provides an abstraction over the host operating system, while the type-1 hypervisor provides an abstraction over the physical machine.

host operating system; it runs directly on the physical machine. Any number of VMs can run on a hypervisor (subject to the resource availability of the host machine), and each VM carries its own operating system. The applications running on different VMs (but on the same host operating system) are isolated from each other, but the applications running on the same VM aren't.

Unlike in a VM, a container doesn't carry its own guest operating system; rather, it shares the operating system kernel with the host. Figure E.3 shows that the containers with the applications run on a Docker layer. But in reality, there's no Docker layer, as the container itself is a construct of the Linux operating system. The containers run on the kernel itself.

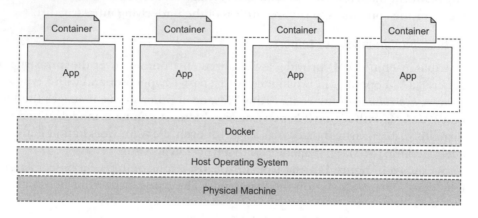

Figure E.3   Each container shares the operating system kernel with the host. Each application runs in its own container, and the applications are isolated from each other.

Docker natively runs on Linux. To run Docker on other platforms, we use a VM with the Linux operating system and run Docker on top of that (we discuss this in detail in section E.1.4). Because a container doesn't carry a guest operating system, but only the bare minimum software packages required to run the application, it's far more lightweight than a VM. That makes containers the preferred option to package and distribute microservices. Also, because a container has no guest operating system, the time it takes to boot a container is far less than that of a VM.

In terms of packaging, we follow the pattern of one application per container: a container represents a single process. Having one process per container helps us address scalability requirements more smoothly. We can't just scale a process with the load, but we can horizontally scale a container, which carries a process. If we have multiple processes running in the same container but with different scalability requirements, it would be hard to address that just by scaling the container. Also, running multiple applications in a single container defeats the purpose of a container, as there's no isolated environment for each application, and this further creates a management nightmare.

When we run multiple processes in a containerized environment, the processes can't talk to each other directly, as each process has its own container. To achieve the same level of isolation with a VM, we need to package each application with an independent VM, creating a huge overhead on the host operating system.

E.1.4 *Running Docker on non-Linux operating systems*

When we run Docker on a non-Linux operating system such as Windows or macOS, the layers in figure E.3 become a little different. Docker at its core uses basic Linux constructs to provide process isolation, and it runs only on a Linux kernel. But a workaround makes it work on non-Linux operating systems. There's some good history on how Docker support for Windows and macOS evolved, but in this section, we focus only on how it works at present.

As shown in figure E.4, Docker for macOS uses an xhyve hypervisor based on HyperKit (a tool kit for embedding hypervisor capabilities in an application on macOS), and Docker for Windows uses a Hyper-V hypervisor, which is built into Windows from Windows 10 onward. Both xhyve and Hyper-V let you boot Alpine Linux (a security-oriented, lightweight Linux distribution) on macOS and Windows, respectively, and Docker runs on top of the Alpine Linux kernel.

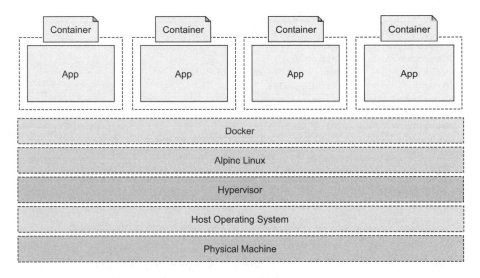

Figure E.4   Docker on non-Linux operating systems runs on a hypervisor. Docker at its core uses basic Linux constructs to provide process isolation, and it runs only on a Linux kernel (in this case, on Alpine Linux).

E.2   *Installing Docker*

Installing Docker on a local machine isn't as hard as it used to be in its early days. Docker has two versions: Community Edition (CE) and Enterprise Edition (EE). In this book, we use Docker CE, which is free and open source. Docker EE and Docker CE share the same core feature set, while Docker EE adds more on top of it at a cost, targeting mostly large enterprises that run mission-critical applications on Docker.

In this section, we don't list Docker installation instructions, because those could change, and there's a risk you'd end up with stale instructions that don't work with the latest Docker version. Docker has clean documentation, explaining how to install Docker on different platforms. Refer to the Docker documentation related to your platform at https://docs.docker.com/install/#supported-platforms. Then follow the instructions to complete the installation. Once the installation is complete, run the following command to find out the details related to the Docker version you're using:

```
\> docker version

Client: Docker Engine - Community
 Version:           19.03.8
 API version:       1.40
 Go version:        go1.12.17
 Git commit:        afacb8b
 Built:             Wed Mar 11 01:21:11 2020
 OS/Arch:           darwin/amd64
 Experimental:      false

Server: Docker Engine - Community
 Engine:
  Version:          19.03.8
  API version:      1.40 (minimum version 1.12)
  Go version:       go1.12.17
  Git commit:       afacb8b
  Built:            Wed Mar 11 01:29:16 2020
  OS/Arch:          linux/amd64
  Experimental:     true
 containerd:
  Version:          v1.2.13
  GitCommit:        7ad184331fa3e55e52b890ea95e65ba581ae3429
 runc:
  Version:          1.0.0-rc10
  GitCommit:        dc9208a3303feef5b3839f4323d9beb36df0a9dd
 docker-init:
  Version:          0.18.0
    GitCommit:        fec3683
```

Docker Enterprise Edition vs. Docker Community Edition

Both Docker EE and Docker CE share the same core, but Docker EE, which comes with a subscription fee, includes additional features such as private image management, container app management, cluster management support for Kubernetes and Swarm (which we talk about in chapter 11), and integrated image security scanning and signing. Explaining each of these features is beyond the scope of this book.

If you're keen on learning Docker in detail, we recommend *Docker in Action* (Manning, 2019) by Jeff Nickoloff and Stephen Kuenzli, and *Docker in Practice* (Manning, 2019) by Ian Miell and Aidan Hobson Sayers. Also, the book *Docker Deep Dive* (independently published in 2018) by Nigel Poulton gives a very good overview of Docker internals.

E.3   *Docker high-level architecture*

Before we delve deep into Docker internals and how it builds a containerized environment, let's have a look at the high-level component architecture. Docker follows a client-server architecture, as shown in figure E.5. The Docker client talks to the Docker daemon running on the Docker host over a REST API to perform various operations on Docker images and containers. (We discuss the difference between an image and a container later in this section; for now, think of a Docker image as the distribution unit of your application, and the container as the running instance of it.)

The Docker daemon supports listening on three types of sockets: UNIX, TCP, and FD (file descriptor). Only enabling TCP sockets will let your Docker client talk to the daemon remotely. All the examples in this appendix assume that the communication between the client and daemon happens over the UNIX socket (the default behavior), so you run both the client and the daemon on the same machine. In chapter 10, we discuss how to enable remote access to the Docker daemon over TCP and secure Docker APIs.

To run an application as a Docker container, we execute the `docker run` command via the Docker client (see step 1 in figure E.5). The Docker client creates an API request and talks to the Docker daemon running on the Docker host (step 2).

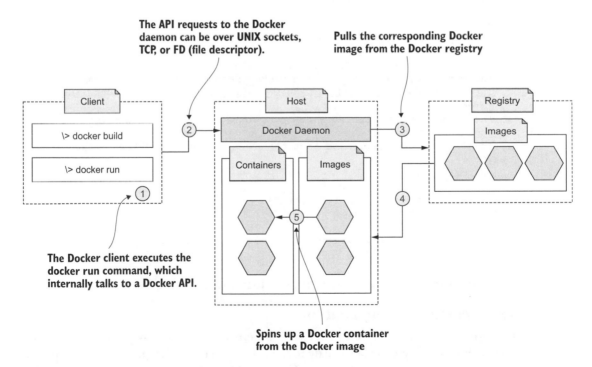

Figure E.5   In this high-level Docker component architecture, the Docker client talks to the Docker daemon running on the Docker host over a REST API to perform various operations on Docker images and containers.

The Docker daemon checks whether the Docker image requested by the client is present locally, and if not, it talks to a Docker registry (a store of Docker images) and pulls the corresponding image and all its dependencies (step 3 and step 4). Then it starts running the image as a container (step 5).

A *Docker image* is the packaging of your application. To share a Docker image with the developers or with the public, we use a Docker registry. For example, *Docker Hub* (https://hub.docker.com) is a public Docker registry. A *container* is a running process. We start a container using an image, and you can use the same image to run multiple containers. In other words, a container is a running instance of an image.

The following command instructs Docker to pull the hello-world image from Docker Hub (when you run it for the first time) and execute it as a container. The process running inside the Docker container prints the message `Hello from Docker` and the rest of the text after that:

```
\> docker run  hello-world

Unable to find image 'hello-world:latest' locally
latest: Pulling from library/hello-world
1b930d010525: Pull complete
Digest:
sha256:2557e3c07ed1e38f26e389462d03ed943586f744621577a99efb77324b0fe535
Status: Downloaded newer image for hello-world:latest

Hello from Docker!
This message shows that your installation appears to be working correctly.

To generate this message, Docker took the following steps:
 1. The Docker client contacted the Docker daemon.
 2. The Docker daemon pulled the "hello-world" image from the Docker Hub.
    (amd64)
 3. The Docker daemon created a new container from that image which runs the
    executable that produces the output you are currently reading.
 4. The Docker daemon streamed that output to the Docker client, which sent
     it
    to your terminal.

To try something more ambitious, you can run an Ubuntu container with:
 $ docker run -it ubuntu bash

Share images, automate workflows, and more with a free Docker ID:
 https://hub.docker.com/
```

For more examples and ideas, visit https://docs.docker.com/get-started/.

E.4   *Containerizing an application*

In chapter 7, you learn about JSON Web Tokens (JWTs) and how to secure microservices with a JWT issued by a security token service (STS). In chapter 10, we revisit the same use case but in a containerized environment. Before running an application (in this case, the STS, which is a Spring Boot application developed in Java) in a containerized environment, we need to first create a Docker image. In this section, we are going to create a Docker image for the STS.

E.4.1   What is a Docker image?

A *Docker image* is a file that packs your software for distribution and is built with multiple layers (we discuss layers in section E.9). If you're familiar with object-oriented programming (OOP), you know about classes and objects. An image in Docker is analogous to a class in OOP. A running instance of a Docker image is called a *container,* and we can create multiple Docker containers from a single image, just as you can create multiple objects or instances from a given class.

E.4.2   Building the application

The source code related to all the samples in this appendix is available in the GitHub repository at https://github.com/microservices-security-in-action/samples inside the appendix-e directory. The source code of the STS is also available in the appendix-e/sample01 directory. Run the following Maven command from the appendix-e/sample01 directory to build the STS. If everything goes well, you should see the BUILD SUCCESS message at the end:

```
\> mvn clean install
[INFO] BUILD SUCCESS
```

Now if you look at the appendix-e/sample01/target directory, you'll find a JAR file, which is the STS that you just built.

E.4.3   Creating a Dockerfile

To run the STS in a Docker container, we need to build a Docker image from the JAR file you created in section E.4.2. The first step in building a Docker image is to create a Dockerfile (see listing E.1). A Dockerfile includes step-by-step instructions for Docker on how to create a Docker image. Let's have a look at the Dockerfile in the following listing (also available in the appendix-e/sample01 directory), which instructs Docker to create an image for the STS with the required dependencies.

> **Listing E.1   The content of the Dockerfile**

```
FROM openjdk:8-jdk-alpine          ← Fetches the Docker image
                                       from the Docker registry
ADD target/com.manning.mss.appendixe.sample01-1.0.0.jar \     Copies the JAR file to
/com.manning.mss.appendixe.sample01-1.0.0.jar         ←       the container filesystem
ADD keystores/keystore.jks /opt/keystore.jks          ←       Copies the jks file to
ADD keystores/jwt.jks /opt/jwt.jks                    ←       the container filesystem
ENTRYPOINT ["java", "-jar", \
"com.manning.mss.appendixe.sample01-1.0.0.jar"]       ←       Copies the jwt.jks file to
                                                             the container filesystem
                          Provides the entry
                          point to the container
```

The first line of this Dockerfile instructs Docker to fetch the Docker image called openjdk:8-jdk-alpine from the Docker registry and, in this case, from the public Docker Hub, which is the default option. This is the base image of the Docker image we are about to create. When we create a Docker image, we don't need to create it from scratch. If any other Docker images are already available for our application's dependencies, we can reuse them. For example, in this case, to run our application, we need Java, so we start building our image from an existing OpenJDK Docker image, which is already available in Docker Hub.

The second line instructs Docker to copy the file com.manning.mss.appendixe .sample01-1.0.0.jar from the target directory of the host filesystem to the root of the container filesystem. The third line instructs Docker to copy the keystore.jks file from the keystores directory of the host filesystem to the /opt directory of the container filesystem. This is the keystore STS used to enable Transport Layer Security (TLS). The fourth line instructs Docker to copy the jwt.jks file from the keystores directory of the host filesystem to the /opt directory of the container filesystem. This keystore contains the private key that STS uses to sign the JWTs it issues. Finally, the fifth line tells Docker the entry point to the container (or which command to run when we start the container). For example, in this case, Docker executes the com.manning.mss .appendixe.sample01-1.0.0.jar file.

E.4.4   *Building a Docker image*

The following command run from the appendix-e/sample01/ directory instructs Docker to use the Dockerfile (see listing E.1) from the current path and builds a Docker image from it. Before executing the command, make sure that you have Docker up and running on your machine:[1]

```
\> docker build -t com.manning.mss.appendixe.sample01 .
```

In this command, we don't need to specifically mention the name of the Dockerfile. If we leave it blank or don't specify a filename, Docker, by default, looks for a file with the name Dockerfile at the current location. The -t option in the command is used to specify the name for the Docker image (in this case, com.manning.mss.appendixe .sample01). The following shows the output of the command:

```
Sending build context to Docker daemon 22.32MB
Step 1/5 : FROM openjdk:8-jdk-alpine
8-jdk-alpine: Pulling from library/openjdk
e7c96db7181b: Pull complete
f910a506b6cb: Pull complete
c2274a1a0e27: Pull complete
Digest:
sha256:94792824df2df33402f201713f932b58cb9de94a0cd524164a0f2283343547b3
Status: Downloaded newer image for openjdk:8-jdk-alpine
 ---> a3562aa0b991
```

---

[1] If you have Docker running on your local machine, the `docker version` command should return meaningful output with the proper versions of the Docker Engine client and server.

```
Step 2/5 : ADD target/com.manning.mss.appendixe.sample01-1.0.0.jar
/com.manning.mss.appendixe.sample01-1.0.0.jar
 ---> 802dd9300b9f
Step 3/5 : ADD keystores/keystore.jks /opt/keystore.jks
 ---> 125e96cbc5a8
Step 4/5 : ADD keystores/jwt.jks /opt/jwt.jks
 ---> feeb468921c9
Step 5/5 : ENTRYPOINT ["java", "-jar",
           "com.manning.mss.appendixe.sample01-1.0.0.jar"]
 ---> Running in 5c1931cc19a2
Removing intermediate container 5c1931cc19a2
 ---> defa4cc5639e
Successfully built defa4cc5639e
Successfully tagged com.manning.mss.appendixe.sample01:latest
```

Here, you can see from the output that Docker executes each line in the Dockerfile in steps. Each instruction in the Dockerfile adds a read-only layer to the Docker image, except for a few specific instructions. We learn about image layers in section E.9. The following Docker command lists all the Docker images on your machine (or the Docker host):

```
\> docker images
```

```
REPOSITORY                            TAG            IMAGE ID        SIZE
com.manning.ms.appendixe.sample01     latest         defa4cc5639e    127MB
openjdk                               8-jdk-alpine   792ff45a2a17    105MB
```

E.4.5   *Running a container from a Docker image*

Now you have a Docker image built for your STS. If you'd like, you can publish it to the public Docker registry or to a private registry so that others can use it as well. Before we do that, let's try to run it locally and see how we can get a token from the containerized STS. Run the following command by using the Docker client from anywhere on the machine where you built the Docker image (to be precise, you run the Docker client from a machine that's connected to the Docker host, which has the image you built):

```
\> docker run -p 8443:8443 com.manning.mss.appendixe.sample01
```

This command spins up a Docker container from the image (com.manning.mss .appendixe.sample01) we created in section E.4.4, starts the STS on the container port 8443, and maps it to the host port 8443. The port mapping is done by the -p argument we pass to the docker run command, where the first 8443 in the command represents the container port, and the second, the host port. Also make sure that no other process is running on your host machine on port 8443. You'll learn why we have to do the port mapping this way in section E.18, when we talk about Docker networking. Once we start the container successfully, we see the following logs printed on the terminal:

```
INFO 30901 --- [main] s.b.c.e.t.TomcatEmbeddedServletContainer :
Tomcat started on port(s): 8443 (https)
```

```
INFO 30901 --- [main] c.m.m.appendixe.sample01.TokenService   :
Started TokenService in 4.729 seconds (JVM running for 7.082)
```

Now let's test the STS with the following `curl` command. This is exactly the same `curl` command we used in section 7.5:

```
\> curl -v -X POST --basic -u applicationid:applicationsecret \
-H "Content-Type: application/x-www-form-urlencoded;charset=UTF-8" \
-k -d "grant_type=password&username=peter&password=peter123&scope=bar" \
https://localhost:8443/oauth/token
```

In this command, `applicationid` is the client ID of the web application, and `applicationsecret` is the client secret. If everything works fine, the STS returns an OAuth 2.0 access token, which is a JWT (or a JWS, to be precise) and only a part of the access token is shown in the following response:

```
{
"access_token":"eyJhbGciOiJSUzI1NiIsI...",
"token_type":"bearer",
"refresh_token":"",
"expires_in":5999,
"scope":"bar",
"jti":"5ed1c472-c3ba-48a3-bab6-bac7c4cca311"
}
```

E.5 *Container name and container ID*

When we start a container from the `docker run` command, we can specify a name for the container by passing the `name` argument. In the following command, we start a Docker container from the `hello-world` image with the container name `my-hello-world`:

```
\> docker run --name my-hello-world hello-world
```

In case we skip the `name` argument, Docker then assigns a generated universally unique identifier (UUID) as the name of the container. In addition to the name, a container also carries an ID (container ID), a randomly generated identifier that can't be changed. The main difference between the container ID and the container name is that we can change the name of a running container (using `docker rename`), but the container IDs are immutable. It's always better to give a container a name that's human readable or easy to remember. This helps you perform certain operations on a running container. Otherwise, if you want to do something on a container, first you need to find out the corresponding container ID or the system-generated container name.

E.6 *Docker registry*

A Docker *registry* is where we store Docker images for distribution. It's a storage and content delivery system for Docker images. A registry has multiple repositories. A *repository* is a collection of different versions (or tags) of a given Docker image (figure E.6). To

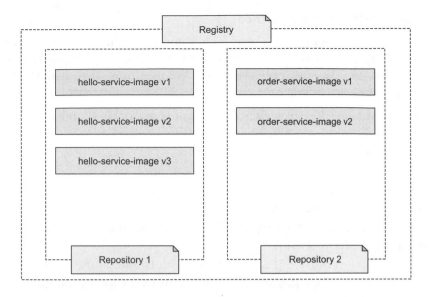

Figure E.6   A Docker registry has multiple repositories, and each repository has multiple versions of a Docker image.

deploy the Docker registry locally in your environment, you can follow the steps defined in the Docker online documentation at https://docs.docker.com/registry/deploying/.

There are two versions of a Docker registry that you can deploy locally. One is the open source community version, and the other is the Docker Trusted Registry (DTR) from Docker Inc. DTR isn't free, however, and the cost comes with a set of additional features like built-in access control (along with LDAP/Active Directory integration), security scans of images, and image signing. To find out more about DTR, you can refer to the Docker online documentation at https://docs.docker.com/ee/dtr/.

E.6.1   Docker Hub

Docker Hub (https://hub.docker.com) is the best-known Docker registry and the default registry in Docker. This hosted service provided by Docker Inc. offers both public and private repositories. Public repositories are free, and an image published to a public repository is accessible to anyone. At the time of writing, Docker Hub offers only one free private repository; if you need more, you have to pay.

E.6.2   Harbor

Similar to DTR, *Harbor* (https://goharbor.io/) is a registry that's also built on top of the open source Docker registry with some additional features (mostly security and identity management). Unlike DTR, Harbor is open source.

E.6.3   *Docker cloud platforms and registries*

Instead of running Docker on your own servers and maintaining the hardware yourself, you can look for a cloud vendor that provides a Docker platform as a service. Multiple cloud vendors are available. All these vendors provide their own Docker registries as a hosted service as well:

- Google Container Registry (GCR) integrates with Google Cloud Platform.
- Amazon Elastic Container Registry (ECR) integrates with Amazon Elastic Container Service (ECS).
- Azure Container Registry (ACR) by Microsoft integrates with Azure Kubernetes Service (AKS). AKS replaced the Azure Container Service (ACS) after it was retired on January 31, 2020.
- OpenShift Container Registry (OCR) by Red Hat integrates with OpenShift Container Platform (OCP).
- Pivotal Container Service (PKS) integrates with Harbor as the Docker registry.
- IBM Cloud Container Registry integrates with IBM Cloud Kubernetes Service (we discuss Kubernetes in appendix J).
- Oracle Container Registry integrates with Oracle Cloud Infrastructure Container Engine for Kubernetes.

E.7   *Publishing to Docker Hub*

In this section, you'll see how to publish the Docker image we created in section E.4.4. We'll publish it to the public Docker registry, which is Docker Hub. First, we need to create a Docker ID from https://hub.docker.com. In this section, we use our Docker ID, `prabath`; you need to replace it with your own Docker ID. Let's use the following command to create a valid login session with Docker Hub and then enter the corresponding password:

```
\> docker login --username=prabath

Password:
Login Succeeded
```

Next, we need to find the image ID of the Docker image we want to publish to Docker Hub. The following command lists all the images in the Docker host machine, and we can pick the image ID corresponding to our Docker image:

```
\> docker images

REPOSITORY                            TAG      IMAGE ID      CREATED       SIZE
com.manning.mss.appendixe.sample01    latest   defa4cc5639e  An hour ago   127MB
```

Now we need to tag the image with our Docker ID, as shown in the following command. (We discuss tagging in section E.8.) In this command, you need to use your own Docker ID. Here `e7090e36543b` is the image ID, and `prabath/manning-sts-appendix-e` is the name of the Docker image, where `prabath` is the Docker ID that you need to replace with your own ID:

```
\> docker tag defa4cc5639e prabath/manning-sts-appendix-e
```

Finally, we push the tagged Docker image to Docker Hub with the following command:

```
\> docker push prabath/manning-sts-appendix-e
```

When we publish the prabath/manning-sts-appendix-e image to Docker Hub, we, in fact, publish it to the Docker Hub registry in the prabath/manning-sts-appendix-e repository. Now anyone having access to Docker Hub can pull this Docker image and spin up a container with the same command we used in section E.4.5, but with the image name prabath/manning-sts-appendix-e:

```
\> docker run -p 8443:8443 prabath/manning-sts-appendix-e
```

E.8 Image name and image ID

When we build a Docker image, it needs a name. In section E.7, we used prabath/manning-sts-appendix-e as our image name. To be precise, prabath/manning-sts-appendix-e isn't the image name, but the name of the corresponding repository (still, many prefer to call it the image name too, which is fine). As we discussed in section E.6, a repository can have multiple versions of a given Docker image. In other words, the registry, the repository, and the image version (or the tag) uniquely identify a given Docker image.

The image version is commonly known as a *tag*. A tag is the same as a version, which we use with other software. If you look at the Tomcat application server image (https://hub.docker.com/_/tomcat?tab=tags) in Docker Hub, you'll find multiple tags. Each image tag represents a Tomcat version number. That's a practice we follow. To pull the Tomcat image from Docker Hub, we have two options: pull the image just by the repository name (without a tag), or pull the image both by the repository name and the tag.

E.8.1 Docker images with no tags (or the latest tag)

Let's see how to work with Docker images with no tags. The following `docker` command pulls a Tomcat image without a tag:

```
\> docker pull tomcat
```

To see the tag of the Tomcat image pulled from Docker Hub, let's use the following docker command:

```
\> docker images tomcat

REPOSITORY    TAG         IMAGE ID         CREATED          SIZE
tomcat        latest      1c721f25f939     11 hours ago     522MB
```

The output shows that the Tomcat image tag is `latest`. This special tag in Docker is also the most confusing tag. If you've published an image to Docker Hub without a tag (just by the repository name, as we did in section E.7), Docker Hub, by default, assigns it the `latest` tag. But this name doesn't mean it's the latest Tomcat image in that repository. It's just a Tomcat image that the Tomcat developers have published to Docker Hub without a tag.

Also, when you use `docker pull` or `docker run` with only the repository name of the image you want to retrieve (without the tag), Docker Hub thinks it's a request for the Docker image with the `latest` tag. That's why earlier, when we used the `docker pull tomcat` command, Docker pulled the corresponding Tomcat image with the `latest` tag. Even if we have a more recent Tomcat image with a tag, Docker still pulls the Tomcat image with the `latest` tag because we omitted the tag in our command. What if all the images in the Tomcat repository are tagged? Then, the command with no tag results in an error.

E.8.2   *Docker images with a tag*

As a best practice, we should tag all the images we push to Docker Hub; at least that will avoid the confusion with the `latest` tag. Let's repeat the steps we followed in section E.7 to publish a Docker image to Docker Hub, but this time with a tag. We're not going to explain each step here, but only the steps that we need for adding a tag.

Before we push the image to Docker Hub, in addition to the repository name (`prabath/manning-sts-appendix-e`), we also need to provide a tag (`v1` in this case). Then we can use the `docker run` command along with the image tag to pull the exact version we pushed to Docker Hub under the `v1` tag:

```
\> docker tag defa4cc5639e prabath/manning-sts-appendix-e:v1
\> docker push prabath/manning-sts-appendix-e:v1
\> docker run -p 8443:8443 prabath/manning-sts-appendix-e:v1
```

E.8.3   *Working with third-party Docker registries*

Although we mentioned in the introduction to section E.8 that the registry, the repository, and the image version (or the tag) uniquely identify a given Docker image, we never used the registry name in any of the commands we've used so far. You might have guessed the reason already! By default, Docker uses Docker Hub as the registry, and if we don't explicitly tell Docker to use a third-party registry, it simply uses the Docker Hub. Let's assume we have our prabath/manning-sts-appendix-e repository in GCR. This is how we use `docker run` to pull our image from GCR. In the command, `gcr.io` is the GCR endpoint:

```
\> docker run -p 8443:8443 gcr.io/prabath/manning-sts-appendix-e:v1
```

To publish an image to GCR, we can use the following commands:

```
\> docker tag e7090e36543b gcr.io/prabath/manning-sts-appendix-e:v1
\> docker push gcr.io/prabath/manning-sts-appendix-e:v1
```

E.8.4   *Docker Hub official and unofficial images*

Docker Hub maintains a set of official Docker images, and the rest is just unofficial images. When you publish an image to Docker Hub and do nothing else, it's becomes an unofficial image. The repository name of an unofficial Docker image must start with the Docker Hub username. That's why we had to use prabath/manning-sts-appendix-e as our repository name, where `prabath` is the Docker Hub username, instead of using manning-sts-appendix-e.

Publishing an official image to Docker Hub requires more work, as defined at https://docs.docker.com/docker-hub/official_images/. A dedicated team from Docker Inc. reviews and publishes all the content in an official image. As a user of an official image, the difference is in how the repository name is constructed. Official repository names don't need to start with the Docker Hub username. For example, the following command pulls the official Tomcat image from Docker Hub:

```
\> docker pull tomcat
```

E.8.5   *Image ID*

We can represent each Docker image as a JSON object, and this object is written to a JSON file inside the Docker image. Let's have a look at it. We can use the following two commands to pull the Tomcat Docker image having the tag `9.0.20` from the Docker Hub and save it to a file called tomcat.9.0.20.tar:

```
\> docker pull tomcat:9.0.20
\> docker save -o tomcat.9.0.20.tar tomcat:9.0.20
```

The `docker save` command creates the tomcat.9.0.20.tar file with all the image content. It's in a TAR compressed format, and we can use a tar utility (based on your operating system) to decompress it:

```
\> tar -xvf tomcat.9.0.20.tar
```

This produces a set of directories with long names and a JSON file. If you find it hard to find the JSON file, you can use `ls *.json` command to filter the file. For our discussion, what matters is this JSON file; it's the representation of the tomcat:9.0.20 Docker image. You can use a tool, based on your operating system, to calculate the SHA-256 digest of this file. SHA-256 is a hashing algorithm that creates a fixed-length digest (256 bits) from any given content. Here, we use OpenSSL to generate the SHA-256 of the JSON file:

```
\> openssl dgst -sha256 \
e9aca7f29a6039569f39a88a9decdfb2a9e6bc81bca6e80f3e21d1e0e559d8c4.json

SHA256
(e9aca7f29a6039569f39a88a9decdfb2a9e6bc81bca6e80f3e21d1e0e559d8c4.json)
=e9aca7f29a6039569f39a88a9decdfb2a9e6bc81bca6e80f3e21d1e0e559d8c4
```

Looking at the output, you might have already noticed a pattern. Yes! It's not a coincidence. The name of the file is, in fact, the SHA-256 hash value of that file. Now the mystery is over! The image ID of a Docker image is the SHA-256 hash of the corresponding JSON file; to be precise, it's the hexadecimal representation of the SHA-256 hash.

Let's use the following docker command to clarify this. It prints the image ID of the given Docker image, which is the first 12 digits of the image ID we got before:

```
\> docker images tomcat:9.0.20

REPOSITORY      TAG               IMAGE ID        CREATED          SIZE
tomcat          9.0.20            e9aca7f29a60    14 hours ago     639MB
```

E.8.6 *Pulling an image with the image ID*

To pull an image from a Docker registry, so far we've used the image name, along with the tag. For example, the following command pulls the Tomcat image with the tag 9.0.20:

```
\> docker pull tomcat:9.0.20
```

We need to be concerned about a few things when we pull an image by the tag. Tags aren't immutable, which means they are subject to change. Also, we can push multiple images with the same tag to a Docker registry, and the latest image overrides the previous image with the same tag. When we pull an image by the tag, there's a chance we might not get the same image all the time. Pulling an image with the image ID helps overcome that issue.

The image ID is the SHA-256 hash of the image. If the content of the image changes, the hash of the image changes as well—hence, the image ID. Two different images can never carry the same image ID, so when we pull an image by its ID (or the hash of the image), we always get the same image. The following command shows how to pull an image by the image ID. The text after tomcat@ in the command is the image ID of the Tomcat image we want to pull:

```
\> docker pull \
tomcat@sha256:\
b3e124c6c07d761386901b4203a0db2217a8f2c0675958f744bbc85587d1e715
```

E.9   *Image layers*

The Docker image we built in section E.4.4 and published to the Docker Hub in section E.7 has six layers. When we run the docker build command to build a Docker image, Docker creates a layer for each instruction in the corresponding Dockerfile, except for a few instructions such as ENV, EXPOSE, ENTRYPOINT, and CMD. For clarity, we repeat the same Dockerfile used in listing E.1 in the following listing.

As per the Dockerfile in listing E.2, the Docker image we create from it should result in only four layers. Even though this Dockerfile has five instructions, no image layer is created for the ENTRYPOINT instruction. But we mentioned before that this

Docker image has six layers. Where does it get the two remaining layers? Those two come from the `openjdk:8-jdk-alpine` base image.

```
FROM openjdk:8-jdk-alpine
ADD target/com.manning.mss.appendixe.sample01-1.0.0.jar \
/com.manning.mss.appendixe.sample01-1.0.0.jar
ADD keystores/keystore.jks /opt/keystore.jks
ADD keystores/jwt.jks /opt/jwt.jks
ENTRYPOINT ["java", "-jar", \
"com.manning.mss.appendixe.sample01-1.0.0.jar "]
```

When we pull a Docker image from Docker Hub, Docker pulls the image in layers. The following two commands pull and inspect the prabath/manning-sts-appendix-e image, and in the truncated output shows the SHA-256 hash of the associated layers:

```
\> docker pull prabath/manning-sts-appendix-e
\> docker inspect prabath/manning-sts-appendix-e

"Layers": [
"sha256:f1b5933fe4b5f49bbe8258745cf396afe07e625bdab3168e364daf7c956b6b81",
"sha256:9b9b7f3d56a01e3d9076874990c62e7a516cc4032f784f421574d06b18ef9aa4",
"sha256:ceaf9e1ebef5f9eaa707a838848a3c13800fcf32d7757be10d4b08fb85f1bc8a",
"sha256:52b4aac6cb4680220c70a68667c034836839d36d37f3f4695d129c9919da9e3a",
"sha256:1fa9ff776ce74439b3437cdd53333c9e2552753cf74986e1f49ca305ad2e3c02",
"sha256:93fc1841ffce641e1da3f3bda10416efcbff73dd9bfe2ad8391683034942dbd5"
]
```

You can also use the tool *dive* (https://github.com/wagoodman/dive) to explore each layer in a given Docker image. Once you install dive in your local machine, you can run the following command to explore the layers of the prabath/manning-sts-appendix-e Docker image:

```
\> dive prabath/manning-sts-appendix-e
```

Each layer in a Docker image is read-only and has a unique identifier. Each of these layers is stacked over the other. When we create a container from an image, Docker adds another layer that's read/write on top of all the read-only layers. This is called the *container layer*. Any writes from the container while it's running are written to this layer. Because the containers are immutable, any data written to this layer vanishes after you remove the container. In section E.12, we discuss an approach to make the container's runtime data persistent, especially the data in logs.

The layered approach Docker follows when creating an image promotes reusability. When you run multiple containers from the same image, each container shares the image (the read-only layers), but has its own independent layer on top of that. Even between different images, if the containers depend on the same image layer, Docker reuses such layers as well.

E.10   *Container life cycle*

A container is an instance of an image. Once we create a container, it can go through multiple phases in its life cycle: created, running, paused, stopped, killed, and removed (figure E.7).

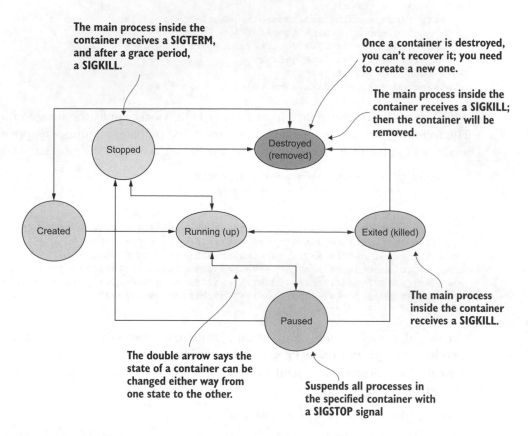

Figure E.7   The status of a container changes from created to destroyed in different phases.

E.10.1   *Creating a container from an image*

Earlier in this appendix, we used the `docker run` command to start a container. That single command does two things: first it creates a container and then it starts it. Instead of that, however, we can use `docker create` to create a container from a given Docker image. The following command pulls the Tomcat Docker image from Docker Hub and creates a container with the name my-web-server. Once the container is created successfully, the command prints the generated container ID:

```
\> docker create --name my-web-server tomcat

d9ad318893e3844695d9f25dd53cb88128329b90d024c86d1774475b81e39de3
```

We can use the following command to view the status of the latest container (`-l`). Here you can see the my-web-server container carries the `Created` status:

```
\> docker ps -l

CONTAINER ID      IMAGE         STATUS         NAMES
d9ad318893e3      tomcat        Created        my-web-server
```

What does it mean that the container is created but not running or up? The `docker create` command takes the corresponding image and, on top of that, adds a new writable layer and then prepares it for running.

E.10.2 *Starting a container*

We can start a Docker container that's created or stopped (not paused) with the `docker start` command:

```
\> docker start my-web-server
```

Once the container is booted up, the following command shows its status as up:

```
\> docker ps -l

CONTAINER ID      IMAGE         STATUS         NAMES
d9ad318893e3      tomcat        Up 7 seconds   my-web-server
```

E.10.3 *Pausing a running container*

We can use the `docker pause` command to suspend a running container. This sends a `SIGSTOP` signal to all the processes running in the corresponding container.[2] What does this really mean?

If we write data to the container's writable layer, that data is still available when we unpause the container. Pausing a container won't remove its writable layer, and the data already written remains unchanged. Docker cleans up the data written to the container layer only when we remove a container from the system (section E.10.6). Even killing a container (section E.10.5) won't wipe out the container layer. Here's the command:

```
\> docker pause my-web-server
```

Once the container is paused, the following command shows its status as paused:

```
\> docker ps -l

CONTAINER ID      IMAGE         STATUS                      NAMES
d9ad318893e3      tomcat        Up About a minute (Paused)  my-web-server
```

---

[2] If a process receives a `SIGSTOP`, it's paused by the operating system. Its state is preserved, ready to be restarted, and it doesn't get any more CPU cycles until then.

We can use the following command to bring back a paused container to its running status:

```
\> docker unpause my-web-server
```

Just as the container layer of a paused container remains unchanged after we unpause it or bring it back to the running status, any data you write to the container's memory also remains unchanged. This is because the docker pause command doesn't make the processes running in the container restart when we unpause the container.

E.10.4 *Stopping a running container*

Once a container is in a running state, we can use docker stop to stop it. This sends the main process inside the container a SIGTERM signal and, after a grace period, the SIGKILL signal. Once an application receives a SIGTERM signal, it can determine what it needs to do. Ideally, it will clean up any resources and then stop.

For example, if your microservice running in a container already has inflight requests that it's currently serving, then it can work on those while not accepting any new requests. Once all the inflight requests are served, the service can stop itself.

In case the service decides not to stop itself, the SIGKILL signal generated after a grace period ensures that the container is stopped no matter what:

```
\> docker stop my-web-server
```

Once the container is stopped, the following command shows its status as Exited with a status code 143:

```
\> docker ps -l

CONTAINER ID    IMAGE      STATUS                      NAMES
d9ad318893e3    tomcat     Exited (143) 3 seconds ago    my-web-server
```

We can use the following command to bring back an exited container to running status:

```
\> docker restart my-web-server
```

Even though the container layer of the stopped container remains unchanged after we restart it, any data you write to the container's memory will be lost (unlike in docker pause). This is because the docker stop command makes the main process running in the container stop, and when we restart it, the process restarts too.

E.10.5 *Killing a container*

We can kill a container that's running or that's in a paused status by using the docker kill command. This sends the main process inside the container a SIGKILL signal, which immediately takes down the running container:

```
\> docker kill my-web-server
```

> **NOTE** To stop a container, we should always use docker stop instead of docker kill, as the stop command gives you control over cleanup of the running process.

Once the container is killed, the following command shows its status as Exited with the status code 137:

```
\> docker ps -l

CONTAINER ID      IMAGE        STATUS                      NAMES
d9ad318893e3      tomcat       Exited (137) 20 seconds ago  my-web-server
```

We can use the following command to return an exited container to the running status:

```
\> docker restart my-web-server
```

Even though the container layer of the killed container remains unchanged after we restart it, as with `docker stop`, any data you wrote to the container's memory is lost. That's because the `docker kill` command makes the main process running in the container stop, and when we restart it, the process restarts too.

E.10.6 *Destroying a container*

We can use `docker rm` to remove a container from the Docker host. We have to stop the running container first, using either `docker stop` or `docker kill`, before removing it:

```
\> docker rm my-web-server
```

There's no way to bring back a removed container. We have to create it again.

E.11 *Deleting an image*

When we pull an image from a Docker registry (or create our own as in E.4.4), it's stored in the Docker host. We can use the following command to remove the copy of the Tomcat image with the tag `9.0.20` stored in the Docker host:

```
\> docker image rm tomcat:9.0.20
```

When deleting an image, Docker deletes all the image layers, unless other images in the system have dependencies to those. Before deleting an image, first, we need to remove the corresponding container using the `docker rm` command (see section E.10.6).

　　　If you want to remove all unused containers, networks, and images, use the following command:

```
\> docker system prune -a
```

E.12 *Persisting runtime data of a container*

Containers are immutable. Any data written to the container filesystem (or the container layer) vanishes soon after we remove the container. Even so, we can't let that happen. Immutable containers are important in a containerized environment, so that we can spin up and spin down containers from a Docker image and bring them into the same state. Still, there's some data we need to persist (for example, runtime logs), and we can't afford to lose that data. Docker volumes and bind mounts help with persisting the runtime data of a container.

E.12.1 *Using Docker volumes to persist runtime data*

When we use Docker *volumes* to persist data outside a container filesystem, Docker uses its own storage in the Docker host filesystem, and Docker itself manages this storage. Let's consider an example to illustrate how to use Docker volumes to share data between containers.

We can have one container that writes logs to a volume, and another container that shares the same volume can read and possibly push the logs to a log management system like Fluentd. In the same way, if you want to store log data in Amazon S3, you can have another container that reads the logs from the shared volume and publishes them to S3. The container, which writes logs to the volume, doesn't necessarily need to know where to publish them or how to publish them: a different container can assume that responsibility. This is a good way of implementing separation of concerns and the single responsibility principle.

Let's look at a simple example to see how volumes work. Here, we're going to spin up a Tomcat container and save its log files in a volume. So, even if we take the container down, we still have the logs. Let's use the following command to spin up a Tomcat container with a volume mapping. The –v argument in the `docker run` command says map the /usr/local/tomcat/logs directory from the container filesystem to the `log-vol` volume in the Docker host, and we use `--rm` argument to instruct Docker to remove this container from the system after we shut down the process (the Tomcat server). If `log-vol` volume does not exist in the system, Docker will automatically create one:

```
\> docker run --rm --name tomcat \
-v log-vol:/usr/local/tomcat/logs tomcat:9.0.20
```

Once the container starts up, we can find all the logs inside the volume we created. Even after we take down the container, the log files still remain in the volume. We can't directly view the files in a volume by checking the Docker host filesystem. One workaround is to use another container, with the same volume, and then list the content of the volume, as in the following command. Here we use the `busybox` Docker image:

```
\> docker run --rm -i -v log-vol:/view_volume busybox find /view_volume
```

In the example in this section, we use –v to do a volume mapping. Instead, you can use the `--mount` option, as in the following command. The –v option was originally intended to use with standalone Docker containers, while `--mount` was used with Docker Swarm (which we discuss in section E.17). However, since Docker version 17.06 onward, you can also use the `--mount` option instead of –v. Here we need to specify the `type` of the `mount` as `volume`. :

```
\> docker run --rm --name tomcat \
--mount type=volume,source=log-vol,target=/usr/local/tomcat/logs \
tomcat:9.0.20
```

The `--mount` option supports two types: `volume` and `bind`. In section E.12.2, we discuss bind mounts. The default mount type is `volume`, so if you want to use a volume mount, you can simply run the following command, skipping the `type` argument:

```
\> docker run --rm --name tomcat \
--mount source=log-vol,target=/usr/local/tomcat/logs tomcat:9.0.20
```

E.12.2 *Using bind mounts to persist runtime data*

A *bind mount* lets you map a directory or a file from the host filesystem to the container filesystem. Unlike with volumes, where Docker itself manages the storage of a volume, in a bind mount, the user has the total control of the storage.

Let's take the same example we used in section E.12.1 to see how bind mounts work. Here, we're going to spin up a Tomcat container and save its log files in a directory on the host machine. So, even if we take the container down, we still have the logs. Let's use the following command to spin up a Tomcat container with a bind mount. The –v argument in the `docker run` command says map the /usr/local/ tomcat/logs directory from the container filesystem to the ~/logs directory in our host filesystem. If you don't have a directory called ~/logs in your host filesystem, the following command will automatically create one:

```
\> docker run --name tomcat \
-v ~/logs:/usr/local/tomcat/logs tomcat:9.0.20
```

Once the container starts up, we can find all the logs inside the ~/logs directory of the host filesystem. Even after we take down the container, the log files remain in the host filesystem. This is only one use case of bind mounts (or even for volumes), where we take data out from a container. We can also use bind mounts (or volumes) to feed in data from the host filesystem to the container filesystem. In chapter 10, we use bind mounts to externalize keys/credentials from a Docker image.

In the example in this section, we use –v to do a bind mount. Instead, you can use the `--mount` option, as in the following command:

```
\> docker run --name tomcat \
--mount type=bind,\
source=/Users/prabath/logs,target=/usr/local/tomcat/logs \
tomcat:9.0.20
```

Even though you can use `--mount` instead of –v, there are some differences. Unlike –v, `--mount` won't create the source directory in the host filesystem if it does not exist.

If you are to pick volumes or bind mounts, what would you pick? We've seen that both options are heavily used, but the recommendation from the Docker community is to use volumes instead of bind mounts. The reason is, unlike bind mounts, a volume does not rely on the structure of the host filesystem, and Docker itself directly manages its storage.

E.13   *Docker internal architecture*

Docker initially used Linux Containers (LXCs) to implement process isolation. Linux cgroups and namespaces are the two fundamental technologies behind LXC. The Linux kernel, but not LXC, implements cgroups and namespaces. When Docker was first released in 2013, it included the Docker daemon, whose implementation was based on LXC. Docker dropped the use of LXC as its execution environment from version 1.10 onward, after making it optional since version 0.9.

Libcontainer, developed by Docker Inc., replaced LXC. Now, libcontainer is the default execution environment of Docker. The motivation behind building libcontainer was to get direct access to the kernel-level constructs to build and run containers, rather than going through LXC (as LXC isn't part of the Linux kernel). Libcontainer is a library that interacts with cgroups and namespaces at the level of the Linux kernel.

In addition to dropping support for LXC, Docker also worked on breaking down the monolithic Docker daemon and taking some functionalities out of it, which was also the motivation behind the Moby project that we discuss in section E.19. Figure E.8 shows the Docker internal architecture.

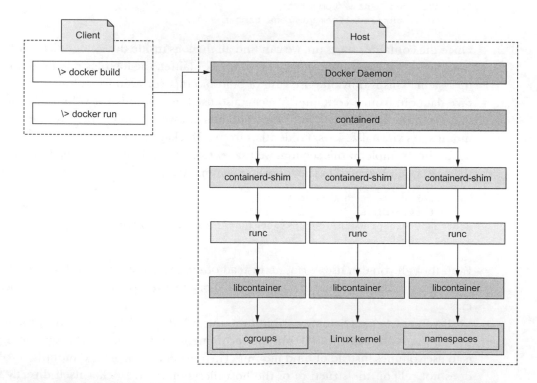

Figure E.8   In the Docker internal architecture, cgroups and namespaces, which are implemented at the Linux kernel, are the fundamental building blocks of Docker containers.

E.13.1 *Containerd*

Containerd is the component in the Docker internal architecture that's responsible for managing containers across all life-cycle stages. It takes care of starting, stopping, pausing, and destroying containers. Containerd finds the corresponding Docker image, based on the image name that comes with the API request and passed to it by the Docker daemon, and converts the image to an Open Container Initiative (OCI) bundle. It then passes control to another component called containerd-shim.

OCI (www.opencontainers.org) is a group that operates under the Linux Foundation, established in June 2015 by Docker Inc. and others in the container industry to develop standards around container formats and runtime. Docker supports OCI specifications from version 1.11 onward.

E.13.2 *Containerd-shim*

Containerd-shim forks another process called runc, which internally talks to the operating system kernel to create and run containers. Runc starts a container as a child process, and once the container starts running, runc kills itself.

E.13.3 *Runc*

Runc implements the OCI container runtime specification. It creates containers by talking to the operating system kernel. Runc uses the libcontainer library to interact with cgroups and namespaces at the kernel level.

E.13.4 *Linux namespaces*

Docker brings in process isolation with namespaces. A *namespace* in Linux partitions kernel resources so that each running process has its own independent view of those resources. While implementing namespaces, Linux introduced two new system calls: `share` and `setns` together with six new constant flags. Each flag represents a namespace as listed here:

- *PID namespace*—Identified by the `CLONE_NEWPID` flag. Ideally, when we run a process on the host operating system, it gets a unique process identifier. When we have a partitioned process ID (PID) namespace, each container can have its own process identifiers, independent of the other processes running on other containers (on the same host machine). By default, each container has its own PID namespace.

  If we want to share a PID namespace among multiple containers, we can override the default behavior by passing the `--pid` argument to the `docker run` command. For example, the following command forces the hello-world Docker container to use the PID namespace of the host machine:

  ```
  \> docker run --pid="host" hello-world
  ```

  And the following command forces the hello-world Docker container to use the PID namespace of the container foo:

  ```
  \> docker run --pid="container:foo" hello-world
  ```

- *UTS namespace*—Identified by the `CLONE_NEWUTS` flag. This UNIX Time Sharing (UTS) namespace isolates the hostname and the Network Information Service (NIS) domain name. In other words, the UTS namespace isolates hostnames, and each container can have its own hostname, regardless of the names that other containers have. To override this default behavior and to share the UTS namespace of the host machine with a container, we can pass the `--uts` argument with the value `host` to the `docker run` command like this:

```
\> docker run --uts="host" hello-world
```

- *NET namespace*—Identified by the `CLONE_NEWNET` flag. The NET namespace isolates the network stack with all the routes, firewall rules, and network devices. For example, two processes running in two different containers can listen on the same port with no conflict. We discuss Docker networking in detail in section E.18.

- *MNT namespace*—Identified by the `CLONE_NEWNS` flag. The MNT (mount) namespace isolates the mount points in the system. In simple terms, a *mount point* defines the location of your data. For example, when you plug in a USB pen drive to your MacBook, the operating system automounts the pen drive's filesystem to the /Volumes directory. The mount namespace helps isolate one container's view of the filesystem from others, as well as the host filesystem. Each container sees its own /usr, /var, /home, /opt, and /dev directories.

- *IPC namespace*—Identified by the `CLONE_NEWIPC` flag. The IPC namespace isolates the resources related to interprocess communication: memory segments, semaphores, and message queues. By default, each container has its own private namespace, and we can override that behavior by passing the `--ipc` argument to the `docker run` command. For example, the following command forces the hello-world Docker container to join the IPC namespace of another container (foo):

```
\> docker run --ipc="container:foo" hello-world
```

- *USR namespace*—Identified by the `CLONE_NEWUSER` flag. The USR namespace isolates the user identifiers within a given container. This allows two different containers to have two users (or groups) with the same identifier. Also you can run a process as the root in a container, while (the same process) having no root access outside the container.

E.13.5 *Linux cgroups*

Control groups (*cgroups*) are a Linux kernel feature that lets you control resources allocated to each process. With cgroups, we can say how much CPU time, how many CPU cores, how much memory, and so on, a given process (or a container) is allowed to consume. This is extremely important in an environment in which multiple containers are sharing the same set of physical resources (CPU, memory, network, and so forth) from the host machine, in order to avoid one container from misusing those.

We can restrict the resource usage of a given container by passing the amount of resources allocated to it as arguments to the `docker run` command. The following command sets the maximum memory usage to 256 MB to the container started from the hello-world Docker image:

```
\> docker run -m 256m hello-world
```

The following command allows the hello-world container to use CPU core 1 or CPU core 2:

```
\> docker run –cpuset-cpus="1,2" hello-world
```

E.14 What is happening behind the scenes of docker run?

When we execute the command `docker run` via a Docker client, it talks to an API running on the Docker daemon (see figure E.9). The Docker client and daemon can run on the same host machine or on multiple machines. Once the Docker daemon receives the API request to create and spin up a new container, it internally talks to another component called the containerd, which we discussed earlier in this appendix.

Containerd finds the corresponding Docker image, based on the image name, which comes along with the API request; converts it to an OCI bundle; and then passes control to the containerd-shim component. Containerd-shim forks a runc process, which internally talks to the operating system kernel to create and run the container. Runc starts the container as a child process, and once the container starts running, runc kills itself. Figure E.9 illustrates the flow of spinning up a container.

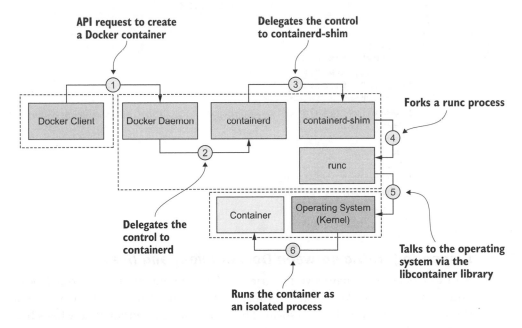

Figure E.9   Behind the scenes of a `docker run` command

In section E.3, we used the following command to run the hello-world process in a container:

```
\> docker run hello-world
```

As you might have already noticed, when we run the container with this command, the console or the terminal where we run the command automatically gets attached to the container's standard input, output, and errors. This way of running a container, known as *foreground mode*, is the default behavior. If we want to start the container in *detached mode*, we need to pass the –d argument to the docker run command. The output will print the container ID:

```
\> docker run -d hello-world

74dac4e3398410c5f89d01b544aaee1612bb976f4a10b5293017317630f3a47a
```

Once the container starts, we can use the following command to connect to the container with the container ID and get the logs:

```
\> docker container logs 74dac4e3398410c5f89d01b544aaee1612bb…
```

The following is another useful command to inspect the status and properties of a running container:

```
\> docker container inspect 74dac4e3398410c5f89d01b544aaee1612bb…

[
  {
    "Id": "74dac4e3398410c5f89d01b544aaee1612bb976f4",
    "Created": "2019-05-22T18:29:47.992128412Z",
    "Path": "/hello",
      "Args": [],
      "State": {
          "Status": "exited",
          "Running": false,
          "Paused": false,
          "Restarting": false,
          "OOMKilled": false,
          "Dead": false,
          "Pid": 0,
          "ExitCode": 0,
          "Error": "",
          "StartedAt": "2019-05-22T18:29:48.609133534Z",
          "FinishedAt": "2019-05-22T18:29:48.70655394Z"
      },
  }
]
```

E.15   *Inspecting traffic between Docker client and host*

All the Docker commands you've tried so far are generated from your Docker client and sent to the Docker host. Let's inspect the traffic between the Docker client and the host by using a tool called socat. This tool helps you understand what's happening underneath.

First, you need to install socat on your operating system. If you're on a Mac, you can use brew, or if you're on Debian/Ubuntu Linux, you can use apt-get. The best way to find the installation steps is to search Google for *socat* with your operating system name. (We couldn't find a single place that carries installation instructions for all the operating systems.) Once you have socat (and all the other dependencies) installed, you can use the following command to run it:

```
\> socat -d -d -v TCP-L:2345,fork,bind=127.0.01 UNIX:/var/run/docker.sock

2019/06/24 23:37:32 socat[36309] N listening on LEN=16 AF=2 127.0.0.1:2345
```

The `-d  -d` flags in this command ask socat to print all fatal, error, warning, and notice messages. If you add another `-d`, it also prints informational messages. The manual (man page) of socat provides these details:

- The `-v` flag instructs socat to write the transferred data to its target streams and also to stderr.
- The `TCP-L:2345` flag instructs socat to listen in on port 2345 for TCP traffic.
- The `fork` flag enables socat to handle each arriving packet by its own sub-process. When we use `fork`, socat creates a new process for each accepted connection.
- The `bind=127.0.0.1` flag instructs socat to listen only on the loopback interface, so no one outside the host machine can directly talk to socat.
- `UNIX:/var/run/docker.sock` is the address of the network socket where the Docker daemon accepts connections.

In effect, the command asks socat to listen for TCP traffic on port 2345, log it, and forward the logs to the UNIX socket /var/run/docker.sock. By default, the Docker client is configured to talk to a UNIX socket. But to intercept traffic between the client and the Docker host, we need to instruct the Docker client to send requests via socat. You can run the following command to override the `DOCKER_HOST` environment variable and point it to socat:

```
\> export DOCKER_HOST=localhost:2345
```

Let's run the following Docker command from the same terminal where you exported the `DOCKER_HOST` environment variable, to find all the Docker images available in the Docker host:

```
\> docker images
```

While running the command, also observe the terminal that runs socat. There you'll find printed request and response messages between the Docker client and host. Without going through the `docker images` command, you can get the same results from the following `curl` command (assuming the Docker daemon and socat are running on `localhost`) by talking to the Docker API:

```
\> curl http://localhost:2345/v1.39/images/json
```

To reset the `DOCKER_HOST` environment variable, run the following command. Now your system will start to function as it was before, and the Docker client will directly talk to the Docker host without going through socat:

```
\> export DOCKER_HOST=
```

E.16   *Docker Compose*

Docker Compose is an open source tool (not part of Docker Engine) written in Python that helps you manage multicontainer applications. For example, your application may have a microservice, a database, and a message queue. Each component runs in its own container. Rather than managing those containers independently, we can create a single YAML file called docker-compose.yaml and define all the required parameters and dependencies there. To start the application with all three containers, we need to run only a single command, `docker-compose up`, from the directory where you have the docker-compose.yaml file.

By default, `docker-compose` looks for a file with the name docker-compose.yaml in its current directory, but you can override the default behavior with the `-f` argument and pass the name of the YAML file (`docker-compose -f my-docker-compose .yaml up`). The following listing shows a sample docker-compose.yaml file.

Listing E.3   The docker-compose.yaml file

```
version: '3'
services:
 zookeeper:
  image: wurstmeister/zookeeper
 kafka:
  image: wurstmeister/kafka
  ports:
  - "9092:9092"
  environment:
   KAFKA_ADVERTISED_HOST_NAME: localhost
   KAFKA_ZOOKEEPER_CONNECT: zookeeper:2181
  depends_on:
  - "zookeeper"
 sts:
  image: prabath/manning-sts-appendix-e
  ports:
  - "8443:8443"
  depends_on:
  - "kafka"
```

This docker-compose.yaml file defines three containers for the application. The STS is a microservice that issues tokens, and it depends on Apache Kafka, which is a message broker. Kafka, internally, depends on Apache ZooKeeper for distributed configuration management. Effectively, to run our STS application, we need three Docker images. We can start all three containers with the single `docker-compose up` command.

A detailed discussion on Docker Compose is beyond the scope of this book. If you're still keen on understanding Docker Compose in detail, refer to the online documentation (https://docs.docker.com/compose/overview/) or chapter 11 of *Docker in Action.*

E.17 Docker Swarm

In practice, when we run Docker in production, we may have hundreds of Docker containers running in multiple nodes. A *node* can be a physical machine or a VM. Also, thinking in terms of high availability of the application we run in a container, we need to have multiple replicas of the same application running in different containers. To determine the number of replicas for a given application, we need to know how much load (traffic) one single container can handle, as well as the average and peak loads that our system gets. It's desirable that we run the minimal number of replicas to handle the average load and then autoscale (spin up more replicas) as the load increases. With this approach, we waste a minimal amount of system resources.

Docker Swarm addresses most of these concerns and more. This feature has been part of Docker Engine since Docker 1.12; prior to that, it was an independent product. Docker Swarm has two main objectives: to manage a multinode Docker cluster, and to act as an orchestration engine for Docker containers. These features are built into Docker with the open source project called SwarmKit (https://github.com/docker/swarmkit/).

Let's revisit the high-level Docker architecture we discussed in section E.3. Figure E.10 (which is the same as figure E.5 shown previously) depicts only a single Docker node. If we want to run a container, the Docker client over an API talks directly to the Docker host to run the container. In a Docker cluster with multiple nodes, it's impractical for our Docker client to talk to multiple Docker hosts and schedule to run a container. This is one very basic limitation, and there are many ways of addressing this requirement, as we discussed at the beginning of this section. The architecture presented in figure E.10 won't work anymore in a Docker cluster.

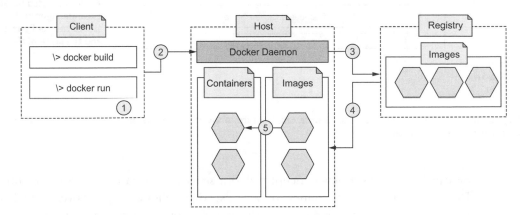

Figure E.10   In this high-level Docker component architecture, the Docker client talks to the Docker daemon running on the Docker host over a REST API to perform various operations on Docker images and containers.

The new architecture that Docker Swarm proposes (figure E.11) introduces a set of manager nodes and a set of worker nodes. In other words, a Docker cluster is a collection of manager and worker nodes.

The *manager nodes* in a cluster are responsible for managing the state of the cluster. For example, if our requirement is to run five replicas of a given application, the manager nodes must make sure that happens. Also, if our requirement is to spin up more replicas as the load goes up, and spin down replicas as the load goes down, the manager nodes should generate the control signals to handle those situations by monitoring the load on a particular application. The responsibility of the *worker nodes* is to accept control signals from manager nodes and to act accordingly. In fact, containers run on worker nodes.

To schedule an application to run on the Docker cluster, the Docker client talks to one of the manager nodes. The set of manager nodes in a cluster is collectively known as the *control plane*.

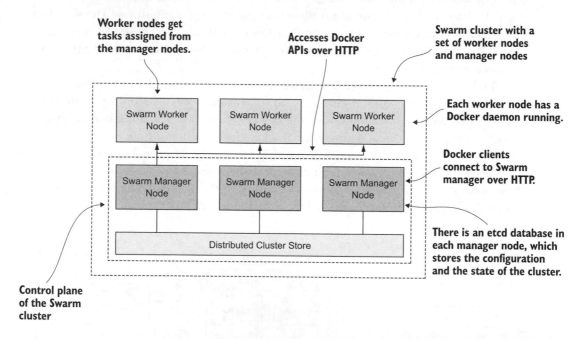

Figure E.11   In this high-level Docker Swarm architecture, a Swarm cluster is built with a set of manager nodes and a set of worker nodes.

Swarm introduces a new concept called a *service*: the smallest deployment unit in a Docker cluster, not a container. In fact, a service builds a wrapper over a Docker container. A container wrapped in a service is also known as a *replica*, or a *task*.

We use the `docker service create` command to create a Docker service. In addition to the image name, port mapping, and other arguments that we use in the docker run command, the docker service create command also accepts other parameters, which you can check with the command docker service create -help. The replicas argument in the following command asks Swarm to create five replicas of the corresponding service (or the application):

```
\> docker service create –name hello-service –replicas 5 hello-world
```

An in-depth walk-through of Swarm is beyond the scope of this book. If you're interested in reading more, we recommend checking out chapter 12 of *Docker in Action*. The online documentation on Docker Swarm is another good place to start; you'll find that at https://docs.docker.com/engine/swarm/key-concepts/.

E.18 Docker networking

As discussed in section E.13.4, the NET namespace in the Linux kernel provides an isolated networking stack with all the routes, firewall rules, and network devices for a container. In other words, a Docker container has its own networking stack. Docker networking is implemented with the libnetwork open source library written in the Go programming language and based on the Container Network Model (CNM) design specification. CNM defines core building blocks for Docker networking (figure E.12), which are the sandbox, endpoint, and network.

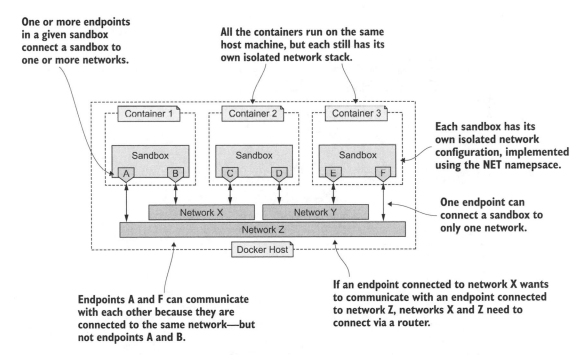

Figure E.12 Docker follows the Container Network Model design for networking, which defines three building blocks: sandbox, endpoint, and network.

A *sandbox* is an abstraction over an isolated networking configuration. For example, each container has its own network sandbox with routing tables, firewall rules, and Domain Name System (DNS) configurations. Docker implements a sandbox with the NET namespace. An *endpoint* represents a network interface, and each sandbox has its own set of endpoints. These virtual network interfaces (or endpoints) connect a sandbox to the network. A set of endpoints that needs to communicate with each other forms a *network*. By default, Docker supports three networking modes: bridge, host, and none. The following command lists the supported Docker networks:

```
\> docker network ls

NETWORK ID          NAME                DRIVER              SCOPE
f8c9f194e5b7        bridge              bridge              local
a2b417db8f94        host                host                local
583a0756310a        none                null                local
```

The following listing uses the network ID to get further details of a given network.

Listing E.4   The details of a bridge network

```
\> docker network inspect f8c9f194e5b7

[
 {
  "Name": "bridge",
  "Id": "f8c9f194e5b70c305b3eb938600f9caa8f5ed11439bc313f7245f76e0769ebf6",
  "Created": "2019-02-26T00:20:44.364736531Z",
  "Scope": "local",
  "Driver": "bridge",
  "EnableIPv6": false,
  "IPAM": {
    "Driver": "default",
    "Options": null,
    "Config": [
       {
        "Subnet": "172.17.0.0/16",
        "Gateway": "172.17.0.1"
       }
    ]
   },
  "Internal": false,
  "Attachable": false,
  "Ingress": false,
  "ConfigFrom": {
    "Network": ""
  },
  "ConfigOnly": false,
  "Containers": {},
  "Options": {
     "com.docker.network.bridge.default_bridge": "true",
     "com.docker.network.bridge.enable_icc": "true",
     "com.docker.network.bridge.enable_ip_masquerade": "true",
```

```
      "com.docker.network.bridge.host_binding_ipv4": "0.0.0.0",
      "com.docker.network.bridge.name": "docker0",
      "com.docker.network.driver.mtu": "1500"
    },
    "Labels": {}
  }
]
```

E.18.1 *Bridge networking*

Bridge networking in Docker uses Linux bridging and iptables to build connectivity between containers running on the same host machine. It's the default networking mode in Docker. When Docker spins up a new container, it's attached to a private IP address.

If you already have the hello-world container running from section E.3, the following two commands help find the private IP address attached to it. The first command finds the container ID corresponding to hello-world, and the second command uses it to inspect the container. The output of the second command is truncated to show only the network configuration:

```
\> docker ps

CONTAINER ID    IMAGE                STATUS            PORTS
b410162d213e    hello-world Up About a minute    0.0.0.0:8443->8443/tcp

\> docker inspect b410162d213e

[
  {
    {
      "Networks": {
        "bridge": {
          "Gateway": "172.17.0.1",
          "IPAddress": "172.17.0.2",
          "IPPrefixLen": 16,
          "IPv6Gateway": "",
          "GlobalIPv6Address": "",
          "GlobalIPv6PrefixLen": 0,
          "MacAddress": "02:42:ac:11:00:02"
        }
      }
    }
  }
]
```

The private IP address assigned to a container is not accessible directly from the host machine. When one container talks to another container in the same host machine with the private address, the connection is routed through the docker0 bridge-networking interface, as shown in figure E.13.

For the communications among containers on the same host machine, an IP address isn't the best option. IP addresses can change dynamically when containers

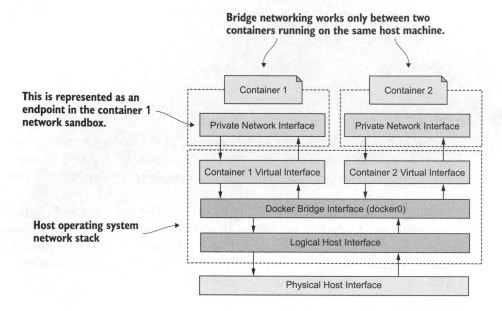

Figure E.13   Containers use the bridge-networking interface provided by Docker to communicate with each other.

spin up and down. Instead of the private address, we can use the container's name itself to communicate among containers. This is one benefit of giving a container a meaningful name (rather than relying on a randomly generated UUID by Docker) at the time we spin up a container.

E.18.2 Host networking

To facilitate communication among containers, *host networking* is the laziest option in Docker. When host networking is enabled for a given container, it uses the host machine's networking stack directly and shares the network namespace with the host machine. To enable host networking, we need to pass the network argument to the docker run command with the value host; for example:

```
\> docker run --network="host" hello-world
```

E.18.3 No networking

No networking mode disables all the networking interfaces available for a given container. It's a closed container. You would need a container with no networking to carry out certain specific tasks; for example, to process a set of log files in one format and then output into another format. To disable networking, we need to pass the --network argument to the docker run command with the value none like so:

```
\> docker run --network="none" hello-world
```

E.18.4 *Networking in a Docker production deployment*

Bridge networking works in only a single host environment or, in other words, only among the containers deployed on the same host machine. In a production deployment, this isn't sufficient, and containers have to interact with each other running on different host machines. Container orchestration frameworks like Kubernetes and Docker Swarm support multihost networking in Docker. Docker Swarm supports multihost container communications with Docker overlay networking, and in chapter 11, we discuss in detail how Kubernetes supports multihost networking.

E.19 *Moby project*

Docker Inc. announced the *Moby project* during its annual user conference, Docker-Con, in 2017. With this announcement, the Docker GitHub project moved from github.com/docker/docker to github.com/moby/moby.

The *Moby project* aims to expand the Docker ecosystem by breaking the old monolithic Docker project into multiple components. Developers from various other projects can reuse these components to build their own container-based systems. You can read more on the Moby project at https://blog.docker.com/2017/04/introducing-the-moby-project/.

appendix F
Open Policy Agent

In a typical microservices deployment, we can enforce access-control policies in either of the following two locations or both:

- *The edge of the deployment*—Typically, with an API gateway (which we discuss in chapter 5)
- *The edge of the service*—Typically, with a service mesh or with a set of embedded libraries (which we discuss in chapter 7 and chapter 12)

Authorization at the service level enables each service to enforce access-control policies in the way it wants. Typically, you apply coarse-grained access-control policies at the API gateway (at the edge), and more fine-grained access-control policies at the service level. Also, it's common to do data-level entitlements at the service level. For example, at the edge of the deployment, we can check whether a given user is eligible to perform an HTTP GET for the Order Processing microservice. But the data entitlement checks, such as only an order admin can view orders having a transaction amount greater than $10,000, are enforced at the service level.

In this appendix, we discuss key components of an access-control system, access-control patterns, and how to define and enforce access-control policies by using *Open Policy Agent* (*OPA*). OPA (www.openpolicyagent.org) is an open source, lightweight, general-purpose policy engine with no dependency on microservices. You can use OPA to define fine-grained access-control policies and enforce those policies at different locations across your infrastructure as well as within a microservices deployment. We discussed OPA briefly in chapter 5. In this appendix, we delve deep into the details. We also assume that you've already gone through chapters 5, 7, 10, 11, and 12, and have a good understanding of containers, Kubernetes, Istio, and JWT.

F.1 Key components in an access-control system

In a typical access-control system, we find five key components (figure F.1): the policy administration point (PAP), policy enforcement point (PEP), policy decision

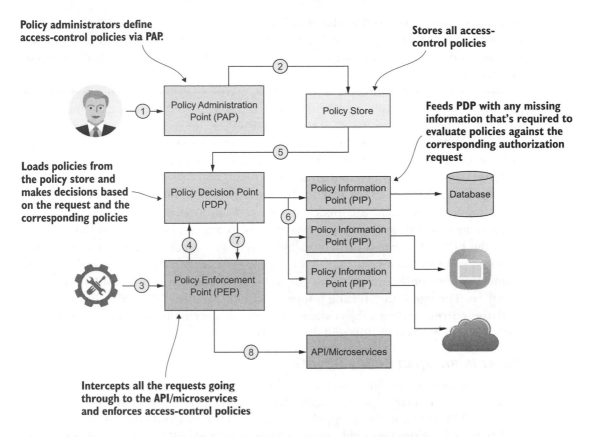

Policy administrators define access-control policies via PAP.

Stores all access-control policies

Feeds PDP with any missing information that's required to evaluate policies against the corresponding authorization request

Loads policies from the policy store and makes decisions based on the request and the corresponding policies

Intercepts all the requests going through to the API/microservices and enforces access-control policies

Figure F.1 Components of a typical access-control system. The PAP defines access-control policies and then stores those in the policy store. At runtime, the PEP intercepts all the requests, builds an authorization request, and talks to the PDP. The PDP loads the policies from the policy store and any other missing information from the PIP, evaluates the policies, and passes the decision back to the PEP.

point (PDP), policy information point (PIP), and policy store. The PAP is the component that lets policy administrators and developers define access-control policies.

Most of the time, PAP implementations come with their own user interface or expose the functionality via an API. Some access-control systems don't have a specific PAP; rather, they read policies directly from the filesystem, so you need to use third-party tools to author these policies. Once you define the policies via a PAP, the PAP writes the policies to a policy store. The policy store can be a database, a filesystem, or even a service that's exposed via HTTP.

The PEP sits between the service/API, which you want to protect, and the client application. At runtime, the PEP intercepts all the communications between the client application and the service. As we discussed in chapter 3, the PEP can be an API gateway, or as we discussed in chapters 7 and 8, it can be some kind of an interceptor embedded into your application itself. And in chapter 12, we discussed how in a service mesh deployment, a proxy can be used as a PEP that intercepts all the requests coming to your microservice.

When the PEP intercepts a request, it extracts certain parameters from the request—such as the user, resource, action, and so on—and creates an authorization request. Then it talks to the PDP to check whether the request is authorized. If it's authorized, the PDP dispatches the request to the corresponding service or to the API; otherwise, it returns an error to the client application. Before the request hits the PEP, we assume it's properly authenticated.

When the PEP talks to the PDP to check authorization, the PDP loads all the corresponding policies from the policy store. And while evaluating an authorization request against the applicable policies, if there is any required but missing information, the PDP will talk to a PIP. For example, let's say we have an access-control policy that says you can buy a beer only if your age is greater than 21, but the authorization request carries only your name as the subject, buy as the action, and beer as the resource. The age is the missing information here, and the PDP will talk to a PIP to find the corresponding subject's age. We can connect multiple PIPs to a PDP, and each PIP can connect to different data sources.

F.2   *What is an Open Policy Agent?*

As we discussed in the introduction to this appendix, OPA is an open source, light-weight, general-purpose policy engine that has no dependency on microservices. You can use OPA to define fine-grained access-control policies and enforce those policies at different locations throughout your infrastructure as well as within a microservices deployment. To define access-control policies, OPA introduces a new declarative language called Rego (www.openpolicyagent.org/docs/latest/policy-language).

OPA started as an open source project in 2016, with a goal to unify policy enforcement across multiple heterogeneous technology stacks. Netflix, one of the early adopters of OPA, uses it to enforce access-control policies in its microservices deployment. Apart from Netflix, Cloudflare, Pinterest, Intuit, Capital One, State Street, and many more use OPA. At the time of this writing, OPA is an incubating project under the Cloud Native Computing Foundation (CNCF).

F.3   *OPA high-level architecture*

In this section, we discuss how OPA's high-level architecture fits into our discussion. As you can see in figure F.2, the OPA engine can run on its own as a standalone deployment or as an embedded library along with an application.

When you run the OPA server as a standalone deployment, it exposes a set of REST APIs that PEPs can connect to and check authorization. In figure F.2, the OPA engine acts as the PDP.

The open source distribution of the OPA server doesn't come with a policy authoring tool or a user interface to create and publish policies to the OPA server. But you

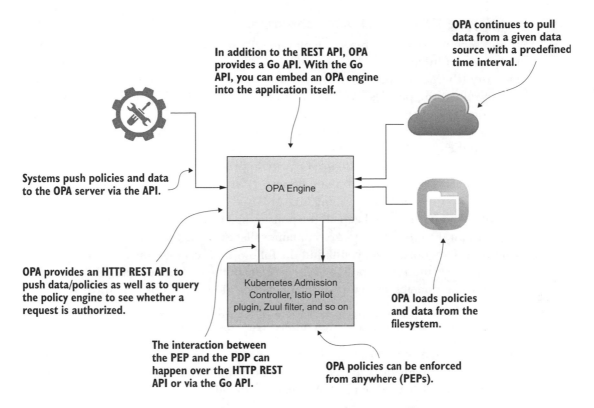

Figure F.2 An application or a PEP can integrate with the OPA policy engine via its HTTP REST API or via the Go API.

can use a tool like Visual Studio (VS) Code to create OPA policies, and OPA has a plugin for VS Code. If you decide to embed the OPA server (instead of using it as a hosted server) as a library in your application, you can use the Go API (provided by OPA) to interact with it.

Once you have the policies, you can use the OPA API to publish them to the OPA server. When you publish those policies via the API, the OPA engine keeps them in memory only. You'll need to build a mechanism to publish policies every time the server boots up. The other option is to copy the policy files to the filesystem behind OPA, and the OPA server will pick them up when it boots up. If any policy changes occur, you'll need to restart the OPA server. However, there is an option to ask the OPA server to load policies dynamically from the filesystem, but that's not recommended in a production deployment. Also, you can load policies to the OPA server by using a bundle server; we discuss that in detail in section F.7.

OPA has a PIP design to bring in external data to the PDP or to the OPA engine. This model is quite similar to the model we discussed in the previous paragraph with respect to policies. In section F.7, we detail how OPA brings in external data.

F.4   *Deploying OPA as a Docker container*

In this section, we discuss how to deploy an OPA server as a Docker container. In OPA, there are multiple ways of loading policies. Importantly, OPA stores those policies in memory (there is no persistence), so that on a restart or redeployment, OPA needs a way to reload the policies. For example, when we use OPA for the Kubernetes admission control, policies are persisted in the Kubernetes API server, and OPA has its own sidecar that loads policies via OPA's REST API. That's roughly the approach we followed in section 5.3. In using OPA in a microservices deployment, the most common approaches are to either configure OPA to download policies via the bundle API (for example, using AWS's S3 as the bundle server) or use volume/bind mounts to mount policies into the container running OPA.

With bind mounts, we keep all the policies in a directory in the host filesystem and then mount it to the OPA Docker container filesystem. If you look at the appendix-f/sample01/run_opa.sh file, you'll find the following Docker command (do not try it as it is). Here, we mount the policies directory from the current location of the host filesystem to the policies directory of the container filesystem under the root:

```
\> docker run --mount type=bind,source="$(pwd)"/policies,target=/policies \
-p 8181:8181 openpolicyagent/opa:0.15.0 run /policies --server
```

To start the OPA server, run the following command from the appendix-f/sample01 directory. This loads the OPA policies from the appendix-f/sample01/policies directory (in section F.6, we discuss OPA policies in detail):

```
\> sh run_opa.sh

{
  "addrs":[
    ":8181"
  ],
  "insecure_addr":"",
  "level":"info",
  "msg":"Initializing server.",
  "time":"2019-11-05T07:19:34Z"
}
```

You can run the following command from the appendix-f/sample01 directory to test the OPA server. The appendix-f/sample01/policy_1_input_1.json file carries the input data for the authorization request in JSON format (in section F.6, we discuss authorization requests in detail):

```
\> curl -v -X POST --data-binary @policy_1_input_1.json \
http://localhost:8181/v1/data/authz/orders/policy1

{"result":{"allow":true}}
```

The process of deploying OPA in Kubernetes is similar to deploying any other service on Kubernetes, as we discuss in appendix J. You can check the OPA documentation available at http://mng.bz/MdDD for details.

F.5   *Protecting an OPA server with mTLS*

OPA was designed to run on the same server as the microservice that needs authorization decisions. As such, the first layer of defense for microservice-to-OPA communication is the fact that the communication is limited to localhost. OPA is a host-local cache of the relevant policies authored in the PAP and recorded in the policy store. To make a decision, OPA is often self-contained and can make the decision all on its own without reaching out to other servers.

This means that decisions are highly available and highly performant, for the simple reason that OPA shares a fate with the microservice that needs authorization decisions and requires no network hop for those decisions. Nevertheless, OPA recommends defense in depth and ensuring that communication between it and its microservice or other clients is secured via mTLS.

In this section, we discuss how to protect the OPA server with mTLS. This will ensure all the communications that happen among the OPA server and other client applications are encrypted. Also, only legitimate clients with proper keys can talk to the OPA server. To protect the OPA server with mTLS, we need to accomplish the following tasks:

- Generate a public/private key pair for the OPA server
- Generate a public/private key pair for the OPA client
- Generate a public/private key pair for the CA
- Sign the public key of the OPA server with the CA's private key to generate the OPA server's public certificate
- Sign the public key of the OPA client with the CA's private key to generate the OPA client's public certificate

To perform all these tasks, we can use the appendix-f/sample01/keys/gen-key.sh script with OpenSSL. Let's run the following Docker command from the appendix-f/sample01/keys directory to spin up an OpenSSL Docker container. You'll see that we mount the current location (which is appendix-f/sample01/keys) from the host filesystem to the /export directory on the container filesystem:

```
\> docker run -it -v $(pwd):/export prabath/openssl
#
```

Once the container boots up successfully, you'll find a command prompt where you can type OpenSSL commands. Let's run the following command to execute the gen-key.sh file that runs a set of OpenSSL commands:

```
# sh /export/gen-key.sh
```

Once this command executes successfully, you'll find the keys corresponding to the CA in the appendix-f/sample01/keys/ca directory, the keys corresponding to the OPA server in the appendix-f/sample01/keys/opa directory, and the keys corresponding to the OPA client in the appendix-f/sample01/keys/client directory. If you want to understand the exact OpenSSL commands we ran during key generation, check appendix G.

In case you're already running the OPA server, stop it by pressing Ctrl-C on the corresponding command console. To start the OPA server with TLS support, use the following command from the appendix-f/sample01 directory:

```
\> sh run_opa_tls.sh

{
  "addrs":[
    ":8181"
  ],
  "insecure_addr":"",
  "level":"info",
  "msg":"Initializing server.",
  "time":"2019-11-05T19:03:11Z"
}
```

You can run the following command from the appendix-f/sample01 directory to test the OPA server. The appendix-f/sample01/policy_1_input_1.json file carries the input data for the authorization request in JSON format. Here we use HTTPS to talk to the OPA server:

```
\> curl -v -k -X POST --data-binary @policy_1_input_1.json \
https://localhost:8181/v1/data/authz/orders/policy1

{"result":{"allow":true}}
```

Let's check what's in the run_opa_tls.sh script, shown in the following listing. The code annotations in the listing explain what each argument means.

Listing F.1   Protecting an OPA server endpoint with TLS

```
\> docker run \
      -v "$(pwd)"/policies:/policies \
      -v "$(pwd)"/keys:/keys \
      -p 8181:8181 \
      openpolicyagent/opa:0.15.0 \
      run /policies \
      --tls-cert-file /keys/opa/opa.cert \
      --tls-private-key-file /keys/opa/opa.key \
      --server
```

Annotations:
- Instructs the OPA server to load policies from policies directory, which is mounted to the OPA container
- The OPA server finds key/certificate for the TLS communication from the keys directory, which is mounted to the OPA container.
- Port mapping maps the container port to the host port.
- Name of the OPA Docker image
- Starts the OPA engine under the server mode
- Private key used for the TLS communication
- Runs the OPA server by loading policies and data from the policies directory, which is mounted to the OPA container
- Certificate used for the TLS communication

Now the communication between the OPA server and the OPA client (curl) is protected with TLS. But still, anyone having access to the OPA server's IP address can access it over TLS. There are two ways to protect the OPA endpoint for authentication: token authentication and mTLS.

With token-based authentication, the client has to pass an OAuth 2.0 token in the HTTP Authorization header as a bearer token, and you also need to write an authorization policy.[1] In this section, we focus on securing the OPA endpoint with mTLS.

If you're already running the OPA server, stop it by pressing Ctrl-C on the corresponding command console. To start the OPA server enabling mTLS, run the following command from the appendix-f/sample01 directory:

```
\> sh run_opa_mtls.sh
```

Let's check what's in the run_opa_mtls.sh script, shown in the following listing. The code annotations explain what each argument means.

Listing F.2 Protecting an OPA server endpoint with mTLS

```
\> docker run \
      -v "$(pwd)"/policies:/policies \
      -v "$(pwd)"/keys:/keys \
      -p 8181:8181 \
      openpolicyagent/opa:0.15.0 \
      run /policies \
      --tls-cert-file /keys/opa/opa.cert \           The public certificate of the CA.
      --tls-private-key-file /keys/opa/opa.key \     All the OPA clients must carry
      --tls-ca-cert-file /keys/ca/ca.cert \          a certificate signed by this CA.
      --authentication=tls \        Enables mTLS
      --server                      authentication
```

You can use the following command from the appendix-f/sample01 directory to test the OPA server, which is now secured with mTLS:

```
\> curl -k -v --key keys/client/client.key \
--cert keys/client/client.cert -X POST \
--data-binary @policy_1_input_1.json \
https://localhost:8181/v1/data/authz/orders/policy1
```

Here, we use HTTPS to talk to the OPA server, along with the certificate and the key generated for the OPA client at the start of this section. The key and the certificate of the OPA client are available in the appendix-f/sample01/keys/client directory.

F.6 *OPA policies*

To define access-control policies, OPA introduces a new declarative language called Rego.[2] In this section, we go through a set of OPA policies (listing F.3) to understand the strength of the Rego language. All the policies we discuss here are available in the

---

[1] This policy is explained at www.openpolicyagent.org/docs/latest/security/.
[2] You can find more details about Rego at www.openpolicyagent.org/docs/latest/policy-language/.

appendix-f/sample01/policies directory and are already loaded into the OPA server we booted up in section F.5, which is protected with mTLS.

Listing F.3   OPA policy written in Rego

> The package name of the policy. Packages let you organize your policies into modules, just as with programming languages.

```
package authz.orders.policy1

default allow = false

allow {
  input.method = "POST"
  input.path = "orders"
  input.role = "manager"
}

allow {
  input.method = "POST"
  input.path = ["orders",dept_id]
  input.deptid = dept_id
  input.role = "dept_manager"
}
```

> By default, all requests are disallowed. If this isn't set and no allowed rules are matched, OPA returns an undefined decision.

> Declares the conditions to allow access to the resource

> The Input document is an arbitrary JSON object handed to OPA and includes use-case-specific information. In this example, the Input document includes a method, path, role, and deptid. This condition requires that the method parameter in the input document must be POST.

> The value of the path parameter in the input document must match this value, where the value of the dept_id is the deptid parameter from the input document.

The policy defined in listing F.3, which you'll find in the policy_1.rego file, has two `allow` rules. For an `allow` rule to return `true`, every statement within the `allow` block must return `true`. The first `allow` rule returns `true` only if a user with the `manager` role is the one doing an HTTP `POST` on the `orders` resource. The second `allow` rule returns `true` if a user with the `dept_manager` role is the one doing an HTTP `POST` on the `orders` resource under their own department.

Let's evaluate this policy with two different input documents. The first is the input document in listing F.4, which you'll find in the policy_1_input_1.json file. Run the following `curl` command from the appendix-f/sample01 directory and it returns `true`, because the inputs in the request match with the first allow rule in the policy (listing F.3):

```
\> curl -k -v --key keys/client/client.key \
--cert keys/client/client.cert -X POST \
--data-binary @policy_1_input_1.json \
https://localhost:8181/v1/data/authz/orders/policy1

{"result":{"allow":true}}
```

Listing F.4   Rego input document with manager role

```
{
    "input":{
      "path":"orders",
      "method":"POST",
```

```
        "role":"manager"
    }
}
```

Let's try with another input document, as shown in listing F.5, which you'll find in the policy_1_input_2.json file. Run the following curl command from the appendix-f/ sample01 directory and it returns true, because the inputs in the request match with the second allow rule in the policy (listing F.3). You can see how the response from OPA server changes by changing the values of the inputs:

```
\> curl -k -v --key keys/client/client.key \
--cert keys/client/client.cert -X POST \
--data-binary @policy_1_input_2.json \
https://localhost:8181/v1/data/authz/orders/policy1

{"result":{"allow":true}}
```

Listing F.5 Rego input document with dept_manager role

```
{
    "input":{
      "path":["orders",1000],
      "method":"POST",
      "deptid":1000,
      "role":"dept_manager"
    }
}
```

Now let's have a look at a slightly improved version of the policy in listing F.3. You can find this new policy in listing F.6, and it's already deployed to the OPA server you're running. Here, our expectation is that if a user has the manager role, they will be able to do HTTP PUTs, POSTs, or DELETEs on any orders resource, and if a user has the dept_manager role, they will be able to do HTTP PUTs, POSTs, or DELETEs only on the orders resource in their own department. Also any user, regardless of the role, should be able to do HTTP GETs to any orders resource under their own account. The annotations in the following listing explain how the policy is constructed.

Listing F.6 Improved OPA policy written in Rego

```
package authz.orders.policy2

default allow = false
                                              Checks whether the value of the method
                                              parameter from the input document is in
allow {                                       the allowed_methods_for_manager set
  allowed_methods_for_manager[input.method] ◄─┘
  input.path = "orders"
  input.role = "manager"                      Checks whether the value of the method
}                                             parameter from the input document is in the
                                              allowed_methods_for_dept_manager set
allow {
  allowed_methods_for_dept_manager[input.method]  ◄─
```

```
    input.deptid = dept_id
    input.path = ["orders",dept_id]
    input.role = "dept_manager"
}

allow {
    input.method = "GET"
    input.empid = emp_id
    input.path = ["orders",emp_id]
}

allowed_methods_for_manager = {"POST","PUT","DELETE"}
allowed_methods_for_dept_manager = {"POST","PUT","DELETE"}
```

> Allows anyone to access the orders resource under their own employee ID

> The definition of the allowed_methods_for_manager set

> The definition of the allowed_methods_for_dept_manager set

Let's evaluate this policy with the input document in listing F.7, which you'll find in the policy_2_input_1.json file. Run the following `curl` command from the appendix-f/sample01 directory and it returns `true`, because the inputs in the request match with the first allow rule in the policy (listing F.6):

```
\> curl -k -v --key keys/client/client.key \
--cert keys/client/client.cert -X POST \
--data-binary @policy_2_input_1.json \
https://localhost:8181/v1/data/authz/orders/policy2

{
  "result":{
    "allow":true,
    "allowed_methods_for_dept_manager":["POST","PUT","DELETE"],
    "allowed_methods_for_manager":["POST","PUT","DELETE"]
  }
}
```

Listing F.7 Rego input document with manager role

```
{
    "input":{
      "path":"orders",
      "method":"PUT",
      "role":"manager"
    }
}
```

You can also try out the same `curl` command as shown here with two other input documents: policy_2_input_2.json and policy_2_input_3.json. You can find these files inside the appendix-f/sample01 directory.

F.7   *External data*

During policy evaluation, sometimes the OPA engine needs access to external data. As we discussed in section F.1 while evaluating an authorization request against the applicable policies, if there is any required but missing information, the OPA server will talk to a PIP (or external data sources). For example, let's say we have an access-control policy that says you can buy a beer only if your age is greater than 21, but the authorization request carries only your name as the subject, buy as the action, and beer as the resource. The age is the missing information here, and the OPA server will talk to an external data source to find the corresponding subject's age. In this section, we discuss multiple approaches OPA provides to bring in external data for policy evaluation.[3]

F.7.1 Push data

The *push data* approach to bring in external data to the OPA server uses the data API provided by the OPA server. Let's look at a simple example. This is the same example we used in section 5.3. The policy in listing F.8 returns `true` if `method`, `path`, and the set of `scopes` in the input message match some data read from an external data source that's loaded under the package named `data.order_policy_data`.

> **Listing F.8   OPA policy using pushed external data**

```
package authz.orders.policy3          ◄─┐ The package name
                                         of the policy

import data.order_policy_data as policies   ◄─┐ Declares the set of statically
                                               registered data identified as policies

default allow = false          ◄─ By default, all requests are disallowed. If
                                  this isn't set and no allowed rules matched,
                                  OPA returns an undefined decision.

allow {                        ◄─
  policy = policies[_]                      ◄ Iterates over values in the policies array
  policy.method = input.method   ◄─┐ Declares the conditions to
  policy.path = input.path          allow access to the resource
  policy.scopes[_] = input.scopes[_]
}
```

For an element in the policies array, checks whether the value of the method parameter in the input matches the method element of the policy

This policy consumes all the external data from the JSON file appendix-f/sample01/order_policy_data.json (listing F.9), which we need to push to the OPA server using the OPA data API. Assuming your OPA server is running on port 8181, you can run the following `curl` command from the appendix-f/sample01 directory to publish the data to the OPA server. Keep in mind that here we're pushing only external data, not the policy. The policy that consumes the data is already on the OPA server, which you can find in the appendix-f/sample01/policies/policy_3.rego file:

```
\> curl -k -v --key keys/client/client.key \
--cert keys/client/client.cert -H "Content-Type: application/json" \
-X PUT --data-binary @order_policy_data.json \
https://localhost:8181/v1/data/order_policy_data
```

---

[3] A detailed discussion of these approaches is documented at www.openpolicyagent.org/docs/latest/external-data/.

Listing F.9   Order Processing resources defined as OPA data

```
[
{                                    An identifier for
  "id": "r1",              ◁────────  the resource path
  "path": "orders",                             The resource
  "method": "POST",                    ◁─────── path
  "scopes": ["create_order"]           ◁─────── The HTTP
},                                              method
{
  "id": "r2",                         To do an HTTP POST to the orders
  "path": "orders",                   resource, you must have this scope.
  "method": "GET",
  "scopes": ["retrieve_orders"]
},
{
  "id": "r3",
  "path": "orders/{order_id}",
  "method": "PUT",
  "scopes": ["update_order"]
}
]
```

Now you can run the following `curl` command from the appendix-f/sample01 directory with the input message, which you'll find in the JSON file appendix-f/sample01/
policy_3_input_1.json (in listing F.10) to check if the request is authorized:

```
\> curl -k -v --key keys/client/client.key \
--cert keys/client/client.cert -X POST \
--data-binary @policy_3_input_1.json \
https://localhost:8181/v1/data/authz/orders/policy3

{"result":{"allow":true}}
```

Listing F.10   OPA input document

```
{
  "input":{
    "path":"orders",
    "method":"GET",
    "scopes":["retrieve_orders"]
  }
}
```

With the push data approach, you control when you want to push the data to the OPA
server. For example, when the external data gets updated, you can push the updated
data to the OPA server. This approach, however, has its own limitations. When you use
the data API to push external data into the OPA server, the OPA server keeps the data
in cache (in memory), and when you restart the server, you need to push the data
again. Nevertheless, this is the approach used within the Kubernetes admission control use case, where there is a sidecar running next to OPA that synchronizes the state
of OPA with external data.

F.7.2 *Loading data from the filesystem*

In this section, we discuss how to load external data from the filesystem. When we start the OPA server, we need to specify from which directory on the filesystem the OPA server should load data files and policies. Let's have a look at the appendix-f/ sample-01/run_opa_mtls.sh shell script, shown in the following listing. The code annotations explain how OPA loads policies from the filesystem at startup.

Listing F.11 Loading policies at startup

```
docker run \
      -v "$(pwd)"/policies:/policies \
      -v "$(pwd)"/keys:/keys \
      -p 8181:8181 \
      openpolicyagent/opa:0.15.0 \
      run /policies \
      --tls-cert-file /keys/opa/opa.cert \
      --tls-private-key-file /keys/opa/opa.key \
      --tls-ca-cert-file /keys/ca/ca.cert \
      --authentication=tls \
      --server
```

◁—— **A Docker bind mount, which mounts the policies directory under the current path of the host machine to the policies directory of the container filesystem**

◁—— **Runs the OPA server by loading policies and data from the policies directory**

The OPA server you already have running has the policy and the data we're going to discuss in this section. Let's first check the external data file (order_policy_data_ from_file.json), which is available in the appendix-f/sample01/policies directory. This is the same file you saw in listing F.9 except for a slight change to the file's structure. You can find the updated data file in the following listing.

Listing F.12 Order Processing resources defined as data with a root element

```
{"order_policy_data_from_file" :[
    {
      "id": "p1",
      "path": "orders",
      "method": "POST",
      "scopes": ["create_order"]
    },
    {
      "id": "p2",
      "path": "orders",
      "method": "GET",
      "scopes": ["retrieve_orders"]
    },
    {
      "id": "p3",
      "path": "orders/{order_id}",
      "method": "PUT",
      "scopes": ["update_order"]
    }
  ]
}
```

You can see in the JSON payload that we have a root element called `order_policy_data_from_file`. The OPA server derives the package name corresponding to this data set as `data.order_policy_data_from_file`, which is used in the policy in the following listing. This policy is exactly the same as in listing F.8 except the package name has changed.

Listing F.13   OPA policy using pushed external data

```
package authz.orders.polic4

import data.order_policy_data_from_file as policies

default allow = false

allow {
  policy = policies[_]
  policy.method = input.method
  policy.path = input.path
  policy.scopes[_] = input.scopes[_]
}
```

Now you can run the following `curl` command from the appendix-f/sample01 directory with the input message (appendix-f/sample01/policy_4_input_1.json) from listing F.10 to check whether the request is authorized:

```
\> curl -k -v --key keys/client/client.key \
--cert keys/client/client.cert -X POST \
--data-binary @policy_4_input_1.json \
https://localhost:8181/v1/data/authz/orders/policy4

{"result":{"allow":true}}
```

One issue with loading data from the filesystem is that when there's any update, you need to restart the OPA server. There is, however, a configuration option (see appendix-f/sample01/run_opa_mtls_watch.sh) to ask the OPA server to load policies dynamically (without a restart), but that option isn't recommended for production deployments. In practice, if you deploy an OPA server in a Kubernetes environment, you can keep all your policies and data in a Git repository and use an init container along with the OPA server in the same Pod to pull all the policies and data from Git when you boot up the corresponding Pod. This process is the same as the approach we discussed in section 11.2.7 to load keystores. And when there's an update to the policies or data, we need to restart the Pods.

F.7.3   *Overload*

The *overload* approach to bringing in external data to the OPA server uses the input document itself. When the PEP builds the authorization request, it can embed external data into the request. Say, for example, the orders API knows, for anyone wanting to do an HTTP POST to it, they need to have the `create_order` scope. Rather than pre-provisioning all the scope data into the OPA server, the PEP can send it along with the authorization request. Let's have a look at a slightly modified version of the policy in listing F.8. You can find the updated policy in the following listing.

Listing F.14   OPA policy using external data that comes with the request

```
package authz.orders.policy5

import input.external as policy

default allow = false

allow {
  policy.method = input.method
  policy.path = input.path
  policy.scopes[_] = input.scopes[_]
}
```

You can see that we used the `input.external` package name to load the external data from the input document. Let's look at the input document in the following listing, which carries the external data with it.

Listing F.15   OPA request carrying external data

```
{
    "input":{
      "path":"orders",
      "method":"GET",
      "scopes":["retrieve_orders"],
      "external" : {
            "id": "r2",
            "path": "orders",
            "method": "GET",
            "scopes": ["retrieve_orders"]
      }
    }
}
```

Now you can run the following `curl` command from the appendix-f/sample01 directory with the input message from listing F.15 (appendix-f/sample01/policy_5_input_1.json) to check whether the request is authorized:

```
\> curl -k -v --key keys/client/client.key \
--cert keys/client/client.cert -X POST \
--data-binary @policy_5_input_1.json \
https://localhost:8181/v1/data/authz/orders/policy5

{"result":{"allow":true}}
```

Reading external data from the input document doesn't work all the time. For example, there should be a trust relationship between the OPA client (or the policy enforcement point) and the OPA server. Next we discuss an alternative for sending data in the input document that requires less trust and is applicable especially for end-user external data.

F.7.4   *JSON Web Token*

JSON Web Token (JWT) provides a reliable way of transferring data over the wire between multiple parties in a cryptographically secure way. (If you're new to JWT, check out appendix B.) OPA provides a way to pass a JWT in the input document. The OPA server can verify the JWT and then read data from it. Let's go through an example.

First, we need to have an STS that issues a JWT. You can spin up an STS by using the following command. This is the same STS we discussed in chapter 10:

```
\> docker run -p 8443:8443 prabath/insecure-sts-ch10:v1
```

Here, the STS starts on port 8443. Once it starts, run the following command to get a JWT:

```
\> curl -v -X POST --basic -u applicationid:applicationsecret \
-H "Content-Type: application/x-www-form-urlencoded;charset=UTF-8" \
-k -d "grant_type=password&username=peter&password=peter123&scope=foo" \
https://localhost:8443/oauth/token
```

In this command, `applicationid` is the client ID of the web application, and `applicationsecret` is the client secret (which are hardcoded in the STS). If everything works fine, the STS returns an OAuth 2.0 access token, which is a JWT (or a JWS, to be precise):

```
{
"access_token":"eyJhbGciOiJSUzI1NiIsInR5cCI6IkpXVCJ9.eyJleHAiOjE1NTEzMTIzNz
YsInVzZXJfbmFtZSI6InBldGVyIiwiYXV0aG9yaXRpZXMiOlsiUk9MRV9VU0VSIl0sImp0aSI6I
jRkMmJiNjNjQ4LTQ2MWQtNGVlYy1hZTljLTVlYWUxZjA4ZTJhMiIsImNsaWVudF9pZCI6ImFwcGxp
Y2F0aW9uaWQiLCJzY29wZSI6WyJmb28iXX0.tr4yUmGLtsH7q9Ge2i7gxyTsOOa0RS0Yoc2uBuA
W5OVIKZcVsIITWV3bDN0FVHBzimpAPy33tvicFROhBFoVThqKXzzG00SkURN5bnQ4uFLAP0NpZ6
BuDjvVmwXNXrQp2lVXl4lQ4eTvuyZozjUSCXzCI1LNw5EFFi22J73g1_mRm2jdEhBp1TvMaRKLB
Dk2hzIDVKzu5oj_gODBFm3a1S-IJjYoCimIm2igcesXkhipRJtjNcrJSegBbGgyXHVak2gB7I07
ryVwl_Re5yX4sV9x6xNwCxc_DgP9hHLzPM8yz_K97jlT6Rr1XZBlveyjfKs_XIXgU5qizRm9mt5
xg",
"token_type":"bearer",
"refresh_token":"",
"expires_in":5999,
"scope":"foo",
"jti":"4d2bb648-461d-4eec-ae9c-5eae1f08e2a2"
}
```

Now you can extract the JWT from the output, which is the value of the `access_token` parameter. It's a bit lengthy, so make sure that you copy the complete string. In listing F.16, you'll find the input document. There we use the copied value of the JWT as the value of the `token` parameter. The listing shows only a part of the JWT, but you can find the complete input document in the appendix-f/sample01/policy_6_input_1.json file.

> **Listing F.16   Input document, which carries data in a JWT**

```
{
    "input":{
      "path": ["orders",101],
      "method":"GET",
      "empid" : 101,
      "token" : "eyJhbGciOiJSUzI1NiIsInR5cCI6IkpXVCJ9... "
    }
}
```

The following listing shows the policy corresponding to the input document in listing F.16. The code annotations here explain all key instructions.

> **Listing F.17   OPA policy using external data that comes with the request in a JWT**

```
package authz.orders.policy6

default allow = false

certificate = `-----BEGIN CERTIFICATE-----          ◁──  The PEM-encoded certificate of the STS
MIICxzCCAa+gAwIBAgIEHP9VkjAN…                              to validate the JWT, which corresponds
-----END CERTIFICATE-----`                                to the private key that signs the JWT

allow {
  input.method = "GET"
  input.empid = emp_id
  input.path = ["orders",emp_id]
  token.payload.authorities[_] = "ROLE_USER"
}
                                                     Verifies the signature of the JWT
token = {"payload": payload} {                       following the RSA SHA256 algorithm
  io.jwt.verify_rs256(input.token, certificate)  ◁──┘
  [header, payload, signature] := io.jwt.decode(input.token)   ◁──  Decodes the JWT
  payload.exp >= now_in_seconds               ◁──  Checks whether
}                                                    the JWT is expired

now_in_seconds = time.now_ns() / 1000000000   ◁──  Finds the current time in seconds;
                                                     now_ns() returns time in nanoseconds.
```

Now you can run the following `curl` command from the appendix-f/sample01 directory with the input message from listing F.16 (appendix-f/sample01/policy_6_input_1.json) to check whether the request is authorized:

```
\> curl -k -v --key keys/client/client.key \
--cert keys/client/client.cert -X POST \
--data-binary @policy_6_input_1.json \
https://localhost:8181/v1/data/authz/orders/policy6

{"result":{"allow":true}}
```

In listing F.17, to do the JWT validation, we first needed to validate the signature and then check the expiration. OPA has a built-in function, called `io.jwt.decode` _verify(`string`, `constraints`) that validates all in one go.[4] For example, you can use this function to validate the signature, expiration (exp), not before use (nbf), audience, issuer, and so on.

F.7.5   Bundle API

To bring in external data to an OPA server under the *bundle API* approach, first you need to have a bundle server. A *bundle server* is an endpoint that hosts a bundle. For example, the bundle server can be an AWS S3 bucket or a GitHub repository. A bundle is a gzipped tarball, which carries OPA policies and data files under a well-defined directory structure.[5]

Once the bundle endpoint is available, you need to update the OPA configuration file with the bundle endpoint, the credentials to access the bundle endpoint (if it's secured), the polling interval, and so on, and then pass the configuration file as a parameter when you spin up the OPA server.[6] Once the OPA server is up, it continuously polls the bundle API to get the latest bundle after each predefined time interval.

If your data changes frequently, you'll find some drawbacks in using the bundle API. The OPA server polls the bundle API after a predefined time interval, so if you frequently update the policies or data, you could make authorization decisions based on stale data. To fix that, you can reduce the polling time interval, but then again, that will increase the load on the bundle API.

F.7.6   Pull data during evaluation

At the time of this writing, the *pull data during evaluation* approach is an experimental feature. With this approach, you don't need to load all the external data into the OPA server's memory; rather, you pull data as and when needed during the policy evaluation. To implement pull data during evaluation, you need to use the OPA built-in function `http.send`. To do that, you need to host an API (or a microservice) over HTTP (which is accessible to the OPA server) to accept data requests from the OPA server and respond with the corresponding data.[7]

F.8   OPA integrations

As we discussed early in this appendix, OPA is a general-purpose policy engine. As a general-purpose policy engine, it can address a large variety of access-control use cases. For example, you can use OPA with Kubernetes and Docker for admission control, with Envoy, Kong, and other popular API gateways for API authorization, with Spinnaker, Boomerang, and Terraform in CI/CD pipelines and with SQLite for data filtering. In this section, we briefly discuss three use cases that are related to a microservices deployment.[8]

---

[4] You can find all the OPA functions to verify JWT at http://mng.bz/aRv9.

[5] Details on how to create a bundle are at www.openpolicyagent.org/docs/latest/management/#bundles.

[6] Details on these configuration options are documented at www.openpolicyagent.org/docs/latest/configuration/.

[7] Details on how to use http.send and some examples are documented at www.openpolicyagent.org/docs/latest/policy-reference/#http.

[8]   You can find more OPA integration use cases at www.openpolicyagent.org/docs/latest/ecosystem/.

F.8.1 Istio

Istio is a service mesh implementation developed by Google, Lyft, and IBM. It's open source, and the most popular service mesh implementation at the time of this writing. If you're new to Istio or service mesh architecture, see appendix K.

Istio introduces a component called *Mixer* that runs on an Istio control plane (figure F.3). Mixer takes care of precondition checking, quota management, and telemetry reporting. For example, when a request hits the Envoy proxy at the data plane, it talks to the Mixer API to see if it's OK to proceed with that request. Mixer has a rich plugin architecture, so you can chain multiple plugins in the precondition check phase. For example, you can have a mixer plugin that connects to an external PDP to evaluate a set of access-control policies against the incoming request.

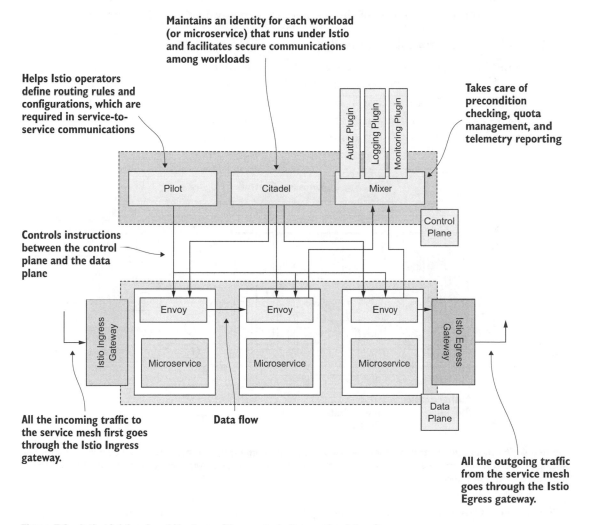

Figure F.3   Istio high-level architecture with a control plane and a data plane

Istio integrates with OPA in two ways: via the OPA Mixer adapter (plugin) and directly with Envoy's check API. You pick one or the other; there is no need for both. For the Mixer integration, when a request hits the Envoy proxy in the data plane, it does a check API call to Mixer. This API call carries certain attributes with respect to the request (for example, path, headers, and so on). Then Mixer hands over control to the OPA mixer adapter. The OPA mixer adapter, which embeds the OPA engine as an embedded library, does the authorization check against defined policies and returns the decision to Mixer and then to the Envoy proxy.[9]

For the second style of integration with Istio, OPA runs as a sidecar next to each instance of Envoy. Mixer is not involved at all. When a request hits the Envoy proxy, it asks OPA directly for an authorization decision, providing the same information it would provide to Mixer. OPA makes a decision, and Envoy enforces it. The benefit to this approach is that all decisions are made locally on the same server as the microservice and require no network hops, yielding better availability and performance.

F.8.2 Kubernetes admission controller

The *Kubernetes admission controller* is a component that's run in the Kubernetes API server. (In section J.18, we discuss how the Kubernetes internal communication works and the role of an admission controller.) When an API request arrives at the Kubernetes API server, it goes through a set of authentication and authorization plugins and then, finally, the admission controller plugins (figure F.4).

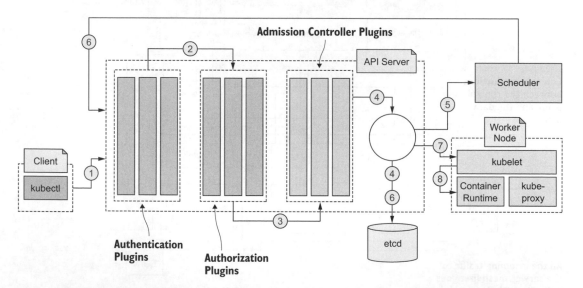

Figure F.4 A request generated by kubectl passes through authentication, authorization, and admission controller plugins of the API server; is validated; and then is stored in etcd. The scheduler and kubelet respond to events generated by the API server.

---

[9] Details on the OPA Mixer plugin are at https://github.com/istio/istio/tree/master/mixer/adapter/opa.

OPA Gatekeeper is a native integration of OPA into the Kubernetes API server that lets you write policies that are enforced via admission control. It lets you control which Pods, Ingresses, Services, and so on, are allowed on the Kubernetes cluster and how they are individually configured. Common policies include ensuring that all images come from a trusted image registry, prohibiting multiple Ingresses from using the same host, and requiring encryption be used on storage.[10]

F.8.3 *Apache Kafka*

In chapter 9, we discuss Kafka under the context of securing reactive microservices. *Apache Kafka* is the most popular message broker implementation used in microservices deployments. To use OPA for Kafka authorization, you need to engage the OPA Authorizer plugin with Kafka. To authorize a request, the OPA Authorizer plugin talks to a remote OPA server over HTTP.[11] In a Kubernetes deployment, you would deploy the OPA server as a sidecar along with Kafka on the same Pod.

F.9   **OPA alternatives**

Since OPA was introduced in 2016, OPA has become the de facto implementation of fine-grained access control, mostly in the Kubernetes and microservices domains. A couple of alternatives to OPA exist, but at the time of this writing, none of them are as popular as OPA.

One alternative, *eXtensible Access Control Markup Language* (*XACML*), is an open standard developed by the Organization for the Advancement of Structured Information Standards (OASIS). The XACML standard introduces a policy language based on XML and a schema based on XML for authorization requests and responses. OASIS released the XACML 1.0 specification in 2003, and at the time of this writing, the latest is XACML 3.0. XACML was popular many years back, but over time, as the popularity of XML-based standards declined, XACML adoption lessened rapidly as well. Also, XACML as a policy language is quite complex, though very powerful. If you're looking for an open source implementation of XACML 3.0, check the Balana project, which is available at https://github.com/wso2/balana.

Speedle, another open source alternative to OPA, is also a general-purpose authorization engine. Speedle was developed by Oracle and is relatively new. It's too early to comment on how Speedle competes with OPA, and at the time of this writing, only Oracle Cloud uses Speedle internally. You can find more details on Speedle at https://speedle.io/.

---

[10] You can find more details on OPA Gatekeeper at https://github.com/open-policy-agent/gatekeeper. How to deploy an OPA Gatekeeper on Kubernetes for a Kubernetes ingress validation is documented at www.openpolicyagent.org/docs/latest/kubernetes-tutorial/.

[11] You can find more details on OPA Kafka Authorizer at https://github.com/open-policy-agent/contrib/tree/master/kafka_authorizer.

appendix G
Creating a certificate authority and related keys with OpenSSL

Anyone who wants to expose services over the web that are protected with Transport Layer Security (TLS) must get their certificates signed by a trusted *certificate authority* (*CA*). Few trusted CAs are available globally, and their public keys are embedded in all browsers. When a browser talks to amazon.com over TLS, for example, it can verify that Amazon's certificate is valid (not forged) by verifying its signature against the corresponding CA's public key that's embedded in the browser. The certificate also includes the hostname of Amazon (which is called the *common name*), so the browser knows it's communicating with the right server.

In this appendix, we show you how to create a CA by using OpenSSL. *OpenSSL* is a commercial-grade toolkit and cryptographic library for TLS, available for multiple platforms. You can download and set up the distribution that fits your platform from www.openssl.org/source. But the easiest way to try OpenSSL is to use Docker. In this appendix, you'll use an OpenSSL Docker image. You need to install Docker, following the instructions at https://docs.docker.com/install/#supported-platforms. The process is straightforward. A deeper understanding of how Docker works isn't necessary to follow along in this appendix (we talk about Docker and containers in detail in appendix E).

G.1 Creating a certificate authority

Assuming that you have Docker installed, follow the instructions in this section to set up the CA. To begin, download the appendix G samples from GitHub (https://github.com/microservices-security-in-action/samples) to your computer. Let's spin up the OpenSSL Docker container from the appendix-g/sample01/ directory.

The following `docker run` command starts OpenSSL in a Docker container with a bind mount that maps the appendix-g/sample01/ directory (or the current directory, which is indicated by `$(pwd)` in listing G.1) from the host filesystem to the /export directory of the container filesystem. This bind mount lets you share part of the host filesystem with the container filesystem. When the OpenSSL container generates certificates, those are written to the /export directory of the container filesystem. Because we have a bind mount, everything inside the /export directory of the container filesystem is also accessible from the appendix-g/sample01/ directory of the host filesystem.

> **Listing G.1 Running OpenSSL in a Docker container**

```
\> docker run -it -v $(pwd):/export prabath/openssl
#
```

When you run this command for the first time, its execution can take a couple of minutes. It ends with a command prompt, where you can execute your OpenSSL commands to create the CA. Use the command in the following listing to generate a private key for the CA.

> **Listing G.2 Generating a private key for the certificate authority**

```
# openssl genrsa -aes256 -passout pass:"manning123" \
-out /export/ca/ca_key.pem 4096

Generating RSA private key, 4096 bit long modulus
```

The generated key file is stored in the /export/ca directory of the Docker container (as specified by the –out argument). Then again, because you mapped the appendix-g/sample01/ directory of the host filesystem to the /export directory, the generated key file is also available inside the appendix-g/sample01/ca directory of the host machine. In listing G.2, the `genrsa` command generates a private key of 4,096 bits and encrypts it with AES-256 and the provided passphrase. We use `manning123` as the passphrase, which is passed to the `genrsa` command under the `–passout` argument.

NOTE The value of the passphrase must be prefixed with `pass:` and must be defined within double quotes.

Next, use the command (`req –new`) in the following listing to generate a public key that points to the already generated private key (`–key`) with an expiration time of 365 days (`-days`).

> **Listing G.3 Generating a public key for the certificate authority**

```
# openssl  req -new -passin pass:"manning123" -key /export/ca/ca_key.pem \
-x509 -days 365 -out /export/ca/ca_cert.pem -subj "/CN=ca.ecomm.com"
```

While creating the public key, OpenSSL needs to know the details related to the organization behind the CA (country, state, organization name, and so on). Of those details, what matters most is the common name (CN). You need to provide something meaningful. The CN may not be important here, but when a client application talks to a TLS-secured endpoint, the client validates whether the hostname of the endpoint matches the value of the CN in the certificate; if not, it rejects the certificate.

In listing G.3, we provide the value of the CN under the `-subj` argument; make sure the corresponding value starts with a `/`. (OpenSSL requires the forward slash.) The `-out` argument specifies where to store the generated public key. Now you can find two files in the appendix-g/sample01/ca directory: `ca_cert.pem`, which is the public key, and `ca_key.pem`, which is the private key of the certificate authority.

G.2   *Generating keys for an application*

In this section, we discuss how to create a public/private key pair for an application and get those keys signed by the CA you created in section G.1. This application can be a microservice, a web server, a client application, and so on. To generate the public/private key pair for an application, you're going to use the same OpenSSL Docker container started in section G.1. Run the command in the following listing to generate a private key for the application.

Listing G.4   Generating a private key for the application

```
# openssl genrsa -aes256 -passout pass:"manning123" \
-out /export/application/app_key.pem 4096
```

This code generates the private key file (app_key.pem) inside the appendix-g/sample01/application directory. When you have the private key for the application, to get it signed by the CA, you need to create a certificate-signing request (CSR) first. Run the command in the following listing in the OpenSSL Docker container command prompt. It produces a file named csr-for-app, which you have to share with your CA to get a signed certificate.

Listing G.5   Generating a certificate-signing request for the application

```
# openssl req -passin pass:"manning123" -new \
-key /export/application/app_key.pem \
-out /export/application/csr-for-app \
-subj "/CN=app.ecomm.com"
```

The OpenSSL command in listing G.6 gets the CSR generated in listing G.5, signed by the CA. The output of the command in the following listing is the signed certificate of the application (app_cert.pem). You can find it inside the appendix-g/sample01/application directory.

Listing G.6 Generating the application's CA signed certificate

```
# openssl x509 -req -passin pass:"manning123" \
-days 365 -in /export/application/csr-for-app \
-CA /export/ca/ca_cert.pem -CAkey /export/ca/ca_key.pem \
-set_serial 01 -out /export/application/app_cert.pem
```

Now we have a private key and signed certificate for the application. For some Java applications (for example, Spring Boot microservices), we need to have this key stored in a Java KeyStore (JKS), which is Java-specific key storage.

In listing G.7, we generate a JKS from the application's private key and the public certificate. In the first command of the listing, we remove the passphrase of the private key (app_key.pem), and in the second command, we create a single file (application_keys.pem) with both the private key and the public certificate. With the third command, we create a keystore of type PKCS with these keys. At the end of the third command, you can find the PKCS keystore (app.p12) inside the appendix-g/sample01/application directory. Finally, in the last command, we use the Java Keytool to create a JKS file from the app.p12 PKCS keystore. There we pass the passphrase of the source (app.p12) keystore under the argument srcstorepass, and the passphrase of the destination (app.jks) keystore under the argument deststorepass. For app.p12, we used manning123 as the keystore passphrase. For simplicity, we use the same passphrase for the destination keystore (app.jks) as well.

Listing G.7 Creating a Java KeyStore with the application's public/private keys

```
# openssl rsa -passin pass:"manning123" \           Removes the passphrase of
-in /export/application/app_key.pem \               the private key: app_key.pem
-out /export/application/app_key.pem    ◀

# cat /export/application/app_key.pem /export/application/app_cert.pem \
>> /export/application/application_keys.pem    ◀    Creates a single file
                                                    (application_keys.pem)
                                                    with both the private key
                                                    and the public certificate
# openssl pkcs12  -export -passout pass:"manning123" \
-in /export/application/application_keys.pem \
-out /export/application/app.p12

# keytool -importkeystore -srcstorepass manning123 \
-srckeystore /export/application/app.p12 -srcstoretype pkcs12 \
-deststorepass manning123 -destkeystore /export/application/app.jks \
-deststoretype JKS    ◀
                                                    Uses the Java Keytool to
                                                    create a JKS file from the
Creates a keystore of type PKCS with the            app.p12 PKCS keystore
keys in the application_keys.pem file
```

appendix H
Secure Production Identity
Framework for Everyone

In chapter 6, we discussed the challenges in key management, including key provisioning, trust bootstrapping, certificate revocation, key rotation, and key usage monitoring. In a typical microservices deployment, each microservice is provisioned with a key pair. In chapter 6, you did that by manually copying Java keystore files to the Order Processing and Inventory microservices.

Doing things manually is not a neat approach in a microservices deployment with hundreds of services, however—everything must be automated.[1] Ideally, during the CI/CD pipeline, the keys should be generated and provisioned to the microservices. In chapter 11, we discussed how to deploy and secure microservices in a Kubernetes environment, and then in chapter 12, we discussed how to secure a microservices deployment with Istio service mesh. In both cases, we relied on Kubernetes and Istio to provision and manage keys of our microservices. This appendix assumes that you have good knowledge of Kubernetes and Istio service mesh, so we recommend you first go through appendixes J and K, and chapters 11 and 12.

When the keys are provisioned to all the microservices, next we have to *bootstrap trust*, or initialize trust, among them. In chapter 6, we bootstrapped trust by manually sharing the public certificates (or the public certificate of the corresponding certificate authority) of the trusted client microservices with the recipient microservice. When a microservice authenticates with mTLS and sends a request to the recipient microservice, the recipient microservice can check whether it can trust the client microservice's certificate.

---

[1] Provisioning and managing keys manually is a poor practice since it's easy for these files to be accidentally or deliberately leaked, thus allowing an attacker to assume the privileges of the corresponding workloads/microservices.

In chapter 12, with Istio service mesh, we used an Istio authentication `Policy` and a set of `DestinationRules` to enforce mTLS among microservices. Then we used `ISTIO_MUTUAL` as the `tls` mode in our `DestinationRules`. With `ISTIO_ MUTUAL`, Istio uses the keys and certificates provisioned to each Pod by Istio itself, and by default all the Pods trust the certificate authority, which issues those keys and certificates.

In addition to bootstrapping trust among microservices, after we provision keys to each microservice, the provisioned keys must be rotated before they expire. If we provision keys manually to our microservices, we have to manually rotate the keys as well. If Istio provisions the keys, Istio itself can rotate the keys. In section 12.6, we discussed how Istio manages keys. In this appendix, we discuss how SPIFFE helps to address key provisioning, trust bootstrapping, and key rotation problems.

H.1 What is SPIFFE?

Secure Production Identity Framework for Everyone (*SPIFFE*) is a project that defines a framework and a set of open standards for a software system (a microservice, in the context of this book) to establish an identity and then communicate with other systems in a secure way. Under the SPIFFE terminology, the microservice, or the software system, is known as a *workload*. In this appendix, we use the words *microservice* and *workload* interchangeably. However, a workload in SPIFFE can be anything (a microservice, an API, an application server, a gateway, a database, a message broker, a security token service, and so on), not necessarily a microservice, and to use SPIFFE it is not a must to run your workload on Kubernetes. SPIFFE has an open source reference implementation called the *SPIFFE Runtime Environment* (*SPIRE*). Istio too implements the SPIFFE specification.

> ### Istio vs. SPIRE
>
> Istio is designed to run within a Kubernetes cluster, and thus has a particularly opinionated view of *workload identity* based on service accounts and Kubernetes namespaces. SPIRE has a much more flexible model of what can be considered a workload, that can include other orchestration frameworks (like Hadoop), provenance from CI/CD pipelines, and clusters of physical or virtual machines.
>
> Istio also includes an out-of-the-box data plane (Envoy proxy) that can enforce authentication, encryption and authorization policies automatically across a cluster, whereas SPIRE requires you to integrate Envoy (or other proxies) yourself.
>
> At the time of this writing, work is ongoing to make different implementations of the SPIFFE specification cross-compatible, such that workloads that have identities provided by one implementation (say, SPIRE) can authenticate, encrypt, and authorize traffic from another implementation (say, Istio).

While helping to establish an identity for each microservice in a given deployment, SPIFFE also solves the trust bootstrap problem, and provides node attestation (verifying the identity and integrity of the machine(s) a workload is running on) and process attestation (verifying the identity and integrity of a specific process running on a given machine) of the workload. In the introduction to this appendix, we defined trust bootstrapping. In general, *attestation* means the evidence or proof of something.

With SPIFFE, you can provision keys (that confer a particular identity) to a given microservice (or workload) only if the corresponding attestation policies are satisfied: our microservice and the node where the microservice runs (figure H.1) must provide enough evidence that they satisfy the corresponding attestation policies, before any keys are provisioned to them. In section H.4, we discuss a couple of sample attestation policies.

The key highlight of SPIFFE is that the keys provisioned to a microservice never leave the node that runs it. A node can be a physical server or a virtual machine, which runs one or more microservices. Figure H.1 shows two nodes in a Kubernetes environment; each node hosts a set of Pods, and each Pod runs a microservice.

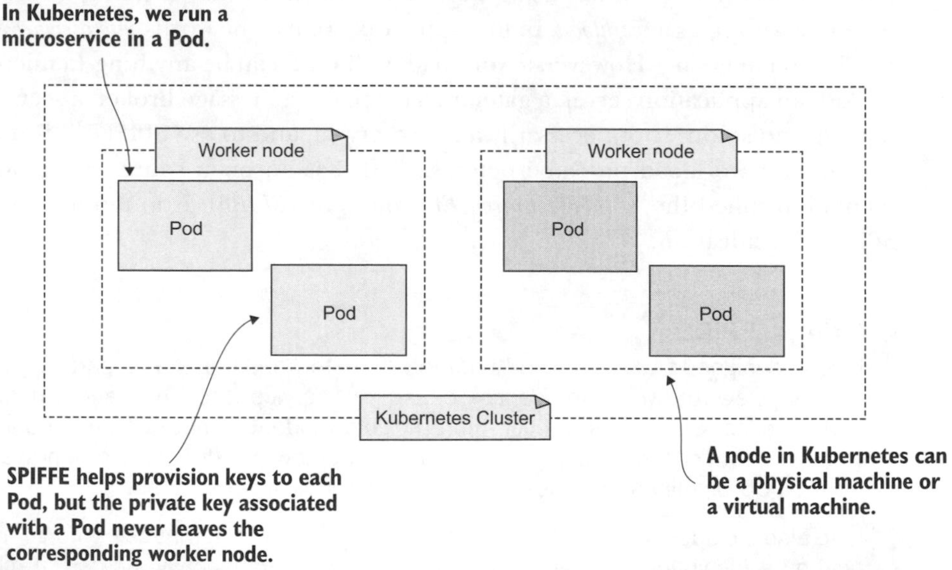

In Kubernetes, we run a microservice in a Pod.

SPIFFE helps provision keys to each Pod, but the private key associated with a Pod never leaves the corresponding worker node.

A node in Kubernetes can be a physical machine or a virtual machine.

Figure H.1   In a Kubernetes deployment, we run microservices in Pods. A given Pod carries one or more microservices. A Kubernetes node hosts one or more Pods. The private key provisioned to a microservice via SPIFFE never leaves the node.

One common way to provision keys to a microservice is, during the continuous delivery phase, to embed a set of long-lived credentials to the microservice. These long-lived credentials can be a username/password pair, an OAuth key, or even a key pair with a long expiration. Then, the microservice uses these long-lived credentials to authenticate to a key server and get short-lived credentials—and it will repeat this process every time the short-lived credentials expire. However, SPIFFE does not require your microservice to have long-lived credentials and doesn't worry about certificate revocation; it relies on short-lived credentials and takes care of key rotation.

H.2 The inspiration behind SPIFFE

The inspiration behind SPIFFE came from three projects at Netflix, Facebook, and Google. Metatron, the Netflix project that we discussed in chapter 6, solves the credential-provisioning problem by injecting long-lived credentials into each microservice during the continuous delivery phase. Facebook's internal public key infrastructure (PKI) project helps bootstrap trust among systems that are secured with mTLS. Google's project, Low Overhead Authentication Services (LOAS), is a cryptographic-key distribution system that helps establish an identity for all the jobs running on the Google infrastructure.

H.3 SPIFFE ID

The *SPIFFE ID* is the unique identifier that SPIFFE provides for each microservice, or workload, in a given deployment. It is a URI in the format of *spiffe://trust-domain/path*. The SPIFFE ID specification at https://github.com/spiffe/spiffe/blob/master/standards/SPIFFE-ID.md shares further details.

A *trust domain* in SPIFFE could represent an organization, a department, an environment (dev, staging, production), and so on. In practice, a SPIRE server (the open source reference implementation of SPIFFE) runs in each trust domain and issues SPIFFE IDs to the microservices running in the corresponding trust domain. For example in the SPIFFE ID spiffe://foo.com/retail/order-processing, foo.com reflects the trust domain, and retail/order-processing is the associated path, and the SPIFFE ID as a whole represents the Order Processing microservice that is running in the trust domain foo.com. However, you can construct the SPIFFE ID in any way you want. But it's always better to make it meaningful and logical.

While constructing a SPIFFE ID, you can create a logical hierarchy that corresponds to how authorization policies might be applied. This makes it easier to write authorization policies later. For example, one might write a policy that says, *any workload with the identity* **spiffe://foo.com/retail/order-processing/*** *can connect to any other identity with an ID that matches* **spiffe://foo.com/retail/order-processing/***. Let's go through a few SPIFFE IDs:

- If you have a database server running with the Order Processing microservice, you could name the database server as spiffe://foo.com/retail/order-processing /*mysql*. To have the name be more meaningful, you may use spiffe://*dev*.foo .com/retail/order-processing/mysql for the database server running in the development environment, and spiffe://*prod*.foo.com/retail/order-processing/ mysql for the database server running in the production environment.

- If you run your microservices in Kubernetes, which we discussed in appendix J and chapter 11, you run each microservice in a Kubernetes Pod. If you are not familiar with Kubernetes, you may revisit this bullet point later, after you go through appendix J and chapter 11. A Pod in Kubernetes runs under a service account, and by default Kubernetes provisions a JSON Web Token to each Pod, which carries the identity of the corresponding service account. For example, the sub claim in the JWT, corresponding to the default service account under the default Kubernetes namespace, looks like *system:serviceaccount:default:default*. So if you group your microservices by Kubernetes service accounts, where a given microservice runs under a specific service account, then rather than going by the service name, you can construct the SPIFFE ID with the service account name. For example, in the SPIFFE ID spiffe://foo.com/ns/prod/sa/mysql, foo.com is the Kubernetes cluster, ns/prod is the Kubernetes namespace, and sa/mysql is the service account name corresponding to your MySQL Pod.

- A given SPIFFE ID has a maximum length of 2,048 bytes. If we want a SPIFFE ID to be self-contained (to carry all the information corresponding to it in the identifier itself), we may find the maximum length to be an obstruction. To overcome such situations, we can use an opaque SPIFFE ID. For example, an opaque SPIFFE ID would look like spiffe://foo.com/0a42aabb-6c87-41c6-9b37-b796983dcbda—and the recipient of the SPIFFE ID can query a metadata endpoint with 0a42aabb-6c87-41c6-9b37-b796983dcbda to find further details.

Let's expand the second bullet point a little. There we encoded a set of attributes corresponding to the workload into the SPIFFE ID itself. This allows you to write authorization policies later based on those attributes. For example, one might write a policy that says, *allow any workload from the prod namespace*. This can be desirable and flexible, but comes with some caveats as listed here:

- You should take care to declare only attributes that have actually been verified by your SPIFFE implementation.
- SPIFFE doesn't provide (at the time of this writing) any formal definition of the attributes (for example, ns is for the kubernetes namespace) or how they are encoded, so you'll need to make one up.
- The length of the SPIFFE ID limits the number of attributes that can be encoded.

H.4   *How SPIRE works*

SPIRE is the reference implementation of SPIFFE. The best way to learn how SPIFFE works is to see how SPIRE works. The SPIRE architecture has two main components: the SPIRE *agent* (also known as the *node agent*) and the *SPIRE server.*

The SPIRE agent runs on the same node where the workload (or the microservice) is running. If you run your microservice on an Amazon EC2 machine, for example, the SPIRE agent runs on the same EC2 node. If you run your microservice in a Docker container, the SPIRE agent runs on the same host machine that runs the Docker container. If you run your microservice on Kubernetes, the SPIRE agent runs on the

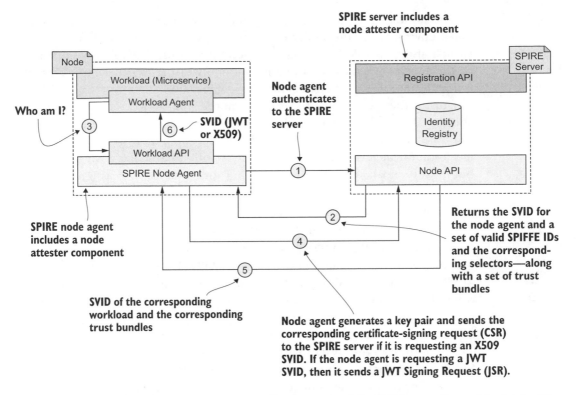

Figure H.2   In this communication between the SPIRE node agent and the SPIRE server, the workload gets either an X.509-SVID or a JWT-SVID via the SPIRE node agent. Both the workload and the SPIRE node agent share the same operating system kernel.

same Kubernetes node. In other words, the SPIRE agent shares the OS kernel with the workload, and a given SPIRE agent can serve multiple workloads running on the same OS kernel or the node.

The following list walks you through the steps defined in figure H.2 to explain how SPIRE works and sets forth its design principles:

1 The SPIRE node agent authenticates to the SPIRE server.

   Authentication happens via a component called a *node attester*. A node attester runs on both the SPIRE server and the SPIRE node agent. If the workload is running on an Amazon EC2 node, for example, the node attester at the SPIRE node agent's end picks the corresponding AWS instance identity document[2] (https:// docs.aws.amazon.com/AWSEC2/latest/UserGuide/instance-identity-documents .html) and passes it to the SPIRE server for authentication. When the document is passed to the SPIRE server, the AWS node attester at the server side validates the signature of the document by using Amazon's public key.

---

[2] The AWS instance identity document is a document signed by Amazon that includes the metadata related to the corresponding EC2 instance. Within a given EC2 instance, you can get only the AWS instance identity document corresponding to that node.

The node attester is an extension point. If your workload runs in a Kubernetes environment, the node agent that runs in the same Kubernetes node (which also runs a Pod carrying the microservice) uses a JWT provisioned to it by the Kubernetes cluster to prove its identity to the SPIRE server. This JWT uniquely identifies the node agent.[3]

During the attestation process, if required, the SPIRE server will look up additional node metadata based on what is attested. If you take the same AWS example we discussed before, the node attester will tell the SPIRE server that it has authenticated the corresponding node with a particular AWS instance ID, but must then talk to AWS to find whether that instance ID is assigned to a particular AWS security group.

2 Once the node authentication completes, the SPIRE server issues a SPIFFE Verifiable Identity Document (SVID) to the node agent.

At a high level, this SVID carries the SPIFFE ID of the node agent in a cryptographically verifiable manner. An owner of a SPIFFE ID can prove the ownership of the corresponding SVID. An SVID can be in multiple formats; at the time of this writing, it can be an X.509 certificate or a JWT. In the case of an X.509-SVID, you get a signed certificate corresponding to the CSR that the SPIRE agent submitted in step 1. We discuss SVID in detail in section H.5.

In addition to the SVID for the node agent, the SPIRE server finds all the SPIFFE IDs corresponding to the node on which the node agent is running, and returns those to the node agent along with a set of selectors.

The process completed with steps 1 and 2 is known as *node attestation*. A registry in the SPIRE server keeps a set of attestation policies that defines the criteria under which a given SPIFFE ID can be assigned to a workload. A registry entry, for example, may say that the SPIFFE ID spiffe://foo.com/retail/order-processing can be issued only to a node running under the AWS security group sg-e566bb82 and a workload with the user ID (UID) 1002. Another registry entry may say that the SPIFFE ID spiffe://foo.com/retail/delivery can be issued only to a node running under the AWS security group sg-e566bb82 and a workload with the UID 1003. In that case, step 2 returns both SPIFFE IDs to the node agent, if the corresponding node runs under the AWS security group sg-e566bb82.[4]

You can define a selector in several other ways, but typically, you use at least two mechanisms: one at the infrastructure level (such as a security group) and the other at the workload level (UID).

Along with the set of SPIFFE IDs and the corresponding selectors, the SPIRE server returns a map of trust bundles. A *trust bundle* carries certificates corresponding to all the CAs (root and intermediary CAs) a given workload can

---

[3] The SPIRE agent runs in Kubernetes in a Pod. Each Pod in Kubernetes runs under a service account. Kubernetes provisions a JWT to each Pod, based on the corresponding service account. It's always better to run the Pod that carries the SPIRE agent under its own service account.

[4] There's no requirement that the SPIFFE ID needs to encode the attributes of the policy that was used to issue it, and in this way allows you to decouple the logical identity of the workload (used to determine authorization policy) from the physical infrastructure that hosts it.

trust, and in the map, each bundle is stored against the corresponding trust domain. In section H.6, we discuss trust bundles in detail.

3 The workload talks to the workload API of the SPIRE node agent and asks for its identity.[5] The workload API is node-local. In the UNIX operating system, for example, it's exposed via UNIX domain sockets.[6] The workload doesn't need to know where it's running. It can be on Amazon EC2, Kubernetes, or any other platform. It simply asks the workload API, "Who am I?"

Each workload (or microservice) can optionally have a SPIRE workload agent, which knows how to talk to the workload API exposed by the SPIRE node agent, on behalf of the workload. In a Kubernetes deployment, this workload agent runs in the same Pod along with the corresponding microservice (or the workload). Strictly speaking, the workload agent directly represents the workload. It might be an agent (like a proxy) acting on behalf of the actual workload, but it must match the preceding attestation policies (step 2), and thus counts as the workload. For convenience, we are repeating figure H.2 as figure H.3 here.

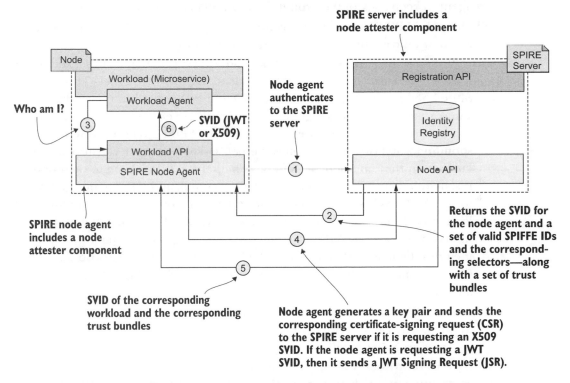

Figure H.3   In this communication between the SPIRE node agent and the SPIRE server, the workload gets either an X.509-SVID or a JWT-SVID via the SPIRE node agent. Both the workload and the SPIRE node agent share the same operating system kernel.

---

[5]   SPIFFE defines the workload API in the specification at https://github.com/spiffe/spiffe/blob/master/standards/SPIFFE_Workload_API.md.

[6]   A UNIX domain socket is a data communications endpoint for exchanging data among processes executing on the same host operating system.

Since the workload API is node-local, the workload does not need to explicitly authenticate to the API. With the attributes attached to the request, the node agent should be able to figure out who the caller is. SPIRE has implemented the workload API as server-side streaming RPC in gRPC. If you are new to gRPC, please check appendix I, where we discuss gRPC fundamentals. With server-side streaming RPC, the workload—or the workload agent—sends a request to the node agent and gets a stream to read a sequence of messages. The workload will keep reading the stream until it finds no more unread messages.

The SPIFFE workload API specification recommends that the workload maintain an open connection with the node agent as long as possible, so it can receive events from the node agent. If the connection drops, the workload should establish a new connection with the node agent as soon as possible. This open connection is used to not only get the corresponding SVID to the workload, but also to enable the node agent to keep the SVID and the trust bundle at the workload updated, before the current ones expire. So, it is the responsibility of the node agent to keep track of the expiration time and to rotate the keys when required.

4 Once the SPIRE node agent receives the request in step 3 from the workload agent, it validates the request and tries to identify the workload.

If the node agent exposes the workload API via UNIX domain sockets, it can find the metadata related to the workload via the OS kernel. This way, the SPIRE node agent can find out the UID and PID related to the workload and can scan all the selectors it got from the SPIRE server in step 2 to find a match. If a match is found, the node agent knows the SPIFFE ID related to the corresponding workload. If you're on Kubernetes, the node agent can also talk to the kubelet on the same node to find out whether the PID related to the workload is scheduled by itself (the kubelet). If all goes well, and if the node agent wants to use X.509-SVIDs, then it generates a key pair for the corresponding workload, creates a CSR, and sends the CSR to the SPIRE server. If the node agent wants to use a JWT-SVID, it generates a JWT Signing Request (JSR), which includes the intended audience of the JWT-SVID—or in other words, an identifier corresponding to the recipient microservice that this workload wants to authenticate with the JWT-SVID.

5 The SPIRE server validates the CSR or the JSR from step 4 and returns an SVID to the SPIRE agent. As we discussed before, an SVID can be in multiple formats; it can be an X.509 certificate or a JWT.

6 If step 5 returns an X.509-SVID, the node agent will pass the X.509-SVID and corresponding private key to the workload. If step 5 returns a JWT-SVID, the node agent will pass the JWT-SVID itself to the workload. Then the workload can use the SVID to authenticate to other workloads. If it is an X.509-SVID, the communications among workloads can be protected over mTLS, and if it is a JWT-SVID, the workload can pass the JWT-SVID as a bearer token to the recipient workload it wants to talk to. In other words, X.509-SVIDs allow workloads to establish

channel authentication and integrity between two workloads, assuming the network infrastructure permits this, while JWT-SVIDs allow for individual messages to be authenticated.

H.5 SPIFFE Verifiable Identity Document

The *SPIFFE Verifiable Identity Document* (*SVID*) is the identity document defined under the SPIFFE specification. It has three basic components: a SPIFFE ID, a public key that represents the workload, and a valid signature by the SPIRE server, which issues the SVID. The SPIFFE ID and the signature are a must, while the public key is optional. The SVID carries the SPIFFE ID in a way the owner of the SPIFFE ID can cryptographically prove the procession of the corresponding SPIFFE ID. An SVID can be in two formats at the time of this writing: X.509-SVID and JWT-SVID.

H.5.1 X.509-SVID

The *X.509-SVID* provides a signed X.509 certificate corresponding to the CSR that the SPIRE node agent submits to the SPIRE server (step 4 in figure H.4).[7] While issuing an X.509-SVID, the SPIRE server acts as a CA, and all the issued certificates must have the corresponding SPIFFE ID in the X.509 Subject Alternate Name (SAN) field. Also the SPIRE server can delegate the certificate-issuing part to an upstream CA.

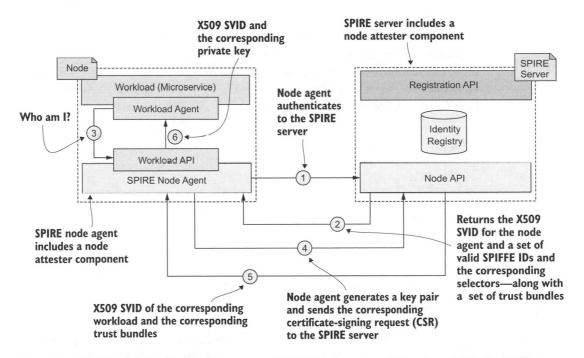

Figure H.4 When the SPIRE node agent requests an X.509-SVID, it creates a CSR and sends it to the SPIRE server.

---

[7] SPIFFE defines the X.509-SVID in the specification available at https://github.com/spiffe/spiffe/blob/master/standards/X509-SVID.md.

In a PKI ecosystem, we find both the root CAs and intermediary CAs. Either CA can sign an X.509 certificate issued to a workload. Both the root CAs and intermediary CAs have their own X.509 certificate as well. The certificate of an intermediary CA is signed by either a root CA or another intermediary CA, while the root CA signs its own certificate. As you can imagine, this builds a chain, or hierarchy, of certificates. At the bottom is the *leaf certificate*, which you have for your workload, and on top of that, you will find a set of certificates signed by intermediary CAs, and finally the chain ends with a root certificate. The following are some of the key points with respect to using an X.509 certificate as an SVID, but we still recommend you go through the X.509-SVID specification if you plan to do any SPIFFE implementations:

- Each X.509 certificate, whether it belongs to a workload or an intermediary CA or a root CA, must have an SPIFFE ID in the X.509 SAN field. If it is a certificate that belongs to a workload, or a leaf certificate, then the SPIFFE ID must have a nonroot path component. In the SPIFFE ID spiffe://foo.com/*retail/order-processing*, for example, retail/order-processing is the nonroot path. If the X.509 certificate belongs to an intermediary CA or a root CA, the SPIFFE ID must not have a path component.

- Each X.509 certificate must carry the Key Usage property and must be marked as critical.

- Any X.509 certificate that belongs to an intermediary CA or a root CA must have the Key Cert Sign set under the Key Usage property. This certificate also should carry the Certificate Authority flag with a value of True or Yes, under the Basic Constraints extension. This requirement is not specific to SPIFFE; figure H.5 shows a sample root CA certificate with those extensions. The value of the Certificate Authority flag in a leaf certificate must be False or No.

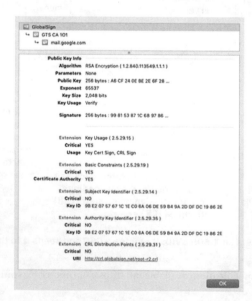

Figure H.5   The X.509 certificate of the GlobalSign root CA. The value of the Key Usage extension contains the value Key Cert Sign, and the Basic Constraints extension carries the property Certificate Authority, with the value Yes.

- Only the leaf X.509 certificates are used for authentication between workloads.
- The leaf X.509 certificate must have Digital Signature as the value of the Key Usage property, and it must not have either the Key Cert Sign or CRL Sign.
- The leaf X.509 certificate should include the Extended Key Usage property, and it should carry the values id-kp-serverAuth and id-kp-clientAuth. These two values indicate that the corresponding X.509 certificate can be used to authenticate both the client and the server in communications over TLS.
- During the validation process of an X.509 leaf certificate, the recipient must validate the certificate path to check whether a trusted CA has issued the certificate. SPIFFE uses a CA trust bundle to distribute trusted CA certificates. Usually, the node agent updates the corresponding workloads with these trust bundles. In section H.6, we discuss trust bundles in detail.

H.5.2   JWT-SVID

The *JWT-SVID* provides a signed JWT corresponding to the JSR that the SPIRE node agent submits to the SPIRE server (step 4 in figure H.6).[8] A signed JWT is a compact serialized JSON Web Signature (JWS). In appendix B, we discuss JWS in detail. The following are some of the key points with respect to a JWT-SVID, but we still

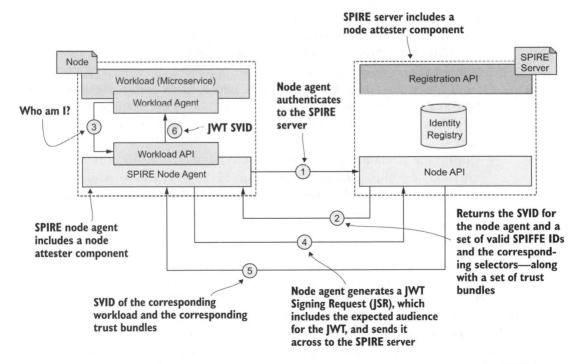

Figure H.6   When the SPIRE node agent requests a JWT-SVID, it creates a JSR and sends it to the SPIRE server.

---

[8]   SPIFFE defines the JWT-SVID in https://github.com/spiffe/spiffe/blob/master/standards/JWT-SVID.md.

recommend you go through the JWT-SVID specification if you plan to do any SPIFFE implementations:

- One key element in a JWT is the value of the aud attribute, or the audience attribute. It defines the intended recipient of the token. The value of the aud attribute can be any string or a URI that's known to the recipient of the JWT. Each workload (or the microservice) that receives a JWT from another workload (or a microservice) during the authentication process as a bearer token must check the value of the aud parameter to see whether it's known before accepting the JWT as valid. In figure H.6, step 3, when the workload requests a JWT-SVID, it passes the intended audience of the token to the workload API of the node agent, and the node agent passes the same to the node API in step 4.
- Each JWT-SVID has an attribute called sub. The sub attribute—also known as the subject attribute—defines the owner of the JWT-SVID or carries the SPIFFE ID of the workload, which owns the corresponding JWT-SVID. As per figure H.6, the JWT-SVID issued by the SPIRE server in step 6 will carry the SPIFFE ID of the workload (which initially asked for the SVID in step 3).
- Each JWT-SVID has an expiration time expressed with the exp attribute. The value of the exp attribute carries the time of expiration in seconds, which is calculated from 1970-01-01T0:0:0Z as measured in Universal Coordinated Time (UTC). Any recipient of a JWT must make sure that the time represented by the exp attribute is not in the past when accepting a JWT (that is, the token is not expired). SPIFFE recommends using a small validity period for the JWT. When you use a small validity period, the impact of someone stealing a JWT is limited to only that time period. In figure H.6, step 3, when the workload requests a JWT-SVID, it passes the intended expiration time of the token to the workload API of the node agent, and the node agent passes the same to the node API in step 4.
- During the validation process of a JWT-SVID, the recipient workload (or the microservice) must validate the signature of the JWT. This workload must also check whether the public key corresponding to the signature is in one of its trust bundles (section H.6).

H.6   *A trust bundle*

As discussed in section H.3, a trust domain in SPIFFE could represent an organization, a department, an environment (dev, staging, production), and so on. In practice, a SPIRE server that runs in each trust domain issues SPIFFE IDs to the microservices running in the corresponding trust domain.[9] The SVIDs issued to all the workloads in a given trust domain are signed by a common signing key, and can be verified with the same certificate chain. A *trust bundle* packs the cryptographic keys of a trust domain, so

---

[9] SPIFFE defines the trust domain and bundle in https://github.com/spiffe/spiffe/blob/master/standards/
SPIFFE_Trust_Domain_and_Bundle.md.

that any workload that carries a trust bundle can check whether any SVID it receives from another workload is issued from an issuer it trusts.

SPIFFE uses a JSON Web Key Set (JWKS) to represent a trust bundle. A JWK is a JSON representation of a cryptographic key, and a JWKS is a representation of multiple JWKs. RFC 7517 (https://tools.ietf.org/html/rfc7517) defines the structure and the definition of a JWK. The following listing shows a sample trust bundle, which carries a key corresponding to an X.509-SVID.

Listing H.1   A sample SPIFFE trust bundle corresponding to an X.509-SVID

Defines the type of the corresponding SVID. If it's an X.509-SVID, the use attribute carries the value x509-svid. If it's a JWT-SVID, the use attribute carries the value jwt-svid.

Defines the key type. RFC 7518 defines the possible values, and the value EC means the key type is Elliptic Curve.

Curve parameter. This is a parameter specific to the Elliptic Curve key type and identifies the cryptographic curve used with the key.

This is a parameter specific to the Elliptic Curve key type, which identifies the *y* coordinate for the Elliptic Curve point.

```
{
  "keys": [
    {
      "use": "x509-svid",
      "kty": "EC",
      "crv": "P-256",
      "x": "fK-wKTnKL7KFLM27lqq5DC-bxrVaH6rDV-IcCSEOeL4",
      "y": "wq-g3TQWxYlV51TCPH03OyXsRxvujD4hUUaIQrXk4KI",
      "x5c": [ "MIIBKjCB0aADAgECA..." ]
    }
  ],
  "spiffe_refresh_hint": 600
}
```

Carries the certificate chain corresponding to the trust domain

This is a parameter specific to Elliptic Curve key type, which identifies the *x* coordinate for the Elliptic Curve point.

Indicates how often the recipient of the trust bundle should check with the bundle publisher for updates

appendix I
gRPC fundamentals

The *gRPC* (https://grpc.io/) is an open source remote procedure call framework (a library), originally developed by Google. In fact, it's the next generation of a system called Stubby, which Google has been using internally for over a decade. gRPC achieves efficiency for communications among systems using HTTP/2 as the transport, and Protocol Buffers as the interface definition language (IDL). In chapter 8, we discuss how to secure communications among microservices over gRPC.

In this appendix, we discuss the fundamentals of gRPC. If you're interested in reading more about gRPC, we recommend *Practical gRPC* by Joshua Humphries, David Konsumer, et al. (Bleeding Edge Press, 2018), or *gRPC: Up and Running* by Kasun Indrasiri and Danesh Kuruppu (O'Reilly Media, 2020).

I.1   What is gRPC?

Many of us are familiar with functions in computer programs. A *function* in a program performs a specific task. A software program usually has a main function that's called by the underlying operating system when the program starts to run. A function in a typical program is invoked and executed by another function (or the main function) running within the same program.

RPC stands for *remote procedure call*. As its name implies, RPC is a protocol whereby a program can execute a function that's running on a remote host/computer on the network. RPC typically involves generating method stubs at the client side that make it look like a local function invocation, as the following example shows, but it's actually remote:

```
Registry registry = LocateRegistry.getRegistry(serverIP, serverPort);
Products products = (Products) registry.lookup(name);
int count = products.getCount();
```

In the preceding example, the object Products is a local variable; its getCount method does a remote procedure call over the network to a method running on a remote server identified by `serverIP` and `serverPort`. The `getCount` method on the server is where the actual business logic of the function resides. The method on the client application is simply a surrogate for the same method on the server application. Figure I.1 illustrates how the client application uses a stub to communicate with the server application.

gRPC has now become the method of choice for communications that happen among microservices. This is primarily because of the performance optimizations it offers compared to other common mechanisms, such as

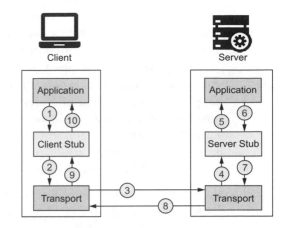

Figure I.1 When communicating over RPC, the client and server both use stubs to interface with each other.

JSON over HTTP. As mentioned in previous chapters, a microservice-driven application has many interactions that happen among microservices over the network. Therefore, whatever optimizations we can achieve at the network layer are realized in several orders of magnitude in real-world applications. Figure I.2 shows interactions among microservices to complete a given user operation.

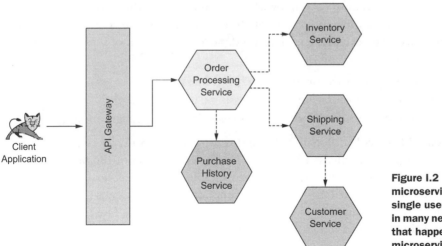

Figure I.2 In a typical microservices architecture, a single user operation results in many network interactions that happen among various microservices.

As you can see, when a user places an order, many interactions happen among various microservices. The Order Processing microservice talks to the Inventory microservice to update the stock information. It also talks to the Shipping microservice for delivery.

The Shipping microservice talks to the Customer microservice for getting delivery information. The Order Processing microservice also updates the customer purchase history by talking to the Purchase History microservice.

Four interactions happen among various microservices to serve a single order operation requested by a user. In this particular use case, because four interactions happen among different microservices, any benefits we gain over JSON/HTTP (measured by time) are realized by an order of magnitude of 4. Similarly, the advantages we gain with much larger applications that can have hundreds of microservices become much more significant. gRPC performs better for microservices compared to JSON/XML over HTTP for two primary reasons:

- gRPC uses Protocol Buffers, also known as Protobuf.
- gRPC uses the HTTP/2 transport protocol as opposed to HTTP/1.1.

I.2   *Understanding Protocol Buffers*

In this section, we introduce Protocol Buffers and explain how these have been essential in the development of gRPC. We also talk about the benefits provided in terms of efficiency in data transfer.

When using JSON over HTTP for communicating messages between clients and servers, the whole JSON message is transmitted in plaintext form. The payload is repetitive and sometimes unnecessary. This is because formats such as JSON/XML have been designed to be human readable. But, in practice, only machines process these messages. While JSON/XML formats make it easier to understand the message structures being passed along the network, when it comes to the application runtime, this isn't necessarily important. Protocol Buffers are a flexible, efficient, and automated mechanism for serializing structured data. You can think of it as JSON or XML but with the following exceptions:

- Much smaller size for representing a given message
- Much shorter time duration for processing a given message
- Much simpler to understand, given its resemblance to programming languages

Google created Protocol Buffers in 2001 to deal with an index server request-response protocol. It was publicly released in 2008. The current version of the language is version 3 (known as proto3). The examples in this appendix use this version.

With Protocol Buffers, you first need to define how your data needs to be structured. These structures are defined in files having a .proto extension. The following listing shows what a simple .proto file looks like when defining a simple `Customer` object.

Listing I.1   A simple .proto file

```
syntax = "proto3";

message Customer {
    string name = 1;
    int32 id = 2;
    string email = 3;
```

```
enum PhoneType {
    MOBILE = 0;
    HOME = 1;
    WORK = 2;
}

message PhoneNumber {
    string number = 1;
    PhoneType type = 2;
}

repeated PhoneNumber phone = 4;
}
```

As you might observe from listing I.1, each message type consists of one or more unique typed (`string`, `int`) fields. Each field has a unique number to identify it. Each typed field in a message has a default value. You can read more about default values at https://developers.google.com/protocol-buffers/docs/proto3#default.

You can also organize your data structure in a hierarchical fashion by using message types within other message types, similar to the way we used the `PhoneNumber` message within the `Customer` message in listing I.1. The Protobuf compiler then uses these structures to autogenerate source code that can be used to read data from streams and populates these structures. The compiler also converts data in these structures to streams. The generated code can be made available in a variety of programming languages supported by the Protobuf compiler.

Let's look at a quick example to understand what this code generation looks like. Before we begin, check out the samples for this appendix in https://github.com/microservices-security-in-action/samples/tree/master/appendix-i/. We're going to generate Java code from a .proto file by using the Spring Boot gRPC module. The following example has been tested on Java versions 8 and 11. You need to have Java 8+ and Maven version 3.2+ installed on your machine to try this. Navigate to the appendix-i/sample01 directory by using your command-line tool and execute this command:

```
\> mvn compile
```

You should see a success message if the compilation is successful, and a target directory as well. Navigate to the newly created target/generated-sources/protobuf/java/com/manning/mss/appendixi/sample01 directory. You should see a file named Customer.java. If you inspect its methods, you'll notice that it has the functions `get-Name`, `setName`, and so on, which perform the manipulation of the fields we declared in the .proto file. The Java programs we implement will use these autogenerated functions to exchange data between clients and servers using gRPC. You can find the compiled form of the `Customer` class in the target/classes directory.

Let's also look at the .proto file we just compiled. Open the appendix-i/sample01/src/main/proto/customer.proto file by using a text editor or an IDE. The `syntax = "proto3";` statement at the top of the file instructs the compiler that we're using protobuf version 3. The package statement, `com.manning.mss.appendixi.sample01;`

specifies the Java package name that should be included in the Java code being auto-generated. You should see the same package statement in the generated Customer.java file. The `option java_multiple_files = true;` statement instructs the compiler to generate separate Java source files for each parent message type. In this example, we have only one parent message type (`Customer`). However, this statement becomes handy when we have multiple messages to build code for, because it neatly breaks the source into multiple files instead of one large file.

I.3   *Understanding HTTP/2 and its benefits over HTTP/1.x*

In this section, we talk about HTTP/2 and how gRPC has benefitted from it to become much more performant, compared to JSON/XML over HTTP. One reason for gRPC's growth in popularity is the performance gains it provides compared to similar alternatives such as JSON over HTTP. gRPC uses HTTP/2 as its transport layer protocol. HTTP/2 provides request multiplexing and header compression, which increase its performance significantly. It also employs binary encoding of frames, which makes the data being transferred much more compact and efficient for processing. Let's take a closer look at request/response multiplexing and binary framing.

I.3.1   *Request/response multiplexing and its performance benefits*

In this section, we introduce the concept of *request multiplexing*, which is used in the HTTP/2 protocol for efficient data exchange among communicating parties. We first introduce the problem with HTTP/1.x, and then look at how request multiplexing solves that problem.

In a client-server communication happening over HTTP/1.x, if the client wants to make multiple requests to the server (in parallel) to improve performance, multiple TCP connections have to be used.[1] This is a consequence of the HTTP/1.x delivery model, where responses are sequential. By default, HTTP/1.x requests that happen over a single TCP connection are sequential as well. However, HTTP/1.x allows a client to send multiple requests to the server on a single TCP connection, using HTTP pipelining,[2] but it involves lots of complexity and has been known to cause a lot of problems. It's therefore rarely in use; sequential requests are the default.

Regardless of whether the client application uses HTTP pipelining or not, only a single response can be sent back from the server at a given time on a single TCP connection. This can cause lots of inefficiencies, which forces applications using HTTP/1.x to use multiple TCP connections even for requesting data from a single host. Figure I.3 illustrates a scenario where HTTP pipelining is in use to make parallel requests to a server over a single TCP connection and shows the sequential nature of responses being sent back.

---

[1]   TCP enables two hosts to establish a connection and exchange streams of data. TCP guarantees delivery of data and guarantees that the packets will be delivered in the same order in which they were sent.

[2]   *Pipelining* is the process whereby a client sends successive requests over a single persistent TCP connection to a server without waiting for responses.

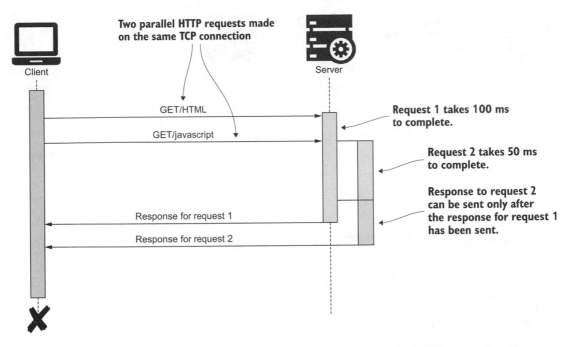

Figure I.3   A client application making two parallel requests to the server over a single TCP connection. The server processes the requests in parallel. Even though the server completes processing the second request first, it needs to wait until the response to the first request is sent before sending the response to the second request.

As you can see, a client application makes two parallel requests to the server over a single TCP connection to render a web page. The server processes the GET /HTML request first and the GET /javascript request next. Preparing the first response takes 100 milliseconds (ms), and preparing the second response takes 50 ms. Given the nature of the HTTP/1.x protocol, responses must be delivered to the client in sequential order. Therefore, even though the server completes preparing the second response much earlier than preparing the first response, it needs to wait until the first response is sent before the second response can be sent. This causes the client application to wait longer than is ideal before it can render the full web page it requested.

This problem is also known as the *head-of-line blocking* problem. As we mentioned earlier, this limitation has forced client applications to use multiple TCP connections in parallel. Figure I.4 illustrates how client applications work around the head-of-line blocking problem by using multiple TCP connections in parallel.

As illustrated in figure I.4, the GET /HTML request and the GET /javascript requests are sent from the client to the server using two different TCP connections. Because the request with lower overhead (GET /javascript) completes first, the server can now send back the response to it without waiting for the other request to complete. This allows the client application to start rendering the web page much earlier than in the previous case (figure I.3), where only a single TCP connection was used.

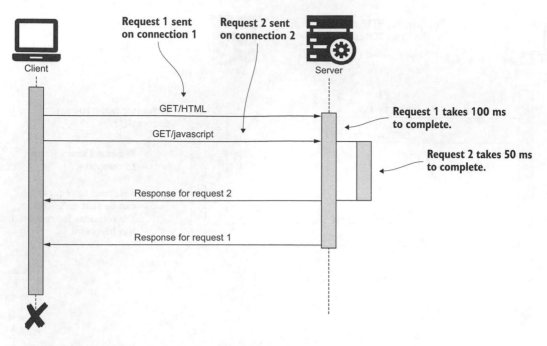

Figure I.4   A client application making two parallel requests to the server on two distinct TCP connections. The server processes the requests in parallel. Responses to requests are sent back to the client in the order of request completion.

Using multiple concurrent TCP connections may sound like the solution to the head-of-line blocking problem. However, when applied in practice, there's a limit on the number of TCP connections that can be created between communicating parties. This is mainly due to the resource limitations including CPU, file I/O, and network bandwidth. A web browser would typically create a maximum of six concurrent TCP connections to a given host (web domain). Therefore, in the context of a web browser, the maximum level of concurrency we can achieve is six. All communications within a given single TCP connection is still sequential.

This is where request and response multiplexing in the HTTP/2 protocol becomes useful. The binary framing layer in HTTP/2 removes the aforementioned limitation in HTTP/1.x by allowing an HTTP message to be broken into individual frames, interleaved, and then reassembled on the other side. Let's take a look at figure I.5 for a better understanding of this capability.

As you can see, with the HTTP/2 protocol, we can transmit multiple messages concurrently. The sending party breaks each HTTP message into multiple frames of different types (DATA frames, HEADER frames, and so on) and assigns them to a stream. The receiving party reassembles the messages based on the streams and starts processing each message as soon as each message completes reassembly. This gets rid of the head-of-line blocking problem with HTTP/1.x that we discussed earlier in this

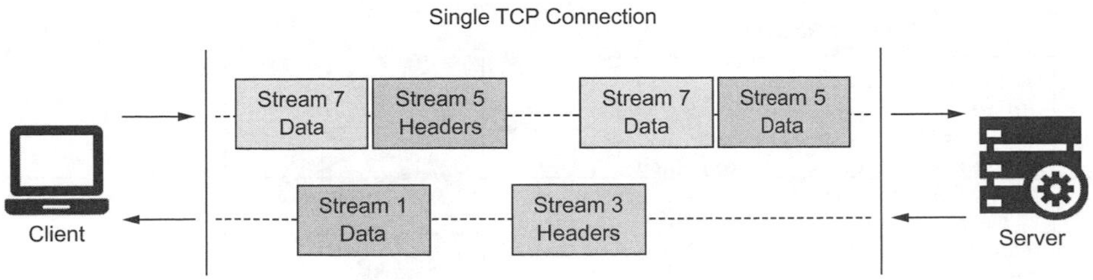

Single TCP Connection

Figure I.5   A client and server communicating using the HTTP/2 protocol. The requests and responses are multiplexed over a single TCP connection so that multiple messages can be transmitted concurrently without a message having to block over another message.

section. The multiplexing capability in HTTP/2 gives us numerous benefits compared to HTTP/1.*x* as listed here:

- Interleaving of multiple requests in parallel without blocking on any one
- Interleaving of multiple responses in parallel without blocking on any one
- Using a single TCP connection between client and server, which massively reduces our resource utilization and also reduces operational costs
- Improving the efficiency of client applications and servers by reducing idle time waiting on one another
- Avoiding underusing our network bandwidth and improving the application efficiency

Binary framing and streaming are the two fundamental concepts that allow HTTP/2 to multiplex requests and responses. Let's take a brief look at what they are and how they have helped the HTTP/2 protocol.

I.3.2   *Understanding binary framing and streams in HTTP/2*

In this section, we look at the fundamental differences in the way messages are encoded and exchanged between the HTTP/1.*x* and HTTP/2 protocols. We discuss in brief the concepts of binary framing and how frames get assigned to streams to allow multiplexing of requests and responses.

HTTP messages are composed of textual information. As the name *HTTP* itself implies (Hyper*text* Transfer Protocol), it includes textual information that is encoded in ASCII and spans over multiple lines with newline delimiters included. With HTTP/1.*x*, these messages were openly transmitted over the network. However, with HTTP/2, each message is now divided into HTTP frames.[3] Figure I.6 shows how an HTTP message is usually broken into frames.

---

[3] A *frame* is the smallest unit of communication that carries a specific type of data; for example, HTTP headers, message payload, and so on.

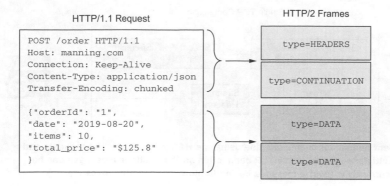

Figure I.6   An HTTP/1.*x* message is broken into multiple frames. The first chunk of headers is put into a frame typed HEADERS, and the consequent header chunks are put into frames typed CONTINUATION. The request body is broken into frames typed DATA.

As shown in figure I.6, an HTTP message is broken into multiple frames. Each frame has a type associated with it, which helps the receiver of the frame interpret the data in it accordingly. HTTP headers are transmitted in a frame typed HEADERS. Consequent headers of the same sequence are transmitted in a frame typed CONTINUATION. The request payload is transmitted in a frame typed DATA. A frame can hold a maximum of 16 megabytes of data. The HTTP/2 standards set the size of DATA frames to 16 kilobytes, by default, and allow the communicating parties to negotiate on higher values if necessary. When initiating a communication channel, a set of events takes place as listed here:

1 The client first breaks the request message into binary frames and then assigns the stream ID of the request to the frames. This way, each frame containing the binary data of the particular request gets associated with a single stream.
2 The client then initiates a TCP connection with the server and starts sending the frames over this connection.
3 Once the server receives the frames, it starts assembling them to form the request message, and then starts processing the request.
4 Once the server is ready to respond back to the client, the server breaks down the response into frames and assigns them the same stream ID as the request frames. Although frames can be transmitted in parallel on a single TCP connection, the stream ID in each frame allows the receiver to identify the proper message each frame belongs to. This scenario was illustrated previously in figure I.5.

You may have noticed in figure I.5 that all stream IDs were odd numbers. This didn't happen coincidentally. The HTTP/2 protocol supports bidirectional streaming, which we talk about in section I.4.6. This basically means that the client and server can both initiate the transmission of frames, unlike in HTTP/1.*x*, where only the client can initiate a transmission to the server.

Client-initiated frames are assigned to streams with odd-numbered IDs, and server-initiated frames are assigned to even-numbered stream IDs. This prevents the possibility of the client and server both initiating a stream with the same ID. The occurrence of such a scenario would have made it impossible for the receiver to properly identify the message a particular frame belongs to.

I.4   The different types of RPC available in gRPC

In this section, we look at the different types of RPC available in the gRPC protocol and the types of scenarios in which each one of them become useful. These include the following:

- Channels
- Metadata
- Unary RPC
- Server streaming RPC
- Client streaming RPC
- Bidirectional streaming RPC

I.4.1   Understanding channels

A gRPC *channel* represents a connection made from a client application to a host and port on a remote gRPC server. A channel has five legal states: CONNECTING, READY, TRANSIENT_FAILURE, IDLE, and SHUTDOWN.[4] Each state represents a particular behavior in the connection between client and server at that moment in time. Clients can specify channel arguments, such as disabling message compression and so on, to modify gRPC's default behavior.

I.4.2   Understanding request metadata

Metadata contains particular information about an RPC call, such as authentication details and so on. Metadata is provided in the form of a list of key-value pairs; keys are usually strings, and the values can be of string or binary types, though in most cases, values are provided as strings. Metadata helps the client provide information about RPC messages to the server, and vice versa. You can think of metadata as similar to headers in HTTP.

I.4.3   What is unary RPC?

Unary RPC represents a typical request-response pattern between client and server. gRPC supports this traditional model in which requests and responses are exchanged in a sequential pattern. In this pattern, the client first calls the stub/client method, which invokes the particular method on the server. The server processes the messages and prepares and sends the response back to the client. In this model, the number of messages exchanged between client and server is equal (one response per request).

---

[4] For the gRPC Connectivity Semantics and API, see https://github.com/grpc/grpc/blob/master/doc/connectivity-semantics-and-api.md.

I.4.4   *What is server streaming RPC?*

In the *server-streaming* model, the server sends a stream of responses for a single client request. Server streaming can be used when it makes sense to send multiple responses for a single client request.

Imagine a scenario in which you place an order in our retail store, and the server starts processing the order by verifying the payment and completing the shipping request. The payment processing and shipping operations can be done in two parallel microservices on the server. Through server streaming, the server now sends an update to the client as soon as each step completes. Once the server has sent all of its response messages to the client, it sends its status details (status code) and optional trailing metadata. The client uses this information to identify the end of the stream from the server.

I.4.5   *What is client streaming RPC?*

Similar to server streaming RPC, gRPC also supports *client-streaming RPC*. In this scenario, the client sends a stream of requests to the server, and the server typically (but not necessarily) sends back a single response. The server waits for the client to send its status details along with any optional trailing metadata before the server starts sending back the responses. Client streaming is useful when the client needs to submit multiple inputs to the server over a period of time before the server can perform its processing or calculations and provide the output.

Imagine that you take a metered taxi ride. The taxi (client) will upload its location data every few seconds or so. The server, upon receiving the location details, calculates the taxi fare based on the distance traveled and pushes an update to the client once every few minutes.

I.4.6   *What is bidirectional streaming RPC?*

In *bidirectional streaming RPC*, again the client initiates the call. The client application starts sending a stream of requests to the server, and the server begins sending a stream of responses to the client. The order in which the data is exchanged is application dependent. The server can decide to wait until it has received all the client request messages before sending back the responses, or the server could send responses while the client is still sending request messages to the server.

appendix J
Kubernetes fundamentals

Kubernetes is the most popular container orchestration framework as of this writing.[1] A *container* is an abstraction over the physical machine, while the *container orchestration framework* is an abstraction over the network. Container orchestration software like Kubernetes lets you deploy, manage, and scale containers in a highly distributed environment with thousands of nodes, or even more.

Kubernetes has its roots at Google as an internal project called *Borg*. Borg helped Google developers and system administrators manage thousands of applications across large data centers in multiple geographies. Borg became Kubernetes in 2014.

A detailed discussion on Kubernetes is beyond the scope of this book. For any readers interested in learning more, we recommend *Kubernetes in Action* (Manning, 2018) by Marko Lukša. Also, *Kubernetes Patterns: Reusable Elements for Designing Cloud Native Applications* (O'Reilly Media, 2019) by Bilgin Ibryam and Roland Huß is a good reference to learn how to use Kubernetes in a production deployment.

In chapter 11, we discuss how to deploy and secure microservices in a Kubernetes environment. If you're new to Kubernetes, this appendix lays the right foundation for following along in chapter 11.

J.1 Kubernetes high-level architecture

Kubernetes follows the client-server architecture. A Kubernetes cluster consists of one or more master nodes and one or more worker nodes (see figure J.1). When we want to deploy a microservice in a Kubernetes environment, we directly interact with a Kubernetes master node, which is also known as the *Kubernetes control plane*. To connect to the Kubernetes master node, we have to run a Kubernetes client on

---

[1] The word *Kubernetes* with ten characters is a little lengthy. In its shorter form, we call it *k8s*, as there are eight characters between *K* and *S*.

499

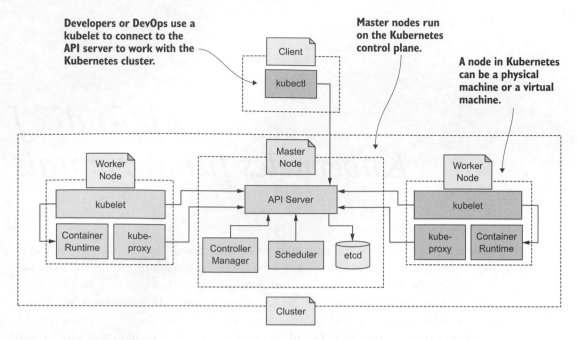

Figure J.1   A Kubernetes cluster consists of multiple master nodes and multiple worker nodes.

our local machine; that's the third component in a Kubernetes environment (in addition to the master nodes and the worker nodes).

J.1.1   *Master nodes*

A *master node* in Kubernetes takes care of almost all the functions in a Kubernetes cluster. A Kubernetes master node consists of four main components: an API server, a controller manager, a scheduler, and an etcd (see figure J.1). In a multimaster deployment, where you have multiple master nodes, each master node will have its own copy of an API server, a controller manager, a scheduler, and an etcd.

The communications among all these components happen via the API server. For example, to deploy a container in Kubernetes, we need to talk to the API server via a Kubernetes client application, which is called a *kubectl*. We discuss all four components in a master node in detail later in the appendix.

J.1.2   *Worker nodes*

Kubernetes runs workloads (containers) on *worker nodes*. When we instruct the master node to run a container (with a microservice) on Kubernetes, the master node then picks a worker node and instructs it to spin up and run the requested container. A worker node consists of three main components: a kubelet, a kube-proxy, and the container runtime (see figure J.1). We discuss these three components in detail later in the appendix.

J.2   *Basic constructs*

To start working with Kubernetes, we need to understand some of its basic constructs. This section covers the most used constructs, but by no means provides a comprehensive list.

J.2.1   *A Pod: The smallest deployment unit in Kubernetes*

A *Pod* is the smallest deployment unit in a Kubernetes environment (see figure J.2). It's an abstraction over a group of containers, so a given Kubernetes Pod can have more than one Docker container. (In appendix E, we discuss Docker containers in detail.) But in a Kubernetes environment, we can't deploy a container as-is; we need to wrap it in a Pod. For example, if we're deploying the Order Processing microservice in Kubernetes, we need to follow these steps:

1 Create a Docker image for the Order Processing microservice.
2 Publish the Docker image to a Docker registry, which is accessible from the Kubernetes cluster.

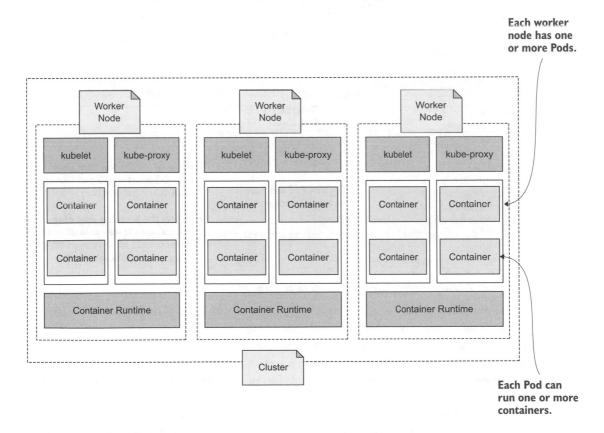

Each worker node has one or more Pods.

Each Pod can run one or more containers.

Figure J.2   A Pod groups one or more containers, and a worker node runs one or more Pods.

3 Write a YAML file to describe the Pod. This file tells Kubernetes which Docker images it needs to pull from the Docker registry to create the Pod. To be precise, we have a Pod within a *Deployment*. A Deployment is a Kubernetes object, which we discuss in section J.3.4; and in section J.14, we discuss Kubernetes objects.

4 Use the kubectl command-line tool to instruct the Kubernetes master node to create the Pod.

Defining constructs in Kubernetes

Kubernetes uses YAML files to represent various constructs. According to the YAML specification (https://yaml.org/spec/1.2/spec.html), YAML is a human-friendly, cross-language, Unicode-based data serialization language designed around the common native data types of Agile programming languages. It's (broadly) useful for programming needs ranging from configuration files to internet messaging to object persistence to data auditing.

Let's have a look at a sample YAML file, which describes a Pod. There, to create the Pod, Kubernetes has to pull the Docker image of the Order Processing microservice from the Docker Hub (a public Docker registry), with the image name `prabath/manning-order-processing`.

Listing J.1   Defining a Kubernetes Pod in YAML

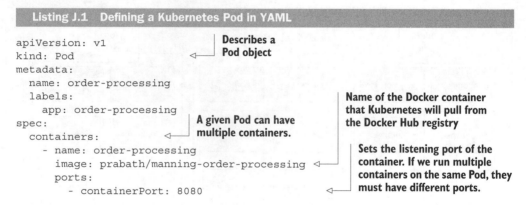

```
apiVersion: v1
kind: Pod                    ⟵── Describes a
metadata:                        Pod object
  name: order-processing
  labels:
    app: order-processing
spec:                        ⟵── A given Pod can have
  containers:                    multiple containers.
    - name: order-processing
      image: prabath/manning-order-processing   ⟵── Name of the Docker container
      ports:                                        that Kubernetes will pull from
        - containerPort: 8080                       the Docker Hub registry
```

Name of the Docker container that Kubernetes will pull from the Docker Hub registry

Sets the listening port of the container. If we run multiple containers on the same Pod, they must have different ports.

J.2.2   *A node: A VM or physical machine in a Kubernetes cluster*

A *node* in Kubernetes is a VM or a physical machine in a cluster. In other words, a Kubernetes cluster is a collection of Kubernetes nodes. When we instruct the Kubernetes master node to create a Pod with one or more containers, it picks the most appropriate worker node and instructs it to run the Pod.

A given Kubernetes cluster has multiple nodes, but all the containers in a given Pod run in the same worker node. We can also instruct the Kubernetes master node to create multiple replicas of the same Pod, and in that case, these replicas could run on different nodes of the Kubernetes cluster. But still, for a given Pod, all its containers run in the same node.

J.2.3 A Service: an abstraction over Kubernetes Pods

Pods in Kubernetes are ephemeral, or short-lived. They can come and go at any time (Kubernetes can start and stop a Pod at any time). For example, when we create a Pod, we can instruct Kubernetes to launch five instances (or replicas) of a Pod to run all the time, but if the load (or the number of requests) coming to those Pods goes beyond a certain threshold value, to increase the number of Pods to eight. This is how autoscaling works in Kubernetes.

With autoscaling, Kubernetes creates more Pods when the load crosses a given threshold and stops certain Pods when the load falls below the threshold. Also, we can ask Kubernetes to run a minimal set of Pods all the time (no matter what), and then, if a Pod goes down by itself (crashes), Kubernetes still makes sure it spins up a new one to maintain the minimal number of Pods we asked it to run.

Because Pods are ephemeral, the IP address assigned to a Pod can change over time, and at the same time, we can't exactly predict in an autoscaling environment how many Pods will be running at a given time and what those are. For these reasons, communications between a client application and a Pod, or communications among Pods, should not be using the IP address assigned to a Pod; instead, use a Service. A *Service* is an abstraction over a set of Pods (see figure J.3). You can create a Kubernetes Service pointing to a set of Pods, and you can think of a Service as a way to route requests to a Pod.

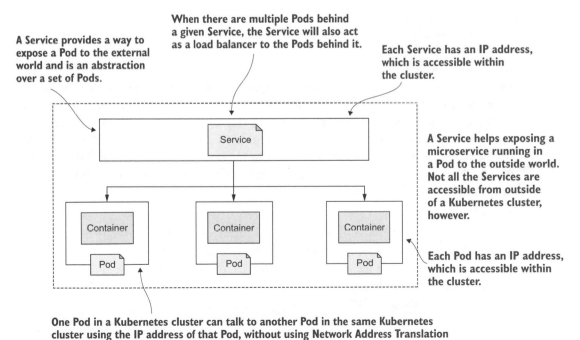

A Service provides a way to expose a Pod to the external world and is an abstraction over a set of Pods.

When there are multiple Pods behind a given Service, the Service will also act as a load balancer to the Pods behind it.

Each Service has an IP address, which is accessible within the cluster.

A Service helps exposing a microservice running in a Pod to the outside world. Not all the Services are accessible from outside of a Kubernetes cluster, however.

Each Pod has an IP address, which is accessible within the cluster.

One Pod in a Kubernetes cluster can talk to another Pod in the same Kubernetes cluster using the IP address of that Pod, without using Network Address Translation (NAT). These two Pods can be in the same Kubernetes node or in different nodes.

Figure J.3 A Service groups one or more Pods and exposes Pods outside the Kubernetes cluster. Not all the Services are accessible from outside a Kubernetes cluster, however.

If the Pod IP address changes over time and if a Pod can come and go at any time, how do we bind a Service to a Pod or to a set of Pods? When we create a Service against a set of Pods, we don't create a static binding between them. We don't tell the Service that these are the IP addresses of the Pods you need to work with. Instead, we use a label to define a filtering criterion so that Kubernetes can filter out the Pods that have to work with a given Service.

If you look at the sample YAML in listing J.2, you'll find the label `app:order-processing` is assigned to a Pod. A *label* is a key-value pair (in this example, `app` is the key, and `order-processing` is the value). All the replicas created from this Pod definition will carry the same label. If we want to create a Service pointing to all the replicas of that Pod, we can use the corresponding label as a filter criterion when defining the Service.

Listing J.2   Defining a Kubernetes Pod in YAML (same as listing J.1)

```
apiVersion: v1
kind: Pod
metadata:
  name: order-processing
  labels:
    app: order-processing
spec:
  containers:
    - name: order-processing
      image: prabath/manning-order-processing
      ports:
        - containerPort: 8080
```

Kubernetes assigns a virtual IP address for each Service. It is interesting to understand how a Service works: unlike a Pod, there is no running *thing* called a Service. A Service in Kubernetes carries a set of configurations that each node can read in order to set up its own iptables rules, so that when a request destined to a Service IP address (and the port) reaches a node, it can be dispatched to one of the Pods behind that particular Service.[2] At the point you create a Service, Kubernetes updates the iptables rules of its nodes.

CLUSTERIP SERVICE

When you create a Service in Kubernetes without specifying any type (or setting the type as `ClusterIP`), Kubernetes creates a Service of `ClusterIP` type; `ClusterIP` is the default Service type in Kubernetes. A Service of `ClusterIP` type is reachable only within a Kubernetes cluster. The following listing shows a sample YAML of a Kubernetes Service of `ClusterIP` type.

---

[2]   Iptables are used to set up, maintain, and inspect the tables of the IP packet filter rules in the Linux kernel (https://linux.die.net/man/8/iptables).

Listing J.3 Defining a `ClusterIP` Service in YAML

```
apiVersion: v1
kind: Service
metadata:
  name: order-processing-service
spec:
  type: ClusterIP
  selector:
    app: order-processing
  ports:
  - protocol: TCP
    port: 80
    targetPort: 8080
```

An optional attribute, "type" defines the type of the Service. If no type is specified, it's a ClusterIP service.

Selects the set of Pods in the Kubernetes cluster by matching labels

The client applications access the Service via this port, along with the ClusterIP.

Each Pod corresponding to this Service listens on the targetPort.

NODEPORT SERVICE

A Kubernetes cluster has multiple nodes. When we want to expose a microservice running in multiple Pods as a NodePort Service, Kubernetes opens a port (which is called the `nodePort`) on each node, which carries the same port number, and binds that port to the corresponding Service. To access a NodePort Service from a client outside the cluster, we need to use a node IP address (each node in the cluster has its own IP address) and the port number (nodePort) assigned to the Service.

When a request destined to a node IP address and a port corresponding to a Service reaches a node, the node can figure out the Service behind it and dispatch the request to that Service. In fact, looking at the iptables rules, the node will directly dispatch the request to one of the Pods behind that particular Service. So, the NodePort Service is accessible from outside the Kubernetes cluster, using the IP address of any of the nodes, and the nodePort of the Service. If a given node is down, the client must detect the failure and switch to a different node. That's one disadvantage in this approach.

If you want to access a NodePort Service within the Kubernetes cluster, you need to use the cluster IP address (not a node IP) of the Service and the corresponding Service port (`port`, not `nodePort`). The following listing shows a sample YAML of a Kubernetes Service of NodePort type.

Listing J.4 Defining a NodePort Service in YAML

```
apiVersion: v1
kind: Service
metadata:
  name: order-processing-service
spec:
  type: NodePort
  selector:
    app: order-processing
  ports:
  - protocol: TCP
    port: 80
```

An optional attribute, "type" defines the type of the Service

Selects the set of Pods in the Kubernetes cluster by matching labels

Within a cluster, the client applications access the Service via this port, along with the cluster IP.

```
targetPort: 8080
nodePort: 30200
```

Each node in the cluster listens on the same nodePort.

Each Pod corresponding to this Service listens on the targetPort.

This YAML creates a Service pointing to all the Pods carrying the label `app:order-processing`. Each Service has an internal IP address (the cluster IP), which is accessible only within the cluster. In this example, the Service listens on port 80, at the internal cluster IP address. Any Pod wanting to access the Service within the cluster can use the Service's internal IP address and the port (80). The `nodePort` (30200) is the port every node in the cluster listens to for any incoming traffic on the node IP address (not the cluster IP), and routes the request to port 8080 (the `targetPort`) of the corresponding Pod. If we don't specify a `nodePort` when creating the Service, Kubernetes internally picks an appropriate port.

LOADBALANCER SERVICE

The LoadBalancer Service type is an extension of the NodePort Service type. If there are multiple replicas of a given Pod, the LoadBalancer Service acts as a load balancer. Usually it's an external load balancer provided by the Kubernetes hosting environment. If the Kubernetes hosting environment doesn't support LoadBalancer services, a Service defined as a LoadBalancer will still run fine, but as a Service of the NodePort type. The following listing shows a sample YAML of a Kubernetes LoadBalancer Service.

Listing J.5   Defining a LoadBalancer Service in YAML

```
apiVersion: v1
kind: Service
metadata:
  name: order-processing-service
spec:
  type: LoadBalancer
  selector:
    app: order-processing
  ports:
  - protocol: TCP
    port: 80
    targetPort: 8080
```

An optional attribute, "type" defines the type of the Service.

Selects the set of Pods in the Kubernetes cluster by matching labels

This YAML creates a Service pointing to all the Pods carrying the label `app:order-processing`. The Service listens on port 80 (the load balancer port) and reroutes traffic to port 8080 of the corresponding Pod. Here, the rerouting works via a `nodePort` (which we discussed in section J.2.2). Even though we don't define a `nodePort` in listing J.5, Kubernetes automatically generates one.

The way routing works is that the external load balancer listens on port 80 and routes the traffic it gets to the `nodePort` of any node in the Kubernetes cluster. Then the iptables of that node reroutes the traffic to port 8080 of a corresponding Pod. Multiple Services can listen on the same port on the load balancer, but each Service has its own public IP address pointing to the load balancer. Then again, this can vary from one Kubernetes implementation to another, especially in the cloud.

J.2.4 Deployments: Representing your application in Kubernetes

Although the Pod concept is fundamental to Kubernetes, in practice, we don't deal with Pods directly (but Kubernetes does). We discussed Pods in section J.2.1. We, as developers (or DevOps), deal with Kubernetes Deployments. A *Deployment* represents your application, which carries multiple replicas of a given Pod. A Deployment is a Kubernetes object that helps with managing Pods. A given Deployment can manage only one Pod definition, however. There can be multiple replicas, but only one Pod definition.

We can use a Deployment to create and scale a Pod. It also helps you migrate your application from one version to another, following a migration strategy that you pick (blue/green, canary, and so on). To create a Pod, instead of using the YAML file in listing J.1, we can use the YAML file in the following listing, which creates a Deployment.

> **Listing J.6 Defining a Kubernetes Deployment in YAML**

```
apiVersion: apps/v1
kind: Deployment
metadata:
  name: order-processing-deployment
  labels:
    app: order-processing
spec:
  replicas: 5                               <-- Instructs Kubernetes to run five
  selector:                                     replicas of the matching Pods
    matchLabels:
      app: order-processing                 <-- An optional section that has multiple
  template:                                     labels. This Deployment carries a
    metadata:                                   matching Pod as per the selector.
      labels:                               <-- Describes how each Pod in the Deployment
        app: order-processing                   should look. If the Deployment defines a
    spec:                                        matchLabels selector, the Pod definition must
      containers:                               carry a matching label under the labels element.
      - name: order-processing
        image: prabath/manning-order-processing
        ports:
        - containerPort: 8080
```

J.2.5 A namespace: Your home within a Kubernetes cluster

A Kubernetes *namespace* is a virtual cluster within the same physical Kubernetes cluster. One Kubernetes cluster can have multiple namespaces. In practice, organizations have one Kubernetes cluster with different namespaces for different environments. For example, one namespace may be used for development, one for testing, one for staging, and another for production. Also, some organizations use two Kubernetes clusters: one for production environments and another for preproduction. The production Kubernetes cluster has one namespace for staging and another for production. The preproduction cluster has namespaces for development and testing. The following YAML file represents a Kubernetes namespace:

```
apiVersion: v1
kind: Namespace
metadata:
  name: manning
```

A Kubernetes namespace has these characteristics:

- The Kubernetes object names (for example, the name of a Pod, a Service, or a Deployment) must be unique within a namespace, but not across namespaces. In section J.13, we discuss Kubernetes objects in detail.
- The names of namespaces, nodes, and persistent volumes must be unique across all the namespaces in a cluster. A persistent volume (`Persistent-Volume`) in Kubernetes provides an abstraction over storage.
- By default, a Pod in one namespace can talk to another Pod in a different namespace. To prevent this, we use Kubernetes plugins to bring in network isolation by namespaces.
- Each namespace can have its own resource allocation. For example, when you share the same Kubernetes cluster for development and production with two namespaces, you can allocate more CPU cores and memory to the production namespace.
- Each namespace can have a limited number of objects. For example, the development namespace can have up to 10 Pods and 2 Services, while the production namespace can have up to 50 Pods and 10 Services.

J.3   *Getting started with Minikube and Docker Desktop*

Minikube provides a single-node Kubernetes cluster that can run on your local machine. It has certain limitations related to scalability, but is one of the easiest ways to get started with Kubernetes. The online Kubernetes documentation provides all the necessary steps in setting up Minikube (see https://kubernetes.io/docs/setup/minikube/).

Docker Desktop is an alternative to Minikube that also provides a single-node Kubernetes cluster that you can easily set up on your local machine. The details on setting up Docker Desktop are available at https://docs.docker.com/desktop/.

J.4   *Kubernetes as a service*

Instead of running Kubernetes on your own servers and maintaining the hardware yourself, you can look for a cloud vendor that provides *Kubernetes as a service*. Multiple cloud vendors offer this service, and most new Kubernetes deployments rely on cloud-hosted Kubernetes deployments. Some popular Kubernetes-as-a-service providers are as follows:

- *Google*—Google Kubernetes Engine (GKE)
- *Amazon*—Amazon Elastic Kubernetes Service (EKS), which runs on AWS
- *Microsoft*—Azure Kubernetes Service (AKS)

- *Red Hat*—OpenShift Container Platform (OCP)
- *Pivotal*—Pivotal Container Service (PKS)
- *IBM*—IBM Cloud Kubernetes Service
- *Oracle*—Container Engine for Kubernetes
- *VMware*—VMware Cloud PKS

Each of these cloud platforms has its own pros and cons, but the fundamental concepts around Kubernetes remain unchanged. In this book, we use GKE for all the samples, except for a few in chapter 12.

J.5 *Getting started with Google Kubernetes Engine*

Google Kubernetes Engine (*GKE*) is a Kubernetes-as-a-service implementation managed by Google. To get started, you need to have a valid Google account, which gives you a $300 credit to try out the Google Cloud Platform. That's more than enough to try out all the samples in this book.

You can sign up for the free trial at https://cloud.google.com/free/ (or search Google for "GKE free trial"). Then follow the straightforward instructions to get started with GKE at http://mng.bz/WPVw. The instructions may change over time, so we avoid repeating them here; always refer to the GKE online documentation to get started.

J.5.1 *Installing gcloud*

Google Cloud Platform (*GCP*) provides a command-line tool to interact with your GKE running on the cloud from your local machine. Follow the instructions corresponding to your operating system to install gcloud, which are available at https://cloud.google.com/sdk/docs/quickstarts. In fact, what you install is the Google Cloud SDK, and gcloud is part of it. Once you have successfully installed gcloud, run the following command to make sure everything is working fine:

```
\> gcloud info

Google Cloud SDK [290.0.1]
Python Version: [2.7.10 (default, Feb 22 2019, 21:17:52)
[GCC 4.2.1 Compatible Apple LLVM 10.0.1 (clang-1001.0.37.14)]]
Installed Components:
  core: [2020.04.24]
  gsutil: [4.49]
  bq: [2.0.56]
Account: [prabath@wso2.com]
Project: [manning-ms-security]
Current Properties:
  [core]
    project: [manning-ms-security]
    account: [prabath@wso2.com]
    disable_usage_reporting: [False]
  [compute]
    zone: [us-west1-a]
```

This output shows only some important parameters. When you run the same command in your local setup, you'll get a different result with more parameters.

J.5.2   *Installing kubectl*

To interact with the Kubernetes environment running on Google Cloud, you also need to install *kubectl* as a component of the gcloud tool, which you installed in section J.5.1. This command-line tool, kubectl, runs on your local computer and talks to the Kubernetes API server running on Google Cloud to perform certain operations. The following command installs kubectl as a component of the gcloud tool:

```
\> gcloud components install kubectl
```

To verify the kubectl installation, run the following command, which should result in meaningful output, with no errors:

```
\> kubectl help
```

J.5.3   *Setting up the default setting for gcloud*

The gcloud command-line tool has an option to remember certain settings, so each time you run a `gcloud` command, you do not need to repeat them. The following example sets the default GKE project ID, an identifier associated with a GKE project that you create from the web-based console. When you set up your GKE account, you also created a project. You need to replace `[PROJECT_ID]` in the following command with your own project ID:

```
\> gcloud config set project [PROJECT_ID]
```

When you create a Kubernetes cluster in GKE, you need to specify under which region, or compute zone, you want to create it. This region indicates the geographical location. All the resources associated with that Kubernetes cluster live in that particular region. The following command sets the default region:

```
\> gcloud config set compute/zone us-west1-a
```

Here, we set the default compute zone to `us-west1-a` (the Dalles, Oregon, US region). In fact, `us-west1` is the region, and `a` is the zone. A *zone* is a location within a region that defines the capacity and the type of available resources. For example, the `us-west1` region has three zones: `a`, `b`, and `c`; and zone `a` has the Intel Xeon E5 v4 (Broadwell) platform by default, with up to 96 vCPU machine types on the Skylake platform. More details on GKE regions and zones are documented at http://mng.bz/EdOj.

J.5.4   *Creating a Kubernetes cluster*

Before we do anything on Kubernetes, we need to create a cluster. You won't do this frequently. The following command uses the gcloud command-line tool to create a Kubernetes cluster with the name `manning-ms-security`:

```
\> gcloud container clusters create manning-ms-security

Creating cluster manning-ms-security in us-west1-a...
Cluster is being configured...
```

```
Creating cluster manning-ms-security in us-west1-a...
Cluster is being deployed
...
Creating cluster manning-ms-security in us-west1-a...
Cluster is being health-checked (master is healthy)...done.
Created [https://container.googleapis.com/v1/projects/kubetest-
232501/zones/us-west1-a/clusters/manning-ms-security]
```

After we successfully create the Kubernetes cluster, we need to configure the kubectl command-line tool to work with the cluster. The following command fetches the authentication credentials to connect to the cluster (`manning-ms-security`) and configures kubectl:

```
\> gcloud container clusters get-credentials manning-ms-security
```

Now let's use the following `kubectl` command to find the version of the Kubernetes client and server. All the commands we run with kubectl aren't specific to GKE, but common across all Kubernetes deployments:

```
\> kubectl version
```

J.5.5 *Deleting a Kubernetes cluster*

You can use the following `gcloud` command to delete a Kubernetes cluster (in our example, `manning-ms-security`) created on GKE, but let's not do that until we finish the examples in this book:

```
\> gcloud container clusters delete manning-ms-security
```

J.5.6 *Switching between multiple Kubernetes clusters*

If you have set up your kubectl tool to work with multiple clusters, you also need to know how to switch between those clusters. Probably you'll connect to GKE and run a local cluster with Docker Desktop or Minikube. The following command lists all the Kubernetes clusters available in your environment:

```
\> kubectl config get-contexts
```

To find the current active cluster, you can use the following command:

```
\> kubectl config current-context
```

To switch the current active cluster to something else, you can use the following command. This command switches the current active cluster to docker-desktop:

```
\> kubectl config use-context docker-desktop
```

J.6 *Creating a Kubernetes Deployment*

There are two ways to create a Kubernetes Deployment: using a YAML file or using the kubectl command-line tool. Even if we use the YAML file, we'll still use kubectl to communicate with the Kubernetes cluster running in the cloud.

In a production deployment, we use YAML files to maintain a Kubernetes Deployment configuration. In most cases, these files are versioned and maintained in a Git repository. A detailed discussion on a Kubernetes Deployment is beyond the scope of this book, so for any readers interested in learning more, we recommend *Kubernetes in Action* and *Kubernetes Patterns: Reusable Elements for Designing Cloud Native Applications*, as noted previously.

In chapter 11, we use YAML files in all the examples to create Kubernetes Deployments, but in this appendix, we use the command-line options. Let's use the following `kubectl run` command to create a Kubernetes Deployment with the Docker image `gcr.io/google-samples/hello-app`. If you run the same command again and again, you'll get an error:

```
Error from server (AlreadyExists): deployments.apps "hello-server"
already exists.
```

In that case, you need to delete the Deployment before running the `kubectl run` command again (check the end of this section for information on the `delete` command):

```
\> kubectl run hello-server --image gcr.io/google-samples/hello-app:1.0 \
--port 8080

deployment.apps/hello-server created
```

When you run this command, Kubernetes fetches the Docker image from the gcr.io Docker registry and runs it as a container on the Kubernetes cluster we just created. The `port` argument in the `kubectl` command specifies that the process running in the container should be exposed over port 8080. Now, if you run the following `get` command, it shows you all the Deployments in the current Kubernetes cluster (under the default Namespace):

```
\>  kubectl get deployments

NAME           DESIRED    CURRENT    UP-TO-DATE    AVAILABLE    AGE
hello-server   1          1          1             1            13s
```

If you'd like to see the YAML representation of the Kubernetes Deployment, we can use the following command, which carries the value `yaml` for the `o` (output) argument. This results in a lengthy output, but carries all the details related to the hello-server Deployment:

```
\> kubectl get deployments hello-server -o yaml
```

In section J.2.1, we discussed that a Pod is the smallest deployment unit in a Kubernetes environment. When we create a Deployment, the related Pods get created automatically, and the containers run inside a Pod. We can use the following `kubectl get` command to list all the Pods running in our Kubernetes cluster (under the default namespace):

```
\> kubectl get pods

NAME                             READY    STATUS     RESTARTS    AGE
hello-server-5cdf4854df-q42c4    1/1      Running    0           10m
```

If you'd like to delete the Deployment we just created, you can use the following `delete` command. But let's not do it until we finish this appendix.

```
\> kubectl delete deployments hello-server
```

J.7   *Behind the scenes of a Deployment*

When we create a Deployment, it internally creates another object called ReplicaSet. For simplicity, we skipped this discussion when we introduced the Deployment object in section J.2.4. As DevOps, we don't directly deal with ReplicaSet, but Kubernetes does internally. In a Deployment, the Pods are created and managed by a ReplicaSet object. The following `kubectl` command lists all the ReplicaSets in the Kubernetes cluster (under the default Namespace):

```
\> kubectl get replicasets

NAME                       DESIRED   CURRENT   READY   AGE
hello-server-5cdf4854df    1         1         1       11m
```

The `kubectl get` command in the following listing gets more details corresponding to the `hello-server-5cdf4854df` ReplicaSet object and prints the output in YAML format.

> **Listing J.7   Defining a ReplicaSet in YAML**

```
\> kubectl get replicasets hello-server-5cdf4854df -o yaml

apiVersion: extensions/v1beta1
kind: ReplicaSet
metadata:
  labels:
    run: hello-server
  name: hello-server-5cdf4854df
  namespace: default
  ownerReferences:
  - apiVersion: apps/v1
    kind: Deployment
    name: hello-server
    uid: c7460660-7d38-11e9-9a8e-42010a8a014b
spec:
  replicas: 1
  selector:
    matchLabels:
      run: hello-server          ◁─┐  Defines the Pod that
  template:                         │  this ReplicaSet controls
    metadata:
      labels:
        run: hello-server
    spec:
      containers:
      - image: gcr.io/google-samples/hello-app:1.0
        name: hello-server
```

```
      ports:
      - containerPort: 8080
        protocol: TCP
status:
  availableReplicas: 1
  replicas: 1
```

The truncated output shows some important sections and attributes. The `spec/template` section defines the Pod, which this ReplicaSet manages.

J.8   *Creating a Kubernetes Service*

The `hello-server` Deployment (which we created in section J.6) listens on port 8080. It's not accessible outside the Kubernetes cluster (it doesn't have an IP address that's accessible outside the cluster). In Kubernetes, a container that carries a microservice (or in our case, `hello-server`) is deployed in a Pod, and Pods can communicate with each other. One Pod can talk to another Pod. Each Pod in a Kubernetes environment has a unique IP address. You can run the following `kubectl` commands to list out all the Pods running in your Kubernetes namespace and then get more information about a specific Pod running within a Deployment:

```
\> kubectl get pods

NAME                             READY    STATUS      RESTARTS    AGE
hello-server-5cdf4854df-q42c4    1/1      Running     0           10m

\> kubectl describe pod hello-server-5cdf4854df-q42c4

Name:             hello-server-5cdf4854df-q42c4
Namespace:        default
Status:           Running
IP:               10.36.0.6
```

The command shows all the details related to the provided Pod (`hello-server-5cdf4854df-q42c4`), but for clarity, only a few important parameters are shown in the output (most important, the IP address). This IP address assigned to a Pod by Kubernetes is accessible only within the same cluster.

In a typical Kubernetes environment for a given microservice (or a container), we run multiple instances of the same Pod to address scalability requirements; each Pod in a Kubernetes cluster has multiple replicas. This helps Kubernetes distribute the requests coming to a given microservice among all the corresponding Pods, or to do load balancing. Remember, Pods in Kubernetes are short-lived. They can come and go at any time, so even the internal IP address assigned to a Pod can change from time to time. This is one requirement for having a Kubernetes Service (see section J.2.3).

A Kubernetes Service provides an abstraction over a set of Pods that matches the given criteria. You don't talk to a Pod directly, but always go through a Service. Let's use the following command to create a Kubernetes Service:

```
\> kubectl expose deployment hello-server --type LoadBalancer \
--port 80 --target-port 8080
```

This command creates a Kubernetes Service over all the Pods running in the `hello-server` Deployment. Here, we create a Service of the type LoadBalancer. Let's use the following command to discover all the Services running in our Kubernetes cluster (under the `default` namespace):

```
\> kubectl get services

NAME          TYPE          CLUSTER-IP     EXTERNAL-IP      PORT(S)        AGE
hello-server  LoadBalancer  10.39.243.41   35.233.245.242   80:30648/TCP   6h8m
kubernetes    ClusterIP     10.39.240.1    <none>           443/TCP        8h
```

The output shows that the `hello-server` Service has two IP addresses. When we access a Service from within a Kubernetes cluster, we use the cluster IP. And for accessing a Service from an external client, we use the external IP. Kubernetes can take a few minutes to assign an external IP address to a Service. If you don't see an IP address assigned to your Service, repeat the command in a few minutes. We can use the following `curl` command to test the `hello-server` Service with its external IP address:

```
\> curl http://35.233.245.242

Hello, world!
Version: 1.0.0
Hostname: hello-server-5cdf4854df-q42c4
```

If you run this sample in your local Kubernetes setup, either with Docker Desktop or Minikube, you won't see an external IP address assigned to it. That is because there is no load balancer associated with your local Kubernetes environment. As you learned in section J.2.3, if we create a Service of NodePort type, we should be able to access it by using the IP address of a node and the nodePort. The following command shows how to create a Service of NodePort type:

```
\> kubectl expose deployment hello-server --name hello-server-local \
--type NodePort --port 80 --target-port 8080
```

If you are running a local single-node Kubernetes setup, your node IP address would be 127.0.0.1, and the following command finds the nodePort of the Service:

```
\> kubectl describe service hello-server-local
```

To test the Service in your local setup, use the following command, where 31587 is the nodePort:

```
\> curl http://127.0.01:31587
```

J.9   *Behind the scenes of a Service*

When we create a Service, Kubernetes internally creates an Endpoints object corresponding to the Service. Before we delve deep into why we need Endpoints, let's use the following `kubectl` command to list all the Endpoints objects in the Kubernetes cluster (under the default namespace):

```
\> kubectl get endpoints

NAME           ENDPOINTS         AGE
hello-server   10.36.0.6:8080    5d18h
```

Each Endpoints object carries a set of Pod IP addresses and the corresponding container ports, with respect to the Pods associated with a given Service. Listing J.8 shows more details of the `hello-server` Endpoints object. The truncated output shows the definition of an Endpoints object with respect to a Service associated with three replicas of a given Pod.

Listing J.8   The truncated definition of an Endpoints object

```
apiVersion: v1
kind: Endpoints
metadata:
  name: hello-server
  namespace: default
subsets:                                                    Name of the node that runs the
- addresses:                                                Pod. Here we can see each Pod
  - ip: 10.36.0.6        ◄─┐ IP address                     runs on a different node.
    nodeName: gke-manning-ms-security-default-pool-6faf40f5-5cnb    ◄
    targetRef:
      kind: Pod                                             Name of
      name: hello-server-5cdf4854df-q42c4    ◄─┘ the Pod
  - ip: 10.36.1.36
    nodeName: gke-manning-ms-security-default-pool-6faf40f5-br1m
    targetRef:
      kind: Pod
      name: hello-server-5cdf4854df-5z8hj
  - ip: 10.36.2.28
    nodeName: gke-manning-ms-security-default-pool-6faf40f5-vh0x
    targetRef:
      kind: Pod
      name: hello-server-5cdf4854df-bdgdc
ports:
  - port: 8080
    protocol: TCP
```

As we discussed in section J.9, a Service finds the associated Pods by matching the corresponding labels. At runtime, for a Service to route traffic to a Pod, it has to know the Pod's IP address and port. To address this need, after we find all the Pods associated with a given Service, Kubernetes creates an Endpoints object to carry all the Pod's IP addresses and the corresponding container ports associated with that Service. The Endpoints object gets updated when there's a change in a corresponding Pod.

J.10   Scaling a Kubernetes Deployment

In our `hello-server` Deployment so far, we have only one Pod. We can use the following `kubectl` command to ask Kubernetes to create five replicas of the Pod within the same Deployment. Kubernetes will make sure it always maintains five replicas of the Pod, and if one Pod goes down, it will spin up a new one:

```
\> kubectl scale --replicas 5  deployment hello-server

deployment.extensions/hello-server scaled

\> kubectl get pods

NAME                          READY    STATUS    RESTARTS    AGE
hello-server-5cdf4854df-c9b4j 1/1      Running   0           52s
hello-server-5cdf4854df-fs6hg 1/1      Running   0           53s
hello-server-5cdf4854df-hpc7h 1/1      Running   0           52s
hello-server-5cdf4854df-q42c4 1/1      Running   0           7h24m
hello-server-5cdf4854df-qjkgp 1/1      Running   0           52s
```

J.11 Creating a Kubernetes namespace

As you learned in section J.3.6, a Kubernetes namespace is a virtual cluster within the same physical Kubernetes cluster. Kubernetes comes with its own set of namespaces. Let's use the following `kubectl` command to view the available Kubernetes namespaces:

```
\> kubectl get namespaces

NAME          STATUS    AGE
default       Active    23h
kube-public   Active    23h
kube-system   Active    23h
```

Each object we create in Kubernetes belongs to a namespace. All the objects created by the Kubernetes system itself belong to the `kube-system` namespace. An object belonging to one namespace isn't accessible from another namespace. If we want to have some objects accessible from any namespace, we need to create them in the `kube-public` namespace. When we create an object with no namespace, those objects belong to the default namespace. Let's use the following `kubectl` command to create a custom namespace called `manning`:

```
\> kubectl create namespace manning

namespace/manning created
```

The following `kubectl` command shows how to create a Deployment in the `manning` namespace. If we skip the `--namespace` argument in the command, Kubernetes assumes it's the default namespace.

```
\> kubectl run manning-hello-server \
--image gcr.io/google-samples/hello-app:1.0 --port 8080 --namespace=manning
```

The following `kubectl` command shows all the Deployments in the default namespace. It doesn't show the `manning-hello-server` Deployment, which we created from the previous command under the manning namespace:

```
\> kubectl get deployments

NAME           DESIRED   CURRENT   UP-TO-DATE   AVAILABLE   AGE
hello-server   5         5         5            5           22h
```

To view all the deployments under the `manning` namespace, let's use the following `kubectl` command (instead of `--namespace`, you can use `-n`):

```
\> kubectl get deployments --namespace manning

NAME                 DESIRED   CURRENT   UP-TO-DATE   AVAILABLE   AGE
manning-hello-server 1         1         1            1           36s
```

J.12 *Switching Kubernetes namespaces*

If we work on multiple Kubernetes namespaces, sometimes it's a pain to switch between them. The kubectx tool lets you switch between multiple Kubernetes clusters and namespaces quite easily.

Installation of kubectx is straightforward when you follow the instructions at https://github.com/ahmetb/kubectx. Once the installation is done, we can use the following `kubens` command (which comes with kubectx) to set `manning` as the default namespace so we don't need to pass the `--namespace` argument with each and every `kubectl` command:

```
\> kubens manning

Context "gke_kubetest-232501_us-west1-a_manning-ms-security" modified.
Active namespace is "manning".
```

J.13 *Using Kubernetes objects*

Kubernetes has a rich object model to represent different aspects of an application running in a distributed environment. Using a YAML file, we can describe each of these Kubernetes objects and create, update, and delete them by using an API, which is exposed by the Kubernetes API server and persists in etcd.[3] For example, a Pod, a Service, and a Namespace are basic Kubernetes objects, as we discussed in section J.2. Each object has two top-level attributes called `apiVersion` and `kind`, and another set of attributes under three main categories: `metadata`, `spec`, and `status`:

- `apiVersion`—Defines the versioned schema of the object representation. This helps to avoid any conflicts in version upgrades.
- `kind`—A string that represents the object type; for example, the value of the `kind` attribute can be `Pod`, `Deployment`, `Namespace`, `Volume`, and so on.
- `metadata`—Includes the name of the object, a unique identifier (UID), the object's namespace, and other standard attributes.
- `spec`—Describes the desired state of a Kubernetes object at the time you create (or update) it.
- `status`—Represents the actual state of the object at the runtime.

---

[3] etcd is a highly available key-value store that Kubernetes uses to persist cluster data. The API server persists the data related to the Kubernetes objects in etcd.

The difference between `spec` and `status` might not be clear, so let's go through an example. Let's revisit the command we used in section J.6 to create a Kubernetes Deployment with the Docker image:

```
gcr.io/google-samples/hello-app
```

This is an example of an *imperative command*. With an imperative command, we tell Kubernetes exactly what to do and give it all the required parameters as command-line arguments to manage a given Kubernetes object (in section J.13.1, you learned about creating Kubernetes objects using a declarative configuration as opposed to imperative commands):

```
\> kubectl run hello-server --image gcr.io/google-samples/hello-app:1.0 \
--port 8080

deployment.apps/hello-server created
```

This command creates a `Deployment` object in the Kubernetes cluster. We can use the following `kubectl` command to get the definition of it (the example shows only truncated output):

```
\> kubectl get deployment hello-server -o yaml

apiVersion: extensions/v1beta1
kind: Deployment
metadata:
  name: hello-server
spec:
  replicas: 1
status:
  availableReplicas: 1
```

Here, we can see that the number of `replicas` under the `spec` category is 1, which is the required number of replicas, and the `availableReplicas` under the `status` category is also 1. Let's use another `kubectl` imperative command to increase the number of replicas to 100. Once again, this is exactly what happens when we use imperative commands: we need to tell Kubernetes how to do everything, not just what we need:

```
\> kubectl scale --replicas 100  deployment hello-server

deployment.extensions/hello-server scaled
```

This command creates 100 replicas of the Deployment, which would probably take a few seconds. We can use the `kubectl` command in the following listing a few times, waiting just a second after issuing the previous command, to get the definition of the Deployment (only a truncated output is shown).

Listing J.9   The truncated definition of the `hello-server` Deployment object

```
\> kubectl get deployment hello-server -o yaml

apiVersion: extensions/v1beta1
```

```
kind: Deployment
metadata:
  name: hello-server
spec:
  replicas: 100
status:
  availableReplicas: 1

\> kubectl get deployment hello-server -o yaml

apiVersion: extensions/v1beta1
kind: Deployment
metadata:
  name: hello-server
spec:
  replicas: 100
status:
  availableReplicas: 14
```

Here, we can see that the number of `replicas` under the `spec` category is 100 all the time, while `availableReplicas` under the `status` category is 1 initially. When we run the same command for the second time, `availableReplicas` under the `status` category has increased to 14. Attributes under the `spec` category represent the requirements, while the attributes under the `status` category represent the actual runtime status of a Kubernetes object.

J.13.1   *Managing Kubernetes objects*

We can use kubectl to manage Kubernetes objects in three ways: imperative commands, imperative object configurations, and declarative object configurations. In the previous section, we used imperative commands. That's a great way to get started, but in a production environment, we shouldn't use those commands. Imperative commands change the state of the Kubernetes objects in a cluster with no tracing. For example, if we want to revert a change we made, we need to do it manually by remembering the command we executed.

IMPERATIVE OBJECT CONFIGURATIONS

With imperative object configuration, we use a YAML file to represent a Kubernetes object (instead of passing all required attributes as command-line arguments), and then use kubectl to manage the objects. For example, let's look at the content of the hello-server.yaml file in the following listing, which represents the `hello-server` Deployment.

> **Listing J.10   Defining a `hello-server` Deployment object**

```
apiVersion: extensions/v1beta1
kind: Deployment
metadata:
  name: hello-server
spec:
```

```
replicas: 1
selector:
  matchLabels:
    run: hello-server
template:
  metadata:
    labels:
      run: hello-server
  spec:
    containers:
    - image: gcr.io/google-samples/hello-app:1.0
      name: hello-server
      ports:
      - containerPort: 8080
```

Let's use the following `kubectl` command to create a Deployment using the object's configuration (from listing J.10). If you ran the previous examples in this appendix, you already have the `hello-server` Deployment. In that case, change the `metadata :name:` in the configuration to another name. You can find the hello-server.yaml file inside the appendix-j/sample01 directory of the samples repo of the book at https://github.com/microservices-security-in-action/samples/:

```
\> kubectl create -f hello-server.yaml
```

```
deployment.extensions/hello-server created
```

To update a Kubernetes object, use the following `kubectl` command with the updated object configuration:

```
\> kubectl replace -f hello-server.yaml
```

One drawback here is the updated hello-server.yaml must carry all the attributes that are necessary to replace the object. You can't do a partial update.

DECLARATIVE OBJECT CONFIGURATIONS

With declarative object configuration, we don't need to tell Kubernetes how to do things, but only what we need. To create a Deployment, first we need to have a YAML file (just as in the imperative object configuration).

Let's use the same hello-server.yaml as in listing J.10 and the following `kubectl` command to create a Deployment using the object configuration in that listing. If you ran the previous examples in this appendix, you already have the `hello-server` Deployment. In that case, change the `metadata:name` in the configuration to another name:

```
\> kubectl apply -f hello-server.yaml
```

When we run the command, we don't ask Kubernetes to create or update the Deployment; we just specify the characteristics of the Deployment we need, and Kubernetes automatically detects the required operations and executes those. Whether we want to create a new object or update an existing one, we use the same `apply` command.

J.14   *Exploring the Kubernetes API server*

The Kubernetes API server runs on the Kubernetes control plane. Let's see how to directly connect to the API server and discover what APIs are hosted there. The following kubectl command opens a connection to the API server. It, in fact, spins up a proxy server on your local machine and, by default, listens in on port 8001.

```
\> kubectl proxy &

Starting to serve on 127.0.0.1:8001
```

We can run the curl command in the following listing to find all the API paths hosted on the API server (here too, output is truncated).

Listing J.11   Listing the APIs hosted in the Kubernetes API server

```
\> curl http://localhost:8001/

{
  "paths": [
    "/api",
    "/api/v1",
    "/apis",
    "/apis/",
    "/apis/apps",
    "/apis/apps/v1",
    "/apis/authentication.k8s.io",
    "/apis/authorization.k8s.io/v1",
    "/apis/authorization.k8s.io/v1beta1",
    "/apis/autoscaling",
    "/apis/batch",
    "/apis/batch/v1",
    "/apis/batch/v1beta1",
    "/apis/certificates.k8s.io",
    "/apis/certificates.k8s.io/v1beta1",
    "/apis/cloud.google.com",
    "/apis/extensions",
    "/apis/extensions/v1beta1",
    "/apis/metrics.k8s.io",
    "/apis/metrics.k8s.io/v1beta1",
    "/apis/networking.gke.io",
    "/apis/policy",
    "/apis/policy/v1beta1",
    "/apis/rbac.authorization.k8s.io",
    "/apis/rbac.authorization.k8s.io/v1",
    "/apis/scheduling.k8s.io",
    "/healthz",
    "/logs",
    "/metrics",
    "/openapi/v2",
    "/swagger-2.0.0.json",
    "/swagger-2.0.0.pb-v1",
    "/swagger-2.0.0.pb-v1.gz",
```

```
      "/swagger.json",
      "/swaggerapi",
      "/version"
   ]
}
```

We can use the `curl` command in the following listing to list all the resources supported by a given Kubernetes API version (output is truncated).

Listing J.12   Listing the resources available in the Kubernetes API v1

```
\> curl http://localhost:8001/api/v1

{
  "kind": "APIResourceList",
  "groupVersion": "v1",
  "resources": [
    {
      "name": "configmaps",
      "singularName": "",
      "namespaced": true,
      "kind": "ConfigMap",
      "verbs": [
        "create",
        "delete",
        "deletecollection",
        "get",
        "list",
        "patch",
        "update",
        "watch"
      ],
      "shortNames": [
        "cm"
      ]
    },
    {
      "name": "pods",
      "singularName": "",
      "namespaced": true,
      "kind": "Pod",
      "verbs": [
        "create",
        "delete",
        "deletecollection",
        "get",
        "list",
        "patch",
        "update",
        "watch"
      ],
      "shortNames": [
        "po"
```

```
        ],
        "categories": [
          "all"
        ]
      }
    ]
}
```

J.15   Kubernetes resources

A *resource* is an instance of a Kubernetes object, which is accessible by a unique URL; in other words, it's a REST resource. We can access the same Kubernetes object via multiple resource URLs. For example (assuming that you have the `hello-server` Deployment still running), the following `kubectl` command retrieves the definition of the `hello-server` Deployment as YAML output:

```
\> kubectl get deployment hello-server -o yaml
```

The following shows the truncated output of the previous command, which includes only some important attributes:

```
apiVersion: extensions/v1beta1
kind: Deployment
metadata:
  name: hello-server
  namespace: default
  resourceVersion: "1137529"
  selfLink: /apis/extensions/v1beta1/namespaces/default/
            deployments/hello-server
  uid: c7460660-7d38-11e9-9a8e-42010a8a014b
spec:
  replicas: 1
status:
  availableReplicas: 1
```

The `selfLink` attribute in the output is the resource that represents the `hello-server` Deployment. As we discussed in section J.14, we can start a proxy locally and issue a `curl` command to this resource URL to get the complete representation of the `hello-server` Deployment resource:

```
\> kubectl proxy &

Starting to serve on 127.0.0.1:8001

\> curl \
 http://localhost:8001/apis/extensions/v1beta1/namespaces/default/\
deployments/hello-server
```

J.16   Kubernetes controllers

In section J.13, we discussed `spec` and `status` as two attribute categories of a Kubernetes object. The `spec` attribute defines the desired status of the Kubernetes object, while the `status` attribute defines the actual status of the object.

The role of the Kubernetes controllers is to maintain the status of the Kubernetes cluster at its desired state. Controllers always observe the status of the Kubernetes cluster. For example, when we ask Kubernetes to create a Deployment with five replicas, it's the responsibility of the Deployment controller to understand that request and create the replicas. In section J.18, we discuss this in detail.

J.17 *Ingress*

In this appendix so far, we have discussed two ways of exposing a Kubernetes Service outside a Kubernetes cluster: NodePort Service and LoadBalancer Service; Ingress is the third way.

Ingress is a Kubernetes object that routes traffic from outside the cluster to a Kubernetes Service over HTTP or HTTPS. It helps to expose one or more Kubernetes Services (say, of the NodePort type) through a single IP address. You can think of Ingress as a level of abstraction over one or more Services (just as a Service is an abstraction over one or more Pods). The following listing defines a sample Kubernetes Ingress object.

Listing J.13 Defining an Ingress object in YAML

```yaml
apiVersion: extensions/v1beta1
kind: Ingress
metadata:
  name: manning-ingress
spec:
  rules:
  - http:
      paths:
      - path: /orders           ◁──┐  Routes a request with the /orders context
        backend:                      to the order-processing-service Service.
          serviceName: order-processing-service  This is a nodePort Service listening on port
          servicePort: 80           80 on its internal cluster IP address.
      - path: /customers
        backend:
          serviceName: customer-service
          servicePort: 80
```

This YAML defines an Ingress object that routes traffic to two backend Kubernetes Services based on the URL pattern of the request. If the request comes to the /orders URL, Kubernetes routes the request to order-processing-service. If the request comes to the /customers URL, Kubernetes routes it to customer-service.

When you create an Ingress resource, it gets associated with an Ingress controller. In fact, you can't have just an Ingress resource; there has to be an Ingress controller too. You can use NGINX as an Ingress controller, for example. GKE uses its own Ingress controller called GKE Ingress. You can read more about GKE Ingress at https://cloud .google.com/kubernetes-engine/docs/concepts/ingress.

If you are running Kubernetes locally, with a single-node cluster, either with Docker Desktop or Minikube, the Ingress controller is not enabled by default. You can see how to set up NGINX as the Ingress controller under Docker Desktop and Minikube at https://kubernetes.github.io/ingress-nginx/deploy/.

J.18   *Kubernetes internal communication*

In section J.2, we discussed Kubernetes master and worker nodes. Each node has its own set of components, so let's see how these components communicate with each other. To check the status of the components running in the Kubernetes master node, or the control plane, let's use the following `kubectl` command:

```
\> kubectl get componentstatuses

NAME                STATUS    MESSAGE               ERROR
scheduler           Healthy   ok
etcd-0              Healthy   {"health": "true"}
etcd-1              Healthy   {"health": "true"}
controller-manager  Healthy   ok
```

When we run the command with kubectl running on our local machine, it simply talks to an API running on the Kubernetes API server, running within the control plane. The API server internally checks the status of all the control plane components and sends back the response. All the kubectl commands we used in this appendix work in a similar manner.

J.18.1   *How kubectl run works*

The best way to understand how Kubernetes internal communication happens is to go through one simple command and see how it works end to end (see figure J.4). In section J.6, we used the following `kubectl` command to create a Kubernetes Deployment with the Docker image `gcr.io/google-samples/hello-app`:

```
\> kubectl run hello-server --image gcr.io/google-samples/hello-app:1.0 \
--port 8080
```

When we run this command from kubectl running on our local machine, it creates a request with the provided parameters and talks to an API running on the Kubernetes API server. The communications among all the components in the Kubernetes control plane happens via the API server.

The following lists the sequence of events in figure J.4 that happen in a Kubernetes cluster after the API server receives a request from kubectl:

1 All the requests coming to the API server are intercepted by an authentication plugin deployed in the API server. This plugin makes sure that only legitimate clients can talk to the API server.

2 Once done with authentication, an authorization plugin deployed in the API server intercepts the request and checks whether the authenticated user has permissions to perform the intended action (not all users are allowed to create Pods).

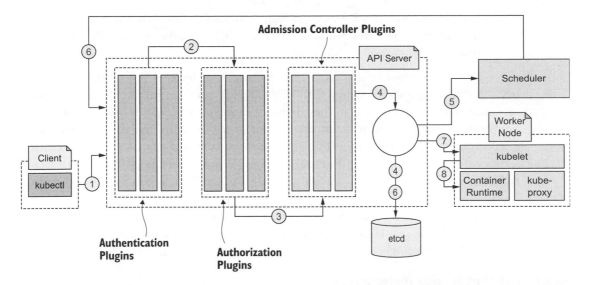

Figure J.4 A request generated by kubectl passes through the authentication, authorization, and admission controller plugins of the API server. It's validated and then stored in etcd. The scheduler and kubelet respond to events generated by the API server.

3 The authorized API request now goes through a set of Admission Controller plugins. The Admission Controller plugins can perform multiple tasks on the API request. For example, the `EventRateLimit` plugin can limit the number of API requests by the user.

4 The API server validates the API request and persists the corresponding objects (corresponding to the API request) in a key-value store, which is etcd. Kubernetes uses this highly available key-value store to persist cluster data.

5 Once the API server performs any operations on an object, it notifies a set of registered listeners. The scheduler, another component running in the control plane and registered with the API server, receives a notification when the API server, as per the API request, creates the new Pod object in etcd.

6 The scheduler finds a node to run the Pod and again updates the Pod definition stored in etcd with node information via the API server. Neither the API server nor the scheduler actually creates the Pod.

7 Once again, the update action performed in step 6 triggers another event. The kubelet component running in the corresponding worker node (where the Pod is supposed to run) picks that event (or gets notified) and starts creating the Pod. Each worker node has a kubelet, and it keeps listening to the API server to capture any events.

8 While creating the Pod, kubelet asks the container runtime (for example, Docker), which is running in the same worker node, to pull the corresponding container images from the registry and start them. At the time of this writing,

Kubernetes uses Docker as its default container runtime, but with the introduction of the container runtime interface (CRI), Kubernetes makes container runtimes pluggable.

Once all the containers in the Pod start running, kubelet keeps monitoring their status and reports to the API server. If the kubelet receives an event to terminate a Pod, it terminates all the containers in the corresponding Pod and updates the API server.

We discussed Kubernetes controllers in section J.16. While the Kubernetes cluster is up and running, the responsibility of these controllers is to make sure the desired state of the cluster matches the actual state. For example, the `ReplicationSet` controller watches the API server to find the status of the Pods it controls. If the desired number of Pods requested at the time we create the Deployment is less than the actual number of Pods running in the cluster, it creates the missing number of Pods by talking to the API server. Then it follows the same flow as explained: the scheduler will pick the Pod creation event and will schedule new Pods to run on a set of nodes.

J.18.2   *How Kubernetes routes a request from an external client to a Pod*

We discussed three ways to open a Pod running in a Kubernetes cluster to an external client. Let's summarize those ways:

- A Service of NodePort type (section J.3.3)
- A Service of LoadBalancer type (section J.3.3)
- An Ingress controller with a NodePort Service type (section J.17)

For simplicity, let's take the second scenario, assuming that we have a Service of Load-Balancer type, and see the sequence of events that happen in the Kubernetes cluster when it receives a request from an external client. The following lists the actions that take place when you create a Service in Kubernetes:

- Each worker node in a Kubernetes cluster runs a component called a kube-proxy. When Kubernetes creates a Service, either of NodePort or of Load-Balancer type, the kube-proxy gets notified, and it opens up the corresponding port (`nodePort`) in the local node. Each kube-proxy component in each worker node does the same. For a Service of `ClusterIP` type, no `nodePort` is involved.
- A kube-proxy operates in one of three modes: userspace, iptables, and ipvs (we keep the ipvs mode out of this discussion).
- If the kube-proxy operates in the userspace mode (figure J.5), it installs iptables rules on the node. This routes the traffic that comes to the `nodePort` (for the Services of LoadBalancer and NodePort type) of the node (via the IP of the node) to the proxy port of the kube-proxy. It also updates the iptables rules to route any traffic that is destined to the cluster IP (for any service type) on a service port to the proxy port of the kube-proxy. The cluster IP is a virtual IP address that Kubernetes creates for all the Services.

- If the kube-proxy operates in iptables mode, it installs an iptables rule that routes any traffic directed to the `nodePort` (for the Services of LoadBalancer and NodePort type) of the node to a randomly picked Pod IP address from the Endpoints object corresponding to the Service object and to the corresponding container port. Also, the kube-proxy updates the iptables rules to do the same even if it receives traffic for a Service destined to a cluster IP on a service port to a randomly picked Pod IP address from the Endpoints object corresponding to the Service object and to the corresponding container port.

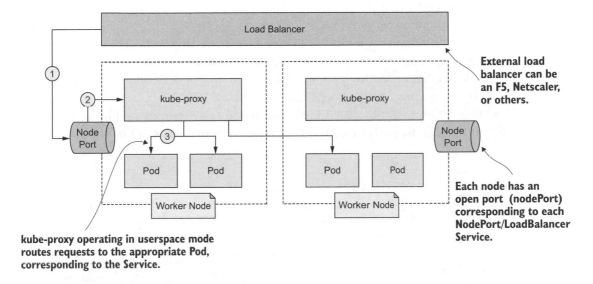

Figure J.5   A kube-proxy operating in the userspace mode routes the requests to an appropriate Pod, which corresponds to the Service.

The following lists the actions that take place when you send a request to a Service of LoadBalancer type:

- The client application, which is outside the Kubernetes cluster, sends a request with the IP address pointing to the load balancer. The load balancer runs outside the Kubernetes cluster and can be an F5, Netscaler, or any other load balancer. When we run the command `kubectl get service` against a Service, the `EXTERNAL-IP` column represents the IP address of the load balancer. Each Service has its own external IP address on the load balancer. Then again, this implementation varies by cloud vendor. On GKE, it generates a different external IP address for each Service.

- Once the request hits the load balancer, and based on the IP address in the request, the load balancer knows the corresponding Service; hence, it can figure out the `nodePort` associated with that Service.

- Based on the load-balancing algorithm, the load balancer picks a node from the Kubernetes cluster and routes the request to the corresponding `nodePort` via the corresponding node IP (step 1 in figure J.5).

- If the kube-proxy operates in the userspace mode, the request routed to the node from the load balancer goes through the kube-proxy, and it finds the corresponding Service by the `nodePort` (each Service has its own `nodePort`) and the appropriate Pod (by default, using a round-robin algorithm) and reroutes the request to that Pod (to the Pod IP address and port). This Pod can come from a totally different node (steps 2 and 3 in figure J.5). The kube-proxy finds the IP address of the Pod by looking at the Endpoints object attached to the corresponding Service.

- If the kube-proxy operates in the iptables mode (figure J.6), the request won't route through the kube-proxy, but according to the corresponding iptables rules in that node, the request is rerouted to one of the Pods associated with the corresponding Service (steps 2 and 3 in figure J.6).

- Once the request hits a Pod, it's dispatched to the corresponding container by looking at the port. In a given Pod, multiple containers can't be running on the same port.

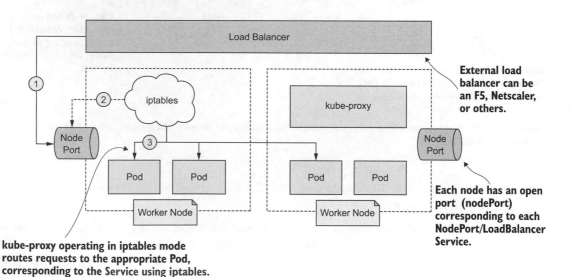

Figure J.6   A kube-proxy operating in iptables mode routes requests to an appropriate Pod, which corresponds to the Service using iptables.

J.19   *Managing configurations*

In a typical Kubernetes environment, configuration data you use within some containers changes from environment to environment. For example, a Pod deployed in the production Kubernetes cluster will have different certificates, database connection details, and so on from the same Pod deployed in a preproduction cluster. First, let's see various ways of carrying out configuration data in a Kubernetes cluster and then see how to decouple the configuration data from the Kubernetes Deployment definition.

J.19.1 *Hardcoding configuration data in the Deployment definition*

The straightforward way to carry configuration data in a Kubernetes Deployment is to hardcode the data into the definition of the Deployment as environment variables. For example, we can modify the command we used in section J.6 to create a Deployment to pass some configuration data as environment variables in the command line:

```
\> kubectl run hello-server --env="name1=value1" --env="name2=value2" \
--image gcr.io/google-samples/hello-app:1.0 --port 8080
```

When you run the command, you'll get an error if the deployment already exists. In that case, you can use the following command to delete the Deployment and rerun the previous command:

```
\> kubectl delete deployment hello-server
```

Let's run the command in the following listing to get the definition of the `hello-server` Deployment in YAML format. You'll notice that the two environment variables we passed in the previous command under the `--env` argument are added to the Deployment definition. The actual code or the process corresponding to the `hello-server` container, which runs inside a Pod within the `hello-server` Deployment, can read the value of the environment variable. For example, if the server wants to connect to a database, it can read the database connection details from these environment variables.

Listing J.14 Defining a `hello-server` Deployment in YAML

```
\> kubectl get  deployment hello-server -o yaml

apiVersion: extensions/v1beta1
kind: Deployment
metadata:
  labels:
    run: hello-server
  name: hello-server
spec:
  replicas: 1
  selector:
    matchLabels:
      run: hello-server
  template:
    metadata:
      labels:
        run: hello-server
    spec:
      containers:              Lists all the environment variables
      - env:              ◁─┘  passed in the command line
```

```
    - name: name1
      value: value1
    - name: name2
      value: value2
    image: gcr.io/google-samples/hello-app:1.0    ◁──┐  Name of the
    name: hello-server            ◁                      Docker image
    ports:                           Name of the container
    - containerPort: 8080           that runs inside the Pod
      protocol: TCP
```

When we create a Deployment as in listing J.14, we couple the configuration data to the Deployment object itself. As we discussed previously, in a typical production deployment, we don't use imperative commands to create a Deployment; instead, we use declarative object configurations (see section J.13). In case of a declarative configuration model, we maintain the definition of the Deployment object (in this case, along with all hardcoded environment variables) in a YAML file and then use the command kubectl apply to create the Deployment.

All the examples we use in chapter 11 follow the declarative configuration model. When we hardcode the environment variables into the Deployment definition, we need to duplicate that definition with different environment values for each production and preproduction environment. Basically, we need to maintain multiple YAML files for the same Deployment! That's not a good approach, and one that's not recommended.

J.19.2   *Introducing ConfigMaps*

A ConfigMap is a Kubernetes object that helps to decouple configuration data from a Deployment. In section 11.2, we use a comprehensive example of ConfigMap. In this section, we discuss various ways of using ConfigMap in a Kubernetes Deployment. If we take the same example as in section J.19.1, we can define a ConfigMap to carry the configuration data as follows.

Listing J.15   Defining a ConfigMap object that carries text data

```
apiVersion: v1
kind: ConfigMap
metadata:                        Name of the
  name: hello-server-cm    ◁──┘  ConfigMap
data:                   ◁──┐  Lists data as name/value pairs,
  name1: value1              where the value is treated as text
  name2: value2
```

This creates a ConfigMap object with a text representation. The following listing shows how to create a ConfigMap with binary data. Here, the value of the key (image1) must be base64 encoded.

Listing J.16   Defining a ConfigMap object that carries binary data

```
apiVersion: v1
kind: ConfigMap
```

```
metadata:
   name: hello-server-cm
binaryData:
   image1: /u3+7QAAAAIAAAABAAAAAQAGand0..
```

Lists binary data as name/value pairs, where the value is base64-encoded

To create a ConfigMap object in Kubernetes following the declarative configuration model, we use the following command, assuming that the hello-server-cm.yaml file carries the complete definition of the ConfigMap:

```
\> kubectl apply -f hello-server-cm.yaml
```

J.19.3 Consuming ConfigMaps from a Kubernetes Deployment and populating environment variables

In this section, we discuss how to consume the configuration data defined in a Config-Map object from a Kubernetes Deployment and populate a set of environment variables. The Kubernetes Deployment reads the configuration data from a ConfigMap and updates a set of environment variables. In the following listing, you can find the updated `hello-server` Deployment, and the code annotations explain how it works.

Listing J.17 Defining a `hello-server` Deployment to read data from a ConfigMap

```
apiVersion: extensions/v1beta1
kind: Deployment
metadata:
  labels:
    run: hello-server
  name: hello-server
spec:
  replicas: 1
  selector:
    matchLabels:
      run: hello-server
  template:
    metadata:
      labels:
        run: hello-server
    spec:
      containers:
      - env:
        - name: name1
          valueFrom:
            configMapKeyRef:
              name: hello-server-cm
              key: name1
        - name: name2
          valueFrom:
            configMapKeyRef:
              name: hello-server-cm
              key: name2
        image: gcr.io/google-samples/hello-app:1.0
        name: hello-server
        ports:
        - containerPort: 8080
          protocol: TCP
```

Name of the environment variable. The corresponding container reads the value of the environment variable using this name as the key.

Instructs Kubernetes to look for a ConfigMap object to read the value of the environment variable

Name of the ConfigMap object

Name of the key defined in the ConfigMap object

With this approach, we've completely decoupled the configuration data from our Kubernetes Deployment. You can have one single Deployment definition and multiple different ConfigMap objects for each production and preproduction environment with different values.

J.19.4   *Consuming ConfigMaps from a Kubernetes Deployment with volume mounts*

In this section, we discuss how to read a configuration file from a ConfigMap object and mount that file to a container filesystem from a Deployment. The following listing shows how we can represent a configuration file in a ConfigMap.

Listing J.18   Defining a ConfigMap object that carries a config file

```
apiVersion: v1
kind: ConfigMap
metadata:
  name: properties-file-cm          ⟵   Name of the
data:                                     ConfigMap entry
  application.properties: |          ⟵   The name of the config file,
    [                                      which carries the content
      server.port: 8443                    within the square brackets
      server.ssl.key-store: /opt/keystore.jks
      server.ssl.key-store-password: ${KEYSTORE_SECRET}
      server.ssl.keyAlias: spring
      spring.security.oauth.jwt: true
      spring.security.oauth.jwt.keystore.password: ${JWT_KEYSTORE_SECRET}
      spring.security.oauth.jwt.keystore.alias: jwtkey
      spring.security.oauth.jwt.keystore.name: /opt/jwt.jks
    ]
```

The following listing shows how to consume the ConfigMap defined in listing J.18 and mount it to the corresponding container filesystem. The code annotations explain how this works.

Listing J.19   Defining a `hello-server` Deployment with volume mounts

```
apiVersion: extensions/v1beta1
kind: Deployment
metadata:
  labels:
    run: hello-server
  name: hello-server
spec:
  replicas: 1
  selector:
    matchLabels:
      run: hello-server
  template:
    metadata:
      labels:
```

```
        run: hello-server
    spec:
      containers:
      - image: gcr.io/google-samples/hello-app:1.0
        name: hello-server
        volumeMounts:
        - name: application-properties
          mountPath: "/opt/application.properties"
          subPath: "application.properties"
        ports:
        - containerPort: 8080
          protocol: TCP
      volumes:
      - name: application-properties
        configMap:
          name: properties-file-cm
```

Defines properties corresponding to each volume mount

Name of the volume

Name of the volume, which refers to the volumes/name element toward the end of the configuration file

Sets the location in the container filesystem (or where to mount the file)

A sub path from the mountPath, so the root of the mountPath can be shared among multiple volumeMounts. If we don't define a subPath here, when we have another volumeMount under the opt directory (the same directory), it would create issues.

Defines a set of volumes that are referred to by name from the containers/volumeMounts section

Name of the ConfigMap object from listing J.18

appendix K
Service mesh and
Istio fundamentals

One key aspect of microservices architecture is the *single responsibility principle,* or *SRP* (https://en.wikipedia.org/wiki/Single_responsibility_principle), which indicates that a microservice should perform only one particular function. In chapter 3, we discussed how to use the API Gateway pattern to take most of the burden from microservices and to delegate security processing at the edge to an API gateway. The API gateway works mostly with *north/south traffic*—the traffic between applications (or consumers) and APIs. But still, in the examples we discussed in chapter 6 and chapter 7, most of the processing while securing inter-microservice communications (or east/west traffic) with mTLS and JWT was carried out by the microservices themselves.

Service Mesh is an architectural pattern with multiple implementations. It deals with *east/west traffic* (the traffic among microservices) to take most of the burden off of the microservices, with respect to security processing and other nonfunctional requirements. A service mesh brings in the best practices of resiliency, security, observability, and routing control to your microservices deployment, which we discuss in detail in the rest of this appendix. This appendix lays the foundation for chapter 12, which focuses on securing a microservices deployment with the Istio service mesh. To follow this appendix, it is a prerequisite that you have some understanding of Kubernetes, which we discuss in appendix J.

K.1   *Why a service mesh?*

A *service mesh* is the result of the gradual progress in implementing the SRP in microservices architecture. If you look at a framework like Spring Boot, it tries to implement some of the key functionalities we see in a typical service mesh today, at the language level as a library. As a microservices developer, you don't need to

536

worry about implementing those functionalities; instead, you'd simply use the corresponding libraries in your microservice implementation. This is the approach we followed in chapter 6 and chapter 7 while securing inter-microservice communications with mTLS and JWT. You can even call this model an *embedded service mesh* (figure K.1) or an *in-process service mesh.*

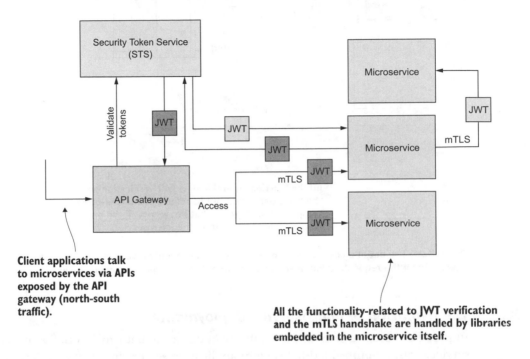

Figure K.1 In an embedded service mesh, each microservice by itself implements security processing with a set of embedded libraries.

The embedded service mesh approach has several drawbacks. For example, if you want to use Spring Boot/Java libraries to implement security, observability, and resiliency features, your microservices implementation must be in Java. Also, if you discover any issues with the Spring Boot libraries, you need to redeploy your entire microservice. At the same time, when there's an API change in the Spring Boot libraries, you need to make the corresponding change in your microservice implementation. All in all, the embedded service mesh approach doesn't quite fit well into the microservices architecture.

In the rest of this appendix when we talk about the service mesh, we mean the *out-of-process service mesh.* In contrast to the embedded service mesh approach, the out-of-process service mesh (figure K.2) runs apart from your microservice, and transparently intercepts all the traffic coming into and going out of your microservice.

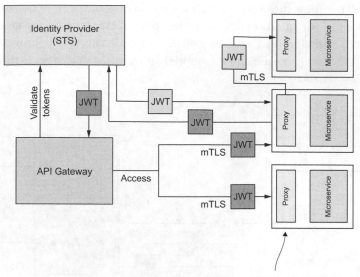

All the functionality-related to JWT verification and the mTLS handshake are handled by an out-of-process component, or a proxy, that intercepts all the requests going in and coming out of the microservice.

Figure K.2   The out-of-process service mesh, which does security processing via a proxy, intercepts all the requests going in and coming out of the corresponding microservice.

K.2   *The evolution of microservice deployments*

In practice, microservice deployments are at different maturity levels. Some run their services with an embedded lightweight application server (for example, Spring Boot) on a physical machine or a virtual machine. This approach is OK if you have just a few microservices and only a few people working on them.

When the number of services increases and more teams start working on those, it becomes harder to live without automation. This is when people start fretting about deploying microservices in containers. It's common for those who are just getting started with containers to begin without a container orchestration framework like Kubernetes. This is now changing with more and more cloud providers starting to provide Kubernetes as a service. When the number of containers increases, the management of those becomes a nightmare unless you have a container orchestration framework (see appendix J).

The next natural step after moving to Kubernetes is to use a service mesh. Kubernetes helps with managing a large-scale microservices deployment, but it lacks in providing application-level, quality-of-service (QoS) features for microservices. This is where the Service Mesh pattern comes in: Kubernetes is like an operating system that has the service mesh (a product that implements the Service Mesh pattern) running on top of it to provide a set of QoS features for microservices on a large scale.

K.2.1   *The Service Mesh architecture*

The Service Mesh architecture consists primarily of two planes: a data plane and a control plane (figure K.3). These planes coordinate with each other to bring in the best practices in resiliency, security, observability, and routing control to your microservices deployment. We'll first look at the data plane.

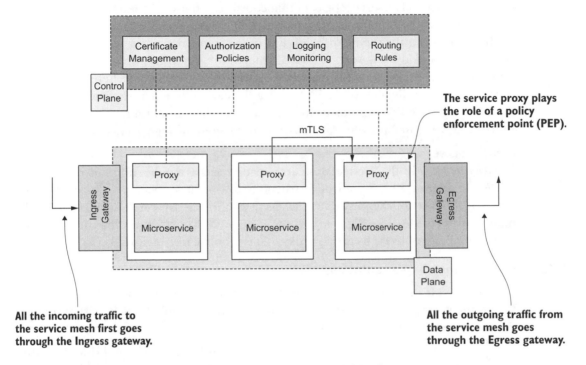

Figure K.3   A typical service mesh consists of a control plane and a data plane.

DATA PLANE

In our Spring Boot examples (in chapters 6 and 7), where we implemented an embedded service mesh with Spring Boot libraries, a Spring Boot handler intercepts all the requests coming to your microservice. In the same way, an out-of-process service mesh uses a proxy that intercepts all the requests coming in and going out of your microservice. We call this a *service proxy* (figure K.3). Because the service proxy is in the request/response path of a microservice, it can enforce security, do monitoring, manage traffic, perform service discovery, and implement patterns like a circuit breaker or bulkhead to support resiliency for all inbound and outbound traffic. The service proxy plays the role of a policy enforcement point (PEP).

> **NOTE**   In this book, we focus only on security in a service mesh. If you'd like to read about other features of a service mesh, such as observability, resiliency,

traffic management, and so on, we recommend that you check out *Istio in Action* by Christian Posta (Manning, to be published in 2021) and *Istio: Up and Running* by Lee Calcote and Zack Butcher (O'Reilly Media, 2019).

In a typical service mesh architecture, each microservice has its own service proxy, and in-and-out traffic from a microservice flows through the service proxy in a transparent manner. The microservice implementation doesn't need to fuss about the existence of the service proxy. The service proxies that coordinate traffic in a microservices deployment and act as PEPs build the data plane of the service mesh architecture.

In addition to the service proxies, two other components are in a data plane: an *Ingress gateway* and an *Egress gateway*. All the traffic entering into the microservices deployment first flows through the Ingress gateway, and it decides where (or to which service proxy) to dispatch traffic. All the traffic leaving the microservices deployment flows through the Egress gateway. In other words, all north-south traffic goes through Ingress/Egress gateways, while all east-west traffic goes through service proxies.

CONTROL PLANE

The *control plane* in the Service Mesh architecture acts as a policy administration point (PAP). It defines all the control instructions to operate service proxies in the data plane and never touches any data packets at runtime. A typical control plane implementation provides an API or a UI portal, or both, to perform administrative tasks and runs an agent in each service proxy to pass control instructions.

K.2.2   *Service mesh implementations*

The Service Mesh architectural pattern has multiple implementations. Of all of these, Istio is the most popular and the one we focus on in this book. Here is a list of some of the more popular implementations:

- *Istio*—An open source service mesh created by Google, Lyft, and IBM. Istio uses Envoy developed by Lyft (written in C++) for the service proxy. In this appendix and in chapter 12, we discuss Istio in detail.
- *Linkerd*—A service mesh developed by Buoyant that has both an open source version and commercial licenses. Linkerd has its own service proxy written in Rust. You can find out more about the Linkerd architecture at https://linkerd .io/2/reference/architecture.
- *HashiCorp Consul*—A service mesh developed by HashiCorp that has both an open source version and commercial licenses. A new feature called Connect, introduced since HashiCorp Consul 1.2, turned Consul into a service mesh. You can read more about HashiCorp Consul architecture at http://mng.bz/D2pa.
- *Aspen Mesh*—A commercial service mesh based on Istio. More details about Aspen Mesh are available at https://aspenmesh.io/what-aspen-mesh-adds-to-istio/.
- *AWS App Mesh*—A service mesh developed by Amazon Web Services. You can read more about AWS App Mesh at https://aws.amazon.com/app-mesh.

- *Microsoft Azure Service Fabric*—A service mesh by Microsoft on Azure. You can read more about Azure Service Fabric at http://mng.bz/lGrB.
- *AVI Networks*—A service mesh by AVI Networks, based on Istio. VMware acquired AVI Networks in June 2019. You can find more about the AVI Networks service mesh implementation at https://avinetworks.com/universal-service -mesh.
- *Red Hat OpenShift Service Mesh*—A service mesh by Red Hat on OpenShift that's based on Istio. You can read more at https://www.openshift.com/learn/topics/ service-mesh.

Even though many service mesh implementations are based on Istio, you'll find some differences when you dig deeper into the details. For example, "Comparing Service Mesh and Istio" (http://mng.bz/B2gr) explains the differences between the upstream Istio project and the Red Hat OpenShift Service Mesh. Also, if you're interested in learning the differences between Istio, Linkerd, and Consul, here's a good reference: http://mng.bz/dyZv. All these service mesh implementations are increasingly evolving projects, so you need to look for the most up-to-date information all the time.

K.2.3 Service mesh vs. API gateway

In chapter 3, we discussed the role of an API gateway in a microservices deployment. The API gateway primarily handles north/south traffic—the communication between the client applications and the APIs. In contrast, in a typical microservices deployment, the service mesh predominantly handles east/west traffic, or the communications among microservices. Then again, we also see some evolving service mesh implementations that handle north/south traffic as well, where some components in the service mesh also play the role of an API gateway.

K.3 Istio service mesh

Istio is a service mesh implementation developed by Google, Lyft, and IBM. It's open source and the most popular service mesh implementation at the time of this writing. The project started in 2016, using Envoy as the service proxy that runs in the data plane.[1] The control plane components are developed in the Go programming language. The Istio code base is available on GitHub at https://github.com/istio/istio.

One of the key metrics when finding the popularity and the adoption of an open source project is the number of GitHub stars. At the time of this writing (May 2020), Istio has almost 22,600 stars. In this appendix, we explain Istio to lay the foundation for what you'll find in chapter 12, where we discuss securing microservices in an Istio environment.

---

[1] For more information, see the Google Cloud whitepaper, "The Service Mesh Era: Architecting, Securing and Managing Microservices with Istio" at http://mng.bz/8pag.

K.4   *Istio architecture*

As discussed in section K.3, a typical service implementation operates in two planes: the data plane and the control plane (figure K.4). In the following sections, we discuss how Istio operates in each of those planes.

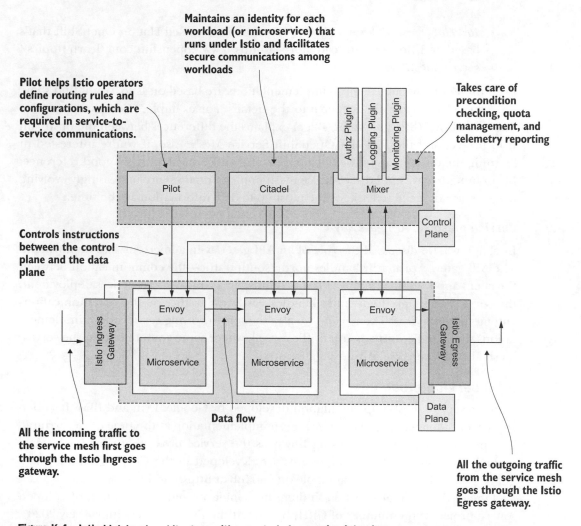

Figure K.4   Istio high-level architecture with a control plane and a data plane

K.4.1   *Istio data plane*

The *Istio data plane* consists of a set of service proxies alongside each microservice, an Ingress gateway, and an Egress gateway. In the following sections, we discuss the responsibilities of each of those components and how they operate in a Kubernetes deployment.

SERVICE PROXY (ENVOY)

Istio out of the box uses Envoy as its service proxy. In a typical Kubernetes deployment, Envoy is deployed in each Pod as a sidecar along with the corresponding microservice.[2] Kubernetes makes sure all the containers in a given Pod run in the same node.[3] Istio also updates the iptables rules in the corresponding Kubernetes node to make sure all the traffic that comes to the container that carries the microservice first flows through Envoy, and in the same way, any traffic that's initiated by the microservice also flows through Envoy.[4] That way, Envoy takes control of all the traffic going in and coming out of the microservice. The following are the core functionalities Envoy supports as a service proxy:

- *HTTP/2 and gRPC support*—Envoy supports HTTP/2 and gRPC for both incoming and outgoing connections. In fact, Envoy was one of the first HTTP/2 implementations. gRPC (https://grpc.io/) is an open source remote procedure call (RPC) framework (or library), originally developed by Google. It's the next generation of a system called Stubby that Google has been using internally for over a decade. gRPC achieves efficiency for communications among systems using HTTP/2 as the transport and Protocol Buffers as the IDL. We discuss gRPC in detail in appendix I.

  HTTP/2 provides request multiplexing and header compression that increases its performance significantly compared to HTTP/1.1. It also employs binary encoding of frames, which makes the data being transferred much more compact and efficient when processing. You can read more about HTTP/2 in appendix I or check out *HTTP/2 in Action* by Barry Pollard (Manning, 2019).

- *Protocol translation*—Envoy is also an HTTP/1.1-to-HTTP/2 transparent proxy; Envoy can accept an HTTP/1.1 request and proxy it over HTTP/2. You can also send a JSON payload over HTTP/1.1, and Envoy translates that to a gRPC request over HTTP/2 and sends it to the corresponding microservice. Further, Envoy can translate the gRPC response it gets from the microservice to JSON over HTTP/1.1.

- *Load balancing*—The Envoy proxy can act as a load balancer for upstream services. When one microservice talks to another microservice, that request first goes through the Envoy proxy sitting with the first microservice (figure K.5). This envoy proxy can act as a load balancer for the second microservice, which is called the *upstream microservice*. Envoy supports advanced load-balancing features including automatic retries, circuit breaking, global rate limiting, request shadowing, zone local load balancing, and so on. You can learn more about

---

[2] A *sidecar* is a container that runs in the same Pod with the container that runs the microservice. A typical Pod can have one main car (which runs the microservice) and multiple sidecars. A sidecar can act as proxy to the main car or as a container that provides utility functions.

[3] A Kubernetes node can be a physical machine or a virtual machine. A node runs multiple Pods.

[4] Iptables is used to set up, maintain, and inspect the tables of IP packet filter rules in the Linux kernel (see https://linux.die.net/man/8/iptables).

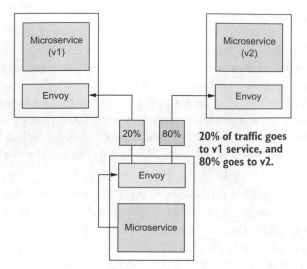

Figure K.5   Envoy carries out load balancing for upstream services.

Envoy load balancing features from the Envoy documentation available at http://mng.bz/rr1e.

- *Observability*—The four main pillars of observability are metrics, tracing, logging, and visualization. Each of these factors is important to monitoring a microservice effectively. In appendix D, we discuss these four pillars and the need for observability in detail.

An Envoy proxy that intercepts all the requests (in and out) from a microservice is in a great position to generate statistics in a transparent manner. It generates stats at three levels: downstream, upstream, and server. The downstream stats are related to all the incoming connections, while the upstream stats are related to all the outgoing connections. The server stats are related to the health of the Envoy proxy itself; for example, CPU, memory usage, and so on. Envoy publishes all the stats it collects to Mixer. Mixer is an Istio control-plane component that we discuss in section K.3.3. Envoy doesn't need to publish stats for each request; rather, it can cache the stats and then (infrequently) push to Mixer.

Unlike in a monolithic deployment, in a typical microservices deployment when a request spans across multiple endpoints, logs and stats are just not enough. There should be a way to correlate logs between endpoints. When an Envoy proxy initiates a request to an upstream service, it generates a unique identifier to trace the request and sends it as a header to the upstream service. When the Envoy proxy publishes its downstream stats to the Mixer, it also publishes the corresponding tracing identifiers. Also, if one upstream service wants to talk to another upstream service, it passes through the tracing identifier it gets from the first downstream service. With this model, when all the stats generated from Envoy proxies are collected centrally, we can build a complete picture of each request by correlating tracing identifiers.

In section K.4.2, you'll learn more about how Istio handles tracing at the control plane. You can read more about the observability support in Envoy at http://mng.bz/Vg2W.

- *Security*—Envoy acts as a security checkpoint or a PEP for the microservice behind it. One of the emerging patterns we see in the microservices security domain is the zero-trust network pattern. In simple words, this says don't trust the network. If we don't trust the network, we need to carry out all the security screening much closer to the resource we want to protect, or in our case, the microservice. Envoy does that in the Service Mesh architecture.

Envoy intercepts all the requests coming to the microservice it backs, makes sure they are properly authenticated and authorized, and then dispatches those to the microservice. Because both the Envoy and the microservice run on the same Pod on the same node, the microservice is never exposed outside the node—and also not outside the Pod! No request can reach the microservice without saying hello to Envoy (see figure K.6).

An Envoy proxy supports enforcing mTLS, JWT verification, role-based access control (RBAC), and so on. In chapter 12, we discuss all the security features Envoy and Istio support. You can read more about the security features Envoy supports from http://mng.bz/xW6g.

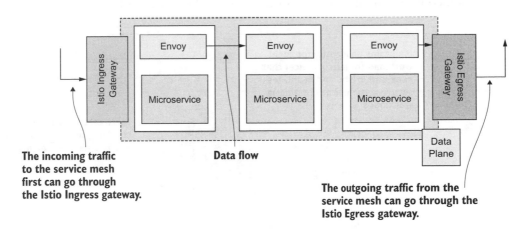

The incoming traffic to the service mesh first can go through the Istio Ingress gateway.

Data flow

The outgoing traffic from the service mesh can go through the Istio Egress gateway.

Figure K.6 The incoming requests to the service mesh can go through the Ingress gateway; any outbound calls can go through the Egress gateway.

INGRESS GATEWAY

Ingress is a Kubernetes resource that routes traffic from outside the cluster to a Kubernetes Service over HTTP or HTTPS. It helps expose multiple Kubernetes Services (say, of the NodePort type) through a single IP address. (In appendix J, we discuss how Ingress works in a Kubernetes cluster.) In order for an Ingress resource to work, we also need to have an Ingress controller in place. Some Kubernetes deployments use NGINX, Kong, and so on as the Ingress controller. Google Kubernetes Engine (GKE) has its own open source Ingress controller (see https://github.com/kubernetes/ingress-gce).

When you install Istio, it introduces its own Ingress gateway (figure K.6). The Istio Ingress gateway is, in fact, an Envoy proxy. All the traffic that enters into the service mesh ideally should flow through this Envoy proxy, and it can centrally do monitoring, routing, and security enforcement.

EGRESS GATEWAY

Similar to the Ingress gateway, Istio also introduces an Egress gateway (figure K.6). All the traffic that leaves the Kubernetes deployment goes through an Egress gateway (if you'd like, you can bypass the Egress gateway as well). Once again, an Envoy proxy runs as the Egress gateway. For example, if your microservice wants to talk to an endpoint outside your Kubernetes cluster, that request goes through the Istio Egress gateway. You can also have your own security policies and traffic control rules enforced at the Egress gateway.

K.4.2 *Istio control plane*

The *Istio control plane* consists mainly of four components: Pilot, Galley, Mixer, and Citadel, as shown in figure K.7. In the following sections, we discuss the responsibilities of each component and how they operate in a Kubernetes deployment.

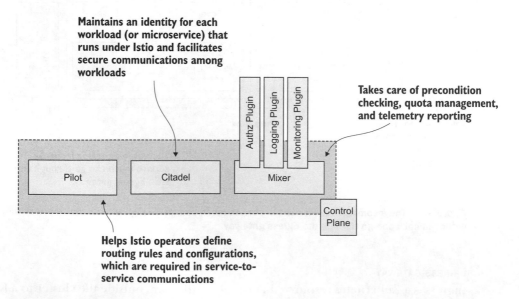

Figure K.7   The Istio control plane consists of four components: Pilot, Galley, Mixer, and Citadel. The Galley isn't shown here because it's internal to the control plane, which deals with only the underlying infrastructure.

PILOT

Pilot helps you define routing rules and configurations that are required in service-to-service communications. For example, you can have a routing rule that says 20% of the traffic goes to v1 (version 1) of the Delivery microservice and 80% goes to v2 (version 2). You can also set up connection time-outs when your service talks to another service, as well as the number of retry attempts. Further, you can define parameters with respect to the circuit-breaker pattern.

When the Order Processing microservice talks to the Delivery microservice, and if the Delivery microservice is down, you can configure a circuit breaker to break the connection between the Order Processing and the Delivery microservices. When the circuit is in an open state (meaning broken), no communication happens between the two microservices, and instead of calling the Delivery microservice, the Order Processing microservice uses preconfigured default values to simulate the response from the Delivery microservice. Then after *n* number of seconds (or minutes), the circuit breaker tries to reconnect to the Delivery microservice, and if it works fine, it closes the circuit (otherwise, it remains open until the next retry).

Pilot exposes an API for Istio administrators (or operators) to define policies and configurations, and another API for Envoy proxies running in the data plane to pull configurations related to them. Once Envoy pulls the related policies and configurations from Pilot, it creates its own Envoy-specific configuration file. The following listing shows an example of how Envoy configures a circuit breaker.

Listing K.1 Envoy configuration for a circuit breaker

```
"circuit_breakers": {
        "thresholds": [
          {
            "priority": "DEFAULT",
            "max_connections": 100000,
            "max_pending_requests": 100000,
            "max_requests": 100000
          },
          {
            "priority": "HIGH",
            "max_connections": 100000,
            "max_pending_requests": 100000,
            "max_requests": 100000
          }
        ]
      }
```

The following is another example of how Envoy keeps connection properties when it wants to connect to upstream microservices:

```
"upstream_connection_options": {
        "tcp_keepalive": {
          "keepalive_time": 300
        }
      },
```

GALLEY

To feed policies and configurations into Envoy, Pilot has to interact with the Kubernetes APIs. *Galley* is a component that runs in the control plane, which abstracts out the nitty-gritty details of the platform underneath. For example, when we run Istio on Kubernetes, the Galley knows how to talk to Kubernetes and find the information Pilot needs, and Pilot can work in a platform-agnostic way.

MIXER

Mixer, which runs in the control plane, takes care of precondition checking, quota management, and telemetry reporting. For example, when a request hits the Envoy proxy at the data plane, it talks to the Mixer API to do precondition checking to see whether it's OK to proceed with that request. The Envoy proxy from the data plane publishes statistics to Mixer, and Mixer can connect to an external monitoring and distributed tracing systems like Prometheus, Zipkin, Grafana, and so on.

Mixer has a rich plugin architecture, so you can chain multiple plugins in the precondition check phase. For example, you can have a mixer plugin that connects to an external policy decision point (PDP) to evaluate a set of access-control policies against the incoming requests.[5]

Mixer has two subcomponents: policy and telemetry. The policy component enforces polices with respect to precondition checking and quota management. The telemetry component handles functionality related to logging, tracing, and metrics.

CITADEL

Citadel is the Istio control plane component that maintains an identity for each workload (or microservice) that runs under Istio. It also facilitates secure communications among workloads. Citadel provisions X.509 certificates to each workload and manages them. We discuss Citadel in detail in chapter 12.

K.4.3   *Changes introduced to Istio architecture since Istio 1.5.0 release*

Prior to Istio 1.5.0, Citadel, Pilot, and Galley components ran as independent services. Since Istio 1.5.0 onward, all three have been integrated into a single binary called Istiod. A blog by Craig Box (https://istio.io/latest/blog/2020/istiod/) explains the motivation and the benefits of this change.

In addition, Istio 1.5.0 introduced another major change with respect to its extensibility model. Up to version 1.5.0, the Istio extensibility model revolved around Mixer. Writing a Mixer plugin that runs in the control plane helps you extend the functionality of Istio. Since 1.5.0 onward, the extensibility model of Istio has been centered on the Envoy proxy, where you can write WebAssembly (WASM) filters to run with Envoy.[6] Envoy proxy provides SDKs to build these filters in multiple languages: C++, Rust,

---

[5] You can find a set of available Mixer plugins for Istio at http://mng.bz/Ed8r.

[6] According to Wikipedia, WebAssembly (often shortened to WASM) is an open standard that defines a portable binary-code format for executable programs, and a corresponding textual assembly language, as well as interfaces for facilitating interactions between such programs and their host environment.

Typescript, Go, and so on. If you are interested in learning more about the motivation of bringing WASM support to Envoy, check out https://github.com/envoyproxy/envoy/issues/4272. With this change, the role of Mixer becomes less important in Istio; Mixer will probably become an add-on in the future that you can add to your Istio environment only if needed.

K.5 *Setting up Istio service mesh on Kubernetes*

The Istio documentation (https://istio.io/docs/setup) explains how to set up Istio in a Kubernetes environment. In this section, we discuss how to set up Istio locally with Docker Desktop and in the cloud with GKE.

K.5.1 *Setting up Istio on Docker Desktop*

Docker Desktop is a popular single-node Kubernetes distribution you can easily run on your local computer. Before you set up Istio on Docker Desktop, you should follow the instructions at https://docs.docker.com/desktop/ to set up Docker Desktop. The resource requirements (in terms of memory and CPU) to run Istio on Docker Desktop are defined at https://istio.io/docs/setup/platform-setup/docker/.

Since the instructions to set up Istio on Docker Desktop could vary from time to time, we have kept those instructions out of the book, and put them in the GitHub repository under the appendix-k directory. You can read the installation instructions from https://github.com/microservices-security-in-action/samples/blob/master/appendix-k/install-istio-on-docker-desktop.md.

K.5.2 *Setting up Istio on GKE*

In this section, we assume you already have access to GKE and have a Kubernetes cluster up and running. If you need help setting that up, check appendix J, which covers how to create a project in GKE and then a Kubernetes cluster. If necessary, you can run the following `gcloud` command to list the information related to your GKE cluster:

```
\> gcloud container clusters list

NAME                   LOCATION     MASTER_VERSION MASTER_IP     MACHINE_TYPE
manning-ms-security us-west1-a 1.13.7-gke.24   35.203.148.5 n1-standard-1

NODE_VERSION     NUM_NODES    STATUS
1.14.10-gke.27  3            RUNNING
```

There are two ways to add Istio support to GKE: either you can install the open source Istio version by yourself (from the scratch on the GKE), or you can enable Istio as an add-on for GKE. In this appendix, we follow the add-on approach. If you'd like to install open source Istio from scratch, follow the instructions documented at http://mng.bz/NKXX.

To add Istio support as an add-on for an existing GKE Kubernetes cluster (in our case, to the `manning-ms-security` cluster), use the following `gcloud` command. Istio support in GKE is still at the beta level, so we have to use `gcloud beta` instead of gcloud. At the time you read this book, if the Istio support on GKE has matured to General Availability (GA), you can skip using beta in the following commands:

```
\> gcloud beta container clusters update manning-ms-security \
--update-addons=Istio=ENABLED --istio-config=auth=MTLS_PERMISSIVE
```

Here we use MTLS_PERMISSIVE as Istio's authentication configuration, which makes mTLS optional for each service or, to be more precise, at each Envoy proxy. In chapter 12, we discuss the authentication options Istio provides. If you want to create a new GKE Kubernetes cluster (rather than updating an existing one) with Istio support, use the following gcloud command:[7]

```
\> gcloud beta container clusters create manning-ms-security \
--addons=Istio --istio-config=auth=MTLS_PERMISSIVE
```

If you have multiple Kubernetes clusters in your GKE environment, and if you want to switch between clusters, use the flowing gcloud command with the cluster name:

```
\> gcloud container clusters get-credentials manning-ms-security
```

The Istio version installed on GKE depends on the version of the GKE cluster. You can find the GKE-to-Istio version mapping at http://mng.bz/D2W0. Also, Istio has multiple profiles, and each profile defines the Istio features you might like to have. When you install Istio as an add-on on GKE, you have limited flexibility to pick which Istio features you want, unless those are officially supported by GKE. Even when you install Istio by yourself on GKE, the recommendation still is to use the default Istio profile. You can find Istio profiles and available features at http://mng.bz/lGez.

K.5.3   Limitations of Istio on GKE

At the time of this writing, all the samples in this appendix and most of the samples in chapter 12 are tested on GKE cluster version 1.14.10-gke.27, which supports Istio 1.2.10. Istio 1.2.10 was released in December 2019, and at the time of this writing, the latest Istio release is 1.6.2, which was released in June 2020. There's always a time gap before GKE supports the latest version of Istio. So, if you are using GKE, you won't be able to test the new features introduced in Istio 1.5.x or later releases. In chapter 12, we talk about some of the new security features Istio introduced in version 1.5.0, and you would need to switch from GKE to your local Istio installation on Docker Desktop to test them.

K.6   What Istio brings to a Kubernetes cluster

Once you install Istio on Kubernetes, you'll find a new namespace, a new set of custom resource definitions, a set of control plane components as Kubernetes Services and Pods, and many others. In this section, we discuss the key changes Istio brings into your Kubernetes cluster.

---

[7]   The list of all available options for the clusters create command are listed at http://mng.bz/Z2V5.

K.6.1 Kubernetes custom resource definitions

A *custom resource definition*, commonly known as a *CRD*, is a way of extending Kubernetes functionality. A custom resource is, in fact, an extension to the Kubernetes API. It lets you manage and store custom resources by using the Kubernetes API via the Kubernetes API server. For example, Istio introduces a set of custom resources like Gateway, VirtualService, ServiceAccount, ServiceAccountBinding, Policy, and so on, and you can use the command in the following listing to list all the CRDs that Istio introduces. The output here shows only a few of them.

Listing K.2 Some of the custom resource definitions introduced by Istio

```
\> kubectl get crds --all-namespaces | grep istio.io

adapters.config.istio.io                  2020-04-15T07:03:49Z
apikeys.config.istio.io                   2020-04-15T07:03:49Z
attributemanifests.config.istio.io        2020-04-15T07:03:49Z
authorizations.config.istio.io            2020-04-15T07:03:49Z
bypasses.config.istio.io                  2020-04-15T07:03:49Z
checknothings.config.istio.io             2020-04-15T07:03:49Z
circonuses.config.istio.io                2020-04-15T07:03:49Z
cloudwatches.config.istio.io              2020-04-15T07:03:49Z
```

Some of the CRDs shown here are deprecated from Istio 1.4.0 onward. For example, CRDs related to ClusterRbacConfig, ServiceRole, and ServiceRoleBinding are now deprecated and are removed from Istio 1.6.0 onward. We discuss these CRDs in chapter 12.

K.6.2 The istio-system namespace

Once you install Istio in your Kubernetes cluster, it creates a new namespace called `istio-system`. All the Istio components that run within the control plane (as discussed in section K.4.2) are installed under this namespace. The following command lists all the namespaces in your Kubernetes cluster:

```
\> kubectl get namespaces

NAME           STATUS    AGE
default        Active    27d
istio-system   Active    14d
kube-public    Active    27d
kube-system    Active    27d
```

K.6.3 Control plane components

Let's use the command in the following listing to list all the Istio components running as Kubernetes Services under the `istio-system` namespace. You will see similar output if you are on an Istio version prior to 1.5.0. From Istio 1.5.0 onward, the set of Kubernetes Services running under the `istio-system` namespace is completely different from the following listing.

Listing K.3   Istio components running as Kubernetes Services

```
\> kubectl get service -n istio-system

NAME                   TYPE          CLUSTER-IP      EXTERNAL-IP
istio-citadel          ClusterIP     10.39.240.24    <none>
istio-galley           ClusterIP     10.39.250.154   <none>
istio-ingressgateway   LoadBalancer  10.39.247.10    35.230.52.47
istio-pilot            ClusterIP     10.39.243.6     <none>
istio-policy           ClusterIP     10.39.245.132   <none>
istio-sidecar-injector ClusterIP     10.39.244.184   <none>
istio-telemetry        ClusterIP     10.39.251.200   <none>
promsd                 ClusterIP     10.39.249.199   <none>
```

Kubernetes exposes all these Istio components as Services. In section K.4.2, we discussed the responsibilities of `istio-citadel`, `istio-galley`, and `istio-pilot`. Let's look at the others:

- The `istio-policy` and `istio-telemetry` Services are part of Mixer.
- The `istio-ingressgateway` Service acts as an Ingress gateway, which we discussed in section K.4.1.
- The `promsd` Service that's based on Prometheus (an open source monitoring system) is used for metrics.
- The `istio-sidecar-injector` Service is used to inject Envoy as a sidecar proxy into Kubernetes Pods, which we discuss in detail in section K.8.1.

From Istio 1.5.0 onward, you won't see separate Kubernetes Services for `istio-citadel`, `istio-galley`, and `istio-pilot`. Instead, you'll find a Service called `istiod`, which aggregates the functionality of all three of those Services.

Something missing in the `istio-system` namespace (listing K.3) is the Istio Egress gateway (section K.4.1). As we discussed in section K.5, when we install Istio on GKE as an add-on, it installs only the default profile of Istio, and the Egress gateway isn't part of the default profile.

Behind each of the Services in listing K.3 is a corresponding Pod. The command in the next listing shows all the Pods running under the `istio-system` namespace. Once again, you will find similar output only if you are on an Istio version prior to 1.5.0.

Listing K.4   Pods related to Istio in the `istio-system` namespace

```
\> kubectl get pods -n istio-system

NAME                                     READY   STATUS      RESTARTS
istio-citadel-5949896b4b-vlr7n           1/1     Running     0
istio-cleanup-secrets-1.1.12-7vtct       0/1     Completed   0
istio-galley-6c7df96f6-nw9kz             1/1     Running     0
istio-ingressgateway-7b4dcc59c6-6srn8    1/1     Running     0
istio-init-crd-10-2-2mftw                0/1     Completed   0
istio-init-crd-11-2-f89wz                0/1     Completed   0
```

```
istio-pilot-6b459f5669-44r4f              2/2    Running     0
istio-policy-5848d67996-dzfw2             2/2    Running     0
istio-security-post-install-1.1.12-v2phr  0/1    Completed   0
istio-sidecar-injector-5b5454d777-89ncv   1/1    Running     0
istio-telemetry-6bd4c5bb6d-h5pzm          2/2    Running     0
promsd-76f8d4cff8-nkm6s                   2/2    Running     1
```

K.6.4 *The istio-ingressgateway Service*

Except for the `istio-ingressgateway` Service in listing K.4, all the Kubernetes Services are of `ClusterIP` type. The `ClusterIP` type is the default Service type in Kubernetes, and those Services are accessible only within a Kubernetes cluster. The `istio-ingressgateway` Service, which is of LoadBalancer type, is accessible outside the Kubernetes cluster, however. Let's examine the `istio-ingressgateway` Service a little further with the following `kubectl` command:

```
\> kubectl get service istio-ingressgateway -o yaml -n istio-system
```

In the output of this command, you can find the `spec/clusterIP`, which can be used by the Services running inside the Kubernetes cluster to access the `istio-ingressgateway`, and `status/LoadBalancer/ingress/ip` to access the `istio-ingressgateway` from external clients outside the Kubernetes cluster. Also notice in the output an array of ports (under `spec/ports`) with different names (listing K.5). Each element in the `ports` array represents a different kind of a Service; for example, one for HTTP/2 traffic, another for the HTTPS traffic, another for the TCP traffic, and so on.

> ### Listing K.5 An array of ports with different names

```
ports:
- name: http2
  nodePort: 31346
  port: 80
  protocol: TCP
 targetPort: 80
 - name: https
  nodePort: 31787
  port: 443
  protocol: TCP
  targetPort: 443
- name: tcp
  nodePort: 32668
  port: 31400
  protocol: TCP
  targetPort: 31400
```

Under each element of the `ports` array, you'll find an element called `name`, `nodePort`, `port`, `targetPort`, and `protocol`. A Service of LoadBalancer type is also a Service of `nodePort` type (see appendix J). Or, in other words, the LoadBalancer Service is an extension of the NodePort Service and that's why we see a `nodePort` element defined under each element in the `ports` array.

Each node in the Kubernetes cluster listens on the `nodePort`. For example, if you want to talk to the `istio-ingressgateway` over HTTPS, you need to pick the value of the `port` element corresponding to the `https` port, and `istio-ingressgateway`, listening on that particular port, reroutes the traffic to the corresponding `nodePort` (of any node the system picks) and then to the corresponding Pod, which is listening on `targetPort`. The Pod behind the `istio-ingressgateway` runs a container with the Envoy proxy.

In section K.10.1, we discuss how to use `istio-ingressgateway` with your microservices deployment, or how to use `istio-ingressgateway` to route requests from external client applications to your microservices.

K.6.5   *The istio-ingressgateway pod*

Let's dive a little deeper into the Pod behind the `istio-ingressgateway` Service. To find the exact name of the Pod, you can use the following command. To filter the Pod, we use the `--selector` flag, which looks for the provided label in the Pod definition. The `istio-ingressgateway` Pod carries the label `istio:ingressgateway`:

```
\> kubectl get pods --selector="istio=ingressgateway" -n istio-system

NAME                                      READY   STATUS    RESTARTS   AGE
istio-ingressgateway-7c96766d85-m6ns4     1/1     Running   0          5d22h
```

Now we can log into the `istio-ingressgateway` Pod by using the following command with the correct Pod name:

```
\> kubectl -it exec istio-ingressgateway-7c96766d85-m6ns4 \
-n istio-system  sh

#
```

In the Envoy filesystem, if you look inside the /etc/certs directory, you'll find the private key file (key.pem) and the corresponding public certificate chain file (cert-chain.pem) provisioned by Istio Citadel (you'll find these files only in Istio prior to version 1.5.0). The Ingress gateway uses these keys to authenticate over mTLS to the upstream service proxies. In chapter 12, we discuss how to enable mTLS between the Ingress gateway and the service proxies. Here are the commands to list the directory's contents:

```
# cd /etc/certs
# ls
# cert-chain.pem key.pem root-cert.pem
```

Also, in the Envoy filesystem, run the following `curl` command to get the Envoy configurations related to routing and upstream connections:

```
# curl 127.0.0.1:15000/config_dump
```

If you want to save the Envoy configuration to a file on your local machine, you can run the following command from your local machine. The corresponding Envoy configuration will be written to the envoy.config.json file:

```
\> kubectl exec -it istio-ingressgateway-7c96766d85-m6ns4 \
-n istio-system  curl 127.0.0.1:15000/config_dump > envoy.config.json
```

K.6.6 *Istio's MeshPolicy*

The MeshPolicy is another important thing that Istio brings to the Kubernetes cluster prior to the Istio 1.5.0 release. Istio introduces a MeshPolicy resource (listing K.6) that is applicable for all the Services in your Kubernetes cluster across all the namespaces. The MeshPolicy resource, with the name `default`, defines a cluster-wide authentication policy. The `mtls` mode of the policy is set to `PERMISSIVE`; this is based on the parameters we passed to the `gcloud` command to add Istio support to the Kubernetes cluster in section K.5.

You can override the global MeshPolicy by defining an authentication policy or a set of policies under any namespace. We discuss authentication policies in detail in chapter 12. From Istio 1.5.0 onward, the MeshPolicy is deprecated and will be removed from a future Istio release.

Listing K.6   Defining the MeshPolicy

```
\> kubectl get meshpolicy -o yaml

apiVersion: v1
kind: List
items:
- apiVersion: authentication.istio.io/v1alpha1
  kind: MeshPolicy
  metadata:
    creationTimestamp: "2019-10-14T22:34:06Z"
    generation: 1
    labels:
      app: security
      chart: security
      heritage: Tiller
      release: istio
    name: default
  spec:
    peers:
    - mtls:
        mode: PERMISSIVE
```

K.7   *Setting up the Kubernetes deployment*

In this section, we create two deployments in a Kubernetes cluster under the default namespace. One is for the security token service (STS) and the other for the Order Processing microservice. These are the same microservices we discussed in chapter 11. In section K.8, we discuss how to engage Istio in these two microservices.

The source code related to all the samples in this chapter is available in the GitHub repository (https://github.com/microservices-security-in-action/samples) in the appendix-k directory. If you're interested in learning more about the YAML files we use to create the two Deployments for the STS and the Order Processing microservice, check out chapter 11.

Run the following command from appendix-k/sample01 directory to create a Kubernetes Deployment for STS:

```
\> kubectl apply -f sts.yaml

configmap/sts-application-properties-config-map created
configmap/sts-keystore-config-map created
configmap/sts-jwt-keystore-config-map created
secret/sts-keystore-secrets created
deployment.apps/sts-deployment created
service/sts-service created
```

Run the following command from the appendix-k/sample01 directory to create a Kubernetes Deployment for the Order Processing microservice:

```
\> kubectl apply -f order.processing.yaml

configmap/orders-application-properties-config-map configured
configmap/orders-keystore-config-map configured
configmap/orders-truststore-config-map configured
secret/orders-key-credentials configured
deployment.apps/orders-deployment configured
service/orders-service configured
```

And run the following command to list the Deployments available in your Kubernetes cluster under the default namespace:

```
\> kubectl get deployments

NAME                READY   UP-TO-DATE   AVAILABLE   AGE
orders-deployment   1/1     1            1           2m
sts-deployment      1/1     1            1           2m
```

K.8   *Engaging Istio to STS and the Order Processing microservices*

Engaging Istio to a microservice results in engaging Envoy with the corresponding microservice at the data plane. Or, in other words, we need to inject the Envoy proxy as a sidecar into each Pod in our microservices deployment so that the Envoy proxy intercepts all the requests and responses to and from the corresponding microservice.

There are two ways to inject Envoy as a sidecar proxy. You can do it manually by updating your Kubernetes Deployment, or you can ask Kubernetes to inject Envoy as a sidecar proxy each time you create a Pod in your Kubernetes Deployment. The Istio documentation available at http://mng.bz/RAND explains the manual process.

K.8.1 Sidecar auto injection

To autoinject Envoy as a sidecar proxy, use the following `kubectl` command. Here we enable autoinjection for the `default` namespace:

```
\> kubectl label namespace default istio-injection=enabled
```

The autoinject doesn't do any magic; it simply adds a Kubernetes admission controller to the request path.[8] This new admission controller listens to the API calls to create Pods in Kubernetes and modifies the Pod definition to add Envoy as a sidecar proxy. It also adds another container as an init container to the corresponding Pod. The role of the init container (which we discussed in chapter 11) is to carry out any initialization tasks before any of the containers start functioning in a Pod. You can use the following `kubectl` command to verify whether `istio-injection` is enabled for the `default` namespace:

```
\> kubectl get namespace -L istio-injection

NAME           STATUS    AGE    ISTIO-INJECTION
default        Active    10h    enabled
istio-system   Active    10h    disabled
kube-public    Active    10h
kube-system    Active    10h
```

When we use autoinject, it doesn't affect any Deployment already running unless we restart it. Kubernetes doesn't have a command to restart a Deployment, but we can use the following workaround. Here, we first scale down the `sts-deployment` to 0 replicas so Kubernetes will kill all the Pods running in that Deployment, and then in the second command, we scale up to 1 replica (or any number of replicas you want). We need to repeat the same for the `orders-deployment` as well:

```
\> kubectl scale deployment sts-deployment --replicas=0
\> kubectl scale deployment sts-deployment --replicas=1
\> kubectl scale deployment orders-deployment --replicas=0
\> kubectl scale deployment orders-deployment --replicas=1
```

Now we can use the following command to find the Pod names associated with the `orders-deployment` and `sts-deployment` Deployments and see what changes Istio has brought into those Pods. Looking at the output here, we can see that two containers are running inside each Pod (`Ready: 2/2`). One container carries the microservice (either the Order Processing microservice or the STS), while the other container is the Envoy proxy:

```
\> kubectl get pods

NAME                                    READY   STATUS    RESTARTS   AGE
orders-deployment-6d6cd77c6-fc8d5       2/2     Running   0          71m
sts-deployment-c58f674d7-2bspc          2/2     Running   0          72m
```

---

[8] An admission controller intercepts all the requests coming to the Kubernetes API server.

Let's use the following command to find out more about the `orders-deployment-6d6cd77c6-fc8d5` Pod:

```
\> kubectl describe pod orders-deployment-6d6cd77c6-fc8d5
```

The command results in a lengthy output; however, we'll pick only independent sections to understand the changes Istio integration has made. We discuss those changes in sections K.8.2 and K.8.3.

To disengage Istio from a given Kubernetes namespace, we can use the following `kubectl` command. Note that the hyphen (-) at the end of the command is not a typo:

```
\> kubectl label namespace default istio-injection-
```

K.8.2 *Setting up iptables rules*

When you look at the Pod description of `orders-deployment-6d6cd77c6-fc8d5` (from section K.8.1), you'll notice the following section that defines an init container with the `proxy_init` Docker image:

```
Init Containers:
  istio-init:
    Container ID:  docker://54a046e5697ac44bd82e27b7974f9735
    Image:         gke.gcr.io/istio/proxy_init:1.1.13-gke.0
```

As we discussed before, an init container runs before any other container in the Pod. The responsibility of the `proxy_init` image is to update the iptables Pod rules so that any traffic that comes in and goes out of the Pod will go through the Envoy proxy.[9]

K.8.3 *Envoy sidecar proxy*

How an Envoy proxy is added into the Pod as a container is another important section you find in the Pod description of `orders-deployment-6d6cd77c6-fc8d5`. This container (`istio-proxy`) listens on port 15090, while the container that carries the Order Processing microservice listens on port 8443:

```
Containers:
  istio-proxy:
     Container ID: docker://f9e19d8248a86304d1a3923689a874da0e8fc8
     Image: gke.gcr.io/istio/proxyv2:1.1.13-gke.0
     Image ID: docker-pullable://gke.gcr.io/istio/proxyv2@sha256:829a7810
     Port: 15090/TCP
     Host Port: 0/TCP
```

The way client applications reach the Order Processing microservice running in the `orders-deployment-6d6cd77c6-fc8d5` Pod is via a Kubernetes Service (we discuss this in chapter 11). You can use the following `kubectl` command to describe the

---

[9] Iptables is used to set up, maintain, and inspect the tables of the IP packet filter rules in the Linux kernel (see https://linux.die.net/man/8/iptables).

orders-service Service (we are still not using an Istio Gateway, which we discuss in section K.10.1.):

```
\> kubectl describe service orders-service

Name:                    orders-service
Namespace:               default
Labels:                  <none>
Selector:                app=orders
Type:                    LoadBalancer
IP:                      10.39.249.66
LoadBalancer Ingress:    35.247.11.161
Port:                    <unset>   443/TCP
TargetPort:              8443/TCP
NodePort:                <unset>   32401/TCP
Endpoints:               10.36.2.119:8443
Session Affinity:        None
External Traffic Policy: Cluster
Events:                  <none>
```

In the output, you'll find that the Service reroutes traffic to port 8443 of the orders-deployment-6d6cd77c6-fc8d5 Pod. The proxy_init init container (as discussed in section K.8.2) updates the iptables rules so that any traffic that comes to port 8443 will transparently be rerouted to port 15090, where our Envoy proxy listens.

K.9   *Running the end-to-end sample*

In this section, we test the end-to-end flow (figure K.8). We need to first get a token from the STS and then use it to access the Order Processing microservice. Now we have both microservices running on Kubernetes with Istio. Let's use the following kubectl command to find the external IP addresses of both the STS and Order Processing microservice:

```
\> kubectl get services

NAME           TYPE          CLUSTER-IP      EXTERNAL-IP     PORT(S)          AGE
kubernetes     ClusterIP     10.39.240.1     <none>          443/TCP          10h
orders-service LoadBalancer  10.39.242.155   35.247.42.140   443:30326/TCP    9h
sts-service    LoadBalancer  10.39.245.113   34.82.177.76    443:32375/TCP    9h
```

Let's use the following curl command, run from your local machine, to a get a token from the STS. Make sure you use the correct external IP address (34.82.177.76) of the STS:

```
\> curl -v -X POST --basic -u applicationid:applicationsecret \
-H "Content-Type: application/x-www-form-urlencoded;charset=UTF-8" \
-k -d "grant_type=password&username=peter&password=peter123&scope=foo" \
https://34.82.177.76/oauth/token
```

In this command, applicationid is the client ID of the web application, and applicationsecret is the client secret. If everything works fine, the STS returns an OAuth 2.0 access token (access_token), which is a JWT (or a JWS, to be precise):

```
{
"access_token":"eyJhbGciOiJSUzI1NiIsInR5cCI6IkpXVCJ9.eyJleHAiOjE1NTEzMTIzNz
```

```
YsInVzZXJfbmFtZSI6InBldGVyIiwiYXV0aG9yaXRpZXMiOlsiUk9MRV9VU0VSIl0sImp0aSI6I
jRkMmJiNjQ4LTQ2MWQtNGVlYy1hZTljLTVlYWUxZjA4ZTJhMiIsImNsaWVudF9pZCI6ImFwcGxp
Y2F0aW9uaWQiLCJzY29wZSI6WyJmb28iXX0.tr4yUmGLtsH7q9Ge2i7gxyTsOOa0RS0Yoc2uBuA
W5OVIKZcVsIITWV3bDN0FVHBzimpAPy33tvicFROhBFoVThqKXzzG00SkURN5bnQ4uFLAP0NpZ6
BuDjvVmwXNXrQp2lVXl41Q4eTvuyZozjUSCXzCI1LNw5EFFi22J73g1_mRm2j-dEhBp1TvMaRKL
BDk2hzIDVKzu5oj_gODBFm3a1S-IJjYoCimIm2igcesXkhipRJtjNcrJSegBbGgyXHVak2gB7I0
7ryVwl_Re5yX4sV9x6xNwCxc_DgP9hHLzPM8yz_K97jlT6Rr1XZBlveyjfKs_XIXgU5qizRm9mt
5xg",
"token_type":"bearer",
"refresh_token":"",
"expires_in":5999,
"scope":"foo",
"jti":"4d2bb648-461d-4eec-ae9c-5eae1f08e2a2"
}
```

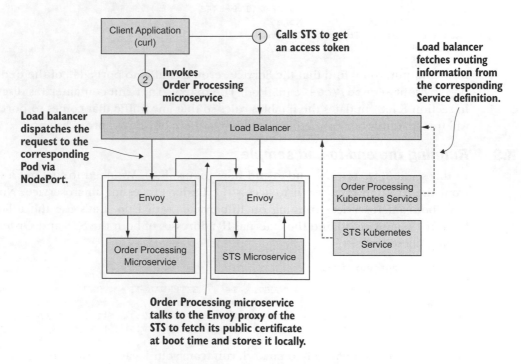

Figure K.8   The client application first talks to the STS to get an access token; then with that token, it talks to the Order Processing microservice.

Now try to invoke the Order Processing microservice with the JWT you got from the previous `curl` command. Set the same JWT we got before, in the HTTP Authorization Bearer header of the request, and invoke the Order Processing microservice by using the following `curl` command with the correct external IP address (35.247.42.140). Because the JWT is a little lengthy, you can use a small trick when using the `curl` command. First, export the JWT to an environment variable (TOKEN).

Then use that environment variable in your request to the Order Processing microservice:

```
\> export TOKEN=jwt_access_token
\> curl -k -H "Authorization: Bearer $TOKEN" \
https://35.247.42.140/orders/11

{
  "customer_id":"101021",
  "order_id":"11",
  "payment_method":{
    "card_type":"VISA",
    "expiration":"01/22",
    "name":"John Doe",
    "billing_address":"201, 1st Street, San Jose, CA"
  },
  "items":[
    {
      "code":"101",
      "qty":1
    },
    {
      "code":"103",
      "qty":5
    }
  ],
  "shipping_address":"201, 1st Street, San Jose, CA"
}
```

The way we implemented the Order Processing microservice doesn't get the full benefits of the Istio service mesh. For example, we do the mTLS validation as well as the JWT validation at the microservice itself, using Spring Boot libraries. Rather, we can delegate those tasks to the service mesh itself. We discuss how to do that in chapter 12.

K.10 *Updating the Order Processing microservice with Istio configurations*

In this section, we update the Kubernetes Deployment we created in section K.7 with respect to the Order Processing and STS microservices with Istio-specific configurations. The only thing Istio has done so far, by engaging with the Order Processing microservice, was to have the Envoy proxy intercept all the requests coming to and going out of the microservice (figure K.8). Both the STS and Order Processing microservices were deployed as Kubernetes Services of LoadBalancer type. When the client application sends a request to the Order Processing microservice, it first hits the external load balancer and then the Envoy proxy, which sits with the microservice. Instead of the requests directly hitting the Envoy proxy via the external load balancer, we want all the requests to the microservices to flow through the Istio Ingress gateway (section K.6.4) first, as shown in figure K.9.

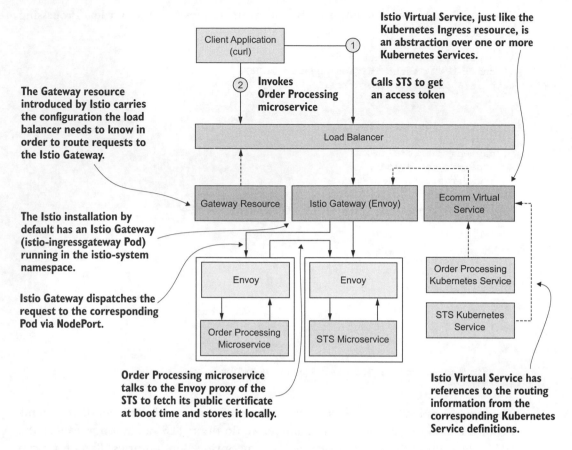

Figure K.9   The Istio Gateway intercepts all the traffic coming into the Order Processing and the STS microservices.

K.10.1 *Redeploying STS and the Order Processing microservices*

In section K.7, we deployed the STS and Order Processing microservices as Kubernetes Services of LoadBalancer type. This would give the external clients the direct access to those microservices. In this section, we are going to change the Service type to ClusterIP, so that the external clients would need to go through the Istio Ingress gateway to access those.

Run the following two commands to delete the current Kubernetes Services corresponding to the STS and the Order Processing microservices:

```
\> kubectl delete service orders-service
\> kubectl delete service sts-service
```

Once both the Services are deleted, run the following two commands from appendix-k/sample01 directory to create the updated Kubernetes Services for the STS and the Order Processing microservices:

```
\> kubectl apply -f sts.updated.yaml
\> kubectl apply -f order.processing.updated.yaml
```

And run the following command to list the Services available in your Kubernetes cluster under the default namespace and make sure both the orders-service and sts-service are of the `ClusterIP` Service type:

```
\> kubectl get services
```

```
NAME             TYPE        CLUSTER-IP      EXTERNAL-IP    PORT(S)     AGE
orders-service   ClusterIP   10.39.245.172   <none>         443/TCP     101s
sts-service      ClusterIP   10.39.251.64    <none>         443/TCP     108s
```

K.10.2 *Creating a Gateway resource*

The Gateway resource, introduced by Istio, instructs the external load balancer of the Kubernetes environment (when there is a load balancer) on how to route traffic to the Istio Ingress gateway. As discussed in section K.6.4, when you install Istio on your Kubernetes cluster, it adds an `istio-ingressgateway` Service and the `istio-ingressgateway` Pod behind it under the `istio-system` namespace. This `istio-ingressgateway` Service is of LoadBalancer type, and the external load balancer of your Kubernetes environment knows how to route traffic to it (or to the Pod behind the Service). The `istio-ingressgateway` Pod runs an Envoy proxy and carries the label `istio:ingressgateway`. Listing K.7 shows the definition of the `ecomm-gateway` (a Gateway resource) that instructs the load balancer to route any HTTPS traffic that comes to port 443 to the `istio-ingressgateway` Pod.

> **Listing K.7   Defining the `ecomm-gateway`**

```
apiVersion: networking.istio.io/v1alpha3
kind: Gateway
metadata:
  name: ecomm-gateway
  namespace: istio-system
spec:
  selector:
    istio: ingressgateway
  servers:
  - port:
      number: 443
      name: http
      protocol: HTTPS
    tls:
      mode: PASSTHROUGH
    hosts:
    - "*"
```

Because the Ingress gateway is running in the istio-system namespace, we also create the Gateway resource in the same namespace.

Binds the Gateway resource to the istio-ingressgateway Pod, which is an Envoy proxy that carries the label istio:ingressgateway

Instructs the Envoy proxy that runs as the Istio Gateway to not terminate TLS, but just pass it through

Instructs the load balancer to route all the traffic coming to any host on port 443 to the Istio Gateway

To create the Gateway resource and the corresponding VirtualService resources for the Order Processing microservice and the STS (we discuss VirtualServices in section K.10.2), run the following command from the appendix-k/sample01 directory:

```
\> kubectl apply -f istio.ingress.gateway.yaml

gateway.networking.istio.io/ecomm-gateway created
virtualservice.networking.istio.io/ecomm-virtual-service created
```

You can use the following `kubectl` command to list all the VirtualService resources available in your Kubernetes cluster under the default namespace:

```
\> kubectl get  virtualservices

NAME                      GATEWAYS           HOSTS     AGE
ecomm-virtual-service     [ecomm-gateway]    [*]       6m
```

K.10.3 *Creating a VirtualService resource for the Order Processing and STS microservices*

The VirtualService resource, introduced by Istio, instructs the corresponding Istio Gateway on how to route traffic to the corresponding Kubernetes Service. A Kubernetes Service (which we discussed in detail in appendix J) is an abstraction over one or more Pods, while an Istio VirtualService is an abstraction over one or more Kubernetes Services. It's quite similar to the Kubernetes Ingress resource that we discuss in appendix J, and the Gateway resource that we discussed in section K.10.1 is quite similar to the Kubernetes Ingress controller.

Listing K.8 shows the definition of the `ecomm-virtual-service` (a VirtualService resource) that instructs the Istio Gateway that we created in section K.10.1 to route any HTTPS traffic with `sni_hosts`[10] `sts.ecomm.com` that comes on port 443 to the `sts-service` (a Kubernetes Service), and traffic with `sni_hosts` `orders.ecomm.com` to the `orders-service` (also a Kubernetes Service).

Listing K.8   Defining `ecomm-virtual-service`

```
apiVersion: networking.istio.io/v1alpha3
kind: VirtualService
metadata:
  name: ecomm-virtual-service
spec:
  hosts:
  - "*"
  gateways:
  - ecomm-gateway.istio-system.svc.cluster.local
```

---

[10] Server Name Indication (SNI) is a TLS extension that a client application can use before the start of the TLS handshake. It indicates to the server which hostname it intends to talk to. The Istio Gateway can route traffic looking at this SNI parameter.

```
tls:
  - match:
    - port: 443
      sni_hosts:
      - sts.ecomm.com
    route:
    - destination:
        host: sts-service
        port:
          number: 443
  - match:
    - port: 443
      sni_hosts:
      - orders.ecomm.com
    route:
    - destination:
        host: orders-service
        port:
          number: 443
```

If the SNI header carries the sts.ecomm.com value, the Istio Gateway routes the traffic to sts-service.

Name of the Kubernetes Service corresponding to the STS Pod

The sts-service listens on port 443.

If the SNI header carries the orders.ecomm.com value, the Istio Gateway routes the traffic to orders-service.

Name of the Kubernetes Service corresponding to the Pod that carries the Order Processing microservice

The orders-service listens on port 443

K.10.4 *Running the end-to-end flow*

In this section, we test the end-to-end flow depicted previously in figure K.9. We need to first get a token from the STS, and then use it to access the Order Processing microservice. Now we have both microservices fronted by the Istio Ingress gateway. Let's use the following two commands to find the external IP address and the HTTPS port of the Istio Ingress gateway that runs under the `istio-system` namespace. The first command finds the external IP address of the `istio-ingressgateway` Service and exports it to the `INGRESS_HOST` environment variable; the second command finds the HTTPS port of the `istio-ingressgateway` Service and exports it to the `INGRESS_HTTPS_PORT` environment variable:

```
\> export INGRESS_HOST=$(kubectl -n istio-system \
get service istio-ingressgateway \
-o jsonpath='{.status.loadBalancer.ingress[0].ip}')

\> export INGRESS_HTTPS_PORT=$(kubectl -n istio-system \
get service istio-ingressgateway \
-o jsonpath='{.spec.ports[?(@.name=="https")].port}')
```

You can use the following `echo` commands to make sure that we've captured the right values for the two environment variables:

```
\> echo $INGRESS_HOST
34.83.117.171
\> echo $INGRESS_HTTPS_PORT
443
```

Let's use the following `curl` command, run from your local machine, to a get a token from the STS. Here, we use the environment variables that we defined before for the hostname and the port of the `istio-ingressgateway` Service. Because we use SNI routing at the Istio Gateway, we also use the hostname `sts.ecomm.com` to access the STS. Because there's no DNS mapping to this hostname, we use the `--resolve` parameter in curl to define the hostname-to-IP mapping:

```
\> curl -v -X POST --basic -u applicationid:applicationsecret \
-H "Content-Type: application/x-www-form-urlencoded;charset=UTF-8" \
-k -d "grant_type=password&username=peter&password=peter123&scope=foo" \
--resolve sts.ecomm.com:$INGRESS_HTTPS_PORT:$INGRESS_HOST \
https://sts.ecomm.com:$INGRESS_HTTPS_PORT/oauth/token
```

In this command, `applicationid` is the client ID of the web application, and `applicationsecret` is the client secret. If everything works, the STS returns an OAuth 2.0 access token (`access_token`), which is a JWT (or a JWS, to be precise):

```
{
"access_token":"eyJhbGciOiJSUzI1NiIsInR5cCI6IkpXVCJ9.eyJleHAiOjE1NTEzMTIzNz
YsInVzZXJfbmFtZSI6InBldGVyIiwiYXV0aG9yaXRpZXMiOlsiUk9MRV9VU0VSIl0sImp0aSI6I
jRkMmJiNjQ4LTQ2MWQtNGVlYy1hZTljLTVlYWUxZjA4ZTJhMiIsImNsaWVudF9pZCI6ImFwcGxp
Y2F0aW9uaWQiLCJzY29wZSI6WyJmb28iXX0.tr4yUmGLtsH7q9Ge2i7gxyTsOOa0RS0Yoc2uBuA
W5OVIKZcVsIITWV3bDN0FVHBzimpAPy33tvicFROhBFoVThqKXzzG00SkURN5bnQ4uFLAP0NpZ6
BuDjvVmwXNXrQp2lVXl4lQ4eTvuyZozjUSCXzCI1LNw5EFFi22J73g1_mRm2j-dEhBp1TvMaRKL
BDk2hzIDVKzu5oj_gODBFm3a1S-IJjYoCimIm2igcesXkhipRJtjNcrJSegBbGgyXHVak2gB7I0
7ryVwl_Re5yX4sV9x6xNwCxc_DgP9hHLzPM8yz_K97jlT6Rr1XZBlveyjfKs_XIXgU5qizRm9mt5xg",
"token_type":"bearer",
"refresh_token":"",
"expires_in":5999,
"scope":"foo",
"jti":"4d2bb648-461d-4eec-ae9c-5eae1f08e2a2"
}
```

Now let's invoke the Order Processing microservice with the JWT we got from the previous `curl` command. Set the same JWT we got in the HTTP Authorization Bearer header using the following `curl` command and invoke the Order Processing microservice:

```
\> export TOKEN=jwt_access_token
\> curl -k -H "Authorization: Bearer $TOKEN" \
--resolve orders.ecomm.com:$INGRESS_HTTPS_PORT:$INGRESS_HOST \
https://orders.ecomm.com:$INGRESS_HTTPS_PORT/orders/11

{
  "customer_id":"101021",
  "order_id":"11",
  "payment_method":{
    "card_type":"VISA",
    "expiration":"01/22",
    "name":"John Doe",
    "billing_address":"201, 1st Street, San Jose, CA"
  },
```

```
  "items":[
    {
      "code":"101",
      "qty":1
    },
    {
      "code":"103",
      "qty":5
    }
  ],
  "shipping_address":"201, 1st Street, San Jose, CA"
}
```

Because the JWT is a little lengthy, we used a small trick when using the `curl` command. First, we exported the JWT to an environment variable (`TOKEN`). Then we used that environment variable in our request to the Order Processing microservice. Once again, here too we used the environment variables that we defined before for the hostname and the port of the `istio-ingressgateway` Service. Because we used SNI routing at the Istio Gateway, we also used the hostname `orders.ecomm.com` to access the Order Processing microservice. Because there's no DNS mapping to this hostname, we used the `--resolve` parameter in curl to define the hostname-to-IP mapping.

K.10.5 *Debugging the Envoy proxy*

With the Istio service mesh architecture, all the requests coming in and going out of your microservices go through the Envoy proxy. If something goes wrong in your microservices deployment, having access to the debug-level logs of the Envoy proxy gives you more visibility and helps troubleshoot. By default, debug-level logs aren't enabled.

You can run the following command with the correct label of the Pod to which the Envoy proxy is attached to enable debug-level logs on the Envoy proxy. Here we use `orders` as the value of the app label, which you can find in the Deployment definition of the Order Processing microservice. If you want to do the same for the Inventory microservice, use `app=inventory`:

```
\> kubectl exec $(kubectl get pods -l app=orders \
-o jsonpath='{.items[0].metadata.name}') -c istio-proxy \
-- curl -X POST "localhost:15000/logging?filter=debug" -s
```

To view the logs, use the following command with the correct name of the Order Processing Deployment. Here, the `istio-proxy` is the name of the container that runs the Envoy proxy:

```
\> kubectl logs orders-deployment-6d6cd77c6-fc8d5 -c istio-proxy --follow
```

If you have a larger log file that takes time to load, you can use the following command to view the last 100 lines of the log file:

```
\> kubectl logs orders-deployment-6d6cd77c6-fc8d5 -c istio-proxy --tail 100
```

To enable debug-level logs at the `istio-ingressgateway`, you can use the following command:

```
\> kubectl exec $(kubectl get pods -l app=istio-ingressgateway \
-n istio-system -o jsonpath='{.items[0].metadata.name}') \
-n istio-system  -c istio-proxy \
-- curl -X POST "localhost:15000/logging?filter=debug" -s
```

index